HEROES

HEROES

John Pilger

JONATHAN CAPE
THIRTY-TWO BEDFORD SQUARE LONDON

First published 1986
Copyright © by John Pilger 1986
Jonathan Cape Ltd, 32 Bedford Square, London WC1B 3EL

British Library Cataloguing in Publication Data

Pilger, John
Heroes.
1. Pilger, John   2. Journalists – Australia –
Biography
I. Title
070'.92'4   PN5516.P5

ISBN 0-224-02301-2

Photoset in Great Britain by
Rowland Phototypesetting Ltd, Bury St Edmunds, Suffolk
and printed by Butler & Tanner Ltd,
Frome and London

For Yvonne, Sam and Zoe, my mother and father,
and the memory of Eric Piper

Contents

Illustrations

Acknowledgments

I would like to thank those who, over a long period, have directly and indirectly helped me with this book. I am especially grateful to my mother, Elsie, for enduring hours of tape-recorded interview and giving us both many laughs in the process; to my father, Claude, for answering unrelenting questions about his early life, always with grace and fine detail in spite of a shoulder injury which made his usual copperplate hand a painful exercise; to Yvonne Roberts for her love and unfailingly wise advice; to Sam, my son, for his interest and for keeping me down to earth; to Scarth Flett for her support and encouragement during our marriage; to Jacqueline Korn and Liz Calder for their care and patience; to Jane Hill for her superb editing; to Martha Gellhorn, Anthony Barnett, Ben Kiernan, Colonel Archimedes L.A. Patti, Colonel Harry G. Summers Jr, Geoffrey Robertson, Jenny Pearce, David Munro, Ken Loach and Matt and Jeannine Herron for reading drafts and offering suggestions and corrections; to Ken Regan, Philip Jones Griffiths, Curt Gunther, Matt Herron, Danny Lyon, Nik Wheeler, Bela Zola, Tom Buist, Andy Hosie, John Schneider, Anthony Howarth and Mathew Naythons for their fine photographs in these pages.

My thanks are also due to Harry Cox and my former colleagues in the library of the *Daily Mirror*; the staff of the BBC's Bush House library; Andrée Wright, Michael Cannon, Henry Reynolds and my cousin Tony Halloran, whose Australian researches I drew upon; also Santosh Basak, Michael Beckham, Phil Braithwaite, Pete and Ronnie Brown, Wilfred Burchett, James Cameron, Paul Chilton, Noam Chomsky, Anna Coote, Hugh Corrie, Ian Craig, Tony Culliton, John Cummings, Mary Dines, Clarice Edwards, John Eldridge, A. U. M. Fakhruddin, Judy Freeman, John Garrett, Ed Harriman, Betty Heathfield, Chris Holmes, Jim Howard, Duong Duc Huong, Joanne Hurst, Mohammed Jarella, Jan Kavan,

Phillip Knightley, Rupert Lancaster, Jim Lawrie, Teddy and Shura Levite, Alan Lowery, John McAuliff, Ranald Macdonald, Linda Mac-Fadyen, Joan McMichael, Humphrey McQueen, Chris Menges, Elizabeth Merritt, John Mitchell, Mon Mohan, Christine Morrison, Liz Nash, Bruce Page, Eric Piper, Bob Saunders, Jeremy Seabrook, Rowan Seymour, Jo South, Peter Stone, David Swift, Do Tuan That, 'Tooby' Thuc, Julius Tomin, Ben Whitaker's Minority Rights Group, Louis Wolf and Arthur Wynn Davies. I owe special thanks to Hugh Cudlipp, Lee Howard, Tony Miles and Mike Molloy who, during our years together on the *Daily Mirror*, gave me rare freedoms to travel, enquire and write. I am grateful to the *Daily Mirror* and the *New Statesman* for permission to publish extracts from my work.

My appreciation goes also to Charles Denton, Richard Creasey, Andy Allan, Richard Marquand, Nicholas Claxton, Bob Phillis, June Peacock, Julie Stoner, Noel Smart, Sue Cameron, Jean Denham, Jonathan Morris, Roger James, Paul Cleary, Mike Nunn, Tim Farmer, Karen Mellor and others at ATV, later Central Television, who made such an enormous contribution to my programmes and who have been my allies. Finally, my thanks to Sue Griffin and Jude Sharpe who, with great care, typed and deciphered these pages.

Preface

On my second day as a journalist I was sent to report on a swarm of bees which was stuck to the windscreen of a car. When I got there it was clear that this was a non-story, and other reporters were putting away their notebooks when somebody walked up to the bees and was stung between the eyes. The following day a rival newspaper's headline read, 'BEES TERROR: MAN HURT'. There was a photograph of the bees and the victim with his head in his hands. It was me.

I have written this book for many reasons, not the least of which has been to show something of the fallibility and absurdity of journalism, as well as its nobility. Having made my way through half a dozen wars and numerous other human upheavals, I have always trusted that, if all my faculties fail, my sense of the ridiculous will remain. War, for me, has two sides: bloody degradation on one side, black farce on the other. How can it be otherwise when, on an Asian battlefield, blonde 'donut dollies' are dropped out of the sky to calm mutinous troops with parlour games of charades and I-Spy; when combat troops are sent into the jungle to win 'hearts and minds' with 5,000 gift-wrapped toothbrushes and party balloons; when ghost sounds are played from a helicopter in order to frighten the enemy; when tens of thousands of scorched dollars rain down on those waiting to be evacuated on the last day of the longest war this century; and when millions of unused banknotes flow in the afternoon monsoon through the streets of a city without food and light? How can it be otherwise when a reporter stands up at a press conference and shouts, 'Three cheers for the victorious general!' And when a director-general of the BBC refuses to lift a ban on a television programme about the iniquity of war because of the effect it might have 'on people of limited mental intelligence'?

Of course it is inevitable, and appropriate, that the farce inherent in human affairs should involve the journalist, although some still refuse to acknowledge this, preferring to ascend to a non-existent nirvana of neutrality. (The religious affairs correspondent of *The Times* recently described this beatific state as 'the automatic habit of non-involvement in other people's crises'.) When I was sent up the River Niger to Timbuktu on a hovercraft with a man called Smithers and another man called Captain Energy, along with crates of teabags and paper underwear, I read, not for the first time, the celebrated *Scoop*, in which my predicament was accurately described. (Moreover, I was later to work for Lord Copper himself.)

All of that, I hasten to say, is not the main reason for *Heroes*. Originally I was asked to write a book about a mining community I knew well in the North of England; and this led me to want to chronicle the lives of those, like the miners, whose struggles I have witnessed in many countries. They are people frequently lost in the broad sweep that is the nature of much television and print journalism; they are dismissed as the minutiae of a news story when they are really the story. Or they are portrayed merely as victims when, in truth, their courage and resilience are often heroic. It is they who are the heroes of this book, which I hope will stand as a tribute to them.

They are those like Jack, a Yorkshire dyehouse worker whose decency and grace and those of his family, in the face of hardship, are seldom reflected in the mirrors held up by the media and established authority; and those like Penn, editor of a small Texas newspaper, who was fire-bombed for upholding the freedom to publish; and those like Lupita, who went under fire to rescue the tortured body of her son in Nicaragua; and Marta, whose songs of freedom in Czechoslovakia have made her a prisoner in her own country; and Cham and Ock, children of Pol Pot's Cambodia who survived, incredibly, and Kuon ('No. 23') who did not; and, in my own country, Yami, blinded by nuclear bombs dropped on his ancient land, who has fought for justice for others and with such magnanimity.

There is another ingredient in *Heroes*. The true nature of many reported events is distorted or lost in public memory, partly because of the sheer volume of the media coverage. The Vietnam war, a famous 'media event', was the only war fought this century by a Western power which did not impose censorship; and yet it was a deeply censored war. I have attempted to explain this and to identify the most common form of censorship, which is the least understood by journalists and public alike. It is censorship by subterfuge: the manipulation of thought and language, such as labels and clichés that deceive and polarise ('moderates' versus 'extremists', etc.) and a conditioned deference to authority and to the 'prevailing view' in the name of objectivity. This is journalism's most insidious restrictive practice. And here the absurdity is Orwellian; for to reject this bias is to be 'controversial' and 'committed' and to invite both direct censorship and the indignation of those whom Robert Louis Stevenson aptly described as 'your sham impartialists, wolves in sheep's clothing, simpering honestly as they suppress'.

Of course there are journalists unaware of their own malleability; I was, and perhaps I still am. 'The censor is no longer at his desk,' the Czech writer Zdener Urbanek told me, 'he is in my head.' And that applies not only in Czechoslovakia but in countries with a so-called free Press. Indeed, it seems perverse to argue, as some do, that while our 'free' Press may be flawed it is better than that in the Eastern bloc. Britain, like the United States, has honourable journalistic traditions. The reporting, for instance, of William Howard Russell in the Crimea set a standard from which journalism should have progressed; but too often the reverse is true. Not only is censorship in its concealed forms (such as the threat of losing a well-paid job) rampant in Britain's 'free' Press, it has become institutionalised in those authorities which exercise direct control over journalism, as in television. At the same time the very notion of a free Press is being undermined by a monopoly which, as general fare, serves up distortion, non-news, violence and soapsuds: anti-journalism.

It seems to me ironic that in the 1980s, as media technology advances, it is not the traditional means of journalism that are becoming obsolete, but the honourable traditions. As secrecy and the deception of governments grow more sophisticated, the need for explanation, investigation and polemic has never been more urgent; equally, there is the need for journalists to make a stand against the bullies of their own industry. I have written this book hoping, perhaps above all, that it will help in the defence of the craft I love. It is no coincidence that among the heroes in the following pages are many journalists, past and present.

JOHN PILGER

London,
March 1986

I

AUSTRALIA

1

Uttering unlawful oaths

Sydney, Australia: November 7, 1821. Just before dawn the barque *John Barry* hove to under full sail off Sydney Heads. In darkness the entrance to the world's greatest natural harbour was easily missed; no less a mariner than James Cook had passed it at night thirty-one years earlier and had had to content himself with a ceremonial flag-raising on the scabrous shores of Botany Bay, unaware that a few miles beyond the dunes lay an anchorage he had sailed an ocean to find. The master of the *John Barry*, Roger Dobson, had recorded making almost the same error on his previous voyage. However, on this voyage he had reason to be pleased; in nine days short of five months, with gales unrelenting from the Great Australian Bight to Van Diemen's Land, he had brought his 520-ton vessel from Cork in Ireland to where the end of the earth was said to be; 'on the very edge of loneliness', wrote another ship's surgeon, 'a place, I should advise, where everything seems weird and wrong.'

When the *John Barry* had passed through Sydney Heads and the first shafts of sunlight had collided with the faces below, pressed to cracks just above the waterline, it was obvious to the prisoners that they had been brought to a 'weird and wrong' place. Almost everything seemed wrong: the shoreline was of rocks shaped like huge teeth and was dark with impenetrable red and ghost-like trees of a variety they had not seen before.

The stillness, like the diamond light, was also 'wrong'. Then suddenly there was laughter – demoniac laughter was it? – then a mocking cackle which reached a crescendo among the trees, and other live sounds that echoed each other. Were these *birds*? And what kind of monster was that? A great body with a rabbit's head, and leaping on two legs! And on the ash-white sand of perfect bays stood erect naked humans so black their eyes seemed painted out. They did not move; then like apparitions, they were gone.

These surely were the savages about whom those below decks of the *John Barry* had heard worrying stories. They 'carried you off to eat the delicate white flesh', was one story. There was much to fear then and I have often wondered what passed through the minds of the Irish men, women and children on that ship that morning. Or perhaps fear had long been replaced by the relief of reaching somewhere, anywhere, after five months of an angular, pitching, at times almost drowning hell of dysentery and pneumonia and scurvy.

Six of them shared a berth of less than six feet square where they lay 'squeezed up against one another, wallowing in each other's filth, sea-sickness and vermin, for the entire length of the voyage. If one wished to turn over in the cramped space, he had to wake the others so that all could roll over in their chains at the same time.'[1] They were fed like pigs, with potato peelings and crusts thrown at them, usually in darkness when the ship was rolling, and if they looked askance, let alone complained, the cruelties visited upon them included whipping with a knotted 'cat', gang-rape for the women and the denial of sustenance until the point of death for children already half-starved. And the final cruelty, which was the twist in those lives resilient enough to survive such a purgatory, was that worse awaited them in the 'weird and wrong' place.

The *John Barry* carried mostly political prisoners from Ireland, the 'inflammable matter', as Queen Victoria called them; and my great-great-grandfather was one of them. His name was Francis McCarthy and he had been convicted of 'uttering unlawful oaths' in his native County Roscommon. This was a charge interpreted in the English courts at that time as 'making political agitation' or 'taking part in seditious conspiracy'. McCarthy was sentenced to transportation to a penal colony for fourteen years, which was double the sentence handed down to the six Tolpuddle Martyrs for the crime of seeking to form a trade union.

To be guilty of objecting to enforced degradation and starvation in Ireland during the first half of the nineteenth century was to be a political criminal. Even before the potato famine, nowhere else in what the Victorians called 'the civilised world' did such uncivilised conditions exist. Absentee English landlords controlled the Irish peasantry; and those Irish people who could not afford a tenancy, or were evicted, were forced to live in holes in the bog: caves of mud without beds or chairs, in which infants lay where animals defecated. Food was dried potatoes and death and disease were on a scale scarcely believable. To these was added the constant menace of English terrorism; if you were convicted or if your crops failed, the Redcoats would arrive to drag away your animals, your last means of survival, and any recalcitrance would lead inevitably to a bloody arrest.

When Francis McCarthy was arrested he was taken to Cork, and when he was convicted, he was led to a blacksmith who fitted him with the standard four-pound leg irons, 'the badge of infamy and degradation rivetted upon me'.[2] He was then confined to a hulk left over from the Napoleonic wars, where he was chained to a berth already occupied by rats, to await transportation on the *John Barry*. He was twenty-six years old and, for that period, unusually tall: five feet eight inches, with a shock of ginger hair and bushy ginger beard. There exists one photograph of McCarthy, who died in 1890. This likeness remains in a certain family archive where the 'secret' of McCarthy's past was locked for many years. He was, according to that source, 'an early land owner' who was 'well acquainted with Government House'. Alas, he was neither. In the register of St Mary's Cathedral, Sydney, he is described as 'a labourer of ruddy face'. That he was convicted of a *political* crime and married a servant girl of 'dark and pocked complexion', herself a convict, only compounded the ignominy.

To an ordinary man like McCarthy, to most Europeans then, the concept of a vast island continent into which numerous Irelands, Englands and Europes would fit was beyond all imagination. Not only were there stories of two-legged monsters and savages who savoured white flesh, but the evidence of convicts swallowed by the sea on their way to this remote Minos was a spectre for those waiting their turn.

There was the *Amphitrite*, in 1833, which was swept by gale-force winds on to a sand bank at the entrance to Boulogne Harbour only five days out. According to a correspondent of *The Times*, the captain and the ship's surgeon had an opportunity to get everybody ashore safely 'but they did not dare without authority to land the convicts, and rather than leave them on board or land them without that authority, they perished with them'. And as the tide rose, reported *The Times*, all 103 female convicts and their twelve children died 'uttering the most piteous cries'.[3]

When the *John Barry* dropped anchor in Sydney the convicts were divided into 'intractables' and those 'prepared to knuckle under'. The intractables were sent to Goat Island, which was within the harbour and from which escape seemed out of the question; these were shark-breeding waters. As the 'intractables' were rowed to Goat Island they were presented with an example of the arbitrary and sadistic brutality awaiting those who might try to escape, and what they saw explained why no nation was born under so cruel a star as Australia.

In a cleft in the rock face there appeared to be a coffin. It had a wooden cover and at one end the upright head of a man was visible. His name was Charles 'Boney' Anderson and he had been transported for theft and drunkenness, even though previously he had been wounded in a naval battle and had suffered a mental disability. On arrival in Sydney Anderson was sent to Goat Island for two months. He escaped, was caught and given one hundred lashes, and another one hundred lashes every month for offences such as 'looking up from work' and 'looking at a steamer on the river'. Again he escaped, and again caught. This time he was given two hundred lashes, and for the next two years he was chained to a rock by a twenty-six-foot chain fastened to his waist. His food was pushed to him at the end of a long pole and at night the wooden cover, with its few air holes, was clamped over him. During the summer months he became something of an early tourist attraction; boat trippers would sail by and throw him bread and dry biscuits. In all, he was given 1,700 lashes. He died insane.

So common was flogging in Sydney then that 'scourgers', those who administered the lash and were trained on dummies in the settlement's Hyde Park, could not meet the demand. A farm overseer described two scourgers 'bespattered with blood like a couple of butchers' while their victim attempted to walk away 'with the blood that had run from his lacerated flesh squashing out of his shoes at every step he took' and a dog licked blood off the 'three sisters' (the flogging triangle) and ants were making off with 'great pieces of human flesh'.[4] It was not surprising that the children of the first great property owners observed the treatment of those who worked in chains for their parents, and, inspired by such ruthlessness, played at flogging a tree 'as children in England play at horses'.[5]

The 'squatters', as the owners were known, soon accumulated what was advertised in England as 'uncommonly large profits' without the drawback of labour costs and the stigma of Negro slavery. My great-great-grandfather was 'assigned' to a Mr Robertson, whose land included part of what is now skyscraper Sydney. He was fortunate, for Robertson was a benevolent man, perhaps not unlike the most paternalistic of the slave-owners in the American Deep South. What was certain was that 'assignment' was slavery by another name, although those historians who sought to convince my generation that the history of Australia was merely an appendage to the imperial history of Britain, and not the unique and rapacious misadventure it was and remains, seldom made mention of slavery, just as the early colonial artists never portrayed such a hell, preferring to contrive idyllic scenes of incongruent gentility from out of the most primitive and harsh landscape in the world. Real Australia and its stains on 'civilisation' did not exist, as if Victorian middle-class England was just over the brow. Such was the beginning of the great

Australian silence which not only emasculated the truth of the past, but distorted the way Australians would come to regard themselves and their nation.

Slavery was abolished throughout the British Empire by the Emancipation Act of 1833. But so powerful was the 'squattocracy', the landed class of Australia, whose labour-free profits were indeed 'uncommon' and whose political friends railed against the 'trimmers, traitors and rosewater liberals' who dared to expose the true nature of the penal colony, that white slavery endured in Australia for more than forty years after it had been abolished throughout the 'civilised' world. 'As the lot of a slave depends upon the character of its [sic] master', reported a House of Commons Select Committee on Transportation in 1838, 'so the convict depends upon the temper and disposition of the settler to whom he is assigned . . . the condition of a transported convict is a mere lottery.'[6]

The day came when Francis McCarthy was ordered to line up with the others in their 'canary' suits of cheap Indian cloth or of a hessian material stamped with arrows, in front of squatters or their overseers. 'Shout out your trade!' they were ordered, and those with skills, blacksmiths, carpenters, coopers and masons, were seized upon.

Ironically, it was this artisan class of 'mechanics', not the 'lowest order', to which McCarthy belonged, that was to suffer most in the wildest terrain. I recently saw in the stables of a homestead in north-western New South Wales a six-foot iron triangle, a 'three sisters', imported from Birmingham and perfectly preserved. On such an instrument the same common folk of England described by William Cobbett as 'the worst used labouring people upon the face of the earth', the debtors, Chartists, unionists and Irish objectors, took their turn to be flogged, though not always into submission.

'Some convicts', wrote Michael Cannon in his brilliant and angry *Who's Master? Who's Man?*, 'took pride in uttering no sound during their flagellation.' Jack Donohoe, the original 'wild colonial boy', was, as Cannon recounts, sentenced to transportation for life at the age of seventeen for the mere *intent* to commit a felony; and when he became a legend as a bushranger and was hunted and finally shot dead in 1834, the ballad of 'Bold Jack Donohoe' was sung in 'all the low public houses through Sydney, but was immediately prohibited by the government'.[7] It was this same underground and melancholy strain of Irish resistance which, eighty-two years later, was to prevent an imperial Australian government from conscripting Australians to die for Britain in Europe's trenches.

On October 12, 1821 Mary Palmer, a scullery servant in a London house, was sentenced at Middlesex Gaol to be transported for life. Her crime is unrecorded. She sailed for Sydney one year and a day later, manacled in the hold of the *Lord Sidmouth*. She was eighteen years old, four feet ten inches tall, with 'dark hair, brown eyes and skin grievously pitted from the disease of smallpox'. She was my great-great-grandmother.

Female convicts were synonymous with whores. The *Sydney Herald* in 1835 commented that so many 'women or prostitutes' were arriving that they added 'pollution even to a society of convicts'. The atrocious treatment of the first women from the 'civilised world' to settle in Australia was largely concealed by Australia's imperial historians. Sir Timothy Coglan wrote dismissively that 'female (convict) labour was never at any time industrially important'. In her 1982 book, *Damned Whores and God's Police*, Ann Summers described conviction of women in Ireland and England as 'transportation plus enforced whoredom'.[8] The first Australian women were enslaved 'legally' in order to sexually service the predominantly male population.

During the voyage out to New South Wales seamen were given 'free access' to the female convicts; the word rape was not used. On arrival those women who were considered the most attractive were each 'assigned' to a man as his servant/mistress; and this was often the only means of getting a decent roof and sustenance. Mary Palmer was not so fortunate.

When she was rowed ashore from the *Lord Sidmouth* she was emaciated, the size of a child, and suffering, like all of them, from dysentery, then a killer. Eyes which had seen so little light remained half-closed; knees which had barely straightened for months remained buckled and crippled. Haggard, broken, bird-like figures were lifted from the longboat to await 'muster' on the Sydney quayside.

Mary Palmer was issued with a heavy brown serge dress to wear in the heat and humidity, and with the other women, some carrying small children and new-born babies, she was marched westward. This forced march, much of it through virgin bushland and along crude roads cleared by male 'iron gangs', was an odyssey of small horrors: adders and other reptiles, flies that stung and ants that clung to flesh. Dehydration, for which there were no medicines and little water, sickened and killed the very youngest by the time the columns reached Parramatta after two days.[9]

Here stood the white stone walls of the 'centre of labour supply and punishment', better known as the female factory. Mary Palmer was put to work spinning yarn and weaving coarse cloth by hand while she waited to be assigned as a live-in domestic, which would mean almost certainly prostitution to master and male servants alike. In the factory itself there was no division by age or crime. According to Charlotte Anley, who was sent by Elizabeth Fry to report on the state of female prisoners in Australia, 'the bad soon became worse, and the most depraved held sway'. She gave the example of one young woman who had resolved to reform and read her Bible and pray. However, on entering the Parramatta factory, 'the blessed Book was torn from her hands, she was scorned and insulted, and left in no peace at all, until she "gave over being sorry".'[10] Roger Terry, an Attorney-General in New South Wales from 1841–3, described how the women in the factory had beaten off 'with a volley of stones and staves' soldiers who had been marched into the gaol yard to quell the 'excessive violence'.[11]

Although female convicts were spared the 'cat', they were given terms of solitary confinement, in total darkness, during which they were starved, or their heads were shaved, or they were subjected to a means of torture which was popular among certain 'penal experts' of the time because it was said not to cause lasting damage. This was the treadmill, a revolving cylinder in which the prisoner had to keep stepping upwards in order to keep the cylinder moving and not fall out. Male convicts were arbitrarily sentenced to weeks and months on the treadmill; women prisoners, although given shorter spells, often suffered intense pain in the groin and heavy menstrual bleeding, so that their dresses were drenched in blood and urine. The guards were male, and other clothes were seldom available.

There was a 'courting day' at the Parramatta factory when the women were placed on view and offer, first to free settlers, then to convicts. The 1838 report of the House of Commons Select Committee on Transportation described the procedure: 'The convict goes up and looks at the women and if he sees a lady that takes his fancy, he makes a motion to her and she steps to one side. Some will not do this, but stand still, and have no wish to be married, but that is very rare. They then have, of course, some conversation together and if the lady is not agreeable, she steps back and the ceremony goes on with two or three more.'

Roger Terry wrote of 'the indifference with which convicts often chose their partners for life . . . passes were sometimes given by magistrates to the ticket-of-leave holders [paroled convicts] "to go to the female factory to choose a wife". The business was sometimes transacted in three days: one day for the journey to the factory; the second day for the courtship and ceremony; the third day back again to the station (property) and the bride.'[12]

In this way Francis McCarthy chose, courted and married Mary Palmer. Both were eventually given their 'ticket of leave' and their names were 'gazetted' in *Her Majesty's Pardons of Exiles*. McCarthy became a miller, then was overseer of a 'horse and buggy bazaar' in Sydney. Mary bore ten children, one of whom was Jane, a replica, it was said, of her tiny mother.

Jane married a man even larger and more imposing than her father. He was Conrad Marheine, six feet six inches tall, his great head enveloped in blond locks as befitting a Hanoverian piccolo-player. On the run from military service in Germany, 'Big Con' arrived in Sydney and joined a German band which played at socials at Government House. It is more than likely he and Jane met at her father's horse and buggy bazaar, for Con was both piccolo-player and master horseman.

Before the railway came and with roads little more than unmarked tracks and subject to disappearance during the floods, bushfires and landslides, Big Con drove the stagecoaches of Messrs Cobb & Co., an American enterprise which began services in 1854 and within two years ran the most extensive coaching network in the world. Riding into the goldfields of New South Wales Con was something of a spectacle, driving a 'six in hand' in his wide-brimmed hat and with his bushy hair, a long-barrelled pistol strapped to his thigh: the latter to assist in 'negotiations' with bushrangers, who regarded the coaches of Cobb & Co. as their private source of plunder.

Con's coach routes covered a region of lawlessness and rebellion which the gold rush of 1851 had spawned and which struck fear into the hearts and ambitions of the squattocracy. 'Prepare for calamities', warned the *Sydney Morning Herald*, 'far more terrible than earthquakes or pestilence. All the intelligent classes have a solemn and urgent duty to counteract and subdue the spirit of excitement. To the labouring classes we can only repeat: Remain steadily at your work and do not be seduced into going into the mines!'[13]

Getting gold safely away from the smaller claims became a logistical challenge to which the 'diggers' rose. A solemn cortège would bear a coffin to Con's stagecoach, to which it would be most securely lashed; for in it would not be the body of an expired Irishman, but gold, although there were, assuredly, occasions when both precious metal and departed digger would ride together.

Con's passengers into the goldfields were more often than not Chinese, who then accounted for one in nine of the Australian population. The Chinese had been brought to Australia in the 1830s as 'indentured labour', which was little better than slavery. Unable to meet the demand for convict labour, the squatters and merchants bought 'consignments of Chows', usually for a five-year period, and worked them more than a hundred hours a week for barely a subsistence. 'The introduction of Asiatic labour', said one Queensland squatter, 'is what machinery is to England.'[14]

Most of the Chinese did not want to stay but they could not afford to leave. At first they were despised for not joining the gold rush, as 'real men' did, but when they confounded their critics by heading for the diggings they were described as 'Mongolian locusts'; and when, unlike many of the white miners, they overcame the challenge of the Australian bush by building dams, working in teams, even forming trade unions, they were attacked; at the diggings at Lambing Flats in 1861 pigtails and scalps were torn off, and children's cradles set alight while a band played 'Rule, Britannia!'

Con and Jane Marheine settled for a while in a frontier town called Berrima, from which Con would drive his 'six in hand' and not return for up to two months. During his absences, Jane endured the extremes of loneliness and bore their three children in quick succession. She was a Catholic, he a Lutheran; and when he returned home the current baby would be duly conveyed to the Protestant pastor for baptism in the family's accredited faith. However, once the German had packed his pistol and piccolo, saluted the busts of the Kaiser and Queen Victoria which he kept side by side on the mantelpiece and was gone again, Jane would summon the Irish priest to ensure that the child was 'properly baptised'. Unfortunately, during one such illicit ceremony, Con returned unexpectedly and the priest was propelled through the door and beyond the hitching posts.

One autumn day in 1860 Con drove his coach and horses into Berrima after six weeks on the road. He passed the cemetery, as he always did to reach their house, and there, prostrate on three fresh graves, was Jane. On the headstones were the names of their three children: Rose, aged five, Charles, three, and Edward, two months. They had all choked to death within a few days of each other during an epidemic of diphtheria.

Con brooded and raged and never again drove for Cobb & Co. He and Jane moved north to Sydney where he eventually got a job driving horse-drawn buses to the city from Waverly, which overlooked a desolate stretch of sandhills and rolling Pacific surf known variously as Bundi, Boondye and, finally, Bondi Beach. It was here that William, my grandfather, was born in 1869.

Shortly afterwards, when the railway had reached Newcastle in the north, the family moved to the Hunter Valley. Con took a lease on fifty acres of thick and unexplored bush and was among the earliest settlers of what is today lush and prosperous countryside; his farm is now the Merewether Golf Course.

Con's family was growing once again, and since such a luxury as a school did not exist, he built one. A fine white weatherboard building, it was not completed in time for William, the eldest son, who was in his teens; throughout his life my gentle, industrious grandfather was dismayed that he could not read and write. And it was the duty of his family to preserve this 'secret', which ranked in importance with the secret of the criminal McCarthy.

Although the depression of the 1890s, an outbreak of swine fever, a flood and a bushfire set Con and Jane back, they survived as only true pioneers could and lived out the rest of their lives as uncomplaining hillbillies. My mother fondly remembers their homestead with its sloping tin roof and vast veranda and the kitchen at the back with its fuel stove always burning the sweet eucalyptus. 'The flies were in the millions', she said, 'and the chooks strolled everywhere. Con and Jane had learned to take life as it came, for life had been hard for them.'

Jane's love of children – she bore another eight – was translated into a legendary role as district midwife. She would say, with pride, 'I never lost a baby'; and that was a remarkable record during days when many were lost. She delivered most of her grandchildren, including all but two of the nine born to William's wife, Caroline. One of them was Elsie, my mother.

These were meant to be momentous days in Australia. January 1, 1901 was the day of Federation when the six Australian states came together as one proud nation: or so we were told. Under inclement skies in Sydney's Centennial Park a minor member of the British aristocracy, the Earl of Hopetoun, rose to his feet with trembling and foreboding (for he was stricken with dysentery, then the 'antipodean scourge') and declared himself the first Governor-General. 'The whole performance', wrote the historian Manning Clark,

> stank in the nostrils. Australians had once again grovelled before the English. There were Fatman politicians who hungered for a foreign title just as their wives hungered after a smile of recognition from the governor general's wife, who was said to be a most accomplished snubber, having trained her eyes to brush the cheek of those who were desperate for a smile, no matter how watery, from an English noblewoman. The snorters at all this imperial tomfoolery, and all the jingo talk about the war in South Africa, where Australian soldiers, so far from being the knights of chivalry, were burning the possessions of Boer women, had to state what they stood for. They had to say what they meant when they declared their loyalty to this Australia that was coming to be.[15]

But no one declared such a loyalty, or said what Australia was meant to be. No one stated a vision, only the fears and the deferential longing of exiles in a 'weird and wrong' place. The 'Asiatic hordes', better known as the Yellow Peril, were now a shadow of the exiles' own creation and haunted them. Worse, the Russian fleet was rumoured to be in the

Tasman Sea; and the Hun, it was said darkly, 'wanted' Australia; and what was Great Britain doing about all this?

As the new year's storm broke over the park, and the 'snubbers' and 'snorters' were drenched indiscriminately, no final, rousing declaration of independence was heard, because the last thing the assembled 'founding fathers' wanted for Australia was independence. What they wanted was Britain to be more loyal to and protective of its empire, of which Australia, according to the novelist C. H. Kirmess, 'was the precious front buckle in the white girdle of power and progress encircling the globe'. So the Earl of Hopetoun, his plumes sodden, declared the proceedings concluded with a few reassurances of imperial fidelity. It was an occasion that is today seldom celebrated in Australia, for still births seldom are.

In the Hunter Valley, a long dirt road, like many other long dirt roads in the new nation, had been named 'Hopetoun Street'. In 1906 William and Caroline decided to take their 'mob', as my mother called her family now grown to nine, north to Hopetoun Street in Kurri Kurri. William was a miner and Kurri Kurri was a pit town. With all the possessions they could carry they set out on the train to Stanford Merthyr, the nearest stop; or so they thought. It was the wrong train and it delivered the family 'somewhere in the bush', through which they walked, with their possessions, following the tracks left by jinkers and wagons until they reached their long dirt road. It was dusk and the dwellings in Hopetoun Street were mostly 'bag humpies', which were hessian bags thrown across a crude frame of tree branches; theirs was a house of weatherboard and iron. A hurricane lamp was lit and the 'mob' fell asleep on recently varnished bare boards to which the girls, with their waist-length hair and plaits, remained securely fastened until the next day.

William went to work at the Pelaw Main colliery, which had been opened in 1900 by John 'Baron' Brown, then reputedly Australia's richest man. Pelaw Main was the largest and richest mine on what were known as the South Maitland fields; apart from the Broken Hill silver-lead mines in the far west of New South Wales, nowhere else was the community based on one industry. It was said of the tumultuous meetings of miners in the Kurri Kurri stadium that you could name the pit where a man worked by his speech: the Welsh at Stanford Merthyr and Paxton, Geordies from England's Tyneside at the Hebburns, Scots at Richmond Main and native-born Australians at Pelaw Main and Abermain.

The miners' lodges supported friendly societies, libraries, Workers' Educational Associations (WEAs), Marxist study groups, hospitals and homes for widows and disabled miners, as well as providing sick pay and funeral 'benefits'. Some of the first silent pictures in Australia were shown at the Kurri Kurri miners' stadium, in the open, rain or shine, for an entry fee of threepence. And out of a pit town with hitching posts, served by bullock and dray, came music: not only music of the miners' brass bands and of the renowned pipe band of the Scots of Abermain, but also the music of eisteddfod winners and of names like Jack Gopinko, formerly of the Warsaw Conservatoire, who became one of Australia's most celebrated teachers of the violin, and Ernie Llewellyn, his pupil, who went from the Kurri Kurri District Orchestra to achieve a worldwide reputation as a violinist and become concert master of the Sydney Symphony Orchestra.

But it was also a menacing place to be. The mine shafts were steeply inclined and the seams were unusually thick, and 'winning' the quality coal was said to be more hazardous than almost anywhere in the world. According to Jim Comerford's history of the area, the coal-face in the South Greta colliery lay almost directly below the miner and 'the skip into which he had to shovel the broken coal was behind him and due to the steepness of the seam he had to throw the coal back and up'. Here, the seam was less than five feet high, which he was expected to drill and 'shoot, fill, timber and tracklay' for a daily output of between seven and eight tons.[16]

At the East Greta pit the main tunnel dipped from the surface at a perilous grade of one in three; and when roofs collapsed, which was often, the miners frequently remained entombed. In these conditions gas was the unseen menace every miner feared; a few months before William and Caroline arrived, Stanford Merthyr had 'exploded like a bomb'. The common graves in Kurri Kurri cemetery bear witness to the miners' long and painful campaign for the most basic safety measures, such as rescue stations, which were denied.

Indeed, theirs was a struggle so prolonged that during twenty-one years of strikes, lock-outs, victimisation and a bitterness described in a miners' ballad as 'like flint off the soul', there developed on the New South Wales coalfields a theatre of civil war and incipient revolution which Australia's imperial chroniclers seldom acknowledged. They preferred to romanticise the short-lived and relatively harmless stand by gold miners at Eureka in the State of Victoria in 1854. My own formal education included nothing about the uprising on the coalfields, which spanned an entire generation.

Governments, state and federal, supported mineowners like Baron Brown and the Australian Agricultural Company, and 'emergency legislation' to defeat the miners and their claims was arbitrary and commonplace. The Coalfields Employees Federation had been formed at the turn of the century; in 1909 its president was Peter Bowling, who was a member of the American-based Industrial Workers of the World (IWW) and the Australian Socialist Labour Party, and these affiliations were perceived as enough of an 'emergency' to arrest and manacle and gaol him for being part of a 'foreign plot' to overthrow 'our British way of life'. So pervasive was the threat of political victimisation that the men were forced to walk long distances into the bush to pay their union dues clandestinely to a lodge secretary and treasurer who would use a tree stump as a desk; thus, union dues became known as 'stump'.[17]

With the Press and politicians condemning the miners as 'treacherous', scabs were used to break strikes and to work in shafts where men had died. From mine to home and home to mine all along the long dirt roads, the scabs would be 'tin-kettled' by women and children. The sound was incessant: 'like the Almighty grinding his teeth', wrote one miner. At dawn and dusk, noon and midnight, the turning of shifts, it was there, an endless echo of contempt.

Caroline, my grandmother, was a strict, God-fearing and shrewd individual of English yeoman stock, who frowned on all discussion of 'politics', the euphemism for the turmoil in the mines. Her reason for this was that William had risen to mine deputy and was responsible for speeding up production in number one tunnel at Pelaw Main. He was a boss. This put the family on the other side of the barricades and 'across the tracks' and afforded them such privileges as an invitation to Baron Brown's annual picnic for his officials and their families. For this event Caroline would make her five daughters white muslin dresses with lace-edged frills, and so on the great day all eleven of the 'mob' would ride in the Baron's train on the Baron's railway line to the Baron's docks and up the Hunter River in the Baron's collier, made clean and resplendent for the occasion, accompanied by the Baron's brass band. On arrival at the Seaham picnic grounds, the wives would picnic and play games with the children and the men would go to a hotel for dinner with 'J.B.'

During the general strike of 1917 miners' lodges were prosecuted under the Master and Servants Act, a standby of owners since the industrial revolution; and an infamous magistrate, Major Crane, began imprisoning miners as if they were felons. As the bitterness deepened so did the anxiety in my mother's family when William went at all hours through empty, hostile streets to the picket line, and into the pit. As a deputy it rested with him to inspect the ventilation and to prevent gas from building up. A ring of resentment would surround him; he was isolated, abused, threatened. He was not merely a boss; worse, his humble origins now made him a scab.

It was probably only my grandfather's self-effacing and humane nature which saw him unscathed through those years. However, the 'difference' his position brought to his family was to have its own reaction on Elsie, who wore the stain of a 'scab's daughter' at school. Later she wrote, 'I

began to spend many hours in Kurri Kurri cemetery counting the
numbers of miners accidentally killed and questioning the justice of their
deaths and of the deity to whom we all prayed under my mother's
surveillance every night.'

Elsie was the only one of nine children to complete her education. Up
before dawn she would catch the train run by the South Maitland Coal
Mining Corporation to the state high school at East Maitland where she
had won a place with the first bursary ever awarded to the little primary
school at Kurri Kurri. At night she would read and study by the light of
a hurricane lamp or a candle under her bed in a room she shared with
her sisters. During weekends she would secrete herself beneath the
water tank which stood on stilts behind the house. Her books were the
first of their kind her family had seen; she was learning to be an outsider.

The 'Great War' with Germany was fed with volunteers from frontier
towns like Kurri Kurri. Elsie sold sprigs of bush wattle for pennies and
knitted balaclavas and mittens for them, as it was a young woman's
patriotic duty then to do, while at the same time she endeavoured to
shield her French-language teacher, Miss Dreher, who was German
born, from abuse and assault, especially during the first two years of
huge British losses.

'War!' intoned William Morris Hughes, then prime minister, 'prevents
us from becoming flabby. War has purged us from physical and moral
degeneracy and decay!'

'Billy' Hughes himself had never fought in a war but devoted much
of his political career to sending Australian youth to an early grave in a
quarrel which did not concern Australia. In April 1915 Australians were
slaughtered at Gallipoli and almost every family on the coalfields was
touched; my mother's cousin died in the landing at Anzac Cove and two
others were maimed. April 25 was thereafter consecrated as Anzac Day,
and every year since it has been the day when columns of old soldiers
march to cenotaphs in the morning and get drunk in the afternoon, when
the police for once are said to 'go easy on the Diggers'. This melancholy
event is the nation's unofficial national day, as if the remembrance of
the undisputed bravery of soldiers and not of the mindless battles they
were sent to fight somehow stands in for the truth that they died in the
cause of imperial Britain, and of nothing. This was the cause in which
Australians gained a form of nationhood: burning Boer farmhouses for
the Brits, detonating chinks and gooks for the Yanks.

But if Australians have died fighting other people's wars, it has not
been without resistance from the people themselves. In 1916 Billy
Hughes returned from Allied Europe concerned that, as the sacrificial
nature of the war was understood, recruiting figures would fall. He
was desperate to send a conscripted Australian force to side with the

'motherland', and in 1916 he held a plebiscite in which people were asked to vote for or against conscription.

The Press supported Hughes and awarded 'Iron Crosses' to those who said publicly they intended to vote against it. The *Sydney Morning Herald* exhorted Irish Australians: 'Remember, the Empire's greatest soldiers were born in Ireland. The Irish are a chivalrous race and the Germans have not one atom of chivalry in their composition.'[18]

In spite of these pressures of blood patriotism, most Australians voted 'no'. An undeterred Hughes tried again with another referendum the following year, when the majority against him was even greater. These were, in my own view, the first and perhaps even the finest hours of Australian democracy: a disturbing of the Australian silence.

Kurri Kurri began to welcome home its survivors. The miners' stadium was draped with banners such as 'Home is Jock the Brave'. The bands paraded; men, women and children, all of them now deeply impoverished as the general strike wore on, were celebrating their wounded diggers' spunk, not necessarily the war. Among those repatriated from the Western Front was a decorated Pelaw Main miner who had enlisted with his two sons. Before the war this miner had stood up for the rights of the union, but he responded when his employer, Baron Brown, called on 'all patriotic Australians to fight the great crusade'. And when the wounded hero returned from that same great crusade, the Baron refused him his job back.[19]

Eleven years later a conservative state government nationalised pits in order to run them with scab labour. A column of miners marched from Kurri Kurri with a pipe band at its head and was met by an armed police force known as 'The Basher Gang'. The police opened fire. Many miners were wounded, and young Norman Brown of New Greta Lodge was shot dead. As one paper announced, the 'war for freedom' was won; the miners had capitulated. Today, all the Hunter Valley pits lie abandoned.

It is ironic that the miners' only political champion of stature was elected to office five months after their defeat. He was Jack Lang, Labour premier of New South Wales, known as 'The Big Fella', after whom the main street of Kurri Kurri is named. Lang became premier during the visit to Australia of Sir Otto Niemeyer of the Bank of England, who toured like an imperial bailiff inspecting the assets. The British government was demanding payment of interest on loans at the rate of ten million pounds a year; and ignoring the soup kitchens, the misery on the coalfields and the lines of unemployed ex-servicemen who had gone to Britain's aid during the First World War, Sir Otto pronounced that Australians were living 'luxuriously' and that the interest would have to be paid and wages come down. Jack Lang saw this demand as a reminder of Australia's continuing colonial civility to Britain. In May 1932 he instructed his state government departments to stop paying money which would supply interest payments. For this, he was summarily dismissed by the appointed Governor of New South Wales, in the name of the King.

After the 1918 Armistice, Elsie left Kurri Kurri for Sydney with a scholarship for a university that was not yet completed. At a boarding house, in a street of English terraces, she met my father, Claude. He was a carpenter and joiner by trade who had also grown up on the northern coalfields and for a time in Kurri Kurri, having left school at thirteen and gone to work in the vineyards at Pokolbin, now the centre of some of the finest wine-growing in Australia.

His job was to 'tie down' the vines, for which the rate was four shillings and sixpence an acre. On his first day he had covered barely half an acre, which was disappointing because it was rumoured that one Ebenezer Mitchell had once tied two acres a day. However, a gift of his father's old watch proved the turning point; he went up to four acres in a single day and his earnings in one week exceeded five pounds, which supported his family handsomely.

Not that they had always been poor. My father's mother, Alice Blick, was the granddaughter of an English surgeon and 'squatter', who, it was said or hoped, had aristocratic links. They lived in a grand property called Belmont overlooking a panorama of vineyards and mountains. In 1854 tragedy overwhelmed the Blicks; five of them were wiped out by 'Asiatic cholera' and the family never recovered its prosperity and station in the colony. One of the surviving daughters, Sarah, was my great-grandmother, and she lived out her life in a humble and isolated house with an unmarried daughter. 'Between them', wrote my father some years later, 'they created an air of gentility and maintained it under all circumstances.' On Sundays, Florence, the daughter, would play the pianoforte and consult the big Bible about 'our ancestors' to the accompaniment of her mother's sighs, which 'somehow conveyed an impression that she had been deprived of her rightful manor house only the day before which, of course, was not the case.'

Claude's father, my grandfather, was born in Berlin. He was Richard Pilger, who read Jules Verne as a boy and decided that he, too, would chart the world. At the age of fourteen he persuaded his father to take him to Stettin, on the southern shore of the Baltic Sea, and to get him 'a good ship with decent officers and a humane captain'. From August 23, 1884, the day he sailed from Germany as a deck boy on the *Leonore*, a barque of 500 tons bound for Wilmington, North Carolina, he did not stop sailing until after he had met Alice Blick on the dockside at Newcastle, New South Wales, at which time, he wrote, he was 'a little conscious of my accent'.

With scarcely any formal education, Richard was a linguist, speaking

English, German, French and Spanish, knowing Latin and classical Greek; he was a musician, a miner, an aesthete and, above all, a sailor. When he died in 1947 among miners in Kurri Kurri he belonged to an élite of sailors known as the Cape Horners, who sailed the tallships around the Horn from east to west; that is to say, *into* the roaring forties. His first rounding of the Horn took six weeks, which he described in his chronicle of the sea, *With Folly on My Lips*. He wrote it in English, the language he loved more than his own, just as he regarded English ships and ports as his own.

'Having tasted the pleasures of Liverpool', he recalled of the 1880s, 'my stock of sovereigns became exhausted and I told Old Tom to look out for a ship for me. One Saturday night, I was in the act of lowering the semi-final one when Old Tom burst into the bar-room . . . "Do you want to ship in a four-masted barque going to Sydney?" he asked. "If you do, you'll have to go straightaway. She is lying out in the stream and the tug is waiting at the pier head. It will be a pier head jump." I said goodbye hurriedly to everyone in general and Lottie in particular, and on arrival aboard I was called aft to sign on.

'"A foreign discharge!" the skipper said somewhat contemptuously, but raised no objection . . . the men in the fo'c's'le were nearly all North Welsh, belonging mostly to Pwllheli, the captain and two mates included. Just the same the conversation was mostly in English – it was considered good manners to do so – though owing to the inflexion in their speech they seemed to me to be in a continual state of excitement.'

The ship was the *Province*, now headed for Cape Horn. 'The weather turned bleak', wrote Richard, 'as we passed Tristan da Cunha, forty-four days after leaving the Mersey. Our cargo consisted of locomotive boilers, rails, girders and other heavy stuff, and we were loaded down to the Plimsoll Mark, with the result that she swung like a pendulum and many times we thought she would roll the sticks out of herself. The "roaring forties" are a succession of westerly gales, and they lash the sea into waves reaching up to forty feet. To the helmsman looking back when the stern was in the trough, the rollers looked like mountains . . . The whole voyage, Liverpool, Sydney, San Francisco, Fleetwood, was completed in the extraordinarily fast time of eleven months and eight days.'

The voyage of the *Monrovia*, fully rigged and 1,500 tons, was very different. She sailed from Barry in Wales in 1894 with coal for Rio de Janeiro and she became a 'hell ship, a death ship'. After starvation, violence and endless storms, wrote young Richard, 'the mate came and ordered us to heave anchor. All hands refused. We'd had enough . . .

'"But men," said the mate, "this is mutiny. You are still on the high seas."

'There was no response. An ultimatum came from the captain: "Return to duty or you will be locked in and starved into submission . . .'''

Rounding Cape Horn the *Monrovia*'s crew began to die, one by one, from the 'black vomit', which was yellow fever. 'The ship was hove to', wrote Richard, 'and at the appointed time we placed the body on the bier, but the bier fell to pieces and poor Bill's sail-wrapped body plumped on deck with an awful crash. After praying under his breath for a few moments, the mate ordered us to put the body on a single plank. Carefully, we rested the plank on the rail, with the body feet first. The captain took his hat off and read the burial service. After the words, "and we commit the body to the deep", we tipped the plank upwards and the body slid off. But instead of shooting into the water like a bolt, it doubled up and then struck the water sideways. No sailor could have made a more ignominious descent to Davy Jones's locker. At that, the mate's long pent up emotions burst forth and we were treated to an unexpurgated version of a vocabulary not found in any respectable dictionary, the gist of it being that in all his seafaring life he had never seen such a rottenly conducted funeral, and his temper was such that no one dared to remind him that he had been the funeral director.'

The mate himself was to die from the fever, and burial services were suspended as bodies were thrown overboard with such frequency, wrote Richard, 'that through these wretched circumstances, the event I had dreamed of for years had actually come to pass; I was practically in command of the ship.'

In 1896, he sailed into Newcastle, New South Wales on the *Marechal Suchet*. It was a Sunday in mid-summer and he was 'at the rail with the mate looking down upon the crowd of sightseers who had gathered around the ship under a canopy of waving parasols.'

'"Aren't you going ashore?" the mate asked, to which I had just replied: "Not today, Mr Linton", when I found myself gazing into the eyes of a most attractive woman. Then I was properly startled when she repeated the mate's question: "Aren't you going ashore?"

'Quite suddenly I found I was off the ship and on the wharf by her side, to our mutual confusion. At last I managed to break an uncomfortable impasse with: "Do you like the ship?" To which she promptly answered: "Indeed and we were wondering where it has come from?"

'Freely forgiving her the "it", I said: "She hails from Liverpool in England. We are 125 days out . . . " Then, a little conscious of my accent, I added: "She's a British ship."'

Six weeks passed, and 'on the 18th February, 1897, my young bride watched our departure from her vantage point on the overhead footbridge at Honeysuckle Railway Station. With binoculars lent to her by the stationmaster, she continued to watch until, topsails set, we rounded Nobbys and passed out of sight, bound for Acapulco, Mexico.'

Alice, my long-suffering grandmother, waved goodbye many times during the years she bore his five children. One of them, Carmen Dolores, was named after another love in Costa Rica where Richard had jumped ship and lived as a fugitive. 'Ramón J. Peralto, birthplace: America' reads one of his discharge certificates. These were the 'false colours' under which he sailed, fearing retribution for his desertion, but this never came.

To be closer to his new home, he sailed on New South Wales coasters, but despised their low breeding. So finally he 'came ashore' and got a labouring job in a sulphide works which he lost at the outset of war in 1914, because he was German. He was one of Australia's first naturalised citizens, yet he and his family suffered terribly because he was considered an 'enemy within', even a 'traitor'. Smear and incipient violence became part of his and my father's lives: in school, in shops, from neighbours. Official propaganda spoke about 'the baby devouring Bosch'.

There were 33,000 German-born citizens in Australia, and many were interned. In 1917 South Australia, the state with the strongest German heritage, prohibited the teaching of German and closed forty-nine Lutheran schools. In spite of this and in spite of having lost his job, Richard took his new Australian citizenship very seriously and joined the Australian Army, which accepted him, and even offered himself for overseas service; but he was then over the age limit of forty-five.

Through a friend he got work at Pelaw Main colliery near Kurri Kurri, working the 'dog watch' from midnight to sunrise, but as the war news worsened, miners' lodges met and the English, Scots and Welsh refused to work with Germans. Richard's concern now was for his brother, sisters and their families in Germany and the privations they were suffering. He scoffed openly at the pretensions of Kaiser Wilhelm and at the Emperor's 'withered arm', a defect he said was due to the in-breeding that occurred in all royal families. His dry, satirical humour also led him to mock the stories of bizarre atrocities widely believed to have been committed by his countrymen. And for this the miners put him out.

He was forced to go 'on the road', picking up miserably paid work where he could find it, then moving on when the accident of his birthplace was revealed. He was 'down south', sewing wheatbags for a German farmer, when his own son, my father, went into the pits.

Claude had just turned fifteen; and of his first shift, he wrote:

> Through the sleeping town I walked with men,
> Who talked of the shift and the coal they had won,
> Of their sweat and their toil and what they might earn,
> With payment at so much a ton.

> One by one my companions left,
> And vanished into the fog,
> My hob-nailed boots and clanking cans,
> Disturbed a day-shift dog.

My father had 'gone on the coal' in direct defiance of Richard's wishes. 'If you go there,' he had warned, 'that's where you'll end.' Reluctantly, Alice had given her approval because the family, now isolated from the community, was hungry and becoming desperate. My father later wrote, 'As I had been brought up on accounts of the great service to the Empire of my illustrious maternal ancestors, the hostility I encountered as the son of a German sowed the seeds of a bitterness which served me ill in later years.'

Fortunately for Claude there were mass redundancies in the pits and miners were 'cavilled out' on the principle of 'last to come, first to go'. So he went; and on Richard's return the two of them went by coastal steamer to Sydney where, in the office of J. C. 'Gentleman Jack' Gardner, Engineer in Charge of the Postmaster-General's Workshops at Darling Harbour, young Claude was apprenticed as a 'junior artisan in training'. Richard returned to Kurri Kurri that same evening. With the Armistice signed, he found a somewhat moderated attitude among the miners and finally got work as a 'wheeler' at Stanford Merthyr, the 'Welsh pit'.

In Sydney Claude won a scholarship which entitled him to membership of the Mechanics' Institute library. He began to read avidly for the first time: Dumas, Dickens, Shakespeare, O'Henry, Marx. He joined the Australian Socialist Party and became a regular at the 'social, political and cultural' lectures given in the Party's rooms by the likes of Moses Baritz, then renowned music critic of the *Manchester Guardian*, who inspired in my father a lifelong devotion to the music of Richard Wagner: an appreciation, alas, I was never able to share.

At that time Elsie would smuggle Claude into the splendid new library at Sydney University, and between them grew, gently, a political conviction: his perhaps influenced by the poverty and bitterness that sprang from the anti-German assaults of his childhood, and hers by the suffering she saw on the coalfields and perhaps also as a reaction against her family's adopted Toryism.

In 1921, while Elsie was away at her studies, her family moved from the Hunter Valley south to Merewether. William, her father, had taken up a lease on a mine which had been worked by convicts and then abandoned. By tracing consecutive numbers on the 'bords' (mine compartments) he came upon candles stuck in bottles, which the convict miners had worn in their hats, and wooden skips which female convicts used to push, fully loaded, to the surface, then unload into bullock drays.

By following these relics he discovered a seam of coal which ran right along the seafront; he called it Happy Valley and went into business with his brother Fred and a local storekeeper called Mr Ralph. And they became rich.

Accordingly, they moved into a large house on a hill. It had luxuries such as the first refrigerator I ever saw, and running hot water, venetian blinds, velvet curtains and French carriage clocks, and it had cupboards of fine dresses and furs. Having acquired the secret of 'getting on', the grandchildren of the manacled gingerman McCarthy and the servant girl Mary Palmer, given a life sentence at Middlesex Gaol, set about becoming the 'Marheines of Merewether', whose respectability would be acknowledged from time to time in the 'society pages' of the Newcastle *Herald.*

In 1922 my mother came home to her family. She had written ahead to say she was bringing Claude with her, and the two of them caught a train from Sydney. At Newcastle station Elsie sensed trouble and suggested that he remain at the station while she went ahead. On the way she met her eldest brother. 'They're waiting for you,' he said. At the big house she found a family court in session. Her father greeted her, then left. 'The other faces', she wrote, 'watched me in silence; then I could hear sobs coming from the bedroom, the sound of my mother.' The disapproval was never expressed, but its source was clear: the only educated daughter had deigned to consider a Bolshie carpenter!

Elsie returned to the station and collected Claude. As it was too late to catch a train back to Sydney, they set out for Kurri Kurri and to the home of Richard, the beached seadog, and Alice. Richard greeted them warmly and a knees-up of singing and flute-playing ensued, for which my mother remains grateful today.

New South Wales then, in the 1920s, was the eastern frontier of a continent about which its white and increasingly urban population knew little. Although the railway had made some bold encroachments into 'the bush', roads were mostly unsurfaced, tortuous or non-existent; the Great Western Highway from Sydney was a ribbon of dust or mud. The state was peppered with solitary communities which had schools and urgently needed teachers; and newly qualified teachers were obliged to go anywhere they were sent: 'outback' or 'down south' or 'up north'.

Elsie was posted to Ballina, more than 500 miles from Sydney in the far north, and as the Department of Education did not consider getting her there its responsibility, she sold her books to pay the fare. The railway line ended in the middle of the night and passengers and luggage were loaded on to a truck with chains on its wheels which found a new line at the end of a bush track. At the Grafton River they were off-loaded again due to the absence of a bridge; and two days after she had left, some time before the dawn, the charabanc stopped and Elsie was told she was in Ballina. 'Sorry, Miss,' said the driver, 'your bag's been dropped off somewhere else.'

In the same clothes and flat broke, she walked into Ballina High School which, along with almost everything in the town, had not long been opened and whose principal was busily inaugurating a pub nearby. He was a man with no eyebrows or recognisable face, a victim of mustard gas on the Western Front. 'What are your subjects?' he asked Elsie, to which she replied, 'French, Latin and perhaps history and English.' 'Oh,' he said, 'then you might as well go back; I wanted a maths teacher.'

She didn't go back. There were only three other teachers in what was meant to be a secondary school. 'Show the brats you're not terrified,' one of them advised, and as so many of the brats had been up since four in the morning, attending the cows, Elsie reckoned, as she told me, that 'a show of authority came second to waking the brats up and shoving into their added bucolic brains Latin verbs, French vocab and algebra.'

After several months in Ballina Elsie received a large dishevelled paper parcel from her family. There was no note, just a bundle of her clothes. She had not been forgiven for her 'crime' which, a year later on her return to Sydney, she compounded. With ten pounds Claude had borrowed, they were married at Parramatta, not far from the white walls of the female factory where Mary Palmer had been incarcerated and had met Francis McCarthy. On her wedding day Elsie sent two one-word telegrams to her still silent family. The first, before they were married, said 'GOING'. The second, after the ceremony, said 'GONE'.

In December 1941, when I was two years old, all of Australia's fears of the Yellow Peril seemed to be coming true. In the aftermath of the Japanese attack on Pearl Harbor, the Labour Prime Minister, John Curtin, defied and enraged Winston Churchill by ordering home two Australian divisions from the Middle East. In a famous radio broadcast on December 26 Curtin said, 'We look to America.' These two actions have been often viewed by Australians as historic moments which at last set the nation on an independent path. Unfortunately, few heard John Curtin rush to qualify his bold stand. 'It is perfectly true', he said, 'that I made a direct and definite appeal to the United States of America. But let it be clearly and definitely understood that the relationships between Australia and the United States are all governed by that one supreme promise of retaining Australia as an integral part of the British Commonwealth of Nations.'

Australia was merely exchanging one protector against the Peril for another, while retaining the trappings of its imperial heritage. And when the new protector's viceroy, General Douglas MacArthur, arrived in

Melbourne, he described the new relationship succinctly. 'It is our race', he said, 'which causes us to have the same ideals and the same dreams of destiny.'[20]

On the moonlit night of March 31, 1942 the Yellow Peril arrived. Three Japanese midget submarines launched from a convoy of mother submarines entered Sydney Harbour. Each carried a crew of two, crouched in a space the size of a telephone box. One sank a ferry, killing nineteen sailors, before being hit by depth-charges. A week later, a mother submarine surfaced off Bondi Beach and fired three shells at my mother's washing. 'It's all right, Elsie,' said a friend as the shells went overhead, 'your name's not on them.' One shell landed in a neighbour's backyard and failed to explode, and the newspapers reported only one casualty: a refugee from Hitler's Germany who broke his ankle leaping out of bed.

But that was quite enough for Elsie, who gathered up my brother Graham, aged nine, and me, aged two, and headed west to a small town called Silverdale.[21] (Claude had tried to enlist but was turned down when the skills of his trade were requisitioned by the Government.) Those were days of much anxiety in Australia, with the 'Japs' about to 'come down' as if by the force of gravity. Japanese planes struck at Darwin in the Northern Territory and in fifty-nine raids flattened most of the town. Stories of panic and looting were suppressed, but people heard about them, as they were to hear about a break-out at a Japanese prisoner-of-war camp at Cowra, New South Wales, where most of the 234 men who had escaped were shot in cold blood.

It was decided, though not spelt out, that half the country would be sacrificed, that an imaginary Maginot Line of resistance would be drawn west from Brisbane. Herds of cattle were driven inland, there was food rationing and the great Australian unthinkable became law: the brewing of beer was restricted.

So it was not a propitious time for Richard to write to Hildegarde, his niece in America. She was a naturalised American employed in Washington as a German code-breaker for the US Army, work for which she was later decorated. Richard's letter to her, written, as he sometimes wrote, in Spanish, was intercepted by the Australian security services. In the letter he expressed a few harmless sentiments about their German family ties, but in doing so he unwittingly breached the censorship laws and was charged under the War Precautions Act. He was convicted and fined. Two Members of Parliament intervened and the fine was eventually remitted, but the conviction stood. And once again, he was ostracised; he lost his job as secretary-manager of the Kurri Kurri School of Arts, and this blow was followed by the loss of his place in his beloved Kurri Kurri Orchestra which, shortly before the war, and under his enthusiastic guidance, had come down to the City of Sydney Eisteddfod and won the championship for amateur orchestras.

The affair got into the newspapers, and in Silverdale my brother Graham was attacked with stones at his primary school and the kind of anti-German abuse his father and grandfather had had to endure during the First World War. Graham bore the terror of the episode stoically but left Elsie in no doubt that he would never go back to that school. So, Yellow Peril or no, we returned to Bondi, where Richard would come to stay and take Graham to hear music and me to gaze at big and little boats, under steam and sail on Sydney Harbour.

At home in Kurri Kurri the old sailor would emerge every morning to check the mercury in the thermometer and the wind on the vane, and watch in mock-imperious silence as Alice talked at the ducks and the cockatoo in its cage. As he got older he seemed to grow more restless, even while struggling against illness. When the war was not long over, he died from cancer. Claude recovered his father's sea chest and spent many devoted hours restoring its cedar finish and repairing the secret locking devices on its labyrinth of drawers. It is now on display in a maritime museum in Newcastle, New South Wales, just down the road from Kurri Kurri, a reminder of one remarkable 'Ramón J. Peralto'.

2

A new Britannia

I grew up in a time known by my Australian generation as the Menzies
Years. They were the 1950s and Robert Gordon Menzies was prime
minister during all of that decade and most of the next, until he was
finally and appropriately elevated to Lord Warden of the Cinque Ports
in his beloved England. Oddly enough, for a society proud of its disdain
for politicians and its irreverent wit, neither was ever really applied to
Menzies; for he was Our Better, the kind of puffed-up authoritarian
figure many Australians secretly admired, and still do. He was our
Statesman, the Queen's Man, who could be trusted not to adjust his
groin or pick his nose in the company of Her Majesty and at those
councils of the world that demanded his presence, which were few.

'Standing at last on Australian soil,' said a young Queen Elizabeth in
1954, 'I want to tell you how happy I am to be amongst you.' (She was
standing at the spot where Francis McCarthy and Mary Palmer and
other riff-raff had been mustered in chains.) Beside her stood the
bell-shaped, florid-faced figure of R. G. Menzies, a name, incredibly,
still bereft of imperial adornments. It was during another of her numerous
Menzies-inspired trips to Australia that the Queen was seen on national
television struggling to control an expression of hilarity after Menzies
had turned to her and said, 'In the words of the old seventeenth-century
poet who wrote those famous words, "I did but see her passing by and
yet I love her till I die".'

Because so much was taken for granted in Australia then, few of us
knew that Menzies was selling off our post-war industries to great
foreign-based companies: the motor industry in its entirety, oil refineries,
minerals. Few of us knew he had conspired with the British to explode
nuclear weapons on our soil, to kill and maim and poison our environment. Few of us knew he was not at all a 'brilliant man' or even a 'great

orator' but a rather petulant, insecure and ruthless figure who smeared and ruined his victims, notably Herbert Vere Evatt, the opposition leader, with bogus allegations at the time of the defection of the Soviet 'spy', Vladimir Petrov. Indeed, in our innocence, we hardly knew that during the 1930s Menzies had regarded Hitler as an inspired leader from whom the democracies had much to learn and whose misdeeds, especially his discrimination against the Jews, had been exaggerated.

By 1961 Menzies felt so assured of his political infallibility that he talked openly of 'one total policy for Australia' – i.e. a one party state. More than any Australian leader, he distorted our image of the world. To him, Asia, our closest neighbour, was merely a great shadow over which one flew with maximum inconvenience on one's aerial progress to London. It was Menzies who, in 1959, re-introduced conscription by playing on fears of an Indonesian threat, which did not exist but which led to secret arrangements with Washington for a conscripted Australian army to join the American assault on Vietnam.

We knew little about any of this because dissenting views had no powerful and persuasive public voice, and the self-image of our society as a second-hand England, a gathering place of 'exiles', was so engraved on all of us that obsequiousness to another people's past and myths was a way of life. How many times as a child was I made to recite the lines, written in 1823, of William Charles Wentworth:

> And, oh, Britannia shouldst thou cease to ride
> Despotic Empress of old Ocean's tide –
> . . . May all thy glories in another sphere
> Relume, and shine more brightly still than here;
> May this, thy last-born infant then arise;
> To glad thy heart, and greet thy parent eyes;
> And Australasia float, with flag unfurled,
> A New Britannia in another world!

At school we sang imperial hymns, celebrated 'Empire Day' on May 24 and were taught a history whose focus was a small cluster of islands on the other side of the planet, a history which terminated with the glories of an imperial victory over Germany and her allies in 1918; events beyond that, as the twentieth century unfolded and the Empire dissolved and most of the world emerged, were not considered history. Australia's own story, especially what was done to the Aborigines, a story in contemporary terms even more rapacious than that of the United States, was frequently dismissed as a joke. Certainly, it was not to be studied for serious purposes such as elevation to higher education.

During the Menzies Years people were admired for their 'English reserve'. This mysterious quality was equated with respectability and therefore cultivated. Menzies was said to have it because he spoke like an English Home Counties Tory, an affectation he would top up during his pilgrimages 'home'. Voices employed by the Australian Broadcasting Commission were widely thought to have it; indeed, a friend of mine took elocution lessons before applying for a job in the ABC Talks Department, but they did him no good. 'You really should go to London for a year or two,' he was advised.

The 'English reserve' was all embracing. Prim houses with red tiled roofs were built with as much sympathy for the Australian climate as igloos, and their male occupants were bound by sartorial conventions which included the wearing of double-breasted serge suits during the long, hot and humid summers. A subtle feature of this mien was the repression of feelings, no matter that your own forebears might have been a volatile bunch or that Australia's sun and light and absence of insurmountable class barriers elsewhere produced a natural informality. In spite of this, a veneer of formality was spread over the most informal of people; and in upholding this fake propriety and avoiding embarrassment at all costs, you did not speak much about religion, race, 'domestic matters', sex or politics. But as this attitude was thoroughly Victorian and hypocrisy was built into it, you spoke of all these things on the sly.

Fortunately the stricture against politics did not apply in my family as both my parents were, and are, Australian socialists, although I instinctively balk at tagging them as such: the word 'socialist', even in its most tepid form, was the great unspeakable in Australia. While teaching at a small private school in Sydney, my mother, then in her twenties, was summoned before the headmistress, who brandished a Labour Party paper she had found in her locker. The headmistress, whose name was Mrs Hunt, harangued Elsie for 'trying to implant *these* ideas in my darlings'. 'Your darlings', replied Elsie holding her breath, 'have not been implanted, because the implanting of any ideas in them would be tantamount to a miracle. Can I have my newspaper back please?'

In 1951, when Menzies tried to outlaw the Australian Communist Party by means of a referendum, and failed, though only just, many people stopped calling themselves socialists in public. Smears became commonplace; Federal Government advertisements 'named' Labour Party stalwarts and trade unionists as 'concealed socialists', which was the euphemism for communists and fellow-travellers. Many of those 'named' were of the most conservative persuasion in the Labour movement, but they and others were silenced or destroyed by a McCarthyite campaign which, though marginally less vociferous than the American original, was as effective in its impact on free speech.

Socialism in Australia had very different roots than in Europe and bore, ironically, a legacy as inglorious as any movement on the right. A main plank of the Australian Labour Party was racism, as expressed through the 'White Australia Policy' and by William Morris Hughes in the first Parliament: 'There is no compromise about it. The industrious coloured brother has to go, and remain away!' Genuine Australian radicalism, without the closed logic of any fear or prejudice, flowed from experience and conditions, rather than from theory or intellectual fashion, which is not in any way to deny its intellectual dimension. During the depressions of the 1890s and 1930s there emerged, among the wool shearers, for example, a peculiarly Australian code of all-for-one-and-one-for-all in the face of mean and frequently thuggish employers.

This has been romanticised as 'mateship' and also derided as such; but an undoubted truth remains that the radical strain in Australian life, of which there is no equivalent in the other immigrants' democracy, the United States, has helped to make decent large sections of Australian life. Australian women were granted the right to vote well before their sisters in Europe or the United States, or indeed anywhere except New Zealand; the first basic wage and child benefit schemes were Australian; the first legislation providing paid sick and long-service leave was enacted in New South Wales. In 1931 the New South Wales Labour Government of Jack Lang, one of Australia's greatest radicals, prepared legislation which included the world's first equal pay for men and women. Like the Whitlam Labour Government forty-four years later, the Lang Government was dismissed by a British viceroy: in Lang's case it was the viceregal Governor of New South Wales, 'King George's Man'.

During the Menzies Years my family lived in what was known as a 'bull-nosed' house, which meant that its corrugated-iron roof hung over the terrace front, apparently like a bull's nose. It was not untypical of Bondi houses; it was small, cramped and dark and the front door opened into the main bedroom until my father erected a plywood screen. This created a sort of passage into the 'lounge room', which was so confined that communal 'lounging' was usually difficult, although there was a precious corner where I would wedge myself and listen to the likes of 'The Search for the Golden Boomerang' and Jack Davey's 'Give It a Go'; Australian radio, then among the world's finest, held many riches for us kids.

On the other side of the lounge room stood an ornate, four-legged gramophone on which my father and brother would play 78 rpm recordings of the works of Wagner and other classical composers with all accompanying solemnity. This would be relieved occasionally by jolly Gilbert and Sullivan, for which silence was not obligatory. Indeed, those who knew the words could sing along while taking care not to get too excited. My father could play the clarinet, my brother the recorder, and I the fool; so a certain balance of talents was achieved.

On Boxing Day 1948 a hailstorm arrived with such ferocity that our bull-nosed abode seemed to be under direct attack from the Peril again, this time with cricket balls. The windows were smashed and the noise of the hail on the tin roof was truly deafening. When the worst had passed, the gramophone was wound up and the fury of the heavens was answered with a ground bombardment of Wagner's *Flying Dutchman*. The customary solemnity was suspended after news had arrived that our 'dunny' at the end of the yard, which normally had a leeward list, was in mortal danger, having been struck by lightning – fortunately while unoccupied.

On Christmas Eve that year the temperature passed 110° Fahrenheit and a side of ham, which my father had won in a raffle, 'went off' in the bath; and on Christmas Day an emu egg, a prized possession the size and shape of a rugby football, exploded in the china cabinet. The smell resulting from both calamities proved a powerful deterrent to a full enjoyment of the festive season. Also, in the run up to these unforeseen Christmas calamities, the annual chook spectacular had taken place. A chook had been decapitated in the next-door neighbour's yard, watched by us kids, then its headless form had engaged in a grand prix with its executioner. No adult ever offered me a satisfactory explanation of this amazing event, and I am still waiting for one.

Our street was Moore Street and a commonwealth of silence guarded it and streets like it. One of our neighbours was a white-haired, cherub-faced old lady whose lover had been killed at Gallipoli and who had retired behind lace curtains to grieve for half a century. We seldom saw her, and after she died her house was left untouched, moribund, the creepers in her window baskets reclaiming her little porch. Old, worried faces peaking from behind lace curtains are as Australian as rubber sandals and zinc cream.

I had a friend then whose father had come home from the horror of fighting the Japanese in New Guinea. This man was for me an object of awe; he weighed barely seven stone, he shook with malaria and was frequently demented. The family had a dilapidated flat on the side of the hill and was very poor; and the ex-soldier would sit in a cane chair, reading comics and boozing and staring at the window and the ocean beyond, and now and then scything the air with the ceremonial sword of a Japanese officer he had killed; or so my friend said, trying hard to be proud of a father he never really knew.

'Giddaymeoldmate,' the soldier would slur to his son, and say not much else. I occasionally saw a woman, who seemed always red-eyed and oblivious to her surroundings. She was my friend's mother.

Outside in the street, we would play a game called 'Aussies and Japs' and hurl lumps of blue metal from the street at each other, until we were shooed by a woman we knew only as 'the reffo' or 'the old Jew'. It was said that most of her family in Poland had been exterminated; but in Moore Street that sort of thing was seldom discussed, for it was incomprehensible.

Then, without warning, the silence would snap and reactions were difficult for everyone. Another friend was Wally, whose father either had been 'killed by the Japs' or was somewhere else. His house was also small and kept dark by wartime 'black-out blinds' which had not been taken down. Wally's mother was a tiny and very kind woman who fussed over her son and welcomed as many of his friends as could fit into their small dirt yard. She had several part-time jobs, and was away a great deal. The same smell of poverty permeated their house, too, with its floors only partially covered by cracked, curling linoleum. As we played she would stand in the doorway watching us, smiling weakly, frowning, gazing at Wally, whom, it was clear, she worried about. Late one night she came home to find that Wally had got a gun, put it in his mouth and blown his head off.

Saturday was the day many of the adult males of Moore Street vanished. My father had become an accomplished tennis player, playing A-Grade competition and once against the great Jack Crawford, the Wimbledon champion. Others went to the races at Randwick or to The Hill at the Cricket Ground, or in winter to the Rugby League, or in all seasons direct to the 'Royal' and the 'Tea Gardens' and 'Billy the Pig's' or their Returned Soldiers' League club. I would watch them go on the 'toastrack' trams, which I 'scaled' illegally to sell the early editions of the evening papers. 'Hereyar, Sunormirror,' I'd yell, 'all the starters and riders or somethingtasiton.'

On a summer's Saturday I would walk down the steep hill of Moore Street, over patches of fresh tar that turned to hot putty in the heat and stuck to my bare feet, through crooked streets and alleys of rusted iron fences, beyond which were 'Bondi semis', faithful copies of the back-to-backs of the north-east of England. The comparison stopped there. Nowhere else was the reflected light so bright it hurt, leaving the eyes with a permanent squint, which became engrained in the Australian face. Nowhere else was the air laced with such an intoxicating fragrance, which was the spray off the South Pacific. And at every turn on the track 'down to the beach' was the impenetrable green of the greatest ocean, caught between red roofs and piles of Aussie Gothic which were pre-war flats and faded posh. All of this was a prop to my precarious happiness then.

I am an inveterate swimmer and I learned to swim when I was very young. A neighbour in Moore Street, Reg Clark, a courtly, few-words man who was a Bondi 'iceberger' and swam in every season, took me with him and made me kick hard through the wash of thirty-foot waves which broke over Bondi Baths during the 'king' tides of Christmas. Racing was not fun at the age of eleven, because winning was too important, although when I managed a close second to Murray Rose, the future Olympic gold medallist, I imagined myself before adoring throngs at the next Olympiad, which was in Finland, wherever that was. What *was* fun was diving into the fist of a wave as it raced towards rocks beside the baths. The trick was to let the wave hurl you along, then cheat it by grabbing a safety rope a dozen feet from the cliffs. Somehow, by taking this risk, I thought I was learning courage; what I was really learning was fear.

'Forget Gallipoli, the Outback and the Aussie battler and other tedious wowser myths from our Anglo-Irish past', wrote Peter Blazey in one memorable piece in the *Australian*. 'The essence of being Australian is, regrettably, doing something much more sensual. It is to lie on warm sand under a carcinogenic sun watching other bodies walking or lying and then to ritually cleanse yourself in the ocean. To Australians, the beach is as holy as the Ganges is to the Hindu. Schoolchildren know this: that is why in summer they sit paralysed at their desks dreaming of Broadbeach, Burleigh Heads, Bondi . . .'[22]

The 'English reserve' *never* applied on the beach. In a monthly journal called *Lone Hand*, one Egbert T. Russell wrote in 1910 that 'one of the strangest features of Sydney surf bathing to the stranger . . . is the casualness of the sexes on the beaches. They are partially naked, but not so unashamed as to notice the fact.'[23]

From an early age I was aware that what happened on and around the beach was a threat to the custodians of civic virtue in Australia and was therefore pleasure. 'Most people have their first sexual encounter on or near a beach', wrote Robert Drewe in his book *The Bodysurfers*.[24] How he researched this he did not say, but I have no doubt he spoke the truth. No matter the serge suits and the dark houses and the Christian 'wowser' Sundays modelled on the Armistice silence, the lascivious Aussie beach was and is a source of good life not known in Europe. In a nation constipated by over-government, Australian egalitarianism is to be found 'on the beach'. And if that is an Australian cliché, so be it; it is true.

When the first Calabrians and Sicilians arrived in the early 1950s, stick thin and as white as ice, I would watch them 'unfold' on the beach, starting with a spectacular lemming-like dash into the Pacific Ocean, unafraid of the surf and the currents and the sharks. They would be duly and cheerfully swept away, then rescued with a large trawling net.

The same ritual would be observed by the Greeks, Lebanese, Turks, English, Chileans and Chinese, as if their immigrants' journey was only complete once they had baptised themselves in the surf of an Australian beach, having taken care to bring with them the necessary burnt offerings: an Esky (portable fridge), a tube of zinc cream, a kid and a gran.

The hero of Bondi Beach during my boyhood was Jack Platt the shark fisherman. Jack owned a dinghy called *Never Fail* in which he and his brother Bill went 'tiger baiting'. During a sweltering overcast day on January 17, 1952 word spread that Jack was fighting a fourteen-foot tiger shark off Ben Buckler rocks; and, as the Sydney *Sun* reported, 'hundreds lined the rocks . . . to watch the monsters struggle . . . Many women screamed when one lunge by the shark almost dragged Jack Platt into the water. Platt recovered his balance and with a wide grin, waved to the crowd.' I was on the beach when Jack dragged his catch up on to the sand, cocked his army slouch hat, leaned on the fin and squinted for press photographers. 'Here y'are, kids,' said Jack and we were each given a lump of the 'monster'. The jawbone and teeth were Jack's prize. He and Bill had a wall full of them in the shed where they kept *Never Fail*.[25]

At the Bondi Road Hoyts Picture Show – long gone like so much fine art deco in Australia – the Saturday matinée provided the pre-pubescent Menzies generation with John Wayne, Randolph Scott, Walt Disney, the Three Stooges and Ronald Reagan. Except for a rare and woefully self-conscious Australian film, usually with the antipodean John Wayne, Chips Rafferty, in the starring role, or an American imported to play an Australian, there were no cinema images of ourselves as we were, there was no mirror to hold up to ourselves, no trove of celluloid fantasy and heroes, as if the society was either bereft or unworthy of them, or both. I cannot think of another modern 'western' society which so deprived itself for so long.

On Saturday evenings, having just seen Ronald Reagan have his legs maliciously amputated in *King's Row* or John Wayne single-handedly win the Second World War, in which a token Australian soldier might pop up like a demented Cockney, I would sit on our 'gasbox', where the meter was kept and redback spiders lived, and try to imagine those other places on which life in Australia was meant to be based. This was often difficult because the distance on the map in my mind to those other places was incomprehensible; they could have been on another planet. And these reflections would be diverted by the weekly parade of the vanished Saturday men coming home, florid or sunburnt and with an uncertain lope, a brace of long-nosed Resch's 'Dinner Ale' under one arm and a raffled chook under the other: the latter a peace offering or 'something for tea'.

At Wellington Street School one of my teachers had an Adam's apple which worked like a barometer. When an attack of 'the mustard gases' was coming on, it would shoot up to his chin and appear to try to get out through his mouth. As a spectacle it ranked with Gary the Greek's playground performance with his double joints. The first moments of the Monday lesson would be given over to my teacher's mustard gas fit, which left him retching and finally hanging his head out the window. He was a truly morose figure haunted by war, from which he still suffered, and by the Peril, whose fiendish image he had plastered on the classroom wall. This was a wartime propaganda poster of an Asiatic devil whose skin was deepest yellow and had plastered across it: 'The gun is at YOUR head. THEY are coming!'

So obsessive were my teacher's fears that on rainy sports days he would show us flickering Japanese atrocity films, which included explicit scenes of babies being impaled on bayonets and Allied prisoners-of-war being decapitated; and they remain today indelible memories. He much admired the Australian 'bush poets', Henry Lawson and C. J. Dennis, both of whom had expressed powerful feelings about the Peril. So when his retching had stopped he would call us to order and begin by reciting something of Lawson's, usually this:

> Beware of the East, O Christian
> For the sake of your fairest and best.
> It is written and written, remember,
> That the tide of invasion goes west,
> You builded a wall, O China!
> To keep your enemies out,
> You builded a wall, O China!
> Let them see that it keeps you *in*!

With his emotions now primed, he would then let forth with C. J. Dennis's:

> Fellers of Australier!
> Cobbers, chaps an' mates!
> Hear the enemy
> Kickin' at the gates . . .

And of course we all knew who the enemy was. His assemblies on Armistice Day, Anzac Day and the King's Birthday were reverential in the extreme. '*Lest we forget!*' he would bellow. '*Amen!*' For all his paranoia, he seemed a soft-hearted man and he never struck anybody, which was unusual then.

On polling days in Bondi Joe Fitzgerald's moon face would look down from telegraph poles. Joe was a dinosaur of the Australian Labour Party and our member in the Federal Parliament. 'She'll be right' was Joe's broad-based message from the steps of the School of Arts, where, as their political bishop, he would pat pensioners on the head. Nobody knew a great deal about what Joe did between elections, but he was a 'good bloke' and he was Irish, and that was enough.

Polling day was the day when the 'tykes' (Catholics) would make a rare crossing of Wellington Street, *en masse*, from 'their' side to 'ours'. On their side were St Patrick's Church, Convent and School; on our side was Wellington Street School, a state institution to which Catholic children would be sent only on pain of purgatory. It was, however, where you went to vote for Joe, who was a good Irish and, more importantly, a 'good Catholic' politician. Bondi certainly was not Belfast, but a 'mixed marriage' did not mean white marrying black; it meant the even more improbable arrangement of a 'tyke' wedded to a 'protty'. 'Where on earth', people would say, in the unusual circumstance of such a union, 'will they send the kiddies?'

Over the hill, in places with faintly effete names like Bellevue Hill and Vaucluse, lived Menzies People. They were not really 'better', it was said in Moore Street, 'just better off'. These people would work assiduously at contriving an 'English reserve', often with hilarious results. The Australian accent, bless its Irish/English rawness, has little tolerance for rounded vowels, but there were those over the hill who tried so hard to round theirs that what came out was: 'GiddayHOWareYOOO'. They would also make excessive use of the word 'actually', pronounced 'exshooly', because it was widely believed over there that the English themselves much preferred this word. They would also try their best not to describe jam as 'flybog' and a shop assistant at David Jones's department store as a 'counter jumper' and a little person as a 'shrimp' and good as 'bewdy' or 'bottler', and the truth as 'dinkum oil'. Over there, getting your face in the *Women's Weekly*, among the blooming pictures of rhododendrons, royalty, raspberry fool and 'personalities from overseas' was not quite the same as an MBE, but almost. Voting for Menzies was much more an article of this snobbery than it was 'political'.

My own family's difficult times were seldom admitted. Elsie, my mother, had given up teaching and there were 'domestic considerations', notably the demise of the relationship between her and Claude, which we knew about, worried about but did not talk about. Her brilliance at classics had no application on the factory assembly lines on which she went to work, making things from model aeroplanes to fake-leather handbags. However, it was work she said she enjoyed because of the friendships she made. She also became a 'house help' to a doctor and his children and, as a further supplement, she took in washing and ironing.

Every year an invitation would arrive for her to attend the reunion of her former pupils at her last school, where she had been revered, but she would put this aside and seldom reply. My father was travelling a lot then; his job was to inspect and advise on post office installations in the western Outback of New South Wales. He would leave with a canvas water-bag strapped to the front bumper bar of his Vauxhall, and each trip, often a minor epic across unsurfaced roads, sometimes on the rim of bushfire and flood, gave him the freedom he cherished.

Elsie had resumed contact with her own family. The Happy Valley Mining Company had made them wealthy and provided a contrast with her own way of life. One of the company principals was her eldest sister May, who now and then would come down to our house in Bondi, but not to stay; we would inspect the diamonds on her fingers and she would take Elsie to lunch at the Australia Hotel. At Eastertime I would be sent for holidays with my cousins, and it was during one of these that an uncle took me down into one of the Happy Valley pits.

'Don't speak to anyone,' he whispered.

'Why?' I whispered back.

'They're all communists,' he replied.

'What's a communist?' I asked.

He put a finger to his lips, then ran it across my throat.

I used to go secretly to LaPerouse, a bleak beach south of Bondi, on the edge of Botany Bay, to play in the forbidden territory of the dunes and to glimpse the strange people who lived there in shacks. The explorer Count de la Perouse had put in to Botany Bay in 1788, only to find the British had claimed it as their own. Such an elegant name, LaPerouse, for a little sideshow of degradation, just down the road from the new crescents of brick veneer and garden gnomes and Sunday sprinklers.

'Man in Australia', explained the *Encyclopaedia Britannica*, 'is an animal of prey; and more ferocious than the lynx, the leopard, or the hyena, he devours his own species . . .'[26] Other works of reference invariably included the opinion of William Dampier, the seventeenth-century English privateer and the first Englishman to sight Australia. The native people of the Great South Land, he noted, 'are the lowest specimens of the human race'.[27]

I would sit on the sand ridge above the Aboriginal 'reserve' at LaPerouse and look at the people standing in the doorways of their rude shelters, made from hessian and iron, fruit boxes and asbestos sheets. There were no paved paths and water ran from communal taps only. The men wore cowboy hats, the women outsized floral cotton dresses. The children would stand stone still when they saw me, and we would inspect each other across an infinity. There was a phantom quality about the Aborigines, which was confirmed by the Australian Constitution. 'In reckoning the numbers of the people of the Common-wealth', ruled Section 127, 'the Aboriginal Natives shall not be counted.'

Outside LePerouse I had seen only one of them. He was a 'half-caste', which was said with a sneer, and he played Australian Country and Western songs on a twelve-string guitar in the great urinal that was the public bar at 'Billy the Pig's' at Bondi Junction. The drinkers seemed kind to him, shouting things like 'Give the poor old boong a fair go', and in return he was effusive in his thanks for the few shillings in his hat; his eyes, however, were opaque and not at all grateful.

The children at LaPerouse had eyes like that, eyes that appeared to be stuck together and had flies on the lids. 'Ain't they dirty, those Abos?' a friend of mine would say, and I would agree. The word 'trachoma' was not used then, but it blinded many of them. I heard about it some years later in Africa, where there is a lot of it, and it occurred to me then where I had seen it first. The children at whom I stared would die from other preventable diseases, like pneumonia and gastro-enteritis. But I knew nothing about that, only the 'fact', which no one challenged, that they were 'dying off anyway'.

During the Great Depression Claude and an unemployed friend had built a house in three weeks, from foundation to finish, on the beach at Patonga, which was literally a one-horse speck on the great Hawkesbury River, north of Sydney. The material for the house came from a Sydney racing stable for which he paid seven pounds. Because it was then not possible to go overland to Patonga the stable was sent by steamer, and when it finally reached its destination it was dumped on the beach and bits of it floated in the bay. These were retrieved with the help of old Mr Hickey, the man who owned the one horse, and a cart with wide iron tyres permitting travel over wet sand at low tide. For a shilling a load old Mr Hickey agreed to take the stable to the far end of the beach where, after countless shilling-a-time trips, it became my first vantage point of an Australia I had never imagined.

Patonga's isolation was Australia's. The sky was greater here, the Southern Cross brighter, the silhouette of hills and of great, misshapen rocks sharper and the silence both wondrous and forbidding. Shortly after a winter's dawn my brother Graham and I would run on sand so hard and cold that the padding of our feet would echo. The river was like a still sea and the parental reason for our not venturing far into it was the danger of sharks, but there was more to it than that; it ran to a depth no one quite knew and, like Patonga itself, held secrets.

The human silence at Patonga had been inflicted, but we never knew about that. Somebody had lived here, at some time, but no one talked about it. In fact, an entire nation had lived around Patonga only a century and a half earlier; the Dhurag, a unique linguistic group of Aboriginal people, had lived in a forty-mile radius of Sydney and all along the banks of the Hawkesbury. When the first white settlers established the town of Windsor to the south-west, on Dhurag land, an epic war began. This war is not recorded in the imperial chronicle of Australia; growing up on one of its principal battlefields, I knew nothing about it. 'The Dhurag', wrote David Denholm in his 1979 history, *The Colonial Australians*, 'resisted the Hawkesbury River settlers for twenty-two years and inflicted on the Hawkesbury settlers a casualty rate similar to that sustained by the Australian armed forces in World War II, about one in thirty four.'[28] As David Denholm explained, the war on the Hawkesbury River was really a contest between Great Britain and a nation which, outnumbered and without guns, went down fighting to the last man, woman and child. In a land of cenotaphs, not one stands for those who fought and fell in their own country.

Sydney High, where I spent most of my adolescence, was an anomaly among schools. It was a member of the 'Great Public Schools' of New South Wales, 'public' being the euphemism borrowed from the English system to describe a private school. The GPS was an élite formed to represent the pillars of New Britannia: the Church of England, the Presbyterian Church, the Roman Catholic Church, the squattocracy, the merchant class and the state, also known as the 'public arena'. All but one of the eight schools sought to copy the likes of Harrow and Rugby and included The King's School, which dressed its boys in uniforms that were part Student Prince and part Light Brigade and were topped by a Boer War-style slouch hat. Many of The King's boys were the sons of wealthy squatters, and at cricket and rugby matches both boys and old boys would shout 'UP *School!'*

The odd one out was Sydney High, which represented the state and was the only truly public school: a fact acknowledged by the public at large, who regarded it as their own and would support it in one of the most competitive and gruelling confrontations of the sporting year: the GPS Head of the River rowing championship. This was an eights race over a mile and a half on the Nepean River which, if it was not running in full flood, was inclined to be as 'dead' as a swamp. To be able to win this race, rowing up to forty strokes a minute, the crews had to train twice a day for up to half the year; and to win it became my clear ambition. It was an ambition which negated, unfortunately or not, most attempts to instil into me the kind of classical education which included the pubescent force-feeding of Shakespeare's *The Tempest*.

Rowing is an exceptional sport, with an elusive combination of factors that makes its devotees go out at night to sweat on oil-slicked rivers.

Sustained grace with power are two of them: the grace of a rhythmical body poised a few inches above the water, driving a pivotal oar so that its 'blade' is just covered by the water, which builds enough pressure to release it. My brother Graham, a superior oarsman, had the style and power I longed to emulate.

For me, the pain required to reach this beatific state was considerable. During one week my body erupted with so many boils that I made the sports pages, under the headline 'CREW HIT BY RECORD BOILS'. The palms of our hands were covered with blisters which would seep and burst and become lifelong calluses. At the end of a twenty-mile row, there was a point past which I would feel a state of disembodiment. Rowing in the dark, when the hard work was done, I would become mesmerised by the phosphorescent explosions of all eight oars striking the water in unison; and this was enhanced one night when a thirteen-foot Grey Nurse shark surfaced beneath us, split the plywood shell and displayed its fin, lit by the phosphorescent glow, within a rigger's reach of our listing craft.

During the years of rowing at Sydney High, I think I learned something about the fragile ways of human beings and about friendship, for ours was the most egalitarian group I have known. Some had already come a long way; Mick Bindley, a No. 2 oarsman whose big heart drove the skinniest of frames, had a background of real sacrifice, and there were many like him in a school representing the 'public arena'. In that respect, we were Australia in microcosm.

In 1957, before a crowd of 50,000 and after a boil- and blister-bursting duel with the blackshirts of Sydney Grammar, we won that damn race. Twenty-seven years later we all met again, and I understood then the meaning of group loyalty and our particular friendship. Brave, skinny Mick had gone into the army and fought and survived in Vietnam while unfailingly standing up for the published views of a friend (me) who had gone to the same war, but in a wholly different capacity.

'Waddyameanyafellasleep?'

Lou D'Alpuget may well have been all dough inside, but from the outside, at that moment, he looked to me like Tyrannosaurus Rex. I had been brought before Big Lou at the end of my shift in the 'police rounds' room of the Sydney *Sun*. I was a seventeen-year-old copy boy and he was the news editor. I had not met a news editor before.

'Howlongyabeenear?' he enquired, bellowing.

'A week,' I replied, terrified.

'You were meant to listen to *everything* on the police radio. Do you know what we've missed because of *you*?'

He produced a first edition of the rival Sydney *Mirror*, whose front page was given over to a picture of what seemed to be a naked body squashed on rocks at a favourite suicide spot called The Gap. The body's flight path was dotted and its landing was arrowed. The headline read: 'CIB PROBE MODEL'S FATAL GAP FLING.'

'*That's* what we missed!' shouted Big Lou.

I passed out.

When I came to, level with Lou's suede shoes, which all news editors wore then, I could hear a voice saying, 'Hey Lou, maybe he's got a weak heart or something. Maybe you've killed him.'

I had entered journalism.

At eighteen I transferred to the Sydney *Daily Telegraph* as a first-year cadet journalist. Australia has an excellent system for training journalists called a cadetship, which is an indentured four-year apprenticeship obliging newspapers to train a quota of cadets, then to hire them as qualified journalists. During my training I went on almost every kind of assignment, wrote features, laid out pages, sub-edited and worked in the composing room. It was one of the happiest periods of my working life.

The *Telegraph* was owned by Sir Frank Packer, former Australian amateur heavyweight champion and one of those newspaper proprietors known as the 'wild men of Sydney'.[29] He was also Menzies's most powerful press patron and, accordingly, the *Telegraph* was extremely right-wing. However, many of its journalists were vociferous supporters and members of the Labour Party; it seemed that writing one thing and believing another was the way the system worked, and to do otherwise was to risk not working at all.

This apparent contradiction, which I soon discovered was universal, left an impression on me. For one thing, it helped to explain why so many young journalists assumed a fake cynicism towards their craft, their readers and themselves. By affecting this cynicism you ordained yourself a 'seasoned' journalist and outfitted yourself in the armoury of the instant 'hack': a description some journalists seem to delight in using, perhaps having long immunised themselves against its true meaning. A veteran once advised me, 'Be sceptical about everything, except what you're told to do.' This philosophy was illustrated by a story told about another of Sydney's wild men, Ezra Norton, owner of the *Daily Mirror*. 'You see, gentlemen,' said Ezra to his assembled executives, 'what I want is less culture and more cunt!' He got it.

In my second week at the *Daily Telegraph* I was assigned to report on the Bees of Bankstown.

For several days the bees had been nesting on the windscreen of a car which was parked in the main shopping street of Bankstown, a suburb of Sydney. The owner of the car was becoming restive; and while the bees were not dropping off, business was. So the police had summoned an apiarist, who was at work in his anti-sting shroud when I arrived. Guided by terror, I forged through the crowd and approached the apiarist. 'Excuse me,' I said, opening my brand-new notebook, 'I'm from the *Daily* . . .' At that, a bee stung me between the eyes.

Endeavouring to pursue the interview while the apiarist beneath his net was trying to spell his Polish name and suggest that I got the hell out, I realised my legs no longer were standing. I passed out. The next morning, the newspapers, including the *Telegraph*, published a picture of the only victim of the Bees of Bankstown sitting in the gutter with his head between his knees.

The *Telegraph*'s chief of staff, a paragon of patience called Tom Mead, summoned me to say he was sending me to cover the Sydney Coroner's Court. 'There', he said mysteriously, 'you will learn about life.' On my first day at the court the cadet journalists were called before the Coroner, Mr Letts, who impressed me as having an ironic, if slightly macabre sense of humour. It was customary, Mr Letts pointed out, for him to take the 'flower of journalism', as he called us, on a tour of his domain. We set out for the morgue.

'Hello Harry,' Mr Letts said to one of the morgue attendants who, as if by a signal, slid open a drawer, revealing a very bloated corpse. 'Fresh out of the drink this morning,' said Harry. I called silently on my legs to stand firm.

'Got a PM under way?' enquired Mr Letts.

'One just finished,' said Harry.

We approached a steel table on which lay a human form with its entrails in plastic bags beside it and the cranium removed. A man was sawing off a foot with a hacksaw. 'Gidday Mr Letts!' he said cheerfully, whereupon the foot dropped to the floor with a thump. I passed out.

The *Daily Telegraph* had a unique and slightly manic style created by its wartime editor, Brian Penton, who decreed that everything had to be written in the active voice, and there could be no exceptions. One good reason for this was to ensure that the source of an item of news was included in the story. The passive 'It is understood' and 'It is believed' were never used because they were judged guilty of fudging the origins of a statement and therefore, ran Penton's argument, its truthfulness. Paragraphs were limited to sixteen words and clichés and 'words of unnecessary length' were banned; 'during', for example, became 'in'.

Although the *Telegraph* was a tabloid, it was then a very serious newspaper, and in the hands of a skilled practitioner the staccato style had a fluency and force of its own, and could be sustained for any length of story. And although it imposed some truly ridiculous constraints ('It rained' became 'The rain fell'), it encouraged in young reporters disciplines of speed and economy of description. Adjectives were treated like gold sovereigns, to be dispensed on special occasions and seldom without the permission of Ray Walker, the chief sub-editor and keeper of the late Penton's purism. In reporting the collapse of a Ferris wheel at a fairground, where several children had been killed, I used the word 'tragic', and applied for dispensation. Ray Walker solemnly considered the context and agreed. 'But don't make it a habit,' he warned. For me then, the power of that lone, pristine word, set among a litany of facts, was immense. When I first saw Fleet Street, festooned with clichés, mixed metaphors and, horror of horrors, the passive voice, I felt like a Trappist monk in Gomorrah.

Since I had begun selling newspapers at the age of eight, thereafter publishing my own paper, *The Messenger*, at Sydney High, I imagined newspaper offices as romantic places, and the pleasant surprise about becoming a journalist, which I regarded as an exalted privilege and still do, was that my imagination was not far out.

The newspaper offices I first knew, mostly of wood panelling, had a distinctive smell, as if each room and cubicle absorbed not only the musty vapours of newsprint and dye from down below, but also something of the speciality practised there. The *Telegraph* offices in Castlereagh Street had such a feel. Ray Walker, guardian of the active voice, wore a green eye-shade and his sub-editors sat around a horseshoe-shaped desk and shouted 'Copy boy!' and, at least once, I swear, 'Hold the front page!' The 'turf office' was frequented by antipodean versions of Sky Masterson and Harry the Horse and smelt and felt like the races. The 'police rounds' room smelt and felt like a central charge room; and the 'shipping room', which was my room at the age of nineteen, might have been a corner of the purser's office on board an Orient liner.

These were stirring times on the dockside at Sydney. On some days four ships would line up at the Heads to enter Sydney Harbour, each with up to a thousand 'New Australians'. The only comparable period in modern history was in the United States at the turn of the century when several million immigrants, the 'huddled masses', passed through Ellis Island in New York Harbour and stirred America's 'melting pot'. In the early 1950s some 30,000 Britons arrived every month under an assisted passage scheme which cost £10 for an adult and £5 for a child, with the condition that they stayed two years. Government propaganda was now crying 'populate or perish'. What this implied was that unless many more white people settled in Australia, even including those of less than Anglo-Saxon credentials, the yellow races would have their way with the great virgin of the south. So the 'White Australia Policy' remained firmly intact. The post-war Labour Government began shipping in '£10 Poms' while refusing to allow Australian occupation troops in Japan to return with their Japanese wives. The Minister of Immigration,

Arthur Calwell, explained this policy succinctly when he said, 'Two Wongs don't make a white.' This racism reached the peaks of absurdity when a constitutional device of a 'dictation test' in any European language was used to deport Asians from Australia: thus, a Filipino, fluent in English, might be given a test in Serbo-Croat or Gaelic. However, this was a time when Australia was moving inexorably away from its reliance on Britain for immigrants, and the ships now came from Genoa, Pyraeus, Bremen, Rotterdam, Malta, Cyprus, Istanbul, Beirut; and their cargoes were changing the nation as never before.

The *Telegraph* shipping correspondent was Bruce Gallard, one of the kindest men I ever knew. Bruce's gentle, conversational way with people taught me much about interviewing, especially those new immigrant families, who were at the point of their greatest vulnerability. Bruce and I would divide the ships between us; and I would leave on a launch shortly after sunrise and clamber up the side of a pitching, rusting, barely seaworthy ship of usually Greek registration.

My first ship was a 'bride ship' packed with teenage brides from Sicily. All had undergone marriage by proxy with Italian men they had never met and who lived in all-male communities, building roads and dams and towns in the Outback. On board, the girls fought for spaces at the railing, each with a photograph of her husband (in which he would be striking a suitably macho pose), and with a glance at that and a glance at the faces looming on the quayside she would attempt to identify the man of her dreams. Equally, there would be a thousand men in their best shoulder-padded suits, pomade and winklepickers, straining against a wire fence erected by the police to prevent them from rushing at their beloveds and into the narrowing gap between the ship and dock. They, too, would be trying to match a flattering image with a face on the deck.

And when the gangways came down and the wire fence collapsed, as it invariably did, young men would run, and stop to look at a photograph, and run again. At the moment of contact they would drop to their knees with a posy of flowers held aloft, or they would shake hands with an almost theatrical propriety and shyness, or they would stand in tears or simply incredulous, as the wife they had never met presented her dowry: a bundle of lira notes, an heirloom, even a carefully wrapped pile of bread her grandmother had baked six weeks earlier; no grandmother could be expected to know that somewhere called Australia, indeed anywhere, was six weeks' journey away. However, the emotion would be of another kind when a husband learned that his proxy bride had fallen for the second engineer during the long voyage. I remember one young woman lying in her blood beside her small bundles. 'She's been stabbed,' said a cop.

When these courageous people left the wharves and went further into

Australia, life was often harsh. Many of the '£10 Poms' were herded into Nissen huts in the hottest and coldest places, a long way from Bondi and the Pacific. The first Greeks to arrive in Melbourne, now the second biggest Greek city in the world, would walk the long straight streets on sepulchral Sundays, on which all manner of simple pleasures were banned, looking for a centre of life that did not exist. So they created it.

In those days there were whispered slurs of 'Dagos' and 'reffos' and 'Balts' and 'Yids', but most immigrants were treated with a curious Australian indifference. They were not compelled to put their hands on their hearts, to salute a flag and promise to bear arms, or to chant a catechism of devotion which by implication would renounce their origins. There was little of the love-it-or-leave-it attitude common in the United States which forced the Ellis Island immigrants to build their tribal fortresses. In Australia, most people were left alone to make their lives in peace; and I have often wondered if this did not touch upon a seam of tolerance deep in a society where in spite of and because of the earlier inhumanity, the majority have been bound together in the search for a refuge. Perhaps the optimism that distinguishes Australian society today flows from that source.

It was 1962, the year the Australian silence began to crack. It was a year in which apparently small events had great significance: the establishment of the first Chair of Australian Literature at Sydney University, the opening of the Australian Ballet School and the publication of the first volume of Manning Clark's *History of Australia*, which offered a powerful challenge to imperium's distortion of the Australian past. It was also the year that the Aboriginal people, the First Australians, having been given the right to count themselves in the human census, were given the right to vote. So, with the ships now arriving full of new faces and energy and hope, had a nation been conceived?

The irony of the ships arriving full was that they were leaving full. Among Australians of my generation there was a migratory urge to go north and for some of us to stay away many years and for others never to come home. Some have been able to state concisely why they left; I have never been able to do so, because I suspect my leaving had more to do with following a moving crowd than any bold expression of individualism. I did want, though, a perspective on the world to which my own small world, a copy, seemed barely connected. And I was twenty-two years old, which was reason enough to go. I am twenty-two years older now, which is reason enough to go back.

Three of us left together: friends and journalists. Bernie Giuliano, ever kind and dry-humoured, was not at all like his infamous antecedent, the Sicilian bandit Salvador Giuliano. Peter O'Loughlin, my rumbustious ally, had fled the navy into journalism. Audacity was meant to keep the three of us going when the money ran out. 'INTEREP', announced the gold-embossed cards which Bernie had had printed for free, 'Representatives of twenty-eight Australian newspapers, magazines and journals. Address all mail to c/o Banco di Roma, Via del Corso, Rome, Italy'. I confess to dreaming up the figure of twenty-eight; as our luck transpired, twenty-eight about equalled our earnings in pounds after six months on the road in Italy. Sadly, INTEREP, although establishing bureaux in a score of youth hostels, *pensioni*, parks, lakesides and haystacks, was not to challenge Reuter.

Our passage to Genoa was in the darkest, dankest abyss of a Greek-owned French-built ship, the *Bretagne*. The fare was about £100 each, and we carried not much more with us, which had to be supplemented by a loan my father arranged with his bookie. This was to be the *Bretagne*'s last voyage; having dropped us off in Genoa, she blew up in Pyraeus harbour, which did not surprise us. What did surprise us was that she crossed three oceans intact, and that she left at all. She was due to sail from Sydney at noon and instead she sailed close to midnight, having mislaid the captain. This left those on board and on shore working shifts of farewells and, when we finally left, almost all of us were drunk.

Elsie had my brother Graham and book-ends of friends, and although I had assured her I would be back in two years, she said to others, 'He's gone for good.' Up along Pitt Street, at the Angel pub, I had said goodbye to Claude, who no longer lived with Elsie and had agreed that it was 'probably best' he did not come to the quay. And when the tugs pushed the *Bretagne* into the harbour and she straightened for the Heads, I felt the excitement I had often glimpsed in those coming the other way. I also felt something of the fear.

II

VISITOR TO BRITAIN

3

Days of hope

'British passport holders straight ahead. Commonwealth to the left. Foreign passport holders wait here!'

Britain's first Commonwealth Immigration Act became law in July 1962, 'restricting the right of entry of persons into the United Kingdom'. After a decade of importing people to run underground trains, buses, maternity wards and other public services, the drawbridge was coming up and officialdom was on enthusiastic guard duty at Dover and the other gates of Britannia. As a citizen of the 'Old Commonwealth', the code for white, I was in under the wire.

The late autumn of 1962 was the harbinger of all the illusions of the 1960s and of the worst winter since the Middle Ages and the last great British smog before the Clean Air Act changed the November sky from black to grey. I was broke, and enticing the crackle of Radio Luxembourg above the musak of a busted cistern in an igloo in Earls Court was fun, but somehow failed to supply the liberating excitement of the soon-to-be-swinging imperial town. So I went to Fleet Street, to an organisation called British United Press, which reputedly hired transient colonials.

My job with BUP was to clip articles from British provincial newspapers, rewrite the first paragraphs and place the regurgitated versions in trays marked INDIA, THE MIDDLE EAST and beyond. Or I would clip pieces from English-language newspapers from India and the Middle East, rewrite the first paragraphs and place them in trays marked BRADFORD and LIVERPOOL. As this activity lacked the ingredients of the journalism I had in mind, I escaped to good grey Reuters; and after a probationary period, during which I was allotted the war in the Yemen and scolded for poor time-keeping, I was sent a kind letter offering me a career and a pension scheme. However, impatience and the wish to work on a newspaper had already led me to the offices of the *Daily Mirror*, then the largest circulating newspaper in the Western world, where I saw an assistant editor just back from lunch in Fleet Street. It was an opportune time.

The assistant editor was a Pickwickian eccentric called Michael Christiansen, a fine tabloid journalist and a kind man, who died as I set out to write this. As he entered his office he leapt at me, gripping an arm and bellowing, 'You're just what we want, an *Australian*!'

He explained that, although winter was almost upon us, there was still a final and crucial game of cricket to be played against the *Daily Express* the following Saturday . . . 'And what do *you* do best, Pilger?'

'I bowl,' I said, 'I spin bowl . . . '

'Splendid,' said the assistant editor. 'You start on the *Mirror* tomorrow.'

'What as?' I enquired.

'Oh, we'll work that out . . . '

He then led me to the news chief sub-editor, who had nothing available, and to the features chief sub-editor, who had nothing available but was a Yorkshireman and asked, 'What does he *do*?'

'He's a spin bowler,' said Christiansen.

'Smashing!' said the features chief sub-editor, whose name was Denis Futrell and who without delay appointed me assistant to the sub-editor in charge of television programmes, gardening, fishing and pets. My career in British journalism had begun. The next day I sent the following craven note to Christiansen:

> Sorry, I don't know a damn thing about cricket. Does this mean a record short innings on the *Mirror*?

Christiansen bore this ill tiding with benevolence; indeed, benevolence was a quality which seemed to pervade the *Mirror*, although some have since called it complacence. The atmosphere on the paper was one for which nothing in my Australian newspaper experience had prepared me. There was a certain grace in the way the *Mirror* was run editorially: hierarchical, certainly, but with an informality and a confidence which arose from the fact that the *Mirror* endeavoured to reflect the lives and hopes of a large body of ordinary British people. As a consequence of this, not to mention the lack of competition, the paper was approaching sales of five million, or some fourteen million readers every day.

Having begun life in 1903 as a journal for ladies of the gentle classes, the *Mirror* changed character radically during the 1920s and 1930s and by the end of the Second World War had established itself as Britain's first truly mass circulation newspaper. In his *English History 1914–1945*, A. J. P. Taylor wrote this of the *Mirror*'s rise:

The war had one important outcome in the newspaper world. For the first time the masses – other ranks in the forces and factory workers – read a daily newspaper, and this carried the *Daily Mirror* to the top of the circulation list. The *Mirror* was popular in a special sense. Previous popular newspapers, the *Daily Mail* and the *Daily Express*, were created by their proprietors, Northcliffe and Beaverbrook, men not at all ordinary. The *Mirror* had no proprietor. It was created by the ordinary people on its staff and especially by Harry Guy Bartholomew, the man who worked up from office boy to Editorial Director. The *Mirror* was, in its favourite word, brash, but it was also a serious organ of democratic opinion and owed its success as much to its sophisticated columnist Cassandra as to Jane, its strip-tease cartoon. The *Daily Mirror* gave an indication as never before of what ordinary people in the most ordinary sense were thinking. The English people at last found their voice . . . [1]

The *Mirror* in the 1960s included some of the most enduring names in journalism: Cassandra (William Connor), Marjorie Proops, Donald Zec and Peter Wilson, 'The Man They Can't Gag', who relished mixing sport with politics and was among the first to explain to the British public the venality of apartheid's role in sport. The editorial director was Hugh Cudlipp, who at twenty-four had been the youngest editor of a national newspaper, the *Sunday Pictorial*. Cudlipp's personality and flair were evident everywhere in the *Mirror*, and such was his influence that, in my opinion, those who have since produced the *Mirror* at its best have done so with that expanse of Welsh forehead and jutting jaw looking over their shoulders, both in reality and in spirit. His understanding of the combined power of words and images – not to be confused with simply big headlines and pictures – was reflected in his classic front pages which, as he intended, helped the *Mirror* 'to create news about itself'.[2]

Cudlipp invented the 'shock issue' in which most of the paper was devoted to one urgent social and political theme. In a shock issue to precede the 1964 election,[3] which was to end thirteen years of Conservative government, the *Mirror*'s front page was simple and eloquent. Beneath a banner headline which read, IS THIS THE PROMISED LAND? was a picture of a woman hanging out washing in her squalid back yard, six feet by nine feet.

Although it was a piece of blatant electioneering on behalf of the Labour Party, that issue of the *Mirror* revealed a truth which lay behind the façade of Britain during those years of never-having-it-so-good, of promise and illusion: a glimpse of the impending betrayal of those British people of patience, modesty and selflessness whose immediate families had suffered a great economic depression and had fought a long war, not only against Hitler but against their own past and for a better life. These were the *Mirror*'s readers, its 'natural constituency', for whom it pledged beneath its masthead, 'Forward with the people', and for whom it spoke on May 11, 1946, ten days after Hitler had died in his bunker: 'There are shining victories to be won in the cause of peace and social justice.'

I was fortunate to be on the *Mirror*. The potential for influencing change, which the paper's circulation and editorial skills held out, was unique in Europe and, if realised, might represent a serious challenge to an established order which, the historian E. P. Thompson later wrote, 'assumes so deeply that it *owns* this island and its inhabitants and that it derives from some antique unwritten charter the prerogative of determining what British interests are.'[4]

Cecil Harmsworth King was of this class. The nephew of Lord Northcliffe, he was, until a boardroom coup in 1968, chairman of the grand-sounding International Publishing Corporation which published the *Daily Mirror*. However, King was an establishment maverick, and it was partly his patronage and a little of his eccentricity which ensured that the *Mirror* remained, as he would say, 'on the side of the underdog'. His magnificent office on the ninth floor, overlooking the dome of St Paul's Cathedral and furnished with priceless *objets*, was about as far from the underdog as it was possible to be; but such is the nature of British paternalism that millionaires are sometimes moved to describe themselves as 'socialists' while holding dear to all that made them millionaires.

I found Cecil King a sincere man who did believe in supporting underdogs, perhaps as part of a wider belief in his own power over the lives of large numbers of underdogs. One of the distractions of working late as a sub-editor (I was now elevated to be *in charge* of television programmes, gardening, fishing and pets) was the sight of the large and stately dinner-jacketed figure of Cecil King sailing serenely across the editorial floor of Britain's only pro-Labour newspaper followed by assorted high priests of the British establishment: the prime minister or at least a cabinet minister, the chairman of a great corporation or of one of the nationalised industries, a state director of the arts or others merely knighted or ennobled.

With Cecil King's blessing it was Hugh Cudlipp who determined where the *Mirror* stood. And where it stood was on the right wing of the Labour Party, whose social democratic faction then was dominant and unassailable and an important prop to what used to be known, prior to Margaret Thatcher's time, as 'the consensus'. This nod-and-wink arrangement between Conservative and Labour governments and the 5 per cent of the population who owned more than 40 per cent of the nation's personal wealth[5] existed so that life in Britain might never *appear* divisive or influenced by the extremes of wealth and poverty.

This largely unspoken, ill-defined, squirearchical and, of course, very British arrangement followed the Second World War. For the ruling class, 'consensus' meant social tinkering which it could tolerate and which would reinforce its power. The fruits of this connivance were made clear when the Attlee Government and successive Labour administrations, especially that of Harold Wilson, willingly mortgaged their policies to Tory assent.

Indeed, for politicians, 'consensus' meant something distinctly cosy, as the Labour MP turned media man, Brian Walden, later described it. Walden wrote:

> The two front benches [in Parliament] liked each other and disliked their back benches. We were children of the famous consensus ... we were spoiled, of course, because the electorate, which was even more irresponsible than we were, could be relied upon to grow bored or disenchanted and turn the opposition into the government. It made little difference, for we believed much the same things.[6]

For working people, the 'consensus' did not have quite the same cosiness, but it did mean that, in exchange for their acceptance of low wages and the acquiescence of their trade union leaders, they were granted reasonably priced housing, clothing and food, as well as basic services such as nationalised health care and the hope of a 'new start' for at least one child.

Hope was the most important ingredient of the 'consensus' arrangement, for without it working people might not work as they had worked for almost a century. One of the profound effects of the Second World War was that the pliancy of ordinary people was no longer assured, and without a modicum of hope people might strike and 'disturb the industrial peace' or, worse, disrupt society.

By the time the 1960s arrived, this hope, as exemplified by 'The Promised Land' in the *Mirror* headline, had converted to specific expectations. These were centred upon the creation of a new consumer world for the young in off-the-shelf, off-the-peg dreams. 'TEENAGERS HAVE FUN ON £1000 MILLION A YEAR!' read a 1962 headline in the *Daily Herald*. Youth was the target; and selling things, lots of things, almost anything, to the previously poor was what Swinging Britain was about. The hope on which the 'consensus' turned, and by which the old assumptions of the 'antique unwritten charter' of power could be preserved, was escape from the drudgery and greyness and imprisonment of class. It was this which was held out so tantalisingly to the young, as long as they spent and spent; and it was this which, in little more than a decade, would be the source of so much 'disruption', when the betrayal implicit in the 'consensus' would be made clear. With hindsight, the quality of the *Daily Mirror* lay in its capacity to warn its readers that the bargain was one-sided, that they were being conned.

In 1963 Harry Hyams, the 'developer', built a skyscraper called Centrepoint and left it empty, and estate agents in West London displayed flats-for-rent signs which read, 'No coloureds' and interesting variations such as 'No coloureds, Irish or Australians'. I saw the thermometer drop below zero for the first time in my life, and I saw snow for the first time. There seemed to be a constant four-foot drift of it outside my front door in Hammersmith, a house rented by a platoon of colonials from a movie star called Gary Raymond, who was away in Hollywood playing John the Baptist in *The Greatest Story Ever Told*. (The house's inventory did not include an original Turner painting, which presumably was worth a fortune. Along with all other wall fixtures, it fell down one night. When told about this, Mrs Raymond said, 'Don't worry. We have poltergeist.')

I rode in a bus whose driver could go no farther in the smog and led us passengers on foot and by torchlight. I attempted to drive my rusting Fiat down The Mall in the smog, turned left, then right, and found myself going in ever-decreasing circles in the front yard of Buckingham Palace until the beams of policemen's torches, like the beams of Davy lamps in a mine, guided me out, accompanied by cheerful words. There was a cheerfulness then and little of the tension that was to come; they were days of hope.

I applied to leave 'TV programmes, gardening, fishing and pets' and to be restored to full life as reporter. Michael Christiansen agreed, and I was sent north for two years, during which time I stayed 'on the road', from Manchester to Tyneside, to the Border, across the Pennines, to the Mersey. It was an assignment which some of my colleagues in London saw as the equal of banishment to Pitcairn Island.

Certainly, during the first drive north, when I stopped for petrol, I failed to understand what the man said, and the farther north I went the more incomprehensible were the voices; but what the people *were* seemed perfectly clear. They were another nation with a different history, different loyalties, different humour, even different values. 'We're the rich who can't get to their money,' someone in Lancashire said to me. In later years I would report from some of the most inaccessible places on the planet, but few of my dispatches would present a more alien picture in the South of England than those sent from the secret society 'north of Watford'.

This was a time when working people were said to be 'speaking out' and even 'taking over'. For example, people whose accents had denied them access to sections of the entertainments industry were now apparently in demand. There had been *Room at the Top* and *Saturday Night and Sunday Morning* and similar films which were said to reflect a new classlessness; but none of them showed people of different classes as equals, at ease with each other or in each other's homes. The principal celluloid 'working-class hero', Albert Finney, came from a lower-middle-class background (like Harold Wilson, who tried hard to cover his tracks with stories about childhood clogs and a devotion to HP Sauce) and only one major working-class actor, Tom Courtenay, broke through.[7] All of them – the Beatles and the many clever cockneys enriched and fêted by the media and the 'old' aristocracy – were absorbed by a fundamentally unchanged class-based society, thus making Britain *seem* more expressive and open and, above all, reinforcing the position of those in charge.

Classlessness was presented as a parade of caricatures: *Coronation Street*, Alf Garnett, even the splendid *Steptoe and Son*. Behind this façade people who came to London from the provinces worked hard to change their accents and obscure their origins and to learn the mannerisms and codes of the middle class. *This* was the momentous change; and these people, who formed new suburbs on new private estates in the South-East, became a 'comfortable class' and a constituency for a new kind of Toryism. When I first met some of these people I was puzzled why they should speak with a certain mockery, tinged with contempt, for those from whom they themselves had come.

During the 1960s the wisdom of the 'consensus' was that everything north of Watford was changing for the best; the North at least was 'modernising'. That this modernising was often merely a process of bringing poverty up to date, of violently distorting and turning back people's lives in the cause of a cult of town planning and of political expediency, was not considered a matter for serious public debate. These were swinging times; progress was progress; the North was a 'land of hope and agony': the agony being a necessary appendage of change, the hope predominant. Those were the words in a headline above an article in the *Daily Mirror* on January 16, 1968, which read:

> Instead of the countless Victorian piles . . . that sat for ages like grim stone Buddhas, great glass towers now rise and are joined to sprawling limbs of new homes that face, not blades of soot, but trees and green. And those fields of rubble seem only in transit; soon people will be living there, with their shopping precincts and post offices and pubs. So have people's faces changed. They are younger now and they wear none of the despair that the North's myths say they should.

Sheffield where, unique on earth, they have built at Park Hill and Hyde Park multi-storey flats, planned to retain something of the neighbourly warmth of the old rotten rows. Here street decks connect the ground with the fourteenth floor so that people can meet and chat, and the milkman can drive straight up to your door and no child need sit forlorn in his boxed isolation, but instead play all around and up and down . . .

Such words embodied the false optimism of the time, denying community traditions in the face of fraudulent 'progress'. They were words which helped to erect the façade beyond which town planners and Labour politicians and journalists did not look, or did not wish to look. The central myth was there; it was youth taking over a new, classless Britain, regardless of huge profit-making from jerry-built human pigeon lofts which, far from retaining 'something of the neighbourly warmth' of people's homes, disfigured much of the landscape and life of Britain. Alas, I wrote the article.

Hugh Cudlipp was an ideas man with few equals. He would think of a framework, such as 'Mirrorscope' and the 'Inside Page', or a series, 'The State of the People', and allow you to change it and adapt it as you wished. In 1967 he dreamt up 'Boom Cities', which was difficult to change or adapt. Either the cities were booming or they were not. Unfortunately, they were not. The 'Boom Cities' series in the *Mirror* was meant to coincide with one of the Wilson Government's seasonal lectures to industry to increase exports. Cudlipp decided that a 'Boom Cities *Mirror*' would be produced in the regional centres of England – Liverpool, Newcastle, Birmingham, Bristol, Manchester, Southampton – and on the evening of publication a spectacular banquet would be held, attended by a cabinet minister at least, various captains of industry, local politicians and others down the established scale.

In Liverpool, the banquet was held on a ship fully dressed for the occasion, complete with Harold Wilson and a real Liver bird. In Newcastle, guests were startled to find a 'tableau' of real steel-plate riveters in their midst. In Birmingham, a motorcycle burst through a screen; and in Bristol, home of the British aircraft industry, the progress of Concorde was discussed over an open line with the co-manufacturers in Toulouse.

All four represented grand illusions. In 1967 Liverpool, docks were falling silent as never before. In Newcastle, shipyard orders were being lost to the Japanese. In Birmingham, the motorcycle industry was in its death throes; and in Bristol, the Concorde was then a magnificent symbol of the British aircraft industry's failure as an international, competitive business.

In all four industries the problems were manifest and similar. The managements were inept, authoritarian and cosseted by a class-founded education system, which looked down its nose on industry, and by pre-war tariff barriers which were the residue of empire. The unions were fragmented and weakened by their own craft and class divisions. In the shipping industry, engineers were deemed 'better' than boiler-makers and drillers were 'better' than fitters, and so on. That management and workers knew almost nothing about each other and shared so little human contact was the canker in British industrial life, the antithesis of 'boom'.

One of the most telling testimonies in the eloquent BBC television series, *All Our Working Lives*, broadcast in 1984, was by Graham Day, a Canadian businessman who, in 1971, was put in charge of the Cammell Laird Shipyard on Merseyside. He recalled:

> I was there before half-past seven which caused everybody great consternation because I guess they did not expect the gaffers until a little later on, and I used to perambulate through the yard most mornings because I was learning and I wanted to talk to people, or wanted them to talk to me so I could listen and start to appreciate what the issues from the shopfloor were. I remember going aboard the accommodation section of a ship we were fitting out, going into a cabin, and there was one of the workmen fitting in a window, and so I said, 'Good morning', and there was no real response and I thought, well, he's not a steelworker so he can't really have a hearing problem, so I raised my voice and said, 'Good morning.' And he turned round and said, 'Are you speaking to me?' And I said yes, and I said we haven't met, and I am Graham Day, and so on. And he said, 'Oh yes, I knew you were here, but I wasn't sure you were speaking to me because I've been here 27 years and you're the first director who's ever spoken to me.'[8]

During my two years' travelling 'north of Watford', and on many sub-sequent trips north, listening to people taught me much and unearthed a bounty of stories of working lives. To be among English people not cultivated to measure their every emotion, indeed who were proud of their ability to express feelings, was a constant pleasure. Almost everybody I met either had a son or an aunt 'down there', in Australia ('You *must* have met Jim; he's in the Wollongong steelworks'), or they once had considered emigrating themselves and had 'sent off for the papers'. In South Yorkshire, strewn with hell's kitchens, were miners descended from the Irish of the Potato Famine who had family in New South Wales; whole collieries had shipped out to the pit towns of the Hunter Valley.

These people knew about such places a world away, yet many had never met a southerner in their own land.

I would find a street, virtually any street, and knock on doors; and what intrigued me then and intrigues me still was that such human warmth, tolerance and forbearance could survive the treadmill of British cities and the hypnotic routine of working lives. For example, Clara Street in 1970 was typical of much of Newcastle upon Tyne. My first view of Clara Street was on a Monday, with the working week ahead. It was half-past two in the afternoon, two hours before the sun was meant to go, and smoke from the six great chimneys of Dunstan Power Station had already seized the November mist and congealed into night. And this 'night' then moved up the hill and settled, like fine silt, in lace curtains and mortar and larders and in the lungs of those who, some hours later, passed as silhouettes along the ribbon of black barracks into doorways of home.

In the very early morning, after a brief interval of telly, food and sleep, the silhouettes moved down the hill, the day's first Woodbines lit up, the first wheezing under way: down into the buses filled with men and women whose skin was ash-grey, and on toward the great chimneys and the brickworks and the steelworks, past the Hydraulic Crane public house and the Forge Hammer and the Moulders Arms, and the Apprentices Welfare Club of 1863, down Gluehouse Lane and Pipe Track Lane. All of that for £16 a week for the men, and less for the women.

At 96 Clara Street lived Bill and Sylvia Clayton and their two children, Kevin, then eight years old, and Sylvia, seven months. Bill took home £21 for a sixty-hour week, driving a lorry. Their ceiling fell in regularly and their walls were like sponges to touch. They had no holidays, no outings; their 'gains', they reckoned, were the Health Service and the television. During the election campaign of 1970 they had seen one politician in their street, a Liberal who came and put up posters and said something inaudible from his Land Rover, and sped away. 'Paying our way' and 'productivity' were newly coined jargon then.

Bill said, 'I'm not political, but I know talk of "paying our way", words the politicians use, is not what's wrong. What's really wrong is the one thing nobody in this country wants to talk about any more. It's people in government not caring how we live, what time we go to work, how long we've got to work just to put shoes on the bairns. We might as well be in Turkey or like that. We're sure as not part of *their* country.'

Peel Street and Gladstone Terrace overlooked the green vales of County Durham, well beyond George Orwell's 'lunar landscape of slag heaps'.[9] This way, the farmland is still grassland, on which Friesian dairy cows and Hereford crosses for beef seem bolted in place. Hawthorn, bramble and wild rose smother the cuttings and embankments of disused railway lines, and the houses with their teafall roofs and lean-to larders are, as Northerners say, 'all pound note and bay window'.

These were village streets with their clubs and pubs and pigeon crees and football teams and the warmth of the inhabitants for each other. Today they do not exist. As almost everywhere else in industrial Britain in the 1960s and early 1970s, there was a Plan. Here it was the Durham Development Plan and among the official paragraphs on ancient monuments and sewage schemes, there was the following: 'Many of the rows of houses which grew up around the pitheads have outlived their usefulness and as uneconomic pits close . . . a gradual regrouping of the population should take place.'

The Plan decreed that 357 towns and villages be classified A, B, C or D. The first three categories meant life; the fourth, D (marked on the maps in scarlet), meant death to 121 villages, mostly mining communities with names like Binchester Blocks, Quaking Houses, Fighting Cocks, Eden Pitt, Burnt Houses, The Slack and Success, all of which were pronounced terminally diseased with unemployment.

According to the Plan, the villagers were not to be moved *en masse* as a community. Instead, they were to be 'phased out' of their Gladstone Terraces and Peel Streets, set in the English countryside, and phased into 'housing estates' close to 'industrial estates', with Western Ways and Central Avenues and without clubs and pubs and football teams. The restoration of their terraces and the inception of bus routes to the industrial estates, which would have preserved the communities, was such an obvious solution that it needed no Plan and was therefore never a consideration. The people were to be moved within sight and smell of industrial compounds, just as people had been moved in the nineteenth century.

In a D category village called Page Bank there was a flood and all the people refused to evacuate, fearing that they might not be allowed back. As the water lapped their tellies, they hung out signs saying, 'NEVER!' and 'GOD IS WITH US'. But He was not.

They were duly regrouped and phased out and into 'new towns', such as Newton Aycliffe, which had a youth club, an ugly rock garden and shops of no character and was flat and bleak: a 'lunar landscape' of jerry-built boxes whose window frames had already burst free and where damp had already risen by the time the first key turned in the door.

4

Country folk

In January 1972 Britain's miners went on strike for a living wage. After seven weeks, they returned to work with a new minimum basic rate of less than £26 a week, which they considered a victory. The expectations of the 'élite' of the British working class were, as ever, almost entirely lacking in greed.

While the miners were out, I went to Dorset to listen to people whose working lives were as remorseless as those committed to the pits, and as vital to the nation, yet even to other working people they were largely unseen and unknown; their wages and conditions were the poorest in the country. For them the hedgerows of Dorset and elsewhere were, in a metaphorical sense, 'north of Watford'.

It was raining hard as I drove up to the country gate and Rosemary Dyer waved, having just returned with a ten-gallon churn of water which she hauled to their caravan every day from the nearest tap, a quarter of a mile away. She said to be careful not to slip on the cow manure and mud which had merged around their door. 'In the winter', she said, 'it gets a nice white frosty coverin'.'

Frank had gone to work at half-past six that morning and would be back shortly for a cup of tea and some bread and butter, his breakfast. He would not finish until about six in the evening, and that was the pattern of his life. Frank Dyer was called an agricultural worker, though in fact he was a dairyman, cowman, herdsman and vet.

Each day he was in sole charge of some forty milking cows; he handwashed them, milked them by machine, recognised the first signs of a range of diseases and treated them with drugs. He was the only worker, apart from the farmer, on a property of seventy acres. As a countryman he had no objection to his hours or to conditions of work that would leave a modern factory shop-steward aghast; his one complaint was that he received just £16.20 a week.

Frank, at forty-eight, had never seen a pay slip. His employer, the farmer, merely made 'the deductions' and handed on the balance. On Saturday mornings he worked from dawn to eleven, for which he was given a pound note. That was called 'overtime'.

Frank Dyer was typical of working people who were no worse off if they did not work, that is, if they could find work. In the 1970s this became known as the 'poverty trap'. Frank's wage was nearly as low as the dole figure he would have received as an unemployed man with a family of four. What burned into him, as he said, was that even after fifty-five hours' work a week his income was below the official poverty line and, in order to survive, he had to collect Family Income Supplements.

He explained this in the twenty-eight-foot caravan in which the five of them lived, with another on the way. His cracked hands were covered with all kinds of dirt and there was no hot water. He rolled one of five cigarettes he rationed himself to every day.

Frank's life was the life of 332,000 agricultural workers who kept aloft Britain's reputation for having one of the most efficient farming industries in the world. Few people worked so hard for so little; and this was a measure of the farmworkers' true progress since the scandal of 1834 when six of them were marched in chains from Tolpuddle, in Dorset, to Dorchester where they were sentenced to seven years' transportation to Tasmania for attempting to establish a trade union.

For years the farmworkers bore mean little myths which refused to die: for instance, that they got a host of supplements, including free food. Rosemary Dyer, surrounded by cows, walked three and a half miles to a supermarket to buy milk in cartons and vegetables in tins. She was not allowed any fresh vegetables from the farm; and she walked because she could not afford the bus fare. The Dyers owned a 1957 Hillman, but they could not afford to pay the road tax. Frank said that some people still believed the tied cottage system was 'a fine perk you've got'.

'I've lived in three tied cottages,' said Frank, 'and each time I was laid off without notice – twice because the farmer found a casual labourer whose stamps he didn't have to pay. I was told, "You're in my house. Get out", and sure enough the bailiffs were right behind, and they'd take the key and that was that: the whole family was out on the road. The last time that happened the Welfare threatened to take away the children.' Rosemary said, with the fourth child coming, they were worried about that threat. 'The Welfare won't like six in a caravan, will they?' she said. They were buying the caravan at £4 a week, and that was why, said Frank, they had sent back the telly, which the children missed.

While we talked, Julia, aged thirteen, sat in her corner of the caravan playing with Patrick, the baby, and a glance at her and at five-year-old Timothy revealed something very poignant about this family. The children's skin was healthy and their clothes warm and neat, while the faces of their parents had skeins of grey: the universal faces of poverty. It was not difficult to know who went without and for whom in this caravan in Dorset.

At four o'clock one morning, before he was due to work, Frank Dyer had sat down and written a letter to the Ministry of Agriculture to say that he was not receiving the overtime due to him. While I was there a wages inspector came to the farm and went first to see the farmer. He then came to Frank and told him that the farmer had said, 'If he works these extra hours that's his business.' Frank replied that the cows did not work to rule; so the official asked for evidence that he worked the hours he did. Frank offered the witness of his wife and children, who 'know when I leave and know when I'm back', and also the woman up the road who greeted him every day. The inspector said he was sorry, but he would need more evidence than that.

The following Saturday, when Frank had worked his overtime, from dawn to eleven, the farmer refused to give him his usual pound note.

In 1985 the farmers' subsidy from the government was estimated at £2,000 million. None of this went to improve the conditions of agricultural workers. The National Farmers Union has repeatedly opposed paying farmworkers a wage comparable with that of workers in industry. In June 1985 the minimum weekly wage paid on British farms was set at £89.70. This has not lifted many agricultural workers' families above the poverty line.

5

The miners

Until 1972 British miners were among the most docile and lowest paid primary industrial workers in the Western world. Since the end of the Second World War hundreds of thousands of miners had left the pits or had been laid off, as hundreds of collieries were closed and their communities lost, many of them for ever. The miners' leaders made few effective protests. The strike in the winter of 1972 was the first official national coal strike since 1926.

Few gains were then made; but two years later, as the cost of living rose sharply following the October war in the Middle East and the oil embargo, the miners again took action, this time banning overtime. They had submitted a claim which sought to raise the minimum basic rate to £35 a week and the minimum for coal-face workers, the highest paid, to £45. During this period, in January 1974, I spent several shifts in a deep seam colliery at Murton in County Durham. It was, for me, the start of a long association with this one mining town and its people.

It was approaching midnight at the pithead, and the first hand I took was a claw. 'It's me . . . Harry,' said its owner, knowing I had failed to recognise him in his helmet, lamp and overalls. His hand, with three fingers gone and a stump, was no guide; so many hands were like that, which perhaps explained why so few were offered. 'Going into F32 are you?' said Harry. 'Aye, you'll know about pit down there.' At the bar of the Democratic Club the night before, F32 was the seam I was told to see; it was not on the 'visitors' run', and it lay a third of a mile beneath Murton and extended about four miles east, almost to the sea.

Harry's voice had filled the lamp room; except for brief, muttered monosyllables and the catching of breath, there was silence as we filled water bottles and strapped on rubber knee-pads and the 'self-rescuer', which is a small metal box with gas mask designed to keep you alive until they reach you. We walked to the cage. We each carried two numbered metal tokens, one to hand to the banksman on the pithead as we went down and one to surrender when we came up. A missing token means a missing man. The banksman frisked us for matches and cigarettes and slammed shut the cage, which rocked with the freezing gale hitting the pithead at seventy miles an hour. There was total blackness now; no one spoke.

Just before one o'clock in the morning we reached 1,100 feet and the shift only now began; this was the time the Coal Board started paying, although most of the men had been at the pit, preparing to go down, for half an hour and more.

Now we were walking downhill through the swirls of stone dust, judging the man in front from the beam of his lamp. Bill Williams, who had been doing this since he was fourteen, bit off some tobacco. 'Aye, that'll catch some of the muck,' he said. He also lifted his ribcage, as someone might hitch up his pants, and attempted to clear his lungs of 'the muck', but without success.

Now suddenly from desert air to tropics: the atmosphere was humid and the pit's first sounds were the hissing of the compression pumps, pumping out 200 gallons of water every minute. We were under old workings, which were completely flooded, and the roof was raining a steady drizzle of white slush, and the ground was silt. We were bent forward at right-angles, and my head slammed into a support. 'Look up, look down, lad,' said a voice from behind.

At two o'clock in the morning we reached the coal-face. Joe Ganning and Doug Walton already wore masks of white clay as they worked a drill at the stone: the noise of the drill was incessant and the sting from the dust and water was relieved only when I lay on my stomach in the slush and crawled under the stone and into the tunnel beside the coal-face, which was three and a half feet high and slightly wider than my shoulders. This was the core of the mine and except for the machinery – the pneumatic drill like a small steam-engine, the coal cutter like a bacon slicer, the conveyor belt – it looked like a scene from a Victorian etching: the men, their bodies doubled, contorted, following the machines, while 'titillating' the roof to test for a fall and moving the hydraulic chocks, as heavy as cannons, which propped up the roof.

They reminded me of troops bringing up artillery under fire. Their lives depended upon how they worked; and in every sense – the clipped commands of the deputy, the tense, planned assault on a stubborn adversary, the degradation of a filthy wet trench and the spirit of comradeship, of watching out for each other – this was another kind of front line.

Bill Williams and Frank Etherington were right up at the face. They were 'rippers'. They were kneeling in coal and slime and water as they shovelled into the conveyor belt. It was cramped where they were and they had to push the coal on to the shovel. They did this for five hours, interrupted only by their 'snap', a twenty-minute meal break for which the Coal Board did not pay. Spam sandwiches and coal dust. 'You breathe it,' shouted Bill, 'you might as well eat it.'

'How long will you keep this up?' I shouted back.

'I've another fourteen years before I'm retired, though I'll be lucky to be at face that long. I'm strong but being fifty-one you can only do so much as you get on. I'll no doubt be pulled back from face work in a few years.'

In 1974 Bill Williams took home the miners' top wage: £29 after deductions. The previous week he had received 42½ pence 'excessive water money'. The week I was there the water was not considered excessive and so, for kneeling five hours in water, he got only the 'wet rate': 11 pence a shift. He said, 'I've been lucky. In thirty-seven years in the pit I've only had a hydraulic pick hit me in the face [he had a prominent scar] and the usual crushed fingers. Many of those who are pulled back have been done in . . . '

We crawled the 220 yards along the coal face. There had been three falls of stone in the past week, leaving just two feet of space for us to slide over them. 'Over there,' shouted another voice behind me, 'our last one was killed; name of Peart. But remember this pit has a fine safety record; only six killed in six years. Peart was impaled by the machine, poor lad. Just not quick enough.'

It was twenty-past eight in the morning. The walk and ride back seemed eternal; the breathing of the men in time with their long steps was metallic. Then at last the cage. *Up!* The cage door sprang open. *Run!*

Now the Coal Board had stopped paying. The young men sprinted for the baths; the older men tried. We passed through the lamp room and Harry Mason, the man with his left hand a claw, whispered, 'This here is where we keep the wounded.'

Harry himself was a dispatcher. Even with three fingers missing he carried on with the heavy, better-paying work for years. When he lost his fourth finger in 1967 he was 'pulled back' to a lower wage. He said, 'When I lost the three fingers I was told that my claim for compensation would be reviewed when I retired – forty-four years later! Fortunately I lost the fourth finger after the Compensation Act came in and I was offered seventeen bob a week or £210. That's the going rate for a miner's little finger and I took the lump sum. You know miners lose fingers and limbs so frequently there's a sliding scale: so much for a leg, an arm. An eye is top whack! Even a finger is divided into joints called digits. For accounting purposes, aye.'

Behind the map room's wire mesh Nick Gowland walked in pain from his smashed hip. He was twenty-two. 'It wasn't thought to be serious at the time,' he said, 'I was only seventeen.' He received no compensation. Bill Wilson lost his left leg below the knee and received compensation of £2 a week. Albert Thompson was hit in the back by a stay which severed a nerve and he received £5.12 a week 'hardship money' and no compensation. British mines were said to be relatively safe. British miners were killed at an average rate of one a week.

There was a human sound I didn't notice at first, which I had heard in the pit, at the pithead and in the pubs and which assumed a certain terrible normality. It was a heaving from deep in the throat, followed by a stuttering wheeze and, finally, a hacking which went on for a minute or for a night, until the black phlegm was brought up. It was called 'the Dust', or pneumoconiosis. There were more than 40,000 registered sufferers of pneumoconiosis and thousands who were not registered, and there were countless others who died from diseases related to or caused by years of breathing in coal dust.

Pneumoconiosis ranged from simple lung damage to extensive scarring of the lung tissues; it developed slowly and did not show up on an X-ray for decades. But that the disease would one day show up was every miner's dread, for it was incurable.

'I knew it would show up sooner or later,' Ron Sugden said. 'It's been difficult to breathe for a long time now, but I'm not much different from other lads of my age. I'm fifty-one, you see. Know what the doctor said to me? He said I'd nothing to worry about until the next X-ray and I should try and keep out of the Dust!'

In the baths everybody had a good laugh at Ron's joke; and when they laughed the hacking reached a crescendo. It was just before nine o'clock in the morning. Black faces and white bodies darted from lockers to showers, along aisles of steam, at the end of which were private shower closets . . . 'for the lads with a bit missing'.

The miners went on strike two weeks later, on February 9. Prime Minister Edward Heath called an election for February 28, which he lost. This was said to be a 'victory' for the miners. If it was, it was one for which they would not be forgiven.

6

A little bit of humanity

In August 1978 a press conference was held in the Fish Room at Admiralty House in London to announce what Jack Ashley, the Labour MP, described as 'the final chapter of a harrowing struggle for justice'. He was referring to the thalidomide drug scandal, then in its twenty-first year. At the top table were Alfred Morris, Minister for the Disabled in the Callaghan Government, Dr Gerard Vaughan, Conservative MP and chairman of the thalidomide assessment panel, Jack Ashley and Sir Alan Marre, a former parliamentary ombudsman and one of the 'great and good'.

Glasses of Niersteiner were sipped in an atmosphere of mutual congratulation as each man rose to tell of the great and good the others had done. On hand were copies of a letter from the chairman of the Distillers Company, John Cater, in which he not only gave his assent to 'the final chapter' but added his own effusive end-of-term congratulations; and for this he, too, was congratulated.

The occasion was the publication of a report by Sir Alan Marre on what to do with the remaining seventy-four youngsters known as the thalidomide 'Y list' who were still awaiting compensation from the Distillers Company, manufacturers of thalidomide, and whose childhoods had slipped away, mostly in poverty, without aids or special comforts or even holidays. The parents of these youngsters had signed a settlement in 1973 with Distillers and, in so doing, had signed away the right to sue the company for negligence, although many of them were unaware at the time that two lists of children had been drawn up, labelled 'X' and 'Y', and that only children on the X list would be compensated.

The 342 children on the X list were made famous by the *Sunday Times*'s tenacious and successful campaign to force the makers of Johnnie

Walker whisky to establish a £20 million trust fund. Theirs was the lucky list, for the selection between X and Y was done by lawyers and was often arbitrary. Being on the Y list meant that these families still had somehow to prove to Distillers that the mother had taken thalidomide during the critical period of pregnancy all those years ago: in some cases, more than twenty years ago.

These mothers lacked written proof; either they had not retrieved the original prescription or their doctor's files had been lost, or their doctor had moved away or had died or did not want to co-operate for fear of implicating himself; or they had been given thalidomide tablets without a prescription. It is not uncommon for doctors simply to pass on a maker's 'sample'.

This stringent condition of proof was applied to the Y group, even though many on the X list had been accepted into the 1973 settlement without such proof. What the X children had in their favour was the approval of one man, Professor Richard Smithells of Leeds University, who 'passed' and 'failed' a number of the children without seeing them and, in some cases, after viewing only a few snapshots. Professor Smithells later protested to me that he had been completely unaware that Distillers was using his judgment to determine the future of each child, and said he was deeply upset by the apparent consequences of any misunderstanding.

By the time the Y list parents knew about the two lists, it was too late; their signatures had indemnified Distillers.

At the time of the 1973 settlement, there were ninety-eight Y list children. In the rejoicing they were forgotten. The legal struggle had been bitter, complex, divisive and expensive; to continue and perhaps to jeopardise that which had been won for the majority of the children, the 'proven' cases, was unthinkable; and most of the Y list families obliged by remaining silent and slipping back into a world of hardship.

Many of them lived in the North of England, in Scotland and in remote rural areas and they could not afford to travel to London; and they were exhausted, having had their hopes raised, then unceremoniously dashed. They were also deeply and justifiably aggrieved. One Y list parent had overheard lawyers saying that they had been instructed to keep the list down to 'no more than 300 kids' which was the figure 'Distillers will agree to'.

It therefore was hardly a coincidence that the lucky and unlucky lists divided in favour of those able to stand up to the outrage of arbitrary and secretive decision-making; those articulate and literate and with access to London lawyers and bank managers and overdrafts, or merely with time and a telephone.

There was a vocal list and a muted list; a list of the strong and a list of the weak. No one dared to say it publicly at the time, but the lists of thalidomide-damaged children divided, with exceptions, just as the nation divided. One who did say it was Olwen Jones, a case worker for the Lady Hoare Thalidomide Trust. 'It's the old story,' she told me. 'The X list families included a strong body of middle-class parents who could get the best legal advice, who knew how to follow the twists and turns and to stay ahead . . . *who knew how to fight.* The Y list families are mostly working-class people, who often find it difficult to deal with a local authority, let alone endless legal matters and who feel betrayed and even ashamed.'

They were not completely forgotten. Olwen Jones had known all the families, X and Y, and had kept case histories on many from the time of birth. Olwen is a woman whose compassion is matched only by her unshakeable determination, and she was incensed at the 'cowardly abandonment', as she put it, 'of those who most needed our help'. She persuaded Jack Ashley, the campaigner for the disabled (he is himself deaf), to convene a meeting at the House of Commons in November 1973. At this meeting Dr Gerard Vaughan, who had chaired the assessment panel, said that sixty of the Y list children 'appear to be thalidomide victims' and he promised that his panel would examine them.

Six months later nothing had happened. With Olwen Jones, I began a campaign in the *Daily Mirror* which ran for four years and ended in the Fish Room at Admiralty House.

Following a highly unusual front page in the *Daily Mirror*, which showed two seriously handicapped children side by side,* one from the X list and the other from the Y list, and with almost identical deformities, Dr Vaughan again committed himself to reconvene the medical panel to see all the Y list children. My own argument for the Y list children to be included in the original settlement was based largely on a long interview I had conducted in May 1974 with Dr David Poswillo, a world authority on birth deformities who had just completed five years' research into thalidomide. He told me that, given two suspected cases, it was impossible to say beyond reasonable doubt that one child was thalidomide-damaged and the other was not. 'Beyond reasonable doubt' was a premise of British justice. Distillers were now beyond reach of the law, but the issue surely was wider.

Here was a multinational company which, although it denied negligence, had continued to market thalidomide after tests in Germany and Britain had shown that the drug could kill laboratory animals and was therefore dangerous.[10] Given this, and Dr Poswillo's statement, it

---

* This was considered something of a 'first' in 1974 as disabled people were seldom seen in mass circulation newspapers and never on the front page.

seemed to me that a clear responsibility rested with the company either to prove that the Y list children were *not* damaged by thalidomide or simply to 'top up' the 1973 settlement so that *all* the Y list children could be included. One thalidomide parent, Alec Purkis, who had struggled to get his daughter Catherine on to the X list and was chairman of the Thalidomide Society, had written a report estimating that this topping-up would cost Distillers less than £3 million after corporation tax. 'It's peanuts,' he said.

But it was the evidence of the children themselves and the suffering of their families which underlined the company's responsibility and which also revealed something of the role of sections of the medical profession in the affair. For example, in 1964 Brian Huckstepp, an East London boy who was then three, was examined by a leading surgeon, Michael Harmer of St Mary's Hospital, London. Harmer wrote in case notes that he believed this must have been a thalidomide baby. Ten years later Harmer reaffirmed this diagnosis in a reply to solicitors acting for Brian's parents. He wrote that he had 'no doubt whatsoever' that Brian Huckstepp's deformities had been caused by thalidomide.

But shortly afterwards Harmer wrote again to say that he had been in touch with Professor Richard Smithells – whose opinion was adopted by Distillers as a verdict – and that Professor Smithells had denied Brian was a thalidomide child. In view of Professor Smithells's opinion, wrote Dr Harmer, he would not be willing to go into the box. The family's confusion was complete.

Brian's father, Harry Huckstepp, told me, 'We knew nothing about thalidomide until the word Distaval [a brand name for thalidomide] leapt at me out of the paper one day. We had kept a bottle of Distaval until we moved house, when it was lost. I went straight to my doctor who was our GP at the time of the birth, but he denied he had prescribed thalidomide . . . but what puzzled me was that he wouldn't say Brian was not thalidomide.'

When I first met Brian he was sixteen and attempting to play football in artificial legs which were old and heavy and caused him much pain. The family had spent everything they had on legal fees and could not afford lighter, specially-made legs. Brian's current GP, Dr John Clougherty, said, 'There appears to be no doubt regarding the presence of thalidomide in young Huckstepp. I cannot for one minute understand the hesitancy of including this unfortunate child in the division of compensation.'

Sandra Allen, whose case was fairly typical, was seventeen. Her mother, Betty Allen, said, 'We hadn't heard of thalidomide until we heard a surgeon say to some students, "This girl is a classic example of the damage done by thalidomide."' When Sandra was eight she was seen by Professor Smithells, who, declared her not to be a thalidomide child. Betty Allen subsequently discovered the remainder of the Distaval tablets she had taken and sent these to Professor Smithells; but by that time Distillers had had his previous opinion and their decision appeared to be final.

By December 1977, more than three years after Dr Vaughan had given his second commitment, few of the children had been examined by the panel and only thirteen of the ninety-eight on the Y list had been transferred to the X list and compensated. Dr Vaughan told me he had passed several cases to Distillers and had asked them to 'exercise a little bit of humanity'.

During the winter of 1977–8 Olwen Jones and I travelled up and down the country interviewing the families, trying to assist them to recollect details such as which neighbour had given them thalidomide tablets 'for depression' or where they might have stored away old papers and perhaps a prescription.

As the years had passed, so the toll of breakdowns and family disunity and divorce had increased. One teenage girl suffered jeers such as: 'We know you're getting a fortune.' She still has received nothing. Both Alfred Morris, the then Minister for the Disabled, and Jack Ashley wrote to the Distillers chairman, John Cater, expressing disquiet that many of the children had not been examined. Cater replied that Distillers had given all the families 'the benefit of the doubt' and that the company 'cannot possibly compensate the thousands of handicapped children born every year'.[11] But nothing of the kind had been suggested. Only the children of those parents who signed the 1973 settlement were eligible for compensation.

However, the company proposed that the families not only submit their cases all over again, but travel to Germany to get the opinion of another specialist. So here were desperate and confused people, burdened by a manifest injustice, yet again being force-marched through a Kafka-like maze. There was no suggestion by Distillers of a final gesture, no act of magnanimity. The profits on the sale of Johnnie Walker, Haig, Vat 69, White Horse and Dewar whiskies, Booth's and Gordon's gins and Cossack vodka had just trebled to £127 million.

In April 1978 I telephoned Ralph Nader in Washington. Nader, who had taken General Motors to court over faulty cars and had won, was supreme at consumer litigation and boycott. He was appalled at the lack of redress under British law against the makers and distributors of unsafe products. 'I thought thalidomide was all wrapped up,' he said. I explained that it was not, and I asked him if he would consider arranging a boycott of Distillers' products in the United States, where the bulk of its profits were made. He agreed in principle and I sent him files on all the children.

When the *Mirror* published news of this impending boycott, I received an anxious call from Distillers, asking for details. A few days later, on January 16, 1978, I wrote an open letter to John Cater, whose picture was prominently displayed above a 1960 advertisement for Distaval. The advertisement showed a small child taking bottles from a bathroom cabinet. It read:

This child's life may depend
on the safety of Distaval . . .

Consider the possible outcome in a case such as this – had the bottle contained a conventional barbiturate. Year by year, the barbiturates claim a mounting toll of childhood victims. Yet it is simple enough to prescribe a sedative and hypnotic which is both highly effective . . . and outstandingly safe. 'Distaval' (*thalidomide*) has been prescribed for nearly three years in this country . . . but there is no case on record in which even gross overdosage with 'Distaval' has had harmful results. Put your mind at rest. Depend on the safety of 'DISTAVAL'.

The open letter asked the Distillers chairman to read again his own advertisement, to consider the salesmanship aimed directly at human vulnerability and fears and the reassuring boast which turned out to be false. It also asked him to consider his recent statement that all the children had been given 'the benefit of the doubt' by Distillers.

Mr. Cater, what benefit of the doubt has ever been given to Brian Huckstepp? Brian was twice declared a thalidomide child by a surgeon who wrote he had 'no doubt whatsoever' that Brian's mother had taken the drug. What benefit of the doubt was given to Andrew Lowe? Andrew's parents fought for sixteen years for justice until their son died last year. Right up until Andrew's death, your lawyers were suggesting that Andrew saw yet another specialist, get yet another 'opinion'. Andrew died a few days before his parents could give him his first real holiday – the first they could afford.

Shortly afterwards Distillers agreed to abide by the recommendations of the enquiry conducted by Sir Alan Marre. This was the way out for Distillers, not for the children. When Sir Alan called me to the enquiry to give evidence, he listened with apparent sympathy, then said he did not wish to be seen 'punishing' Distillers. In his report, Sir Alan wrote:

My inquiry has satisfied me that, in general, Distillers has tried to apply fairly the test of the balance of probabilities in deciding whether a Y list child should be accepted as thalidomide damaged . . .

The families regarded this statement as unbelievable. What 'fairness' had been applied to any of them? Sir Alan had consulted none of the experts, like Dr David Poswillo, who held that the onus of proof ought to be on Distillers. Incredibly, he produced two more lists: this time the unlucky list was called 'A category' and the lucky list 'B category'. Forty-nine youngsters were offered a derisory £10,000, only twenty were included in the 1973 settlement and five were told they must 'await further reports'. It was not surprising that Distillers all but sent a sprinter with their congratulations.

What was it about the thalidomide affair in all its stages that brought out in so many of those involved a bias against these families? It was a bias which at times bordered on institutional spite. Was it that the Y list families, however self-effacing, were living reminders of twenty years' manoeuvre and duplicity, collusion and ineptitude by public men, corporate men, lawyers and assorted licensed do-gooders?

Was it that the Y list families posed questions which were all too revealing and embarrassing? Questions such as: What *were* the deals that lawyers did with Distillers? Why *did* so few doctors speak out for the children, particularly doctors who had known them as patients? Why did Dr Gerard Vaughan (who went on to become a junior health minister) let four years elapse before honouring the public commitment he made that the panel, for which he was responsible, would examine all the children? These were years during which, for most of the children, their adolescence was spent in dire poverty. And why did no government order an open public enquiry into what surely was one of the most unremitting scandals of the post-war period?

The established order is masonic; when it is challenged, it closes ranks and sends emissaries to smile weakly. The gentile celebration in the Fish Room at the Admiralty was such an occasion.

7

Invisible people

The war is an illusion; it is more often than not merely 'the Troubles'. The most recent Irish war that is not a war began more than four years before Joe was born, and he was eleven when I met him. Apart from a flesh wound caused by a ricocheting plastic bullet, he bore no visible scars of the battles fought outside his front door. Like all the children on his estate in Belfast, he was said to be 'okay' and 'tough'; but he was seldom well, as the rising and falling of his small chest indicated.

He and his brother Sean, aged nine, and his sister Liza, aged seven, were like ferrets, forever on the lookout, usually for rats which walked not ran, on the balconies and the window sills and inside, beneath the kitchen sink and the beds, and which now were immune to the poison laid for them. There was no heat in their flat, except a single electric bar, and this was exposed and liable to be touched. Water was restored to the lavatory after an absence of eight weeks; there was no other water, except the flood water, which seeped regularly through the cracks in the roof.

The stomach pains of dysentery were to Joe and Sean and Liza, and to countless other Northern Irish children, what the sniffles of a common cold were to children in England. They lived in the Third World, in the United Kingdom. The real tragedy for them, and for all of Northern Ireland, seemed too obvious to be noticed; it was not so much the war or the sectarianism as it was an all-pervasive poverty that was the disgrace here. An understanding of this poverty was central to a solution to the war in the North of Ireland, which perhaps explained why so little was heard about it.

I first saw this poverty in 1963 before the present war began. In the intervening years Irishmen would come to London and sit in the foyers of Fleet Street newspaper offices and describe the impoverished conditions enforced by a sectarian regime at Stormont to junior reporters whose job it was politely to get rid of them. In 1969 when I reported this poverty from Belfast and Derry, a minister in the Stormont Government demanded the right of reply in the *Daily Mirror* and accused me of using 'the language of Chinese communism at its worst'.[12]

Today, the quality of the political debate about the North of Ireland is not much improved and the poverty is overseen directly by the British government. 'Outrages' continue to happen and are reported with weary indignation; the instrument of British power, the Army, moves morosely in and out of its corrugated-iron forts and is hated by the Catholics it was sent to protect and accused by the Protestants of not doing enough to protect them. The current British prime minister remains the IRA's best recruiting agent. British ministers in Northern Ireland and 'across the water' are regarded, at best, with cynicism by both sides. There is no genuine movement; no durable policy for peace and reconciliation.

However, there is an economic plan: that of deprivation. Not only does every Government 'cut' in Britain have a disproportionately cruel effect in Northern Ireland, but millions of pounds are being withdrawn from housing schemes and the social services, which in some areas have been withdrawn altogether. Unemployment is frequently higher than 50 per cent.

The war's catalyst was this poverty, mostly Catholic poverty. Today, as Protestant-dominated shipbuilding and engineering decline, the same poverty does not discriminate between faiths. But people in Northern Ireland still fight the wrong fight, encouraged by British politicians who see Northern Ireland as a security problem and political problem with religious overtones, rather than a problem of poverty with religious distractions. One in three households existed on an income below that considered by the Government to be 'essential to meet basic needs'. One in three pensioners lived on or below the poverty line. About half of all the children in Northern Ireland live in accommodation officially considered to be 'unfit or lacking basic amenities such as a flush lavatory or hot and cold water supply'.[13] Infant mortality is the highest in the United Kingdom.

How many British politicians and how many civil servants, seconded to Northern Ireland and living in quiet middle-class areas, have ever seen how 'those damned Irish' are forced to live and understood the meaning of the statistics of their lives? The answer is few. The people around them are invisible, and to successive governments which have tolerated accelerating poverty on the mainland, the level of poverty in Northern Ireland is acceptable: an issue no longer worthy of 'policy consideration'.

Almost everybody I have spoken to in Northern Ireland, Catholics and Protestants, agrees that housing, statistically the worst in Western Europe, was the one issue on which progress could be made. And yet the Northern Ireland Housing Executive built only 4,042 houses in 1983; and the number of families on the housing list has remained at 30,000, with the majority of them classified as 'in acute need'.

In Belfast, on estates I know well, action committees compile dossiers for housing officials they seldom see and the questionnaires are more often than not ignored. The estate where Joseph, Sean and Liza lived with their sparrow-like mother, Moragh, is lit up only when the Army turns on its floodlights. In the flat below, Rosie Nolan hanged herself and an action committee was formed to force the authorities to move people out. Rosie had a handicapped child and could not bear the strain of a modern form of serfdom created by endlessly deepening debts and punished by a law unique to Northern Ireland. This is the Payments for Debt Act which was introduced by the Unionists at Stormont and extended by the Callaghan Government. It allows the authorities to 'claw back' debt from the very poorest; rent, rates, gas and electricity can be deducted from wages and state benefits, often regardless of hardship. If the electricity supply is not cut off, a 'limiter' is installed. This allows only one light or two rings on an electric cooker. To watch television, the electric fire has to be switched off.

In the Divis flats it was noon in November and dark on the catwalks. Candles flickered in those flats where the front room was used as an impoverished shop: a snapshot of the 1930s, when Catholics and Protestants joined in hunger riots. Gerry Downs, who ran the Divis community centre, said, 'We have 4,000 people crammed on to fourteen acres. Unemployment is, at least, 80 per cent. The rats play in the playgrounds. In that flat there was an old fellow who was dead a week before we found him.'

In a city of murals the most ironic is the one of the Divis which depicts a cosy, taunting picture of street life as it was in the old Loney district. On the Protestant Shankill Road there is a derelict swathe where blocks of 'modern' flats once stood; built for human battery hens in 1971, demolished in 1981. Joe, Sean and Liza slept in one bunk because their mother believed they were safer there if the room flooded or if there was not enough water pressure in the lavatory and sewage rose from the ground outside.

Governments cannot erase the Battle of the Boyne or the bigotry taught in schools, and money is not the whole answer; what is certain is that there can be no solution without it. The building of decent homes instead of a £30 million motorway and the abolition of the Payments for Debt Act, which perpetuates the stigma of poverty as if it were a crime, would raise the morale of people and attack the siege mentality from which sectarianism flows.

The governing authority in London can absorb the violence on either side of the water, be it the bombing of Harrods or the Grand Hotel, Brighton or a knee-capping on the Falls Road. Indeed, such violence also serves to shore up the 'stalemate': the real instrument of control.

What is more threatening to the British government is the kind of liaison which occurred in Belfast on the night before the IRA martyr Bobby Sands starved himself to death. Then, Catholics and Protestants marched together, calling for an end to their punitive housing conditions. It received little media attention. Once again, all too briefly, they had fought the right fight.

8

Anne Frank with a telephone

In the heart of London one family stays together in their one large room, overlooking the street. They do not go outside after seven o'clock at night, neither do they go downstairs after dark. Only the dog, a worrying beast called Soldier, is downstairs, in the front room which was to be the father's tailor's shop and is now barricaded, on the urging of the police, who say they can do nothing.

The mother sits beside the window in the large room. She seldom moves from this watching position. Her bed has been moved there, beside the window; and when she talks her eyes remain fixed on the street below. Beside her is a plastic box filled with a variety of medicines, most of them anti-depressants and sleeping tablets and others for the relief of asthma. As each siege begins or appears imminent, she calls out names, names which are familiar to all the family. They are the names of their tormentors, led and inspired by fascist and racist groups, some of them dating back to January 1983 when the family moved into the house.

'They go in circles,' said the eldest daughter, Nasreen, who is sixteen. 'They go round and round. Or maybe they just sit, and do nothing at all. Or maybe they just hit the door or just throw rocks . . . '

'And shit,' said her father, trying to smile.

'And shit,' said Nasreen.

I met this family in the winter of 1983 when the attacks were most intense, and since then I have kept in regular contact with Nasreen. She is the voice of her parents, who came to Britain from Pakistan twenty-one years ago, and of her teenage sister and brother, who, like her, were born and brought up in the East End of London. The conversations I have with Nasreen on the telephone run to a pattern. 'Nasreen 'ere,' she says in her cockney accent. 'They're at the door now. Hear 'em? I've called the police and they're comin', they say . . . that's all. Bye.'

She may ring back to say they are all right. She may ask me to ring Newham Council the next day and occasionally the police that night, but more often than not she asks nothing; she is merely making contact with the world outside her barricades. She always reminds me of Anne Frank, the Jewish girl who hid in the attic of her home in Amsterdam during the Nazi occupation and kept a diary of her life. She is Anne Frank with a telephone.

Nasreen's diaries are material for future historians who wish to look beneath the 1980s surface of British society, of which her father's family, before they came from the Punjab, used to speak as 'a place of free dreams'. The first entry in Nasreen's diary was during the week they moved in, having invested all their savings and taken out a mortgage; this was to be a new life.

On the night of January 25, 1983 a gang of forty attacked. They threw stones, smashing the shop windows and missing the family by inches. They daubed swastikas and gave Nazi salutes and chanted, 'Fucking Pakis out!' They did this for six straight hours. Nasreen wrote this in her diary:

> When the trouble started, we phone the police, but they never came. Then again we phone the police, but they never came. Then my father went to the police station to get the police . . . we had a witness. The police said they didn't need a witness.

The entries in the diary for the days and weeks that followed, often written by candlelight or in freezing darkness as the family huddled in an upstairs room, were repetitive and to the point: 'Trouble. Got no sleep. Had no telephone . . . three or four of them throw stones at our window.'

Today, the family is still prevented by menace and violence from opening the shop they own. For a time her father worked in the most secure room, in the back. Then a stone narrowly missed his head and he became ill. He seldom comes downstairs at all now, and in the winter and autumn they are usually all inside by five in the afternoon. Nasreen describes her life as 'sort of like living under a table'.

The casual brutality this family has experienced is typical of that endured by numerous families of Asian origin and has now reached a level reminiscent of the racist attacks on East End Jews in the 1930s. The Home Office has estimated that Asians are fifty times more likely to be attacked than white people,[14] although few of these attacks are reported in newspapers or on television, let alone to the police.

Newham police told me they gave the family 'special attention' but that it was impossible to mount 'a twenty-four-hour guard'. Had they, I asked, prosecuted anybody in connection with the attacks? A senior officer said that it was difficult to prosecute because 'They are mostly juveniles.' This was an unconvincing explanation as more juveniles are being prosecuted now than ever before, with racist bullies the exceptions.

Alongside Nasreen's diary is a growing file of correspondence with the police, the Home Office, the local authority, the local MP and the prime minister. She has tried to make the nominal system of accountable government and law work to protect her family. She began by writing a sheaf of letters to Arthur Lewis, then the Labour MP for Newham North-West. She was fourteen then. She wrote:

Dear Mr. Lewis,
   We are an Asian family under attack by the National Front and similar group. My mother has not slept for the last two months and has had to go to hospital for several days. We cannot furnish or decorate our home because we are too busy looking out through the window day and night, ensuring nobody attacks our house. The police seem to come only when you either phone them or write to them, or when they feel they are being watched by people such as you. Since the attacks began they failed to arrest one person, even though they know who they are. You say in your letter that our problem is housing. We have a house, Mr. Lewis, and we want to stay in the house. I ask you for your help [and the] local Labour Party members to come and defend us. People have died this year, by attack, and the police never protected them.
                                                    Yours sincerely,
                                                    Nasreen

On March 29, 1983 Arthur Lewis told the House of Commons that the family had been 'smashed about by skinheads'. Mrs Thatcher replied that the then Home Secretary, William Whitelaw, was 'taking up the matter'. Mr Whitelaw is now in the House of Lords. The matter was never taken up. In the meantime Nasreen had written to Newham Council housing department saying, 'We cannot go on living under attack all the time.' Her mother, on one rare expedition to the shops, was surrounded by a gang and spat at.

The Council offered the family a house, but they could not afford both to rent it and pay their mortgage, and while their present house was barricaded and smothered with graffiti, they could not sell it. They were trapped. Two 'average' days in Nasreen's diary read:

9.10 p.m. There was a knock at the door. [Almost every night there is a knocking or the thud of a boot or the crash of a bottle.] I got out of bed and looked out the window. A driver shouted at us . . .

10 p.m. There were two boys sitting in the car park throwing stones at us . . . no sleep again.

In May 1983 Nasreen wrote to Mrs Thatcher:

Dear Margaret,
    I understand that you were able to raise these matters when he deputised for you at Question Time . . . I am sorry to tell you that you don't understand our matter, Mrs. Thatcher. You don't care if we get beaten up, do you?
    My mother has asthma and she has to stay to 11 a.m. watching through the window because me and my brother and sister has to go to school. I can't stay home to look after my mother because I got exams to worry about, My father has blood pressure and if he loses his temper, what are we going to do? He is the only man to feed us. We have no money to repair our house since the kids in the street have damaged it. We are asking for your help, not your money, Mrs. Thatcher.
                                    Yours sincerely,
                                    Nasreen

An extraordinary reply came, not from Mrs Thatcher but from a Mr C. D. Inge at the Home Office. Mr Inge urged the family to keep reporting every attack to the police 'even if the police are unable to take effective action'. In his final paragraph Mr Inge said:

I am sorry that I am not able to give you a more helpful reply, but let me take this opportunity to assure you that the Government does care about the incidence of racial attacks and is committed to a multi-racial society in which all can go without fear of racial violence or abuse.

This 'commitment' has yet to take effect. It is difficult to find an Asian family in East London who has not been attacked in one form or another. Nasreen's family have weathered their siege better than most. Not far from them lives an eleven-year-old Asian boy who wrote this essay at school:

The day we moved into the new house, we got up at six o'clock. We came to the estate, to wait for the electricity man. The neighbours came out and shouted, 'Get those people out of here.' The big boys shouted, 'Send them out. Send them out. Send them out.' These boys says, 'Look, there's bugs in their bed and in the chairs.'

The essay ends abruptly because its small author had to retreat inside his new home when a mob arrived. The mob consisted of adults leading teenagers and children and it blockaded the family's flat, taped up the door and let loose a German shepherd dog. The police were called and arrived after a long delay. They demanded to see the father's rent book to see if he was 'legal' – that is, legally entitled to be in Britain – which he was. Then they left; nobody was arrested. Most families under siege are too frightened to call the police for fear of being prosecuted themselves.

In 1982 the London region of the Fire Brigades Union asked its eleven divisions for details of the fire attacks on ethnic minorities. Walthamstow fire station listed thirteen cases, the most common being petrol poured through the letter box followed by a lighted paper. One of these incidents had appeared in the local press; none had featured in the national papers or on television. They happen in a world little known to most journalists and to those who live in places of suburban privacy. In a society kept divided and mutually antagonistic, the Asians serve a dual purpose. Part of the Asian population forms a new working class with many of the old illusions and expectations intact and so remains politically pliant; others fulfil their old imperial role as a shopkeeper class, allegedly Mrs Thatcher's favourite people. In Handsworth in 1985 this group felt particularly betrayed when their property was not protected. In both cases they serve as scapegoats for the frustrations of working-class people – white and black – whose expectations have long been undermined.

On the night I last visited Nasreen's family not much happened. The usual tormentors were there. Soldier, the dog chained in a room meant to be a tailor's shop, barked on cue. Nasreen ventured half-way down the stairs, but would go no farther. A stone smashed against their van, and there were human yowls outside their door. Later, when I had returned home and she phoned me as usual, not much more had happened. They got to sleep at one o'clock, when at last there was nobody down there.

9

Cashing in

When the Conservative Government of Margaret Thatcher took office in May 1979, the term 'consensus' was replaced by a new jargon word, 'reality'. In the mid-1980s this means that more than a quarter of school-leavers cannot get work[15] and that long-term unemployment is higher than it was in 1932, the peak year of the Great Depression. It also means that 3,500,000 children or a third of the youngsters of Great Britain are living in poverty.[16]

There is an abundance of this 'reality' in the River Streets area of Birkenhead, across the Mersey from Liverpool, where unemployment reaches up to 60 per cent. Of course, to those who do not go to places like the River Streets, which were built on a vast rubbish dump in the 1940s, the image of poverty remains rooted in the 1930s and therefore 'real' poverty no longer exists in Britain and comparisons with previous hard times are merely emotive. It is true that many comparisons with the 1930s no longer apply and this makes all the more remarkable those that do.

For example, the Thatcher Government's Social Security has achieved what even the hated National Government of the 1930s balked at doing: it has cut unemployment and sickness pay in real terms. It has also dismantled many of the defences erected for the poor as a result of the indignities of the 1930s. During the Great Depression council schools used to issue old shoes to children who had none. This was called the 'boots for the bairns' fund and the children of the unemployed had to demonstrate their need in order to qualify for such charity. Social Security legislation now so severely restricts clothing (and shoes) grants that the primary school attended by many River Streets children has had to retreat to standards of forty years ago.

In 1980 the headmistress, Jean Farrell, began filling a room with old shoes and clothes. She told me, 'It's simply not possible to teach a child who is uncomfortable, who comes to us without breakfast, shaking with cold, who can't write with fingers that are blue. More than half my children are from unemployed families who try very hard, but after they eat they often have nothing but debts.'

An icon of the 1930s was the photograph of a miner and his son scavenging for coal. In the 1980s the unemployed and their children scavenge on a twenty-acre rubbish tip near the River Streets known as Bidston Moss. They slither and climb on their hands and knees over hills of filth, fish finger packets, bacon rind, tea bags and dead dogs in their search for saleable scrap: a discarded telly, an old copper, wearable clothes. Only the polythene bags tell you this is the 1980s, not the 1930s.

To observe distinctly 'modern' poverty in the River Streets you need to look for what was once expected and only briefly or never gained: telephones, a Sunday joint of meat, a hi-fi, warmth in winter, holidays, a night at the pictures, an outing anywhere. These are now as rare as chest ailments and rats are common again; even rickets has returned. What is less obvious is the sense of loss, of having been duped, that is felt profoundly by the young, and especially so as reminders of the old, broken promises remain.

On Merseyside I am always struck by the bizarre billboards which exhort the young to buy £20-a-bottle French brandy, to smoke cigarettes out of a packet that looks like a gold brick, to talk to 'the listening bank', to eat colourfully packaged junk, to take holidays in the Caribbean and to drive 'Supercat', a Jaguar car worth more than £20,000. These are scattered, mysteriously, as if to taunt, around lifeless docks and in streets where public services are such that women have formed groups to attempt to collect refuse.

For five years the people of the River Streets struggled for urban grants to build a community centre. Before, they did not even have a pub. Now they have a small prefabricated building and officially defunct skills of men and women, pensioners and teenagers are concentrated here, painting and decorating, organising keep-fit classes and a football team.

When they heard that Prince Charles was to visit Liverpool, they sent Charlie Wright to see if the Prince would open the centre. Charlie, the club secretary, said, 'We were offered half an hour of the Prince's time and told to submit a route with the quickest way in and out.' As the day of the Prince's visit approached, Wirral authority miraculously found funds to sandblast 'distasteful' graffiti from walls and to paint bridges and to lay turf. Rubbish was collected for the first time in weeks, and twenty wagons appeared one morning to sweep, hose and scrub the streets.

As it turned out, Prince Charles was unavailable, and Prince Michael came instead. The Prince's motorcade passed by what used to be Terry and Pauline Quigley's house. I met Terry and Pauline when I first visited the River Streets. They were both twenty-two. The roof in their council house had just fallen in directly above their baby's cot and the wreckage of the ceiling remained unrepaired and ignored by Wirral authority. It had been nine months since the North-West Gas Board had disconnected their gas supply, because Terry, unemployed, had been unable to pay £126 in arrears. Their house was a spick and span igloo.

All through the 1979 winter the Quigleys had slept on one damp floor beside a single electric bar: a year in which gas profits exceeded £600 million. The children had 'bad chests' and Terry was waiting to go to prison for twelve days because he had been caught without a television licence and had no means of paying the fine. They said the TV detector van often prowled the River Streets, where people were an easy catch.

One year later I found their house empty and gutted after a fire. Neighbours said an electrical fault had started it, which was likely, considering the damp in the house. The Quigleys apparently had escaped just in time, and they were now 'down South somewhere, looking for work'.

Nearby lived Norma Hampson and her family. Norma was a teenager in the 1950s, a shop assistant and a trainee nurse. And she was a young woman in the 1960s when, to the beat of Elvis, almost anything seemed possible. 'The difference with my parents' time was the hope,' she said. 'You could touch the hope. Before I got married, well, I always imagined my kids would break through, definitely. They'd work in offices, live the lives you saw on telly.'

Norma's husband and three daughters, all unemployed, listed the places where they had looked for work like auctioneers calling the offers to hand. 'My Debbie', said Norma, 'longs to work with children, to be a children's nurse, to train and everything. But she'll never do that. She's up at four in the morning doing things about the house, little jobs, anything to keep busy. She's lost some of her hair because of nerves, because of never getting a job.'

Debbie, her sisters and their friends gathered in Birkenhead Park, a manicured Victorian landscape on which New York's Central Park was modelled. They sat and watched rubbish swirl through the railings, from which many of the steel spikes are missing, having been torn from their mountings in 1932 when the one serious uprising during the Great Depression took place in Birkenhead. Today, for all the pockets of youthful violence, such as at Toxteth, Handsworth and Tottenham, and at football games, *outward* violence is still not widespread: indeed in most of Britain it is rare.

One reason for this is that in a Britain whose popular, inspirational images are almost all those of wealth and acquisition and where authority and most of the media now 'blame' people who are unable to live up to these images, the violence is directed *inward*. And it is this internalised violence, which is manifest in ill health and reliance on drugs and in the disintegration of relationships and families, that is widespread.

There is, for example, much 'reality' in the coroners' courts these days. For the past three years – since unemployment passed three million – I have been collecting reports of coroners' inquests in which unemployment has been mentioned as a principal factor in suicides. Taken mostly from provincial newspapers, the inquest stories are of a kind virtually unknown a few years ago. They have headlines such as 'REDUNDANCY BLOW LED TO DEATH' and 'SUICIDE OF JOBLESS MAN WHO LOST WILL TO LIVE' and 'DEATH LEAP BY MAN WITH JOB LOSS FEAR'.

This survey is, of course, a superficial one; much research investigating the causes of suicide needs to be done. But the trend is very clear and is supported by an increasing number of specialist reports on the subject. For example, in *New Society*, author Martyn Harris published research which concluded that more than half of all men who attempted suicide were out of work.[17] In August 1983 Dr Stephan Platt, an Edinburgh University research sociologist, found that men out of work for longer than a year were nineteen times more likely to commit suicide than those with jobs. 'The long term unemployed are clearly at risk,' Dr Platt told me, 'but the Government denies there is a problem.'

Mr William Bell had something to say about this in a letter he wrote to the *Daily Mirror* in March 1984. Mr Bell's son, Gordon, looked for work for two years; in the week he killed himself, in October 1983, he had been turned down as a salesman. He was twenty-six. In his moving letter Mr Bell wrote:

There were many factors which drove my son to such a tragic thing, but I can state categorically that if he had had employment he would still be with us today. He was intelligent, ambitious, full of drive and initiative, and prepared to work hard in any career. These qualities are not enough in Maggie Thatcher's New Britain. I am left wondering what sort of person can pursue political dogma relentlessly at the cost of so much human misery, despair, degradation and even life itself.

I cannot condone my son's action in taking his own life, but I can understand the depth of his despair and hopelessness and his refusal to accept the loss of dignity and pride which long-term unemployment entails. The increases in suicides or attempted suicides have roughly corresponded over the past seven years or so, and one would have expected this superficial relationship to have sufficiently been marked to have moved the government to investigate the matter with some urgency. Instead Mrs. Thatcher claims there is no evidence of any such relationship and dismisses the subject out of hand. How dare she!

When the *Daily Mirror* published Mr Bell's letter, I received some seventy letters, most of them from people suffering the loss of a loved one. From one town in Britain, which my correspondent asked me not to name, a widow wrote that 'unemployment suicides are so common around here that they're almost a joke in the pub'. This woman had lost both her husband and her brother-in-law. There were other kinds of letters. This following one, unsigned, touched me deeply.

I have recently experienced a different kind of death on the dole, the death of a once happy relationship. I have lived with my man for eleven years. He has been out of work for three of those eleven years, and slowly, painfully, our relationship has deteriorated. It was once full of happiness, of planning and looking forward to a good future together; now it is dead because my husband couldn't get a job. He is unskilled and 35 and nobody wants him. He couldn't stand the humiliation of not being able to provide for me and our two children. We clung to every straw, desperately trying to keep our small family a happy one, but then we could fight no longer. He's gone now and I am left with only the pain. Our love never died, but the struggle, with no end in sight, was too much for him to bear. Being unemployed destroyed not one, but four lives. I hope the people responsible for this can rest easy in their beds at night. I know I cannot.

There is also much 'reality' these days in the field of housing. Since 1979 spending on housing has been more than halved, and fewer houses are being built in Britain now than at any time since the Second World War.[18] Put another way: in 1975 equal amounts of tax money were spent on defence and housing; in 1984 five times as much was spent on the military services and on war material.[19] Britain no longer has a national housing programme.

While this policy has created more and more homeless people, a phenomenon has emerged. It is the British Welfare State bank-rolling the exploiters of the homeless and the unemployed to the extent of more than £120 million a year.[20] This windfall now enriches the owners of so-called hotels and hostels, most of them squalid, where victims of the recession are sent by local authorities and by the Department of Health and Social Security. These are the workhouses of the late-twentieth century.

'Guests' at these places sometimes have a choice. They can sign the backs of their Social Security cheques and hand them directly to the owner, or they can take a receipt for payment to the local DHSS office and be reimbursed. Either way, the hotel or hostel owner is paid promptly, and virtually any amount he wishes to charge will be accepted as a 'ceiling' by the DHSS and paid. Local authorities often have no choice but to send people to these places, as they are now prevented by central government from funding the building and restoration of homes.

This wholesale diversion of public money is one of the fastest ways of becoming rich in Britain today. In every city newspapers carry advertisements seeking, almost pleading for, 'unemployed guests'. In Bristol, where I posed as homeless and unemployed, the system moved smoothly into action. One hotel manager told me to get a 'lilac and blue B1 form' from the Social Security office and was so keen to have my head on one of his beds that he offered to send me to get the form in a taxi. This must be one of those rare moments when the unemployed feel themselves wanted, when their poverty is the source of such easy profit.

London is where the big money is to be made: London with its mutilated inner-city life, bursting housing estates and transient people still believing that their version of Spanish gold is to be found there.

At the time of writing I know of two children living in the heart of London, just across the park from Buckingham Palace, who have stopped eating. They are both two years old. The doctor attending them is Richard Stone and he described their condition to me as 'a phenomenon of the times we are living in'. These children, he said, 'are far from unique. Today children are picking up their parents' emotions, their sense of hopelessness; they are withdrawing into themselves and losing the will to thrive. Can you imagine a one-year-old apathetic about life? What we have is malnutrition, a Third World problem, here in Britain.'

Dr Stone's family practice is in Bayswater, in an area of seedy, flea- and cockroach-infested bed and breakfast hotels where local authorities as far afield as Brent and Camden send homeless families. Brent authority, prevented by central government from allotting money to a housing programme, has a constant 19,000 homeless families and in 1985 spent an estimated £5,600,000 on keeping many of them in bed and breakfast hotels; the profit to the hotel owners can only be imagined.

Outside these hotels are kerb-crawlers and prostitutes, and even with their babies in their arms homeless mothers are harassed. Cookers are not legally allowed in the rooms, and families often have no choice but to live on hamburgers, pizzas and chips which fatten and depress: the sustenance of modern poverty.

Kathy and her six-month-old baby Darren were in one of these rooms.

Darren could not crawl and explore. He had to be kept strapped and still in his cot, away from the electrical points and the window and the boiling kettle. He had a 'bad chest' and diarrhoea, and he screamed. Kathy could not imagine doing it herself, but, she said, 'I now understand how some mothers are driven to batter their babies.'

My symbol of the 1980s is not the micro-chip; it is Princes Lodge. A cavernous, granite slab, standing like a Colditz on a corner of Commercial Road in Tower Hamlets, East London, Princes Lodge was completed, appropriately, during the Great Depression. It became a British nightmare.

In February 1984 I slipped past the bouncers who guarded it and found up to five hundred people inside, an under-class of cowed humanity. They included many young children, over whom I had to step as they played in the damp filth of carpets in darkened corridors; there was nowhere else for them to play. Some of the residents had complained, but not for long; several were evicted, with all their possessions and their children at night, or poverty had its own debilitating effect upon them, converting them into 'trustees' who ran the place for a few extra pounds in hand. Having been rejected by the 'reality' outside, they had become dependent on a landlord, his 'wardeness' and his 'minders'.

There was another group at Princes Lodge. These were people who had done what the then Secretary for Trade and Industry, Norman Tebbit, had advised the unemployed to do: to 'get on your bike' and find work. They had got on their bikes and into trains and coaches and old cars and looked for work which did not exist and had ended up in London, in places like this.

Jim and Kay McKirdy and their six children had set out from Glasgow, and Princes Lodge was the end of their fruitless travels and their hopes. They had two rooms. One room was twelve feet by six feet and had a cooker, kitchen utensils, two beds, a television, all the family's clothes and all their belongings. It was not really a room; it was an extended cupboard.

Their six children, aged from three to eleven, slept in another room, six feet by fifteen feet. They had four bunks and they slept in shifts. There was room for one adult between the bunks. Jim and Kay maintained the rooms as a feat of order and dignity. They could do nothing about the vermin. For accommodating the McKirdy family, the owners of Princes Lodge received public money of £195.85 every week.

Princes Lodge is owned by Namecourt Ltd, which made more than £250,000 profit on the sale of its previous slum hostel in Earls Court.[21] From the beginning, Namecourt's directors included members of a wealthy London family, the Agrans, who are well known in the property, television and film worlds and in the Conservative Party. Albert Agran is a Justice of the Peace who sits on the bench at Redbridge Magistrates' Court.

In January 1984 the Agrans pulled out of the company and left it to two Scots, Paul Cowie and Alan Gill, who had run an Oxford Street 'accommodation bureau' enterprise. It was Cowie who collected the rent at Princes Lodge every Thursday when the Social Security cheques arrived. With the Agrans out and the enterprise now his and Gill's, Cowie doubled the rents for children under the age of eleven and increased by six times the rents for those up to fifteen years old. The local DHSS office accepted the increases, the new 'ceiling' imposed by Cowie, and proceeded to tax the residents accordingly. One man with three children was told in a letter from the DHSS, 'As you are probably aware, since Princes Lodge have seen fit to increase their board and lodge charge . . . we are unable to allow a meal allowance for children under eleven years.'[22]

The increase gave Cowie's company up to £250,000 extra on its current income, and Cowie has become a millionaire. In County Durham he has spent £750,000 restoring an eighteenth-century Gothic castle which, until the local council rejected his planning application, he intended to turn into a profitable old people's home.[23]

According to Councillor Paul Beasley who was leader of Tower Hamlets authority for ten years, 'Princes Lodge managed to slip through the net of our planning regulations. We have been against it from the word go.'

From 'the word go', in 1979, Tower Hamlets Council knew about conditions at Princes Lodge and, apart from a drawn-out correspondence with Cowie about 'constructive discussions . . . in an attempt to maintain some degree of flexibility',[24] the Labour Council did nothing to end the misery in its borough.

Several worried councillors did not manage to get into Princes Lodge, but the Council's own health officers were able to make a number of visits, and nothing changed. Professional warnings of the risks to health and life at Princes Lodge came from independent sources outside the Council. In 1984 two independent health officers found only sixteen lavatories for 500 people, no hot water in the bathrooms, no radiators working, broken glass on the stairs, open dustbins in the hallways, surrounded by rubbish and vomit, as well as exposed asbestos, filthy communal kitchens, half the fire extinguishers missing and 'the very real possibilities of fire tragedies'.[25]

The paediatrician at the nearby London Hospital, Dr R. J. D. Harris, wrote to Councillor Beasley:

For some years now the families living in Princes Lodge have been causing anxiety. The number of hospital admissions is disproportionately high for the number of children resident in the lodge.[26]

Dr Harris and his staff had conducted a survey and found that of nine babies admitted during a five-month period, six had serious respiratory and stomach infections. He described infants with the same strain of food poisoning, and one little girl who was admitted to hospital six times. He wrote:

> When I am faced with a newborn baby destined to live at Princes Lodge I tend to keep mother and child in hospital longer than would otherwise be necessary . . . I cannot take the risk of discharging a baby . . . and therefore place its life in jeopardy.

No council officer had reported the possibility of such serious risks to children. No council officer had reported the extreme conditions under which sixteen Vietnamese refugee families were forced to live in the top floors of Princes Lodge; no doubt these were 'problem families'. A case worker for the British Refugee Council, Romily Gregory, described the conditions to me as 'unbelievable . . . In the common toilets you were up to your ankles in urine and water. The people tried so hard to make civilised order out of this, but it was impossible. In one room there are badly disabled old people, two of them paralysed. They couldn't go anywhere. Tears streamed down their cheeks when I was there . . . I've not seen such desperation.'

On the contrary, a council environmental health officer had reported that 'the premises, whilst far from five star hotel standards, are in reasonably clean condition, bearing in mind some of the individuals and problem families who stay there'.[27] The implication was clear: the people, not Princes Lodge, were the 'problem'. This was reminiscent of Poor Law attitudes which were not difficult to promote in devastated communities encouraged to seek scapegoats rather than political action.

Princes Lodge, which has hundreds of counterparts all over Britain, existed as a landmark a few miles from the City of London. Neither Paul Cowie nor Paul Beasley would discuss it with me. Beasley, having relinquished his leadership of the Labour group in 1984, became a busy man as 'special projects adviser' to a Turkish multi-millionaire financier, Asil Nadir, who has interests in Tower Hamlets.

Paul Cowie carried a plastic shopping bag containing a monkey mask which he would put on and run whenever he arrived at and left Princes Lodge. So anxious had he been to conceal his features from the Press that he would open the door of his flat in Victoria wearing the mask.

The day after I published Jim and Kay McKirdy's complaints, Cowie's bouncers evicted them and their six children and two other families who had complained.

It was March 13, Budget Day. While the Chancellor was intoning his portfolio of tax favours in the Commons, fourteen people, including nine children aged from three years, attempted to assemble their belongings on a traffic island in front of Princes Lodge. An icy wind sluiced Commercial Road. It was rush hour and employed people on their way home stopped to watch. They seemed bemused and entertained as if what they were witnessing was the filming of a street scene in a movie. The bouncers brought out the families' personal things in black plastic bags, several of which split. There was a birdcage, an ironing board, a television. Jason McKirdy, aged four, asked his mother where they would sleep that night. Kay replied, 'Oh, we'll know soon.'

They were thrown out at dusk, just as the Council's homeless persons unit was about to close. When I got to the Council Offices, I received a dissertation from an official on whether or not the Council had 'statutory obligations' to the families. I finally left with the addresses of two hotels whose gain of the three families was Cowie's financial loss; the system was simply recycling them. All three families were eventually rehoused by the Greater London Council.

Princes Lodge was important because it represented much of what had happened to working people since the days of hope in the 1960s. What its conditions vividly expressed was the failure of the 'old guard' of the Labour Party in local government, in Parliament, in the institutions, to protect the very people for whom the Party was meant to exist; and by not protecting them, and by consorting with their enemies, and playing tactical political games rather than *opposing* and fighting back with ideas and commitment, they have betrayed and effectively disenfranchised up to a third of the population.[28] It is they who are a major source of bitterness in Britain.

Tower Hamlets is traditional, old guard Labour ground. My experience of the ruling Labour group was best summed up by the former mayor, Councillor John O'Neill, whose health and consumer services committee had resisted to the end all attempts to serve Namecourt Ltd with a control order under the Housing Act. O'Neill said to me, 'It's all right you writing these melodramatic reports. Cowie's got rights, too.'

The end came on May 3, 1984 when Tower Hamlets Council was forced by public pressure to serve the first statutory control order in the borough's history. This was the direct result of a campaign led by a coalition of unemployed people, including former residents of Princes Lodge, Tower Hamlets Law Centre, the Campaign for the Single Homeless (CHAR) and the Houses in Multiple Occupation Campaign, together with teachers, priests, vicars, bishops, doctors, nurses, trade unionists, the Greater London Council (which has since rehoused most of the residents of Princes Lodge) and myself.

This remarkable campaign, for which I can recall no precedent, raised spirits and dispersed apathy at meetings and rallies in the East End of London. Outside Princes Lodge itself, a great 'LIVING HELL' banner was raised. On one memorable night hundreds of us crowded into or stood in the rain outside the Old Poplar Town Hall where, in the 1920s, the radical politician George Lansbury had made his impassioned speeches against the levying of punitive rates on the stricken borough, and went to gaol for his pains.

Sixty years later the coming together of so many from across the divides of class, race and creed was an echo of that struggle. And, of course, there was more to it than the closure of one slum. It was a revivalist meeting whose energy derived from a wider frustration and a deeper anger.

Indeed, the Princes Lodge campaign was part of a resistance; and resistance is the appropriate word at a time when many in the governing authorities regard large sections of the population as 'enemies within'. Those who resist believe, with evident justification, that democracy is no longer open to them.

10

Fighting back

One of the most visible and positive examples of the resistance has been the work of and support given to the Greater London Council under its final administration before closure by government manoeuvre. As the Tammany Labour Party continued to identify itself with the pretensions of the establishment, the GLC presented an alternative model to the fake and passive pluralism upon which Labour had previously assumed power. Behind what at times seemed like an anarchic façade, the GLC raised almost to an art form the notion that every group in a multi-racial society ought to have its say in an arena of public discussion and negotiation.

'Consensus' taboos were placed in the public domain: Northern Ireland for one, on which Labour and Tory parties in government had conspired to agree. Oases were created in shabby London; parks were used to renew the capital's popular cultural life and great staged events, from black gospel concerts to the 'Thames Day' celebrations, became celebrations of people, sometimes with a defiant edge.

In this same atmosphere institutionalised racism has been challenged on the streets, although this is not widely known because it is not reported. On a winter's afternoon outside Walthamstow Senior High School for Girls in London I watched a gang of bullies gather to wait for the school to come out. They unfurled racist slogans, hoping to provoke the large number of black pupils. They were breaking the law, of course, but there were no police on hand to arrest them or move them on.

What transpired was described by one of the girls, who happened to be white. 'We didn't really have to say much,' she said. 'More than 300 girls turned up and stood right up to them. There was white with black. And there was this white girl with a black girl on her shoulders and we were all chanting, "We are black, we are white. Together, we are dynamite!"'

All the strengths of youth – idealism, resourcefulness, rebellion – were on show. These young people despise the moral vacuity of so much of present-day politics and their energy has yet to be siphoned off into the premature cynicism necessary to run a 'Taiwan economy' devoted to servicing the few. In Britain in recent years the fastest-growing movement of young people, apart from the unemployed, has not been 'punks' or football hooligans, but the youth wing of the Campaign for Nuclear Disarmament, which has recruited up to 500 young people a month.

The resistance grows mostly by word of mouth. As the 'caring' society has been usurped by the 'blame' and 'bootstraps' society, it is far easier for the media 'communicators' to blame the victims of poverty than to call the rest of us to admire their dignity in the face of impossible odds. There are few opportunities to explain, for example, that the Welfare State has been redefined by governments and today increasingly provides neither 'benefits' for people nor ammunition in the fight against 'Want, Squalor, Disease and Ignorance', as Lord Beveridge identified the 'common enemies of us all'. In the years of 'reality' the Welfare State's bureaucracy has imposed on people manipulative and punitive control.

This control was demonstrated clearly to me in July 1984 when I returned to the pit town of Murton in County Durham, where I had gone down to the coal-face ten years before. With the miners' strike at its height the Department of Social Security maintained a public fiction that miners were 'deemed' to be receiving strike pay, which they were not; in this way, benefits were withheld punitively.

I met Patrick Warby, a Murton miner whose five-year-old daughter, Marie, had been born with a bowel deformity. Marie needed a special high-fibre diet; otherwise she was in constant pain. Her father explained, 'I went to the DHSS with a letter from my doctor which said that if I didn't have something extra to buy the food for her, she'd block up. The official told me, "Come back when that happens."'

He appealed to a tribunal which, according to a record of the hearing,[29] accepted the fact that Marie had a medical condition for which she required 'a special diet' and 'accordingly, an additional requirement for a special diet was appropriate'. But because Marie's father was 'affected by a Trade dispute', this additional requirement could not be made. In other words, because a man is on strike his child must physically suffer.

It was this common, insidious kind of punishment, more than the riot shields and batons, which stiffened miners as traditionally cautious as the men of Durham. In 1984 and 1985 resistance on a national scale was left to those who put their lives at risk every day to produce Britain's most basic primary energy. They were the bedrock upon which the industrial society was built and their communities were among Britain's most precious assets. The miners' strike was about preserving these assets and preventing further encroachment by the rim of an industrial dustbowl. It was a protest against the notion of Two Nations, which the Thatcher Government flaunted. Above all, it was an acknowledgment that the 'consensus' had been bogus, and they had been betrayed.

It is a liberal platitude that vigilance is the price of liberty, for it has not been the liberals who have fought for, established and re-established basic liberties in Britain; it has been ordinary people and their prosaic and frequently scorned and brutalised organisations ... Peterloo in 1819, Bloody Sunday in 1887, the free speech struggles in Manchester in 1896 and the campaign at the turn of the century against the courts' hostile interpretation of laws establishing trades union rights.[30]

The 1984–5 miners' strike was such a struggle from below. Perhaps that is why the question of 'violence on the picket lines' was debated with such hypocritical zeal; one of many studies all but ignored by the national media found that most arrested miners had committed no offence, that most of the arrests were illegal or contravened the Judges' Rules (failure to caution an arrested person; the use of threats and intimidation) and that most magistrates gave blanket 'political' bail conditions, regardless of the merits of each case.[31]

In Ollerton and other Nottinghamshire towns I found dozens of striking miners who, away from the picket lines and the television cameras, had been taken by policemen in boiler suits and beaten so efficiently they are unlikely to work again. They held their press conferences, reporters listened sympathetically and took notes, and nothing appeared that evening or the next day. That the police and the courts belonged to the government of the day was a truth not 'moderate' enough for public consumption.

The trade union establishment hoisted the white flag of 'consensus' long before the end. In February 1985 I happened to be visiting Murton when the television news showed the recently retired Trades Union Congress leader, Len Murray, doffing his cap three times to Lord Hailsham as 'Lord Murray of Epping Forest' took his seat in the unelected upper chamber. It had been Len Murray who, together with Margaret Thatcher, had called for an attitude of 'reality' from working people. Translated, this meant collaboration with the makers of deliberate policies of mass unemployment.

On a freezing night in the Murton miners' institute, such a spectacle of ritual betrayal caused an embarrassed silence among the men I was with. Either they were too incredulous, too exhausted or too generous to say what was in their minds. 'There goes Len', said one of them finally.

Murton remained almost solid until the last few weeks. 'A strange thing happened,' said John Cummings, secretary of the mechanics. 'The banks and the finance companies began to turn the screws all at once. We couldn't go on bleeding, we could give no more.'

Since the miners were forced back to work colliery closures have gone ahead exactly as the union leadership warned. More than 30,000 jobs are likely to be lost and the 'Plan for Coal' abandoned, all of which the National Coal Board said would never happen. Elsewhere, the Government has abolished the minimum wage for workers under the age of twenty-one. This was a protection dating back to 1909 when the Asquith Liberal Government sought to deal with post-Victorian sweatshops. What amounts to a vendetta against the vulnerable young is being pursued. Not only are the young being required to bear a disproportionate burden of mass unemployment but those with no hope of finding work are being forced to keep moving around the country, often sleeping rough, by new regulations which stop the payment of Social Security benefits in any one place for a certain period, no matter that you may have grown up in that place. This is how the Victorian Poor Laws operated.

A triumphant police force has, in full public view, attacked groups of citizens, from miners at Orgreave to students at Manchester to black women in their homes in London, two of whom died as a consequence. To reinforce future police requirements, the Government has proposed new public order legislation which, it is predicted, will bring about the greatest reduction of political freedom in nearly two centuries. Public dissent, even in the form of static demonstrations, will become potentially illegal, and the initial arbiters of legality will not be the courts but senior police officers in their new role of political commissars.

Following the miners' strike the resistance spread to education. Teachers unable to subsist on their salaries resigned or began to take action. Maintained by both Conservative and Labour governments as forever the poor relation of private education, the state system is on the way to demoralisation, in spite of its very considerable and unsung achievements of cutting by half the number of children gaining no academic attainments[32] and in widening and enriching the curriculum of study for all children.

In 1984 a senior Department of Education official warned in a report that legislative powers might be necessary to change and 'rationalise' the schools' curricula. 'We are in a period of considerable social change,' he wrote. 'There may be social unrest, but we can cope with the Toxteths. But if we have a highly educated and idle population we may possibly anticipate more serious social conflict. *People must be educated once more to know their place.*'[33]

The process of educating people 'once more to know their place' may face insurmountable difficulties. Civil disturbances in those parts of Britain where Government policies of 'de-industrialisation' together with institutional racism have left fewer than 10 per cent of the young with any prospect of a practical purpose in their lives have become commonplace. Following the riots of Handsworth, Brixton and Tottenham in autumn 1985 the political 'consensus' was briefly reinstated as Labour Party leaders joined with the Government to focus the public's attention on the criminality of what had happened, not on the causes. A gloating speech by Enoch Powell, calling again for repatriation – sending the victims of Government policies and of racism back to where most of them had not come from – was described by the prime minister as 'very interesting' and 'worth reading very carefully indeed'.[34]

In 1986 the hope of British politics lies in its volatility. The miners were beaten, but their struggle spawned a popular front which could transcend the capricious 'solidarity' of the traditional labour movement and force a historic realignment of opposition forces. Women, farmers, teachers, shopkeepers, civil servants, pensioners, clergymen, Irish people, ethnic people and peace movement people went to remarkable lengths to help the miners. The depth of their improbable alliance was seldom reported and remained a 'secret' of the strike. People for the first time, wrote Hywel Francis, 'began to take control of their own lives'.

For example, when the South Wales Striking Miners' Choir entertained an entirely black audience in Walsall one of the choristers paid tribute to the 'ethnic minorities' who had been so outstanding in their support during the strike. To which a black leader responded, 'The Welsh are the ethnic minority in Walsall!' And both audience and choristers stood and cheered. 'The strike', wrote Hywel Francis who recounted this story, 'has begun to teach all of us that none of us are minorities.'[35]

It was good to be in Britain then, to meet women who stood with their men with a vitality and courage which humbled those of us who visited their front line. The shadow over them, and over all who might resist in the future, is that the centralised state, now progressively shorn of countervailing power and of many civil liberties, was far more powerful than they. And yet people are never still.

On the morning the Murton miners went back to their pit, their prize brass band emerged from the mist with the women marching first. This had not happened before. Regardless of future events, what their long and heroic action meant, at the very least, was that ordinary men and women had stood and fought back. And that, for me, is Britain at its best.

III

AMERICA

Heroes
Saviours
Un-Americans

11

Heroes

CHASING THE DREAM

In his speeches, notably during his election campaigns, President Reagan has described America as 'that God-given place between two oceans . . . a shining house on the hill . . . a beacon to all the world'. America is the only nation 'to have a government, not the other way around' and 'the only place on earth where freedom and dignity of the individual have been available and assured'. In his inauguration speech of 1981, Reagan went further. 'We are unique,' he said. 'This transition of power [from President Carter to himself] is a miracle!'

This kind of rhetoric might well have come from B-movie Hollywood, which spawned Ronald Reagan and that other celebrated symbol of American idealism, the late John Wayne. Just as Reagan has exhorted Americans to 'stand tall' against malevolent forces, so Wayne's celluloid heroism inspired many of a generation's young men to go willingly to a war they did not understand. His example on the screen, always tough, vigilant and moral, provided a simplistic model to which many aspired.

What Reagan and Wayne also had in common was that neither man ever had to 'stand tall' in the defence of his country. Both remained in Hollywood during the Second World War. Indeed, Reagan was then busy halting the premature decline in his acting career by informing on 'communists' for the studio bosses Jack Warner and Louis B. Mayer, and went to considerable lengths not to put on a uniform, devoting himself instead to making wartime propaganda films.[1] And that alone might help to explain the manufactured nature of the idealism which, packaged and promoted for television, has become the almost uninterrupted voice of America.[2] Having lived and worked in America, and admiring much about American life, I find myself resentful of such a distortion. It is as if genuine, popular response to idealism has been manipulated by a powerful group whose belligerent sense of moral superiority, not to mention paranoia, actually runs against the grain of ordinary, unwarlike American decency.

I travelled a great deal in America during the 1960s and 1970s, a period of upheaval but also of hope. Black people in the old southern confederacy had begun to demand their civil rights, the ghettoes of Los Angeles, Detroit and Washington erupted, Martin Luther King, Malcolm X and Robert Kennedy were assassinated, the Vietnam war was executed to disaster and a visible and active movement, whose roots were idealistic, held the imagination of millions of Americans. Martha Gellhorn, the war correspondent, described them as

> . . . that life-saving minority of Americans who judge their government in moral terms. They are the people with a wakeful conscience, the best of America's citizens . . . they can be counted on, they are always there. Though the government tried viciously, it could not silence them.[3]

To many of them, the notion of conscience itself was not exotic, as it sometimes seems today; and moral concerns had not become so rare that they seemed eccentric. They understood the nature of their country's longest war and they rejected 'manifest destiny': their government's self-given right to coerce and assault small nations. They believed that America ought to behave abroad according to the democracy its leaders claimed for it at home. They resisted what they saw as the one-dimensional, often venal politics of those who possessed so much of their country's public life and whose propaganda frequently claimed to express its patriotism. At times their own political aims and energy seemed fatuous and ephemeral, yet their movement was briefly powerful enough to influence, marginally, the American media, political process and scholarship and to reach beyond the limits of American liberalism, making radical change seem possible.

Matt and Jeannine Herron were two such Americans. Jeannine's family were Quakers, originally from Kansas where her father had attracted the disapproval of their small community by registering as a conscientious objector during the First World War. In 1962 Jeannine had helped to found 'Women's Strike for Peace' which, although it had no organised political base, had a powerful and spontaneous effect on women all over the United States. 'On the day the call went out across the country', said Jeannine, 'thousands of women in their home towns refused to go to work and stood in public in protest against nuclear testing. We collected baby teeth and had them analysed for Strontium

90 and we decided to send a delegation to Geneva to lobby at the arms control talks. None of us had done anything like this before.'

Jeannine was one of those who went to Geneva. On her return she and hundreds of other women travelled to Washington in support of Dagmar Wilson, one of the Strike leaders, who had been called to testify before the House of Representatives Un-American Activities Committee, once the inquisition of Senator Joe McCarthy into communist influence in American public life. Jeannine said, 'The hearing room was jammed with us women and children – lots of babies-in-arms, diaper bags and flowers. We stood and cheered every time Dagmar politely refused to answer a question. And when she was asked who the officers of the organisation were, she replied that they had not had time to elect anybody. "We're not very well organised," she said, as babies were crying and everybody was laughing.'

In June 1963, the Herrons were living in Philadelphia when Jeannine received a telephone call from a friend in Jackson, Mississippi. Medgar Evers, a leader of the National Association for the Advancement of Colored People, had just been murdered. Her friend asked her to come down for the funeral and to 'see what's going on in the South and maybe help us'. Jeannine went. On the day of Evers's funeral tension was high in Jackson. As white and black mourners left the church to begin a procession through the town Jeannine became separated from the others. 'Just then', she said, 'an old black woman stepped beside me and took my hand. "Don't be afraid," she said, "I'll walk wi' you. We glad you came."'

Mississippi was then little different from South Africa. Segregation was the rule in housing, schools, hospitals, restaurants, transport. 'Nigras' knew their place and their place was literally and figuratively 'in the back of the bus'. Burning crosses, lynchings and other forms of racial violence associated with the Ku Klux Klan had continued into the 1960s, often unreported and covered up by complicit police forces. Between the autumn of 1962 and the spring of 1963 the US Civil Rights Commission received more than 100 serious complaints of 'lawless conduct and defiance of the Constitution' on the part of the Mississippi state authorities.[4] These ranged from local politicians denying the vote to blacks, to welfare officials impounding federal government food meant for impoverished black children, to the fire-bombing of the homes of whites sympathetic to black emancipation.

Matt Herron was a photo-journalist whose picture essays in *Life*, *Look* and the *Saturday Evening Post* were to become a distinguished chronicle of the decade. His outspokenness against the Korean war during the height of McCarthy's witch-hunting had led to strained relations with his own conservative family and prepared him for difficult years in the

South. When Jeannine returned from Mississippi, 'we decided to put our money where our mouth was'; and she and Matt and their children Mathew and Melissa packed a few household possessions and set out in their old van for Jackson, Mississippi.

This was the beginning of the exodus to the South by northern civil rights activists seeking to enforce a 1954 Supreme Court Ruling against racial segregation. The Herrons stayed at first with a native white Mississippian, Ed King, who was first on the Ku Klux Klan death list and received constant calls threatening his life: the minimum price paid by those southern whites who spoke out against segregation. Matt later wrote:

> Southerners know far better than northerners that a whole social order is at stake. Like every battle, this one has produced its heroes – sung and unsung. Ed King was one of the white heroes. Among the many black heroes was Hartman Turnbow who wanted to be the first Negro in Holmes County to get on the voter registrar's list. That same evening, as a reward for his uppityness, he had to stand-off a posse of white men who shot up and tried to burn down his house. Turnbow drove them off singlehanded, but when he reported the incident next day, he was arrested – for arson![5]

One of the earliest civil rights actions was an attempt to integrate Jackson's churches. Teams of blacks and whites would go up to the doors of the white Baptist church and be turned away by the church elders, or arrested or beaten up, or both if they persisted. It was the afternoon of November 22, 1963 when Jeannine and Matt heard white schoolchildren chanting, 'One down, two to go! One down, two to go!' and a man at a newsstand said to Jeannine, 'Well, you hate to see a dog lying in the middle of the road, but the world's better off for it, isn't it?' John Kennedy had been shot in Dallas, Texas. (One of the Herrons' rich assortment of friends was the heroic Penn Jones Jr, editor of the *Midlothian Mirror*, near Dallas (weekly circulation: 850). Penn wrote, produced and printed every issue of his newspaper, which achieved fame, and a Pulitzer prize, for publishing evidence of an official cover-up of the circumstances surrounding the murder of President Kennedy. His office and printing press were fire-bombed, but in the highest tradition, he never failed to bring out the *Mirror*.)

For more than two years the Herrons 'chased the dream', as they once described their commitment and that of their friends, in the South. During that time they braved shotguns protruding from pick-up trucks, fire-bombings and a constant menace wherever they went, from the towns to the roads through the jungles of the river country to the vastness of the Delta. In 1964 Matt set up the 'Southern Documentary Project in Photography', a team of eight young photographers whose work attempted to go beyond the standard 'good' news pictures of violence and record the real images of change in a society that had remained stable for more than a century and was now rapidly dissolving. They achieved this with, above all, a sympathy for the South, black and white, and by living with people, marching with them, being beaten with them, even facing the possibility of dying with them; three civil rights workers were kidnapped and murdered that summer.

Matt Herron's pictures and those of his photo team brought to the attention of many Americans outside the South a situation they had never imagined and injustices they would not tolerate in their own lives. I worked with Matt on many similar assignments; his pictures were frequently displayed across 'Mirrorscope' in the *Daily Mirror*, and I never ceased to be struck by the humanity in them. It was often a subtle quality, expressed in the shadows of people's faces, in the way they stood, in their humility and defiance; and it contrasted sharply with the 'human interest' contrived in so many Press pictures. (Almost exactly the same quality is in the pictures of another great American photographer, Ken Regan, with whom I have also worked.)

The civil rights workers made many gains, based solidly on the initial courageous acts of rural blacks. They established, for example, more than 100 'freedom schools' across Mississippi. This was an astonishing achievement, which grew out of the need to provide both academic and political education for black children whose only contact with formal learning was the sub-standard, white-run, segregated schools of the state. The new schools set out to change the way black children had been taught to see themselves: as happy, childlike, fundamentally inferior people whose only culture was a second-rate one borrowed from the white man. The 'freedom' teachers were often young, inexperienced, northern college students. Their classes met in churches, community halls, on porches and in open fields; and when the church housing a freedom school at Gluckstadt, Mississippi, was fire-bombed and burned to the ground, the children and their teachers turned up the next morning and set up their chairs in the smouldering ashes.

When President Johnson's 'Great Society' reforms finally reached the South, it was a programme devised by Jeannine Herron which eventually brought the first organised preschooling to some 5,000 children in Mississippi. And when Johnson signed the Civil Rights Act in 1964 and the Voting Rights Act the following year, both a direct result of the work and courage of black Americans and their white allies, one victory in a long, continuing struggle was won.

THE BOYS OF BEALLSVILLE

Beallsville, Ohio: June 1970. The first hot winds of summer blew through the American heartlands, where the town of Beallsville had slept beneath its magnolias and elms for two centuries, ever since George Washington himself farmed here. There is one main street, which is also State Highway 556, coming in from the hills of Appalachia, West Virginia, going on to Jerusalem, Hannibal and Cincinnati. Some seven hundred people live here, beneath scarred slopes and in sour little hollows over which hangs the fleck of coal: the 'dust of darkness' as an eloquent soul wrote on a memorial near the pit-top at the Ogilby-Norton mine.

There are two major sources of income: the mines operated by the North American Coal Company and the Ornet aluminium plant in Hannibal, where the 'swing shift' (through the night and dawn) is worked by poor dirt farmers. During the 1960s and early 1970s the plant thrived on making shells for the war in Vietnam. In 1970 40 per cent of the families of Monroe County, which has Beallsville at its centre, subsisted below the official government poverty line of $3,000 a year.

For this reason Beallsville is not attractive in the style and manner of so much of small-town America. It has a few splendid multi-gabled buildings, but most are of gaunt grey and white clapboard, like a western film-set about to blow down. There is a general store run by Dewey and a barber shop run by Kelly and a hairdresser's over which hangs a sign, 'Dior wigs made to order'.

And beyond the junkyard is the high school from which fewer than 3 per cent of the pupils go on to college; the rest go to the mines or to the service industries of Cincinnati or are idle. In 1970 they went to the military draft, and when the seventeen young men of the 'senior class of '70' received their diplomas, they strode ritually across the football field and up the hill, to where many of the classes of '65, '66, '67 and '68 were enshrined: in the graveyard.

Jack Pittman and Bob Lucas, Charlie Schnegg, Rick Rucker and Duane Greenlee: all of them born here and grown up here; all of them killed in places their parents could never pronounce. At the height of the war in Vietnam the national ratio for Americans killed was one in 6,000. For Beallsville it was one in ninety.

'We've already lost the goddamn war,' said the mayor, Ben Gramlich, who also ran the 'JFK recreation center' for the town's teenagers. 'I'm not against it, but we're running outta young'uns to give.'

The unique severity with which the war came home to Beallsville made this one small community a microcosm of the deep confusions which racked much of middle America during the war. In a place where it was heresy to question duty to God and country, fear seemed to be everywhere; for patriotism itself had been violently challenged by the suspicion, much of it still unspoken, that their sons had died in the cause of nothing.

When Bob Lucas was brought home in summer 1969 and everyone filled the streets for his funeral – everyone, except his father who had a heart attack on the day – Keith Harper got up and said angrily, 'Enough is enough! The way they're decimating our boys just isn't right.' As Beallsville's undertaker, Keith Harper had buried all five boys, and the day after the Lucas funeral he called up the county treasurer Ray Starkey, and said, 'Ray, you got to do something.' And Starkey called up Congressman Clarence E. Miller who said he would see if he could 'get the boys moved around the war zone a little bit, to save lives'. And Congressman Miller called up Washington and was turned down.

'I just felt it was one helluva toll to take out of a little place,' recalled the undertaker. 'Why, down in Woodsfield – that's the county seat – the biggest part of them goes to college and gets a deferment, whereas our boys are too poor to go.'

Between 1965 and 1970 Beallsville gave thirty-five young men to the draft and most of them went to Vietnam and were wounded or killed. At the time of Bob Lucas's death, there were no more to give. Jack Pittman, aged nineteen, was the first to die. He was an only child who lived with his parents in a two-storey house which leaned with the wind opposite their peach orchard. Earl Pittman worked the afternoon shift at the aluminium plant. 'I got to,' he said. 'The price of peaches ain't changed in twenty years.'

After Jack was killed, in July 1966, his mother left his room as it was and they seldom went upstairs. 'We keep his trophies down here,' said Maegene Pittman. 'He was captain of both the football *and* basketball teams at Beallsville High. Why, he even took a little team of eighth graders under his wing to teach them basketball. He was a good Christian boy.'

She read me a letter Jack wrote from Vietnam on March 18, 1966: 'They gave me a machine gun and a pistol today. I'm not sure what I'm to do, Mom, because I'm only a radio man . . .'

That afternoon he was ambushed and shot in the head.

'The first news we had was a telegram saying he had been critically wounded,' said his mother. 'Then nothing for a week. Earl and I nearly went insane, so eventually I said, "I'm going to call Washington." Well, the man on the phone at the Pentagon just didn't understand. He said, "Listen, lady, what's happened to your boy is an everyday account. I can't trace every kid who's got hisself hurt out there."

'I said, "You listen to me, bub, if you were on this end of the line, in this house, you wouldn't consider it an everyday account. He's *our boy*."

'Well, the next thing a sergeant came around and told us Jack had died in an army hospital in San Francisco. He said, "I'm sorry, but that's war." And I guess I just stood there cryin' and bellowin', "God, it's their war, not our war."'

Maegene Pittman had never heard of Vietnam when Jack was called up. 'I thought it was somewhere near Panama: real close and threatening,' she said. The Pittmans refused a military funeral. 'It didn't seem right,' said his father. 'That uniform was just rags of death. We buried him in his graduation suit.'

A mile and a half away, down Rural Route 1, lived Kenneth and Betty Rucker, whose son, Rick, also nineteen, was killed on May 30, 1968, Memorial Day. 'Bernie Decker who runs the gas station brought the telegram,' said Mr Rucker, an electrical linesman. 'Bernie's had two boys out there and I knew by the look of him what it was. The telegram said Rick had been killed by a "friendly rocket while storming a Vietcong bunker".'

Mr Rucker tapped some tobacco into a small patch of paper, curled it, wet it, and lit up. He was smiling and crying. Betty Rucker shooed the other children out into the fields. 'You see I could tell from my boy's last letters that he was going to die,' she said.

May 8

Hello everyone. Well the shit is really happening here. I didn't want to tell you but I'm tore up bad mentally. My buddy Frank got zapped the other day, right next to me. He was all over me. He had 13 days to go.

May 21

Got ambush patrol tonight. Ugh! They won't let you out of this field until you drop. I haven't had a real break since I got here, wherever here is. The leeches got all my blood now. Covered with sores and mud ...

May 29

Some of us were thinking of refusing to go in tonight, but they'll only send us to jail. Hell, why am I here? Do you know? Guess all I can do is go for broke and kill as many gooks as I can . . . Hope you got a good price for my car.

The next day Rick was killed.

The Ruckers reluctantly agreed to a military funeral, which provided their ordeal with a brutal finale. The officer sent to organise it was drunk most of the time and could not be found to give orders to the honour guard. 'Guess, he'd done one too many,' said Betty Rucker with infinite generosity.

At the funeral they met a young soldier who had been with Rick when he died. There was no Vietcong bunker, he told them: 'just a bunch of guys sitting around in a latrine area' when someone, somehow, accidentally blew them all up. 'They was having a crap,' said Kenneth Rucker. 'Nothin' more than that.'

From a small boy, Duane Greenlee had wanted to be a marine and his mother knew it was the only way out of the poverty which paralysed the family of eleven. So Duane enlisted in the marines when he was eighteen and was still eighteen when they brought him back home in a box marked, in heavy type, 'UNVIEWABLE' and 'THIS WAY UP'. Duane had been wounded once before he died, said his mother, and the bandages meant he could not wear a helmet. All the same, he was sent in to fight and a sniper shot him in the head.

Mary Greenlee moved house after her son's death and it was dusk when I found her, working in a bar twelve miles away in Claringtown, on the coal ridge just above the Ohio River.

'Duane's father and I separated soon after our boy's death,' she said. 'I guess we couldn't stand what losing him did to us. Duane, that's Duane senior, moved out to Bellaire, while my three other boys and my four girls just picked up the pieces around here. I knew all the Beallsville boys who died. They'd come round to our house; Duane and them were all friends. I wanted to go to each one of their funerals but I just couldn't. I just stayed away and thought about them like they were my own boys.

'Duane really wanted to go to the war, but when he got there he didn't know why he'd been sent! Out there he didn't see no sense in any of it. We were so proud of him. I got a son thirteen coming up and he can't wait to get in the marines. Isn't that something?'

I returned to Beallsville exactly ten years later and looked for the Pittmans, the Ruckers and Mary Greenlee. Mary, I learned, had taken her flock deeper into Appalachia, looking for work. Kenneth and Betty Rucker had long ago parted. 'The strain of Rick dyin' in the way he did', said a neighbour, 'just got too much for them.'

Earl and Maegene Pittman had moved, and Earl would only speak to me through the flyscreen door. 'Thank you for sending them photographs of us,' he said. 'I can't let you come in because my wife is dyin' in here.' They had, he said, moved Jack's room intact from the old house. 'Nothin's been disturbed,' said Earl Pittman. 'We ain't never forgettin' him.'

Five years later, on the tenth anniversary of the end of the war in Vietnam, some of Beallsville's people took up a collection to pay for a memorial shaped like a huge American flag. They raised only $1,030 and the idea lapsed.

'SUCKERS'

The American public believes by a two to one margin that the veterans of the Vietnam war 'were made suckers of, having to risk their lives in the wrong war in the wrong place at the wrong time'.

Harris opinion poll, November 1979

On patrol, in the drumming rain, with each step requiring a superhuman effort to reclaim a boot from the sucking mud, a hand would reach back to beckon or drag me forward, followed by a reassuring voice: 'C'mon man, let's go.' The voice would come from a street corner in the Bronx, a rural town in the Confederacy, a steel mill in Pennsylvania: little America.

The only drinking water would be brackish and polluted, which meant that you got sick and slept in it. Leeches were ritually pulled from each other's arms and backs in the dark: 'jungle rot' it was called, and it served to relieve the hours of waiting for seconds of terror.

Then, in a field suddenly ablaze, a stunned face lay with someone trying to stem a crescendo of screams. Confusion; panic; timidity; bravery; stoicism; and more waiting until the burst of a flare and the swishing of rotors as a ruined nineteen-year-old was delivered to the medevac helicopter.

Bob Muller endured all that. For him, the price was a shattered spinal column and two useless legs.

I never met Bob Muller in Vietnam, which is not surprising as 3,700,000 Americans served there. When I did meet him I realised I had seen him at the Republican Party's convention at Miami Beach in 1972, booing the candidate for President, Richard Nixon. He and other protesting Vietnam veterans had been thrown out, in their wheelchairs.

Five years later I saw him again, out in the sun on the steps of City Hall, New York. It was Memorial Day, the day America remembers its 'foreign wars'. There were medals and salutes and dignitaries, then former Lieutenant Robert O. Muller of the United States marines, a much decorated American hero of the kind John Wayne never was, took the microphone and from his wheelchair brought even the construction site beyond the crowd to an attentive silence. He said:

> There are 280,000 veterans of Vietnam in New York alone and a third of them can't find jobs. Throughout America sixty per cent of all black veterans are unemployed. Almost half of all Vietnam veterans have problems with alcohol and drugs, and just as many are probably dying now from the effects of poisons we dumped over there as died on the battlefield.
>
> You people out there, who didn't go, ran a number on us, right? Your guilt, your hang-ups made it socially unacceptable to mention the fact that we fought in Vietnam. We wear artificial limbs so *you* won't know we're disabled veterans.
>
> Why do we feel like we just held up a bank when someone asks about our wounds? Why do we feel that we must be guilty for letting America down or, if we're critical of America, we can't explain even to ourselves why we went over there and needlessly killed civilians?
>
> Eight of my friends, with dead legs like these, killed themselves when they got home; we've got the highest suicide rate in America . . . that's all I want to say to you today.[6]

The following year flags throughout America flew at half-mast for the eight soldiers killed in the failed attempt to rescue the American hostages in Iran. President Carter visited most of the families of the fifty-two hostages and there was a patriotic parade in their honour. Two years later the hostages themselves were welcomed home in one of the greatest American parades of all. They, of course, were officially approved heroes, who would embarrass no one with accusations of collective guilt or confessions of failure: 'victory' in their case having been bought conveniently with money.

There was no great parade for America's greatest army, which went to Vietnam; they were GIs who, unlike the 'doughboys' of 1919 and the 'johnnies' of 1945, never marched home. They returned individually. 'We slunk home,' many of them told me. More marines died in Vietnam than in all of the Second World War, yet it was not until 1982 that a monument to the dead of the nation's longest war was erected in Washington and it was not until 1985 that New York, which traditionally honoured America's returning troops, laid on a ticker-tape parade.

Contrary to myth and unlike the Second World War, 80 per cent of America's soldiers in Vietnam were volunteers. They came mostly from working-class America, and they had no student deferments with which to evade the draft; anyway, their evangelical patriotism put that out of the question.

I found Bob Muller in an almost bare office at the seedy end of Fifth Avenue in New York. He is a slight, grey figure whose appearance belies his booming eloquence and deep sense of irony. He said that in 1976, when he formed Vietnam Veterans of America in order to help, as he put it, 'my invisible comrades', he was briefly fashionable:

I was constantly being wheeled out for all kinds of establishment groups. Carter had made a big deal of human rights and I was probably the most convenient, most accessible human right around. I was invited to a meeting with all the big names of Exxon, the Chase Manhattan Bank and so on. They said, 'We're going to bring you vets right back into the mainstream; we're going to put things right for you.'

Just look at this letter I wrote to one of them, David Packard, one of the ten richest men in the country, whose corporation made a fortune out of the war. The day after Packard took his brotherly arm off my shoulder I wrote a letter to him, requesting some help for the vets: pretty modest stuff, like administration costs. That was six months ago and I haven't had a reply. We can't even pay our office phone bill. Of course we weren't completely friendless. The editor of the *Washington Post* agreed to see me and said, 'I'm gonna go to bat for you guys.' Well in the course of a year he published a total of thirty-six editorials and columns about us and at the end of the year, he said, 'I've never conducted an editorial campaign as I have on behalf of you Vietnam veterans and had such a silence in response. It's unprecedented and it's stunning . . . '[7]

Perhaps the most important reason for this stunning silence, as well as for the studied neglect of America's 'invisible' army, was that the Vietnam veterans held the secrets of the war: that is, they understood the true nature of the war.

Mike Sulsona was a marine who 'loved all the John Wayne movies as a kid'. He reminded me of those GIs I knew who had deliberately fired over the heads of an enemy they came to respect more than their own officers.

'We're not much worse in America than people anywhere,' he said. 'But we're not much better either, and there's the problem for us. We've got too many myths to live up to, as if our national moral life is forever hanging in some kind of uneasy balance, slanted toward violence but checked by decency.'

I met Mike in 1978, two years after President Carter had commissioned a study which called for the creation of 100,000 jobs for Vietnam veterans; during those two years 136 jobs had been found. Out of 21,000 seriously disabled veterans, 500 had been offered work. A mere £5 million had been set aside to help disturbed veterans: the equivalent, as Bob Muller told Carter himself, 'of five days' shelling of one lousy hillside in Vietnam long abandoned by the enemy'.

The contrast with the treatment of Second World War and Korean war veterans was striking. The earlier veterans had been rewarded with a 'GI Bill' which gave them automatic rights of employment, education and medical care for life. President Johnson re-introduced, reluctantly, the GI Bill in 1966, but with a catch: it gave Vietnam veterans some $3,000 *less* than their fathers had received a generation earlier. In 1972 President Nixon vetoed the Veterans Medical Care Expansion Act, another extension of the GI Bill, which it was now clear had been drafted for different heroes coming home from a different war.

Mike Sulsona received no compensation for a crippled hand and for deafness caused when a land mine blew off both his legs. He was nineteen then. Like most of the veterans I met, Mike would not talk much about the war itself and expressed no self-pity. 'I gave my Bronze Star to the kid next door,' he said. 'He likes to play soldiers with it.'

Mike lives in Brooklyn, New York, in a faded area which used to be a Jewish ghetto. At the end of his street is Coney Island, once the world's greatest funfair, where he played as a child, and which is now shuttered and rusting.

'All the nine-to-five jobs I applied for needed someone who could get about,' he said. 'I can't do that for long with artificial legs and a cane. But I've got lucky! The Italian mob who run the collision trucks heard about me and said, "No problem, we'll fire somebody." They're like that, those Italian boys.'

A funny and bitter little story about Mike's struggle with bureaucracy says much about an attitude which many Vietnam veterans have had to face. Sitting in his small kitchen with Beryl, whom he met and married on his return from the war, he said:

Right from the start I was determined never to go out in the wheelchair. I didn't want people recognising me as a vet; I just didn't want any arguments about the war. Either I'd wear the damn tin legs, no matter how much they hurt, or I'd drive my car.

I figured that losing my legs in the service of my country gave me at least one extra right: to drive my car and park where best I could and not have to pay any parking fines. I didn't want any parades or any of that bullshit; all I wanted was the freedom to park my old Volkswagen!

Well, you guessed it: nine years later I had $7,000 worth of parking tickets piled up, more than my car was worth. Again and again I'd explained my case, but still the tickets kept coming. Then when they took away my car registration that was it! Beryl and I went down to the courthouse, walked right into the judge's chambers and I took off my legs and put them on his desk. The judge went red, his secretary went red and both of them just got the hell out leaving me sitting there in my underpants.

Some official came in and tried to explain to me their situation. I understood their situation, but they didn't understand mine. They said, 'Pay us $5 and we'll give you your registration.' I said, 'I'm not paying a penny of those fines.' So I just sat there – underwear, legs on the desk and all – until they started to lock up.

Well, finally they agreed to reduce it from $7,000 to $75, and I weakened and accepted it. As I was leaving I said to the lady dealing with the matter, 'Don't you know I'm a Vietnam veteran?' 'Yeah,' she replied, 'unfortunately you were in a war that nobody really cared about.' I said to her, 'Okay lady, but keep it to yourself, will you?'[8]

Mike is a sculptor. His major work is a seven-foot figure of a veteran with one leg which took him two years to complete. 'The statue can't talk back,' he said. 'It doesn't have to feel it's a scapegoat ... It's my gift to the memory of friends who didn't make it back.'

It was 1968 when Jay Thomas made it back and both the war and the anti-war movement were at their height. To some of the American 'new left', enlisted soldiers were, at worst, baby killers and, at best, dupes now obsolete; and the latter represented an attitude shared by many of the middle ground and the extreme right in America.

Jay Thomas, a marine, was severely wounded in the arm and neck and, like many veterans, had become addicted to heroin in Vietnam. He described his first day back in America:

I was hitchhiking home from Philadelphia naval hospital and I had my uniform on, and I was walking with a cane and my neck and arm were in a brace. I was a sight, I can tell you.

This van went past me and stopped about twenty feet ahead and signalled they would pick me up. Well, just as I reached it I got ketchup and Coca-Cola and whatever all over my uniform and face. Then they pulled away.[9]

When Bob Muller first went to the White House, as founder of the Vietnam Veterans of America, he overheard a presidential aide telling a reporter, 'You have got to understand these guys are a no-votes situation.' When he met President Carter he tried to explain that a third of Vietnam veterans were suffering from something called 'delayed stress syndrome', which was distinct from 'shell shock' and 'combat fatigue' and needed the urgent attention of the commander-in-chief himself, the president.

'What did the president say?' I asked.

'He told me he loved me.'

When Bob Muller first met President Reagan it was at a Veterans' Day ceremony at the White House. The President spoke about the lessons of the American War of Independence, about the First and Second World Wars and the Korean War; he said nothing about the nation's longest war. As he was leaving, Reagan found his way blocked by Bob Muller's wheelchair. Bob recounted the incident to me:

I said to him, 'Mr President, when are you going to listen to us, the veterans of Vietnam? Before you build up your defence budget, when are you going to listen to us tell you what war is really like these days, with all these new weapons . . .'

It was unbelievable. He missed the point completely and said, 'The trouble with Vietnam was that we never let you guys fight the war the way you could have done and should have done and so we denied you the victory all the other veterans in this country have enjoyed . . . It won't happen like that again, Bob.'[10]

On August 18, 1980, during the presidential campaign, Ronald Reagan attacked the Carter administration's 'stingy' approach to the Vietnam veterans. 'It is time we recognised', he said, 'that ours was, in truth, a noble cause . . . and [that] we have been shabby in our treatment of those who returned . . . They deserve our gratitude, our respect and our continuing concern.'[11]

Seven months later Reagan, as president, asked Congress to cut programmes designed specifically to help Vietnam veterans find jobs, complete their education and be treated for drug addiction and alcoholism, both scourges of the war. He also proposed closing ninety-one counselling centres which, after a long resistance by the veterans' bureaucracy in Washington, had been established in the poorest parts of cities and towns, where most Vietnam veterans live. These 'storefront' centres were considered by many casualties of Vietnam as the 'last line' in their struggle to come to terms with the aftermath of the war and with an America which apparently did not want them. As a direct result of the president's intervention, many of the centres closed and others continued only with meagre resources.

The story of Roy Benavidez illustrates much of this cynicism. In 1968 the former Army sergeant sustained a '90 per cent disability' of his abdomen, back, thighs, head and arms when he was clubbed from behind during a Vietcong ambush. Regardless of his wounds he led the rescue of American troops trapped in downed helicopters which were still under attack. He was later credited with having saved the lives of eight comrades and was awarded America's highest military decoration, the Medal of Honour. At an emotional ceremony at the White House, President Reagan told Benavidez that he had shown 'conspicuous gallantry and intrepidity'. Later, addressing a hispanic audience in Austin, Texas, Reagan cited the award as an example of his administration's recognition of hispanic citizens. When soldiers like Roy Benavidez, declared the president, 'place their lives on the line for us, we must make sure that they know we're behind them and appreciate what they are doing.'

Two weeks later the Reagan administration cut Social Security payments to disabled veterans and Roy Benavidez was one of the first victims. The seriously incapacitated hero was deemed to be 'capable of some kind of work'.[12]

Bob Muller, the paraplegic ex-marine, went back to Vietnam with a group of other veterans in 1981. The trip came as a shock to them all. In the old enemy capital of Hanoi, on which the Americans had dropped a greater tonnage of bombs than the Germans had dropped on Britain during the entire Second World War, they were astonished to find not a metropolis reinforced by war industry but a small Third World town of relentless poverty.

'For the first time,' said Bob Muller, 'I saw the Vietnamese as people: people with tears in their eyes, like me. I found no animosity, only generosity and interest. People stopped me and asked where I had got my wounds, and when I told them, we would end up by lifting our shirts and comparing the scars. I know they have terrible post-war problems, but for them to be able to look upon us not as the enemy any longer but as human beings and hopefully as friends means the war's over for them. In this country we're still fighting it and portraying the Vietnamese as the bad guys and doing what we can to continue to frustrate their efforts of recovery. Until we end the war and really effect the peace, we'll never get that off our backs: our soul will be captive over there.'

58,022 Americans were killed in Vietnam. According to one estimate, more than 50,000 Vietnam veterans have killed themselves since their return from the war.[13]

12

Saviours

BOBBY

California: June 1968. The candidate was due in the vineyards the next morning. He himself would walk these unsurfaced streets which were joined together by power lines sagging almost to porch level and strewn with the wrecks of Detroit's fantasies, the fins and dashboards meticulously stripped of chrome. The people here had celebrated his coming for weeks; most of the huts bore a poster I had seen in half a dozen states: 'KENNEDY. THE NAME YOU KNOW AND TRUST. VOTE FOR BOBBY ON JUNE 3.' The face on the poster was the familiar image: tousled hair, resolute, eternal youth applied for.

One of the huts displayed a montage which had been preciously culled from magazines and laid out on flattened fruit cases and protected by sheets of plastic, in which Robert Kennedy and his assassinated brother wore haloes and were depicted as being under the patronage of the Madonna, whose arms were about them both. The most graphic image had Robert Kennedy wearing a starched, luminous white shirt and a red, white and blue tie, kneeling beside a chicano (Mexican-American) grape picker who was vomiting into the furrowed earth beside large clusters of grapes. The name of a local grower appeared beneath this, next to a skull and cross-bones, and an exhortation, in Spanish, to vote for Robert Kennedy.

I found a hotel, whose staircase was apparently supported by a defunct Coke and Sprite machine and whose communal television had a ketchup-stained paper napkin taped across its screen: the equivalent, I assumed, of a shroud drawn respectfully over the countenance of a newly departed corpse. There was nowhere to eat so I went to bed with *Time*, which quoted the polls as saying that Kennedy would narrowly win Tuesday's presidential primary: a win that was essential if he was to steal the Democratic convention in Chicago from Vice-President Hubert Humphrey. Kennedy, the poll predicted, would capture more of southern California's 'volatile suburbs' (meaning places where the politics ranged from the sweet banalities of Hippy Lotusland to the belief that Reds were both under beds and in them) than the poet-senator Eugene McCarthy who, with the inspirations of Thomas More said to guide him, had won the New Hampshire primary solely on the issue of the discredited war in Vietnam and, in so doing, had humiliated President Johnson and forced his abdication. Just a few days previously, McCarthy had won again in Oregon.

McCarthy's visible strength was his youth following, the 'children's crusade'; and Kennedy, who had announced his presidential candidacy only after McCarthy had successfully mined the deep seam of feeling in the nation against the war and against LBJ, had mounted a strategy which largely bypassed youth and concentrated on the 'true Kennedy constituency', as his people liked to say. These were the minorities: the poor, the blacks, the Indians and the chicanos who, if they could be persuaded to go to the polls, would vote overwhelmingly for almost anyone with the name Kennedy, or with a Kennedy's public blessing.

Calexico, on the banks of a trickling sewer called the Rio Nuevo, was the perfect place for a Kennedy to come and talk of 'hope' and 'justice' and 'a new direction for this great compassionate country', for the message would go forth on prime-time television in a state which, if considered as a country in its own right, would be the sixth wealthiest in the world and where workers could find conditions that paralleled those in Britain before 1872, the year the first union of agricultural labourers was formed. The *Fresno Bee* had carried the story of a girl of eight who worked a seventy-hour week on a 'grape ranch'. Nor was this unexceptional in the San Joaquin valley where US laws relating to the employment of young children were held openly in contempt; the largest California grower, Guimarra Vineyards, had been tried and convicted on forty violations of child labour and health laws; and the fine, a mere thousand dollars, had been suspended.

Early that morning, Adam Walinsky was at work in the Royal Suite of the Ambassador Hotel in Los Angeles. As a political aide Walinsky enjoyed something akin to the rank of colonel. He wrote most of Robert Kennedy's speeches; the candidate would be content to pencil in his own thoughts in the margin, but even these would be little more than perfunctory remarks underscoring Walinsky's points. Walinsky was to Robert Kennedy what the ubiquitous 'high-flyer' Richard Goodwin had been to John Kennedy: a fine tuner of public utterances that would appeal to most people at different times and say everything and nothing. It was Goodwin who was said to have coined 'the New Frontier' for John

Kennedy's campaign and later, for Lyndon Johnson, 'the Great Society'.

Robert Kennedy's people came in two clearly defined packs: the 'sodbusters' and the 'cattlemen'. The sodbusters were the veterans of the New Frontier and wore a 'PT 109' tie-pin, which was a miniature of the PT boat commanded by John Kennedy in the Second World War. They included brother Ted Kennedy, brother-in-law Stephen Smith, authors Arthur Schlesinger Jnr, Theodore Sorensen and Theodore White, speechwriter Richard Goodwin, Pierre Salinger, who was John Kennedy's press secretary, and crowd-arranger and political prankster Dick Tuck, who coined the unforgettable anti-Nixon slogan, 'Would *you* buy a used car from this man?' and had it translated into Chinese and hung across Powell Street in San Francisco's Chinatown on the day that Nixon came to seek the 'ethnic vote'.

The sodbusters believed in an America described in an unguarded remark by the New Frontier's poet laureate, Robert Frost, as the country you left only when you went out to 'lick another country'. None of the sodbusters would have put it so crudely, of course; and the banality of the remark was uncharacteristic of Frost. But beneath their rumpled Brooks Brothers shirts and PT 109 tiepins, they longed for the old JFK days of constant crisis, of interruptions at Georgetown dinner parties and summonses to the Oval Office or the Situation Room, of 'eyeballing' the Russians and the State of Mississippi, of saving people, wherever they were, from themselves. That was what they as ascendant liberals were there to do.

Walt Rostow and Max Millikan, theorists of the New Frontier, had spelt out this liberalism. 'The nation's sense of world mission', they had called it. John Kennedy used the expression often. A sense of mission surely equalled 'morality', and morality was the President's justification for fuelling a war in Asia, 'the football game', as they used to call it, and for intensifying the cold war. The sense of mission, the morality, the football game: *that* was what they missed. Now they could not believe their luck; Robert Kennedy promised an action-replay.

The 'cattlemen', on the other hand, were post-JFK people, fresh-out-of-law-school-or-IBM people who, unlike the sodbusters, drank little, were young and forever earnest. They were of the Sixties generation, whose 'revolution' was at its peak. They were of the same age as the hippies, but they despised the hippies' nihilism which – and perhaps they did not realise this – was also a reaction against the John Kennedy years of near-apocalyptic mission they wished to repeat. For they, too, were missionaries. They, too, wanted the opportunity to show the world what was right from wrong. They, too, wanted a piece of the Situation Room action. Their leader was Adam Walinsky, thirty-one years old, a Yale man.

From March 16, the day Robert Kennedy announced his candidacy in the wake of Eugene McCarthy's New Hampshire victory, it was clear to those who had helped to sell JFK and would now sell his brother that Robert Kennedy had an image impediment. One of his first jobs had been as a counsel for Senator Joe McCarthy on his witch-hunting committee investigating 'un-American activities'. Robert Kennedy had admired Joe McCarthy and had incurred his brother's anger by going out of his way to attend his funeral. Even so, he became President Kennedy's Attorney-General and he soon gained a reputation for ruthlessness – although, unlike his work for McCarthy, his targets were not infrequently those who deserved little pity: segregationist Southern politicians and the mobster Jimmy Hoffa who led the Teamsters' Union. But Robert Kennedy also had the unfortunate reputation of threatening to 'get' people; and at times it did not seem to matter to him whether they were crooks or vacillating Minnesota delegates needed for their votes at a Democratic Party convention. He also defended American military action in Vietnam, as if there was an American solution to the 'problem' of Indo-China. After John Kennedy was assassinated, Robert Kennedy used his brother's name and political machine to help him win election as a junior senator for New York. By March 1968 he was in much of the public mind as a carpetbagger.

All this had to be changed before the California primary on June 4; during two months of following Kennedy to California I watched the process as it was changed. The Speech, as conceived by Walinsky and with variations to account for geography, class and colour, was swallowed with minimal indigestion by the 'Boys on the Bus', who were those of us travelling in his press caravan. It did not matter to us that in Indiana and Nebraska Kennedy sounded like George Wallace, with his prolific references to 'law and order', the euphemism for keeping the blacks in their place. It did not matter that he flew especially to Philadelphia to laud the notorious James Tate as 'one of the greatest mayors in the United States'. He promised tax incentives to big business, so that jobs might be created in the ghettoes, though he seldom talked about levelling the ghettoes, or rebuilding the schools and hospitals. Instead, he would 'return government to the people', offer the oppressed 'dignity' and, of course, 'hope' and 'justice'.

'As Bernard Shaw once said', he would say at the end of the Speech, 'most men look at things as they are and wonder why. I dream of things that never were and ask why not?' His audience may or may not have been inspired; it did not matter; this was his signal for us all to run for the bus. Once, he substituted Aristotle for Shaw – 'It is they who act rightly who win the prize' – and left us in confused hilarity. It was such fun. Indeed, how could we reporters write ill of a man who, on these

jolly outings, was freely available to us all. In the process of change he
almost always got a good press.

So the old Bobby was buried and the new 'liberal' Bobby arose.
Occasionally we would brush the Nixon campaign in the Midwestern
states, and although few realised it at the time, there was an irony in
this; by similarly orchestrating the media in *his* caravan, Richard Nixon,
also an old McCarthyite witch-hunter, shed his 'old Nixon' image and
became the 'new Nixon', a national healer with a slogan promising a
New Day.

In early May 1968 Robert Kennedy arrived in California for the run
up to the primary. He sat in the forward compartment of his campaign
jet, a speech on his lap, his eyes closed and his face set like a totem,
rather like a small boy struggling to memorise his catechism. Softly he
addressed himself as he would the people waiting for him at Los Angeles
airport. 'I have come to this great state to ask you all to help me chart a
new direction for America,' he said. 'I do not believe we have to accept
the gap that exists between the generations and the races. I do not believe
we have to accept the concept that young Americans should die in Asia
while others starve to death in . . .'

'No!' said Walinsky, whose words they were, 'let's start with Ethel and
how much you both wanted to come back here.'

'Yes,' said the candidate and again he spoke only to his memory. 'My
wife was so glad when I told her that I had decided to run for President
of the United States. She said, "Doesn't that mean we'll be going to
California for the primary?" I said, "Right!" You see, we were here just
after our honeymoon . . . ' He repeated this, then spoke of Vietnam and
the gap between the generations and so on, then turned the page and
stopped. 'What's this, Adam?' he said to Walinsky. 'I can't read this;
we've got to get it typed.'

'It's Jefferson,' said Walinsky. '"We are the last and the best hope of
the world." I think you should end on that.'

On June 2, with two days left to polling day, Robert Kennedy travelled
south in California, starting in the San Joaquin valley, stopping at Delano
and Turlock and reaching Calexico that evening, just as the pickers were
coming home. The hysteria with which he was greeted left those in his
caravan open-mouthed, and the candidate himself anxious. People came
like a great wave at his car and swept him out of it, and he bobbed on
the sea of them, his hands fastened to people's lips. The Old Saviour
was an abstraction which these people worshipped, but here was a New
Saviour, who could deliver.

'Kennedee! Kennedee!' The chorus was plaintive and it said, 'Save
us; lead us; give us all those things to which we, as honorary Americans,
are entitled!'

Eighty per cent of these people lived in slums. Few of their children attended high school. The average income of a grape-picker was about £450 a year for eighty-two days' work. They had no rest periods, no time off with pay for sickness, no health insurance and no pensions. Their leader, Caesar Chavez, had called them the niggers of ten years ago. The United States government had refused to recognise Chavez's United Farmworkers' Union, which had organised the first strikes against the worst employers among the winegrowers and a national boycott of their products. Chavez had told a congressional inquiry that, of 774 grape-pickers who were tested, only 121 showed no symptoms of pesticide poisoning.

Kennedy was swept on to a vineyard nearby and, in one of those moments which silence even circuses, he was confronted by a woman crouching beneath the vines, vomiting. 'Spray sickness', it was called. 'That has got to change,' he said, looking around, as if for someone to change it.

After his usual sixteen-hour day, the candidate boarded his chartered DC6 propellor plane and flew back to Los Angeles. I sat opposite to him and Ethel, who was now button-eyed with fatigue. Kennedy held a can of beer in one hand and his last speech of the day in the other. Even as we took off, the windows were filled with brown faces, many of them crying with joy.

'These people love you,' I said.

His voice was tremulous. I said I didn't hear him.

'Yes, yes, sure they love me,' he said. 'I love *them!*'

'If you become the President, how will things improve for them?'

'I'll break the Teamsters' power in the valley . . . I'll see that Chavez gets a square deal.'

'How?'

'I'll use the law . . .'

'You didn't say anything about that today.'

'I don't want to raise their hopes.'

'But your presence alone does that. Why do you think you're such an inspiration to these people?'

'They remember what President Kennedy stood for. They know I'll do the same for them.'

'But Senator, surely their situation didn't change one bit under President Kennedy.'

'Their voice was heard, wasn't it?'

I asked him how he would describe his political philosophy. 'In your speech,' I said, 'it's the one thing that doesn't seem to come through.'

'My philosophy?' he said, almost puzzled. 'My philosophy is based on

a faith in this country and I believe that many Americans have lost this
faith and I want to give it back to them.'

'That's what you say in your speech. Surely the question is: How?'

'How? . . . by charting a new direction for America.'

'What direction are you thinking about?'

'Well, that's difficult to explain. But what I want to do is give people the
feeling that *they* are running the country, not the people in Washington. I
want individuals and neighbourhoods to feel independent and important.
I want America to go back to what she was meant to be: a place where
every man has a say in his destiny.'

I said, 'You used to dismiss blacks as immigrants. Now you're their
champion . . . '

'Well, that's what I mean by change. I didn't dismiss black people. I
was just ignorant; I admit that. I was from ignorant Irish immigrant
stock! I had no idea what was *really* happening in Mississippi until I
became Attorney-General. Well, I know now. Maybe I can never suffer
like the blacks, the Indians and the chicanos do. But, Jesus Christ, I'm
the one to stand up for them.'

'Why?'

'I can be the President of the United States.'

'So can Hubert Humphrey or Richard Nixon.'

'They can't be President Kennedy . . . '

The rabbit smile now enveloped his face and momentarily discharged
his fatigue. I asked him if he wanted me to leave him alone now. 'No,
no, go ahead,' he said. He reached under his seat for two beers. Ethel
was in a deep sleep.

'Senator,' I said, 'aren't you possibly unique? You have had little
experience and there are no achievements to your name, and yet you
enjoy a reputation among a large proportion of the population as a
political saviour. Why is that?'

'Most politicians, the successful politicians, listen to what people have
to say. President Kennedy did that and he added a dimension; he tried
to tap their dreams. The name is a lot, I know. I've confessed many
times, right? But for me personally, the answer to your question is, "I
don't know".'

'Didn't your father once say he was going to sell the Kennedy name
like you sell soap?'

'He said that?'

'I read it somewhere. I think President Kennedy quoted it. Don't you
believe it?'

He belly-laughed. 'Sure . . . I believe it.'

He dog-eared a page in his speech. 'I have to work at this,' he said.
'Why don't you see Dick Tuck and maybe come along to The Factory

with us after the results are through Tuesday night?' (The Factory was a Los Angeles discothèque.)

'Thank you,' I said. 'Are you going to be the next president?'

'Nothing,' he replied, now with his head down, 'can stop a good man, who has faith in the people, from becoming President of the United States; okay?'

It was a line from the Speech.

On June 4, polling day, Robert Kennedy and friends went to Malibu Beach where they surfed until dusk. At seven o'clock that evening he returned to the Ambassador Hotel to watch the first returns on television. His prodigious family were represented there: Ethel, four of his children, David, Michael, Courtney and Kerry, his sister Jean and brother-in-law Stephen Smith. Their rooms were directly across the hall from the Royal Suite where Walinsky and other aides and friends, including the astronaut John Glenn, his wife and daughter, were gathered around the television. There was a help-yourself bar.

At 9.35 the television projections began to point to a Kennedy victory and the candidate strolled out into the hall, leaned against the wall and kicked at the carpet with his heel. A voice shouted from the Royal Suite, 'Hey, Bob, Gene McCarthy's on the tube sounding more like an angry politician than an intellectual . . . how about that?'

At eleven o'clock Los Angeles County went for Kennedy by a large margin and Walinsky said, 'That's it . . . we've got it!' The elation grew quickly and John Glenn said, 'Huntley and Brinkley have Nixon saying he can beat you easier than Humphrey.'

I pushed downstairs and through the crowd in the Embassy ballroom to the press enclosure which was to the left of the podium where the candidate would speak. Press tags were given to almost anybody who wanted them; reporters drifting over from the souring McCarthy cele-bration at the Beverly Hilton picked up their 'accreditation' without having to say who they were. Others interviewed Kennedy in the hallway; there was virtually no 'security'. A few hotel guards tried to question people as they streamed into the ballroom but, overwhelmed by the exuberance of the crowd, they soon gave up; American officiousness is so often admirable for its lack of stamina.

There were no police in the hotel. Kennedy despised protection and his two bodyguards were old friends; Rosie Greer, an enormous ex-football star, and Bill Barry, a former FBI agent, performed more as stewards rescuing a pop idol from his fans than as guardians of a possible future president. Greer had complained good-naturedly, 'If I can get the Senator through a crowd with his pants on, then I've done my job. I don't bother to go back for the cuff links.'

In the press area, George Gale, then the *Daily Mirror*'s columnist, Jon

Akass of the London *Sun* and I were befriended by a young Kennedy volunteer, Susan Harris, who kindly insisted upon delivering drinks to us from a bar on the other side of the hotel. To avoid the crush in the ballroom, she had found a short cut through the hotel's kitchen and serving pantry and had twice said to us, 'There's a little guy in there who keeps looking at me kind of funny: just staring as if he's waiting around for something.'

The little guy was a Palestinian immigrant called Sirhan Bishara Sirhan who, in spite of his industry and intelligence, had failed in the concrete of Los Angeles. As a Palestinian he bore a hatred for the oppressors of his people in the Middle East and their patrons in the United States. Robert Kennedy, not surprisingly for a man seeking the presidency of the United States, had courted the 'Israel Vote' and, only a week previously, wearing a Jewish skull-cap at a rally in Portland, Oregon, had pledged himself to support the Israelis' occupation of Palestinian land on the West Bank of the Jordan, where Sirhan Bishara Sirhan was born.

It did none of us credit – those who heard Susan Harris's words of unease and those who themselves had taken the short cut through the kitchen – that no one attempted to find out who the staring little man was. If one of us had heeded Susan's warning, we might have changed, quite literally, the course of American history.

At 11.35 Pierre Salinger heaved his portly self and large cigar up on to the podium, tapped the microphone and said into it, 'Oh yes, oh yes, he's a comin' now!'

Robert and Ethel Kennedy left their room and walked down the hall; Kennedy, now filling up with the sense of his victory, said to the aides and friends jockeying beside him, 'Ethel asked me if we should take Freckles [their dog] down there with us, but I said no, because the newspapers will only say we used a dog and an astronaut to win.'

It was just after midnight and a delirium of cheers greeted 'the next President Kennedy', as Pierre Salinger announced him. The candidate thanked a list of helpers by name and 'all my friends in the black community' and 'all those loyal Mexican-Americans who have given me their trust and support'. He ended with, 'We are a great and compassionate country . . . now it's on to Chicago and let's win there!'

Kennedy jumped down from the podium, shook more hands and, with Rosie Greer cutting a swathe through the crush, headed for the kitchen. Inside the pantry serving-area, he shook hands with a chef in his big white hat and with others of the kitchen staff, who were mostly blacks and chicanos; and then, before thought and sound could be synchronised, there were reports like balloons bursting or flash bulbs popping; they were not shots, I thought, because that surely could not happen again.

The unreality persisted, until a woman collapsed at my side with blood trickling from her head. She had been shot. Several had been shot, including Senator Kennedy.

The staring little man in the kitchen had taken a .22 revolver from underneath his yellow jacket, jumped on to a table and taken aim; Kennedy had seen him, screamed, 'No!' and half-glanced for a space against the wall, anywhere, to escape. He had been shot still smiling that rabbit smile of his, and he lay beside a refrigerator with a chicano dishwasher kneeling over him. Ethel flailed out with her fists, her lips sucked in with the horror and shock, and for a brief time she prevented anybody, even friends, from touching her husband. 'Where's the doctor?' she shouted; and when a brooch fell from her dress on to Kennedy's chin, she put her face close to his and said, 'I'm sorry, my darling, please forgive me . . . '

From somewhere a priest appeared and said, 'I must be with Senator Kennedy. You *know* that!' Rosie Greer, tears flowing with rage, lifted Sirhan Sirhan off his feet, smashed his hand and disarmed him. Others attempted to beat their fists on his small body, but Greer protected him in a stranglehold that might have dispatched him there and then had four policeman not arrived and run with him from the hotel.

Outside in the ballroom mobile TV cameras raced like stockcars at the kitchen entrance, which was too narrow for them to enter; in trying, one of them ran over a girl lying face down and pounding her head on the floor. The lights, which must accompany them, fell or ricocheted dementedly back and forth. Photographers fought each other for space in which to take a picture, any picture. Harry Benson of the *Daily Express* was propelled bodily from the kitchen. Stephen Smith, Kennedy's brother-in-law, took the microphone on the podium and pleaded, 'We must have a doctor! Please, will a doctor come forward?'

On the television monitors, NBC's studiously urbane commentators Chet Huntley and David Brinkley were droning about 'the trends' in Los Angeles and the crumbling McCarthy lead in northern California. A large woman bent over one of the sets and beat on the screen, as if to batter the pundits out of their self-possession – '*For Christ's sake, haven't they heard?*' Robert Kennedy, along with several other wounded, was taken to hospital, with a bullet in his brain.

A young girl wearing a Styrofoam Kennedy boater ran into me and when I tried to let her pass she let out a sob that silenced the ring of barking people around us. Somebody took her from me; there were many who quietly performed that kind of chore, who gathered grieving young people into groups and talked softly to them. (I recalled this some years later when I saw the celebrated film *Nashville* whose political assassination scene depicted an audience, meant to represent the

American people, as being unmoved by the death of their heroine. For me, having known the reality, the film's lie made no sense.)

Time cartwheeled; surely only minutes had passed, but, no, it was already one o'clock. Like a fool, I asked a witness in the kitchen to spell his name at least a dozen times. 'M-u-r-r-a-y,' he said, over and over and over again, as we stood locked in an absurd little sideshow, neither of us hearing the other, or wanting to.

Robert Kennedy died the next day. No buses left Calexico for the vineyards for almost a week; instead, people gathered around them every morning, like patients at a shrine. And the assassin said in a television interview, 'I loved him . . . he was the hope of all the poor people in this country. I'm not rich, otherwise I wouldn't be here on this programme. I had no identity, no hope, no goal to strive for. Everyone in America loves a winner, and I was a loser.'

GEORGE

Montgomery, Alabama: July 1968. The sky over Goat Hill was pewter, except for occasional shafts of filtered sunlight which caused the waiting folks to squint painfully and to mop large, creased necks. It was on Goat Hill in 1861 that Jefferson Davis proclaimed the Confederacy with the cry, 'To war, you all, for Dixie!' and the rebel flag still flies above the Alabama State House and the bleached flat roofs of the capital, Montgomery.

The folks seemed to come in two sizes: some of them perilously thin, like human grasshoppers or the victims of a malignancy, and others like Buddhas with blood pressure, the women with vast pumpkin-like breasts. These very fat folks, especially their very fat children, seemed to grip the familiar red can – pronounced 'Co'-Cola' in the South – in the same protective way that chain-smokers nurse their cigarettes, which perhaps explained their shape. Their opaque eyes and monotone voices had other origins, of which a clue was to be found in the country music of this part of America, in which the theme of loss and of being put upon by 'them' was constant. Curiously, only in Alabama was I never asked the standard American question: 'Whereyafrom?'

'Ladeees and gen'lemen!' bellowed a man on Goat Hill. 'The next President of the Yew-nited States, Alabama's own George C. Wallace, is now approachin', so ah'll have to ask y'awl to sing along! Yo' ready with them geetars, yo' fellas?' So they sang:

> Stand up for Alabama!
> Like a pebble in the bay,
> He's become a way of saving
> The entire U-S-A!

George Corley Wallace was the little Southern man who in his inauguration address as Governor of Alabama had blared against 'a mongrel unit of one under a single all-powerful government' and had pledged, 'From this very heart of the great Anglo-Saxon Southland ... in the name of the greatest people that have ever trod this earth ... I say,

"Segregation now! Segregation tomorrow! Segregation for ever!"' That was in January 1963; and when he stood 'in the schoolhouse door' of the University of Alabama and prevented the enrolment of the first black students under the Kennedy administration's desegregation laws he earned the international infamy he now relished as he set out to 'save the entire USA'.

George Wallace was running for president and it was appropriate that his caravan on its way north should first review his own beloved folks gathered at his spiritual seat of power. 'George, You Are Going to the White House. Do You Hear Us?' read a home-sewn banner held aloft as the little man arrived, cigar in mouth, Secret Service protectors at his side, one hand outstretched to shake another or slap a back or clutch at a neck, the other holding a red, white and blue rent-a-car bag on which were the words, 'George C. Wallace, the White House, Washington, DC'.

George Wallace, the presidential candidate, was not, as some syndicated pontiffs of the American Press had us believe, a bad joke. It was true he had no chance of winning a majority of the 270 Electoral College votes at the election in November, but he had every chance of dividing the country and the national vote in such a way that no candidate, Republican or Democrat, would win, and the House of Representatives would then be forced to choose the president. In this respect Wallace was, in 1968, potentially the most powerful politician in America; for he would be in a position to strike a deal with one of the two main candidates: a deal in which Wallace would withdraw and release those votes pledged to him in return for the kind of 'concessions' which might begin to unravel many of the reforms of the early 1960s.

As America's most uncertain political year for a generation grew older and more uncertain, so the appeal and power of George Wallace multiplied. During June and July, according to Gallup, his national support doubled. 'I may not become President of the United States', said the candidate, 'but I sure am goin' to have my say on who becomes the President: yessuh!'

What was fascinating about Wallace was that he represented for more than a decade something called the 'new populism' in America: a label which itself fostered an illusion. As the old *émigré*/unions/blacks coalition which had made up the Democratic Party's 'New Deal constituency' broke apart in the late 1960s, and the issue of 'law and order' (i.e. race) became predominant, an air of disgruntlement and persecution hung over the 'little folks' (i.e. the little white folks). The evidence for such a claim lay in those millions of Americans who abandoned venerable political alliances and supported George Wallace well into the 1970s, then transferred to the embrace of Ronald Reagan. When Wallace said in 1968, 'Soon you gonna see this whole country Southernised, from Boston to Los Angeles. And when that happens, we gonna seem like a Sunday school down here,'[14] he was being prophetic. And more than most, he made that come true; and more than most, he created present-day political America, 'Reagan's America'. Reagan, of course, is the preferred image of the ideological revival in America; he presents himself as a nice guy, ignorant but with a certain grace, while Wallace, although of the same species, eschews all niceness and grace. 'George is not so much openly indecent', wrote Wallace-watcher Garry Wills, 'as indecorously honest.'[15]

It is perhaps ironic that in a society said to venerate 'winners' the disaffection of so many potential 'losers' should inaugurate the successful Wallace/Reagan movement. George Wallace said he believed in many things – 'Fascism over communism for one . . . why, at least a fascist believes in God!'[16] – but what he believed in most of all was that he, George Wallace, had had a raw deal, and it was this feeling of being a loser which made him so convincing to all the other losers looking for something and someone else to blame. This, of course, had its contradictions; he kept winning by being a loser, a spoiler, which meant that if he ever really won he would probably be lost. I suspect he understood that.

The first of many trips I took with George Wallace was in that high summer of 1968, to Ohio. He is not an easy man to hate. 'Do correct me if I'm wrong', he said to me, 'but it's my guess you'll be printin' pictures of me lookin' like Simon Legree, or a mean-faced mule. Well now, let me help you out . . . '

He squared in his seat and pulled a face at Matt Herron's camera. 'This is my Jimmy Cagney bad guy face,' he said. 'Now this here's my Mickey Rooney mean look. Did you catch that? Now allow me to curl up my lip at the corner so's your readers can really say, "I hate that George Wallace", and thereby cleanse themselves of the things they really hate; like the things I'm battlin' against . . . '

He shouted across the aisle to a six foot six inch jug-faced man in cowboy boots: 'Say, Two-Storey, how'm I doin'?'

'Just fine, Guv'nah,' shouted back Two-Storey, 'you're lookin' real despisable. They sure gonna hate you in old England.'

I said that he was best known for his stand on race segregation and, if he became president, would he attempt to segregate all of the United States?

'Now shee-it you've never heard me say a bad word against any nigra. Why, my little wife, Lurleen, carried one county on the votes of nigras and you remember that Selma march of Dr King, whose death, I might say, was a regrettable tragedy . . . why, when that march was over, me and my wife had some of them protestin' nigras over for iced tea, and we all set down and talked, real friendly.

'Nigra folks knows I holds nothin' against them. They knows that under Governor George Wallace, why, everything's just fine, long as they stay in their required places and we, of the Caucashun race, stay in ours.

'The trouble with your country is like the trouble with my country: both of us has got too many beatnik bureaucrats and pointy-headed pseudo-intellectual traitors and liberal sonofabitches skulking around where the power is. I tell you what I'm goin' to do with that gang when I'm President of the United States: I'm gonna throw every briefcase belongin' to a bearded bureaucrat in the Potomac River, and the first protester, white or nigra, I see layin' down in front of my automobile I'm gonna run straight over him, yessuh! And anyone riotin' can expect the same treatment!'

He raised his arms holding an imaginary rifle. 'Nigra or white starts lootin' and bam, bam, I'd have 'em shot on the spot. Yessuh, there'd be orders to shoot to kill if anyone so much as hurls a rock at a police officer. "Don't shoot any chillun" I'd tell 'em. "Just shoot that adult standin' beside the kid that throws the rock." That may not prevent the burnin' and lootin' but it sure will stop it after it starts ... shee-it, nothin' surer.'

At Dayton, Ohio, where the cash register was invented and the Wright Brothers are said to have dreamt up their aeroplane, there was a 'patriotic rally' in a covered stadium. A country and western group, who had come with us from Montgomery, dispensed a deafening 'Mule Train'; and when they struck up 'Stand up for Alabama' we knew the little man was approaching. Two and a half thousand people were in the stadium: decent rabble ready to be roused.

'The common man', said the candidate, 'has had enough. He's been pushed around *too long*. He's had to settle for second class in his job, in the schools his kids attend, in the hospitals he's paying for and he's the one payin' the taxes. It's them in Washington that's been ripping the little man off, and it's them big city socialists like the Rockefellers who can ride around in big black limousines because of what they're takin' outta *you*!'

Rapturous cheering greeted this dose of 'them' and 'us'. But which was George Wallace himself: a 'them' or an 'us'? A reporter from the *Dayton Daily News* remarked, 'Jesus, these people are suckers.'

Many reporters believed that George Wallace was a phoney; but few wrote it or said it, or were able to. Many reporters knew that in almost every area in which Wallace declared himself a champion of little folks, he was nothing of the kind, and indeed the very opposite. Under his administration, Alabama remained one of only nine states in the Union without a minimum wage law, and workers' compensation was the lowest in the land. During his time as governor the proportion of his constituents living below the poverty line rose to 24 per cent, double the national average, and most of them were white.

Wallace invariably mentioned 'your schools' because state education has been the very poor and working-class family's ticket up the American ladder: no thanks, however, to the Governor of Alabama. When Wallace took office, Alabama ranked forty-eighth among the fifty-one states in money spent per pupil. After ten years under the 'new populist' Alabama ranked fiftieth. His mental hospitals were described by a federal district court judge as 'barbaric'.[17] His state legislature, according to the Citizens' Conference on State Legislatures, was simply 'the worst in the country';[18] and he raised taxes higher than in any other state. The tribune of the persecuted was a double agent. But what Wallace *had* done was keep the blacks in their place, an achievement whose symbol was Montgomery's segregated drinking fountains: unique in all America.

'We are gonna restore some sanity,' said Wallace from his bullet-proof podium, 'if I have to put 30,000 troops on the streets, one every five feet apart, with a three-foot bayonet . . . '

Ecstatic cheering now. They knew what he meant. He meant keeping the blacks back and down; and Dayton was 25 per cent black. Now he was the articulator of their reasons for feeling their bigotry justified.

'And let me assure you good folks that nobody's gonna take away your guns . . . '

The crowd was on its feet.

'Finally, I wanna say that we're gonna take the handcuffs off the police and let them get down to their work the best way they know how . . . '

There was now the almost sensual roar of a mob rampant, of people saying, 'Yes, yes, George, you got it, that's it!' At that moment, as if on cue, a group of students ran towards the podium and unfurled a banner reading WALL-ASS IS A RACIST. Big men came out of the crowd to rip the banner and stamp on it and push the students against the stage. Police in their Smokey the Bear hats and toolkit belts arrived with batons drawn, like small baseball bats, and prodded the students in the chest. The front rows of little folks were now baying for blood; an old woman threw her shoes into the mêlée, which spilled on to the stage. Caught in mid-invective, Wallace, their hero, was bundled off the stage by Two-Storey and his other 'aides'; he wore a curiously detached expression of fascination and awe.

On May 15, 1972, 'Crazy' Arthur Bremer shot George Wallace in a shopping mall in Maryland on the day he won the Democratic primary elections in that state and in Michigan, which gave him a remarkable 35 per cent of the national Democratic vote. Six weeks later, in Miami for the Democratic Party's presidential nominating convention, George Wallace, now a paraplegic, was pushed into a press conference by his second wife, Cornelia. 'Shee-it,' he said, minus the old harsh inflection. 'Let's get on with this thing, fellas. Nothin's changed, d'yer hear?'

During that summer Wallace was widely believed to have done a deal with President Nixon that he would not run as an independent candidate in the election in November, thus surrendering the five states he had won in 1968 and giving Nixon his huge majority. When I asked him about this, he replied, 'On the record, boolsheet. Off the record I ain't sayin' nothin'.'

'Boolsheet' or not, George Wallace's power as a spoiler increased markedly as the 1976 presidential campaign began, and it was clear that in the wake of Watergate and the 'loss' of Vietnam, a 'new populist' stood a real chance of defeating Gerald Ford, the bumbling caretaker in the White House. But *President* Wallace? Was this really a prospect? Well no, but ...

'I'd just like to say', said Senator Edward Kennedy, standing beside George Wallace's wheelchair on a stage in Decatur, Alabama on July 4, 1973, 'that Governor Wallace and I might not see eye to eye on some matters, but we are agreed that they have corrupted the spirit of our Founding Fathers and they have hounded the working man with higher taxes.'

Here were the two populists of the Democratic Party uniting to smite 'they', the oppressors in government and big business and to shore up their own opportunism. Would-be President Ted and would-be Vice-President George: the alleged left and right of American politics. But was there ever real and substantial difference between the two of them, apart from style? As Wallace himself had said, 'The pretence of liberalism has always been that ours is a politics of givin'. But liberals know, just like I knows, that politics is about *gettin'*. They just dress it up kinda different ... '

Indeed, after Kennedy's pilgrimage, the other great names of American liberal politics – Ed Muskie, Hubert Humphrey – came south to court the man they once described as representing everything venal in the American system. For his part, Wallace obliged by dramatically adjusting his image. During his campaign for re-election as governor in 1974, he stopped at the all-black town of Tuskagee and sat quietly in his wheelchair in front of an all-black audience while the mayor, a black man called Johnny Ford, put his hand on the candidate's shoulder and said, 'Now this man may have been on the wrong track, but now he's on the side of the little guy, white *and* black. Brothers and sisters, what I am sayin' is this is the man with the *power* and we gotta vote for him.' They clapped politely, and the candidate said something about everybody being 'God's chillun' and that 'no bureaucrats in Washington ever pushed the folks in Tuskagee around, nosuh!'

In their quest for a more respectable façade for their man, Wallace's managers set out, as one of them put it, to 'de-kook' his campaign. A 120-page campaigners' manual was drawn up, warning Wallace workers to stay away from those with a single 'pet issue' (i.e. race). But in the end it was Cornelia, First Lady of Alabama, former beauty queen, racing-driver and water-ski champion, tall and cool, always dressed in blazing red with cheeks to match, who assumed the role of Beauty couthing the Beast.

Cornelia had taken over George from his first wife Lurleen, who died from a lingering cancer shortly after Wallace had run her for governor so that he could rule Alabama, in effect, for a third consecutive term. Cornelia's ambition was, like her make-up, incandescent. 'I guess you know', she told me at the Governor's mansion in Montgomery, 'that I've been called the Jackie Kennedy of the rednecks. Now I don't really care for that.' Still, she watched with satisfaction as I wrote it down.

Cornelia stopped George reaching into his trousers in public and scratching his crotch. She issued an instruction that he could be interviewed 'only if his table manners are off the record'. She also had much to do with the fashioning of his new image on race, often against his will. While I was in Montgomery she invited a group of retarded children, black and white, for breakfast. 'When George came home he was *aghast*,' she told me. 'He took me aside and whispered, "Honeybunch, I don't think it looks right for us to eat with an integrated group at the Guvnah's Mansion." To which I replied, "Well my darlin', *you* don't have to eat here!"' And it was Cornelia who lifted him out of the depressions which followed his shooting and persuaded him to try acupuncture and faith healing and who every morning, as he struggled to heave himself along parallel bars, shouted, 'Keep at it baby! Don't look back now honey!'

Sitting with Cornelia, George and his entourage in the Montgomery High School during speech day 1974, one could feel the candidate's new propriety. Up at the podium a preacher intoned, 'We pray, O Lord, that you deliver these children from evil and temptation and, seein' that he's come among us, you might also, Lord, deliver our fine boy, George C. Wallace, to the White House and allow him to restore the goodness to this great country that is threatened by tides of moral decay . . . Amen . . . and now folks, here's the one and only Grandpa Jones . . . '

Grandpa Jones, who was a genuine grandpa and toothless, skipped on to the stage with a banjo and bellowed that old favourite, 'Son, go git the lamp, I think I've knocked one of ma's eyeballs out'. Propriety was clearly at risk.

'Hey grandpaw,' shouted someone from the back, 'sing "Run, nigger, Run".'

That did it. Cornelia gave a whispered instruction to Two-Storey to 'git that asshole outta here', while the candidate himself struggled not to smirk.

Later I asked him if he had forgotten his pledge of 'segregation now . . . today . . . for ever'.

'I ain't gone mella, if that's what yo' mean,' he replied, 'and I ain't gone yella. I made that statement in the context of the times, and the times have changed. Now take your British Empire. That changed, didn't it? Hell, that just vanished and I personally grieve its loss and I hope you British solve yo' problems cos you know how much I've always admired yo' awl.'

No story about George Wallace is complete without Kissin' Jim Folsom, Cornelia's uncle, who was twice Governor of Alabama and who, according to George, 'taught me everythin' about folks and votes'.

On my last trip to Alabama I drove from Montgomery to the one-street town of Elba, where Kissin' Jim was to be found rocking on his porch, chewing his cud and projecting it through the picket fence, a folksy, malevolent gleam in his good eye. Elba, he explained, was historic for two reasons: 'It's named to honour Napoleon and it's where George Wallace grow'd up. Now *there's* two folks with the same ideas o' grand-yaw. Now the difference between George and Napoleon is that George is a whole lot smarter because he would always go over to the enemy and smile and get folks on his side, even if he'd spoken indiscreetly about them folks in the past, get me?'

He was referring, of course, to blacks. Today George Wallace is still Governor of Alabama, on the vote of many blacks. He has softened his language and wooed them with gestures of 'little guy' solidarity. Of course, he never did get to the White House; but then Ronald Reagan, who is better looking, not crippled and doesn't slurp his food or scratch his crotch in public, did, and he is the embodiment of everything George stood and fought for. 'Anybody who thinks communists will disarm just because we disarm ought to have his head bored for a holler-horn' is pure George, but it could be Ronnie . . . 'I'm against helping people ten thousand miles away who just spit on us in the UN. The UN's a kind of Playboy Club' is also pure George, but it could be Ronnie. The crudeness of the sentiments have merely been refined by Reagan in office.

George Wallace was of course right when he said almost twenty years ago that 'you gonna see this whole country Southernised, from Boston to Los Angeles; and when that happens, we gonna seem like a Sunday school down here'. Reagan has 'southernised' much of America, pushing black Americans back to levels of unemployment and deprivation not known since George Wallace was sitting at Kissin' Jim's knee.

JOHNNIE AND TIM

Omaha, Nebraska: August 1972. I was forty-six feet underground and an eight-ton steel door had closed behind me. The door was guarded by a man wearing a white silk scarf, a revolver and a Mickey Mouse watch. I passed through more doors, and was ushered finally into a room shaped like an airport control tower which overlooked a darkened arena called 'the Computerised Coliseum'.

I sat. Directly in front of me, through tinted blastproof glass, were four huge screens on which were projected vistas of numbers and equations and weather maps and words like ZIMPOC, ZULU, BATTLE and PLAN HERO and, above them all in winking red neon, PEACE IS OUR PROFESSION.

Beneath me were rows of control panels flashing lights of many colours, including candy stripe; and beside my leather chair were two telephones, one blue, one gold. The gold phone rang.

'Hello,' I said.

'Mr Pilger?'

'Yes.'

'You are speaking on the President's line.'

'I see. Is that the President?'

'No. My name is Captain Baumberger ... Mr Pilger, first may I welcome you, on behalf of the United States Air Force, to Strategic Air Command headquarters, Omaha, home of the nation's ever-ready nuclear strike force. And, second, may I point out that you, sir, are sitting in the very chair from which the United States and the United Kingdom and the entire Free World will be defended in the unfortunate event of nuclear war!

'Through that telephone, the one now in your hand, the commanding general of SAC will receive an order from the Chief of Staff – maybe even from the President himself! – and on the basis of that Emergency War Order, or EWO, he will war game the situation with computers, and then, sir, he will order our missiliers to say go to their birds.'

The voice's tone was now Very Serious Indeed.

'Sir . . . you will understand that we at SAC are always in the cocked configuration and you will have to excuse us if, during this briefing, we are interrupted by a priority call.'

'You mean . . .?'

'Sorry, sir . . . that information is classified. Thank you for coming and have a nice day.'

I replaced the gold phone; the steel doors swung open; the man with the Mickey Mouse watch saluted; and I ascended into a windowless foyer which was dominated by a brass bust of General Curtis ('Let's bomb 'em back to the Stone Age') Lemay, founder of the Stratcgic Air Command and sire of its Doomsday machine.

Having thus been 'briefed', I flew west to Missouri, to the 351st Strategic Missile Wing base (Motto: Sentinels of Peace); and with hot dust blowing in from the plains outside, the Wing Commander greeted me in his 'particle free' arctic-cooled, nuclear-sealed, flag-draped office. Colonel William J. Grossmiller III . . . handsome, greying at the temples, beribboned son of a preacher, said, 'I've been in missiles right from the beginning and I'd just like to say that we have some of the coolest heads on the block out here!'

Colonel Grossmiller III commanded four 'squadrons' of 200 Minutemen Intercontinental Ballistic missiles which were buried over 16,000 acres of farmland. Each missile could cause destruction equal to that of two Second World Wars, Hiroshima and Nagasaki included. The squadrons were divided into 'flights' of ten, and these were launched by just two men, cocooned in a steel capsule fifty feet underground.

These 'missiliers' would 'press the button'. To fire each missile, according to the official story, each man would take a key, about the size of an ordinary latchkey, from a red metal box and insert it into the control panel in front of him and turn it. After they have turned their keys, another two-man team in another capsule several miles away would follow the same procedure. Each of the four missiliers would then verify the 'launch order'. An order to launch the missiles would be transmitted in code, and the code was said to be changed every hour.

At 8 p.m. Johnnie Conner, newly promoted to launch commander at the age of twenty-five, kissed his pregnant wife Fran goodbye and left to begin his regular shift of two nights and a day in his capsule. At 8.25 he reached the Operations Building, where he greeted his deputy, Lieutenant Tim Hough, and they collected two locks which they would fit to the red box in their capsule. Inside the box, in a plastic envelope, were the two launch keys and coded documents telling them how to authenticate an order to launch, 'even how to identify the voice giving the order', said Colonel Grossmiller III.

The road was deserted and moonlit as we set out to drive the thirty

miles to the launch capsule. Johnnie pointed out a missile silo which was
no more than a concrete lid surrounded by a chain fence. He said it was
one of 'his'. Near the town of Windsor we passed the High Point Baptist
Church and the Gouge Funeral Home, then turned right into Smith
Street and five miles along there was a gate with a steer's skull on it.

Floodlights picked us up; Johnnie spoke a coded number at the
intercom and the gate opened electronically. This was 'Missile Flight
Foxtrot'.

Inside the guard post, a non-commissioned officer, Sergeant Trumble,
said to Johnnie, 'Only one malfunction tonight, sir. The ice-making
machine is broken.'

Johnnie and Tim each collected a .38 Colt revolver and loaded it
inside a metal barrel. 'We don't want to zap anyone by mistake,' said
Tim. The reason for the guns was unspoken: if one went berserk, the
other had to shoot him.

Tim filled a tray with Coca-Cola, corn flakes and Kentucky Fried
Chicken. As we rode down in the lift he revealed that he suffered from
chronic indigestion and flatulence. 'I got so much gas,' he said, hitting
his chest, 'it really burns me up.' At this, he belched loudly.

The lift doors parted and revealed a thing shaped like a Thermos
flask, suspended from the ceiling by four gigantic shock absorbers. The
capsule door swung open and the launch commander from the preceding
shift, a moonfaced man with freckles, said, 'How, man, no war tonight
. . . so far!'

The capsule appeared to be the latest in computerised tombs. Controls
cluttered the walls and roof, leaving just enough space for shelves of red
folders marked TOP SECRET, a bed, a plastic lavatory (acquired, curiously,
from San Quentin prison) and two aeroplane seats with safety belts – 'in
case of turbulence under normal conditions,' said Johnnie. 'Normal
conditions' meant nuclear war: that was the jargon.

'You see how far apart Tim and I are seated,' he said. 'It would be
physically impossible for him to turn his key and then hustle over here
and turn mine in time to fire a bird.'

'But,' I said, 'isn't it a fact that all the information and equipment
required to start a nuclear war is known to each of you?'

'Yes,' they chorused with a certain pride.

'Hey, no sweat,' said Johnnie. 'We've both been put through the
Human Reliability Programme, which means we've been cleared as sane
and, anyway, one of us would know if the other was going bananas!'

At midnight all 200 missiles in the squadron were shown on the
console under green lights. 'They are 100 per cent ready to go,' said
Johnnie. But now there was a red light flashing and I was told to face
the wall while the two men checked their red folders and consulted a

computer to find out what was wrong. Within seconds a teleprinted reply was received.

'Hey, no sweat,' said Johnnie. 'It's just a maintenance party working on a bird in Flight Oscar.' He tossed the reply into a brown paper bag marked TOP SECRET WASTE and folded the top so that I could not see inside.

Into the early morning, with the hours dragging, Johnnie said, 'Monotony factor is always high down here.'

Tim, who had belched and farted with precision, sat back and lit a cigar. 'You know, you can never trust the Russians,' he said. 'Look what happened in 1962 over Cuba. All our guys were on "go" then. The tension must have been really something. Hell, I was only thirteen at the time.' There was a longing in his voice. 'There isn't a lot of glamour in this job,' he said. 'Pilots have all the glamour.'

'It's a thankless task we're performing here,' added Johnnie.

'That's right,' said Tim, 'a thankless task.'

To Tim's left and Johnnie's right were the two keyholes under transparent plastic covers. A launching, said Johnnie, would be 'deceptively quiet and undramatic'.

They would simply lift off the plastic covers and tick off a check list which would take three and a half minutes from the time the Emergency War Order had been authenticated.

'I guess', said Tim, 'the only weak link will be the President himself. He may have only a few minutes to decide his war plan. But at least he'll have all the alternatives worked out for him by the experts . . . generals, people like that. And we sure as hell won't fire a bird until the war has been authorised by somebody.'

They practised:

Johnnie: 'Launch keys!'

Tim: 'Deputy's key launched.'

Johnnie: 'Conference call' (to other capsules in the squadron).

Tim: 'Accomplished.'

Johnnie: 'Commit keys on my mark, 5 . . . 4 . . . 3 . . . 2 . . . 1.'

The two men rotated their keys half a turn to the right and held them while Johnnie counted again: '1 . . . 2 . . . 3 . . . release!'

In 1983 the American investigative columnist Jack Anderson revealed the following:

On November 19, 1980, Capt. Henry Winsett and 1st Lt. David Mosley were conducting a reliability test of their Titan missile at McConnell Air Force Base near Wichita, Kan. The drill was to be a simulated launching. To fire the liquid-fueled Titan, both missile officers in the command capsule must turn keys simultaneously after receiving the proper 'enabling' code. This unlocks a butterfly valve, allowing two chemicals to combine and ignite, launching the missile. This time, when Winsett and Mosley went into their prescribed drill, strange things started happening. 'We had a green light on the butterfly valve lock control that was not supposed to have a light at all,' Mosley recalled. The two officers turned the keys.

'Instead of giving us the lights that said the test had begun, it said, "Launch OK" and "Launch Sequence Go", which means you're actually in the launch sequence,' Mosley said. In desperation, Winsett shut the missile down – pulled the plug. It was the only way to keep the thing from taking off, he said. The incident was confirmed by both men. Mosley said they couldn't be absolutely certain the missile's guidance system would have steered it to a target in the Soviet Union, which would have invited certain retaliation. But he said that 'it probably would have gone north'. It was a close call that still gives Mosley the tremors. As he puts it, he and Winsett 'saved the world' that day.[19]

JERRY

Lynchburg, Virginia: October 1980. It was Sunday morning. I was sitting on my Holiday Inn bed, watching television. The face on the television screen was appealing to sufferers of arthritis, deafness, peptic ulcers, rotting wisdom teeth, ingrown toenails and 'exposed cancers' to press the 'relevant ailing part' to the television screen so that 'God might bestow his glory and heal you for Heaven's sake'. (There was no special guidance on how to get your peptic ulcer into position.)

It was not easy to imagine millions of Americans contorting themselves around their TV sets, but they were 'out there', the rest of us were assured. And with that, 'the Reverend Jerry' called on God 'to bestow your glory and heal, heal, heal!' This was followed by a hymn sung by a choir dressed in powder-blue smocks whose totem faces and flat eyes contrasted with the fervour of their voices.

At this point, the Reverend Jerry pressed his own face to the other side of the screen and asked his people to give a tenth of their incomes, or $200 to be going on with; and for that they would get a 'Training for Christ' certificate and a 'Jesus First' lapel pin or bracelet or brooch and a message such as this: 'Maybe your financial situation seems impossible. Put Jesus first in your stewardship and allow Him to bless you financially!' In a warehouse almost a block long, guarded day and night and known locally as 'the counting house', a phone bank receiving pre-paid calls would take at least $100,000 a day and up to a million dollars a day at Christmas. And these 'pledges' would be pursued by computerised, 'personalised' letters sent to some seven and a half million 'fund-raising families'. In the 'stewardship and development' department of the Reverend Jerry's operation, specially-trained employees would keep an eye on people who had indicated they might leave God a little something in their wills, like a piece of prime real estate.

In all, some $72 million pours in every year to the Reverend Jerry's 'Old Time Gospel Hour', broadcast on 392 TV stations across America. He receives separately $12 million for his Moral Majority Incorporated, the political crusade whose latest 'cause' is support for the regime in South Africa.

Jerry Falwell springs from a rich American tradition. More than a century ago all Protestants considered themselves evangelicals, in the sense that they believed that God had given them North America as a base for erecting an evangelical empire. America was 'God's country' and the American Way of Life, or American*ism*, was a religion in all but name.

The Founding Fathers had not planned it that way, of course. They were men of the Enlightenment and they wanted a government of laws, not gods. Indeed, God appears only twice in the Federalist papers, as Gore Vidal observed:

> ... they should have known that on a vast empty continent (save for Indians to be converted or killed or both), superstition, the zanier the better, would be the only glue that could hold together so many disparate elements ... divinely inspired, we began to invent new religions: Mormon, Christian Science, Scientologist. Today the US is a teaming bazaar of fundamentalist-style religions, united only by a common hatred of satanic Communism and, alas, of our lovely *reasonable* eighteenth-century Constitution and its intolerable freedoms.[20]

Modern evangelists like Jerry Falwell preach that the world is an evil place from which revivalists must rescue souls, one by one. This essentially American view assumes that the Apocalypse is near, that only after Christ's return in glory across the wastes of the encroaching 'evil empire' will there be a just and truly 'glorious' society.

The resurgence of evangelical Americanism during the 1970s co-incided with the post-Watergate period when it became fashionable to portray the United States as 'leaderless' and 'humiliated' following events in Vietnam and Iran. People all over the world, it was said, were spitting on the American Flag. Godless communism (the Soviet version, not the Chinese) was taking advantage of American 'weakness'. By 1980 more than 65 million Americans were willing to describe themselves as 'born again Christians', including President Jimmy Carter.

However, it was not Carter but Ronald Reagan who became both beneficiary and herald of born-again Americanism. Whereas Carter's presidency seemed to smack of blundering and weakness, even appeasement – an ironic situation for the hapless Carter, who did more than his share of 'standing up to the Russians' following their invasion of Afghanistan – it was Reagan who demonstrated true revivalism.

Americans had cause to be proud of the Vietnam war, he said, not bowed 'before our God'. Reagan did not wave a Bible as Jimmy Carter had done, but his language was clearly evangelical. Communism was *always* 'Godless' and, as he told Robert Scheer of the *Los Angeles Times*:

> . . . the reason for the godlessness with regard to communism – here is a direct teaching of the child from the beginning of its life that it is a human being whose only importance is its contribution to the state – that they are wards of the state – that they exist only for that purpose, and there is no God, they are just an accident of nature.[21]

For some years Reagan had referred to the approaching Apocalypse and to the Book of Revelation and had repeated that 'retribution will be ours unless we put the world in order'. This side of the homey cowboy actor was little noticed; and by the time he was running for president in 1980, he was tempering his fire-and-brimstone. There were Catholic and Jewish voters who might get the wrong idea.

Falwell could express in raw terms the primitivism which Reagan, the presidential candidate, now had to try to measure. The Moral Majority Inc. had been established partly for this purpose: to say, as Falwell told me, 'the things that gotta be said and said and said', as well as to rally the 'moral vote' for Reagan. 'We are God's guerrilla army,' Falwell told me with a sense of satisfaction. At the time I met him, his guerrillas were working through a 'hit list' of thirty-six senators and congressmen whom the Moral Majority regarded as too liberal and therefore anti-God and anti-American. Many of these 'liberals' were to lose as a result of Moral Majority campaigns, including smears aimed at the candidates' views on 'the family', divorce, abortion, homosexuality and the Sovet Union. It was a Moral Majority campaign which effectively buried the Equal Rights Amendment for women.

At first sight Lynchburg is a neon-lit outpost in a jungle of circular, elevated banking ribbons of concrete apparently designed to get people around and out of Lynchburg as expeditiously as possible. The town bears the name of Colonel Charles Lynch who delighted in personally hanging loyalists to the Crown following the War of Independence: thus the term lynching. Today it makes ChapStick (for dry lips), Fleet's Enema, General Electric products and parts for nuclear weapons. However, Lynchburg's most famous industry is based in the former Donald Duck Cola factory, now a Baptist church and the headquarters of 'The Old Time Gospel Hour'. 'It was Donald Duck before the Reverend Jerry took it over,' said Jerry Falwell's Media Co-ordinator. 'Right now it's God's house.'

There was much excitement down at the former Donald Duck Cola factory when I was there. Ronald Reagan, then in the last two weeks of his campaign, was due in Lynchburg the next day 'to meet and pray with the Reverend Falwell' and to receive the Good News, in advance, of God's endorsement.

God's advance man was clearly a big wheel. He not only had a media co-ordinator, he had a 'public affairs administrator' and a 'chief of stewards' and his jaw-jutting picture, like a candidate's poster, almost covered the walls. He also had men who talked into their suits and had wires coming out of their ears, just like the Secret Service agents who guarded the President of the United States. Of course the Reverend Jerry did not speak to anyone. 'London, England', said the media co-ordinator, 'will get you top of the line. The Reverend Jerry *loves* England. He always says that the only thing that would make him split from Ronald Reagan was if Reagan bombed England.'

As it turned out, the Reverend Jerry's motorcade (he had just flown in from Washington) had gone instead to the Holiday Inn where he would conduct a national press conference. Neither the media co-ordinator nor the public affairs administrator nor the chief stewards seemed to be aware of this, which is the lovable side of American madness. 'Larry's screwed this one,' said the media co-ordinator.

In the 'ballroom' of the Holiday Inn the Reverend Jerry sat eating his way through a trayful of 'Danish' (sticky buns). He was a portly businessman-looking person with red, watery eyes who spoke in lip-smacking, modulated tones, occasionally dropping to a powerful baritone.

During the press conference he was asked about his connections with Ronald Reagan. 'In an ideal world', he said, 'we'd have God for President. Nothing less is appropriate for this nation. But that's not to be, so He will speak to His supporters in the polling booths and advise them of His Chosen Man.'

'Okay Reverend,' said a television reporter, 'on a scale of one to ten, and with the Devil as ten, how would you – I mean God – rate Ronald Reagan?'

Positioning his profile to the camera and putting his hand on his heart, Falwell replied, 'Why, candidate Reagan is a *fine* man. He believes what the Moral Majority believes, what *God* tells us. He's regenerated ... born again! He's for Adam and Eve and he's against what they call the Theory of Evolution. He's for the family and against sex education in schools. He's against homosexuality and abortion and feminism and all that welfare. What's more, he's for America being number one again, having the strongest military since Creation. To answer your question, sir, why I'd say that Ronald Reagan and the Devil are at *opposite* ends of the scale.'

'London, England' saw me through the ranks of my colleagues and into a room where the Reverend Jerry sat with another sticky bun. I asked him why Jimmy Carter, the most public born-again Christian in America, had not warranted his support.

'Born again Christians', he replied, 'gave Jimmy Carter his razor-thin majority in '76. He's let us down; he's shown himself to be a volatile liberal, so we're aiming to reverse that!'

I asked him in what respect was Jimmy Carter a volatile liberal.

'Look around,' he said. 'Is America what it used to be any more? Do people in England feel reassured by America's position in the world nowadays? Jimmy Carter tore the courage out of this proud land of ours.'

I asked, 'How do you propose to swing the election for Reagan?'

'I have four million registered Americans who did not vote last election, and their time has come. I can say to them direct, "Ronald Reagan is the Man of Destiny" and I know they'll vote for him.'

I asked him if he had ever wondered if God was right-wing or left-wing.

'Capitalism,' he said, 'is enshrined in the Book of Proverbs. Of course God is *right*, but with a small "r" – do you get me?'

I did, but I wondered how important money was in his work for God. 'Money?'

'Yes, you rake in ... I beg your pardon ... you are sent millions of dollars, and all religious contributions are tax free. You live in a great mansion, you have a private plane. It seems you have become very rich doing God's work.'

A pause followed, during which I produced a recent issue of *Newsweek* and I read out a quotation attributed to the Reverend Jerry. 'Material wealth is God's way of blessing people who put Him first.'[22]

'That was taken out of context,' he said.

We moved on to Jews. 'Did you not say', I asked, 'that God does not answer the prayers of Jews?'

'That was a theological statement made by another member of the Moral Majority. I love Jews. I *love* 'em.'

I broached war. 'From Genesis to Revelation,' he said, 'the message is clear ... there will be a nuclear holy war over Jerusalem and the Russians will come out second best ... *if we are ready for it*. The issue here is survival. Jesus was not a pacifist. He was not a cissy ... okay, you got enough? You have a nice day and God bless you.' He placed a stubby bejewelled hand on my shoulder; it bore the largest diamond ring I have ever seen.

The next day presidential candidate Reagan duly arrived in Lynchburg and made a speech to the Liberty Baptist college of which Jerry Falwell is the founder. The college, surrounded by Bible-quoting guards, has 3,000 students who are said to represent a vision of Jerry Falwell's America. It is like a tableau of the 1950s. The grey, scrubbed young men wear suits, ties and regulation haircuts; the young women petticoats and dresses. Jeans, make-up, dancing and movies are banned, and there is a curfew. There are no poor and no blacks.

The Reverend Jerry introduced the next President of the United States as a 'great Christian who is going to rejuvenate America and the world'. The candidate spoke about being born again 'out there on the range' and about the moral pits the world was in, and he warned that 'if we don't get our house in order we're not going to be able to stop the Apocalypse because we're going to deserve all we get . . .'

Later, before the television cameras, the candidate seemed more than a little worried about what Jerry was supposed to have said about the Jews. 'Gosh,' he said, 'Jews and Gentiles are all Moses' people', a statement which may or may not have appeased the New York vote.

After Jerry and Ronnie had departed to the strains of 'Onward Christian Soldiers', we reporters were given a press kit with 'JERRY FALWELL' on the cover and, inside, a picture of the Reverend Jerry, jaw jutting, on the steps of the US Capitol Building. It all seemed to say that God might, just might, send Jerry himself to Washington one day.

'It's in the Book of Psalms,' the Reverend Jerry had replied when I asked him about this. 'God is judge. He putteth down one and setteth up the other.'

THE ROCK

New York: February 1981. It was almost midnight and the Beast was due. Underground, on a New York subway station, the expectancy of ambush seemed as routine as the trains. Passengers hurrying home or simply taking part in New York's parade from nowhere to nowhere, shared one physical characteristic: their eyes were like small frosted windows. Only Getting There mattered.

Now the commander-in-chief approached. 'It is da Rock,' said Finger. 'Get straight for inspection you jerks.'

The Rock wore a cavalry twill overcoat like a cape, pin-striped trousers and black leather gloves, and a shoulder holster made for a snub-nosed revolver and now bearing his wallet and three autographed pictures of himself. A gold star medal hung from his red beret and he would reveal an emblazoned T-shirt, for cameras or cops or hoods, the way Clark Kent exposed his Superman chest prior to an assignment in pursuit of universal goodness.

'The Rock,' proclaimed Finger, who was one of his captains and reputedly could split a wooden board with one finger, 'the Rock has intelligence and class. The Rock is clean and pure right through. No smokin'; no booze; one chick. The Rock is a scholar, right? He's got spiritual eyes. He can feel you behind him, and breakin' ass is what he does to jerks who mess with the good people of this city. Right, Rock?'

The pay phone on the platform rang. The Rock picked it up and listened while engaged with his own reflection. A little adjustment of the coat collar maybe; a little movement of the eyebrow for the camera. 'Greeneyes!' he said into the phone, 'I wanna know what you did with da crowbar ... Yeah ... okay ... so you stripped the jerk, and you made a citizen's arrest, right? You got witnesses? Good Angel. Now get your patrol over here to Lexington and 59th. I want you with me on the Beast tonight. We're riding it right out to Gunsmoke. I got the London *Daily Moon* doin' an interview.'

The Beast is a subway train that runs into an area of Brooklyn where the going price for burning a tenement block is $100 (three times that if people are living in it) and twelve-year-olds can earn up to $2,000 a score selling heroin to other twelve-year-olds. Unemployment and disaffection from Ronald Reagan's America are total.

The Beast stops at a station called Rivonia Avenue, better known as Gunsmoke because many of the 82,000 New Yorkers who are mugged every year are mugged or murdered there. According to those who have to travel on the Beast, the transit police have given up in the war against the muggers and the last line of defence is that provided by the Guardian Angels, who claim to have grown from a mere 'Magnificent 13' to a 600-strong force patrolling, in four-hour shifts, all 760 miles of the city's subway system.

'I want to tell you boys,' said a commuter, touching the sleeve of the Rock, 'when I see you Angels on my train, I sleep. Can you imagine that? I sleep all the way home. And I'm one of the 14 per cent with chronic insomnia! You're *beautiful!*'

According to the Rock, the Guardian Angels would be nothing without him; and on that, Finger and Big Man and Apache and Cherokee and Savage and Snake and Space and Lightning concur. To these and the other mislaid souls from New York's streets, who are Puerto Rican, black and white both male and female (Toni Tucker, a boxer, leads an all-girl patrol), Curtis Silwa is inspiration itself. The Rock is a name Curtis acquired after legendary ass-breaking activities as a bouncer at a McDonald's in the Bronx and as a gas station 'jockey' on the night shift. So many people drove off without paying that the Rock would station himself in front of each car and hurl metal weights through the windshield if the driver attempted a getaway. 'Jerks', he said, 'started paying.'

Above all, the Rock is good. This is confirmed in the publicity put out by the Rock's mother, who is the Angels' public relations director. The approved life story is as follows:

By the time he was five, Curtis lusted after achievement and began by leading thousands of pre-schoolers in reciting the Pledge of Allegiance to the Flag of the United States on a TV show called *Romper Room*. By the time he was nine he was reading Voltaire and Edmund Burke and *How to Handle People*, and writing letters to President Johnson. By the time he was fourteen he was, alas, bounced from a Jesuit school for attempting to 'democratise the Catholic faith'. One year later he had redeemed himself by collecting sixty tons of rubbish and storing it in his backyard, 'as part of the ecology movement', but no one picked it up and the neighbours complained about the stink.

Breakthrough came when he was invited to the White House to receive the Newsboy of the Year award from President Nixon. The citation said he had saved six people from a burning house on his paper delivery round. And now, at twenty-five, with the medal on his beret awarded in gratitude by the Workers of the United Nations who travel on the subway and come under Angel protection, the Rock confounds and divides New York officialdom by the popularity of his Angels.

'These Angels are not vigilantes,' said New York Lieutenant-Governor Mario Cuomo fulsomely at a dinner in honour of the Rock. 'These youngsters have decided, at great risk to themselves, to perform a major public service. They are the best society has to offer.'

The Mayor of New York, Ed Koch, did not agree. He denounced the Angels as 'paramilitary'. But such was the commuters' indignation at this slander on their saviours that the mayor had to recant and offer the Angels auxiliary police status, which the Rock rejected. 'The cops are stigmatised,' he said. 'We are not cops. We are of the citizenry.'

As for the cops, according to the Rock, 'two off-duty jerks took me for a ride out to Jones Beach and threatened to grease me if the Angels didn't stop what they called cheap labour scabbing. That's all they care about: their lousy jobs.'

There must have been something to this because the District Attorney posted two of his own 'good' cops to protect the Rock from the city's 'bad' cops, who referred to the Angels as 'the goon squad' or, in the words of one senior officer, 'those haemorrhoids in berets'.

'Significantly,' said the Rock, 'two Angels have been killed in the line of duty: one fighting off a mugger, the other shot dead by a cop who didn't even tell the Angel to freeze or nothin'. They just shot him. Cops are assholes. Everybody knows that.'

The Beast approached. It had the look of a munitions train having just completed another run to the front. One carriage was a blackened shell, the rest were graffiti-splattered and smelled of urine. The Angels entered through the last car, as they always did, and marched up towards the front of the train, peeling off at every door, eyes darting. 'We are like minnows moving across a pond,' said the Rock in one of several literate and literary bursts. He took a seat as befitted a commander-in-chief and acknowledged the admiring nods of the commuters.

The Angels say they are unarmed and that everybody is frisked before a patrol. 'I've cashiered a hundred jerks for insubordination,' said the Rock 'Nobody gets into the Angels who's got a record of violence. It was Voltaire who said, "Nothing violent is intelligent".'

'Right, Finger?'

'Sure, Rock.'

At the 167th Street station another patrol came aboard. It was led by the Chinaman, who saluted his leader. 'You see these guys?' said the

Rock. 'I had to hold consultations with da Ghost Shadows, biggest gang in Chinatown, before any Oriental could join the Angels. Those Chinese wanted assurances I was not out to control turf. It was the same with the deaf mutes.'

'The deaf mutes?'

'Yeah, we got an élite patrol comprised exclusively of deaf mutes who were in a Bronx gang and are currently with us. Some jerk might shout out "nigger" or "spik" and they don't get provoked because they can't hear. But, man, those guys can smell trouble, and two of them got black belts.'

We got out at the next stop because the Rock was expecting a phone call and, right on cue, the pay phone on the platform rang. It was his mother, the public relations director, with a message from the Rock's lawyer, Mr Schwartz, who also handles entertainers. 'Mr Schwartz is a wunnerful man,' said the Rock. 'He's got a TV movie made about the Angels and, in particular, about my life story. But he's got problems because someone has taken liberties. But we ain't suin' yet.'

There was no gunsmoke that night at Gunsmoke Station, which was in semi-darkness because electricians refused to work there. 'Right at this point I fell seventeen feet off a bridge trying to get a shotgun off a guy,' said the Rock. 'Hey Apache! Cover that old man going up the steps!'

Like a whippet, Apache did what he was told. He had skull-shaped knuckledusters on both fists. 'If you ever see a jerk with skulls on his face,' said the Rock, 'you know Apache has taken care of him.'

'What about Voltaire', I reminded him, 'and violence not being smart?'

'Apache never read Voltaire. He reads Batman. All he knows is that more people in New York get hurt crossing the road when the lights are with them than when the lights are against them. Apache's just a city schmuck who gets his good impulses from me.'

I lit a cigar. 'Excuse me sir,' said Finger, 'but smoking in the subway is illegal.'

We returned to midtown Manhattan and emerged into the dawn. New York confronted us, glittering walls against a sky the colour of roses, garbage blowing like tumbleweed down Park Avenue. I was escorted to a taxi by the Rock and Finger and Apache and a platoon of Angels whistling 'Colonel Bogey': a scene which, I suggested to the Rock, ought to be in his movie.

'Right,' he said, and made a note on a pad held by Finger. 'Hey, you know I met this English clergyman and he said we could be the toast of London, workin' the subway over there. Waddya say?'

Recalling a quotation in the Rock's life story (written by his mother)

I replied, 'The only thing necessary for the triumph of evil is for good men to do nothing!'

There was the hint of a first smile. 'Now don't tell me . . .' said the Rock, 'but did you not just speak the very words of Edmund Burke. Or was it Batman?'

13

Un-Americans

FOR GOD AND COUNTRY

New Mexico: October 1968. Sunrise had just begun on Route 66 and the man and his wife sat as one in the dust beside the long, black road, his broad-brimmed hat over his eyes, her shawl cocooning them both against the cold. They did not move or speak. They waited.

Behind them, in an infinity of screaming colours, lay their America, an America known only to them and not to those who drove thunderingly by; a silent and beautiful land without cities or shopping malls or billboards, just the Painted Earth and its mountains and mesas, rivers and lakes and canyons and great red rocks, like cathedrals; and trees, stillborn and black. And beyond that, the sun.

This is the desert: the America of the First Americans, who call themselves simply *Dineh*. The Spanish conquistadores knew them as *Apaches de Navajo* and the settlers called them redskins; and they have been waiting beside this long road for a century or more, since Colonel Kit Carson came with his United States Army, marching against them into the Canyon of Death, destroying, as he went, their mud homes and their livestock and starving them into surrender and into signing treaties, which granted them no more than the worst of their own lands, renamed, with ignominy, reservations.

No other people have been more mythologised than they – what pre-computer age Western child had never heard of Sitting Bull and Geronimo? – and yet no other people are more forgotten. And nowhere does this irony echo louder than among themselves. Dressed like cowboys, they have waited, wasted and watched their children play that interminable game based on themselves, but with plastic bows and arrows and the strongest among them always the triumphant white man.

It was a national television programme that persuaded me to go to the south-west of the United States, to Arizona and New Mexico, where the Navajo, the largest tribe, live. It was a late show broadcast from New York and one of the guests was a young Indian girl, bedecked in feathers and beads and aching with shyness. The compère said: 'Well, folks, we have a *gen-u-ine* Indian princess for you tonight, just like Hiawatha. Let's hear it now for Miss American Indian of 1968!'

He put on an Indian head-dress and danced a bizarre dance in front of her and the audience laughed.

'Tell me, honey,' he said to her, 'why you come here to heap big paleface pow-wow?'

There was a long silence before she said, 'I have been sent to ask for jobs for my people and for food for our hungry children and for freedom and honour.'

The compère was speechless; a commercial followed quickly.

The average income of an Indian family is less than half that of even a black family, and in remote areas, in the 1960s, it was not uncommon for five people to attempt to survive on the equivalent of £250 a year, or less. Then, an Indian could expect to be dead at forty-three, or twenty-seven years sooner than a white American, and an Indian child was twice as likely as a white child to die during infancy. Diseases under control in white America are rampant still on the reservations. Tuberculosis, which has all but extinguished a whole tribe in the State of Washington, is ten times the national average.

There is little work of any kind on the reservations. And because there is no work, one of the few ways they can make money is to sell hand-made jewellery and pottery to white tourists, the descendants of those who lured tribes off their land with trinkets and trade. Nowadays, many Indians are uneducated, untrained, illiterate; many live in less than slums, in dome-shaped structures of mud and wood, called hogans, and in tarpaper shacks and shelters made of leaves and tents. A high proportion of Indian families are divided because there is no transport into the outposts and the government boarding schools are far away and sometimes in another state. A statistic frequently used by Robert Kennedy, who was briefly and tenuously their champion, was that the suicide rate among Indian teenagers was one hundred times that of the rest of the country, and suicide occurred as early as eight years old.

I drove on to Navajo land at dawn when the desert is spectacular. The old man and woman huddled by the road were glad of my offer of a lift; they had been there all night, and they spoke no English, and in haphazard Spanish they said they wanted to go to a trading post to buy food.

The man was blind and had skin like baked liver and he wore a shirt with a great oval hole in the front; for a moment it was inconceivable that they were Americans, of perhaps a hundred generations, and I was the foreigner. Ten miles on, they got out, bade me, '*Haa gone!*' – Godspeed – and they disappeared into the trading post, over which hung a sign: 'War Bonnets 59 cents. Send One Home!'

At Window Rock, the administrative capital of the reservation, I needed a 'clearance'. Window Rock was a forlorn settlement of Nissen huts and trailers in which the Bureau of Indian Affairs, the BIA, and the ONEO and the PHS and a dozen other acronyms of officialdom did their work. The BIA public relations man who was to 'clear' me had previously been with NASA, the space agency.

'Can I tell you something?' he said. 'There's oil and gas and all kind of wealth on this reservation and it belongs to the Indians. They're rich! Some of them just don't know how lucky they are! Well, let me whisper, maybe a few of them are kinda indolent. Maybe that's their problem: they're rich and they're indolent.'

Margaret Boyd was a beautiful old woman, like a slender oak trunk. She was, in many ways, typical of her tribe. She lived without a light in a wood and mud hogan, fourteen feet by five, where she slept on a damp dirt floor, wrapped in a sack beside an old pot-bellied stove which smoked. The sack, she said, had once held fertiliser. She had no water; the nearest was a spring, half a mile away on a ridge which she climbed in spite of her bad heart. She was aged somewhere between fifty and seventy; she would not say where. Her food was the Indian staple: corn and bread fried in black grease, and occasionally mutton.

Margaret Boyd was unusual because she could speak English and she did not object to her picture being taken. 'I come from Colorado', she said, 'so I am civilised. Ha! I used to stand in trading posts long hours and listen to Anglos talk because I know if I talk like an Anglo I get served quick smart. Ha!'

Just across the Arizona border was a one-street oasis called Tuba City. It was in Tuba City that I met the remarkable Mr Max H. Hanley, Snr. Mr Hanley knew his people like an ant knows the earth: for years he tape-recorded their songs and prayers and memories, in order to resurrect some of the tribe's fading history. He also raised money to send young people to 'college', a choice available to very few Navajo.

Mr Hanley was able to do this work by going regularly to California to dance, like a fool, before businessmen's luncheon clubs where he was advertised as 'The Dancing Warrior' although he was at least seventy years old. In return they gave him bundles of cast-off clothing and some cash. 'Yes, I am truly the white man's clown,' he said. 'But there is no other way. We are only beginning. We do not have the Negroes' numbers.'

Mr Hanley's proudest achievement was that he had persuaded the

US Public Health Service to send a doctor, twice a month, into the moonscape around Tuba City, where previously only medicine men treated the sick. 'If ever a chunk of Heaven fell,' he said, smiling wide, 'it was that doctor coming. Why, our Navajos used to go a hundred miles to find one an' that's some walkin' in this rough country, especially if you're pregnant or what-not. Why, even in a spring wagon that's a lot of distance when you're sick.'

Seven thousand feet up on Red Mesa Mountain the derricks of the El Paso Oil Company sucked the earth like great nodding crows seeking ever elusive worms. As the public relations man had said, 'The land here is rich, rich, rich.' For every eight barrels of oil the oil company drew, the tribe received just one. For every ton of coal mined on the reservation, the tribe received the equivalent of tenpence, and perhaps a promise of jobs for some, while the majority waited for their welfare cheques, and for the tourists.

Outside Sam Chief's hogan I sat and talked with the old man and his grandson. On about £35 a month Sam Chief helped support his ten grandchildren, who lived with their mother, Mrs Grace Moody, in a shelter made from bark and leaves and furnished with two large burst mattresses, two home-made chairs and a picture of John F. Kennedy, with the caption, 'A Leader of Men'. She said she was embarrassed to have me inside because it was not her cleaning day.

As we sat in the sun a car pulled up in the distance and a woman in checked Bermuda shorts and hairnet and tennis shoes walked across to us, loading an instamatic camera.

'Well, hello there! My sister and I were just wondering . . . do you folks actually live in *that*?'

Sam Chief and Grace Moody said nothing.

'Why, heaven to Betsy, you *do*! We thought it was a storehouse or somethin'. You don't mind if I get a picture, do you? I mean with you all in front?'

Sam Chief shook his head. 'Two dollars, one picture,' said his grandson.

'You want me to pay? Oh, I couldn't do that, I mean it's the principle . . .'

As I drove into the outpost of Shiprock, on the northern edge of the reservation, a halo of peach light burned around the great rock itself and, in the town, smoke curled up from ripe wood fires and children squealed and old women nodded and dogs fought. A banner of flapping calico announced, 'Navajo Fair Today. All Welcome.'

The fair was an annual event and people had come from all around, in old trucks and on horseback, to show their prize corn and fabrics and beads of silver and turquoise and to watch the parade, which had just begun.

There were school bands, with drum majorettes, and a display float of arts and crafts sponsored by the Distant Drums Launderette of Fort Defiance and cars with the slogans of white people seeking the Indian vote to make them county judges and tax collectors, and a tableau entered by the Bureau of Indian Affairs depicting 'A Century of Navajo Progress', over which someone had scribbled 'Century of Programs'.

And, inexplicably, there were two white men carrying a banner proclaiming arguably the most racist group in America, the John Birch Society. 'For God and Country', it read, and in cruel procession behind them came a wagon on which were wreaths and names of some of the Red Americans who had died in the war in Vietnam . . . Johnnie Bigwater, Private First Class, Jimmie Bearchild, Corpsman, Thomas Dakota, Sergeant . . .

PYRAMID LAKE IS DYING

Nevada: October 1976. Four years earlier I had met at Wounded Knee in South Dakota Red Cloud, Chief of the Sioux. He had patiently written down for me a quotation which his grandfather had addressed to his people in tones of scornful irony more than eighty years before:

> You must begin anew and put away the wisdom of your fathers. You must lay up food and forget the hungry. When your house is built, your storeroom filled, then look around for a neighbour you can take advantage of, then seize all he has. That is the way of the white man, the victor.

On January 10, 1844 Lieutenant John Fremont, of the US Army Corps of Topographical Engineers, sighted what was believed to be an inland sea in the Nevada desert; 'a sheet of green', he wrote, 'breaking upon our eyes like the ocean ... The waves were curling in the breeze and their dark-green colour showed it to be a body of deep water ... It was set like a gem in the mountains.' Fremont noted strange shapes, formed by carbonate deposits precipitated from the water, which resembled castles, minarets and domes. One of them, more than three hundred feet high, 'presented a pretty exact outline of the great pyramid of Cheops', Fremont wrote. 'This striking feature suggested a name for the lake, and I called it Pyramid Lake.'[23]

Fremont was greeted by Paiute Indians who, he wrote, 'appeared to live an easy and happy life' on the shores of the lake. One reason for this was the abundance of a species of salmon trout found nowhere else in the world, which grew to a length of two feet. In 1970 Alvin M. Josephy Jr, an editor of *American Heritage* and author of *The Indian Heritage of America*, described Pyramid Lake as 'one of the few remaining unspoiled natural wonders in the American West'. He wrote:

> The color of the lake, deep blue, green, or gray, changes to reflect the hues of the desert sky but depends also on the density and

movement of concentrations of plankton in its waters. Along the shore there are still few signs of development or of man's presence, and the great sheet of water and hills around it are overwhelmingly quiet save for the sounds of wildlife. California gulls, caspian terns and blue herons flap and soar across the sky. Ducks ride the swells and approximately 7500 white pelicans, probably the largest colony of that species in North America, nest on Anaho Island, three hundred yards off the eastern shore.[24]

My own impression of Pyramid Lake, having driven from Reno over the ridge of hills which encircles a vast prehistoric basin, was that I had come upon a place of such intense beauty and solitude that it might have been unique in the United States. It was a secret place. But when my eye followed the sweep of the lake to its immediate foreshore, I could see there was something wrong.

In photographs taken early in the century the 'pyramid' outcrop had been an island; now it was visibly joined to the shoreline, which receded beyond banks of dry white silt. These, too, had formed a lake, once about thirty miles long and fed by water overflowing from Pyramid Lake. This lake, Winnemucca, had entirely dried up and disappeared or, as the Indians who live around it said candidly, 'It was murdered.' And what befell Lake Winnemucca was happening to Pyramid Lake.

Pyramid Lake has only one principal source, the Truckee River, which starts at Lake Tahoe almost 100 miles to the south-west. In 1905 the Department of the Interior built Derby Dam across the Truckee, diverting part of the river into an irrigation project for settler-farmers around the town of Fallon. The result has been dramatic; eighty feet of water have been lost and every year the level of the lake drops by ten feet. Sandbars clog the mouth of the Truckee so that fish can no longer get up the river to spawn. The unique Lahontan trout described by Fremont are already extinct. Alvin M. Josephy Jr predicts that when Pyramid Lake is about 70 per cent of its present size 'the water will be too saline for fish ... and Pyramid will be a dead salt lake'.[25] Certainly, by the turn of the twenty-first century the lake will be past the point of recovery. 'This is one of the blackest pages in the history of American fisheries and wildlife', wrote Thomas J. Trelease, an official of the Nevada Fish and Game Commission in 1967. '[It] represents what must be close to the ultimate in greed and lack of foresight ... a grim, humiliating sermon in selfishness on one hand and public apathy on the other.'[26]

In 1859 the federal government set aside Pyramid Lake for the Northern Paiute people as part of an otherwise desolate reservation. The lake provided their livelihood, and the courts confirmed the tribe's legal ownership. But this did not stop the Derby Dam project. Without ever being consulted, the Indians had their water stolen from them.

Ironically, though not uncommonly, the arm of government charged by law to protect their rights, the Department of the Interior, was responsible for diverting the water. The Department stood squarely for the interests of those whites 'opening up' the West and its bureaucrats generally believed that their conflict of interest would be resolved by the early demise of the 'vanishing' Paiutes. Inconveniently, the tribe did not vanish, but increased in number and began to fight back with the weapon of a 1972 Supreme Court ruling which established the Indians' first-priority water rights on all reservations. The court also ordered that water should be diverted back to Pyramid Lake. The response of those whites who used and operated the Derby Dam was that the court's decision had nothing to do with them.

The Indians were left with only one course of action: they had to sue each of the water users, at a cost of millions of dollars and years in time. However, any action they decided to take had to be via their 'protectors', the compromised Department of the Interior. At the same time local white politicians erected a tangle of statutes and regulations against them, and the political *coup de grâce* was administered on July 6, 1969, when Governors Ronald Reagan of California and Paul Laxalt of Nevada discussed the future of Pyramid Lake at a meeting on Lake Tahoe in a cruiser owned by the Reno gambler, William Hurrah.

'Without consulting the Indians', wrote Alvin M. Josephy Jr, 'they agreed that engineers should hasten Pyramid Lake's gradual decline by draining it down to the level at which it would stabilise.'[27] As Vine Deloria Jr, Indian author of *Custer Died For Your Sins* and a former executive director of the National Congress of American Indians, recounted: 'It was the same logic used by the Army to destroy a Vietnamese village – "We had to destroy the village to save it". It naturally followed that the only way to save Pyramid Lake was to drain it.'[28]

One cold, diamond-bright morning I sat on the shore of Pyramid Lake with Warren Toby, whose people had lived in that place for more than four thousand years. A Paiute, he was the longest-serving member of the tribal council; he remembered Lake Winnemucca as being twenty miles long and 'full of fish and a sanctuary for waterfowl'. He also remembered the year of its death.

'It was 1938,' he said. 'I watched the Tooey fish – the ones that don't breed anywhere else on the earth – just lie on the shorelines, some of them already dead, some of them just barely moving and some of them you could see turning inside out. That was the end for them, gone for ever. The waterfowl left the next year, over to the still water that had been stolen from Winnemucca for the irrigation scheme at Fallon. That's where the ducks are now, and they have a duck club there where you have to join before you can hunt down there. I've never hunted down there. They took the water, then they took the wildlife that went with it. That's the way they did it.'

Nowhere was the extravagant waste of Pyramid Lake's water more obvious than around the town of Fallon, centre of the irrigation scheme. Only a sixth of the irrigated land had been cultivated, and much of the diverted water was used to create a so-called sportsmen's reserve, to which the wildlife of the dying lake were migrating. For all the hardship it had caused the Indians, the irrigation scheme was a spectacular failure.

In Nevada, a desert state with virtually no water controls, the biggest user of water in the Fallon area was a ranch of 1,400 acres owned by State Senator Carl F. Dodge. Senator Dodge's solution was a pay-off.

'Assuming they've been wronged,' he said, 'the federal government should pay them damages.'

But money, I pointed out, would not preserve what they wanted to keep: their identity and their lake.

He replied, 'No, but it's a case of balancing the interest . . . that's what I think we have to consider at this point in time, because we use it for multiple purposes here. We got swimming, boating, water skiing, picnicking, overnight camping, that sort of thing.'[29]

A modern school was built on the edge of the Pyramid Lake reservation in the 1960s because white families living nearby demanded it. The school emphasises the white way of life. According to the headmaster I met, a man of measured cynicism, 'We honour one of the principal aims of the Bureau of Indian Affairs' nineteenth-century charter, which stated that Indians should be alienated from their culture and their language.'

Indian elders, known as 'consultants', come to teach the children bead work and how to prepare Paiute fried bread. When I was there, the Paiute children were participating in a 'Tom Tom dance' which was not Paiute in origin; the drummer was a social worker from another tribe, as foreign to the Paiute as the Greeks are to the English. Thus, the children of Pyramid Lake were being taught to adapt to the Hollywood image of Indians.

Kate, whom I knew briefly, was a Paiute in her seventies. Kate seemed to be the lone repository of the memory of the crimes against her homeland and her people. She worried obsessively that 'If we complain too loud of what they did to us they're gonna come and terminate us.' I asked her what she meant by 'terminate'. 'They'll close down the reservation', she said, 'and send us out into *their* America, and we'll go the way of the Negroes then. We'll be terminated.'

Kate could be found most days contemplating Pyramid Lake from a makeshift bench near the graveyard where her husband and son were buried. Her husband had been a 'doughboy' in General 'Blackjack' Pershing's expeditionary force to France and had died of his wounds there. Why, I asked her, did so many Indians volunteer to fight in foreign wars, more than any other group of Americans?

'We're just like ordinary people anywhere,' she replied. 'The young think they're fighting for their country. In a way, I guess they are.'

Most of the headstones are of Paiute teenagers who died in Vietnam. 'We tried not to cry when they went', said Kate, 'because the older people always told us that if we cried or felt bad, our boys would be killed. That was the saying they had. So I didn't cry when my eldest boy went. I just gave him dinner and he left with the rest of them. I guess he must have died for his country.'

ON THE ROAD

Los Angeles, California: February 1983. In John Steinbeck's classic novel, *The Grapes of Wrath*, poor farmers evicted from their land in dustbowl Oklahoma in the 1930s were advised to drive to a land of plenty, untouched by the Depression:

> Why don't you go on west to California? There's work there and it never gets cold. Why, you can reach out anywhere and pick an orange. Why, there's always some kind of crop to work in. Why don't you go there? And the owner men started their cars and rolled away.[30]

In the 1980s much of America is back on the road: not on protest marches, but in a procession of old cars and campers, heading west once again to where the 'American Dream' is believed by many still to be held in trust, regardless of the hard times.

The families in the cars and campers, now living out their lives in caravan parks and in tents, in cardboard shacks and under bridges, are not at all like those of the 1930s. There are some small farmers, forced off their land by rising interest rates, but the majority are skilled workers in the new middle class for whom there is no longer anything on offer in an economy increasingly polarised between the high-paying new-technology and the low-paying service industries. Indeed, as America's 'smokestack industries' have contracted dramatically since the 1970s, taking away the competitive advantage the United States once enjoyed as if by right in manufacturing automobiles, rubber, steel and machinery, so the foundation of the 'middle income' class formed since the Second World War has eroded; in some parts of the country, such as in Pennsylvania, Michigan and Ohio, it has retrenched altogether. 'MIDDLE CLASS SHRINKS AS POVERTY ENGULFS MORE FAMILIES', announced a headline in the *New York Times*, as though an article of faith had been excised from the Constitution.[31]

Profound economic and demographic changes in America began to occur well before the Reagan years, but since Ronald Reagan became president in 1980 they have accelerated, making life more desperate for the old poor, while creating a new breed of 'loser'. These are people who never imagined that one day they might not be able to pay off a mortgage or a car or their American Express bills, and would find themselves shuffling forward in a queue to receive government surplus food or Salvation Army soup.

In 1976 in Detroit, America's 'Motown' and once the harbinger of the dream of full employment, I interviewed Henry Ford, whose father is sometimes credited with having invented the consumer society. Henry, the son, guided me to the panoramic windows of his office in the Ford Building, and as grist to his argument that 'one day soon almost all of America will be rising middle class', he indicated the points on his compass of prosperity.

'Over there', he said, 'is the East Side of Detroit right up against Grosse Pointes. The East Siders have got too much crime and their living standards are not high enough by far. The Grosse Pointers give their kids home computers and violin lessons. Now these two places are divided down the middle by Alter Road. You know what they call Alter Road? They call it the Berlin Wall. Well, let me tell you that before I'm a dead man that wall is going to be down and the East Siders will be on their way up. And that's no dream.'

Henry Ford is not dead, but his prophecy is. In the decade since he expressed that optimism unemployment in Detroit has trebled, reaching 70 per cent in some places; and since 1982 the city has declared itself to be in a 'state of unemployment and hunger emergency'. Not only have the East Siders lost all promise of 'upward mobility', but under new Reagan laws the maximum period for which they can receive unemployment benefit is fifty-five weeks, and the poorest families are now denied all welfare if the father leaves home to look for work; thousands more are no longer eligible for free school meals, summer 'feeding programs' and medical check-ups.

Meanwhile, on the other side of the 'Berlin Wall', those who struggled their way into the middle class via the assembly lines of General Motors, Chrysler and Ford have begun to lose what they assumed was theirs for ever. When Henry Ford pointed down at their neat streets, in the mid-1970s, almost all their cars, he said with pride, were 'new and expensive'. Now the names of the grills are a roll-call of obsolescence: Coupe de Villes and Caprice Classics and Henry's own Thunderbirds and station wagons in various states of decay. Every week now, usually on a Sunday morning before sunrise and before the neighbours are up, more Thunderbirds and station wagons pull away and head west.

John Wyatt[32] and his family reached Phoenix, Arizona at three in the morning, having camped two nights in the desert in temperatures below freezing. They had almost no cash. They had driven first to Texas and stayed in the 'Almost Heaven' campsite near Houston, where John had found a job on a construction site for four dollars an hour; but this would not feed his family and, unlike Michigan, Texas has no general welfare programme. So they came further west.

There were so many like the Wyatts, looking for shelter, food and gasoline to keep them going, that the Salvation Army had set up a marquee at the approaches to the city. The tent was filled to capacity when the Wyatts arrived, but the Salvation Army major on duty found John, his wife Carol, and their children, Pat, aged eleven, and Donna, nine, a basement room for the night in a cheap hotel.

'The problem here in Phoenix', said Lieutenant-Colonel Muriel Collier, 'is that we've got a city council that wants nothing to do with these folks. They're hostile to them. They've just rushed through an ordinance making it illegal to sleep on a city street or even to forage through garbage in a public place. You read the letters in the paper; people don't want reminders of hard times; and quite a few of them want the police to run these migrant families out of Phoenix.'

John Wyatt had been an engineer, about to be promoted to foreman, he thought, when he was made redundant at Pontiac, near Detroit. 'From that day', he recalled, 'everything ran out like water from an empty tank . . . my credit, my medical and hospital cover, my mortgage payments, my stereo payments, my vacation fund payments. I guess I decided it was time to go when I found myself lining up at a food bank and being handed a parcel marked "From the auto workers of Western Germany to the auto workers of America".'

When the Wyatts arrived in Trabuco Canyon, California, they bought a vintage caravan with broken louvres and a hole in the roof. They lived on a vacant allotment with other families who had come west, many of them single-parent families. Carol got a job cleaning in a House of Pancakes and John split wood several days a week for a retirement home. Between the two of them they made ten dollars above the limit for claiming benefit for their children, whom the state welfare authorities were threatening to take from them. This had also happened to them in Texas; it is the *Catch-22* of modern poverty.

At four o'clock one February morning they drove into Los Angeles, where at the St Vincent De Paul mission on West Ninth Street, the federal government was giving away cheese. This was surplus cheese which the government had bought as a form of subsidy in order to keep the price up and the politically powerful dairy lobby happy. The Catholic Church had paid the shipping costs; and at nine o'clock a convoy of trucks turned off the freeway into West Ninth Street, which was filled with several thousand people in an orderly coiled line, each of whom would receive five pounds of cheese and a priestly blessing. These were not 'Bowery people'. They were John and Carol Wyatts: steelworkers from Ohio, a shoe salesman from Trenton, New Jersey, an ex furniture store manager from Syracuse, New York.

Shortly afterwards John Wyatt answered the following newspaper advertisement:

WANTED!
Unemployed people who want to change their lives on TV's newest, most original game show. Apply Group W Productions . . .

The newest, most original game show was called 'Help Wanted!' and the producer was Charlie Colarusso. I spoke to Charlie. 'What we're creating', he said, 'is reality entertainment broadcasting. These are *real* people competing on air for a *real* job. It's a situation we can all relate to. We have two finalists for one job, and the audience votes on who should get the job. We've got jobs for a dog groomer, a dipper and packer in a chocolate factory and a supermarket checker. The winner gets the job and the loser gets $250!'

John Wyatt put himself up for the dipper and packer in the chocolate factory, but he did not pass the audition. It was clear that what Charlie Colarusso wanted was not an ex foreman with a skill but an attractive girl. When John was turned down, Carol Wyatt, a normally taciturn person, described what was happening to them as 'like being raped from within'.

In 1985, according to a congressional study, almost one American child in four lived in a family whose income was below the official poverty line.[33] On 14th Street in Washington, nine blocks from the White House, 'Bread for the City' hands out food to more than a thousand people a month. These new hard times, which have been imposed not on the wealthy but on a nation of ordinary people who seek only to get by, are in some ways harder than when Franklin Delano Roosevelt was elected president in 1933 in the depths of the Great Depression.

Hard times were news then. They are not now. If there was shame and anger, it was likely to be shared then; new divisions make that difficult now. Today the imagery of television, of an all-powerful consumer world, reflects overwhelmingly the world of the 'winners', in which cities like Detroit are disposable, 'losers' cease to exist and the vision and humanity that come from true political leadership are as obsolete as an old Coupe de Ville.

IV

VIETNAM

14

Dreamland

Saigon: June 1966. I arrived in Saigon during an electrical storm, trying to feign nonchalance. However, the American next to me on the flight from Bangkok was the model of nonchalance and the contrast was obvious. He was so drunk that when the tail of the flaking Caravelle was struck by lightning on the approach into Saigon, his small, shaven head grunted serenely and vomited in my lap without waking. This was genuine nonchalance; he was clearly an 'old Asia hand'.

I was young and owl-eyed. Through the wet, Saigon's military and civilian airport, Tan Son Nhut, appeared as a metallic jungle whose silhouetted peaks and slopes represented machines of a number and variety I had not imagined; Saigon had recently taken over from Chicago as the world's busiest airport. The pitch and variation of the noise – the whining of fixed-wing aircraft, the thudding syncopation of helicopters – induced a fear which did not leave me for almost a decade.

Outside the terminal building waited fat Chevys and Fords, pick-ups and jeeps, their Vietnamese drivers barely visible. There always seemed something menacing about Detroit cars and trucks in Saigon; they would plough imperiously through the bicycles and insect-Renaults, and if their foreign occupants were in a hurry or bored with the traffic, one of them would hold a flashing light on the roof and tell the Vietnamese driver to 'gun it'. Into one of these climbed Nonchalance himself, now awake and sucking on a cigar. Into the others went men similar in build and swagger, heavy, ponderous men who were contract workers and on US government business. A mighty, winged Pontiac saw me to the Hotel Hope.

In the late nineteenth century the French had laid out Saigon with tamarind and eucalyptus trees so that they might be reminded of Nice. They had built in the centre their colonial piles, the post office and the zoo and the Customs House, from which radiated streets of villas with verandas and pink wash on the stucco walls. One of these had been gutted by fire and the skeleton had become the Hotel Hope, run by a family of Chinese who accommodated on its four floors numerous transients, dope addicts, prostitutes and a man who stood motionless, framed in the doorway of his room, who was to shoot himself early one morning. My arrival as a genuine 'guest' so bemused the *mama san* that she gathered from somewhere a group of young and old women, each with a painted death mask, to view the new boy and to assess the degree to which my stay would support their debilitating industry.

The Hope and the Dreamland were indivisible, drawn together by an umbilical cord of corrugated iron and children. The Dreamland was no more than a shed lit by purple neon, although inside it might have been any bar on any truck route in the American Midwest: high swivel vinyl stools, jukebox, temperature just above freezing. This was an American cocoon, one of many from which Vietnam was viewed as fun city: a war, a screw, a joint, a suspended life. Here melancholy men would try to forget they were 'in-country' and surrounded by 'gooks', 'slopes' and 'dinks'. They knew less than little about the Vietnamese and their Confucian society, about their past and the roots of the war. Some did not know quite where on the globe they were; and this ignorance, at once cheerful and invidious, remained a phenomenon of the American experience in Vietnam until the last hours of the last day.

It was a phenomenon compounded by delusion on a giddy scale. Every evening, in the windowless blockhouse at Tan Son Nhut known as 'MACV' (Military Assistance Command Vietnam), senior officers would sit at a long polished table facing a lectern flanked by the United States flag and two wall-length charts and listen to a briefing major reiterate that which they and their predecessors had heard many times: that the blue bits on the plastic relief map of South Vietnam (areas controlled by US and allied forces) were 'dominant' and the pink bits (areas controlled by communist forces) were relatively insignificant and the white bits ('movement areas') were indeed moving 'in the direction of our disposition'. Vietnam was a war, not a country.

'I'm getting out of here as soon as I can,' Randy, the Dreamland's owner, would pretend, knowing that Vietnam gave him what he could never have back home: a bargain basement life, provided by a PX card, which was a season ticket to the military's Post Exchange, an Ali Baba's cave of tax-free everything. Vietnam also offered something more elusive than Budweiser on the cheap. Women. Beautiful, compliant refugee women were readily available in Saigon, where a 'round-eye' (a white man) was viewed as a strolling money tree, a means of support for a family of a dozen or more. And in return for this 'security', in times of constant insecurity, the 'temporary wife', the woman who went to live with an American for a price, provided a servitude which not even money could buy 'back home in the world'.

Randy was a former GI, a kindly and garrulous failure from Tucson, Arizona whose temporary wife was called 'Suzy-boo'. She was Vietnamese, French and Thai, and she would see to it that the girls from the Hope massaged the huge backs of the 'boys' at the bar while a blue movie flickered on to a stiffened towel above the bar. The girls, she would whisper, were 'nice and clean'; a Listerine swill every Friday was mandatory (and useless).

On my second night in Saigon, Flipper appeared. He had what Randy called 'his routine'. He would sing, over and again, 'You got-ta live a lit-tel, love a lit-tel . . .'; and he would follow this with a kind of soft-shoe shuffle, then a circuit with a rusted Coca-Cola can tied around his neck. 'Hey, Flipper number one, eh?' Then Suzy-boo would throw him out; he lived not far away in a colony of shacks made from flattened American beer cans. He was once a soldier fighting in the Army of Ngo Dinh Diem, the dictator installed and assassinated in a CIA-engineered coup in 1963. He had lost both arms at one of the sacrificial places coloured blue on the map at MACV. He still wore his Army fatigues and, at the end of his 'routine', before he begged, he would draw himself to military attention, his gaze straight ahead. At first I found it difficult to look at him; he seemed to embody the degradation and humiliation of people damaged by the war and forced to live in and off its garbage. But the more I saw him, the more I detected that not only was his dignity intact – his eyes were proof of that – but his capacity to survive was nothing less than heroic. His patrons would not have seen it that way. 'Why, Flipper's like a mascot to us,' said Randy.

Not far from the Hope and the Dreamland was vacant land cluttered with stalls and debris. In the midst of this was a *dinh*, a shrine. I came upon this one day by accident, and was intrigued by its attraction for people of all kinds: soldiers, bargirls, old people. When I enquired I was told that a *xa*, a village, had stood there some years earlier, before Saigon had swollen with war refugees, and that families were buried there and their remains were 'the source of life itself'.

Enveloped in petrol fumes, sluiced by monsoonal mud, the shrine symbolised the coherence of a society enduring a cataclysm. Shortly afterwards, in the countryside, I watched an old man refuse to leave his paddy fields, which had been designated an area to be mined, a 'free fire zone'. On the bank of the paddies was the familiar family *dinh*, bullet- and shrapnel-scarred from battles that had gone on around it, in which the old man had lost his wife and sister-in-law. Not only was this shrine sacred, the old man protested to those wanting to hurry him into a waiting helicopter, but the land itself could not be desecrated, for it belonged to the dead, his ancestors, 'the source of life'. The Vietnamese translating his words knew precisely what he was saying; the American responsible for getting people out of the area was aghast at such obstinacy. Hands on his hips, he looked at the old man across an abyss. Their perspectives were irreconcilable.

'We can't *make* him save his own ass,' said the American. 'So we'll have to leave him.' And they left him.

For a reporter, the 'Green Machine' began at the Joint United States Public Affairs Office, or JUSTPAO, with a smiling President Johnson framed above a bored marine at the door. The President had been to Vietnam a few months earlier and had told his men 'to come back home with that coon skin on the wall'. Here I was fingerprinted, 'accredited' and provided with a small laminated card which read:

NOTICE: The bearer of this card is a civilian noncombatant serving with the armed forces of the United States. If the bearer of this card shall fall into the hands of the enemies of the United States he shall at once show this card to the detaining authorities who shall entitle him to the same treatment and privileges as a Major of the US Army.

With this laminated card I could fly almost anywhere 'in-country' on the world's greatest airline, operated by the American military. I could present myself at a 'departure lounge', where there were racks of war comics and Harold Robbins books, and Hawaii posters and Muzak, and soft drink and candy machines. What fun this was! I was going to a place called Can Tho, in the Mekong Delta, where there were more red bits than blue bits on the MACV map. With my boarding card and my Hershey bar, I might have been flying to Miami. The soldier at the check-in desk even pointed out the arrival of my aircraft. It taxied to a halt and a truck backed up to its open belly to receive cargo. The loadmaster emerged and shouted, 'Where's the man from the KIA Travel Bureau? I ain't handling these dudes alone out here!' [KIA stood for Killed in Action.] A soldier came running with a clipboard and checked every item of cargo until the truck was full. 'That's it,' he said, to which the loadmaster replied, 'Oh no you don't; one more here, baby.' This item of cargo had split open – it was a green sack – and a corpse slid down the loading tray. It was trussed and the face looked like one of those clean-living young Mormons who prowl the world's suburbs. The loadmaster and the man from the KIA Travel Bureau struggled to return the corpse to its sack, their efforts accompanied by the Muzak, which was interrupted so that we could be told to have a nice flight.

Almost anywhere a reporter went in Vietnam there was a Press and Information Officer, or PIO, to meet and 'brief' him. In 1966 many

1 University of Sydney graduation day, Bondi Beach, 1920. Elsie
  Marheine, later to become Elsie Pilger, is third from the right.

2 Richard Pilger, alias 'Ramón J. Peralto', fourth from the left in the
  back row, on one of his ships, *c.* 1890

3 Frank Dyer, agricultural worker, Dorset, 1972 (*Photograph: Bela Zola*)

4 Joe Cardy, Murton colliery, County Durham, 1974 (*Photograph: Tom Buist*)

5 The homeless McKirdy children in their one room in Princes Lodge hostel, London, 1974 (*Photograph: Andy Hosie*)

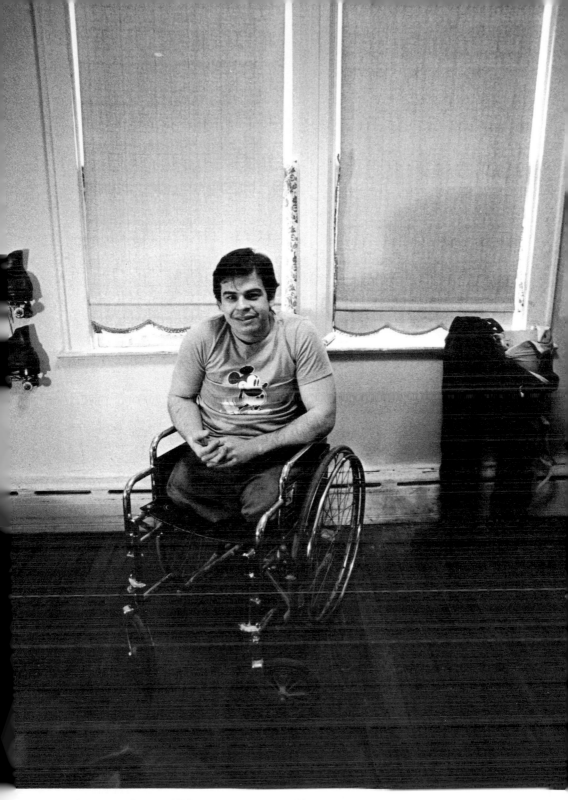

6 Mike Sulsona, former US marine wounded by a mine in Vietnam, at
home in New York, 1980 (*Photograph: Ken Regan*)

7 Civil rights campaign poster, Georgia, *c.* 1963 (*Photograph: Danny Lyon*)

PIOs held an almost evangelical belief in the correctness of the American 'crusade' and in what their version of the MACV chart told them. The captain who briefed me at Can Tho wore silk basketball shorts and the trophies in his hut confirmed that his passion was basketball. Covering one wall was the MACV chart. 'This here's the VC,' he said. 'This here's the ARVN [Army of the Republic of Vietnam – Saigon regime] and this here's us. Now I'm not going to give you any of the military's platitudes, shit like that. All I want you to discern is that, although the VC are present around here, this area right across here has been pacified. The people *know* the VC are their enemy. In other words, we got Charlie sucked dry.'

That night, while the captain was elsewhere, his hut, his chart, his basketball trophies and his 'on-base' newspaper duplicating machine were destroyed by a VC rocket. The attack came early in the morning while I was asleep in the dispensary of Can Tho's civilian hospital. The rockets did not hit the town, only the American base, but all the next day the hospital shook from the reprisal bombing of villages a few miles away which were said to have spawned the attackers. That evening the wounded and dying arrived from these villages on the veranda of the hospital.

'I guess he's around ten years old,' said the young American civilian doctor. Before us was a boy whose nose and chin had merged, whose eyes could not close and whose skin, once brown, was now red and black and papery, like frayed cloth. The doctor said that if I touched the skin it would cling to my fingers or would turn to powder. He said he bothered to mention this because it had happened to him. 'It beats me how these kids live through all that shit out there,' he said. 'This one's been burned with Napalm B. That's the stuff made from benzene, polystyrene and gasoline. It usually sticks to the skin and is impossible to get off, and either burns the victim to death or suffocates him by using up all the oxygen.' An American photographer appeared and said he had come from My Tho, which had also been rocketed. The photographer launched into a manic monologue about the kind of weapons and tactics he had seen deployed. He spoke in military acronyms mostly, and he seemed to be addressing the single light bulb above the terribly wounded boy, now swathed in intravenous tubes. 'Nothing here,' he said finally, and left without taking a picture.

The next morning the captain who loved basketball gave me a briefing from a makeshift chart, meticulously drawn with red and blue crayons, like a child's craft project. The area around the town, where the charred boy had come from, had been coloured red before the Napalm B was dropped. It was now coloured blue. The boy died.

15

History as illusion

When I began to write this, in 1985, ten years after the end of the war in Vietnam, I heard the results of an opinion poll in which people in the United States were asked how much they could remember about the war. More than a third could not say which side America had supported and some believed that North Vietnam had been 'our allies'.[1] This reminded me of something a friend of mine, Bob Muller, a former US marine officer paralysed from the waist down as a result of the war, told me. As president of the Vietnam Veterans of America, Bob speaks on college campuses where he is asked as a matter of routine, 'Which side did *you* fight on?'

This 'historical amnesia' is not accidental; if anything it demonstrates the insidious power of the dominant propaganda of the Vietnam war. The constant American government line was that the war was essentially a conflict of Vietnamese against Vietnamese, in which Americans became 'involved', mistakenly and honourably. This assumption was shared both by 'hawks' and 'doves'; it permeated the media coverage during the war and has been the overriding theme of numerous retrospectives since the war. It is a false and frequently dishonest assumption. The longest war this century was a war waged by America *against* Vietnam, North and South. It was an attack on the people of Vietnam, communist and non-communist, by American forces. It was an invasion of their homeland and their lives, just as the current presence in Afghanistan of Soviet forces is an invasion. Neither began as a mistake.

So it is not surprising that many Americans are today confused about who their 'allies' were during the war, because in reality they had none. Clients yes, allies no. The difference is as critical as the difference between 'attacked' and 'became involved', for it is the clear division of truth from propaganda.

The war in Vietnam was the first television war, watched by millions year after year. But the news became a mockery, telling so much and explaining so little. And such is the obsolescence today of unpalatable, 'forgotten' events that a reminder of some of them seems important if mendacity and illusion are not to be transmuted into history: a process now well under way.

On my first trip to Hanoi I was intrigued by the following familiar words on a plaque in the Museum of History:

> All men are created equal. They are endowed by their creator with certain inalienable rights, among these are life, liberty and the pursuit of happiness.

It was with these words that Ho Chi Minh had proclaimed the Democratic Republic of Vietnam on September 2, 1945. Standing on a hastily-erected wooden platform opposite the French Governor-General's palace and with the flag of the new republic above him, Ho had gone on to acknowledge the source of 'these immortal words', as he described them. They were taken, he had told the crowd,

> from the Declaration of Independence of the United States of America in 1776. In a larger sense, this means that all the people on earth are born equal; all the people have the right to live, to be happy, to be free.

In the crowd had been a group of American officers, led by Major Archimedes L. A. Patti of the Office of Strategic Services (OSS), the forerunner of the Central Intelligence Agency. Major Patti's work as a US government 'liaison officer' in Hanoi during the summer of 1945 represented the first direct American involvement in Indo-China. He remains one of the crucial witnesses to and participants in the war's gestation period and was for many years the keeper of its early secrets. It was not until 1980 that Major Patti's book *Why Viet Nam? Prelude to America's Albatross* was published, even though the manuscript of his story was ready in 1954. McCarthyism had taken hold in America and he was threatened with 'disciplinary action' if he disclosed what had happened during his time in Vietnam.[2]

When we met in Los Angeles in 1983 Major Patti described the 'extraordinary pro-American spirit that was everywhere at the birth of Ho Chi Minh's Vietnam'. 'They didn't regard America as an imperial power,' he said. 'They thought we were different from the Europeans and they were desperate not to be associated with international communism, not with the Chinese or the Russians, but with *us* in America. What an opportunity it was. I remember when Ho Chi Minh called for me and said he was drafting Vietnam's declaration of independence. He asked if I could remember how the American text went and said, "The same declaration is appropriate because Americans and Vietnamese believe in the same anti-colonialism." Well, that was fine, but my problem was that I couldn't remember it word for word!'

The ironies then multiplied. Also in Hanoi that day was the French Commissioner for Indo-China, Jean Saintenay, who was to accuse Patti and the United States government of 'infantile anti-colonialism', and of endorsing 'this communist takeover of Indochina'.[3] The French bitterness was understandable; not only had they been humbled in their own colony as quislings of the Japanese, but now the Americans, the liberators of Paris, had arrived to help not them but the Vietnamese nationalists, the Vietminh, who were led by a communist called Ho Chi Minh. Moreover, President Roosevelt had already vilified France which, he said, had 'milked' Vietnam for a hundred years. 'The people of Indo-China are entitled to something better,' the President had said, and the United States supported their 'independence and self-determination'.[4]

Ho Chi Minh liked Americans. He told his friend Wilfred Burchett, the Australian journalist, that he enjoyed 'the openness of Americans . . . the way they get things done. They didn't seem [in 1945] to be prisoners of the past, not like the French.'[5] Ho perhaps had a personal reason to like Americans. In June 1945 *Life* magazine published a family album-style picture of members of an American OSS team who had parachuted behind Japanese lines to supply the Vietminh. In the centre was Ho Chi Minh; on his left was a young American holding a pith helmet, Paul Hoagland, who had found the Vietminh leader seriously ill and had nursed him with sulphur drugs and quinine and, as Ho himself later acknowledged, had saved his life.

Ho Chi Minh was the antithesis of other emerging communist leaders in one respect: he wanted his people to open themselves out to other societies, communist, capitalist and non-aligned. Like Tito in Yugoslavia, he knew that this was the only way his people could survive as a national entity. Indeed, so anxious was Ho for American support for his fledgling republic that he addressed twelve separate appeals to President Roosevelt, to his Secretary of State, Cordell Hull, and to the Senate Foreign Affairs Committee. Major Patti later wrote that Ho 'pleaded not for military or economic aid',

> . . . but for understanding, for moral support, for a voice in the forum
> of western democracies. But the United States would not read his
> mail because, as I was informed, the DRV Government was not

recognised by the United States and it would be 'improper' for the President or anyone in authority to acknowledge such correspondence.[6] [DRV stood for Democratic Republic of Vietnam, later known colloquially by the Americans as 'North Vietnam'.]

Ho Chi Minh saw America's post-Second World War strength as a counterweight to China and went so far as to propose that Vietnam should be part of an 'American Commonwealth' in Asia with a trusteeship status similar to that of the Philippines. That the Philippines then was effectively an American colony apparently did not concern him; for this was an expedient. Unless Vietnam survived in the shadow of the most populous nation, independence would never be realised.

As for relations with the Soviet Union, Ho had spent fifteen years in Moscow and expressed himself well aware of the tenuous and highly conditional nature of Soviet 'friendship'. He told Patti, 'I place more reliance on the United States to support Vietnam's independence, before I could expect help from the USSR.'[7]

During the summer of 1945 Ho Chi Minh would hold a press conference every morning at ten o'clock in his office in Hanoi, although he would ask most of the questions and direct them at a young American, Ed Hoyt, the correspondent of United Press. 'When is the United States going to do something about Mr Roosevelt's promises?' he would ask. Ed Hoyt reported Ho's enthusiasm for siding with America, only to discover later that an employee in the United Press relay office at Chungking was an agent of Chiang Kai-shek's secret police and had rewritten his dispatches to suit China's foreign policy. 'So all Uncle Ho's pleas for help from Uncle Sam never got past Asia,' Hoyt later lamented, with only slight exaggeration. 'So much for journalism as history.'[8]

In September 1945 Vietnam was a country of artificial, overlapping, foreign-imposed divisions. The French had divided Vietnam into three, all sub-divisions of its colony in Indo-China. The Allies divided it between two military commands headquartered in China and South-East Asia. On September 4, 1945 Major-General Douglas Gracey, a British colonial officer, entered Saigon with the 20th Indian Division and took the surrender of the Japanese. He immediately rearmed them and ordered them to put down the Vietminh, who had already formed an administration in the South. Like the Vietminh in the North, they were a popular movement of Catholics, Buddhists, small businessmen, communists and farmers who looked to Ho Chi Minh as the 'father of the nation'.

By January 1947, thanks largely to Gracey, the French *colons* were back in power in Saigon. Ho Chi Minh still hoped for an alliance with Washington and appealed again to President Truman while insisting to

Patti that he was 'not a communist in the American sense'. Although he had lived and worked in Moscow, Ho considered himself a free agent; but he warned that he 'would have to find allies if any were to be found; otherwise the Vietnamese would have to go it alone'.[9] And alone they went until 1950 when Ho Chi Minh believed he could no longer delay accepting the formal ties and material assistance under offer from the Soviet Union and especially from China. It was the success of the Chinese revolution in 1949 that was to give the Vietminh the means to defeat the French: military training, arms and sanctuary across an open frontier.

In 1950, with the Korean war under way, the American view of monolithic world communism prevailed. The sentiments of Roosevelt about opposing colonialism had long been blown away by the Zeus-like figure of John Foster Dulles, whose fundamentalist crusade against 'Godless communism' guided American foreign policy during the 1950s. Dulles bracketed Vietnam north of the seventeenth parallel with 'Red China', without regard to the complex and fragile relationship which had existed between the two nations for several thousand years and which always had a potential for enmity.

Of course at the root of Dulles's evangelism was a practical, imperial concern which, wrote Noam Chomsky,

> ... was over strategic resources of Southeast Asia and their signifi-
> cance for the global system that the US was then constructing,
> incorporating western Europe and Japan. It was feared that successful
> independent development under a radical nationalist leadership in
> Vietnam might 'cause the rot to spread', gradually eroding US domi-
> nance in the region and ultimately causing Japan, the largest domino,
> to join in a closed system from which the US would be excluded . . .
> The idea that US global planners had national imperialist motives is
> intolerable to the doctrinal system, so this topic must be avoided in
> any history directed to a popular audience.[10]

Having declared a policy of 'containing communism' in Asia, the American government in 1950 gave $10 million to assist the French in winning back their colony in the North. Within four years the Americans were paying for 78 per cent of a colonial war directed by the same French whom President Roosevelt had castigated. For Washington, the French surrender following the siege in the valley of Dien Bien Phu ought to have forewarned them of the fighting qualities of the Vietnamese, but it did not. The front page of the *New York Times* of April 6, 1954 read: 'DULLES WARNS RED CHINA NEARS OPEN AGGRESSION IN INDOCHINA.'

What the 'warning' did not say was that Dulles was preparing for an 'all out war' against China, using nuclear weapons.[11]

The rout of the French in the North by the Vietminh took place while an international conference on Indo-China was convened in Geneva in July 1954. The final declaration divided Vietnam 'temporarily' at the seventeenth parallel into two 'national regrouping areas'. North and South would be reunited following free national elections on July 26, 1956. There seemed little doubt that Ho Chi Minh would win and form Vietnam's first democratically elected government. Certainly President Eisenhower was in no doubt of this. He wrote: 'I have never talked . . . with a person knowledgeable in Indochinese affairs who did not agree that . . . 80 percent of the population would have voted for the Communist Ho Chi Minh as their leader.'[12]

The Geneva conference held many secrets. One of them was the part China played in the division of Vietnam. It was a role of exquisite duplicity which owed nothing to the solidarity of 'world communism', the current Western bogey, and was pursued with the same fervent self-interest which has seen the 'Chinese communists' embrace a galaxy of disparate allies, from Pol Pot in Cambodia to General Pinochet in Chile. Chou En Lai, the Chinese premier, had gone to Geneva with the hope of ending China's diplomatic isolation and the aim of 'neutralising' Indo-China. The latter meant keeping the Americans away from China's southern borders and dividing the growing nationalist movement in Vietnam. According to Anthony Barnett:

> Chou secretly informed the French that he recognised the reality of the South Vietnamese government they were attempting to construct. His plans misfired – with the ironic result that his country's diplomatic isolation was only ended when the war that followed between Vietnam and the United States looked like being won by a Vietnamese party no longer beholden to Peking.[13]

(In his book *Caveat*, Alexander Haig described a trip he made to Peking in January 1972 to prepare for President Nixon's 'opening to China' that year. Haig wrote that Chou En Lai 'touched on every subject that was of interest to our two countries but he dwelled on one in particular – Vietnam . . . I reported to President Nixon that the import of what [Chou] said to me was: don't lose in Vietnam; don't withdraw from Southeast Asia.')[14]

Dulles refused to sign the Geneva accords and less than a month after the protagonists had returned home from Geneva, according to the *Pentagon Papers*,[15] the United States moved in secret to 'disassociate France from the levers of command' in southern Vietnam and to assume direct American control. This task was assigned to the newly formed CIA which, during the summer of 1954, invented a 'republic of Vietnam' with Saigon as its capital. This was known by those assigned to the task as 'creating the master illusion'.

Ralph W. McGehee was for twenty-five years a career officer in the CIA and one of the creators of such illusions. He was an expert in 'black propaganda', which is known today as 'disinformation'. In an interview with me in 1983 he described the war in Vietnam as 'the Agency's longest and most successful disinformation operation'.[16] In 1977 McGehee retired, not as renegade, but with the CIA's highest honour, its Medal of Commendation. He was disillusioned, he said, because the CIA had become 'not an intelligence gathering organisation but a covert operations arm of the Presidency'. In 1983 his book *Deadly Deceits*[17] was published. In the following passage he describes how the CIA not only installed a regime of its choice in Saigon, its 'master illusion', but changed the demographic map of South-East Asia:

To make the illusion a reality, the CIA undertook a series of operations that helped turn South Vietnam into a vast police state. The purpose of these operations was to force the native South Vietnamese to accept the Catholic mandarin [Ngo Dinh] Diem, who had been selected by US policymakers to provide an alternative to communism in Vietnam. It was a strange choice. From 1950 to 1953, while Ho's forces were earning the loyalty of their people by fighting the French, Diem, a short, fussy bachelor, was living in the U.S. in Maryknoll seminaries in New Jersey and New York.

Diem arrived in Saigon in mid-1954 and was greeted by Colonel Edward Lansdale, the CIA's man in South Vietnam and the head of the Agency's Saigon Military Mission (SMM). Diem was opposed by virtually all elements of South Vietnamese society – Bao Dai's followers, the pro-French religious sects, the Buddhists, the remnant nationalist organisations, and, of course, the followers of Ho Chi Minh. He had no troops, no police, no government, and no means of enforcing his rule. What he did have was the complete support of Colonel Lansdale and all the money, manpower, weapons, training, propaganda, and political savvy in the CIA's covert-action war chest.

To create Diem's government, Lansdale's men, operating in teams in North Vietnam, stimulated North Vietnamese Catholics and the Catholic armies deserted by the French to flee south. SMM teams promised Catholic Vietnamese assistance and new opportunities if they would emigrate. To help them make up their minds, the teams circulated leaflets falsely attributed to the Viet Minh telling what was expected of citizens under the new government. The day following distribution of the leaflets, refugee registration tripled. The teams spread horror stories of Chinese Communist regiments raping Vietnamese girls and taking reprisals against villages. This confirmed fears of Chinese occupation under the Viet Minh. The teams distributed other pamphlets showing the circumference of destruction around Hanoi and other North Vietnamese cities should the United States decide to use atomic weapons. To those it induced to flee over the 300-day period the CIA provided free transportation on its airline, Civil Air Transport, and on ships of the U.S. Navy. Nearly a million North Vietnamese were scared and lured into moving to the South.

Lieutenant Tom Dooley, who operated with the U.S. Navy out of Haiphong, also helped to stimulate the flow of refugees to the South. At one point he organised a gathering of 35,000 Catholics to demand evacuation. A medical doctor, Dooley was a supreme propagandist whose message seemed aimed largely at the U.S. audience. He wrote three bestselling books, and numerous newspaper and magazine articles were written about him. Dr. Dooley's concocted tales of the Viet Minh disembowelling 1,000 pregnant women, beating a naked priest on the testicles with a bamboo club, and jamming chopsticks in the ears of children to keep them from hearing the word of God, aroused American citizens to anger and action. Dr. Dooley's reputation remained unsullied until 1979, when his ties to the CIA were uncovered during a Roman Catholic sainthood investigation.

The Agency's operation worked. It not only convinced the North Vietnamese Catholics to flee to the South, thereby providing Diem with a source of reliable political and military cadres, but it also duped the American people into believing that the flight of the refugees was a condemnation of the Viet Minh by the majority of Vietnamese.

Now the scene had been set and the forces defined. The picture drawn to justify U.S. involvement was that the Communist North was invading the Free World South. The CIA was ordered to sustain that illusion through propaganda and, through covert operations, to make the illusion a reality. Its intelligence, with an occasional minor exception, was only a convenient vehicle to sell the lie to the U.S. bureaucracy and people. Unfortunately, nearly everyone, including later policymakers, was deceived by this big lie. While the plan was never detailed in a single available document, an examination of the *Pentagon Papers*, plus other related information, demands this conclusion.

The terror which the regime of Ngo Dinh Diem inflicted on people living south of the seventeenth parallel is conclusively documented. The main instrument of terror was a 50,000-strong civil guard, or secret police, which had been set up and trained by teams from the CIA and

Michigan University. In 1959 the Diem regime passed a law requiring the death sentence for those found guilty of speaking out or 'spreading rumours' against the government. This was the model of a 'free world democracy' which the United States was committed to defend against the 'communist threat' and on whose behalf President Kennedy, by clear implication in his inaugural address, had called on his countrymen to lay down their lives. Colonel Lansdale, on the other hand, was more candid; in a secret memorandum to the Secretary of Defence in 1961 he wrote: 'I cannot truly sympathise with Americans who help promote a fascistic state and then get angry when it doesn't act like a democracy.'[18]

In 1960 the Front for the Liberation of South Vietnam (FSLN, better known as the NLF*) was established out of the old organisation of the Vietminh. It came about partly as a result of a decision by the Vietnam Workers' Party (Lao Dong) in the North, but also in response to intense pressure from southern cadres. Like the Vietminh, its membership included Catholics and Buddhists, city and country people, communists and non-communists. Two years later, in a clandestine congress, Nguyen Huu Tho, a non-communist Saigon lawyer, was elected NLF president and remained in that position after the capture of Saigon on April 30, 1975. The NLF wanted primarily to free Vietnam from the control of foreigners and those of their countrymen courted and bought by foreigners. Inevitably, by its massive presence of up to half a million men under arms, the United States ensured the alienation of those who were not communists and reinforced those who were.

In 1961 Diem's troops and their American advisers drove large numbers of the rural people of southern Vietnam into what became known as 'strategic hamlets'. These were concentration camps, surrounded by wire and watchtowers, whose purpose was to 'protect' the people from the Vietcong. Those who objected to being 'protected', and who resisted, were murdered and tortured. Such 'excesses' and the nepotism of the Diem family received wide publicity in the United States, and it was clear that 'Asia's George Washington', as Diem called himself, was becoming an embarrassment to President Kennedy. In November 1963 Diem was overthrown by a triumvirate of his generals, organised by the CIA.

One of the generals was Duong Van Minh (the Americans called him 'Big' Minh because he was six feet tall), a devout Buddhist who had approached the NLF seeking a ceasefire and negotiations toward a 'neutralist' non-communist coalition government in Saigon. According to a study by George Kahin, based on extensive interviews, the generals,

* Vietcong, meaning Vietnamese communists, was an American term.

who were 'seeking a negotiated agreement among the Vietnamese parties themselves without American intervention', regarded the NLF as 'overwhelmingly non-communist' and 'sufficiently free of Hanoi's control to have made [a political settlement in South Vietnam] quite possible'.[19]

The Vietnamese were never allowed to choose. The historian David G. Marr wrote that the generals' mere countenance of peace negotiations

> . . . was one of the main reasons why the US government, or at least the US military commander in Saigon, encouraged their overthrow in turn only three months later. From then on, every Saigon military officer knew that contacts with the NFLSV, or even internal discussion of negotiation options, risked vigorous American counteraction. Some were still prepared to take that risk, but with the arrival of US combat troops in early 1965 the historical opportunity vanished. Henceforth the US government had the means . . . to ensure that no 'neutralist'-inclined RVN officer came close to power.[20] [RVN stood for Republic of Vietnam – Saigon regime.]

The creation of more 'illusions' and a legal justification for an expanded war now became an urgent necessity. American planes were already 'secretly' bombing Vietnam on its border with Laos, and American 'advised' sabotage teams were operating north of the seventeenth parallel. But to the American public the war was still a remote and perplexing affair, and domestic politics and civil rights upheavals preoccupied the news. President Johnson was then running for re-election against Barry Goldwater, an Arizona conservative whom the Democrats had succeeded in casting as a dangerous hawk in contrast with the 'statesmanlike' Johnson. However, to counter Goldwater's charge that the President of the United States was going soft on communism, Johnson needed ritually to demonstrate how 'tough' he was. The remarkable events that followed were to justify the coming American invasion of Vietnam.[21]

During the spring and summer of 1964 the United States organised commando raids from the South against the North, using South Vietnamese and landing them from the sea. Hence, Washington was already engaged in unprovoked hostilities against Vietnam. An American spy ship, the USS *Maddox*, took part in this action. On August 2 the *Maddox* fired on two torpedo boats off the coast of North Vietnam in the Gulf of Tonkin. The boats had neither attacked the *Maddox* nor returned its fire. Two days later Captain John J. Herrick, on the bridge of the *Maddox*, noticed two 'mysterious dots' on his radar screen and concluded they were torpedo boats. It was a blustering, stormy night and visibility was nil. Again, no attack materialised. However, Herrick had sent an emergency call to his headquarters in Honolulu and this was passed quickly to President Johnson, who was 'furious' and wanted to order the bombing of North Vietnam immediately. A few hours later a cable arrived from Captain Herrick. It read:

> Freak weather effects on radar and over eager sonar men . . . No actual visual sightings by *Maddox*. Suggest complete evaluation before any further action taken.

President Johnson asked his Defence Secretary, Robert McNamara, for urgent 'clarification' while he prepared to address the nation. Captain Herrick cabled back that there was 'a confusing picture', although he was now certain that the report of an attack was 'bona fide'. What he did not say, until 1985, was that this confirmation of a 'bona fide' attack was based on 'intercepted North Vietnamese communications' which he had not seen. Johnson's television speech was now written; America was going to war. But a third cable now arrived from the *Maddox* in which Captain Herrick reverted to his original doubts. Half an hour after this was received, and ignored, the President was on networked television telling his fellow Americans, 'Renewed hostile actions against United States ships on the high seas have today required me to order the military forces of the United States to take action in reply.'

This became known as the 'Gulf of Tonkin Incident' and as a direct result, a resolution was sent by the White House to Congress seeking authority for the United States to invade Vietnam. Seven years were to pass before the *Pentagon Papers*, the official 'secret history' of the war, would reveal that administration officials had drafted the 'Gulf of Tonkin Resolution' two months *before* the alleged attack on the *Maddox*.

On August 7, 1964 Congress authorised President Johnson to take 'all measures' to protect US forces from 'any armed attack'. American-planned sabotage attacks increased against the North. Six months later the State Department published a White Paper[22] whose centrepiece was the 'provocation' of the 'Gulf of Tonkin Incident', together with seven pages of 'conclusive proof' of Hanoi's preparations to invade the South. This 'proof' stemmed from the discovery of a *cache* of weapons found floating in a junk off the coast of central Vietnam. The White Paper, which would provide the legal justification for the American invasion, was, in the words of Ralph McGehee, a 'master illusion'. McGehee told me:

> Black propaganda was when the US Government spoke in the voice of the enemy, and there is a very famous example. In 1965 the CIA loaded up a junk, a North Vietnamese junk, with communist weapons

– the Agency maintains communist arsenals in the United States and around the world. They floated this junk off the coast of Central Vietnam. Then they shot it up and made it look like a fire fight had taken place. Then they brought in the American press and the international press and said, 'Here's evidence that the North Vietnamese are invading South Vietnam.' Based on this evidence two Marine battalion landing teams went into Danang and a week after that the American air force began regular bombing of North Vietnam.

The bombing was code-named 'Operation Rolling Thunder' and was the longest campaign in the history of aerial bombardment. Few outsiders saw its effects on the civilian population of the North. I was one who did. Against straw and flesh was sent an entirely new range of bombs, from white phosphorus (1966) to 'anti-personnel' devices which discharged thousands of small needles (1971). North Vietnam then had no air force with which to defend itself. The scale of the American bombing in the mid-1960s, both in the North and South, together with the American-directed terror of the South, eventually persuaded Ho Chi Minh to send regular army units south in support of those South Vietnamese opposing the American invasion.

This was not how propaganda in the United States explained the origins of the war. Neither is it how many people remember the war today. In the opinion poll quoted at the beginning of this chapter, in which more than a third of those questioned expressed confusion as to who were 'our allies', almost two-thirds said they were aware that the United States had 'sided with South Vietnam'. As Noam Chomsky has pointed out, this is the equivalent of being aware that Nazi Germany sided with France in 1940 and the Soviet Union now sides with Afghanistan.

The accredited version of events has not changed. It is that non-communist South Vietnam was invaded by communist North Vietnam and that the United States came to the aid of the 'democratic' regime in the South. This of course is untrue, as documentation I have touched upon makes clear. That Ho Chi Minh waited so long before sending a regular force to resist the American attacks seems, in retrospect, extraordinary; or perhaps it was a testament to the strength and morale of those South Vietnamese who had taken up arms in defence of their villages and their homeland. In 1965 the American counter-insurgency adviser, John Paul Vann, wrote in a memorandum addressed to his superiors in Washington that 'a popular political base for Government of South Vietnam does not now exist' and the majority of the people in South Vietnam 'primarily identified' with the National Liberation Front.[23]

When the US marines finally 'stormed ashore' at Danang in central

Vietnam on March 6, 1965 they were bemused to find that there were no 'Vietcong' defending the beaches, dug in like the Japanese in all those Second World War movies. Instead, there were incredulous fishermen and curious children and beautiful girls with flowing black hair, wearing silk dresses, split at the waist, and offering posies of flowers. Men in white shirts had supplied the flowers and they watched from a distance as the press photographers and the film crews recorded this moving illusion of welcome, while the jungles and highlands beyond cast a blood-red shadow no one saw. Ten years, one month and eighteen days were to pass before the last marine left, pursued by an embittered mob up the stairwell in his country's fortress embassy.

During those years the United States dispatched its greatest ever land army to Vietnam, and dropped the greatest tonnage of bombs in the history of warfare, and pursued a military strategy deliberately designed to force millions of people to abandon their homes, and used chemicals in a manner which profoundly changed the environmental and genetic order, leaving a once bountiful land petrified. At least 1,300,000 people were killed and many more were maimed and otherwise ruined; 58,022 of these were Americans and the rest were Vietnamese. President Reagan has called this a 'noble cause'.

16

Hearts and minds

Danang: August 1967. The invasion had been under way for more than a year now and Danang, where the first marines had landed, had been transformed into the biggest single military base on earth. In the briefing room a Press and Information Officer was announcing with enthusiasm the establishment of a 'free fire zone' near An Hoa. 'Thanks to our fellows who hacked it right around the clock,' he said, 'we got the people out of those insecure villages. We got them right away from the enemy. We denied the enemy . . . and we saved those people. Like Chairman Mao wouldn't say [grin], we removed the water from the fish!'

I asked him if the people had expressed their 'insecurity' and desire to be saved from 'the enemy'. He replied that he did not understand the question and I should put it in writing to JUSTPAO. I asked him what time had elapsed between the dropping of leaflets informing people where to assemble for their helicopter ride to 'security' and the firing of the first rounds of artillery, which were known in military parlance as 'mad minutes'. He replied, 'Between six hours and one hour.'

So more than 3,000 people had as much as six hours and as little as one hour to relocate from what had been, for many of them, a modestly prosperous life dependent only on the seasons, to another life in a town and in peonage to the needs and whims of a foreign army whose ubiquitous presence underwrote an 'economy' based upon the services of maids, pimps, whores, beggars and black-marketeers. Unlike Saigon, also a refugee city but which had maintained a certain brittle sense of itself predating the coming of the GIs, Danang was wholly victim. Where there had been fishermen, there were now the human consequences of 'removing the water from the fish'. The upheaval caused was universal among poor farmers and those already on the margins of city life. Between 1964 and 1966 2 million Vietnamese were made homeless by such a strategy. By 1968 a *third* of the population of South Vietnam were refugees.

The ruin of lives was at once brutal and subtle. Families and networks of friends, once guardians of compassion, grace and sensuality, seemed to dissipate in the streets without sewers and tap water; fear, neurosis, casual brutality and avarice corroded lives beyond repair. People rammed each other in the markets; sons duped fathers; the elderly were neglected; rape entered the language and venereal disease entered bodies and brains, along with serious drug addiction. The Americans called the nightmare they created 'Dogpatch'.

'HISTORY IS WHAT'S HAPPENING' read the words on the 'hospitality jeep' at the gates of the American base at Danang, the greatest cocoon. The base was a small American city, with its own generators, water purification plants, hospitals, cinemas, bowling alleys, ball parks, tennis courts, jogging tracks, supermarkets and bars, lots of bars, with Budweisers and burgers and little plastic 'wooden' shingles among the bottles on which were written, 'Confucius say: Grab them gooks by the balls and their hearts and minds will follow!' And restaurants risen out of the mud, with New York cut steaks served by Filipino waiters beneath plastic chandeliers and with large signs in fluorescent lettering: 'NOTICE: Your cardiac pacemaker may be subjected to magnetic influence from the Food Preparation Facility.' And a radio station where the 'Wolfman of Nam' opened his programme thus:

> Goooooooodmorning! . . . Now here's a little advice regarding our Vietnamese friends. Never pat a Vietnamese on the head. Stand on low ground when you talk to them. Make it a golden rule, okay?

During the monsoon much of the country west of Danang looked like caramel. Life was mud; humans walked like storks; the mud engulfed all dreams. And when the rain stopped, there was dust: powder-fine red dust which blinded you and gutted your throat and crept up your arse. Containing your fear, not so much of the war as of being afraid, was most difficult at a point of departure which was a vortex of dust and searing, thudding noise. I hated the helicopters; I loathed the obese Chinook, which carried men to and from their death. There was also a practical reason for fearing these machines; seldom a day passed when one did not burst its bolts in the air. Those who flew them knew this and did not seem to mind. They drove them like souped-up Mustangs. They were nineteen and twenty years old and to them 'contour flying' meant 'skiing' on the treetops and tall grass. I never knew where their adolescence ended and their bravery began, but when they more than once picked me up under fire, judging, measuring, waiting, brave they were.

My helicopter did not go as far as Tuylon. The last twenty miles was by jeep through 'Indian country' and past a point of recurring ambush known as 'Gook Hill'. By day the marines would clatter through the villages on their 'search and destroy' sweeps, the tracks of their armoured personnel carriers churning the rice harvests. For the most part the NLF would fight only when they were assured of victory. When big operations came they were warned well in advance by intelligence from inside the Danang base, or by runners or by the noise of approaching armour or, as an NLF officer told me, by the 'strong sweet smell of American after-shave'. The guerrillas would fall back across the paddies or hide in tunnels, in holes under the fireplaces of their huts and in ponds and canals, breathing through bamboo. At night they would move back into the villages, many of which welcomed them, or, at worst, regarded them with indifference. Unlike the Saigon-appointed 'village chief', the NLF cadre and soldiers were usually local people, for which the struggle was one of educating others by example.

This did not mean the NLF aspired to be saints, as some have wished to portray them. Saints do not wear well in war. The 5 to 15 per cent of a rice harvest the NLF collected as tax was hardly popular among farmers who were forced to pay tax to the Saigon regime and to give 30 per cent to the church which owned the dam and 20 per cent to the man who owned the pump. And by their presence the NLF would expose a village to the indiscriminate fire of American helicopter 'gunships' and to the legacy of unexploded munitions in the paddies. But these notwithstanding, the NLF's recruits were peasant people who, according to an American cliché, were 'non-ideological' and 'wanting only to be left alone'; and one reason for the high level of recruitment lay in a lesson the Americans and their surrogates never learned from the French.

The French had allowed the disparity between city and country to grow to the point where, by the mid-1960s, up to 80 per cent of the rural people of South Vietnam owned only 12 per cent of the land. Landless farmers had been treated harshly by the French colonial administration and by the Catholic regime of Ngo Dinh Diem. And such was American ignorance or misunderstanding of the Vietnamese colonial experience that it did not seem to occur to them until it was too late that genuine land reform won 'hearts and minds' in Vietnam.

But, as Frances Fitzgerald has pointed out, the issue was not that simple; land reform was only part of the people's grievance, which had as much to do with the control of credit by the Saigon banks and the misuse of the available national wealth by city black-marketeers and a nepotic élite. It also had to do with the shift of political power away from the villages and districts. In the South the authority of local government had eroded during the post-Second World War French period and accelerated under the Americans. The NLF understood the implications of this; paradoxically perhaps for revolutionaries, they also understood the attachment of rural people to the traditional way of life, known as the *Tao*. This centred upon the respect for ancestral lands and burial places and for the Confucian structure of society. The Vietnamese revolution was once described to me by an NLF cadre as 'change and disturbance by stealth'.

Change and disturbance by stealth were not in the brief of Sergeant Melvin Murrell and his marines when they dropped into Tuylon with orders to sell 'the basic liberties as outlined on page 233 of the Pacification Program Handbook' and at the same time to win the hearts and minds of the people as described on page 86 under 'WHAM'. On that morning, recalled Sergeant Murrell, they saw no one, 'not a child or a chicken'.

'Come on out, we're your friends!' Sergeant Murrell had shouted through a loud-hailer; not a shadow moved. 'Come on out everybody, we got rice and candy and toothbrushes to give you!' Sergeant Murrell had cooed into the hot silence. 'Listen, either you gooks come on out from wherever you are or we're going to come in there and get you and maybe kill you!'

So the people of Tuylon came out from wherever they were and queued to receive packets of Uncle Ben's Miracle Rice, chocolate bars, party balloons and 7,000 toothbrushes; and in a separate ceremony befitting his station, the district chief was presented with four portable, battery-operated, yellow flush lavatories. 'If these are right for your requirements', said Sergeant Murrell, 'there will be more where they came from.' And when it was all over and the children cheered on cue, Sergeant Murrell noted in his log of the day:

> At first they did not appear to understand that we had come to help them. However, they were persuaded otherwise, and at this time they are secured and on our side. I believe they respect our posture of strength and humanity. I believe the colonel will be pleased.

Sergeant Murrell commanded a CAC unit, or Combined Action Company, which meant that their role was both military and civil. A CAC unit would move into a village known to be 'under threat' from the NLF and 'secure and protect' it, whether or not the villagers asked or wanted to be secured and protected. They would dig trenches and lay booby traps and erect barbed-wire fences. Then they would declare the village 'friendly' and set about selling 'the basic liberties as outlined on page 233 ... ' The flaw in this strategy was that the marines had been trained to fight and kill Vietnamese rather than sell them basic liberties. Melvin Murrell and his men had been assigned to hearts and

minds duty in order to wind them down from a stretch in the war's
hellfire, its 'Somme': the Demilitarised Zone at the seventeenth parallel.
Marines who had been on the 'DMZ' had translucent eyes and appeared
to be asleep standing up. Dug into exposed hills, utterly isolated in
warrens of mud or dust, lying painfully on their sides and often in their
own shit and blood, they were under orders not to advance an inch but
to 'sustain' the artillery, mortar fire and rockets which pummelled them
day and night. Their frustration was intolerable; they were targets, not
soldiers. There were more marines killed in Vietnam than during all of
the Second World War. I have never known men to have demonstrated
such raw courage in the cause of nothing.

Melvin Murrell had been twice on the DMZ and twice wounded. He
was twenty years old. Like many blacks he loved 'Nam' because, as he
put it, 'here I'm *somebody* . . . not just some street nigger who's nothin'.'
Here he was not only telling a bunch of 'honkies' what to do – there was
only one other black in the unit – but the colonel was proud of him and
had made him King of Tuylon! And round his realm he would swagger,
all six foot four of him, stripped to the waist, Colt .45 on his hip, proud
that the NLF had a 'price' of $750 on his head.

But how did he know that? Like the others, he spoke no Vietnamese.
A boy called Dang had told him. 'He's our spy,' Murrell said. Dang,
whom I met, was a fretful teenager whose sister had been killed in
crossfire, and he had built a shrine to her with her photograph and
cosmetics and fine bamboo necklaces arranged around two candles which
he lit every night at the hour of her death. He blamed his sister's death
on the VC, and said he would do anything for the Americans because
of her. So he was their friend, and his heart and mind were won. Or so
they thought.

When the colonel arrived from Danang, Murrell was all spit and
polish. This was his moment.

'How is everything here, Murrell?' said the colonel. 'How is the
hygiene programme coming along?'

'Toothbrushes went down a dandy, sir, but as for getting people to go
to the bathroom and all that . . . well I'm afraid these people been doin'
it otherways for thousands of years and they seem to like it that way.'

'Okay, what's your kill ratio?'

'Well sir, got two last night.'

'Okay, sounds good. Book yourself down for two.'

'Well thank you, sir.'

The colonel left before night came to Tuylon. We sat on sandbags
and ate canned corn and canned bread while frail young faces stared at
us through the camp's perimeter wire.

'They think I'm the devil 'cos I'm black,' said Murrell.

'Well ain't you?' said a white corporal, who was called Fats. He was a thoughtful man who seemed to have taken deliberate steps to protect his compassion. On a walk through the village that afternoon he had accidentally knocked over a food storage jar, which shattered. Children came to stand and gaze at his inept attempts to make amends and mollify the owner, a crippled old woman. He collected the pieces and tried to fit them together, saying 'they have a special adhesive in Danang' and he would have it sent out. But the old woman kicked the pieces into the dust and Fats, now on his knees, apologised profusely in GI Vietnamese and paid her many times that which the jar was worth, and she snapped the money from his hand. For him, the point about this incident was clear. 'No matter what we do', he said, 'we'll gain nothing here. This is the china shop and we're the bulls.' Fats had three weeks left in Vietnam; in his hooch was a calendar with the days crossed off. 'I don't want to have to love these people; I don't want to have to hate these people,' he said. 'I just want to go home.'

We slept until just after midnight when the NLF came through the wire and the night erupted. Like an apparition in ebony Sergeant Murrell burst into my tent and tossed an M-16 on to my blanket. 'Use it when they come, man,' he said.

'No,' I replied.

'Okay . . . ' And he lay on his belly outside, firing at the moon, it seemed. He was protecting me.

The next morning a bleached and suffering face lay in a trench in which were stacked boxes of toothbrushes and party balloons, still awaiting distribution. It was Fats. He had been shot in the back and could not be moved until the medevac arrived.

On the other side of the wire, in what was Tuylon's main street, lay two bodies. One of them belonged to Dang, the fretful boy who had said the marines were his friends. He wore black and an ammunition belt, and a marine issue M-16 lay beside him. The other body was that of a woman about thirty years old and pregnant and now peppered with splinters. She had been a victim of mistake, although whose mistake was not known. And as soon as a crowd gathered, Dang's corpse disappeared; and people poured rice wine on the woman's body until the funeral cart came to take it away: heart, mind and all.

Tay Ninh province: September 1970. In June the US Senate had repealed the Gulf of Tonkin Resolution which had provided a rationale for

President Johnson's land invasion. Now Johnson had retired in political ignominy and the illusion his administration had created was of no further use. Moreover, President Nixon had replaced it with his own, which he called 'peace with honour'.

When I returned to Saigon it was clear that the war was going badly for everybody. The NLF had suffered grievous losses in the Mekong Delta. The saturation 'firepower' of the Americans, combined with the use of 'anti-personnel' technology, had so damaged NLF infrastructure that former strongholds had fallen silent. For the United States, the damage was from within; its army was beginning to unravel. A minority of troops in Vietnam were combat soldiers, and most of these were 'grunts': men conscripted not only from working-class America but from among those who regarded their presence in Vietnam as anything but their 'patriotic duty'. These were sometimes known as the 'Chicago Generation', an allusion to the bloody battle fought by anti-war protesters and police outside the Democratic Party's convention in summer 1968.

This was the era of the 'drug culture' and by 1968 it was unusual to meet an American drafted soldier in Vietnam who was not using drugs. Getting stoned in your hooch made the war go away. Getting stoned on patrol made the enemy go away; and if this turned out not to be so, what difference did it make? Just as much of American society was then divided between the 'straight world' and those in or on the fringe of the anti-war movement and its attendant drug culture, so the Army was now divided between career men, known as 'lifers', and drafted men who openly displayed peace signs, beads, long hair, insubordination and not infrequently a smouldering joint of choice 'Laotian gold'. And some grunts' way of dealing with lifers who made drafted men 'hump the big pack to the boonies and get blown away' was occasionally to lob a live grenade into the officers' hooch. This was known as 'fragging'.

The US Army's 1st Air Cavalry Division was proud of its history at war and its colours celebrated its origins under General George Custer whose 'last stand' against the Sioux at Little Big Horn was an appropriate legacy in 1970. Cut off by road and under siege from both the NLF and PAVN [People's Army of Vietnam or 'North Vietnamese' Army] regular troops, 'Firebase Snuffy' might have been Little Big Horn revisited. The difference was that Snuffy was itself coming apart. Mutiny had been declared, mostly in the form of a sullen resistance by drafted men to the daily functions of the 'Green Machine'; weapons were not cleaned, latrines were not emptied, clothes were not washed, salutes were not given. A 'long-range' patrol meant venturing beyond the perimeter of the base, sitting down, lighting up, getting stoned, giggling, waiting, and returning with tales of 'contact'.

How the NLF viewed this farce, which they must have known about, was not recorded. They certainly did not ambush as often as they could, perhaps because a 'body count' was irrelevant to their struggle. To them, destroying the enemy's morale was paramount, and this was being done for them. At Snuffy I interviewed men who had 'fragged' two officers and shot another in the back. As we spoke, an officer ordered the men to report to him at the double. They ignored him; one man jerked a finger in the air. 'We'll get him later,' he said. The officer walked away.

The 1st Air Cavalry Psy-Ops (Psychological Warfare) officer was a captain, although he might have been Sergeant Bilko; he wore black horn-rimmed glasses and a banana grin. He was a stereo-and-speakers buff and what he loved to do was to fly in a helicopter low over the jungle and play his tapes to the enemy. His favourite tape was called 'Wandering Soul', and as we lifted out of Snuffy he explained, 'What we're doing today is psyching out the enemy. And that's where Wandering Soul comes in. Now you've got to understand the Vietnamese way of life to realise the power behind Wandering Soul. You see, the Vietnamese people worship their ancestors and they take a lot of notice of the spirits and stuff like that. Well, what we're going to do here is broadcast the voices of ancestors – you know, ghosts – which we've simulated in our studios. These ghosts, these ancestors, are going to tell the Vietcong to stop messing with the people's right to live freely, or the people are going to disown them.'

The helicopter dropped to within twenty feet of the trees. The Psy-Ops captain threw a switch and a voice reverberated from two loudspeakers attached to the machine-gun mounting. While the voice hissed and hooted, a sergeant hurled out handfuls of leaflets which made the same threats in writing. The captain picked up an unopened box of leaflets, grinned and shouted that 'Maybe I'll be lucky and hit a VC on the head and then I won't have to worry about changing *his* mind.' He threw the box out and we watched it fall into the trees.

Saigon: December 1972. In August the last American combat troops had left Vietnam. In October, shortly before President Nixon's re-election, his National Security Adviser Henry Kissinger announced that 'peace is at hand'. Kissinger had negotiated an agreement with the Vietnamese in Hanoi, but the president of the regime in Saigon, General Nguyen Van Thieu, refused to sign the draft. Neither Kissinger nor Nixon had bothered to inform Thieu, their frequently uncompliant client, that it had been agreed that PAVN troops could remain south of the seventeenth parallel. Thieu believed that he had been betrayed, and he was right. For their part, Kissinger and Nixon were simply casting aside the 'sovereignty' of Saigon and dealing with the reality behind it; and the reality in 1972 was the same as it had been in 1962 and in 1952; the countryside belonged to those who opposed the dictatorship of Saigon. Thieu's objections led to further revisions demanded by Hanoi and the talks foundered there. Kissinger put the blame on 'communist intransigence' and Nixon ordered the bombing of Hanoi. During twelve days over Christmas, 100 B-52s and 500 other aircraft attacked the suburbs of Hanoi and its port, Haiphong.

I flew to Saigon from Sioux Falls, South Dakota, where in the Holiday Inn I had watched the last hurrah of George McGovern as he conceded to Nixon the greatest electoral defeat in twentieth-century America. McGovern won only one state, yet he was the first presidential candidate to commit himself unconditionally to ending the war in Vietnam. On the eve of his defeat, at a party for the small group of journalists who had followed his campaign right across America, including places where reporters were his only audience, I asked McGovern to imagine his first morning as President of the United States: what would he do? It was a pleasant fantasy which we all enjoyed, for the candidate was an honest and humane man who deserved better than humiliation.

'On the first day', he replied, 'I will use every authority at my disposal to withdraw every American and every dollar that are directly or indirectly causing the war to continue. I will stop the damn thing; I will stop it; I will stop it.'

George McGovern's political demolition seemed to me to negate any contention that the American public had been turned against the war by the media and the street demonstrations. Now that Americans were no longer dying in Vietnam, and those who were dying on their behalf were only brown stick figures on the TV news, American interest in Indo-China appeared to have declined sharply.

From Saigon I drove north along Highway 15 towards An Loc, where PAVN artillery and American B-52s competed for the ashes of the rubble that remained. An Loc was claimed as a victory by both sides, and there seemed to be no one to decide who was right. Two miles away three ladders curved in the sky, and as each rung reached the ground there was a plume of fire and a sound which welled and rippled rather than exploded. These were the bombs of three B-52s flying in formation, unseen above the clouds; between them they would drop seventy tons of explosives in a 'long box' pattern. Everything that moved inside the box would be destroyed. This was 'Operation Arc Light'. Unlike the dropping of 'soft ordnance', such as Napalm, the spectacle was precise, contained, unreal. A street would be replaced by a crater; people a hundred yards from the point of contact would leave not even their scorched shadows, which the dead had left at Hiroshima. Here in the South, the American ally, people inside the box were being destroyed in order to save them. In the North, the American enemy, they were being destroyed for less altruistic reasons.

On the way back to Saigon, along roads unnaturally empty of refugees, I found in a roadside bunker an American major whose job was to call in low-level air strikes. He was alone and looked like the surviving member of an expedition which had penetrated too far into nowhere. His tape deck played country and western music. His pipe collection was arranged on a bamboo frame he had carved himself. Next to it was a photograph of his three sons. His name was Dale. He puffed on an outsized corn cob and shouted into and at his radio equipment. He said his problem now was flags. He produced a map and explained, 'Every house here has got to display the GVN [Saigon government] colours since the peace talks got serious. If they don't, they get classified as bad guys. Problem is that on Wednesday we went right into those villages and asked people why they weren't displaying the flags we'd issued them on Tuesday. Well what they said was that bad guys come into the village at night and take down the flags.'

That afternoon Dale's bunker was attacked with mortar, and he lay seriously wounded while people walked across the paddy land to look at him. And by the time the medevac helicopter reached him, he was dead.

Quang Ngai: March 1974. The Paris peace agreement had been signed more than a year earlier. Article 4 specified: 'The United States will not continue its military involvement or intervene in any way in the internal affairs of South Vietnam.'

Illusion still triumphed. The Americans had not gone, merely changed costumes. Senior officers, pilots and technicians were now disguised as civilians or as US embassy officials. As a cover for this 'secret army', sixty American companies were contracted by the Pentagon. The 'Management Services Division' of the Lear Siegler Corporation of Oklahoma City effectively ran General Thieu's air force; Kentron Hawaii ran his radar and surveillance bases; and Computer Services Incorporated ran his secret police force. The MACV blockhouse was renamed the 'Defense Attaché's Office of the United States Embassy'; the sign on the door of the War Room was changed to 'Readiness Room'. During fifteen months of the 'ceasefire' some 70,000 soldiers and civilians were killed, and

American planes dropped a greater tonnage of bombs on Indo-China than was dropped during all of the Second World War.

In March 1974 President Nixon asked Congress for $2 billion in 'aid' to the Saigon regime. Less than half of 1 per cent of this would assist the millions of people uprooted, orphaned and maimed: the war's 'collateral damage'. South Vietnam, which had become a nation of amputees, had only three hospitals equipped to treat the limbless. The best of these was run by the American Friends Service Committee, the Quakers, at Quang Ngai. Under the Paris accords the United States had agreed to remove its unexploded munitions and 'anti-personnel' devices, which had been scattered like confetti in the Delta and the central highlands. These included a bomb two inches across, the shape of a tiny envelope. If you stepped on it, it blew your foot off. Children would lose a leg and they frequently died. It was designed to lower the morale of people who supported the communists. None of these bombs was removed. During the period of 'peace with honour' people were blown up in the paddies and grasslands every day, often several people a day. On some mornings, from the hospital veranda at Quang Ngai, you could hear the muffled explosions as people walked into the fields.

South of Quang Ngai was a fishing village called Son Tra, whose population had been moved *en masse* one night in 1966 after the Americans had declared their nearby paddies a free fire zone. This was another example of removing the water from the fish: the fish being the NLF. Few outsiders had been to Son Tra; I was taken there by Earl Martin, whose American Mennonites, like the American Quakers, were held in trust by people on all sides. Earl, a gaunt, bearded, measured man, was the antithesis of those of his countrymen who ran the war. He spoke not only Vietnamese but understood their indirect, oblique language, the nuances and mannerisms which are the seams of Vietnamese communication. He also knew, in relationships with people, 'when to go forward, when to wait and when to drop back'. There were a few Americans in Vietnam like Earl, who never carried a gun, and whom some Vietnamese will always remember with affection.

The people of Son Tra had been twice punished. The American-inspired strategy decreed that, having removed them, the people's new home be made more 'secure' by denuding it of all basic vegetation. This, the strategy declared, would 'deny cover to any infiltrating enemy elements'. So Son Tra was sprayed with defoliant herbicides as part of 'Operation Hades' which was later re-named 'Operation Blue Skies' and 'Operation Ranch Hand', as these labels were considered friendlier. The defoliants included Agent Orange which contained an impurity called dioxin, the cause of foetal death, miscarriage, chromosomal damage, congenital defects and cancer. In January 1970 the US government

banned the marketing of the herbicide 2,4,5-T, which contained Agent
Orange, following a campaign by small farmers in the United States who
claimed that the spray poisoned water and turned young trees to powder
as well as causing paralysis and blindness among their livestock and
impotence in themselves. The 1970 ban applied only to the United
States. The principal manufacturer, Dow Chemical, continued to make
the spray for the Pentagon.

By 1970 a pattern of deformities began to emerge in Vietnam: babies
were born without eyes, with deformed hearts and small brains and with
stumps instead of legs. In August 1970, in a report to the US Senate,
Senator Gaylord Nelson wrote that 'the US has dumped [on South
Vietnam] a quantity of toxic chemical amounting to six pounds per head
of population including women and children'.[24]

The impact on the environment was devastating. A mangrove forest
which had taken at least twenty years to rise, where people drew harvests
of birds, honey and wood for charcoal, had been destroyed. Decaying
plant matter had robbed the water of oxygen and reduced the catches of
fish and crabs by as much as 80 per cent. The land around had salinated
and was rock hard and good for nothing.

When we arrived at Son Tra many people were visibly distressed and
hungry. They explained to Earl that they had neither the money nor the
resources to buy expensive imported rice. When he asked if they could
fish in the bay, he was told, 'Yes, but at our peril.' Part of each
catch invariably contained chemical agents and caused frequent sickness
among the very young and old. They could not fish further out to sea
because they had no fuel; and their boats were mostly coracles suited
only to calm waters. In a district which once had been one of the richest
rice producers in South-East Asia, the staple in this village of former
rice farmers was the leaves of sweet potato plants. In 1974 South Vietnam
was the single largest beneficiary of American food aid in the world.
Large quantities of this food was sold on the open market for hard
currency and for arms and ammunition.[25]

17

The last day

Saigon: April 1975. At dawn I was awake, lying under my mattress on the floor tiles, peering at my bed propped against the french windows. The bed was meant to shield me from flying glass; but if the hotel was attacked with rockets, the bed would surely fall on me. Killed by a falling bed: that somehow made sense in this, the last act of the longest-running black farce. I had returned to Vietnam at the beginning of April with my right arm in a sling, the result of my efforts to fend off a rubbish truck in the London traffic; it seemed an appropriate 'war wound' to bear at the end.

Even now, past my vertical bed in the first light outside, one of the original cast performed. Flipper, the armless Vietnamese veteran and mascot of the Dreamland bar, sang his one refrain. A policeman, dozing in a hammock, waved a listless arm for Flipper to shut up; but the veteran was having none of it. Since Randy had closed the Dreamland and fled with his 'temporary wife', Flipper and flotsam like him had gravitated to the centre of Saigon, to Lam Som Square, Tu Do and Le Loi, to watch the last 'round-eyes' go, and to wait for the end.

The long-awaited drive by the legatees of Ho Chi Minh to reunify Vietnam had begun at last, more than twenty years since the 'temporary' division imposed at Geneva. On New Year's Day, 1975, the PAVN surrounded the provincial capital of Phuoc Binh, seventy-five miles from Saigon; one week later the town was theirs. Quang Tri, south of the Demilitarised Zone, and Phan Rang followed, then Bat Me Thout, Hue, Danang and Qui Nhon in quick succession and with little bloodshed. Danang, once the world's greatest military base, was taken by a dozen NLF cadres waving white handkerchiefs from the back of a truck. A United Press wirepicture of an American punching a South Vietnamese 'ally' squarely in the face as the Vietnamese tried to climb on board the last American flight from Nha Trang to Saigon held a certain symbolism. By mid-April, the end was in sight as the battle for Xuan Loc unfolded thirty miles to the north-west of Saigon, which itself was already encircled by as many as fifteen PAVN divisions armed with artillery and heat-seeking missiles. The PAVN was now probably the most experienced army in the world, and, together with sapper units of the depleted NLF, it seemed to be sitting, waiting for all the Randys to go.

Watching them go was like watching a closing pageant of the American war. During April more than 3,000 'non-essential' Americans and their dependents were evacuated every day from 'Dodge City', the code-name for MACV, the old American command cocoon at Tan Son Nhut airport. Saul, a former US Army major, left with twenty-two dependents: his wife, her parents, her grandparents, her sisters and brothers and three alleged creditors. 'I reckoned on taking six along', he said, 'and all these folks turned up. All I can say is everybody back home is in for a surprise: now that's for sure.' Some of these Americans had paid bribes of hundreds and thousands of dollars to get passports, exit permits and tax clearances for their dependents. Many need not have bothered. Since President Ford's order to get them out, they and their flocks had only to enter Dodge City in the morning to be 'processed' and flown away by nightfall. But this was slowing down now. Fighting between Saigon troops and NLF units had spread to within range of the airport and the waiting time for aircraft to complete their round trips to the Philippines and Okinawa became a day, then two days, then three; and those with cause to be worried were becoming alarmed.

'Now hear this please,' said the loudspeakers in the gymnasium and the bowling alley at Dodge City. 'Each American and each dependent is entitled to one can of Seven-Up or Sprite but only one unit per person, please!'

It seemed that anyone could go, as long as he, or more usually she, was 'sponsored' by an American. Familiar faces of whores from Tu Do Street appeared in the crush, affecting demure expressions and wearing Barbie-doll dresses.

'What's *her* status?' said the processor.

'She's my wife,' said a giant called Les who wore a peasant's conical hat on his head, cameras around his neck, a ceramic elephant under one arm, and 'Miss Nhu', a beautiful young woman of perhaps seventeen, under the other.

'Okay,' said the processor, 'read this and sign it.'

'I certify,' said Les, 'that I am legally free, without any encumbrance, to assume responsibility for . . . I'll put your name in here sweetheart . . . commensurate with the responsibility normally accorded a spouse. Spouse? What's a spouse? Sounds like a bird dog.'

There was a faster, almost VIP procedure for another category of 'high risk' passenger. President Ford had called these people 'endangered Vietnamese'; they were all murderers. American processing officials had been told not to talk about them, but one of them did. 'Bye, bye to the Phoenix special,' he said acidly as he watched them go, some of them still clutching their Seven-Up or Sprite issue. All of them had worked, at one time or another, for the CIA's Phoenix Programme: 'programme' being the euphemism for death squad. They and their predecessors had murdered as many as 50,000 district and village chiefs and others who had been considered less than totally loyal to the Saigon regime. Some of these evacuees were destined for Niceville, Florida.

What people in places like Niceville really wanted was babies. The demand in the United States and Europe for Vietnamese 'war orphans' was fostered by famous people paying large sums of money for 'their' orphans and by Christian organisations, which 'saved' and 'supplied' the children, and by the White House, which encouraged the notion that only the 'civilised' world could do something to rescue the mites of South Vietnam from the Red hordes and the revenge to be exacted on children fathered by the enemy. The point was that, far from taking 'revenge' on children of a former enemy, the Vietnamese had already integrated generations of half-French children. 'Operation Babylift' was to have the patronage of the President of the United States, who would personally greet the first 'orphan' to be 'rescued'.

Since early in March President Ford had been having difficulty persuading Congress to renew American aid to the collapsing regime in Saigon. Around the same time the deputy prime minister of South Vietnam, Dr Phan Quang Dan, wrote in a letter: 'The departure in large numbers of orphans will cause deep emotion in the world . . . favourable to South Vietnam. The United States Ambassador will assist me in making sure they leave in large numbers.'[26]

Frank Snepp, a CIA analyst who was stationed in the US embassy in Saigon at the time, was in no doubt about the purpose of Operation Babylift. In his book *Decent Interval* he described it as a 'conspiracy' designed to 'arouse sympathy for the South Vietnam cause around the world . . . Operation Babylift was a fraud from the start, for few of the children who were to benefit from it were refugees. Most of them, in fact, had been languishing for years in Saigon's orphanages . . .'[27]

In the last week of March, when Dr Phan Quang Dan wrote his letter, foreign aid workers in Saigon became concerned about some 4,000 children who had been evacuated to Saigon from the central highlands. Most of the children were not orphans at all and had been placed in the care of the Ministry of Social Welfare, which was the direct responsibility of Dr Phan Quang Dan. But when the first American airlift of 'orphans' was announced on April 2, these children 'simply disappeared', according to a British agency worker. Two days later the first aircraft of Operation Babylift, a Galaxy, took off from Saigon carrying 243 children. The huge plane had not cleared the runway when it crashed, killing 206 of the children and forty-four adults. Charred infants were fished from nearby paddies. A soldier holding up a dead child by one arm stood stiffly to attention as he was photographed; it was this one image which, for me, symbolised the tiers of suffering of the Vietnamese people.

Meanwhile, a British version of Operation Babylift was being organised in great haste by the London *Daily Mail*. The *Mail* announced 'Operation Mercylift' and chartered a Boeing 707 to 'rescue' 100 children. Reporters, doctors and nurses flew on the 707 to Saigon, including the editor of the *Mail*, David English, who was photographed at Saigon airport holding an 'orphan'. The subsequent rejoicing in the columns of his newspaper mentioned only some of the difficulties he and his team had encountered. The *Mail* had relied on a Christian evangelical charity, Project Vietnam Orphans, to find quickly and deliver the 100 children. But verifiable orphans, with legal clearance to leave the country of their birth, proved hard to find, and the *Mail's* rescue mission was on its way from London before enough children had been found to fill the 707.

One of the suppliers of children to the *Mail's* enterprise was Victor Srinivasin, who ran two homes in Saigon known as 'Hope One' and 'Hope Two'. I knew him and his homes well. Srinivasin's children were mostly those whose mothers had been forced into prostitution or other desperate means of supporting a fatherless family. Some of the children were simply being held 'in care' and were visited regularly by their mothers and relatives. Only a very few were genuine orphans who were considered truly alone in the world. The *Mail* claimed that all the 'orphans' it flew out of Vietnam were 'scheduled for adoption by the British organisations looking after them'.[28] Helen Jacobus, then a relief worker for the Ockenden Venture, the agency which helped to resettle the children in Britain, spent several years after the war trying to trace the children. Writing in the *New Statesman*,[29] she concluded that most of the children were not orphans at all, and most of them had not been 'scheduled' for adoption. She wrote:

> PVO [Project Vietnam Orphans] knew at the time that some of the children had living mothers. Roy Clarke, the man who now runs Christian Outreach, as PVO has become, says that he remembers 'quite a tearful scene' at the airport as a mother of one of the children waved goodbye.

On April 20, Xuan Loc was captured by the PAVN. Only Saigon was now left. Among the ribbons of refugees heading away from the fighting were embittered ARVN troops, whose president and commander-in-chief, General Thieu, had acknowledged their defeat by fleeing to Taiwan with a fortune in gold.

On April 27, General Duong Van ('Big') Minh was elected president by the National Assembly with instructions to find a way to peace. It was 'Big' Minh who in 1963 had helped to overthrow the dictator Ngo Dinh Diem and had sought, with his fellow officers, to negotiate a peace settlement with the NLF. When the Americans learned about this they bundled Minh out of office, and the war proceeded.

It was now eight o'clock and long spokes of sunlight spread from my hotel, the Caravelle, across Lam Som Square to the National Assembly, which the French had built as an opera house, to the beautiful Continental Palace Hotel and the most appropriately ugly statue on earth. The statue, in the centre of the square, was meant to depict two South Vietnamese soldiers advancing bravely into battle, but to jaundiced eyes it represented an American pushing his reluctant Vietnamese 'ally' into the fight. I watched it being built within the space of a few days by students, using 'Kwik-set cement' sprayed over a swaying iron frame, with green paint added to give it a weathered bronze effect. Alas, the effect was that of papier mâché. It was hollow, of course. Some terrible things happened beneath that monster: dissenters from General Thieu's wisdoms were beaten and shot; penniless and maimed veterans were clubbed from their wheelchairs as they demonstrated peacefully for a pension. The previous week a man had come to attention beneath it and slit his throat. 'His wife or the war,' said a policeman, scuffing dust into blood, 'one or the other, it got too much for him.'

I walked across the square to get some coffee. Flipper had gone; the policemen were out of their hammocks, stretching and lighting up; and the two loudspeakers in front of and behind the monster had begun their daily, mindless clamour. For a month now they had been playing martial music and telling people not to panic. Then the night before, shortly before midnight, they had opened up with three long whines from a siren; this, as if we did not know, was to tell us that Saigon was under rocket attack for the second night running. The rockets made a hissing sound, which was more frightening to me than the thud and shake of shells and bombs. The previous night's rockets, like the rockets the night before that, were launched by NLF units encamped less than a mile away on the other side of Saigon. They were meant to persuade Minh to hurry up in getting the last Americans out of his country and to surrender. Four rockets fell and caused havoc among the poorest of Saigon, killing many of them: how many it was impossible to tell in the ordinary chaos in which they were forced to live.

As I left the hotel to look for the damage I was greeted by 'the Interpreter'. This person was a moon-faced, voluble, leering man whom it was difficult to like, for when asked his name, he would say only, 'I am the Interpreter. Please come quickly.' He had said this on many other occasions, whether or not there was a need to 'come quickly'. He was a bit player in the black farce. As recently as three months before he had been a tourist guide leading bands of Westerners who came to Saigon to get the stamp in their passport and to take the 'all city tour' which included the zoo and the botanical gardens, the monstrous Kwik-set statue, the basilica, the public buildings and the covered market where their pockets were duly picked. The Interpreter said, 'Some American ladies very sad . . . they come to see what their son died for, and all they see are the girls in Tu Do and these poor crabs . . . ' He pointed to a legless soldier who had slithered out from a doorway to beg with his Coca-Cola can.

I asked the Interpreter to take me to where last night's rockets had fallen, and we packed into a small Renault taxi which was built in 1945, the year that the British marched into Saigon and re-armed the Japanese so that they could put down the Vietnamese nationalists. 'On your left', intoned the Interpreter, 'is the Saigon Town Hall, built at end of the nineteenth century and a fine example of . . . and on your right, the Presidential Palace, more recent, also fine modern architecture . . . over there, typical street food sellers, selling very good little fish . . . ' I asked him to stop, but he was possessed. 'This now Cholon . . . colourful Chinese part of Saigon; many Chinese, Chinese everywhere; Chinese all over streets.'

One rocket had fallen near here and the Interpreter stopped the taxi and pushed through the crowd along an apparently endless alleyway. The faces stared; a few smiled; during all the American years, few Americans had penetrated here. 'Over here typical Vietnamese home,' droned the Interpreter. 'Please watch the typical grandmother with children, and the Buddha on the wall.' Did this manic man, leading me to a scene of terrible destruction, actually imagine I was a tourist? His madness now seemed touching and he was no longer difficult to like. As his imaginary tour came to an end, he romped ahead, climbed on to a crumbled wall and, in a theatrical gesture, swept a hand in front of him and said, '*Monsieur, voici la guerre!*'

My preoccupation with the Interpreter's madness and my reluctance to view any more of this war's suffering had persuaded me that the rockets had hit an empty building or had landed on open land. But no. This one rocket had cut a swathe through half an acre of tiny, tightly packed houses, and the fire storm which followed had razed the lot.

There were people standing motionless, as if in a tableau, looking at

8 Betty and Kenneth Rucker, with the decorations awarded to their son Rick who was killed in Vietnam, Beallsville, Ohio, 1970 (*Photograph: Matt Herron*)

9 Robert Kennedy interviewed by John Pilger shortly before his assassination, California, 1968 (*Photograph: Curt Gunther*)

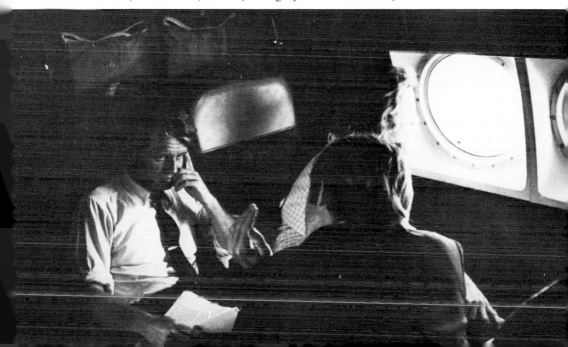

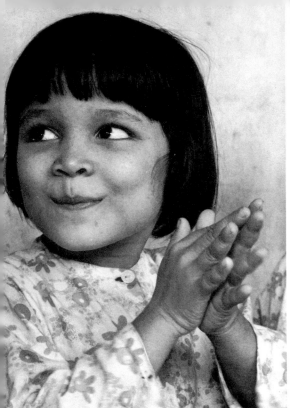

10 Daughter of an American GI, Saigon, 1978 (*Photograph: Eric Piper*)
11 Child burned by Napalm, Vietnam, 1966 (*Photograph: John Schneider*)

12 The bombed ruins of Hongai, Vietnam, 1975 (*Photograph: John Pilger*)

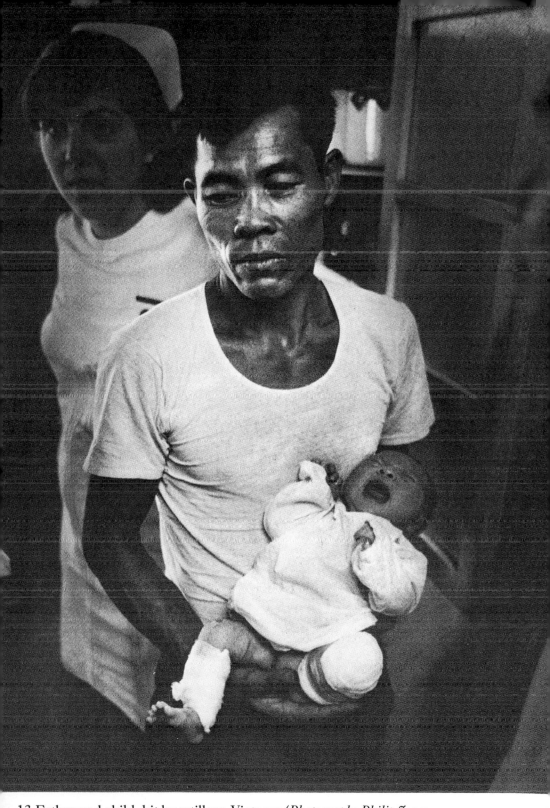

13 Father and child, hit by artillery, Vietnam (*Photograph: Philip Jones Griffiths*)

14 US Army, Vietnam (*Photograph: Philip Jones Griffiths*)

15 American soldier and 'suspected Vietcong', Vietnam (*Photograph: Philip Jones Griffiths*)

the corrugated iron which was all that remained of their homes. There were few reporters; yesterday's rockets were news, the first to fall on Saigon in a decade; today's rockets were not. A French photographer blundered across the smouldering iron, sobbing; he pulled at my arm and led me to a pyre that had been a kitchen. Beside it was a little girl, about five, who was still living. The skin on her chest was open like a page; her arms were gutted and her hands were petrified in front of her, one turned out, one turned in. Her face was still recognisable: she had plump cheeks and brown eyes, though her mouth was burnt and her lips had gone completely. A policeman was holding her mother away from her. A boy scout, with a Red Cross armband, clattered across the iron, gasped and covered his face. The French photographer and I knelt beside her and tried to lift her head, but her hair was stuck to the iron by mortar turned to wax by the heat. We waited half an hour, locked in this one dream, mesmerised by a little face, trying to give it water, until a stretcher arrived. The Interpreter had fled.

Following the rocket attacks the American Ambassador, Graham Martin, appeared on Saigon television and pledged that the United States would not leave Vietnam. He said, 'I, the American Ambassador, am not going to run away in the middle of the night. Any of you can come to my home and see for yourselves that I have not packed my bags . . . I give you my word.' America's last proconsul on the continent of Asia, he was a private, strong-willed and irascible man. He was also very sick; his skin was sunken and skeined grey from long months of pneumonia; his speech was ponderous and frequently blurred from the drugs he was taking. He chain-smoked, and conversations with him would be interrupted by extended bouts of coughing.

To describe Graham Martin as a hawk would be to attribute to that bird qualities of ferocity it does not have. For weeks he had told Washington that South Vietnam could survive with an 'iron ring' around Saigon supplied by B-52s flying in relays back. During a convalescence he told a friend in Washington that if Watergate hadn't happened, President Nixon would have bombed. Since then Martin had sifted the ashes of the American débâcle for anything he might use to persuade Congress to re-arm the Saigon forces. After the 'fall' of Danang he told a senator that the 'orphans issue' was important. But Martin could not ignore completely what he saw; he knew it was his job, and his job alone, to preside over the foreclosure on an empire which had once claimed two-thirds of Indo-China, for which the greatest army in the history of the world had fought, and his own son had died, nine years before.

A tree, one of many mighty tamarinds planted by the French a century before, dominated the lawns and garden outside the embassy's main foyer. The only other open space big enough for a helicopter to land had the swimming pool in the middle of it. The helipad on the embassy roof was designed only for the small Huey helicopters. If 'Option Four' (a helicopter evacuation) was called, only the marines' Chinook and Jolly Green Giant helicopters would be able to fly large numbers of people to the Seventh Fleet, thirty miles offshore, within the course of one day. The tree was Graham Martin's last stand. He had told his staff that once the tree fell America's prestige would fall with it, and he would have none of it.

Tom Polgar was the CIA station chief. Unlike many of his predecessors, he was extremely well informed and he despaired openly of the Ambassador's stubbornness. When Thieu locked himself in the bunker beneath the presidential palace for three and a half days, refusing to resign or even to take any phone calls, it was Polgar, together with the French Ambassador, Jean-Marie Merrillon, who finally persuaded Graham Martin that he should intervene. To Martin, the felling of Thieu became like the felling of the embassy tree: a matter of pride and 'face', for himself and for America. The United States government had solemnly committed itself to Thieu and the American taxpayer had given him billions of dollars. Moreover, his own son had died so that Thieu's South Vietnam could remain 'free'.

On April 19 Graham Martin received a note from the Provisional Revolutionary Government, the NLF's politicians, through the International Commission of Control and Supervision in Saigon. It said that now that Thieu had gone there could be a 'political solution': a hint that the PRG might agree to the setting up of a 'tripartite government of conciliation and concord' under the terms of the Paris agreement. Martin showed the note to Polgar, who argued that it was a smokescreen, that the PRG wanted an unconditional surrender and nothing less. Martin disagreed.

Saigon now seemed like a dream. At the Cercle Sportif tennis courts were fully booked, and there was consternation that the 'boys' on the rollers had dared to disappear. During the long Gallic lunch and rest period, the sun beat down on a city as outwardly languid as Graham Greene had found it in the early 1950s. Then suddenly, for no apparent reason, the traffic would build up and become frenzied; people would drive and ride aimlessly, three cars and a dozen Hondas abreast, blocking intersections. The Vietnamese, who are open about their sorrow, are subtle and oblique in their anger and bitterness; and Saigon's traffic, where the prizes of its non-productive consumer society were on display, seemed to be making one more frenetic dash down Le Loi and Tu Do before the end of 'all that'. But just as suddenly as it had erupted, the mood would subside and the city would return to its alternate state of resignation.

On April 28 there was reason for frenzy. The NLF had raised their flag on Newport bridge, three miles from the city centre. I waved down a vintage taxi and immediately recognised the driver; it was Tran, the same cackling face who used to drive me to the Reuter office and run a finger across his throat whenever we passed the presidential palace. He was a Buddhist, a supporter of 'Big' Minh, and he had loathed Thieu. But now he was subdued and nervous and kept glancing in his rear-view mirror, trying to build words and courage for a question he wanted to ask me.

'VC in Saigon now, right?' he said.

'Yes,' I replied, 'they're in Saigon.'

More nervous silence. 'So they take over soon, right?' he said.

'Yes.'

'Please tell me, what become of me, a Buddhist, a taxi man, always driving Americans . . . what happen to me; they hurt me, eh?'

The rear-view mirror showed a guttered, nicotine-stained face now suddenly soft and afraid. I held his bony old shoulder and said that which I could not guarantee: 'No one's going to hurt you. Don't be afraid.'

'Out, out!' Mortar shells were suddenly landing a few dozen feet away and in his fear Tran had put the Renault into a culvert. Crouched behind it, I was able to see clearly for the first time in years the bush hats and black pyjamas and bandoliers of ammunition of the National Liberation Front. There was less than a company of them, perhaps two platoons; they had set up mortars on the other side of the bridge, but it seemed they were here only to raise the flag. Twice they ran up the red and blue with gold star, and each time it was shot away by a determined nest of ARVN defenders. An ARVN soldier, overloaded with kit in the American style, charged past me and hurled two grenades at his black-pyjamaed brothers on the other side. Then he dropped on one knee, swung his M-16 rifle into position and was firing his first burst when he was blown away like human confetti. In old-fashioned wars, such an act would have been worthy of a medal to the order of a Victoria Cross, for he had gone to rescue a wounded comrade in the middle of the bridge. With politicians and generals and colonels now scuttling the country, this one soldier chose to die like that.

A television crew picked up Tran and me in their winged Pontiac, then reversed at speed to below the brow of the bridge, where we were stopped by the swell of people pouring across and under the bridge and along the riverbank. Some had come all the way from Xuan Loc, thirty miles away, and their suffering was like a plague; a baby dehydrated and silent in the arms of a father whose feet were bound in newspapers, and bloodied; a family of five on a Honda, which finally gave up, spreading children and burst bags of rice in the path of others who did not stop.

It was five o'clock. The monsoon had arrived early and Saigon now lay beneath leaden cloud; beyond the airport were long, arched bolts of lightning and the thunder came in small salvoes as President Minh prepared to address what was left of his 'republic'. He stood at the end of the great hall in the presidential palace, which was heavy with chandeliers and gold brocade, and he spoke haltingly, as if delivering a hopeless prayer. He talked of 'our soldiers fighting hard' and only, it seemed, as an after-thought did he call for a ceasefire and for negotiation. As he finished speaking a succession of thunderclaps drowned his last words; the war was ending with a fine sense of theatre.

I walked quickly along Tu Do as the lightning marched into the centre of the city. Half a dozen shops had closed since the day before, their owners having evacuated themselves to the bowling alley and gymnasium at Dodge City, where they paid handsomely for a place in the queue. The Indian tailor at No. 24 Tu Do, 'Austin's Fine Clothes', was morosely counting his dollars and cursing his radio for not picking up the BBC World Service news. It was an unusual show of emotion for him, for, like his cousins from Bombay, who were Saigon's tailors, hotel door-openers and black-market money dealers, he was the most pragmatic of men. I had known the tailor at Austin's for a long time, and our relationship had always been one of whispers and comic furtiveness, involving the handing over of one green note, which would be fingered, snapped, peered at and put up against the light, and the receiving of a carrier-bag filled with best-British Vietnamese piastres. (Britain's greatest export to South Vietnam was banknotes.)

'What's the rate today?' I asked.

'If this bloody radio will give me the news I will be able to tell you,' the tailor replied.

'I can tell you the news,' I said. 'Minh has asked for a ceasefire.'

'A ceasefire! My friend, you shouldn't have told me that; the rate has just gone down. Only 2,500 to the dollar.'

'But', I countered, 'the VC will never accept it, will they? They will attack Saigon, won't they?'

He listened with interest. 'Okay, for you the rate has just gone up by 300 piastres.'

Thunder now pulverised the city. The tailor continued to count his money; he had at least $5,000 in that drawer, today's and yesterday's takings, and his Indian passport protruded from his shirt pocket. 'Communists respect passports,' he said, patting his without knowing what they respected. He had once had a shop in an American air-base selling American comics, which he imported from a cousin living in Atlanta, Georgia, and he now worried if this would qualify him as a 'collaborator'.

He said Saigon would not fall for at least a month, which caused the Vietnamese assistant, whirring at his sewing machine behind the curtain, to laugh.

The thunder had a new sound, dry and metallic. It was not thunder; it was gunfire. The city seemed to be exploding with weapons of every kind: small arms, mortars, anti-aircraft batteries. 'I think we are being bombed,' said the tailor, who flinched from his counting only to turn up the volume on his radio, which was tuned to the Voice of America's 'Oldies and Goldies' hour. He instructed one of his Vietnamese staff to close the steel shutters, which they did, but only after gathering in their Hondas from the street, which was now sluiced with bullets.

'They'll be killed out there,' I said.

'Then they and their Hondas will die a glorious death together,' he replied, by way of a little joke.

For the next half-hour the shop itself seemed to be a target and I ensured that two walls stood between me and the street. The tailor, however, remained at his post and counted his dollars while the Voice of America played 'Cherry Pink and Apple Blossom White', which was barely audible above the gunfire. It is a profoundly witless song, but I sang along with the tailor, and I shall probably never forget the words. In a far corner, like a wounded bird, an old Vietnamese woman clawed at the wall, weeping and praying. A joss-stick and a box of matches lay on the floor in front of her; she could not strike the matches because her whole body was shaking with fear. After several attempts I was able to light it for her, only then realising the depth of my own fear.

The loud noises, including the thunder, stopped, and there was now only a crackle of small arms fire. The Voice of America had moved on to 'Bird Dog'. 'You are most fortunate,' said the tailor. 'Thanks to the gentlemen who have bombed us the rate has just risen a thousand piastres . . . but only 100 dollar bills, please.' He opened the steel shutters, looked out and said, 'Okay . . . run!'

It seemed that all of Saigon was running, in spasms of controlled, silent panic. My own legs were melting, but they went as they never had before, and were given new life by an eruption of shooting outside the Bo Da café. A military policeman, down on both knees, was raking the other side of the street, causing people to flatten or fall; nobody screamed. A bargirl from the Miramar Hotel, wearing platform shoes, collided with the gutter, badly skinning her legs and her cheek. She lay still, holding her purse over the back of her head. On the far corner, opposite the Caravelle Hotel and outside a gallery which specialised in instant, hideous girlie paintings, a policeman sprayed the sky with his M-16 rifle. There was a man lying next to him, with his bicycle buckled around him.

Saigon was now 'falling' before our eyes: the Saigon created and

fattened and fed intravenously by the United States, then declared a
terminal case; capital of the world's only consumer society that produced
nothing; headquarters of the world's fourth greatest army, the ARVN,
whose soldiers were now deserting at the rate of a thousand a day; and
centre of an empire which, unlike the previous empire of the French
who came to loot, expected nothing from its subjects, not rubber or rice
or treasure, only acceptance of its 'strategic interests' and gratitude for
its Asian manifestations: Coca-Cola and Napalm.

Having flattened the Indian door-opener with the urgency of my entry
into the Caravelle Hotel, I was accosted by a man with a walk-on part
in the farce now dissolving into tragedy. He introduced himself as the
representative of a church adoption agency in Texas and asked if I knew
where he could lay his hands on thirty children 'by tomorrow'. I asked
him if he was serious and he seemed hurt. 'I am on a humanitarian
assignment,' he said. I replied that there had been many humanitarians
looking for orphans lately. However, there was a place on Le Loi with
children who, as they say in the orphans business, were difficult to place.
The children were mostly black and had impediments, such as harelips
and crippled limbs, *and* they were half-American. He said he did not
think that was funny. And he was right.

That night I walked to the Miramar Hotel, waving to the teenage
militia boys who, with their old Armalite rifles, policed the eight o'clock
curfew. It was now half-past eight. For five dollars they would not shoot
you; in a city of bribes this one represented value for money. Inside the
Miramar, where five dollars would buy a woman, the air was stiff with
neurosis. The bargirls sat huddled at one end of the bar; only one was
going through her robot's routine of stroking the vast back of a customer.
A few had already gone and the others did not know what to do. They
clustered around Peter Hazelhurst, *The Times* man in Saigon who was
their friend and confessor. Peter, a very caring man, was often chided
for trying to 'save' the girls; it was he who listened to their fears for
hours on end and tried to reassure them that they would be all right if
only they would go home to their town or village or to a relative
somewhere.

Peter had at one time introduced me to Phuong, who had tried
unsuccessfully to cultivate a sour little smile. She was a kind of shop
steward to the girls, and she worried about what would happen to them,
although she probably worried more about her mother and sister finding
out that she was a whore, not a waitress as they believed. A few weeks
earlier Phuong had been beside herself with worry; her sister, a nurse,
had arrived in Saigon and wanted to stay with her. Phuong had feigned
illness, the sister went home slightly confused, but the crisis had passed.
Like all the girls, Phuong supported a large family with her earnings: in

her case eight. Her father had been killed a long time ago. He was an NLF soldier and this was her secret, which was common enough among families fending for themselves. She said he used to come back to see her, but was almost caught the last time, and she had not seen him for four years when she heard of his death. Sadly, she now worried what the NLF would do with her, 'just a hooker'.

Phuong was missing from the bar that night. 'She in monkey cage,' said one of the girls. 'She was very unhappy, very scared, like all of us.' The 'monkey cage' was an attic room next to the hotel laundry. It was about twenty feet square and it was where the girls stayed through the curfew if they had not gone to a client's room for the night. On a slow night, when most of them had to go back to the monkey cage after the bar closed at one o'clock, there was sleeping room for only a few; the others crouched in a corner, some of them still in their paint and doll's dresses.

I met Phuong on the stairs to the monkey cage. Her hair was pulled back with a rubber band and she wore no make-up. She said in a mock-tough voice, 'Not long go now, eh? Not long to VC coming, eh? I go tomorrow. Tonight, after bar, I cut hair and Luy Am . . . you know her: girl with frown . . . she and I leave Saigon. You know, I have black pyjamas up there in monkey cage right now. So goodbye to you.'

The restaurant at the top of the Caravelle was full, a picture of normality. As we ate, a window banged open and the curtains blew in; the waiters, normally the most serene of men, struggled to shut it against the wind. When several of us went to their assistance the *maître d'hôtel* screamed, 'Please, we must shut it! The planes . . . ' The window then closed of its own accord, the *maître* covered his eyes and said, 'I am sorry . . . please forgive me.'

Most of the staff at the Caravelle were Catholics who had come south after the Geneva conference. One of them kept a leaflet which the US Air Force had dropped in the spring of 1954. It read: 'BEWARE! THE VIRGIN MARY HAS FLED SOUTH. FOLLOW HER OR BE SLAUGHTERED BY THE BARBARIAN COMMUNISTS.'

There was no bloodbath, and the Catholic Church survives if not prospers in the North, among young and old, yet those of us staying at the Caravelle were asked constantly by waiters and receptionists, 'Will the VC harm us?' It was impossible to reassure them, for their fear had been fashioned for too long. The previous Sunday Catholic priests and Buddhist monks had gathered at the basilica, Saigon's cathedral, for the first joint service ever held in South Vietnam. Prayers were offered, in the words of one of the monks, 'to seek harmony and protect and help the Vietnamese people. It would be very good to help us sufferers'.

A French woman journalist entered the restaurant trailing two children. The eldest turned out to be a heroin addict who begged from us in the square; the other a flower girl, who sold us chains of jasmine. The first girl was Phan Thieu Kieu and I did not realise I had known her for years until Bruce Wilson, the correspondent of the Melbourne *Herald*, said, 'Don't you recognise her? No, you probably don't, because she looks pretty bad now.' She was in a terrible state. 'Oh, mister, oh, mister,' she convulsed at no one in particular. 'I kill, you kill, all die, all kill.' Kieu was seventeen and looked ten years older. In the fluorescent light of the restaurant, she appeared more damaged than I had imagined; I had seen her mostly in shadow, begging from a doorway. Now the sores and ulcers on her legs, caused by injecting herself with filthy and rusted needles, were on show. She was hushed and comforted by the Frenchwoman and sat at a table until a reporter, between courses of *pâté de foie gras* and *fruits de mer*, objected to her presence. She and the flower girl, who gripped the last unsold chain of jasmine as if it was life, were taken to a room where they spent the night.

At one o'clock in the morning Graham Martin called a meeting of his top embassy officials to announce that he had spoken to Henry Kissinger, who had told him that the Soviet Ambassador to Washington, Anatoly Dobrynin, had promised to pass his (Kissinger's) message to Hanoi requesting a negotiated settlement with President Minh's government. Martin said Kissinger was hopeful that the Russians could arrange this. He said he wanted the evacuation by fixed-wing aircraft to continue for as long as possible, perhaps for twenty-four hours.

Dodge City, the blockhouse at Tan Son Nhut, was surrounded by marines, most of them outside the twenty-foot wire fence which had been electrified in the 1960s. The marines were deployed in pairs; each carried an M-16 rifle, four grenades, a grenade launcher, a .45 revolver, a hunting knife and four canisters of Mace, a riot control gas which paralysed the muscles. They lay on their stomachs, with rifles balanced on their packs in front of them. There was some small arms fire a mile or two to the east and the occasional crackling sound of masonry falling in the Nissen-shaped aircraft shelters damaged during the bombing the night before. Inside, in the gymnasium, the bowling alley and the cinema, 3,000 Vietnamese and their American sponsors, who were due to catch their evacuation flights when the bombing began, sought to contain their fear with sleep, gentle talk, card games and trips to the Coke machine. A teenage boy played his tapes; the processor slept at his desk; a small boy urinated in the gutter of the bowling alley; a marine, in combat kit, stood by the door, sucking on a can. In the cinema, a poster advertising the last month's movie, read: 'THIS WILL KILL YOU . . . DON'T MISS THE DAY THE EARTH TURNED INTO A CEMETERY.'

Down a long featureless corridor, through a warren of offices and signs such as 'PRIVATE: HUMAN AFFAIRS OFFICE', was the operations room. The sign on this door said 'READINESS ROOM'. There was the long table, the swivel chairs, the flag and the wall-length charts from the days of hearts and minds. The difference was that the blue and pink and white bits on the charts had been replaced by thick black flight-paths in and out of Saigon: the escape routes.

It was shortly after four o'clock in the morning when scores of rockets fell on Tan Son Nhut airport, followed by a barrage of heavy artillery. The waiting was over; the battle for Saigon had begun. The sun rose as a ragged red backdrop to the tracer bullets. A helicopter gunship exploded and fell slowly, its lights still blinking. To the east, in the suburbs, there was mortar fire, which meant that the NLF were in Saigon itself, moving in roughly a straight line towards the embassy.

Graham Martin was awakened at his residence, three blocks from the embassy. He phoned General Smith, who could not be found; he phoned the embassy, where a marine officer told him that Saigon airport was under full attack. He dressed and phoned Jacobson, the counsellor, instructing him to get everybody together for a meeting in the embassy at six o'clock. As they talked, the Irish voice of Father Devlin from Yeu Do Street broke into the VHF frequency and asked if the evacuation was on. 'How do I get to the helipad?' he pleaded.

The 6 a.m. meeting between Martin and his top officials was a disaster. All of them, except Martin, agreed that they should start the evacuation immediately. Martin said no, he would not 'run away', and announced to their horror that he would drive to Tan Son Nhut to assess the situation for himself. There was no more than a suspicion among the embassy staff that the last proconsul of the empire might, just might, have plans to burn with Rome. When the meeting ended in confusion, Polgar ordered that the great tamarind tree be chopped down.

At 7.30 a.m. on April 29 Graham Martin left his residence for Tan Son Nhut in his bullet-proof Cadillac. The Cadillac had served the two previous Ambassadors and its age and slightly worn appearance had concerned Graham Martin for some time. He believed an American Ambassador should look like one, right down to the chrome on his limousine; he was a man much concerned with 'dignity', both of action and appearance. In 1974 he had sent one of his angrier messages to Washington about a new car, and was told that a brand-new, Secret Service-approved Cadillac was on the way. When the central highlands, Hue and Danang fell, he was told that his Cadillac had been diverted to Israel, where the 'security needs' of the American Ambassador, the proconsul for the Middle East, were more pressing. Graham Martin was sorely offended; to him, the cancellation of his car was yet another signal that Washington was preparing to scuttle Vietnam without consulting him. He sent several more messages demanding a replacement car, but they were all turned down. The Cadillac, like the great tamarind tree, had become to Graham Martin a symbol of his and America's credibility, which he called prestige.

He was alone in the back of the Cadillac, with his bodyguard and the Vietnamese driver in the front. The anxious voice of Jacobson, the counsellor, came on the open VHF network, to which most of the journalists in Saigon were listening: 'Tell the Ambassador to proceed with utmost caution. There's some incoming fire between the road and the DAO . . . a bus has been hit . . . '

The tree-cutters assembled, like Marlboro men run to fat. These were the men who would fell the great tamarind; a remarkable group of CIA officers, former Special Forces men (the Green Berets) and an assortment of former GIs supplied by two California-based companies to protect the embassy. They carried weapons which would delight the collector, including obsolete and adorned machine guns and pistols, and a variety of knives. However, they shared one characteristic; they walked with a swagger that was pure cowboy: legs slightly bowed, right hand hanging loose, fingers turned in and now and then patting the holster. They were issued with axes and a power saw, and secretaries from the embassy brought them beer and sandwiches. They were cutting down the Ambassador's tree.

At the same time, a fleet of cars and trucks pulled into the market outside the Botanical Gardens and Zoo, and quickly discharged their cargo: frozen steaks, pork chops, orange juice, great jars of pickles and maraschino cherries, cartons of canned butter beans and Chunkie peanut butter, Sara Lee cakes, Budweiser beer, Seven-Up, Wrigley's Chewing Gum, Have-A-Tampa plastic-tipped cigars and more, all of it looted from the Saigon commissary, which had been abandoned shortly after an NLF sapper unit strolled in Indian file past its rear doors. To the Saigonese, stealing from their mentors and patrons had become something of a cultural obligation, and there was a carnival air and much giggling as fast-melting T-bones were sold for a few cents. A pick-up truck discharged a dishwashing machine and a water cooler was quickly sold and driven away in a tri-shaw; the dishwasher was of the Blue Swan brand and on its box was the Blue Swan motto: 'Only the best is right for our customers'. The dishwasher was taken from its box and left on the road. Two hours later it was still there, unsold and stripped of vital parts, a forlorn monument to consumer enterprise in Vietnam.

Saigon was now under a twenty-four-hour curfew, but there were people in the streets, and some of them were soldiers from the 18th ARVN Division which had fought well at Xuan Loc, on Highway One. We had been expecting them and awaiting the first signs of their anger as they watched the Americans preparing to leave them to their fate. That morning, when they first appeared in the centre of the city, they merely eyed foreigners, or robbed them, or fired into the air to relieve their frustration.

At the Reuter office, a lone Vietnamese telex operator converted words into perforations on reams of tape: words, thousands of them, bound for the United States, Europe, Japan, Australia, South America, words which described his fate and speculated upon his future. I watched him. He did not look up. He seemed to be working so hard to transmit these words, and although I was thankful, I could not understand his dedication. How could I understand? During all the time I had sent my dispatches from here, I had not bothered to meet him.

I walked back to the Caravelle Hotel where I was to meet Sandy Gall of Independent Television News; Sandy and I were the 'evacuation wardens' for the 'TCN Press', which meant Third Country Nationals, which meant everyone who was not American or Vietnamese. For some days Sandy and I had concerned ourselves with the supremely eccentric task of trying to organise those representatives of the British, Canadian, Italian, German, Spanish, Argentinian, Brazilian, Dutch and Japanese Press who wanted to be evacuated. The American embassy had distributed a fifteen-page booklet called 'SAFE' – short for 'Standard Instruction and Advice to Civilians in an Emergency'. The booklet included a map of Saigon pinpointing 'assembly areas where a helicopter will pick you up' and it listed four colour-coded alerts: white, grey, yellow and red. When the red alert came it was everybody to the assembly points: 'You should bring along two changes of clothing, a raincoat, a sewing kit, an umbrella, a can opener, insect repellent, your marriage certificate, a power of attorney and your will . . . but unfortunately you must leave your furniture and your automobile behind.' There was an insert page which read:

> Note evacuational signal. Do not disclose to other personnel. When the evacuation is ordered, the code will be read out on American Forces Radio. The code is:
>
> THE TEMPERATURE IN SAIGON IS 112 DEGREES AND RISING. THIS WILL BE FOLLOWED BY THE PLAYING OF 'I'M DREAMING OF A WHITE CHRISTMAS'.

The Japanese journalists were concerned that they would not recognise the tune and wondered if somebody could sing it to them. Philip Jacobson, the correspondent of the London *Sunday Times*, obliged, rendering his Bing Crosby to the incredulity of both his oriental and occidental audience.

At the Caravelle Sandy Gall and I had nominated floor wardens who, at the first hint of yuletide snow in Saigon, were to ensure that reporters who were infirm, deaf, asleep, confined to a lavatory or to a liaison, would not be left behind. There was more than a modicum of self-interest in this arrangement; I had, and have, an affliction which has delivered me late for virtually every serious event in my life.

The door was open to the room next to mine. It was as my friend Michel Laurent had left it five days earlier. He had driven to Bien Hoa, where there was fighting, and no one had heard from him. There was a report that his car had been hit by a rocket and that he had been seen lying nearby, wounded. I had known Michel in many places and I admired him. He was a photographer for the Gamma agency in Paris who had produced some of the finest pictures of the war: not of battles but of the agony of civilians. He had come back to Vietnam reluctantly; he was Gamma's only man with a valid visa in his passport. He was a thin, freckled man who seldom wore combat kit, but took more risks than most of us. Over dinner the night before he left he had said, 'I take pictures of wars for the simple reason that I want people never to forget how horrible they are.' I learned later that Michel had been killed.

Two C-130 Hercules aircraft from Clark Air Force Base in the Philippines were over Tan Son Nhut. They were ordered not to land. Scouts sent to the perimeter of the airport reported that two platoons of PAVN infantry had reinforced the sappers in the cemetery a mile away; a South Vietnamese pilot had landed his F-5 fighter on the runway and abandoned it with its engine running; and a jeep-load of ARVN were now ramming one of their own C-130s as it tried to take off. 'There are some three thousand panicking civilians on the runway,' said General Homer Smith on the VHF. 'The situation appears to be out of control.'

Graham Martin, alone in his office, watched the tree fall and heard his CIA Station Chief cry, 'Timberrrr!' When Kissinger phoned shortly afterwards, in compliance with President Ford's wish that the American Ambassador should take the final decision on the evacuation, he listened patiently to an exhausted and ailing Graham Martin. At 10.43 a.m. the order was given to 'go with Option Four' [the other options had involved evacuation by sea and by air]. But Martin remained steadfast in the belief that there was 'still time' to negotiate an 'honourable settlement'.

At 1.20 that afternoon an unfamiliar voice came over the scrambled circuit at the National Military Command Center in Washington, ordering the helicopters not to land at Tan Son Nhut at the scheduled time of two o'clock, but one hour later. In the confusion only the lead helicopter carrying Marine Brigadier General Richard Curry received the correction, while the thirty-five other helicopters went into a holding pattern over the sea, losing valuable daylight time. The identity of the voice which gave the order was never confirmed.

The Caravelle emptied without the knowledge of the Unofficial Joint TCN Warden. Nobody told me. Bing Crosby did not croon on my radio. When I emerged, the rooms looked like the *Marie Celeste*, with clothes, papers, toothbrushes left. In the foyer the French housekeeper was shouting, 'Everyone has gone. It is the end of the war, good God. My cashier – this man over here – he says he want to shoot himself. Thank goodness he has no gun. Please, should I laugh or cry?'

It was a question I was about to ask myself. I ran to my room, gathered my typewriter, radio and notes and jammed them into one small bag; the rest I left. Where had I hidden my money? In the bathroom, on top of the cistern, of course. Two room attendants arrived and viewed my frantic packing, bemused and slightly in awe. One asked, 'Are you checking out, sir?' I said that I was, in a manner of speaking. 'But your laundry won't be back till this evening, sir.' I tried not to look at him. 'Please . . . you keep it . . . and anything else you see.' I pushed a bundle of piastres into their hands, knowing that I was buying their deference in the face of my graceless exit. After nine years, what a way to leave. But that I wanted to leave was beyond question; I had had my fill of the war.

The French housekeeper had her face in her hands as I blundered past her. I owed for two nights but if, as she said, the cashier wanted to shoot himself, he would be in no mood to receive my money. Outside, Lam Son Square was empty, except for a few ARVN soldiers slouched in doorways and in the gutter. One of them walked briskly up Tu Do, shouting at me; he was drunk. He unholstered his revolver, rested it on an unsteady arm, took aim and fired. The bullet went over my head as I ran.

'Hey, where the bloody hell is everybody?' The antipodean voice belonged to my old friend George James, with whom I had worked my apprenticeship in journalism some seventeen years earlier on the Sydney *Daily Telegraph*. George was now a television director with the Canadian Broadcasting Corporation and he and his crew had just returned from filming at Tan Son Nhut, and now wished, like me, to leave. They had a jeep, whose driver was heaving with fear.

'Number 35 Gia Long Street,' we told the driver.

'What is that, please?' he said.

'We hope it's a building with a helicopter on the roof.'

'I see . . . okay, I take you if you take me with you.'

The jeep went in a wide circle and we quickly realised that if 35 Gia Long existed, it would be deserted by now. We told him to take us to the American embassy.

There was a crowd pressing at the gate of the embassy; some were merely the curious who had come to watch the Americans' aerial Dunkirk, but there were many who gripped the bars and pleaded with the marine guard to let them in and waved wax-sealed documents and letters from American officials. An old man had a letter from a sergeant who a long time ago had run the bar at the Air Force officers' club in Pleiku. The old man used to wash dishes there, and his note from the sergeant, dated June 5, 1967, read, 'Mr Nha, the bearer of this letter, faithfully served the cause of freedom in the Republic of Vietnam.' Mr Nha also produced a toy Texas ranger's star which one of the pilots at Pleiku had given to him. He waved the letter and the toy Texas ranger's star at the marine guard who was shouting at the crowd, 'Now please don't panic . . . please!' For as long as they could remember, these people, who worked for the Americans, had been told to fear the communists; now they were being told, with the communists in their backyards, that they should not panic.

The old man attempted to slide through the opening in the gate and was pushed to the ground by the marine who was telling them not to panic. He got up, tried again and was tackled by a second marine who propelled him outside with the butt of his rifle and hurled the Texas ranger's badge over the heads of the crowd. As I struggled through the crowd, pushing and using my strength in order to get my free ride away from the war, I felt only shame.

Inside the embassy compound the marines and the cowboys were standing around the stump of the great tamarind tree. 'Okay, you tell me what we're gonna do about this immovable bastard?' said one of the cowboys into his walkie-talkie. 'Take it easy, Jed,' came an audible reply, 'just you and the boys level it down by at least another foot, so there's plenty of room for the rotors. And Jed, get all those shavings swept up, or sure as hell they're gonna be sucked into the engines.' So the marines and the cowboys went on swinging their axes at the stump, but with such mounting frustration and incompetence that their chopping became an entertainment for those both inside and outside the gate, and for the grinning French guards on the high wall of the French embassy next door.

'Now I want to make this very clear to you,' said Lieutenant-Colonel Harry Summers through a loud-hailer, with his words translated into Vietnamese by an American missionary, Tom Stebbins. 'Every one of you folks is going to get out of here. Let me repeat that. All you people here with us today are going to be flown to safety and freedom. Not one of you will be left behind. I will go only after the last one of you has left. And the United States Ambassador has assured me he will leave right at the end, after you and me. On that we give you our solemn word.'

Colonel Summers was one of three officers who had been negotiating with Hanoi on prisoners-of-war and Americans missing in action; when events overtook them he was ordered to oversee the evacuation from the embassy. He got down from the soft drink stall, where he had addressed the people crowded on the lawn around the swimming-pool, and walked among them, saying, 'Now don't you worry' . . . 'Sure you'll get a job in the States', as though he had taken it upon himself to sweep up some of the dust of America's honour in Vietnam. He was, it was plain to see, a man of honour and compassion, which were qualities unknown to many of those to whom he had just given his word.

There is in the Vietnamese language, which is given much to poetry and irony, a saying that 'only when the house burns, do you see the faces of the rats'. Receiving Colonel Summers's reassurances was Dr Phan Quang Dan, former deputy prime minister and minister responsible for social welfare and refugee resettlement, who had tried his best to exploit the 'orphans issue', a man seen by Washington and by Ambassador Martin as the embodiment of the true nationalist spirit of South Vietnam. An obsessive anti-communist who was constantly making speeches exhorting his countrymen to stand and fight, Dr Phan Quang Dan was accompanied by his plump wife sweltering under a fur coat and by a platoon of bagmen whose bags never left their grip.

The 'beautiful people' of Saigon were also there, including those young men of military age whose wealthy parents had paid large bribes to keep them out of the Army. Although they were listed as soldiers on some unit's roster, they never reported for duty and their commanding officers more than likely pocketed their wages. They were called 'ghost soldiers' and they continued to lead the good life in Saigon: in the cafés, on their Hondas, beside the pool at the Cercle Sportif, while the sons of the poor fought and died at Quang Tri, An Loc, Xuan Loc and all the other places.

'Look, it is me . . . let me in, please . . . thank you very much . . . hello, it is me!' The shrill voice at the back of the crowd outside the gate belonged to Lieutenant-General Dang Van Quang, regarded by his countrymen and by many Americans as one of the biggest and richest profiteers in South Vietnam. The marine guard had a list of people he could let in, and General Quang was on it. With great care, the guard helped General Quang, who was very fat, over the fifteen-foot bars and then retrieved his three Samsonite bags. The General was so relieved to be inside that he walked away, leaving his twenty-year-old son to struggle hopelessly in the crowd. There were two packets of dollars sagging from the General's jacket breast pocket. When they were pointed out to him, he stuffed them back in, and laughed. To the Americans, General Quang was known as 'Giggles' and 'General Fats'. When Thieu

dismissed him as commander of ARVN troops in the Mekong Delta it
was a blow to Mrs Quang, who had her own extensive business interests
in the Delta.

Among the Americans in the embassy compound there was a festive
spirit. They squatted on the lawn around the swimming-pool with
champagne in ice buckets looted from the embassy restaurant, and they
whooped it up; one man in a western hat sprayed bubbly on another and
there was joyous singing by two aircraft mechanics, Frank and Elmer.
Over and over they sang, to the tune of 'The Camp Town Races':

> We're goin' home in freedom birds,
> Doo dah, doo dah;
> We ain't goin' home in plastic bags,
> Oh doo dah day.

'This is where I've come after ten years,' said Warren Parker almost in
tears. 'See that man over there? He's a National Police official . . .
nothing better than a torturer.' Warren Parker had been, until that
morning, United States Consul in My Tho, in the Delta, where I had
met him a week earlier. He was a quiet, almost bashful man who had
spent ten years in Vietnam trying to 'advise' the Vietnamese and puzzling
why so many of them did not seem to want his advice. He and I pushed
our way into the restaurant beside the swimming-pool, past a man saying,
'No Veetnamese in here, no Veetnamese', where we looted a chilled
bottle of Taylor New York wine, pink and sweet. The glasses had already
gone, so we drank from the bottle. 'I'll tell you something,' he said in
his soft Georgia accent, 'if there ever was a moment of truth for me it's
today. All these years I've been down there, doing a job of work for my
country and for this country, and today all I can see is that we've
succeeded in separating all the good people from the scum . . . and we
got the scum.'

The first evacuation helicopter had reached Tan Son Nhut and there
was pandemonium among the people waiting in the bowling alley and
the gymnasium. They had swarmed on to the runway when the two
C-130s had attempted to land and their panic had put an end to any
hope of an orderly evacuation by conventional aircraft. Many would not
get out, because there were not enough seats, and their American
'sponsors' knew it. So big men slipped away from their 'fiancées' and
their families, swiftly and unceremoniously, even from women with
whom they had lived for years, some even from wives and children. Now
it was every 'round eye' for himself.

At 3.15 p.m. Graham Martin strode out of the embassy lift, through
the foyer and into the compound. The big helicopters, the Jolly Green

Giants, had yet to arrive and the stump of the tamarind was not noticeably shorter, in spite of the marines' and cowboys' furious chopping and sawing. Martin's Cadillac was waiting for him and, with embassy staff looking on in shock, the Cadillac drove towards the gate, which was now under siege. The marine at the gate could not believe his eyes. The Cadillac stopped, the marine threw his arms into the air and the Cadillac reversed. The Ambassador got out and stormed past the stump and the cowboys. 'I am going to walk once more to my residence,' he exclaimed. 'I shall walk freely in this city. I shall leave Vietnam when the President tells me to leave.' He left the embassy by a side entrance, forced his own way through the crowd and walked the four blocks to his house. An hour and a half later he returned with his poodle, Nitnoy, and his Vietnamese manservant.

People were now beginning to come over the wall. The marines, who had orders not to use their guns, had been up all night and were doped with 'speed' – methedrine – which provides a 'high' for twenty-four hours before the body craves sleep. But methedrine also whittles the nerve ends, and some of the young marines were beginning to show the effects. As the first Chinook helicopter made its precarious landing, its rotors slashed into a tree, and the snapping branches sounded like gunfire. '*Down! Down!*' screamed a corporal to the line of people crouched against the wall, waiting their turn to be evacuated, until an officer came and calmed him.

The helicopter's capacity was fifty, but it lifted off with seventy. The pilot's skill was breathtaking as he climbed vertically to two hundred feet, with bullets pinging against the rotors and shredded embassy documents playing in the downdraft. However, not all the embassy's documents were shredded and some were left in the compound in open plastic bags. One of these I have. It is dated May 25, 1969 and reads, 'Top Secret . . . memo from John Paul Vann, counter insurgency':

> . . . 900 houses in Chau Doc province were destroyed by American air strikes without evidence of a single enemy being killed . . . the destruction of this hamlet by friendly American firepower is an event that will always be remembered and never forgiven by the surviving population . . .

From the billowing incinerator on the embassy roof rained twenty, fifty and one hundred dollar bills. Most were charred; some were not. The Vietnamese waiting around the pool could not believe their eyes; former ministers and generals and torturers scrambled for their bonus from the sky or sent their children to retrieve the notes. An embassy official said that more than five million dollars were being burned. 'Every safe in the embassy has been emptied and locked again,' said the official, 'so as to fool the gooks when we've gone.'

The swishing of rotors now drowned the sounds of the dusk: the crump of artillery, the cries of women attempting to push young children over the wall. Two marines watched a teenage girl struggle through the barbed wire. At first they did nothing, then as her hands clawed the last few inches one of them brought his rifle butt down on one hand, while the other brought his boot down on the other. The girl fell, crying, back into the mob. Somehow, most of one family had managed to get over the wall: a man, his wife, and her father. Their sons and his grandmother were next, but the barrel of an M-16 spun them back to the other side. The wife pleaded with a marine to let the rest of her family over, but he did not hear her.

At least a thousand people were still inside the embassy, waiting to be evacuated, although most of the celebrities, like 'Giggles' Quang, had seen themselves on to the first helicopters; the rest waited passively, as if stunned. Inside the embassy itself there was champagne foaming on to polished desks, as several of the embassy staff tried systematically to wreck their own offices: smashing water coolers, pouring bottles of Scotch into the carpets, sweeping pictures from the wall. In a third-floor office a picture of the late President Johnson was delivered into a wastepaper basket, while a framed quotation from Lawrence of Arabia was left on the wall. The quotation read:

Better to let them do it imperfectly, than to do it perfectly yourself, for it is their country, their war, and your time is short.

From the third floor I could see the British embassy across the road. It was being quietly ransacked now. The Union Jack, which had been spread across the main entrance, perhaps to ward off evil spirits, had been torn away and looters were at work with little interference from the police. I derived some small satisfaction from the sight of this. It was there, a few days earlier, that the British Ambassador, a spiffy chap called John Bushell, had shredded his own papers and mounted his own little evacuation without taking with him a dozen very frightened British passport holders. Before he drove away, Mr Bushell gave an impromptu press conference.

'We are pulling out for reasons of safety,' he said. 'Our main responsibility is the safety of the British community in Saigon.'

I asked him about people who were waving their British passports outside the gates of the British embassy. Why were they not even allowed into the compound?

'Look here,' he replied, 'we gave ample warning. We put advertisements in the local papers. The trouble with these people, as I understand it, was that they didn't have tax clearance, which takes ten days, as well as exit visas from the Vietnamese government.'

Exit visas? Tax clearances? But wasn't this an emergency evacuation for reasons, as he had just said, of protecting life?

'Well, yes,' he replied, 'but we really can't break the rules laid down by government, can we?'

But surely this government had ceased to exist and there might be anarchy and a great deal of danger, which was why he was getting out?

'That may be true,' said the Ambassador, 'but we gave these people a reasonable time to get the paperwork done, and you really can't expect us to help them at such short notice . . . look here, the Americans surely will pick up any stray palefaces.'

But 'these people' were Indians and Chinese. The Ambassador looked confused.

'Oh, you mean Hong Kongers,' he said. 'They should have heeded our warnings . . . they'll have just to work hard at it, won't they?' At this, he turned to another British official and said, 'How many coolies . . . Vietnamese . . . are we leaving, do you know?'

The official replied, 'Coolies? Oh, about thirty-six in all.'

At 6.15 p.m. it was my turn for the Jolly Green Giant as it descended through the dark into the compound. The loadmaster stopped counting at sixty; people were in each other's arms. The helicopter tilted, rose, dropped sharply, then climbed as if laden with rocks; off to the starboard there were shots. We flew low over the centre of the city, over the presidential palace where 'Big' Minh awaited his fate, and the Caravelle Hotel, where I owed for two days, then out along the Saigon River, over the Rung Sat, the 'swamp of death' which lay between the city and the sea. The two gunners scanned the ground, as they always used to, looking for 'Charlie'. Some of us had on our minds the heat-seeking missile which had brought a helicopter down as we watched in the early hours. There was small arms fire around us, but they were letting us go; and when the South China Sea lay beneath us, the pilot, who was red-eyed with fatigue and so young he had acne, lit up a cigarette and handed the packet around. In the back of the helicopter there was a reminder of what we had left: a woman, who had left her daughter on the other side of the wall, cried softly.

It was approaching midnight in Saigon. The embassy compound was lit by the headlights of embassy cars, and the Jolly Green Giants were now taking up to ninety people each. Martin Garrett, the head of security, gathered all the remaining Americans together. The waiting Vietnamese sensed what was happening and Colonel Summers appeared once again to reassure them. Outside the wall a grenade exploded in the crowd and a marine reported on his walkie-talkie, 'Many wounded here.'

It was 2.30 a.m. on April 30 when Kissinger phoned Martin and told him to end the evacuation at 3.45 a.m. After half an hour he emerged with an attaché case, a suit bag and the Stars and Stripes folded in a carrier bag. He met Tom Polgar, George Jacobson and Conrad LaGueux at the lift and they went in silence to the sixth floor where a helicopter was waiting.

'Lady Ace 09 is in the air with Code Two.' 'Code Two' was the code for an American Ambassador. The clipped announcement over the tied circuit meant that the American invasion of Indo-China had ended. As his helicopter banked over Highway One, the Ambassador could see the headlights of trucks of the People's Army of Vietnam, waiting.

At 5.20 a.m. Martin Garrett ordered all those supervising the evacuation to assemble inside the embassy building. Colonel Summers reminded him that there were more than 500 'endangered' Vietnamese still waiting to be evacuated. Garrett replied that the pilots had been flying for fourteen hours and the President had said that the evacuation must end. He said to tell the marines to wait at least an hour, then to walk slowly, casually, back to the embassy reception hall and then to lock the door to the stairwell behind them. This they did, and at that moment people streamed over the wall and past the stump of the great tamarind tree and the embassy cars with their engines running and their headlights on, marking a landing zone of no further use.

The last marines reached the roof and fired tear-gas canisters into the stairwell. They could hear the smashing of glass and desperate attempts to break open the empty safes. The marines were exhausted and beginning to panic; the last helicopter had yet to arrive and it was well past dawn. They fired Mace, the gas which disables muscles, into the stairwell. Colonel Summers could see people still waiting in a long orderly queue, still believing that their turn for evacuation would come, because he had told them again and again that he would not leave without them. Even men of the Saigon fire brigade, who had worked for twelve hours to protect the helicopters, were still at their posts; he had given the same undertaking to them. But now he was going without them, having learned only by accident that the Ambassador had left three and a half hours earlier. 'I will be the last man to leave this embassy,' Graham Martin had told him in his office. 'You have my solemn word on that.' When he landed on the USS *Okinawa* in the South China Sea, Colonel Summers was, he told me later, 'so ashamed that I could cry . . . but I was too damned mad to cry and too tired to yell.'

Three hours later, as the sun beat down on an expectant city, tanks flying NLF colours entered the centre of Saigon. Their jubilant crews showed no menace, nor did they fire a single shot. One of them jumped down, spread a map on his tank and asked amazed bystanders, 'Please direct us to the presidential palace. We don't know Saigon, we haven't been here for some time.' The tanks clattered into Lam Son Square, along Tu Do, up past the cathedral and smashed through the ornate gates of the presidential palace where 'Big' Minh and his cabinet were waiting to surrender. In the streets outside, boots and uniforms lay in neat piles where ARVN soldiers had stepped out of them and merged with the crowds. There was no 'bloodbath'. The war was over.

Two days later, May Day 1975, my last glimpse of Vietnam was from the deck of the aircraft carrier *Blue Ridge*, command ship of the US Seventh Fleet. It was the kind of tropical dusk of which matinée travelogues used to be made. Sailors, marines and pilots lounged; reporters moped, like homeward-bound conventioneers; Nitnoy, the poodle belonging to Ambassador Martin, took its evening walk among the F-5 fighters and the Jolly Green Giants, accompanied by the Ambassador's manservant, who hovered with a plastic trowel; Tom Polgar, the last CIA station chief in Saigon, who had struggled on board with an illicit cache of whisky, stared Buddha-like at the horizon. Helicopters which had cost the American taxpayers at least half a million dollars each were thrown unceremoniously overboard like rejected fish. Officers of the South Vietnamese Air Force had made their escape in them. There was nothing mechanically wrong with them. They were, like South Vietnam itself, simply redundant.

For some this was not a time of brooding. Round and round the deck jogged a platoon of playful marines, spurting at each exhortation from their sergeant for 'a big dirty dozen, you guys!' A rock band prepared for the evening's celebrations, while jolly chefs hoisted slabs of steak on to mobile barbeques and sailors arrived with crates of Coke and Diet Cola, but no booze: American naval ships are 'dry' and this fact was bemoaned over the public address system by the admiral himself, a jovial, obese man who looked and spoke like Andy Devine, the late Hollywood actor. Said the admiral, 'Well folks, that just about wraps up Vietnam. So let's all have a party and get outta here, so we can mosey on back to Subic Bay and get ourselves a *genuine* Budweiser beer!'

The admiral's voice, the joggers' heavings, the rock band's discord and the clatter of feast preparations all but drowned a persistent knocking at our stern, as if somebody was trying to bring us all to order.

'Damned if it ain't *them*!' said a marine major, peering over the side. 'Damned if it ain't the gooks.'

As many as fifty Vietnamese huddled below us in a listing, rusted landing craft; they were mostly the families of ARVN soldiers and about a third were children. During all of that day, in the still heat, an old man had swung a boathook laced up with pots and pans against the carrier's side, while another attempted to heave a length of rope up on to the deck; it barely reached the railing.

As the first steaks were devoured and the rock band struck up, the *Blue Ridge* shuddered and moved forward, leaving the faces in the rusted craft still pleading to be taken on board. A box of Diet Cola was thrown down to them, but it missed and sank. They had been given, we were assured, five days' supply of fresh water and a map. That their wretched craft was already sinking and the people would go nowhere, except down, was acknowledged; but still we steamed away. In one last, disconsolate gesture, which is embedded in my memory, a woman stood up and held out her baby as if to say, 'At least take him!' then she slipped, and they both fell into the sea.

We reported that small finale, but it was published in only a few papers. By the time we reached the Philippines and telex machines and got ourselves a genuine Budweiser beer, Vietnam was indeed 'just about wrapped up'. The world's first media war had run out of ratings. And this generally happened when only 'the gooks' were involved.

18

The price

Hanoi: May 1975. Two weeks after the American evacuation of Saigon I flew to Moscow to catch a flight to Hanoi. In the departure lounge at Moscow there were three Vietnamese, two men and a woman, wrapped like mummies against the cold. They were being seen off by a wedge of Soviet officialdom, and the unease and false conviviality between the two groups was self-evident. There was something all too familiar about this scene. Peel away the scarves, the greatcoats and fur hats, and the Russians could have been Americans. Even the carousing of the big Russians who boarded the flight and proceeded to drink their way through the night and dawn to Pakistan and Indo-China was reminiscent of Americans flying to Saigon and wishing they were anywhere but there.

I had waited six years for this: years of letters of application, of tea parties at embassies, of paralysing courtesies and interminable appeals to my patience: years of reporting the war from the other side of the seventeenth parallel, where the black farce had played to packed houses. In Ho Chi Minh's Vietnam it played to outsiders who said they were keepers or friends of the faith and to mavericks like Wilfred Burchett and James Cameron. Ho and his peers had decided long ago to endure a bombardment greater than that suffered by Germany, Britain and France combined without the rest of the world watching. They had journalists working at the war, but these were not reporters as the term is understood in the West. For all their talent at myth and legend-making, such as the cultivation of Ho's beatific 'Uncle Ho' image, the Vietnamese of the Red River were as Confucian as they were communist, secretive and purist. They left much of the telling of their story to others; even today the case they wish to make to the world is invariably better than their propaganda. There is an interesting comparison with the British use of propaganda during wartime. In 1940 and 1941 the Ministry of

Information dispatched to the United States dramatic film of the Royal Air Force fighting the Battle of Britain. The propaganda message was clear: here was the British people 'standing alone': David versus Goliath. By contrast, remarkable film of the American blitz on Hanoi during Christmas 1972, which Vietnamese cameramen shot by the light of burning buildings and showed the flaming torches of B-52s being brought down, was seldom shown outside Hanoi and never, to my knowledge, in the West. When I enquired why, I was told that it was 'not for theatres, but for history'.

Beside the runway at Hanoi airport the words 'Dai Thang' were emblazoned on a hoarding raised on the rim of a bomb crater so large it had been improved with steps. *Dai Thang* means 'Great Victory'; and 'Welcome to the Great Victory' was a greeting which had entered the official language on April 30, 1975, although it was already losing popularity as the realities of the war's aftermath chastened the memory of that heady day when the people of Hanoi gathered in the streets following the brief announcement that their thirty-year war was finally over. There were few other signs that they were the nominal victors in a struggle against two imperial powers. On the contrary, arriving in the North was like stumbling upon the appendage to some great and unrecorded disaster. For all the media saturation of the war in the South only half the war and half the story were reported; I, for one, had not imagined what had happened here.

I found much of North Vietnam a moonscape from which visible signs of life – houses, factories, schools, hospitals, pagodas, churches – had been obliterated. In some forests there were no longer birds and animals. There were truck drivers who would not respond to the hooting of a horn because they were deaf from the incessant sound of bombs; the Vice-Minister of Health told me that 30,000 children in Hanoi and Haiphong had suffered permanent deafness during the bombing at Christmas 1972.

And yet there was also something intangible which impressed itself upon all of us who saw the North in the immediate post-war days. It was the truth that people here have prevailed not as Oriental Prussians under the spell of an ideology, but as a peasant people who developed their ingenuity and patience to the extreme human limits and were united in their sense of community and history. Above all, it was this extraordinary presence of history – or national myth, call it what you will – during which they had repelled and absorbed invaders from the North, East and West, that had dominated every move they made; and that remains true today.

One of the most poignant stories I was told came from a Frenchman who was in Hanoi during the 1972 bombing. 'I took shelter in the

museum,' he said, 'and there, working by candlelight with the B-52s overhead, were young men and women earnestly trying to copy as many bronzes and sculptures as they could. They told me, "Even if the originals are destroyed, something will remain and our roots will be protected."'
In Hanoi zoo, the wreckage of one of the twenty-three B-52s shot down during Christmas 1972 was kept in a cage under a conventional zoological sign showing a map of the United States and the words 'Great Ferocious Beast'. Children peering through the bars at it chorused 'Beefeetytoo!' and made a mock growling noise. Nothing, certainly not the power of irony, was wasted here.

And yet all this seemed unreal because Hanoi was no more than a small, monkish place of controlled poverty. There were no beggars, no limbless soldiers coming at you, no child prostitutes, no back-street orphanages, as in Saigon; but if you threw away the stick of your ice lolly it was likely that a hovering person would retrieve it and wash it and press it into some other service: that was how they survived.

Thirty years of war had exterminated private cars and taxis. This was a city silent with the bicycle, the most venerable of which is mounted in a corner of a museum; on it 300 kilos of supplies were pushed distances of up to 500 miles at Dien Bien Phu where the French were finally driven from Indo-China. A bicycle repair shop is to Hanoi what a pub is to London. It is where people stop, talk, squat, mull. And the people live in streets laid out as if in the Middle Ages, on a craft basis; there are streets of workers in ivory, brass and leather, streets of tinsmiths and streets of coffin-makers. These streets, not the spacious, French-built centre, were the B-52s' main target and 'carpets' of bombs were laid down them with sustained accuracy.

One evening I walked along Kham Thiem Street where at ten minutes past ten on the night of December 26, 1972, a bomb had struck every third house; and every day since an old nicotine-stained figure had kept a vigil at one of these gaps. His name was Hoang Van Dung and he alone survived where 283 died in a crushed block of flats. 'We were mostly the old, women and children. There was no time to reach the shelters,' he said. Then he asked, 'Are you Russian? German?' I said I wondered what he would say if I said I was American. At this, the small crowd that had followed me pressed forward to hear his reply. 'If you are an American,' he said, 'I shall ask you to inform your presidents that before they bomb us again, they should remember that a reed has two choices: it must bend or grow stronger. Some of us died, but we did not bend. And one other thing. Your presidents should not forget about the singing. All through the night we sang. All the children and me with my terrible old voice. Singing, you see, is louder than bombs.' And without so much as a signal the crowd began to sing, and two five-year-olds stamped in a circle like toy soldiers, and the old man shook my hand with both of his and others did the same.

In Hongai, a provincial capital 140 miles from Hanoi on the Gulf of Tonkin, Dr Luu Van Hoat estimated that 10 per cent of the town's children were deaf. 'The planes used to come from ships at seven o'clock in the morning and bomb us until late at night,' he said. 'It was as if a great drum was being beaten in our heads.'

We were standing on the veranda of the hospital overlooking Hongai, which is a coal-mining and fishing town on the shores of beautiful Ha Long Bay. For three days in June 1972, American fighter-bombers flew fifty-two sorties against Hongai, round the clock. This is believed to be something of a record. Dr Philip Harvey, of St Stephen's Hospital in London, who had travelled with me to Hongai, was one of the few foreigners who witnessed what happened. He belonged to a British organisation, Medical Aid for Vietnam, which had provided a lifeline of drugs and medical equipment to Hanoi during the war when almost all Western humanitarian aid went to the South. The efforts of Medical Aid's secretary, Dr Joan McMichael, led to the establishment of a British-funded hospital at Ky Anh, near the old division of North and South Vietnam. To the Vietnamese, Joan McMichael, who has just turned eighty, is rightly a heroine.

'Many people, including myself, were evacuated to the caves,' Dr Harvey said, 'but the pilots seemed to want to pulverise the ruins. They were using a new type of pellet bomb, the size of a grapefruit which exploded into millions of fragments.'

At the school in Hongai, which was flattened, I found a letter pinned to a classroom wall. It was written by a young girl called Nguyen Thi An. 'The children wrote many letters to themselves in those days,' said a teacher.

My name is Nguyen Thi An. I am fifteen years old. This letter comes to you from Hongai, where I was born at the foot of the Bai Tho mountain and in the murmur of the sea-waves lapping against the shore. I had just done the seventh form in the Cao Thang school. It was a sunny, glorious day and my mother had just told me to lay the table. My father had come from his work. The next thing I heard the air raid siren and I hurried to the shelter nearby. I could hear the engines of the planes and then the explosions. When the siren went again I came out. My mother and father were lying there, my brother, Nguyen Si Quan, and my sister, Nguyen Thi Binh, were covered in blood. My sister had pieces of metal in her and so did her doll. She kept shouting, 'Where is mother and father? Where's my doll?' My street, Ha Long Street, has fallen down now. The houses have no roofs; the school and the Pioneers' Club are destroyed. This is the end of my letter.

The street where the Nguyen family lived was hit by pellet bombs which sprayed darts. The darts entered Thi An's sister, Binh, and continued to move around in her body for several days, causing internal injuries from which she eventually died an agonising death. The darts were of a type of plastic difficult to detect under X-ray. They were first tested on Hongai.

The bombing of Hongai was one of the heaviest and most concentrated that has ever happened. There was almost nothing about it in the world's Press at the time; and when the North Vietnamese released their account of the bombing, it was heavy with jargon and was largely dismissed as propaganda. When I visited Hongai, two and a half years later, much of the town still lay in its debris, a Pompeii of war. Two schools, a kindergarten, a nursery, a clinic and a market were rubble. A block of miners' flats were pocked with cannon blast; the Corinthian columns of the miners' club sagged like broken matchsticks and the rest was a pile. St Mary's Catholic Church, in the saddle of a hill, was an altar and a steeple and no more. It had taken a direct hit; none of the other churches stood at all. In the alleyways, many of them still dammed with brick and masonry, there were the inevitable banners, sodden in the monsoon drizzle. One of them proclaimed, 'The human being is evergreen'. These were words I was to see and hear again and again. Another banner, its red and gold running in the rain, announced that the people of Hongai had won a great victory over the USA and that nations all over the world would draw lessons from it, so that such a terrible war would never happen again. The moss-overgrown ruins of this impoverished backwater, and of all the other backwaters we knew nothing about, made gentle mockery of that.

Such places existed along Route One, going south, which was known as the 'Street of No Joy' by the American pilots who blitzed it and by those who depended on its convoys. There were no surface-to-air missiles here, just militia of local people who would put up a curtain of small arms fire as the F-105s and the Phantoms came in at 200 feet; and when the planes had gone, small groups of mostly women and children would swim the pontoons into place to allow the trucks through, then dismantle them before dawn and hide them in the paddies. Many villages established their own museum of US Air Force scrap: a pilot's helmet, a boot, a Batman comic. On the hillside at Dong Loc, which was bombed back to the Stone Age and beyond, leaving craters which merged into a swamp, were the graves of the entire anti-aircraft militia, all young women . . . Vo Thi Than, aged twenty-two, Duong Thi Tan, aged nineteen. Dong Loc and a place called Ham Long ought to be as famous as Dresden, because they were bombed more than Dresden: every week, sometimes every day, on and off for four years, from five in the morning till two in the afternoon.

During this onslaught, life proceeded in astonishing ways. What now look like archaeological digs were underground hospitals: wards, operating theatres, baby delivery rooms. Every village in North Vietnam had its own crêche, and as the planes swept in from the sea the infants were lowered on a cord and pulley device four at a time in a padded basket, into deep shelters just below their cribs; and in every classroom, beside every desk, was a trap door so that within seconds a class of fifty children could disappear. In this way, casualties outside the towns were kept low. It is the tradition in Asia that the youngest look after the water buffaloes, and because draft animals are life to people here they became a popular 'sundowner' target for the American pilots. Today, in the corners of the paddies there are many gravestones of their small keepers.

In Vinh, a mining town, the layer upon layer of bombing penetrated underground so that not even the foundations of buildings remained. Vinh is surrounded by hills and evoked for me the haunting photograph of Hiroshima taken on the first anniversary of the atomic bombing. In 1975 people were living under straw; and through the streets of straw rumbled a seemingly endless convoy, coming up from the south, bringing home young soldiers who cheered as we passed them, their legs dangling through the sideboards of the trucks, their transistor radios and Marlboro cigarettes newly acquired in the thieves' markets of Saigon and Danang.

Three years later, in May 1978, I travelled again down Route One and heard no mention of the 'great victory'. Floods, two disastrous crop failures and the enforced union of the two alien economies of North and South had thrown food distribution into disarray. The people of Vinh, still living under straw, were now rationed to just six pounds of rice each per month and were on the edge of famine. On the day I returned to Vinh a military convoy drove through the streets. But this time the soldiers in the trucks were not cheerful faces homeward bound, but troops going to the border with Cambodia, to another war.

I had not been back to the South since the American evacuation. The old South Vietnam began at Quang Tri on the seventeenth parallel, where the hills, once crowned with American 'firebases', looked like miniature extinct volcanoes. As with so many places in the South I had known during the war, the realisation that I had been here before was slow in coming. There was nothing to indicate that this was the 'Demilitarised Zone' and that for five years thousands of US marines had occupied and died in these hills. Now there was not a single grave, not a helmet or a boot, as if what had happened had never happened.

The graves begin a few miles beyond these hills. Not American graves; there are none in Vietnam. Not even graves with human remains. At the end of the war, the Hanoi leadership gave priority to a cosmetic operation which may have been unique in its intent and scope. Throughout South Vietnam there are now hundreds of military cemeteries which did not exist in 1975. These cemeteries are phoney. They were prefabricated in the North and transported to battlefields on which the People's Army of Vietnam had fought and lost many men. Each new headstone had the name of the soldier purported to be resting beneath it; but he was not. The PAVN was meticulous about gathering up its dead, and had units trained for the job, so that the Bo Dai ('Soldiers of Liberation') could be buried with honours in the North. The cemeteries in the South are symbols both of grief and defiance. One of them was raised on a bulldozed American base, whose garbage of spent tyres, shell casings, a Coke machine, a volleyball net, were swept into one neat tip.

At Hue, the old imperial capital for which the PAVN and the Americans mauled each other and the civilian population for thirty-six days and nights during the Tet offensive in 1968, my guide refused to walk with me through the citadel. He said he would cross the moat but not enter the garden. He was a tolerant, melancholic man called Do Tuan That. As a lieutenant in the PAVN he had fought here and clearly regarded his survival as a miracle; he was terribly scarred and embedded with shrapnel. It was not difficult to understand his reluctance. The citadel was left as though a swarm of virulent locusts had descended upon it and savaged every tree; even the ancient walls appear to have been 'eaten'. One landscaped terrace, where the first line of PAVN troops were dug in, has resisted all attempts to replant it, and is now considered to be poisoned for the foreseeable future.

I had a room in a hotel directly opposite the citadel, across the Perfume River, built in 1962 for the first American advisers to the regime of Ngo Dinh Diem. The long padded bar was now frequented by a few cadres but mostly by Russians, East Germans and Cubans who, with unwitting irony, used the same vocabulary of derision to describe their hosts as the Americans had used before them. One Russian technocrat I met even looked like his American predecessors: crew cut, tailored safari suit, patent shoes, fine Samsonite attaché case. He did not use the word 'gooks', but his sentiments were clear.

'These people', he said, '*infuriate* me; they are lazy, dirty, incompetent, ungrateful and they will not listen when you tell them how to manage themselves. And the controls! They have people spying on us everywhere, telling us how to do this, do that. I despair of them. Look at my position;

I am here to help them, but they are full of suspicion; they restrict my movements. I am fed up with them . . . aaah!' A Cuban seated beside him approved of this diatribe. 'They're impossible,' he said, 'they won't be told anything.' All this was most interesting, because it suggested that the basic lesson of Vietnam's long struggle was still to be learned by her allies, as it was learned painfully by her adversaries: that the Vietnamese passion for independence, coupled with a fear of subjugation by war or by aid with strings, transcended 'fraternalism'.

A dozen miles west of Danang, where the US marines had stormed ashore Hollywood-style in 1965 and where a pen of dislocated humanity fled from 'free fire zones', I brushed against raw bitterness. In a paddy beside the road defeated soldiers heaved and ploughed through the mud. Most were of 'the generation of America', as a Vietnamese friend used to say. They were battle wise, street wise, helicopter wise and Coca-Cola wise, but nothing in their lives had prepared them for the type of toil which, to many of their fathers, had been life itself. Three years earlier they had been members of the Army of the Republic of Vietnam, the ARVN, which the Americans had created and built into the fourth largest military force in the world. For most of the war the ARVN was scorned as incompetent and corrupt, even craven. The soldiers were, of course, the same Vietnamese as those in black pyjamas, whom the Americans came to regard as anything but incompetent and craven. The American brass would say that their allies in the ARVN 'lacked motivation', without digesting the implications of that truth. And when the Americans withdrew their land army in 1973 they invented 'Vietnamisation', which meant that they could continue to run the war without shedding more of their own blood; the despised ARVN would shed it for them. Rumbling about in their armoured personnel carriers, often ill-trained and led by senior officers with Mafia-style business enterprises on the side, the ARVN soldiers were sitting ducks. In the last year of the war, in their vast cemetery on the road between Saigon and Bien Hoa, burials were timed at one every fifteen minutes.

Now here in this paddy field were the survivors, deserted by those in whose cause they had been pressed to fight and labouring without joy or much hope in a 'New Economic Zone'. These zones had a dual purpose; they were to produce food and to 're-educate' former soldiers and servants of the Saigon regime, hucksters and others left by the tide. When I looked at the faces in the paddy all but one of them turned away. This man glanced to see if the guard was looking, then he rammed a finger in the air and mouthed, 'Fuck you!' and 'You number ten!'

Only when I drove away did I realise where I was. Nearby was the village of Tuylon where, more than a decade before, I had camped with Sergeant Melvin Murrell's WHAM unit and watched awed peasant farmers receive packets of Uncle Ben's Miracle Processed Rice, comics, party balloons and 5,000 toothbrushes in return for 'protection'. WHAM stood for Winning Hearts and Minds, or re-education by other means. Both were versions of the same game.

It was difficult to find out who had been sent to the countryside to be 're-educated' and when they would be released. One young woman I met in Saigon told me that her father, an Army surgeon, had been taken away a few days after the capture of Saigon and the family still had no news of him; their repeated requests for confirmation that he was alive had gone unanswered. However, her brother-in-law, an architect, had returned after two years of re-education, leaner but otherwise well, and was allowed to resume his profession. She said he had played the re-education game skilfully by not complaining and by fabricating 'confessions' of past political allegiances, and after a while the family was permitted to write a letter to him every two months. They were given a number and a postcode and in their letters they always included effusive words of praise for Uncle Ho's wisdoms; they hoped this would speed his release. On his return he described a rigorous ten-hour day clearing land near the border with Cambodia. The food was frugal: a mush of rice and animal fodder; and he slept in barracks he had helped to build. There was little brutality, he said, but suicides among the oldest were not uncommon, and there was much suffering from untreated dysentery and malaria.

The rationale behind the zones was not only political and punitive. The food situation was critical; the beginnings of famine I had seen in Vinh, in the North, presented a danger for much of the country. Moreover, Vietnam's area of cultivation is today about the same as it was some 4,000 years ago; but the population has leapt to 50 million, to which a million and a half mouths are added every year. During the war years North Vietnam subsisted like a Trappist practising self-denial, while South Vietnam, the former 'rice bowl', sustained an exodus to the cities and was fed intravenously by the Americans. Before 1975 South Vietnam had been the biggest single recipient of American food aid in the world. That changed on April 30, 1975, when the US Trading with the Enemy Act was made to cover all of Vietnam, former enemy and ally alike. There was now nothing coming from outside to compensate for food production lost during the war. Those without access to the land or the black market became desperate. Bankrupt small businessmen became 'volunteers' for the New Economic Zones. They had no choice but to plead poverty to the authorities who then directed them to the convoys of trucks leaving for the countryside before sunrise every morning. Many of these desperate people became 'boat people'.

In the South people talked obsessively about food, or the lack of it. I was told about one neighbourhood 're-education' session in Saigon where there were muffled complaints about the new bureaucracy's poor record of distribution. 'You should not complain,' said a humourless cadre, 'it's better than before when the Americans ate the flesh of your babies!' An old woman leapt to her feet and shouted, 'Rubbish! We all know the Americans only eat out of cans!' The audience burst into laughter and cheering. Re-educating millions of like-minded heretics will not be easy.

In Saigon, I attended an 'evening of revolutionary culture' in the former National Assembly. The tableaux of song and dance had the repetitive theme of liberation fighters entering the city to an ecstatic welcome by the populace, which of course did not happen. During the intermission a young man hovering close to me whispered, 'Do you like our revolutionary theatre?' 'Yes,' I responded, dutifully. 'Well, mister,' he said, 'I'm glad you do because these actors are the only Vietcong you're going to see.'

Whenever I put the question, 'What has happened to the National Liberation Front [the Vietcong]?' the response was 'They are in positions of responsibility' or, less obliquely, 'A great many of them died in the liberation struggle.' It was impossible to know how many of the former southern revolutionaries were in control in the South, but their decimation was certain. According to one estimate,[30] the party membership in Saigon had been reduced to 400 by the end of the war, compared with 3,000 in 1954 when the city had half its present population. The Americans' 'Phoenix Programme', which saw to the murder of thousands of NLF cadres, had succeeded. If there are northerners now running the South, the years of American assault on those southerners who had defended their homeland had helped to put them there.

A former NLF cadre took me to a place I had heard many rumours about during the war, including one that it did not exist: the NLF's 'central staging point' at Cu Chi, fifty miles from Saigon. This was the junction of a network of tunnels, 200 miles of them, through which whole regiments slid like snakes during daytime, emerging at night to resupply and ambush. The Americans were never able to find or destroy the main tunnels, and 'Operation Hades' was conceived in the 1960s to root out the subterranean enemy. Tracts of forest were defoliated and crops were poisoned by the wholesale spraying of Agent Orange. When I first came to Vietnam in 1966 I flew over Cu Chi and was told that the leaves on the trees would grow again in eighteen months. Four years later I flew over the same area; most of the trees, the pines, birch, hawthorn and hickory, stood like grey needles, twisted and broken and held aloft by choking vines. By that year, 1970, an estimated quarter of South Vietnam's forest had died as a result of 'defoliation'. The US

Army's Handbook for South Vietnam attributed the 'degradation' of earth which had been sprayed three times over to 'the combination of iron oxides [in the spray], plus the effect of rain and sun results in the soil setting like cement'.

When I arrived at Cu Chi a bizarre and touching scene presented itself. Within sight of a bomb, a wrecked American tank, a shallow grave and a crippled child drawing water with a Napalm canister, a lunch table was being laid. The tablecloth was white linen, silver cutlery was wrapped in pink napkins, beer stood in ice buckets and cold towels were dispensed by a waiter who saw off the flies and mosquitoes. A nugget of a man with two red stars on his collar greeted me. 'My name is Minh Number Four,' he said.

Minh Number Four – that was his military codename – had the eyes and ways of a hypogeal creature recently released into the light. This was not surprising for he and his men had lived and fought in darkness for a decade. Crouching in a narrow shaft Minh said, 'During the daylight the Americans would be directly above. We could smell their shaving perfume. To shoot them we often had to trip them up first, to get the right aim. We killed them one by one. They should not have dismissed us as children. They took too many risks because they thought we were stupid and inferior. That was a shame for them.'

The tunnels are today inhabited by insect mutants, created by the constant spraying of herbicides. The mutants cling like tiny primeval bats to walls of rock-hard earth, while outside the same lifeless earth extends without greenery or topsoil to a shimmering horizon broken only by silhouetted figures bent over their ploughs. This was where the forest I had flown over twelve years earlier had stood. In the villages nearby there are children with spina bifida and cleft palates and the rate of miscarriages is said to be higher than average: none of which is surprising in an area saturated in Agent Orange. When General William Westmoreland, the American commander in Vietnam, wrote in his book of 'some of the most imaginative and successful expedients and innovations to cope with the unusual nature of the enemy and the war that any military force has ever brought to bear',[31] he was referring to the use of Agent Orange.

I returned to Saigon to find the city like an old whore with a hangover. The greatest consumer society in the world producing nothing still wore its steel skin and flaking mascara and tight white pants, preserved for the liberating Army, though at much reduced rates and for a limited season. At the Caravelle Hotel the Catholic waiters who had worried about a communist bloodbath were the same men doing the same work for less pay. The hotel cashier, who had threatened to kill himself as the Americans left, was still the cashier. 'You did not shoot yourself?' I said.

'No,' he replied, 'I got drunk instead.' 'How is life now?' I asked. He waggled his hand from side to side. 'Not enough money, not enough food, and I sold my watch. But, we live . . . '

The CIA's Saigon headquarters had been converted to a Disneyland of carnage. Every devilish thing that was dropped on the Vietnamese was here including a sort of miniature neutron bomb which sucked the oxygen from the air, killing people and leaving buildings intact. There was a weed developed by American scientists to prevent normal vege-tation from growing. There was a CIA relief map of Saigon's brothels, which lit up. There was a reconstruction of the 'tiger cages' of Con Son Island and a beautiful, crippled young woman called Tao, who told me that cold water was thrown into her cage during winter and quick-lime in summer. 'When I heard the war was over', she said, 'you can't imagine . . . my mind flies!'

When Tran Van Tuyen heard the war was over, did his mind fly too? He was chairman of the National Assembly and one of the most tenacious democrats I ever met. A radical lawyer of the 'Third Force',[32] he championed Thieu's political prisoners until he too was imprisoned in the tiger cages and tortured, which included being buried to his neck in sewage. I was told that when the war ended he was classified as 'obstinate' and was dispatched to some miserable place for 're-education'. I have no confirmation of this; but I have heard nothing of him since.

If such Stalinist barbarity is one of Vietnam's many sides today, the fate of her children is surely another. Wherever I went in Vietnam after the war, I found abundant evidence that children orphaned or handicapped were being well cared for by the state, and with a sensitivity which covered the small nation left behind by the former enemy. Many of these 'Amerasian' children have been told that their fathers were foreign soldiers who had to go home; there seems to have been no mention of war crimes or 'imperialist aggressors'; they have even been taught some 'American culture', and Donald Duck shares the wall above their beds with Uncle Ho. And if their mother can be found and she has an address in America, the children are encouraged to write to their fathers. Today, those who are completely on their own and whose fathers want to care for them are allowed to leave the country, accompanied to America by a group of former GIs devoted to establishing a rapport with their former enemy and who themselves represent the best of their country. There are delays and misunderstandings, but the good faith is there. This does not in any way qualify as a happy ending, but it demonstrates the possibilities.

At the Young Flower orphanage in Saigon I asked the name of a black curly-headed jumping ball with big Chicago eyes. 'My name is Tran,' he said. 'I am nine.' I asked him, 'What are the words of the song you have just sung?' He looked gravely at the floor, as children do, and his words left the interpreter shaking her head. She repeated slowly, 'The war is gone . . . planes come no more . . . do not weep for those just born . . . the human being is evergreen.'

19

The boat people

Kelantan, Malaysia: July 1979. I missed the 'shooing operation', as the Malaysian authorities called it, but saw the little boat's outsized and ragged sail on the horizon and the silhouettes of many heads beneath it. The 'shooing' had occurred before dawn when the tourists were asleep and were observing the nocturnal habits of turtles or were still at the Happy Times disco, whose barrage would have covered any cries from the beach. Fortunately, a Malaysian Army officer assured me, there weren't any cries. 'The illegal immigrants generally go quietly,' he said, 'and really it's only the children who muck up a bit when it's time. Shooing these people is very different from shooting them, you know, and we are definitely not shooting them.'

The Malaysians had refined their deceit. The soldiers would at first pretend to be friendly as they fitted everybody in, laying the wispy old people and the children and mothers with infants on the breast like human carpet over the hull, the way slave ships were loaded. The officers would calm the refugees by assuring them they were merely being towed to 'another safe haven', from which their passage to America could be arranged. Only when the towlines were abandoned and the people faced the open sea did they know they had been tricked.

That evening I sat on my hotel balcony and watched a storm rise with high winds from the west. The boat which had been 'shooed' twelve hours earlier was a converted trawler. It was overloaded, listing and in the hands of amateurs. It would not have lasted.

Perhaps as many as a quarter of the 'boat people' who fled Vietnam after the war ended in 1975 drowned at sea or were murdered by pirates. Every country in the region prepared an excuse for rejecting them; Malaysia was not a signatory to the United Nations Convention on Refugees and insisted that its brutal policy broke no law. Thailand did nothing seriously to discourage the rapacity of its pirate fishermen whose treatment of the boat people seemed at times unbelievable. In Singapore prime minister Lee Kuan Yew said, 'If you don't have calluses on your heart you will bleed to death.'[33] In Hong Kong and Taiwan Chinese fat cats, both regular and communist, made fortunes by supplying unseaworthy craft. In Vietnam, *apparatchiks*, usually at the level of neighbourhood committees, extracted their share in gold and bribes. In Washington, London and elsewhere righteous and punitive voices preferred to ignore their own complicity in the circumstances which had produced this latest surge of refugees from Indo-China. That much of the suffering could have been avoided was barely a footnote to the last 'big story' of the war.

I was in Vietnam in the spring of 1978 when the first exodus of boat people began. The years immediately after the war had been harsh. In the South the American life support machine had been switched off. In the North rations had fallen to below the wartime level. Two crops had failed in 1976 and 1977, and by January 1978 the ricelands in the 'Parrot's Beak' area of southern Vietnam were under constant attack by the Chinese-supported regime of Pol Pot in Cambodia.

The government in Hanoi had been wholly unprepared for its 'great victory' in 1975. The speed of the Thieu regime's disintegration surprised even old eagles like the defence minister, General Vo Nguyen Giap, and the commander in charge of the final campaign, General Van Tien Dung. The leadership had reckoned on two to three more years of attrition before forming a peacetime administration and preparing officials to run it. Many of the most skilled people had been killed; in the South the NLF was bloodied and destitute of experience. It seemed predetermined that the government's first post-war economic measures would fail. On March 23, 1978, 'bourgeois trade' was nationalised and a disaster ensued.

The most seriously affected were the Chinese population in the South, known as the 'Cholon Chinese' of Saigon, who had presided over the mosaic of corruption that had been the South Vietnamese economy. The richest of them had left with their gold before the final collapse of Thieu, but the rest continued to control the Mekong rice trade for almost three years, regardless of the complexion of the new regime.

This was also a time of rapid deterioration in the relations between China and Vietnam. Their previous fraternalism had concealed Vietnam's objection to being part of China's geopolitical 'back yard'; a Chinese 'Eastern Europe'. Vietnam, standing astride the land bridge to South-East Asia, was the barrier between China and its 'sphere of influence'. From April 1975 to December 1978 Cambodia was well within the Chinese sphere, with some 10,000 Chinese advising on Pol

Pot's increasingly frequent attacks against Vietnam's southern border. In the North, Chinese troops and armour had moved into position in the mountain passes overlooking the road to Hanoi. Following the March 23 announcement ending 'entrepreneurial' – in effect Chinese – control of the rice markets, the Peking government accused Hanoi of racial discrimination against its 'nationals' in the South, while drawing its own racial distinction by insisting that the Chinese of Vietnam were not Vietnamese at all but 'people of the motherland'. Broadcasts from China exhorted the Cholon Chinese to flee, which they did; and as they panicked the Vietnamese authorities confiscated their property and gold as the price for permission to reach the open sea. It was a squalid episode in which natural justice and international law were set aside. Many of the Chinese were ordinary workers who had no accumulated wealth, and they and their families found themselves packed in the least seaworthy boats. At the same time the Hanoi government, unavailingly, gave Peking an opportunity to mount an orderly evacuation of its 'nationals'; but this was ignored.

John McAuliff, whose American Friends Service Committee has had long and honourable experience in Vietnam, has pointed out that 'had the United States been prepared to negotiate a mass orderly departure between the end of the war in 1975 and 1978 immense suffering and loss of life could have been avoided.'[34] It was during this period that Hanoi had on numerous occasions proposed to Washington that 10,000 refugees a month could be flown out in an 'airbridge' similar to that which operated beween Havana and Miami during the 1960s allowing 700,000 people to leave Cuba without loss of life. The Vietnamese request was ignored. Moreover, it was one of numerous attempts by Vietnam at reconciliation with the United States, none of which succeeded. This is an extraordinary chapter in recent Indo-Chinese history and one which is little known because, until the first wave of boat people appeared, the Western media had abandoned Vietnam as surely as the last helicopter had abandoned those waiting in the embassy below.

As soon as the war was over the Hanoi leadership began to extricate Vietnam from the embrace of the Soviet Union and to look to the West. They rejected both the Soviet view that ASEAN (the Association of South East Asian Nations) was an 'imperialist creation' and Moscow's offer of a 'treaty of collective security'. Much to the Soviets' chagrin the Vietnamese also resisted joining COMECON, the Eastern bloc economic alliance, and instead Hanoi took the Saigon regime's seat in two pre-eminent capitalist institutions, the World Bank and the Asian Development Bank. To underline its independence the Vietnamese barred Soviet ships from using port facilities at the former American base at Cam Rahn Bay. To those who see the world in 'blocs' and small countries as 'dominoes'

Vietnam's stance must have seemed puzzling; the Soviet Union, after all, had been Hanoi's principal weapons supplier. But communism was no more than a tool of Vietnamese nationalism and the rejection of one communist ally in favour of overtures to the West was entirely consistent with Vietnam's past. Once again they were unravelling themselves from somebody else's quarrel which, in the 1970s, was the war of attrition between China and the Soviet Union. Ho Chi Minh had foreseen the dangers of being too closely tied to any bloc and his successors were simply proceeding with his wishes to 'internationalise' Vietnam as the means, no longer of breaking the bonds of colonialism, but of surviving in the shadow of the most populous nation on earth.

In 1977 the Vietnamese government announced an investment code under which foreign companies would be offered attractive terms in joint enterprises with Vietnam. It was, ironically, a policy similar to that which present-day 'pragmatic' China is offering to the West. A long line of American, Japanese and European bankers, businessmen, oil men and travel agents was invited to Hanoi. While I was there in 1978 a fraternal delegation from Cuba was moved out of the best hotel to make way for a fraternal delegation from the Chase Manhattan Bank, New York. Congressmen came to discuss diplomatic recognition; a prospective American embassy in Hanoi was renovated, even a flag-pole put in place. Finally, the Vietnamese let it be known that they were dropping all claims to the $3.4 billion in reparations promised to them in the Paris accords of 1973. 'Normalisation' of relations with the United States *without conditions* was now policy in Hanoi; and this included resolution of the Missing in Action (MIA) issue to the satisfaction of the Carter administration and an orderly departure of all Vietnamese previously associated with the United States.

During 1978 the Vietnamese foreign minister, Nguyen Co Thach, and the US Assistant Secretary of State, Richard Holbrooke, met on numerous occasions and the Americans were said to be enthusiastic for such a 'historic reconciliation'. Nguyen Co Thach recalled:

> We accepted the US position on normalisation. We agreed to defer other problems until later. We agreed on the number of embassy staff, where the embassies would be located. Everything was agreed. I waited in New York through October and then I had to go home. In November I got a message that there was now 'a question of Cambodia'.[35]

The 'question of Cambodia' meant the increasing attacks mounted by the Pol Pot regime on Vietnam and the Vietnamese counter attack in December, which led to the retreat of the Khmer Rouge and an end to the genocide in Cambodia. But to the Americans, this was really 'a

question of China', for the American romance with Peking was deepening. That China happened to be underwriting Asia's Hitler, Pol Pot, was
one of those unfortunate impediments one tolerates in a bridge of such
promise. In any event there was a cover story. President Carter's National
Security Adviser, Zbigniew Brezezinski, had visited China in May 1978
and received a warning from Deng Xiaoping that Vietnam was an 'Asian
Cuba', or little more than a satellite of Moscow.[36] This convenient
description was accepted by those in the Carter administration who, like
Brezezinski, had little time for a 'historic reconciliation' with Vietnam
and instead viewed 'normalisation' with China as a new and potent
cold-war weapon against the Soviet Union. When, in summer 1978,
Deng Xiaoping visited the United States he informed the Americans of
Peking's intention to teach Vietnam a lesson and sought Washington's
tacit approval of a Chinese invasion of Vietnam. He got it.

On February 18, 1979, more than 600,000 Chinese troops – more
than the Americans ever had in Vietnam – attacked Vietnam from the
North. It was a massive assault, destroying dykes and canals which had
withstood Chinese invasions for 2,000 years and more recently American
bombing. The most painful blow was the systematic sabotage of the last
reserve stocks of rice, to which Chinese sappers had been led, claimed
Hanoi, by scouts recruited from among the *Hoa*, the ethnic Chinese of
Vietnam's northern provinces.

The *Hoa* were mostly skilled workers who had blended into Vietnamese
society and were important to the economy of the North. Recognising
this and as a counterweight to Peking's campaign against 'racial persecution' in Vietnam, Hanoi had offered the *Hoa* economic incentives
to stay at their jobs. But this spirit of accommodation evaporated as the
Chinese campaign against Vietnam became more and more shrill. As a
result, whole mining communities left for China, and it seems likely that
farmers and fishermen living in areas of strategic importance, such as
the invasion routes south, were expelled. Peking had demonstrated its
ability to manipulate the loyalties of the *Hoa* and this, combined with the
apparent betrayal of some *Hoa*, rebounded unjustly on all members of a
minority who found themselves pawns in a struggle between their
homeland, Vietnam, and China. On the one side Chinese troops reportedly killed those *Hoa* who refused to collaborate. On the other side, the
Vietnamese gave those who had maintained Chinese citizenship the
choice of crossing into China, or of going to 'New Economic Zones' far
from the northern frontier and far from the eastern coast where the next
Chinese invasion was expected. A third option was the sea voyage to
Hong Kong.

Is it mere hindsight to write now that this need not have happened?
Perhaps; but in the long parade of lost opportunities in Indo-China,

the overture by Vietnam to its former enemy, the United States, was outstanding in the multiple possibilities it offered. Had the United States responded, the international embargo on and the state of siege in Vietnam would have lifted. Reconstruction would have begun. Spare parts for American machinery would have arrived, together with other props to a southern economy built by and dependent upon United States aid. Many Western-trained Vietnamese might have stayed. Certainly, that was the impression I gained when I interviewed some of the first groups of boat people awaiting resettlement in the United States in 1976 and 1977. Many of them loathed the 'old Vietnam' as much as they distrusted and feared the communists. Had the United States been part of the solution to Vietnam's post-war problems, rather than a primary source of them, people who had wanted to go to America could have done so in safety. The Americans could have had their *rapprochement* with China *and* with Vietnam.

Such hindsight could, of course, serve the notion that the United States gained nothing by isolating China for more than twenty years and that the same 'tragic error' or 'perversity' determined American policy towards Vietnam in 1978 and 1979. There was nothing accidental or perverse about American actions. Indeed, it could be argued that by isolating China, America in the end 'gained' China. The excesses of the Cultural Revolution were a symptom of China's isolation and the inevitable reaction in China provided the opportunity for the Nixon 'opening' to Peking in 1972. This is known as 'divide and rule'.

In February 1979, President Carter renewed the economic embargo against Vietnam, refusing an appeal by a mission sent to Vietnam by Senator Edward Kennedy that American humanitarian aid should go directly to Vietnam 'as a single act of magnanimity to a people suffering the most severe privations as a consequence of thirty years of war'. Members of the mission had expressed shock at the malnourished state of many Vietnamese children. The Carter administration heeded none of this and instead pressed the World Bank to suspend all aid to Vietnam, thus sabotaging a 60 million dollar loan for an irrigation project which would have increased food production.

The implications of this bore on American policy elsewhere in the world. President Carter, on assuming office, had confronted one central foreign policy problem: how to clean up the image of the United States so that American foreign policy could proceed on its *unchanged* course. Carter's selective human rights campaign was part of the solution; and without denying the positive side-effects of that policy, especially in the Eastern bloc, the tragic events of Indo-China were its greatest 'success'. By adopting the flight of the boat people as a singular human rights crusade, without reference to American complicity in the causes of the exodus, the Carter administration was able to begin to clear the way for its repetition, in Asia and other places.

Among the American public there was a confusion of views about the boat people, some of them resentful towards the refugees themselves, many of them charitable. The flight of the boat people was perceived as a phenomenon of the Vietnam war, 'that mess we got into', and of 'the spread of communism'. But of course it was no phenomenon; it had all happened before, as illustrated by the irony implicit in the following extract:

EXODUS OF THE LOYALISTS

When the British evacuated Boston in 1776 and Philadelphia in 1778, thousands of Loyalists went with the troops, and it was reported in 1777 that two thirds of the people of Cumberland County, North Carolina, were moving. How many left the United States permanently is impossible to determine; the number has been estimated as high as a hundred thousand.

They went to all parts of the empire, but mainly to Canada; especially to the region around Nova Scotia and New Brunswick, and to the British Isles. Their departure deprived the United States of a goodly percentage of the wealthy and cultured classes, but at the same time took away a group that had been constantly at odds with the new American conceptions of government and democracy. They were not only victims of British defeat, but of their own failure to keep abreast of the times.[37]

As John McAuliff has pointed out, '100,000 Tory refugees were about four percent of the population of the American colonies; a similar proportion of departures from post-war Vietnam would be more than 2,000,000 people'.[38]

In July 1979 Margaret Thatcher had been in power in Britain for less than two months. One of her first foreign-policy decisions was to suspend British humanitarian aid to Vietnam, the bulk of which was to be £4 million worth of food, including milk powder for children. This action contrasts with her reluctance in 1985 to impose economic sanctions on South Africa. Roused by what British government press officers called Mrs Thatcher's 'humanitarian initiative' on behalf of the boat people, the European Community stopped the shipment of 100,000 tons of food to Vietnam, including 15,000 tons of milk powder for children. The Ministry of Health in Hanoi reported that the country's stocks of skimmed milk were depleted; there was none. Applying further constraint to an economy already in ruins from the war would of course ensure the departure of more boat people. As if to encourage them, the Voice of

America broadcast daily the movement of 'friendly' ships in the South China Sea. This was like pointing out a mirage in the desert, for ships' captains were now deliberately changing course rather than pick up boat people and bear the responsibility of finding a haven for them.

The boat people received a lot of media attention during the summer of 1979, the period of the second and greatest exodus following the Chinese invasion of Vietnam. But three important elements were often missing from the 'story'. The first was an international conference on refugees in Geneva at which the Vietnamese delegates agreed on an 'orderly departure programme' by air, to be supervised by the United Nations High Commissioner for Refugees. The second was that many more exit visas were granted in Vietnam than there were governments willing to accept them. The third was the haemorrhage of refugees elsewhere in Asia. For example, 320,000 'road people' had fled from Pol Pot's Cambodia into Vietnam where they were given refuge, with minimal international assistance. This number was greater than all the categories of boat people combined. And during the same period more Chinese refugees arrived in the British Crown Colony of Hong Kong, often by the hazardous sea route, than arrived from Vietnam. Most of these were sent back to China without international opprobrium being directed at Hong Kong or at Britain; returning refugees was, after all, a longstanding policy of the colonial administration. As for political iniquities and poverty in China which had caused their people to flee, these were overshadowed by the Western 'opening' to China, which was no longer 'Red China' and was therefore exempt from pillorying as a repressive regime.

Coincidentally or not, the bold cynicism which was a feature of some Western governments' approach to the issue of the boat people was best illustrated in Hong Kong. Unlike Malaysia and most of the region, Hong Kong did not turn away or 'shoo' boat people. In 1979 more than 95,000 refugees were allowed to land at Hong Kong, presenting an opportunity for swift compassionate action by those who had proclaimed solidarity with communism's cast-offs. Unfortunately this did not happen. In July 1979 a UNHCR official in Hong Kong told me that 'what we have here is nothing more than a human meat market, and a buyer's market at that'. No government gave refuge to people simply because they were refugees and helpless; there was no 'orderly queue'. The UNHCR official in Hong Kong showed me a copy of each country's 'guidelines', which determined the refugees who were 'acceptable' and those who were not. The United States 'Parole Program' listed five categories. The 'acceptable' categories demanded a proven association with America, as well as skills and means. Category Five was for people who had been 'inspected' by other countries and turned down, such as a fisherman and his family of seven whom I interviewed, who had failed to 'qualify' for anybody's compassion and who are, to my knowledge, still behind wire in a Hong Kong 'closed camp'. The fisherman's disabilities were many: he did not have well-off relatives in America or Europe, or a bank account in California, or gold stashed away, and he did not train in Vietnam as a doctor or a helicopter engineer or a computer programmer. Worse, he and his family were not Christians.

Germany's quota was restricted to 'those Vietnamese with previous links with the Federal Republic'. The Japanese, however, beat them all. 'A Category One Japanese Government Approved Refugee', read the Japanese guidelines, 'will prove that he or she has Japanese relatives and/or is part Japanese.' Those enjoying a reputation in Hong Kong as the most liberal in their 'processing' methods were the Canadians. A Canadian 'processor' described his job to me. 'I zoom into this camp,' he said, 'then it's on to that camp, pick up a dozen here, grab a few there. I feel bad about it man, real bad ... but listen, if a refugee can say "Hello Joe" that's good enough for me; they're down in my book as "English-speaking". And, hey, I take aunties! I don't care if they can't write their names. The Brits and the Americans won't take aunties, but I take 'em ... I just said to those refugees over there, "Listen, if you've got an auntie you want to throw in, let's have her!"' I asked him if they had had an auntie to throw in. He replied, 'Nah, all they got is cousins, and we don't take cousins.'

Since the end of the war in 1975 the United States has taken 560,000 refugees, Canada 94,000 and Australia 91,000. Britain, whose prime minister has spoken out frequently about the 'rights' of the boat people, has accepted fewer than 16,000 refugees from its own colony. At the time of writing there are 6,500 refugees left in Hong Kong, the victims of a disease known among governments and aid agencies as 'compassion fatigue'. David Pallister, reporting in the *Guardian*, was close to the truth when he described the boat people stranded in Hong Kong as 'victims of a cleverly contrived inertia in Whitehall'.[39]

According to a report by the British Refugee Council,[40] these forgotten people are confined in prisons and in concentration camps surrounded by wire fences and rolls of barbed wire. Hundreds of families are forced to sleep in a former warehouse on tiers of steel platforms. At least one camp is run by Chinese prison warders who display their enmity for the Vietnamese by imposing twenty-eight-day 'solitary confinement' as punishment for 'disruptive' refugees. Evangelical Christian organisations are given exclusive access to the refugees and operate a system of rewards in return for the refugees' commitment to a set of religious beliefs at odds with their own. Every morning and evening queues form to watch the television news in Cantonese, a language none of the refugees can understand, with some of them hoping there will be news about their own plight; there seldom is. 'Unless the situation changes', reported the House of Commons Home Affairs Committee in 1985, 'there will shortly be children of school age who have spent their entire lives in closed camps.'

The British government's treatment of these people is in contravention of the United Nations charter on refugees and of international law on human rights, and it bears comparison with the Vietnamese government's persecution of them; the difference is that Britain has not emerged from thirty years of war. When Mrs Thatcher signed the 'historic agreement' handing back Hong Kong to China, no mention was made of the people trapped in Britain's concentration camps who are now said to place their last hope in China's assumption of power in Hong Kong in 1997. Should the unlikely occur and the British government agree to take them, one more irony for the boat people may be the bitterest. The following is a recent news item from *The Times*. At the time of writing such items are not uncommon.

Vietnamese refugees living in south-east London are living in fear of racial attacks, Mr. Lloyd Henry, Chairman in Community Aid for Victims of Crime in Lewisham, said at a conference at the weekend. Children have been kept from school to prevent them being beaten in the streets and parents had been assaulted . . . One refugee returning from hospital was cornered by white youths, and he begged them on his knees not to hurt him, but he was still beaten up, Mr. Henry said.[41]

20

Follies

In August 1981 the magazine *Encounter* published an article entitled 'How to Lose a War: Reflections of a Foreign Correspondent'. The author was Robert Elegant, a former Vietnam war reporter. Elegant wrote:

> For the first time in modern history the outcome of a war was determined not on the battlefield but on the printed page and, above all, on the television screen . . . never before Vietnam had the collective policy of the media – no less stringent a term will serve – sought by graphic and unremitting distortion the correspondents' own side.

Setting aside Elegant's delusion of a media conspiracy with 'the enemy', his view is important because it encapsulates two of the most durable and influential myths about the Vietnam war. The first is that the Americans 'lost' the war because the media coverage in the United States, notably on television, undermined the military and political effort. The second is that most journalists and broadcasters opposed the war. Neither is true. Indeed the truth may well be the very opposite of Elegant's stricture: that on the whole the American media, while questioning the way in which the war was being fought, supported what Stanley Karnow, formerly of the *New York Times*, has since called 'a failed crusade'.[42]

In his classic study of war correspondents,[43] Phillip Knightley described the reporting from Vietnam during the early 1960s as

> . . . not questioning the American intervention itself, but only its effectiveness. Most correspondents, despite what Washington thought about them, were just as interested in seeing the United States win the war as was the Pentagon. What the correspondents questioned

was not American policy, but the tactics used to implement that policy . . .

David Halberstam, formerly of the *New York Times*, who was considered the *bête noire* of the Kennedy administration for his critical reporting from Vietnam, later wrote, 'We would have liked nothing better than to believe that the war was going well, and that it would eventually be won.'[44] Knightley related a revealing story about *Time* magazine's chief correspondent in South-East Asia in 1963, Charles Mohr. Mohr had co-authored an article which began, 'The war in Vietnam is being lost . . . ' When the piece appeared in *Time* this line had been deleted and the article said the opposite: that the war was going well and '[Saigon] government troops are fighting better than ever'. Mohr had also co-written an article defending the American Press corps in Saigon, who were then being accused in Washington of painting too bleak a picture of Ngo Dinh Diem, the South Vietnamese tyrant imported from exile in America by Colonel Edward Lonsdale of the CIA. *Time* not only refused to publish this second article but replaced it with a version rewritten by its managing editor; once again, it said the opposite of the original. When Mohr was refused equal space to reply, he resigned, only to find that his stand against *Time* had made him something of an anti-war hero; and this embarrassed him. 'Everyone thought I left because I was against the war,' he said. 'I just thought it wasn't working. I didn't come to think of it as immoral until the very end.'[45] Moreover, wrote Knightley, 'Mohr's commitment was such that, back in Vietnam for the *New York Times*, he took part, armed with an M-16, in the American re-taking of Huc Citadel after the Tet offensive.'

In news agency offices in Saigon there were photographs of dismembered bodies, of soldiers holding up severed ears and testicles and of actual moments of torture. These were the atrocities few wrote about. In the Associated Press office, pinned on the wall, was a photograph of an NLF soldier being tortured; above the torturer's head was a stick-on comic strip balloon which said, 'That'll teach you to talk to the press.' The question came up whenever visitors caught sight of these pictures: why had they not been published? A standard response was that the agency would not distribute them, because newspapers would not publish them, because their readers would not accept them. And to publish them, without an explanation of the wider circumstances which produced them and of the nature of the war itself, was to 'sensationalise'.

I myself accepted the apparent logic of this when I first arrived in Vietnam; atrocities surely were aberrations by definition. But this did not explain 'collateral damage' and 'circular error probability': civilians killed, maimed, made homeless and sent mad by bombs dropped and artillery trained on villages, paddies, schools and hospitals. It did not explain children burned to a bubbling pulp by Napalm or farmers killed during helicopter 'turkey shoots' or 'suspects' thrown out of helicopters or dragged down country roads, roped from neck to neck, by jeeps filled with doped and laughing soldiers, or dead 'suspects' laid out like rabbits. It did not explain the soldiers who kept human parts in their wallets and the Special Forces officers who kept human skulls in their huts, enscribed with the words, 'One down, one million to go'.

Philip Jones Griffiths, a Welshman with whom I worked in Vietnam and one of the most compassionate and incisive photographers of the war, told Knightley about women and children huddled together, waiting to be killed by American artillery in a 'search and destroy' mission. When he tried to stop it, he was told by an American officer, 'What civilians?' He told Knightley, 'If I had gone back to Saigon and into one of the agencies and had said, "I've got a story about Americans killing Vietnamese civilians", they would have said, "So what's new?" It was horrible, but certainly not exceptional, and it just wasn't news.'[46]

In 1983 I interviewed General Winant Sidle, the chief spokesman for General Westmoreland, the American commander in Vietnam at the height of the war. He told me, 'A lot of what we did just wasn't newsworthy. Take collateral damage. Of course that's a term that tends to deceive, although the reporters and the military men using the term knew what it meant. I know a lot of military terms were misunderstood, like "search and destroy", which was an unfortunate choice of words because "reconnaissance and force" would have done the job, and it's exactly the same operation . . . but, gee, war is hell, and if a civilian doesn't want to get killed in the battle zone, he should leave.'[47]

Atrocities were neither isolated nor aberrations. It was the *nature* of the war that was atrocious; this was the 'big story' of the war, but it was seldom judged to be 'news' and therefore seldom told, except in fragments. Atrocities were reported as 'mistakes' which were 'blundered into'. Behind this acceptable version appalling events could proceed as part of a deliberate and often efficiently executed strategy, contrary to the popular misconception of 'blundering' generals and policy-makers. For example, one of the earliest atrocities was the herding of people into concentration camps which were known initially as 'strategic hamlets'. The coercion and terror employed and the subsequent deliberate dislocation of millions of lives was a carefully formulated strategy. In April 1967 Robert ('Blow Torch Bob') Komer, the American 'pacification' expert, recommended that the United States 'must step up refugee programs deliberately aimed at depriving the VC of a recruiting base.'[48] His recommendation was acted upon, at incalculable human cost; but this was not reported as an atrocity.

'Pacification' was a term which became familiar to many newspaper readers and television viewers but was seldom understood. 'Pacification', like 'collateral damage', was part of the distortion of language employed to preserve the war's façade. It meant killing as many people as possible in a given area within a given period of time. In 1971, for example, Kevin Buckley and Alex Shimkin of *Newsweek* happened on an old military 'handout' which said the US Ninth Infantry Division had killed 11,000 of the enemy in a 'pacification' campaign called 'Operation Speedy Express'. The flaw in this story was that only 700 weapons had been captured. Buckley and Shimkin were told by an American official that 5,000 'non-combatants' had been killed. If this was true, it was mass slaughter, officially condoned and covered up. *Newsweek* balked at publishing the story, telling its reporters that it would be 'a gratuitous attack on the [Nixon] administration at this point'.[49] Six months passed before a 'savagely cut' version of the truth was finally published, almost four years after the event itself.

Most experienced reporters knew that Operation Speedy Express was not unusual, although some preferred to pass it off by describing its perpetrators, the Ninth Division, as 'notorious'. What it represented, however, was the war itself: an all-out assault on the Vietnamese people, regardless of whether they were communist or non-communist. But the war was not presented in this way, rather as teams: 'good' teams and 'bad' teams. The Americans were on the side of the good team, the South Vietnamese, who were defending themselves against 'aggression' by several bad teams of 'communists'. Not surprisingly, this version excluded the fact that the Americans had killed tens of thousands of their South Vietnamese 'allies' and had destroyed their homes and crops, levelled their forests, poisoned their water and forced them into 'refugee programs'. The propaganda version also excluded what American intelligence had known from the beginning: that the regime America had installed in Saigon, complete with the machinery of mass terror, had no popular base.[50]

The standard version never satisfactorily came to terms with exactly who 'the communists' were. If the NLF, or Vietcong, were South Vietnamese how could they possibly 'invade' their own country? Words had to be found to describe what were, in effect, the actions of people defending their country against an invasion by the United States. The words chosen were 'internal aggression'. The propaganda also had difficulty with the 'North Vietnamese' who were said to be attacking the South. There had been no North Vietnam and no South Vietnam until the Geneva conference on Indo-China in 1954 'temporarily' divided the country to await national elections in 1956, which the Americans refused to allow, knowing that Ho Chi Minh would win hands down. Not only was Vietnam one country, but there were southerners in the Hanoi leadership in the North and northerners in the southern-based NLF. The first units sent south by Ho Chi Minh to support those resisting the foreign invaders were composed entirely of southerners.[51] So, once again, the South Vietnamese were 'invading' their own country!

This was confusing to reporters (myself included) and reducing it to shorthand was a formidable task, if not an impossible one; and not many of us tried. The easiest way was to adopt the jargon, euphemisms, acronyms, the whole language of propaganda on which, sadly, so much bad reporting was based. Criticism of events, individuals and even policies was not uncommon but this dissidence rarely exposed the false assumptions which underpinned the American war. Moreover, criticism which did not go 'too far' and which remained 'objective' and 'unemotional' and incorporated the principles of the official line served to strengthen the impression that the war was being reported vigorously and entirely free of censorship. General Sidle told me, 'Two delegations of bureau chiefs called on me in 1968, asking me to please impose censorship. They were getting confused about what they could do, what they could say and what they couldn't say.'[52]

Behind this fiction the essence of the war could be pursued without serious examination. 'Anti-personnel' technology was deployed with impunity; the bombs which sprayed needles into flesh and organs and were difficult to detect in X-rays created little fuss. Although millions of gallons of Agent Orange were dumped on Vietnam during the 1960s, the outcry about its genetic and environmental effects came only as the war was ending. In the daily flow of 'news' the victims of the war, such as refugees, became almost non-existent, like phantoms. The news instead concentrated on contrived American slaughter-fests such as the siege of Khe Sanh and the battle for 'Hamburger Hill'. 'We deal in facts, not judgments' was the motto of some tough, impartial scribes who witnessed all the war's dimensions and reported only one. Their 'facts' invariably omitted the racist nature of the war, as expressed by the common usage of 'gooks', 'dinks', 'slopes' and 'slants' and by the military's obsession with the 'body count' and 'kill ratio'. The good old blundering 'green machine' was a murder machine.

Death squads, which were to prove so effective in Central America, were expertly organised in Vietnam. An estimated 50,000 South Vietnamese were systematically murdered by assassins working for the CIA's 'Phoenix Programme'. The most decorated American soldier of the war, Lieutenant Colonel Anthony Herbert, wrote in his book, *Soldier*, 'They wanted me to take charge of execution teams that wiped out entire families and tried to make it look as though the VC themselves had done the killing.'[53] Like Agent Orange, the Phoenix Programme was not a 'story' until the war was ending. Like Operation Speedy Express, the massacre of between 90 and 130 men, women and children at the village of My Lai on March 16, 1968, was not a story until long after it had happened. For more than a year a soldier who had heard about the My Lai massacre tried to interest *Newsweek* and others, without success. Finally, the story was 'broken', not by any of the 600 reporters in Vietnam, but by a freelance in the United States, Seymour Hersh, who regarded the murder of unarmed civilians by American soldiers as both shocking and important. Only then did the correspondents in Vietnam tell their own atrocity stories. There was a cataract of them. Everybody, it seemed, knew about or had witnessed at least one; and everybody had either not reported it or pleaded that their office had 'spiked' the story they had sent.

The My Lai massacre eventually made the cover of *Newsweek* under the banner headline 'AN AMERICAN TRAGEDY', which invited sympathy for the invader and deflected from the truth that the atrocities were, above all, a *Vietnamese* tragedy. Although other atrocities seemed to be surfacing by the hour, the effect of the reporting of the My Lai massacre was to present it as an isolated, if 'significant' incident. After that, wrote Phillip Knightley, the media began to lose interest in Vietnam. The war was now obsolete, 'peace with honour' was being pursued by Nixon and Kissinger; so what else was there to say?

Yet as the reporters left Vietnam – by 1974 there were only thirty-five permanent correspondents in Saigon – the war was intensified. More bombs were dropped during this period than at any time before: a fact relentlessly and courageously pointed out by a Boston-based columnist, Anthony Lewis of the *New York Times*.[54] One year after the Paris peace accords in 1973 the US Senate Refugee Committee noted that 818,700 new refugees had been created in Vietnam and an average of 141 people were being killed every day. As Lewis pointed out, the Vietnamese had suffered more in one year of peace with honour than America had experienced in a decade of war. This was the time of 'Vietnamisation', which meant that Vietnamese troops were dying on America's behalf, 'supported' by American bombers which continued to destroy their country. But this did not qualify as a 'big story'.

Vietnam was said to be the first television war. That the television coverage 'lost' the war for the Americans always seemed to me a thoroughly ridiculous charge because 'good television' – a term which has since become a parody of itself – was, with honourable exceptions, one-dimensional and offered no threat to the 'consensus' view of the war. In the early stages the arrival of the hand-held camera allowed television to concentrate on dramatic battle scenes reminiscent of Second World War Hollywood films, regardless of the purpose and achievement of the action. Indeed, this reinforced the 'consensus' view and may well have played a part in prolonging a war which was said to be 'lost' some seven years before it was finally abandoned. Television news, not documentary, was dominant; the 'bang-bang', the endless shots of helicopters, even occasionally of pain and bloodshed, were generally allowed to dictate their own terms and, once edited, became, in the jargon, 'slugs' (action film) and 'sound-bites' (very brief interviews).

Images usurped the judgments of experienced reporters who affected the roles of innocent bystander and caption writer. Public attitudes flow from perspectives; by allowing the false 'neutrality' of television images to dominate the coverage of the war, journalists allowed misconceptions to become received truths. The first casualties were truth and context; bang-bang and contemporary history were deemed not to blend on the screen. That the Geneva peace conference in 1954 had been undermined by Washington, that communist China was no friend of communist Vietnam, that the NLF had sought the establishment of a non-communist, neutral coalition in South Vietnam – these truths went unremembered and unconnected.

In an American CBS 'special' during the Tet offensive in March 1968, Walter Cronkite said, 'The only rational way out . . . will be to negotiate not as victors but as an honourable people who lived up to their pledge to defend democracy and did the best they could.' That this distinguished journalist could speak to a mass audience, presumably with a straight face, about defending 'democracy' in Vietnam said much about the entire news industry of which he was the paragon. According to Amnesty International, the 'democracy' which the Americans had created and were 'defending' at that time incarcerated more than half the world's known political prisoners and allowed 'systematic' torture. Few other regimes can claim a comparable record of brutality and repression of the democratic process.

In my view, the television coverage of the war, far from contributing to 'the victory of the enemies of the correspondents' own side', as Robert Elegant charged, confused and anaesthetised and dulled memories. The results of two surveys (among many) struck me as being particularly relevant. The first, for *Newsweek* in 1967, found that television did not cause 64 per cent of viewers to recoil from the 'reality' of the war, but encouraged them to support the war and to 'back up the boys'. Only 26 per cent of those polled were moved to call for an immediate end to the war. Five years later, during a period of sustained American bombing, a follow-up survey found that the American television audience had developed an immunity to all the pictures of horror and fireworks from far-off Asia. Without meaning, context, analysis and the 'judgment' often scorned by reporters who saw themselves only as 'witnesses', the images of the war were said to have merged with all the other 'fireworks' on television, such as in war movies, *Kojak, Starsky and Hutch*, etcetera.

The Vietnam war was perhaps the only war in history in which correspondents were free to go almost anywhere on the battlefield and were provided with an efficient means of doing so. You could fly from American cocoon to cocoon, officers' club to officers' club, hot shower to hot shower, Budweiser to Budweiser, latest movie to latest movie. After a long day being splattered with mud or covered with dust, shot at, bitten or just bored, a 'Hi-how-ya-doin'?', plus the shower and the Budweiser, could cast a certain spell. On the most remote firebase there was always a joint of marijuana on offer to calm the twilight. The unit Press and Information Officer might not inform, but he would surely entertain with a manic whirl round his briefing map of red bits and blue bits. He and most of the others I met were usually pleasant men who marked off the days until their return to 'the world' and for whom it was easy to feel sympathy. Indeed, on American bases in Vietnam I often felt as I had when I lived briefly in New Orleans. The weather was similar, and the folks had a lovable side and a lethal side.

The Vietnamese had every reason to fear the lethal side, which would express itself in human target practice and the arbitrary expenditure of ammunition, known as 'mad minutes'. The lovable side, the can-do *bonhomie*, street wit and frequent acts of kindness, had a profound effect on young reporters sent by Midwestern papers to do hometown-boys-out-there-in-'Nam stories and on the numerous foreign journalists whose travel to and from Vietnam, plus generous expenses, were paid by the United States Information Service and other US government agencies. I used to run into these junketeers, who in the midst of a nasty confusing war would feel secure and grateful in the American cocoon, and this would be reflected in what they wrote or broadcast. With no formal censorship and with such available largesse, and such nice guys dispensing it, it was at times impossible for all of us not to become part of an unseen and powerful propaganda machine.

In Saigon every day there was the 'Five O'Clock Follies', the military's press briefing. 'News' of the latest bodies counted, paddies bombed, arms caches captured, enemy soldiers 'rallied' and gleams glimpsed at the end of the metaphoric tunnel, was handed out here. I once asked Morley Safer, the veteran CBS network correspondent, to compare the Saigon 'Follies' with its equivalent at the Ministry of Defence in London during the Falklands war. He said, 'Well, during the Falklands Mr Ian McDonald would give a press conference and be absolutely confident that no one in the room knew more than he did. Now in Vietnam the poor old briefer knew that everyone in the room knew more than he knew . . . *at least those of us who'd been out of Saigon at all.*' [My italics]

Unlike Safer, relatively few journalists did leave Saigon. According to General Sidle, out of 649 correspondents accredited in March 1968, fewer than eight went regularly into the field. What this meant was that the 'Follies', which experienced reporters like Safer regarded no more seriously than 'sport at the end of a long day', was often the only source of information for the representatives of certain agencies, newspaper chains and other publications whose readership ran to millions. Near the end of the war the correspondent of the London *Daily Telegraph*, which devoted many column inches to Vietnam, was one John Draw. At least, his byline said that. In reality he was Captain Nguyen Ngoc Phach, aide to the Chief of Staff of the Army of South Vietnam. As Saigon began to 'fall' in 1975 the captain reported the retreat of his own Army and *Telegraph* readers were none the wiser.[55]

So rare were those like Safer, who would describe in his reports what *he* as well as the camera saw, that he was accused of being 'anti-American': the catch-all tag for those who stepped even briefly outside the consensus view. When in 1965 Safer's CBS crew filmed marines burning down a village with Zippo cigarette lighters, President Johnson himself intervened. David Halberstam related what happened, in his book, *The Powers That Be*:

'Frank,' said the early-morning wake-up call, 'are you trying to fuck me?' [Frank Stanton was then the president of CBS.]

'Who is this?' said the still sleepy Stanton.

'Frank, this is your President, and yesterday your boys shat on the American flag,' Lyndon Johnson said, and then administered a tongue lashing: how could CBS employ a Communist like Safer, how could they be so unpatriotic as to put on enemy film like this? Johnson was furious, he was sure that Safer was a Communist and he sent out a search party to check his past, and the Royal Canadian Mounted Police checked out everything about Safer, including his sister, finding that he was indeed totally above suspicion and law-abiding. (Johnson was insisting that Safer was a Communist, and when aides said no, he was simply a Canadian, the President said, 'Well, I knew he wasn't an American.')

He was also, and this was more serious because it suggested some of the paranoia that was to come, absolutely convinced that Safer had bought the Marine officer, that he had bribed him to do this. 'They got to one of our boys,' he told his staff. He immediately called through to the Joint Chiefs to launch an investigation of the officer in charge, to make sure that he had not been bribed by a Communist reporter, that he had not taken money, and even after a serious investigation brought back the report that there was no bribing, it was just one of those things, those trick press people had fooled a green young officer, the President of the United States believed there had been a conspiracy.[56]

Safer's 'crime' had been to give a mass American audience a glimpse of the real war. When British journalist James Cameron and cameraman Malcolm Aird raised their own finance to make a filmed report from Hanoi in 1965, they were castigated as communist dupes, a charge, Cameron later told me, he relished. 'Only when they called you a dupe, not a communist outright, but a dupe,' he said, 'did you know you'd broken the great mould that covered the reporting of the Vietnam war and that maybe you'd got it right!'

In one respect it was easy for the likes of me in Vietnam; I came and went. I always sympathised with journalists based in Vietnam because I knew that the longer you stayed, the more you contrived to remain aloof from the suffering and criminal stupidity of it all and the more difficult it became to protect your compassion. If you stayed too long you were in danger of being able to walk into a hospital and hover over a human form sticky with burns and say, 'Nothing in this.' If you stayed too long you were able to take pictures of suffering people and not think to help them and to cause people to be hurt by your presence and not realise it. If you stayed too long you did not look many Vietnamese in the eye.

Murray Sayle, the former correspondent of the London *Sunday Times*, has said that the war overwhelmed him. I often felt the same, and when I did I would plan to leave, and I could not get to the airport at Tan Son Nhut fast enough. These became moments of inexplicable panic; and I would wonder later if the war was beyond me and us all: beyond journalism. It is an interesting thought, because one work of fiction, Graham Greene's *The Quiet American*, written in the 1950s, still stands as perhaps the definitive 'reporting' of events and attitudes which fuelled the American war. It is regarded as such by many journalists who knew Vietnam and who, like myself, would ritually hand over a battered copy to those who wanted to know how and why such an apparently pointless endeavour could be sustained. Did we realise when we passed on the book that it contained perhaps a mirror of ourselves? Robert Scheer, the distinguished *Los Angeles Times* reporter, believes *The Quiet American* is 'the best thing written about Vietnam'. He told me, 'Greene got it right because he described that American personality that says, "We're going to save you from yourselves", who is totally insensitive to the history of another people, totally disrespectful of the idea that they may have aspirations of their own and who believes you can instantly learn about their society. Greene's Quiet American was a CIA agent, but it could have been some of our best reporters who went over there and went along with the war until the war stank so much you couldn't do your job *and* go along with it.'[57]

That said, I admired many of my colleagues, and most of all those who battled against monsters in their home offices, and against their own dismay at the turn of events, as well as their confusion and fear and the insidious pressure to join the 'pack' and its deferential consensus view. They included Richard Hughes, the young American who gave up being a journalist to care for the 'dust of life' children of Saigon, the photographers Philip Jones Griffiths (whose superb book, *Vietnam Inc.*, encapsulated more about the nature of the war than years of news reports), Don McCullin and the late Michel Laurent, the journalists Gloria Emerson, Victoria Brittain, Jack Laurence, Murray Sayle, James Cameron, Wilfred Burchett, Harrison Salisbury, Martin Woollacott, Morley Safer and others, alive and dead. For me, the greatest American reporter in Vietnam was Martha Gellhorn, who had covered the Spanish Civil War, China during the Japanese invasion, Finland, Italy and Britain during the Second World War and Dachau at the moment of liberation. She had gone to Vietnam as a freelance in the mid-1960s and her first published dispatches were my own brief when Hugh Cudlipp, then editor-in-chief of the *Daily Mirror*, sent me to report the war. (I corresponded with Martha Gellhorn for seven years before I met her. We are now close friends and she is godmother to my Zoe, born in 1984.)

From Qui Nhon provincial hospital, where wounded civilians were being treated 'under conditions suitable for the Crimean war', Martha Gellhorn wrote:

> We, unintentionally, are killing and wounding three or four times more people than the Vietcong do, so we are told, on purpose. We are not maniacs and monsters, but our planes range the sky all day and all night, and our artillery is lavish and we have much more deadly stuff to kill with. The people are there on the ground, sometimes destroyed by accident, sometimes destroyed because Vietcong are reported to be among them. This is indeed a new kind of war.

Her reports were published by the *Guardian* in 1966. Of all the American newspapers she approached, only the *St Louis Post-Dispatch* bought the series, but refused to print the angriest piece which had raised the forbidden question about American motives in Vietnam. She was subsequently refused a visa by the regime in Saigon and was unable to return there.

The following passage is from her article banned in the United States.

She had visited a refugee camp, 'a dump heap' she called it, where she found some of the million people made homeless in the previous two years. She wrote:

These peasants had survived the Vietcong since 1957, on whatever terms hostile or friendly, and the war however it came to them. But they cannot survive our bombs. Even the Catholic refugees did not leave their hamlets until the bombs fell. We are uprooting the people from the lovely land where they have lived for generations; and the uprooted are given not bread but stone. Is this an honourable way for a great nation to fight a war 8,000 miles from its safe homeland?[58]

21

A noble cause

On my wall is a photograph of what appears to be a swamp, which I took a few weeks after the end of the war in Vietnam in May 1975. I had been standing in a hillside cemetery among the graves of a town's entire anti-aircraft militia, all of them young women . . . Vo Thi Than, aged twenty-two, Duong Thi Than, aged nineteen . . . and I had asked where the town itself was. I was told I was looking directly at it, or rather where it had been. It was now a swamp, which on closer inspection was a series of overlapping craters. On the far side of the largest crater I could see a small pile of bricks, the foundation of something. There were no paddies, no shrines, no rickety high fences of bamboo, no draft animals. There were no people, of course. They were dead or gone.

Dong Loc, north of the seventeenth parallel, had been a farming community of several thousand people, whose 'strategic importance' was that it stood close to Highway One, the 'Street of No Joy', running along the curved spine of Vietnam. Dong Loc was one of hundreds of such places. There is no longer farming nearby where chemical agents dropped on the earth have caused it to salinate and set, in some places like stone, and it has yet to regenerate. Much of Vietnam today endures this twilight of devastation, unique, unseen, and perhaps infinite, in which the poisons run through the soil, water and genes: legacies of a 'noble war'.

President Reagan has described it as such and that is to be expected. But more than a decade after the 'fall' of Saigon, 'noble war' is gaining a certain currency as the revisionists work quickly, although 'revisionism' is not entirely apt because it implies new facts are to hand, demanding a change of perspective, when the old facts remain at bay, in shadow, unheeded. This is known as the 'new Vietnam scholarship'. 'New' Vietnam scholars include the familiar, discredited faces and the 'new' facts they present are familiar, discredited lies. At the time of the tenth anniversary of the end of the war, in 1985, the London *Sunday Times* gave Henry Kissinger most of a page to justify his claim that 'the ultimate political goal of America was noble: to enable a distant people to resist tyranny . . .'[59] To Kissinger, 1985 model, the media were to blame for 'failing to distinguish between what was inherent in modern weaponry and what represented deliberate cruelty'. Pushing people out of helicopter gunships was, of course, not deliberate but 'inherent in the weaponry'. Or in Kissinger's case, the consequences of the secret and unconstitutional dispatch of B-52 bombers against peasant Cambodia were not deliberate but 'inherent in the weaponry'.

There is a *chic* implied in this 'new scholarship', which has both the dress of academic sophistication and the attention of media eager to be seen absolving themselves of any guilt in 'losing' the war. In a major article in its Sunday magazine, the *New York Times*[60] chronicled the 'new' sombre reflection and diligent research. The cover showed pre-eminent 'new scholar' Douglas Pike presiding over his 'Indochina Studies Program' at the University of California at Berkeley. On the blackboard behind Pike was the word 'ideology'; it was misspelt: a fitting symbol. For much of the war Pike was a senior *apparatchik* of the United States Information Service (USIS) in Saigon and the leading US government propagandist on the Vietcong. His zeal in promoting the American cause was rare even among like-minds. During the 1960s he directed propaganda against the 'threat' of a political settlement among the Vietnamese themselves, because, as he put it, the American-backed 'minnow' would be swallowed by the enemy 'whale': in other words, the will of the Vietnamese majority would prevail.[61] According to the author of the *New York Times* article, Fox Butterfield, himself a former Vietnam war reporter, 'Mr. Pike's presence at Berkeley is testament to Vietnam's having quietly made the transition from controversial public issue to history.' Translated, this 'quiet transition' is from propaganda to history, from 'master illusion' to accredited truth. It is classically Orwellian.

The epitome of the 'new scholarship' is a 700-page history of Vietnam which Pike has described as 'more objective' than earlier 'angry' works. This is Stanley Karnow's *Vietnam: a history*,[62] which is described on its cover as 'a companion to the PBS Television series' intended for students as well as the public. Although Karnow was 'chief correspondent' of the series his book bears little relation to the excellent documentary films shown in the United States and Europe in 1983. All the conservative and liberal myths are paraded arm in arm in Karnow's 'history'. His readers are told that the war was a 'failed crusade' conducted for the 'loftiest of intentions', that the communists were 'terrorists' who were 'merciless' and 'brutal' in contrast to the Americans who were 'sincere' and 'earnest' and whose 'instincts were liberal'. Good guy Lyndon Johnson, 'mistakenly imputed [American] values to the communists', believing that 'they would respond like reasonable people' (to American threats to demolish their towns) but of course these communists were 'rarely troubled by heavy human tolls'. Karnow gives the My Lai massacre one line, but tells the moving story of how Robert McNamara, secretary of defence under Johnson, expressed his 'anguish', not for the enforced uprooting of millions, not for the mounds of victims of American bombing: no, McNamara's 'voice broke' as he described 'the futility, the crushing futility of the air war'. Like many 'new' historians Karnow justifies the war by pointing accusingly at the absorption of the southern resistance movement by the leadership in Hanoi. In other words, as Noam Chomsky pointed out, 'this consequence of US savagery [is] exploited as a justification for it, a propaganda achievement that Goebbels would have admired'.[63]

At the level of popular culture, always the vanguard in matters of national redemption, the post-war propaganda has worked assiduously to celebrate the invader and to reduce the invaded to their wartime status of commie stick figures on celluloid. The multi-Oscared Hollywood creation *The Deerhunter*, which according to *Time*-speak 'articulates the new patriotism', was the first prime example. It arrived at America's box offices in the late 1970s when little was being spoken publicly about the war. This was said to be wound-licking time, though complicated by Jimmy Carter's obsession with the humiliation of the American hostages in Iran. A Hollywood catharsis was required urgently. Certainly, few movies have been better timed than *The Deerhunter*, and few have enjoyed such ecstatic pre-publicity. In Britain, Derek Malcolm in the *Guardian* insisted that it should be seen 'at all costs'; the *Daily Mail* described it as 'the story they never dared to tell before . . . the film that could purge a nation's guilt!'; Milton Schulman of the *Evening Standard* was left 'quivering and shattered', and Alexander Walker wrote in the same paper that here was a film that 'says things that needed saying'. Lady Delfont, wife of the film's British backer, Bernard Delfont of EMI, announced that she had wept openly at a preview.

There was much to weep about. The producers had spent $14 million of EMI's money packaging the war for Hollywood as a movie which would reincarnate the triumphant Batman-jawed Caucasian warrior ('liberal by instinct') and present a suffering people as sub-human Oriental barbarians and idiots. The American heroes managed to wipe out a houseful of barbarians, M-16s rotating from their lean hips. None of this, of course, was new; it was how Hollywood created the myth of the Wild West, which was harmless enough unless you happened to be an American Indian; and how the Second World War and the Korean

War were absorbed into box office folklore, which was harmless enough unless you happened to be a dumb Kraut or an unspeakable Nip or a commie chink; and of course, *The Deerhunter* was harmless enough unless you happened to be a gook.

The film's dramatic pitch was reached during recurring orgiastic scenes in which the American heroes were forced to play Russian roulette by their Vietnamese captors. In all my time in Vietnam I never heard about this 'game'. I asked others who had been there if they had heard about it and they had not. Interviews with returning American prisoners-of-war never mentioned it, and these surely would have been seized upon at the time as confirmation of the enemy's inhumanity. The director of *The Deerhunter*, Michael Cimino, insisted that the Russian roulette was authentic. But Cimino's original script had been simply cameos of ex-GIs recalling their time in Vietnam, which was rejected by the potential backers in Britain as unexciting and potentially unprofitable. So Cimino discarded his cameos and on his travels across the Atlantic came up with a script which centred upon the gratuitous violence of games of Russian roulette, which he had invented. Linda Christmas of the *Guardian* wrote that Cimino had told her, 'During the making of the film, I certainly had the sense that we were doing something special. It was such an agonising experience both emotionally, physically – the tropics, the heat, the humidity. I can't shake off *The Deerhunter* even now. I have this insane feeling that I was there, in Vietnam. Somehow the fine wires have got really crossed and the line between reality and fiction has become blurred.'[64]

Although Cimino said he had 'this insane feeling that I was there, in Vietnam', he was never there. He told Linda Christmas, and Leticia Kent of the *New York Times*, that he was called up shortly after the Tet offensive in 1968, and was a medic attached to the Green Berets. He 'missed' Vietnam because, he said, he had a job 'involved in defence and classified. Something to do with that'. The Defence Department records tell a different story. Cimino was in the Army reserve before draftees were sent to Vietnam and was pursuing a career in advertising at the time of the Tet offensive. These discrepancies might not have mattered had the director not insisted that his film's most dramatic moments were based upon fact – 'meaningful horror', he called them – and had his film not been regarded virtually as documentary and had he not been elevated to a champion of America's 'new patriotism'. President Carter reportedly saw *The Deerhunter* three times and was moved by its 'genuine American message'. Another 'master illusion' had triumphed.

Francis Ford Coppola, unlike Cimino, was already a director of some distinction, and his film *Apocalypse Now* was, as they say in Hollywood and Cannes, 'long awaited'. Also set in Vietnam, *Apocalypse Now* had exceeded its budget by many millions of dollars, partly because of an absurdly inflated fee demanded by Marlon Brando. Like Cimino, Coppola was one of the first directors to exploit the special effects technology developed during the 1970s and his film was acclaimed as a spectacle true to its subject. That he had reduced the Vietnamese and Montenard peoples to stereotypes of Oriental viciousness was generally passed over by the critics. Coppola claimed in his film that NLF soldiers hacked off the arms of children to discourage a vaccination programme and implied that this was the reason why the United States invaded Vietnam. When an American journalist wrote to the screenwriter, John Milius, asking where the children's severed arms story had originated, her letter was returned by Milius with the US Special Forces death's head drawn on it, together with these words:

> We must burn them,
> We must incinerate them,
> Press after press,
> Pen after pen,
> Pencil after pencil,
> – No dialogue with communist criminals[65]

In another acclaimed film, *The Killing Fields*, scenes which showed the Vietnamese as the liberators of Cambodia in 1979 were cut. These cuts included, according to the shooting script I saw, Vietnamese soldiers handing out food and 'doing their best to minister to the needs of the Cambodian people' following the holocaust of Pol Pot – all of which is documented and is anathema to the 'revisionists' who have worked hard to confuse the Vietnamese role with the genocide of Pol Pot.

In 1985, with the remembrance of the tenth anniversary of the end of the war, a rash of films about heroic 'rescues' in Indo-China were released. They were mostly about Americans missing in action and surviving in jungle hells against all odds. *Missing in Action I*, *Missing in Action II*, *Uncommon Valour* and *Battle Rage* all performed well at the box office; but none approached the popularity and profitability of *Rambo: First Blood Part II*.

'Rambo' is Johnny Rambo, a wedge-shaped Vietnam veteran and psychopath (played by Sylvester Stallone) who is sent into post-war Indo-China to rescue GIs held in bamboo cages by loathsome Oriental communists supported by loathsome Russians. And although he is betrayed by Washington, he wins through in the end, pectorals gleaming, the blood of others flowing. It is one of the most violent films ever made. *People* magazine calculated that Rambo slaughters somebody every 2.1 minutes during the film. This time there is no 'meaningful horror', no masquerading as art. Among the film's promoters was President Reagan. 'After seeing *Rambo* last night', he said, 'I know what to do the next time this happens.'[66] He was referring to the hijacking of an American airliner to Beirut in July 1985. Three months later he sent American warplanes to force down an Egyptian airliner carrying the Palestinian hijackers of an Italian cruise liner. Headlines in Britain read, 'RAMBO REAGAN' and 'RAMBO STRIKES BACK!'.

The film turns the truth of Vietnam inside out. In spite of a 1976 Congressional Select Committee report that 'no Americans are still being held alive as prisoners in Indo-China' and a commission of enquiry sent by President Carter to Hanoi which agreed with the Select Committee's findings, the 'MIA issue' has exerted considerable influence on many Americans' emotions and politics. There are 2,477 officially listed 'MIAs', most of them pilots who went down with their aircraft. Compared with 78,751 American soldiers still 'missing' from the Second World War and 8,177 MIAs from the Korean War, the Vietnam figure is very low and may be the lowest this century. Since 1975 the Vietnamese have returned the remains of more than 100 Americans.

Nevertheless, the MIA families have had their hopes raised by various 'sightings' of prisoners, none of them confirmed, and by President Reagan himself. Since Reagan was elected there has been a 'National POW/MIA Recognition Day' and the families have been flown to Washington in military aircraft to hear their President pledge 'the highest national priority' to bring the POWs home. He has made these gestures in the face of evidence from his own Defence Intelligence Agency that it is highly unlikely there are any POWs left in Vietnam. Clearly *Rambo* is enough evidence for him.

Most of these films have transferred to the mass audience video-leasing market and have also been sold to television. *The Deerhunter* and *Apocalypse Now* were shown on peak-time television in Britain during the run-up to the tenth anniversary; the latter was described in the *Radio Times* as a film which 'proved to be one of the definitive studies of men in war'.[67] My own view is that these films have become by default a kind of popular history of Indo-China because the ubiquitous television coverage failed to provide context and meaning, unlike the 'meaningful horror' of *The Deerhunter* and the 'patriotism' of *Rambo*. That the truth is not permitted to intervene in such 'new' and packaged history is of course by the way; what matters is the strength of the purgative. Like any propaganda, its long-term effects are difficult to forecast.

In literature, Michael Herr's 1978 best-seller *Dispatches* made respectable the narcissism of a breed of war-lovers. On the cover of the book's first edition are comparisons with Dante, Erich Remarque, Crane, Orwell, Hemingway and Francis Bacon. Robert Stone is quoted: 'I believe it may be the best journal about war, about any war, that any writer has ever accomplished.' John le Carré is quoted: 'The best book I have ever read about men and war in our time.'

Herr glamorised a group of English and American 'war freaks'. These freaks included Herr himself, a reporter for *Esquire* magazine, and Sean Flynn, son of Errol and a photographer who, wrote Herr,

> . . . could look more incredibly beautiful than even his father, Errol, had 30 years before as Captain Blood, but sometimes he looked more like Artaud coming out of some heavy heart-of-darkness trip, overloaded on the information, the input! The input! He'd give off a bad sweat and sit for hours, combing his moustache through with the saw-blade of his Swiss Army knife.[68]

The former war correspondent James Fenton was one of the few reviewers who did not eulogise such insights. In the *New Statesman* Fenton described Herr, Flynn and the other war freaks as 'boring, spaced-out sadists hitching a lift with Murder . . . [To them] the American side of the thing was glamorous, manly, absorbing. The gooks' side was of no interest whatsoever. The enemy gooks were of no interest; the "friendly" gooks were of no interest.'[69]

Like many 'liberal by instinct' Caucasians who went to Vietnam, Herr was itching to use a gun on a human target. He got his chance:

> One night . . . I slid over to the wrong end of the story, propped up behind some sandbags at an airstrip in Can Tho with a .30-calibre automatic in my hands, giving cover for a four-man reaction team trying to get back in. One last war story.
>
> The first night of the Tet Offensive we were in the Special Forces C Camp for the Delta, surrounded as far as we knew, and with nothing but bad news filtering in: from Hue, from Danang . . . from Saigon itself, 'lost' as we understood it at that moment, they had the embassy, they had Cholon, Tan Son Nhut was burning, we were in the Alamo, no place else, and I wasn't a reporter, I was a shooter.[70]

The next morning there were a dozen Vietnamese dead in the area where Herr had been firing. He wrote that he could not know whether or not he had killed any gooks, but 'I couldn't remember ever feeling so tired, so changed, so happy'.

Having possibly killed people, Herr had 'lost' his innocence. 'Lost innocence' is a constant theme of the 'revisionists'. During the tenth anniversary gush, *Newsweek* described the American political establishment which prosecuted the war as 'by and large idealistic, if sometimes naive, defenders of democracy ... to many minds, that innocence can never be fully recovered'.[71] I am not so sure; as the American Indians learned, and the Nicaraguans are learning, such lethal innocence has a life force of its own.

When President Reagan was asked about the analogy of America's war in Vietnam with its current war in Central America, he said the comparison was 'totally unjustified' because 'North and South Vietnam had been, previous to colonisation, two separate countries'. He said that at the 1954 Geneva conference provisions had been made that 'these two countries could by a vote of all their people decide together whether they wanted to be one country or not'. He said that Ho Chi Minh 'refused to participate in such an election'. He added that American military advisers were sent to South Vietnam to work in civilian clothing and without weapons until they were attacked with 'pipe bombs'. Ultimately, said the president, John Kennedy had authorised the 'sending of a division of marines'.[72] What was striking about this piece of 'new' history was that it was apparently believed by reputedly the most powerful person in the world and that none of it was true. He was wrong on every score. To give one example, it was President Johnson, not Kennedy, who sent in the marines.

Perhaps in the near future President Reagan will order an invasion of Nicaragua. It is not inconceivable; it is his obsession, just as Vietnam was Lyndon Johnson's obsession. The similarities are many. There is even a debate in the United States between the conservative and liberal wings of the establishment, the so-called 'hawks' and 'doves', about whether Nicaragua poses a military threat to the United States. Like their predecessors during the American invasion of Vietnam, the 'doves' say the threat is exaggerated, but they do not deny that a threat exists.

However, these 'opinion leaders' are not the American people. Two polls conducted in the United States in 1978 and 1982 produced, in my view, highly significant results. In both years the polls found that 72 per cent of the American public felt that 'the Vietnam war was more than a mistake; it was fundamentally wrong and immoral'.[73] If this is true, it means that a majority of Americans have failed to succumb to years of indoctrination. It means that a chasm exists between the policy-makers and the public on the issue of other Vietnams, such as El Salvador and Nicaragua, and it helps to explain why so many normally pliant congressmen have opposed Reagan's attempts to intervene directly in Central America. Nicaragua may yet be spared.

The results of these polls are, of course, complementary to the 1985 study cited earlier, which found that a third of Americans could not remember which side the United States had supported in Vietnam. The *New York Times* described this as 'ignorance', which is rather like *Pravda* dismissing as ignorance the failure of Soviet citizens to grasp which side the Kremlin supported in Afghanistan. My own experience of being in America during the Vietnam war was that many people did not believe what they were told by their government or by their 'opinion leaders' in the media and the intelligentsia. The information industry saturated them with the official line, relieved by an occasional show of dissidence within the establishment; and yet the public remained unconvinced. This was known as the 'Vietnam syndrome'. In 1985, when this disturbing condition seemed on the verge of becoming an epidemic, Noam Chomsky identified its symptoms as 'an understanding of the facts of the real world, opposition to massacre and aggression and sympathy for the victims . . . Great efforts have been made to overcome this malady, but it persists, imposing constraints on the resort to violence in Central America and elsewhere'.[74] For example, when the British/American/ French television production *Vietnam* was shown in 1983 the American public's response appeared to be overwhelmingly in favour of the series' generally honest and critical appraisal of the war and its origins. The producers won nineteen American awards and their films are still being shown in schools and colleges: a potent antidote to the 'new scholarship'.

Post-war propaganda in both the United States and Vietnam is reconciled on one point: that America was 'defeated' in its war in Asia. But this is not true. The United States gained a significant, if partial, victory. As Chomsky has pointed out, American policy was never concerned with Vietnam alone, just as it is not concerned with Nicaragua alone. In Vietnam the short-term 'threat' came from a nationalist leadership concerned with domestic needs rather than with the transcendent demands of the United States. The long-term 'threat' to America was that of a development model which other states might have followed; and precisely the same is true of the Nicaraguan 'threat'. Far from being vanquished in South-East Asia, the United States has devastated, blockaded and isolated Vietnam and its 'virus' and has subordinated to American interests almost every regime in the region. Not even Hollywood has understood the scope of this achievement.

22

Revenge

In April 1980 a delegation of Americans went to the White House with a petition requesting the United States government to allow humanitarian assistance to be sent to Vietnam. They met Roger Sullivan of the National Security Council, who told them, "To put it in terms of a Chinese dialectic, United States policy is exactly to squeeze Vietnam to rely on the Soviet Union: then Vietnam will find the Soviet Union cannot meet all its needs ... If Vietnam suffers economic hardships, I think that is just great.'[75]

When the 1973 Paris peace agreement was signed there was a great deal of secrecy surrounding the detail of the negotiations. For example, Article 21 included the pledge that 'in pursuance of its traditional policy, the United States will contribute to healing the wounds of war and post-war reconstruction ... '; but there appeared to be no specific commitment, and in 1978 President Carter was able to state that 'the damage was mutual' and 'we owe them nothing'.

This was false, as Joel Charney and John Spragens Jr have documented.[76] In December 1975 the Vietnamese disclosed to visiting members of the US Congressional Select Committee on missing persons in South-East Asia that President Nixon had agreed to post-war reconstruction assistance 'in the range of $3.25 billion'.[77] Nixon's promise was contained in a letter to Pham Van Dong, prime minister of the Democratic Republic of Vietnam (North Vietnam), dated February 1, 1973. The State Department later confirmed the authenticity of the letter and of the agreement, details of which ran to eight, single-spaced pages, specifying the forms American aid would take. Eighty-five per cent of the money would be spent in the United States; American firms would tender for contracts to build industrial plants and commodities, including a thermal power station.

On April 30, 1975, the day the war ended and two years after the agreement on reparations was signed, the US Treasury Department froze Vietnamese assets of $70 million. Two weeks later the Commerce Department classified Vietnam a 'Category Z' country, requiring all exports there to be approved by the State Department. These controls are stricter than those applied to Cuba and the Soviet Union. The policy was now revenge.

Almost every year since the end of the war there has been a natural catastrophe in Vietnam. On October 18, 1982, Typhoon Nancy struck north central Vietnam and demolished acreages of maize, sweet potato, citrus and coffee crops; once more, people were beginning to starve. In 1982 the EEC embargo on powdered milk had been in force for three years. In April of that year the director of research at Saigon's Paediatric Hospital No. 2, Dr Duong Quynh Hoa, told Alfred McCreary, representing the World Council of Churches and Christian Aid, that the milk ban had been 'devastating'. The price of a kilo of milk powder had risen to ten times that of a kilo of meat; and based on World Health Organisation measurements, a survey had found that 30 per cent of children under five were suffering from malnutrition. In Dr Hoa's children's hospital, McCreary witnessed 'distressing scenes of deprivation . . . I saw children stunted and malnourished, and babies who were blind due to a lack of Vitamin A'.[78] The EEC was then supplying large quantities of its surplus food to repressive regimes in Haiti, Uruguay and Chile. 'Our primary adversary in Vietnam was the Soviet Union', wrote the former US secretary of state, General Alexander Haig.[79] The United States was then supplying large quantities of its surplus food to the Soviet Union, which it denied to Vietnam.

Since 1981, under the Trading with the Enemy Act, a legacy of the First World War, American voluntary agencies have been denied export licences for humanitarian aid to Indo-China. This banned aid has consisted of modest amounts of seed-processing and storage equipment which Oxfam America promised to an agricultural co-operative in Vietnam and assistance in setting up a small bee-keeping co-operative designed to supply honey as a food supplement to pre-school and kindergarten children.

Revenge as policy has been internationalised. For six months the US government fought to stop the United Nations Development Programme from helping to rebuild Vietnam's broken railways. American officials argued that twenty-six locomotives for the southern region would allow the Vietnamese to move freight 'right up to the Cambodian border'. The UNDP pointed out that not only were railways essential to the restoration of an agricultural economy, but that there was no line running towards or near the border with Cambodia or on the other side of the border.

The loan was eventually approved, but American lobbying had succeeded in delaying it for a year. Similarly, other international financial institutions with which Vietnam had or might have had an arrangement found their very existence jeopardised by the threat of withdrawal of American funds.

At least a million Vietnamese are believed to be suffering from the effects of Agent Orange. In 1983 American veterans who had been sprayed with the herbicide received an out of court settlement of $180 million. The Vietnamese received nothing. During the litigation the National Cancer Institute in Washington conducted extensive research into the effects of the herbicide and reached a number of important conclusions; little of this knowledge has reached Vietnam, where a group of distinguished Hanoi doctors, led by Professors Lang, Tung, Van and Tuyen, has investigated, with minimal resources, the symptoms and long-term effects of Agent Orange, especially on children. They have no computers or other modern statistical services; even their microscopes are old and few. In the South much of the modern medical equipment is American and in need of spare parts, which are embargoed.

There are myriad problems of economic management, war ruin, reconciliation and human rights outstanding in Vietnam today. There are thousands of political prisoners still held without trial in 're-education camps', most of them former military officers and officials of the old regime and some of them nationalists of the 'third force' who have continued to be 'obstinate'. Reconciliation, not revenge, almost certainly would set free those in the camps.

There are many in Vietnam who wish to see, as one of them once said to me, 'our country step forward from the shadows'. They believe that forty years of cold war between the Eastern and Western blocs offer the opportunity of creating a new synthesis, perhaps an Asian Yugoslavia, but that enforced dependence on the Soviet Union unbalances the equation. It is no paradox that Americans are welcomed in the streets of Hanoi while Soviet benefactors are often regarded with less equanimity.

But they are also welcomed for reasons of simple generosity. How can it *not* be generosity in the circumstances? 'We have smashed the country to bits', wrote Telford Taylor, chief United States prosecutor at the Nuremberg trials, 'and [we] will not even take the trouble to clean up the blood and rubble. Somehow we have failed to learn the lessons we undertook to teach at Nuremberg.'[80] He was referring not to Germany, of course, but to Vietnam.

V

AFRICA

23

Skin deep

Cape Town: January 1967. Meish and I had flown from Johannesburg on the morning South African Airways Boeing, whose blinding tangerine and gold upholstery, along with the preposterous Bavarian-style hats of the stewardesses, complemented my growing depression: such had been the events of the night before. A friend of mischief and courage, Meish Levin was a star muckraker on the Johannesburg *Sunday Times*, a man whose love of his country was equalled only by his loathing for its political system, whose passions were brandy and exposing the iniquities of the ruling Nationalist Party and coming up with a scandalous morsel in time for his Saturday deadline, and who once distinguished himself by striding up to Johannes Vorster, then Minister of Justice, at Jan Smuts Airport and bellowing at him, to the horror of assembled notables, 'You're nothing but a fucking Nazi, man!'

Meish had said, in a lunchtime bar, that it was time he broke the law again and that we should go to Soweto, the African township ten miles from Johannesburg. I had not been there, although it was South Africa's largest city.

'We'll go by train,' he said, and patted the flask of brandy in his hip pocket. 'Fuck 'em, man.'

Our taxi stopped at the main entrance, which was palatial and shining clean, as railway stations are not meant to be, and almost empty; the few people were white, save a sprinkling of blacks at the end of brooms. We bought tickets, returned to the forecourt and walked to the back of the station where the white faces evaporated. Here black South Africans went home in what was less a commuters' rush hour than an evacuation.

'Hey, where are you two goin'?' shouted the only white man, a railway guard.

'Up you man!' replied Meish, as we leapt over a turnstile, waving our tickets.

The train shuddered, whistles blew; people fought to get on board, using knuckles, boots, bags. Meish, a small, hunched man with bifocalled eyes like a crayfish, put an elbow into the human wall, opened a crack in it and we boarded and left with the train.

Our carriage, a decrepit, airless container, was for non-whites only, and our intrusion into this world was now under consideration by our fellow passengers, who it was clear had not seen white men playing this game. Packed like livestock, and with people hanging from the open door and other people hanging on to them and others on to them, we sweated. Outside the train, it was a normal sticky summer's evening: inside it was a kiln. The face not an inch from mine decanted sweat, filling the eyes so they could not close, splashing on to the neck. Every long summer's night this happened to him.

This was the last train of the day to Soweto. For a black man or woman to miss this train and to be in 'Jo'burg' after dark without a special stamp in his or her pass-book, which the law required Africans to carry at all times, meant the risk of arrest, a beating, a fine of three weeks' wages or a month in gaol or, worse, another stamp in the pass-book which meant exile in an alien, distant Bantustan or 'homeland', without work. 'The native should only be allowed to enter the urban areas', pronounced a Transvaal Government Commission in the 1920s, 'when he is willing to minister to the needs of the white man and he should depart therefrom when he ceases so to minister.' And that was still the law in 1985. The fear of missing this train, of 'crossing the police', was such that murderous brawling before and during the journey was not uncommon; and bodies found beside the track seldom prompted more than perfunctory police enquiries.

'If this is what life in the lovely suburbs is all about, you can fucking well keep it!' announced Meish to our fellow travellers. Meish's belligerent humour knew neither shame nor fear. But it worked, breaking the hostile silence which had enveloped us since we had bullied our way into the carriage. The face pressed close to mine brought up a laugh from the belly, and a chorus of guffaws followed. Exhausted, drenched, apprehensive to say the least and with my money clip stolen, we climbed out at Soweto.

The man who had laughed was called Daniel. He was in his thirties and worked eleven hours a day, six days a week, building luxury flats in the white suburbs, for which he was paid £4. He, and a million Africans like him, were the staple of 'booming' South Africa: mere units of work capacity which could be trundled anywhere, without recourse from a society that divided their families and imposed sub-human living conditions on them in order that they could 'minister to the white man'. In 1973 Adam Raphael reported in the *Guardian*,[1] 'On the outskirts of Johannesburg in Alexandra, 24 vast tower blocks are being constructed to house 60,000 migrant workers strictly segregated according to sex. The structures have no lifts and no heating. Instead they are equipped with such amenities as electronically-controlled steel doors, charge offices and built-in cells.' Daniel counted himself lucky. He had the treasured stamp in his pass-book that allowed him to work in Johannesburg and live nearby with his family, all of which could be revoked if he missed the train.

It was now dark and there were no lights at the station. We stumbled along on an unmade road running beside the barbed-wire fence that surrounds Soweto and entered the township at a large sign which read, in English and Afrikaans, 'Bantu township prohibited for members of other races. Special permission may be obtained from the Bantu Administration'. The sign was lit up by one in a network of stadium-type floodlights.

Daniel befriended us. It was clear he enjoyed Meish's unyielding, cussing cynicism. There was a bunched-up fist in both of them and, anyway, Meish had passed him his brandy.

People sat in doorways and on the road, seeking respite from the heat compressed beneath their low corrugated-iron roofs. On sight of us they stared, mumbled, whooped; no policemen would stagger in like this, led by a six and a half foot black man, and whites with or without permits simply did not come here at night, for one good reason that the last year alone had seen an average of fourteen murders a week.

Daniel's wife, Minnie, assumed we were officials of some sort and assailed us with a litany of complaints about her life, and in particular her fruitless attempts over the years to secure a pass which would allow her to work in Johannesburg. One of their four daughters, Sylvia, pored over schoolbooks at a desk in the concrete kitchen, beneath one anaemic light bulb which dangled on an unravelling flex. 'She'll get right out of here one day,' said Daniel affectionately, clasping her neck. The one obsession Africans share with Afrikaners is education; but because in many areas the standards are kept deliberately low, a minority of black schoolchildren get beyond the first four years of lower primary schooling and they are fortunate if they get three hours' schooling a day.

Sylvia had on an English-style school uniform, with a school tie and white blouse that had been cared for meticulously. Above her, Sellotaped to the wall, was a newspaper picture of John Kennedy at his desk in the White House, the then universal symbol of hope acceptable in a country where the real heroes, the incarcerated Mandelas and Sobukwes, would surely have taken pride of place, if that were permitted.

Daniel listened impassively to his nagging Minnie; he said theirs had been a 'shilling-marriage', a marriage of convenience, which was common because only married men could qualify for a job in Johannesburg and a house in Soweto.

'She's good; she's got problems. Her TB is maybe fixed now, I don't know,' he said as we walked the half-mile to the nearest *shebang* where everybody, it seemed, got lit up or mindless on a thick, pink, stinking poison that came in cardboard boxes. They called it beer. One glimpse of us was enough to stop the talk. A man with his arms fixed rigidly in his jacket pockets lurched at us, fell across our table, got up and stammered angrily, something about a hospital and blood.

'He's saying', said Meish, 'that his father may die because he had to wait a day for a blood transfusion. There was plenty of white blood but the black blood had run out. It's a common complaint.'

A young man in a suit and tie approached. 'Who are you?' he said.

'I am a reporter from Britain.'

'What are you doing here?'

'I wanted to see for myself how black people have to live in South Africa.'

'What will you do with all this you have seen?'

'I'll write about it for my newspaper.'

'For white people to read?'

'Yes.'

He smashed a fist down in front of me, walked back to the bar, picked up a bottle and was disarmed before he could throw it. 'Go, man,' said Daniel. 'Go *now*.'

On our return to Johannesburg, by way of an exorbitant taxi ride, Meish and I went into the only bar we could find open, a ten-shilling-a-dance dive operated by a Greek. It was not long before a barfly overheard us, told us about his Scottish heritage and wanted to know what we were doing, where we had been. So we told him.

'Man you don't buy that bullshit of the Kaffir being badly off, do you?' Without waiting for an answer he shouted to the Greek behind the bar, 'Hey, Nick, bring out your Kaffir!'

A black man, of indeterminate old age, emerged and the barfly crooned at him. 'Here, boy, get me some Rothmans from the machine over there.' The old man got the cigarettes, and handed him the change, which the barfly threw on the floor. 'That's yours, boy,' he said, 'all of it! See my friends, see how good we treat Kaffirs!'

The old man went down on his knees and scooped up the change. What was remarkable, or perhaps not, was that almost exactly this performance had been played to me the previous year in a bar in Johannesburg.

Cape Town was a relief after Johannesburg; the difference is a delusion, of course, as familiarity quickly shows. I suppose Cape Town reminded me a little of Sydney, my home town: the bleached, surfy, seemingly relaxed way of the whites, most of whom were 'trying to get a colour up' on beaches where people whose colour was already up were banned. Cape Town was where Meish was based, with his wife Doreen, who was an equally spunky journalist, and a group of decent, intense friends, such as the artist Sue Mountain, who worked to maintain vital contacts with the 'other side': keeping nursery schools integrated, covering for black servants who lived illegally with their wives who also worked in white households, clinging to tenuous links of solidarity with the coloured (mixed race) community in District Six, whose belated, total disaffection was fast approaching after the government had announced plans to reclassify their homes as a white area and to remove them from the city.

For years, people with 'mixed' on their birth certificates had lived almost as whites in Cape Town. They broke the law every day by sitting in whites-only seats in buses, attending whites-only cinemas and concerts, staying at whites-only hotels and holding whites-only jobs. For those who found this continuing round of deceit too much and wanted to put the final official seal on their honorary white status – those who, in a poignant local expression, wanted to 'try for white' – there was an incredible body called the Race Classification Board: incredible, that is, to outsiders, but both credible and vital to those who had thrown their life's chips on white and now faced the prospect of all their winnings being expropriated. If they could prove to a tribunal of three that they appeared physically to be white and that they were generally accepted by the public as white, the Board had the power to alter the race classification on their identity card, which was a ticket to a lifetime of privilege or humiliation. Black-skinned people, of course, need not apply.

But the South African parliament had recently passed the Population Registration Amendment Bill, which tightened apartheid as never before by placing the emphasis in an appeal against race classification on descent and not on 'appearance and acceptance'. The new law now said that coloured descent meant coloured for life, no matter the 'whiteness' of skin. With typically meticulous devotion to detail, the legislators of apartheid made the amendment cover the 353 people waiting for their race to be reclassified.

In the week I left London a Cape boxer called Ronnie van der Walt received a letter from the Ministry of the Interior which read, 'In terms of the Population Distribution Act, you are hereby classified as a Coloured Person.' Ronnie van der Walt was a local hero, the welterweight who had beaten Willie Ludick, the South African champion and leading contender for the world title, and he was widely tipped to be the next champion. And van der Walt was an Afrikaner; his name and language were the products of Afrikanerdom; he was the proud grandson of Johannes van der Walt, one of South Africa's greatest wrestlers. He had gone to whites-only schools, fought on the whites-only circuit – coloured boxers, no matter how good, were lucky to get the equivalent of five pounds a fight – and, most important, he regarded himself as a white man with the Afrikaner's added, ingrained sense of exclusiveness. Naturally, he was a lifelong supporter of Dr Verwoerd's Nationalists, the party of apartheid.

To official eyes that had followed his career and the rapid growth of his popularity, however, Ronnie van der Walt was suspect. He was swarthy, as many Afrikaners are: due more often than not to prolific sexual contact with blacks during the Voortrek from the Cape to the Transvaal. Van der Walt was due to fight in a tournament at Cape Town's Green Point Stadium on the day he received the letter from the Ministry, a copy of which had gone to the Cape Boxing Control Board. Van der Walt's name was promptly deleted from the programme and wall posters with his picture were torn down. 'We had to do it', the secretary of the Board, Sydney Beck, told me, 'or Ronnie would have been fined or gaoled. The law says coloureds and whites can't step into the same ring and Ronnie, the poor bastard, is now a coloured.'

In fact, Ronnie van der Walt had been anxious and confused for months, since he had received an earlier letter from the Race Classification Board summoning him to Room 33 in the Old Training College Building and instructing him, in a handwritten postscript, to bring his wife and children.

Ronnie told me, 'I saw two men at different times. They tried to be polite, but it was difficult because they asked me questions like, "Who are your friends? Are they white?" I told them that nearly all my friends were white. One of them said, "All right, then, what are your fans? Aren't they your friends?" I said some of them were, but, man, I can't help it if coloured people like to watch a good fight. Why shouldn't they? The other man walked round Rachel, my wife, and the kids peering at us from every angle like you do when you buy an animal. He said nothing, just looked. Then he said, "Don't worry, I'll do my best for you." The children didn't understand, of course, but, man, we all cried when we got outside.'

To Ronnie, the shame of being declared a coloured man meant wearing a hat for the first time in his life, wide-brimmed, and pulled down over his eyes. 'In the bus today', he said, 'I compared my bare arm with the man in the seat next to me. If I'm black, I must be dreaming . . .'

The van der Walts' ordeal in Room 33 was mild compared with that
of others who were summoned or who asked to come before the Race
Classification Board. Theirs was also one of the few cases which, because
of Ronnie's standing in the sporting world, reached the Press. Even
when a case went on to the Supreme Court for further appeal, no names
were published. The hearings were secret, claimed the government, out
of respect to people who, in their desperation to be classified white, were
forced to renounce everything of which their ancestors might have been
proud. Such humanitarian concern might have been laudable if it were
not charlatanry. The proceedings in Room 33 were secret and it was
here that apartheid, as Meish put it succinctly, 'presents its arsehole'.

After transacting a bribe of considerable amount with a civil servant
subverted by Meish, I sat at the back of Room 33 during a hearing. The
Old Training College Building is in Queen Victoria Street, Cape Town.
On the second floor is Room 33, which is laid out like a magistrate's court,
with a witness box and tables for counsel representing the 'applicants' and
the Ministry of the Interior.

It was just after nine o'clock when the first family of the day was
ushered in. They were a middle-aged man, his wife and their two sons,
aged ten and eight. They were veld Afrikaners and their case was not
uncommon: the youngest son had been born with Negroid features and,
although he had been registered at birth as white and baptised as white
in that bastion of apartheid, the Dutch Reformed Church, the whispers
in the town had reached such a crescendo that the principal of the boy's
school was moved to write the following to his parents:

I can no longer ignore the concerns of other parents and, with the
authority invested in me by the Education Department, I must inform
you that your son must be withdrawn from this school until the status
of his European race has been made clear.

The following are excerpts from a translation of the Afrikaans dialogue,
which I recorded.

Magistrate to father: 'Tell us about your background . . . the line of
your family . . . your wife's family.'

Father: 'I worked at a garage. I am on the board of the rugby club . . .
I played in our First XV and injured myself seriously while playing . . .
my father played for the club . . . '

Magistrate: 'Yes, yes, that's very interesting, but to your knowledge,
did your father or grandfather co-habit with a Bantu?'

Father: 'No, certainly not . . . they were elders of the church . . . how
can you speak like that?'

Magistrate: 'I can speak like that because your neighbours, maybe people who know your family well, accuse your boy of having Bantu blood, and we must decide here and now what's to become of him. I must not only ask you, "Have you ever co-habited with a Bantu?" I must also ask you, "Is this *really* your boy?"'

Father: 'God help me, how can you say that in front of us . . . my boy standing here? Of course he is mine. I have the papers . . . '

Magistrate: 'Yes, yes we have seen them . . . ' (and now addressing the mother) 'It is my duty to ask you if your mother, to your knowledge, ever went with a Bantu? Or have you . . . ?'

Mother: 'Have I what?'

Magistrate: 'Have you ever been impregnated by a Bantu? . . . one of your boys?'

Mother (now crying): 'Stop this. What are you saying?'

Magistrate: 'Madam, we have to establish if there has been some intrusion into the genes.'

Mother: 'Genes? I don't know what these genes are.'

Magistrate to mother: 'I must say you look a little on the dark side. Is that the sun? Or is there a coloured . . . Bantu line there? You must not keep anything at all from us.'

Mother: 'Please, I am before God . . . of the church . . . white . . . ' She wept.

The cross-examination of the parents continued for an hour and a half, during which time the father admitted, on the point of tears, that his maternal grandfather had had the reputation of being 'a ladies man . . . a free spirit . . . he shunned the church'.

The son was called forward.

Magistrate: 'Do you feel you are a white?'

Son: 'Yes sir . . . I don't know any Bantu . . . only our boys . . . I am good at rugby, cricket. I do my lessons and pray . . . ' (He was intoning, as if trying to remember lines in a school play.)

Magistrate: 'Do your friends regard you as just like them . . . do you use the toilet when they go in there?'

Son: 'Yes, I have lots of friends at school . . . but some . . . some of them don't speak to me. Since this business began they say bad things . . . '

Magistrate: 'What do they say to you?'

Son: 'I . . . they . . . call me a white Kaffir . . . and treeboy.'

After the lunch break the three magistrates stepped down from the bench and called again to the son to come forward. One of them produced a comb, which he ran through the boy's hair, over and over again, after dipping it in a clear solution in a labelled bottle. When he had finished doing this, he lifted the boy's eyelids and inspected his gums. Finally, he ran both hands round the base of his skull. The three magistrates then muttered solemnly and concluded the proceedings by thanking everyone concerned.

Outside I asked the father what he would do if his son was classified coloured. 'What can I do,' he replied, 'but make him a house servant or something like that, otherwise he won't be able to live with us, will he?' The mother implored me not to use their names: the 'shame', she said, would destroy them.

Three months later, the Board upheld the family's appeal on the basis of descent and the son retained his white classification. But such was the stigma and hostility in their town that the family had to move away from the place where all of them had been born.

Ronnie van der Walt also lodged an appeal with the Board and his friends began to prepare a case that would prove his white descent. But they were aware that Rachel, his wife, had a coloured ancestry that could be traced. So even if Ronnie was reclassified white, he might not be able to live with his wife, because they would be contravening the Immorality Act, which then prohibited co-habitation between people of different racial classification. With his fight career ruined, Ronnie van der Walt did not wait for the appeal hearing. He took his family to Britain and, to my knowledge, has never returned to his beloved South Africa.

Shortly after my return to London I received a letter from the South African embassy banning me from the country. No reason was given.

In 1973 Meish Levin died with too much brandy and too much anger inside him.

In 1975 a message was passed to me that the new head of information at the South African embassy would like to meet me. His name was Christopher van der Walt, Ronnie's name. It is a common name in South Africa but how ironic, I thought. We met three times, during which he told me how much he hated apartheid and the 'old guard' and assured me that the young, enlightened Afrikaners, like himself, were taking power. Then he came to the point. 'Journalists like you who have been naughty in the past', he said in the curiously coy South African way, 'should have a go and apply for a visa. And when you get your visa, I shall give you a list of names of the right people, the *enlightened* people, to interview.' He said I would not know South Africa from my visit in the 1960s. 'The situation has changed out of all recognition,' he said.

I was still awaiting a reply to my visa application when the black rebellion broke out in Soweto in June 1976.

The following January the Johannesburg *Rand Daily Mail* published a list of 499 names of black people who were known to have died during the uprisings. Most of them had been shot by the police, some were children as young as four years old, many had been shot in the back and many were wounded, thrown into heaps by the police and deliberately left to die.

The uprising in the black township flared again in 1984 and 1985 and, at the time of writing, it has not died down. Untold hundreds have been killed and wounded, including many of those blacks drawn into the governing process of apartheid. A state of siege exists in most black townships, which are known locally as 'free zones' and are regarded by the white authorities as 'no go' areas.

However, the rulers of apartheid retain ubiquitous power of oppression, and perhaps the most profound change has been psychological, among both blacks and whites. Helen Suzman, the voice of white liberalism in South Africa, has told me that some whites are for the first time becoming frightened, now that the system appears to be in danger, and 'a lot of young people have left which is a very distressing part of it all'. Joe Slovo, military planner of the African National Congress, believes that 'the century-old African feeling of impotence has faded and there is the beginning of a feeling – I put it no higher than that – that the white monolith can be cracked'.[2]

24

Smithers of the river

St Louis, Senegal: October 1969. I lay out of the sun beneath a portico announcing *La Maison d'Esclaves*, the House of Slaves, a bleached little ruin listing into the Senegal River and lapped by sewage and the green foam of a fertiliser factory's waste. The Portuguese are believed to have been the original architects, with the French adding the stucco. Both nationalities, and the English, used it as a way station to Goree Island, the African Alcatraz, lying just off The Hump, where the best young men and women were packed like dried fish into the holds of ships and dispatched to the auction blocks of the Americas. The dungeons, which had ceilings no higher than a child, are now open and the long steps down into them are concave, having been worn by the weather and those human feet which survived the river journey from their village to the sea, and waited here, in chains, until a number was bellowed and a final inspection was made; lameness, disease or death meant an early freedom. Old Black Joe, Harlem, Watts, 'We Shall Overcome' sung on the roads to Alabama, freedom rides, Martin Luther King's 'dream': all that began here.

Facing the House of Slaves, where the river became suddenly a great moving belt as wide as a lake, was a graveyard of nineteenth-century river boats, rusted *African Queens*, exquisite things with their woodburners like periscopes and the name-plates visible: *Mary Queen of Scots* and *Hallelujah*. Directly behind me, across the only road, people had gathered to watch our expedition make ready at the stone jetty: some of them under trees and some standing like cranes, raising each foot alternately from the new asphalt turned to molasses by the sun, and some of them mourners, in procession to another graveyard. These people wore white sheets, giving the impression of black Romans, and they waited patiently to bury the day's quota of dead, which were carried in coffins or in containers made of fruit boxes and flattened Fanta cans or wrapped in palm leaves, depending on the station of the deceased; and when their turn came they did their job so quickly that the corpses lay barely beneath the ground, just peppered with dirt and each with a stick or a broomhandle as a headstone, forming, as night came, a horizon of contorted silhouettes. Many of them, I was told, were diseased and malnourished children; a reminder perhaps, to those members of our expedition who complained of the stench, of what Africa does to its people, as a matter of longstanding routine.

I had gone to the House of Slaves to seek refuge from my leader, David Smithers. There would only be one more escape before Timbuktu, though there would be other attempts; but from dawn the next day I would be incarcerated with Smithers of East Grinstead, with Captain Energy and a mysterious American called Bob, and with a detachment of the British Army who were meant not to exist and whose real identities I was sworn by my leader not to report. There were also the scientists: notably Hans Jergens, a German anthropologist whose speciality was the shape of human heads. The French had sent a parasitologist, the British a biologist/botanist and a geographer and an 'aeromedical survival expert'. In addition, there was a United Nations guide who did reckonings with a twelve-inch school ruler, a German writer, a BBC television crew and photographer Peter Stone, whom the *Daily Mirror* had sent with me. In all there were nineteen of us assembled at St Louis, where we were to fill a hovercraft.

It was a vintage hovercraft recently repossessed after punishing and unprofitable service on the Bay of Naples, and it would take us on 'the most audacious inland journey since Stanley crossed the Congo and Mungo Park sailed the River Niger to Timbuktu'. At least that was how I reported our departure then and although I am tempted now to delete audacious and insert ridiculous, I believe the description was correct, though for reasons of which I was completely unaware at the time I wrote it.

The expedition was sponsored by Harold Wilson's fabulous failure, the Ministry of Technology, and by Shell, the British Hovercraft Corporation, the BBC and Cecil King's International Publishing Corporation, which not only published the newspaper I worked for but ran an 'IPC Exploration Unit' from a fifth-floor office of its Holborn Circus headquarters, headed by the enigmatic Smithers. I was assigned to report the expedition's progress or, perhaps more to the point, to justify the money-raising and public relations campaign mounted by David Smithers. I was, in this last respect, an unwise choice, although I suspected that the then editor of the *Mirror*, Lee Howard, a man with a gentle sense of mischief, knew what he was doing.

In Lee's office, after Smithers had excitedly unveiled voluminous maps and charts of the Rivers Senegal, Niger, Benue, Logone, Chari, Oubangui and Congo, and had finished his lecture, with the aid of a pointer, on what the exhibition would achieve – 'We shall open up the great trans-African water route which eluded the explorers! . . . We shall now show the way for hovercraft hospitals! . . . hovercraft schools!' – Lee leaned on his braces and said, 'If that's all true, then it's a story. If it isn't true then I suggest one of you gentlemen is sacrificed to a crocodile. We'll at least get *that* in the paper.'

On the morning we left St Louis, David Smithers, the wind wagging the peak of his red baseball cap as he bestrode the bows acknowledging the tom-tom dancers hired for the occasion, told me that one of the principal backers had threatened to withdraw much of its support for the expedition if I was to be the reporter on board. When I asked why, he held a 'can't tell' finger to his lips. However, the reason for the Corporation's concern soon became apparent as we set out to hover 7,000 miles from the Atlantic to the centre of Africa, and back to the sea. This, I wrote at the time, had never been done before in a hovercraft; neither, on reflection, had it ever been done on roller skates.

The commander of the hovercraft was Peter Ayles, a former pilot and a great, ruddy and genial bundle of professionalism, who, it seemed, was the only one on board who knew where we were going, having most of that year flown, rowed and walked over the route. Behind Ayles sat Smithers, son of a missionary and luminously pallid. Smithers' publicity handout for the expedition noted that he had walked from Benghazi to London, lived with cannibals in the rain forests of Brazil and intended to stand as the Liberal candidate for East Grinstead.

Whatever Smithers had been, his immediate past was known to Bob Saunders, the BBC's producer on the expedition. Saunders, who made *World About Us* programmes, had filmed the first Smithers hovercraft expedition up the Amazon against considerable odds. Saunders remembered Smithers as being inseparable from his little spade, which had been issued to all members of the expedition with orders to use it as part of the ritual of crapping in the jungle. In spite of such precautions, poor Smithers succumbed to a fever, the lasting effects of which were sporadic screams in the night; we would hear these screams, often with frightening clarity, over our campsites all the way to Timbuktu.

At the first stop, a riverside town called Richard Toll, the expedition established a pattern of greeting. The Beast would thunder around a bend, up the bank and ease its remarkable flatulence with one almighty hiss, having showered the assembled municipal notables with dust and mud. Our departure would mean another brown cascade for all; and although the people in the towns and villages showed much good nature, it was clear that we left many of them in a state of confusion as to the precise nature of our mission.

We would come in our hissing, heaving, detonating contraption, rather like a rich boy showing his noisy new toy to the poor boy next door; we would soak the citizens, disturb the fishing, ruin the washing, and disappear. The deeper into the continent we went, the sillier it all became. I shall not forget the faces of fishermen in one impoverished village, who might well have been interested in some assistance in improving the strain of their catch or in combating the river blindness of their children but instead were shown the wondrous irrelevance of a Polaroid camera. Meanwhile the eminent geographer took his notes and the Kew Gardens biologist/botanist pressed his flowers and the German anthropologist inspected the shape of heads and the French parasitologist jotted down the names of myriad parasites likely to be in the distended bellies all about him. In addition, a truly bizarre figure, sweating painfully in a version of an astronaut's suit, observed the reactions of us hovering explorers. Known affectionately to us as 'Captain Energy', he was a 'human resources expert' whose job was to report on how we adjusted to our environment and how we got on together, as we hovered along. He carried stopwatches and gauges and clipboards of questionnaires, and his own body, as gaunt as a pipe-cleaner, played guinea-pig under his masochistic costume. The impoverished fishermen surveyed him, and all of us, with mounting incredulity. Their faces, smiling and pitying, were just visible through our departing spray.

David Smithers had a routine at each stop, to which I very much looked forward. He would leap ashore, grasp the local, now drenched mayor by the hand and, with his red baseball cap over his heart, make a little speech which went like this:

> We have come only in peace! We have come from colder climes and your sun has warmed our hearts! We bring greetings from Her Majesty the Queen, and His Royal Highness the Duke of Edinburgh! And we bring gifts all the way from Great Britain!

The gifts were not quite beads. They included boxes of sweets called Spangles, boxes of teabags, and boxes of paper underpants, which were regulation issue to us; these were the expressions of our esteem. Then the drummers would form around Smithers, and as the primitive beat came in salvoes, our leader's gaze would seem to recede into the last century.

At Podor, still in Senegal, our leader inspected a most remarkable guard of honour. Standing impeccably to attention, each man carried a gilt-fringed flag on which was inscribed '*Anciens Combattants de*

Podor' – Old Soldiers of Podor – and each wore a chest of medals on his robes, and none was younger than eighty. Here a generous feast was held by moonlight and a whole sheep produced: a particular delight for those whose meat is never rare enough. For dessert, we had festive cakes about which Smithers was so ecstatic he decided to make another speech. He asked the interpreter, 'By the way, what were the ingredients?'

'Flour and human semen,' was the reply.

Because a hovercraft is like an aircraft in design and temperament, its payload must be carefully weighed. Peter Ayles reckoned that we were now overweight by a ton. After one overnight stop, and with the villagers convinced of our collective lunacy, we jettisoned tents, stoves, lamps, Spangles, paper underpants and teabags. Peter Stone and I arrived at this ceremony just in time to see our leader about to cast off a crate of whisky, but our pledge to do extra Little Spade duty went straight to his heart. He paused just long enough for me to wrest the whisky from him.

In the seats behind David Smithers sat the men of the British Army who were meant not to exist. But enquiries revealed that their leader, Don Patterson, was a captain and the others were non-commissioned officers. They were systematic, hard-working and likeable men, but when I questioned Don Patterson about their role in the expedition, his reply was that whatever I did I must not say they were Army. 'It could wreck the whole thing,' he said. He would not say why, nor explain what 'the whole thing' was.

Behind the Army men sat Bob, the uncommunicative and diffident American, whose source of employment was obscure and who received, at every major town where we stopped, a 'drop' of US Army C-rations (hot dogs, canned bread, Coke) and dispatched his copious film and tapes via the same courier system. Bob was being resupplied with amazing efficiency right across the African continent. But Bob, said Smithers, was merely doing 'research'. When we entered the Republic of Mali, which is strongly nationalist and aided by the communist world and then did not encourage visits or extended travel by Americans, Bob would aim his motor-drive camera, not at flora and fauna but at Chinese and Soviet installations. He shot bags of film.

'Are you from the CIA?' I asked Bob.

'Gee, I'm sorry,' he replied with a smile, 'I can't really say anything to you.'

Early the next morning we hissed into Kayes, in Mali, reputedly the hottest point on the African continent. Here we would leave the Senegal River and our four tons of capricious technology would be taken apart by the Army men and lifted, without a crane, on to a train that would carry it 250 miles to Bamako, Mali's capital, and to the River Niger. When I asked the Army captain, Don Patterson, why there were no special tools for dismantling the hovercraft, he said, 'It's all part of the exercise . . . it's never been done before, you see . . . hush, hush.' It was indeed all part of the exercise and Don and the Army boys accomplished it brilliantly by jacking one end up and then the other, and then the other.

One morning, as the hovercraft's torso lay in the centre of Kayes, awaiting the train, a small but significant drama unfolded. The hovercraft carried some of the most spectacular radio equipment I have seen and every day Don Patterson would tune into and chat to a chirpy, whizzo voice at the Ministry of Defence Establishment at Lee Slip, Isle of Wight.

'Good morning, Don. How goes it?' said Whizzo.

'Good morning . . . wait on, closing down now . . . bit of an emergency . . . over and out.'

A Soviet-made jeep full of Malian soldiers approached us. 'Stow it, for Christ's sake,' said Patterson, and our mighty radio telescoped into the guise of a normal VHF. Jolly gesticulations were exchanged with the Malian troops and our boys wiped their foreheads.

'No more contact with base till we're on our way,' said Patterson sternly to his men.

Time in Kayes passed like a snail with a stroke. Bob Saunders, his BBC cameraman Butch Calderwood, the sound recordist Peter Smith, Peter Stone and I moved into a former prison, now run as a hotel by Monsieur Lamez. A bulbous, stone-like figure with almost nothing to say, he was one of six Europeans left behind when the French abandoned this regional centre of their West African empire. In the early morning, between six and seven, Monsieur Lamez would talk to his monkeys. At dusk he would sit facing his great prison gate and stare through the bars at nothing. And at night he could be heard tap-tapping with his cane, round and round the old exercise yard. Whenever we enquired about other guests, Monsieur Lamez would say, '*Cet hôtel est tout complet*'; but all the windows were shuttered and we saw no one. It was pointed out that Monsieur Lamez had been in Kayes forty-one years.

The only light in the only paved street of Kayes was that of the only bar, 'The Guys with Dolls'. The proprietor was a young man who attempted to affect the style of the then popular Super Fly: shades, Afrocut, yellow shirt, black bell-bottoms. Shades had his place rigged for hi-fi, and the flamingos around the next bend of the river might well have heard the beat; but sadly, he possessed only two records, an early album by James Brown and the Mali National Anthem. He played them alternately. Few of his customers stayed to listen, preferring to drink their beer down by the river. One who did stay in the bar, as if transfixed, was Jesse Davis, a former insurance salesman and clarinetist from Madison, Wisconsin: a decidedly melancholy figure who would sit over a soft drink at the only table outside nodding to the beat of James Brown and staring impassively through the Mali National Anthem.

'Are you an American?' he asked me one night, and when I said no, he was visibly disappointed. He was an American, intelligent, highly articulate and still living in the 1960s. He told me he had come to Africa at the height of the 'Back to Africa' movement in the United States. 'I came as a pilgrim,' he said. 'It was the year Watts exploded. It was when American blacks were knocking down every myth about themselves and, of course, picking up new ones. Africa was no longer the primitive, heathen dark place which blacks never spoke about, except in white society's terms of Tarzans and savages. Africa became the place to extol, to copy and dream about seeing for yourself. For me, I wanted to be in a racial situation that counted me *in* instead of *out* . . . I came with a lot of people, Black Panther people, people like that, who I guess have since gone home; there were problems and there still are, but I'm hanging in here a while yet.'

I asked him how Africans had accepted him, a black man from America. 'The first surprise was *not* being accepted,' he said. 'When the Africans I met couldn't sort out my tribe, my language and my back-ground, they either left me alone or treated me like an American tourist or a white man. They called me "Mr Jesse"! I had my movie camera stolen, like any dumb tourist; and what rubbed in the salt was the reaction of the whites, who didn't reject me because of my blackness but accepted me on the basis of my American background. I'd be in somebody's nice house and he'd say, "The boy will get you a drink." What I've learned is that a black American is not an African; he is an American; no, he is an *exaggerated* American.'

The hovercraft was now lashed to rolling stock of the Republic of Mali Railways, which had exhumed a passenger carriage of Crimean vintage without light, food or water: a bare black metal box. Indeed, of all the trains I have known, the Night Train to Bamako will remain the most sinister and the silliest. The station master, a biblical figure in his puce and blue *bou-bou* robes, bade us farewell with a solemn salute which he did not relax until we were out of sight, and the train's driver, Monsieur Rubens, an elegant young Malian in a tailored pink safari suit, sounded his horn in order to clear the track of sheep and shepherds. Except for a weaver bird falling and ascending and an eagle mesmerised on the branch of a dead tree, there was no other life, no movement but ours. Wildlife in most of West Africa, the elephants, lions, giraffes, hippos, had succumbed to drought or had been shot.

It was now dark and raining as if from the lip of falls directly above us. The black metal box, which had long discarded its windows, was filling with water. David Smithers sat cross-legged on the floor, with the water rising towards his knees and a tape recorder held to his ear on which he played Bach at full volume. The train stopped. From out of the bush two hooded apparitions lurched and climbed aboard. One was robed in black, the other in white – monks, we thought – and they stood before us, saying nothing. When our leader offered them each a packet of Spangles, they shook their heads, then they jumped from the train, screaming, and were gone.

Eric Verg, the German writer travelling with us, took advantage of this unexplained stop to return from the front of the train where he had met the engineer, a Russian. 'He saw me and he sobbed,' said Verg. 'He said he had been running this train for eight months. He was a pitiful sight.'

The rain had a steel-hammer rhythm now and the train was drowning. Our leader comforted us with more Bach. Twenty-two hours later we reached Bamako, where I found the *General A. Soumare* at anchor. I wasted no time in planning my passage to Timbuktu, my escape.

I have known few journeys to compare with that of the *General A. Soumare*, one of the last great river steamers in Africa, having been made in Germany in 1918 and brought overland in pieces by donkey and train. The *General*, as the steamer is known affectionately in Mali, sails every now and then along the River Niger: north through the great lakes and the threadlike canals, the sandbanks and islets of papyrus, to the river's Great Bend and on to Timbuktu.

I told David Smithers that I would catch up with the hovercraft in Timbuktu and sailed that evening in the company of a young Malian, Minkeila Dallo, who worked for the government. At twenty-three he spoke seven languages and was typical of a generation of young Africans who sought a way for themselves and their country between those of Europe and the tribe. He was going home on leave to his Songhay village near Gao, former capital of the Songhay empire and one stop past Timbuktu. In one of Minkeila's history books I came upon a passage which reflected the pride being chronicled retrospectively in Africa. It read:

in 1066 William of Normandy crossed the English Channel to conquer Anglo-Saxon England. What would have been his chances if, instead, he had fought the imperial armies of Africa. But, of course, no one knew of Africa, her law courts, her Islamic universities, her Golden Age . . .

The *General* was a floating carnival. At each stop her loudspeakers offered a broadside of the Beatles, while a cargo of millet, water, leather, brass bedsteads and cloth flecked with gold was exchanged for a clutch of Baptist missionaries, half-drowned in a sea of Islam. On the fourth night, as if by a signal, black Africa slipped away and with it all green. We had tied up at Kabara, the port of Timbuktu, and the crowd was different: quiet, intense and mostly Tuaregs, the descendants of the Moors and enemy of the Songhay. They wore encrusted daggers at their waists and had faces like foxes.

Timbuktu stood almost as it had been when it was founded fourteen years after the Battle of Hastings. In 1828 the explorer René Caillé wrote after he first sighted Timbuktu, 'The sky was pale red . . . and the most profound silence on earth prevailed.'[3] Except for the wail of the devout, Timbuktu seemed, indeed, a city without sound. There were no cars and the streets were white streams of moving sand. The houses were flat and square and the colour of sand, which was also the colour of the sky, so that they appeared to merge and were broken only by the spires of three mosques and by the red turrets of a fort which the Foreign Legion had garrisoned.

Timbuktu's reputation, apart from being for Europeans the symbol of the inaccessible, was as a centre where gold was exchanged for salt, which still arrived, in slabs, by caravan and camel train. Tuareg women still weighted their ears with gold; old men and children still searched the mud for gold. Today, if you have salt, you can have gold. Minkeila pointed out a group of young men in rags, drawing water from a well in goatskin bags. 'They are *Bella*,' he said. 'That means slaves. They are free now, of course, but few of them will ever leave the families to which their fathers and grandfathers were bonded.'

In the bar of my hotel, which has to be rebuilt every decade as the sand begins to cover it, behind a Glenlivet bottle and a Hennessy bottle standing alone and almost empty between little piles of sand, there was a telephone. It had a long, ornate receiver and legs of gold in the shape of lions' paws. On my second evening in Timbuktu the hotel experienced a major upheaval. The telephone rang. The manager was summoned to answer it – no one else appeared to dare – while Peter Stone and I, and the others in the doorway who had heard the strange sound, watched with interest.

'Hello,' said the manager. 'Who?' he said. And then to me: 'I believe it is for you.' A telephone had rung in Timbuktu and someone had asked for me; I knew no one in Timbuktu. 'Hello?' I said. But whoever it was had hung up.

The hovercraft arrived in Timbuktu, heaved out of the Niger and began its run toward the town and the Sahara, creating a sand storm that blew over a salt-laden camel. It got almost as far as the '*Bienvenue à Timbuctou*' sign when its great rubber skirts began to sag.

'Sorry, old boy, she won't do the desert,' shouted the indomitable

Peter Ayles to David Smithers. And there the Beast remained until the expedition turned south-east, toward Lake Chad.

Answering a selenic call from my editor, I caught the weekly Dakota to Bamako and flew on to Casablanca and London. Peter Stone escaped in Chad, but only after his wife had pleaded for his release on humanitarian grounds. Captain Energy, the 'human resources expert', was flown home suffering from exhaustion. Bob, the suspected CIA man, continued to slip away into the bush and desert and to exchange his film and tapes for hot dogs and canned bread. The hovercraft detonated its way to Kinshasa on the Congo, and the following January it reached the Atlantic where it was wrecked by a large wave.

Back in London, I was commissioned to write the commentary for two of Bob Saunders' three BBC films about the expedition. When the films were previewed, David Smithers enlisted IPC's lawyers to persuade the BBC to delete all mention of an incident which, for me, summed up the whole gruelling farce: the hovercraft's destruction of fields of precious ripened corn being harvested by poor farmers in Niger, who were compensated, begrudgingly, with a pittance. Most of the episode remained in the film.

At a banquet in the Guildhall David Smithers celebrated his triumphant return to London. A telegram of congratulations from Prince Philip was read out and Harold Wilson made a speech in which he agreed with David Smithers that 'the hovercraft will now be finding its place in developing countries in exploiting resources and opening new regions'.

Sixteen years later no such thing has happened, or is planned, or is likely to happen. The expedition produced learned articles and learned lectures and a book about plants by Nigel Hepper, the Kew Gardens biologist/botanist. It also helped to fill the British Hovercraft Corporation's order book for special, jungle-tested hovercraft for the US Army in Vietnam. Within a year I was to see this military version in action on the Mekong River, on other 'audacious' journeys, strafing villages, killing people, 'finding its place' in a developing country.

25

'No story down there'

As I began to write this chapter, on the eve of the greatest 'natural' disaster in modern history, the 1983–5 famine in Africa, a group of disconsolate journalists returned to Khartoum from Eritrea, where 32 million people have been resisting extinction for almost a quarter of a century. The journalists had seen no set-piece battles and taken no dramatic pictures of war. 'All that hassle for nothing,' said one of them, a veteran of Vietnam. 'There's no story down there.'

When I first went to Eritrea, in the spring of 1978, the war was in its seventeenth year. For longer than he could remember Gebreab Tmarian had amputated a limb, 'every other night' by candlelight, relying entirely on his memory of surgical operations at the American Hospital in Asmara where he had once worked as a scrub nurse. His precious hoard of anaesthetics had run out completely and he was forced to operate using only a saw, surgical spirit and a mouth gag. In his 'hospital', as in others in Eritrea, stocks of blood, antiseptics, antibiotics and anti-malarials had been exhausted and were not replenished; as a consequence a policy of *triage* was introduced. Under *triage*, a term coined by the French during the carnage of the Somme, the most seriously ill were allowed to die because the drugs which might possibly have saved them were kept for those with at least an even chance of survival.

Thus, the victims of cluster bombs were allowed to die. The cluster bombs used against Eritrea were made in the United States, supplied by Israel and dropped by Soviet aircraft which were piloted by Ethiopians and occasionally by Cubans. They carried a device which sprayed minute needles designed to 'swim' through flesh and organs and were difficult to detect, even by X-ray. This type of bomb was developed for 'anti-personnel' work in Vietnam, where I saw its effects on civilians.

Of the thirty-three wars fought since 1945, Eritrea's is the only war to which none of the reporter's shorthand labels will stick. 'Pro-West', 'Pro-Soviet', 'Marxist', etcetera: all are seen to be meaningless because Eritrea's enemies have come at her from over every ideological horizon, from both 'imperialist' and 'revolutionary' Ethiopia, from both the United States and the Soviet Union and their respective clients, Israel and Cuba. The struggle of this nation of beleaguered people is not only heroic in the classic sense but a negation of the hoary, though still fashionable, Kissinger view that all the world is a chess game in which the small, resource-impoverished nations are pawns and can be moved at will, or declared expendable. Having been systematically duped, terrorised, starved and bombed, as well as shunned by most of the international relief organisations (with honourable exceptions, such as Britain's War on Want), the Eritreans have fought back and have regained 90 per cent of their homeland, including 600 miles of some of the most strategic coastline on earth: that slim neck of the Red Sea through which pass much of Western Europe's raw material.

Since 1961, in spite of a poverty harsh even by the standards of the poor world, the Eritreans have begun to build – in isolation – a self-reliant, humane and literate society in which the national burden is shared by most and the seeds of industrialisation have taken root on peasant land. They are achieving this unaided, except for a modicum of Arab cash and a right-of-way through Sudan. Most of their arms, trucks, machines and tools either have been captured from the Ethiopians or are the products of their own ingenuity, made on underground assembly lines without equal in the Third World. Even their dogma, a stewpot of basic Marxism, has been usurped by years of bloody experience and betrayal. 'It may sound preposterous to you', a teacher who had studied in Britain told me, 'but we have no left-wing and no right-wing. These are European concepts which have no application in Eritrea, or probably anywhere in Africa. How can we possibly use these stupid terms? We have been let down too often. We are ourselves: and we have no political debts.'

The Eritreans have never had to convince each other that their home-grown socialism is the right way for them, because there has been no other way to survive. Neither has Arab or Muslim nationalism any place in Eritrea, for the Eritreans are equally Muslims and Christians. All of this perhaps explains why the leadership of the main revolutionary group, the Eritrean People's Liberation Front, has remained relatively obscure and has changed constantly, without sustained upheaval. There is no Fidel Castro because, the EPLF say, there is no need: and they pay only lip service to an international socialist fraternity. With good reason. The Soviet Union used to trumpet the Eritreans' right to independence until strategic opportunities in Africa presented themselves to Moscow; and the Cubans, who armed the first guerrillas of the EPLF, have built airfields from which Ethiopian jets drop Napalm and cluster bombs.

Eritrea caught my imagination in the early 1960s when their struggle was new and I met, in Port Sudan, a man who had endured indescribable tortures at the hands of the Ethiopians, yet retained grace and humour and a commitment to what seemed then, to me at least, a fruitless cause. I wanted to know why they fought and held out against such odds, who they were and why so little was understood about their struggle. They were something of a mystery.

Eritrea lies at the intersection of Africa and the Middle East. It is bordered by the Red Sea in the east, Sudan in the north and west and Ethiopia and Djibouti in the south. After the collapse in the seventh century of the Axumite civilisation, which had integrated Semites with the original Negroid population, the area fell into a long succession of internecine wars between feudal kingdoms, Christian highlanders, Muslim lowlanders, slavers and others, until the arrival of the Turks and Egyptians and finally the Italians in the late nineteenth century. The Italians did what all the colonialist powers did; they exploited and they defined a nation; Eritrea is an Italian word. They built factories, organised the land and educated the few, and they drew borders. In 1941 they were driven out by the British.

A treacherous John Bull appears on the posters of the EPLF, yet the British still hold pockets of goodwill in Eritrea. From 1941 to 1950 some of Britain's best colonial administrators went to Eritrea and are remembered with nostalgia by the older generation as the first foreigners to recognise the strength of the Eritrean case for independence. After the Second World War, the British government and two international commissions agonised about what to do with Eritrea. In 1952 Britain finally fell in with a United Nations decision, backed by America, to 'constitute an autonomous unit federated with Ethiopia'.

The Americans had promoted the federated solution as part of their cold war policies and with little regard to the merits of the case, as the US Secretary of State, John Foster Dulles, made clear when addressing the Security Council in 1952. He said that regardless of 'the point of view of justice' the strategic interest of the United States in the Red Sea basin and considerations of world peace 'make it necessary that the country [Eritrea] has to be linked with our ally, Ethiopia'.[4]

The Emperor Haile Selasse had dutifully supplied an Ethiopian brigade to fight in the Korean war, and the Americans wanted to shore up his regime, for much the same reasons that the Russians are helping to prop up his successors. For the Americans then, the immediate prize was the Kagnew communications station in the Eritrean capital of

Asmara. For the Russians now, it is the deep-water port of Massawa on the Eritrean Red Sea coast. For those in power in Addis Ababa – be they the courtiers of the Lion of Judah or the 'revolutionary Marxist' leadership of the Dergue, the Ethiopian military junta – Eritrea has represented a route to the sea: a tract of necessary earth inhabited by unnecessary people. And genocide by attrition has been their common strategy.

A member of the British administration in Eritrea, Sir Kennedy Trevaskis, wrote in *The Times*:

> In the circumstances of a country which was then almost evenly divided between Moslems who were demanding independence and Coptic Christians who wanted union with Ethiopians, it [the federation with Ethiopia] was not an unreasonable decision. Nevertheless . . . a blatant Ethiopian campaign of bribery, blackmail and intimidation was later launched against the newly-constituted Eritrean legislature enabling the Emperor, Haile Selasse, to annex Eritrea in 1962 with its ostensible consent. The Eritreans were left to seek their own salvation.[5]

In fact, the Eritrean parliament 'voted' for absorption into Ethiopia with Ethiopian guns trained on them from the galleries. The Emperor's troops immediately occupied Eritrea, the main Eritrean languages of Triginaya and Tigre were banned, leading partisans were murdered, thousands were imprisoned and a war of resistance began.

Ethiopian bombs, which did not distinguish between those of different faiths, quickly dissolved any Christian desire to join the Emperor. Thus, Christians are now prominent in both liberation groups, the EPLF having broken away from the more conservative Eritrean Liberation Front. The warring between the two groups has been one of the unfortunate diversions of the Eritrean struggle. That the ELF is supposed to be 'more Muslim' and the EPLF 'more Marxist' is regarded as an irrelevance by many Eritreans, for whom the only issue is the justice of their nationalist cause. In April 1978, as I set out for Eritrea, the two groups announced a joint command and called on Ethiopia to open negotiations without conditions. The reply from Addis Ababa was a trenchant call to 'annihilate the treacherous secessionists'.

From Khartoum to Port Sudan on the Red Sea I was passed between nocturnal 'contacts', each not identifying himself or indicating how I would next proceed, but always arriving at precisely the promised time. From Port Sudan I was driven the thirty-five miles to Suakin, where the road south ends and the desert, literally, begins, and where, I was told, a convoy would pass at two in the morning. It did.

There were four large Fiat trucks, still with their Ethiopian markings.

16 Hoang Van Dung, the only survivor of 283 people who lived in a
block of flats destroyed by a direct hit from a B-52 bomber, Hanoi,
1975 (*Photograph: John Pilger*)

17 and 18 A helicopter belonging to the South Vietnamese Air Force is thrown over the side of the aircraft carrier USS *Midway* on the day after the end of the war in Vietnam, 1975 (*Photograph: Mathew Naythons*)

19 The wreckage of an American B-52 bomber in its 'cage' in Hanoi zoo, 1975 (*Photograph: John Pilger*)

20 Bargirls of Saigon (*Photograph: Philip Jones Griffiths*)

21 The devastation caused by a Vietcong rocket attack on Saigon a few days before the end of the war, 1975 (*Photograph: Nik Wheeler*)

22 Graves of the entire anti-aircraft militia of Dong Loc, Vietnam, all of them young women, 1975 (*Photograph: John Pilger*)

They carried ammunition, food and tins of powdered milk given by
Kuwait. The driver of my truck was a gentle, taciturn and suffering
young man called Suleiman, who drove by the slant of the sun and at
night by his instincts; here and there tracks appeared, but there was no
road and no map. He ate and drank little. He slept for only a few daylight
hours when the squadrons of insects allowed. Malarial sweat steamed
down his face and on several occasions, once during a sandstorm, he
paced the length of his truck until the shaking had stopped. He accepted
my anti-malarials, bemused; he had never seen such things before. His
concern for me and for the other passengers was unqualified; he insisted
that we should rest when he would not, that we should retreat to the
shade of a thorn bush while he and the other drivers dug their vehicles
out of the dunes.

Suleiman was to drive as far south as the Asmara road, a spine-gutting
journey of five nights, turn around and then follow the same punitive
route back to Port Sudan. And so he would go on and on, until the
seasonal rains filled the riverbeds. He and his comrades did this with a
cheerfulness and an old fashioned *esprit*. Only after we had parted did I
learn that he carried a piece of shrapnel in his neck. Like the victim of
torture I had met years before, he epitomised the Eritrean will.

Clinging to our load was what I first took to be a family. In fact, each
was the sole survivor of a family. One young woman had been sent to
Port Sudan for hospital treatment. 'Why are you coming back?' I asked
her. 'To fight,' she replied, 'what else?' Her parents had been killed in
the shelling of Masawa by Ethiopian and Soviet naval ships and her
sister had been killed accidentally during the evacuation of 40,000
civilians from the city. A third of all Eritreans were refugees. She, too,
shook with malaria; they all seemed to have it, just as one child in every
family had tuberculosis or trachoma, or both. My travelling companion,
the photographer Eric Piper, cared for this huddled group with his
customary kindness. He would go back to them at each stop with his
water canteen, and he gave them most of his precious antibiotics.

Eritrea began at a crumbling brick-and-stucco police post, manned
by a Sudanese sergeant and shaded by a giant margossa tree brought
from India as a seedling by the British. Here, during the Second World
War, the British post commander would alternately lunch with and snipe
at his Italian counterpart from across the river. Or so goes the story. The
old Italian post has flown the pale-blue Eritrean flag since the Ethiopian
garrison was overrun: the first in a chain of successful sieges, which
almost certainly would have climaxed in the fall of Asmara, the capital,
had the Russians stayed away.

Beyond here, the landscape was extreme, outsized, almost grotesque:
mountains rose in the shapes of primeval creatures or of giant waves

about to break. We continued at night for fear of strafing and on roads dug by hand that coiled around the mountains into mist. On either side, on spilling terraces, were circles of raised stones, like curious miniatures of Stonehenge; the headlights never lost them and the deeper we went into Eritrea the more commonplace they became. They were graves. They were the graves of people killed from the sky – lone shepherds and nomads, and whole communities as the larger patterns of stones indicated – and of people who had died from disease and hunger; the Sahel famine of 1973–4 was severe in Eritrea and deaths were disproportionately high. Not a drop of the relief that finally trickled out of Addis Ababa ever reached here.

The shock upon reaching Eritrea was the illusion that there were no people. Then, out of the ground they came, flashing torches, embracing the drivers. A generator somewhere in the scrub thudded into life, a fuel line materialised, arc lights were slung across the stumpy trees and mechanics swarmed over the trucks. Spokes of light picked up vegetation that was neatly singed. Napalm had been dropped here that morning and a shepherd and a child had been killed. Behind a tent, their charred remains lay covered by a tarpaulin, awaiting removal.

This was a nation of the night. The guerrillas carried out their ambushes in the early hours and retrieved their dead and wounded before the planes came at first light. Children went to school in the early evening and farmers worked in their fields by moonlight. In the north, an astonishing, complete industrial town had been built underground. At the end of tunnels and mine-shafts were factories and foundries, insulated by Ethiopian parachutes and powered by captured Birmingham-made generators. Here, self-taught men and women, many the sons and daughters of farmers and nomads, had organised their own small industrial revolution. In the 'gun factory', weapons of every nationality, from antique Brens to modern Kalashnikov rifles to huge artillery pieces, were stripped, studied and duplicated. Manuals were written from scratch; the Kalashnikov, for example, had been modified so that it was lighter and easier to control. 'It used to have a mind of its own,' said the foreman. 'Now it is truly an Eritrean weapon.'

In the 'metal shop', an entire Soviet MiG-21 fighter-bomber, which had crash landed almost intact, had been recycled into guns, buckets, ovens, kitchen utensils, ploughs, hoes, X-ray equipment and machine tools. In the 'electronics plant', copies of Sanyo and Hitachi radios were produced on an assembly line. In the 'woodwork factory' school desks were laid out with rows of crutches and artificial limbs; and in the 'textile factory' disabled soldiers, many of them amputees, sat at modern Singer machines (captured during a raid on Asmara) making uniforms and children's clothes and flags to fly on 'independence day'.

The traditional system of land tenure in Eritrea used to be known as *diesa*, whereby heads of families in the villages had equal rights to the land, which was redistributed every seven years. But this had long been corrupted by private landlords. In the 1960s the EPLF abolished large private holdings and resurrected and reformed the *diesa* system. Women are now allowed to own their own plots.[6] Indeed, the most radical change has been in the position of Eritrean women, who previously had neither political nor social rights; girls as young as eleven were 'given' to older men and female circumcision was universal. All of that has been reversed by EPLF legislation; and although traditional attitudes remain, women now are mechanics, engineers and teachers and make up a third of the Army. Here a bleak irony intrudes. 'We have no use of birth control,' a young woman teacher told me. 'We cannot get enough children to replace those who die or are killed. We actually encourage big families. That is the reality of our situation. But no young person becomes a fighter until he can read and write and understand why he may die that day.'

Her school was a cave. One notebook and two pencils were shared among a class of fifty; crayons, paints, chalk and toys were unknown. The children were taught many strange but useful things. They were taught that if they were caught in an air-raid in the open they must squat in single file, so that only some in the line would be hit. When they reached the age of fourteen they were asked to volunteer to be fighters, as their soldiers are called; and fewer than half of them escaped death or injury. Almost all of Eritrea's fighters have been born since the war began. Every school in Eritrea is an orphanage and the physically and mentally handicapped are scattered among every crowd of youngsters.

The Eritreans say that the Ethiopians, with their Soviet armour and their American cluster bombs and their Soviet and Cuban advisers, will never roll them back, and they may well be right; no demoralised, conventional Army, such as Ethiopia's, would last long in the mountains. But they freely admit that, while their morale and even their supply of arms are not in question, they could 'vanish'. And 'vanish' is a word they use frequently.

Since the severe drought of 1973–4 they have watched the weather with increasing anxiety. When I was there wells were down to 100 feet and almost dry, and the sand shifting across eroded fields and the desiccated remains of livestock were unmistakable signs that there was worse to come. Even the preciously irrigated citruses in the lowlands were beginning to die; while I was there most of one plantation was finished off by a lone marauding Ethiopian F-5 fighter aircraft and three canisters of defoliant gas.

Starvation had begun again. And starvation was what the Eritreans had in common with the peasant soldiers of the Dergue whom they regarded as fellow victims and took prisoner-of-war according to the Geneva Convention, of which they had copies, and regardless of the strain this placed on their own meagre supplies. One morning I watched the EPLF engage a battalion of Ethiopians and beat them. Of all the images of war, none is more indelible than starving teenagers fighting each other.

Food was not the only concern. There was the prospect for the wounded and sick. The most basic medicines were not being replaced. I have not seen field hospitals attempting to function with so little. At one hospital, so called, there was not a complete first-aid kit left and there was only half a bottle of blood. Outside in the heat, beside a malarial steambog, bloodied bandages were being scrubbed in cooking pans to be used again and again, applied inexpertly but with tenderness by a squad of children known as 'the dressers'. At this hospital the 'wards' were in dank crumbling tunnels; and infection was the main cause of death among the wounded. There were three surgeons and thirteen physicians for Eritrea's three and a half million people. They operated without many surgical instruments, such as forceps, and treated with drugs that were out of date or with none at all.

I stood beside Dr Simon Haile, a worn and wise man in his twenties, while he tried to decide which of two people should be given the only antibiotics available: a teenage boy, pocked with shrapnel, or a fleshless child with tuberculosis. The boy had the best chance of survival and it was decided that he should be treated. The child died.

As I left the hospital a sound like a high frequency whistle made people stop, then run and take shelter. Gaunt and graceful and ordered, they were like figures in a slow-motion film; they had performed this routine many times before. Two Napalm canisters exploded against a hillside, erecting a fence of fire directly in front of us. They had come from a MiG aircraft which twice before had aimed for the hospital; now it had missed a third time, but it was getting closer.

Eric and I hitchhiked back across the desert to Port Sudan and flew on to Khartoum, where the Hilton Hotel, rising out of the city's former rubbish dump, awaited us. In the bar was a group of competing foreign salesmen. Among them were spruce fellows from British Aerospace who were there seeking to persuade the Sudanese government to buy a complete missiles system; the Rapier, I understood it to be. If the sale was successful, they said, it would put the Callaghan Labour government's export of arms over the billion pound mark. Most of this money was provided, in one form or another, by poor countries.

While amputations proceeded in Eritrea without anaesthetics, while armies of the starving fought each other, that seemed to me most relevant.

In February 1982 'Operation Red Star' was mounted by the Ethiopian regime against the Eritreans. An estimated 100,000 Ethiopians were conscripted to join the 30,000 troops already in Eritrea. It was the sixth major military attempt by Addis Ababa to defeat the 'secessionists'. There were initial reports of heavy losses in Eritrea. However, by April it was clear that the EPLF, fighting against huge odds and at terrible human cost, had blunted the Ethiopian advance. No foreign journalists were present.

In January 1984 the EPLF counter-attacked and captured a string of Ethiopian garrisons in southern and eastern Eritrea. At the Red Sea town of Mersa Teklai the Eritreans used for the first time a mechanised brigade-level force with tanks captured in previous battles from the Ethiopians. According to a Norwegian observer this decisive battle lasted two days and resulted in more than 4,000 dead, most of them Ethiopians. Around the same time the Eritrean towns of Nacfa and Tessenei were bombed to rubble. Again no journalists were present.

By December 1984 there was at last a 'story down there'. Although famine conditions had prevailed in the Horn of Africa for most of that year, and Western governments and the Soviet Union were well aware of the scale of the famine, as indeed was the United Nations Food and Agricultural Organisation, there was no international alert and 'the story' was not widely publicised until a BBC cameraman filmed some of the most harrowing pictures ever to be shown on television. Help then began to arrive in Ethiopia along with the general assumption that it would reach the northern territories of Eritrea and Tigre, which were among the worst affected. Such was the international ignorance of Eritrea's (and Tigre's) struggle that this assumption continued into 1985 until those who understood that starvation was being used as a weapon of war were heard.

George Galloway of War on Want estimated that 1,750,000 Eritreans were at risk and required a minimum of 20,000 tonnes of food every month. 'Thanks to Western pusillanimity', he wrote, 'they are currently receiving fewer than 2,000 tonnes which leaves nine out of ten people getting no assistance at all. The Eritrean people now stand on the brink of disaster, with mass starvation now a reality.'[7]

At the time of publication, Eritrea is receiving only intermittent supplies across the Sudanese border. Voluntary agencies like War on Want are doing their best; but when I asked the Foreign Office what the British government could possibly do to help the Eritreans, I was told, 'Eritrea is not a recognised state.'

VI

JOI BANGLA!
(Long live Bengal!)

26

Lakhs and crores

Hatya, East Pakistan: November 1970. A cable, garbled in transmission, had arrived in the wire room of the *Daily Mirror* in the early hours of Sunday, November 15. It read, 'Five lacks gone. Definite. Possible one crone. No souls sighted Patuakhali. Wave thirty feet. Minimum one crone cattle done for Noakhali. Terrible state affairs. Respectfully request most urgentest immediate attentions government and newspaper. Topmost priority. Come quick. I am here. – Sorrows. Fakhruddin.'

Abdul Umarah M. Fakhruddin was the *Mirror*'s 'stringer' (local correspondent) in East Pakistan. His 'lack' and 'crone' translated as lakh and crore, terms used in the sub-continent for 100,000 and one million. He was saying that between half and one million people had died in a cyclonic tidal wave that had rolled into the Bay of Bengal at midnight on the previous Friday, a natural disaster with few equals.

I flew to Dacca, the capital, and following A. U. M. Fakhruddin's advice, journeyed on to Chittagong. Together with a man called Kamal and a local headmaster organising relief, I chugged westward in Kamal's ageless country boat, to which he had recently added a lovingly reconditioned Morris Oxford engine. We carried what relief was available: six kerosene cans of drinking water, a bundle of dried fish, bandages, a box of lime, an old fashioned antiseptic cream and, inexplicably, vaccine but no syringes.

There was no wind, the sun was a blazing torch and the water, dark with silt, moved in such erratic currents that Kamal was kept hard at his tiller. The great cataract brought by the tidal wave had receded but the Delta, explained the headmaster, was 'still dancing in its aftermath'. The mightiest rivers of the East, the Ganges and the Brahmaputra, merge here. Seen from the air, the whole of the countryside south of Dacca looks like a vast jigsaw puzzle set afloat on a placid lake and then shaken gently apart. Where it fringes the Bay of Bengal and is broken up into islands and islets, the land is extraordinarily low-lying. If the water's edge recedes more than a few feet, the people who attempt to live and farm here call it 'high land'. Rice is grown and cattle are grazed here all year round, in spite of the fact that twice during the year, the tides are so high that many of the islands are submerged and the probability of cyclones is perhaps greater than anywhere in the world.

But in November it was harvest time and so great was the need of food in a nation of 75 million, then with an average income of less than £20 a year, that people had to live where no people should be, sheltering behind trees planted in a single elevated line across the middle of each island as a pitiful rampart against the storms. This was an extremely dangerous place: a geographical coffin.

The storms come whirling up the Bay of Bengal, smashing into this corner, this huge dead end, where the coast of the sub-continent swings through more than a right angle to become the coast of Burma. The tidal wave that heralds it runs over the level land and is advertised only by its own roaring and by the lights of the country boats carried on its crest.

That was what happened at midnight on Friday, November 15, 1970. One survivor who reached Dacca, the only member of the Manpura district council to live, described a hollow, rolling roar accompanied by a cold, luminous glow, ' . . . like a piercing ray. I had to squint in its glare.' The wave was between twenty and thirty feet high, perhaps higher, and after its first onset, the water rose enough to drown the feeble houses built on stilts above the covered paddies and to drive the first survivors into the upper branches of the few trees that remained upright. For two hours the water hung, poised. Then the wind came howling in at speeds of 100 miles per hour, tearing all but the strongest from their handholds. And as the wind subsided, all the accumulated water went rushing back into the Bay, taking most of the dead with it.

The first island we approached was Hatya. About 2,000 people had lived on it, but now it appeared like a polished coin, save for one leaning house with a grey shadow on its southern rim. As we drew closer Kamal leapt to his feet.

'People!' he shouted. 'All people!'

The shadow was dead people. Some of them were sitting upright; some were holding each other.

'There was a primary school right here,' said Kamal. 'Where is it?'

There had also been one decent street of kiosk shops, a police post and a jetty with a petrol pump. There was nothing now, except the leaning house and behind it, now visible, a tree bent into a U-shape.

Kamal anchored near the breakwater formed by the bodies, of which there were several hundreds. The headmaster surveyed his relief boxes, then picked up the lime and trudged into the sludge. We followed, going calf-deep through sand and silt that looked as though it had been swept by a giant rake. We halted where a wedge of children's bodies lay. The headmaster threw lime on them, cursed and threw the box to the side. It seemed such a perfunctory, inhuman act, but it was not; tears streaked his face.

The house on its own was a monument to the impossible; the reason why it had not been swept away with everything else was soon evident. There may have been fifty bodies inside; heaven knows how many. They were people who had heard the roar and had huddled together in the most secure house, and somehow their combined weight had kept it upright. In the branches of the tree behind there was the body of a child.

We stopped at two more islands. One was wiped clean, except for a few carcasses of cattle; the other, miraculously, had lost only two families, although half the houses had been flattened or carried away. The people had the expressions of those who have walked away from a crashed aeroplane. The headmaster gave them all the supplies we had; the drinking water was gone within minutes. Then he sat on one of the empty kerosene cans and held court; Bengali bureaucracy had arrived. In three school exercise books he noted, in an excruciatingly laborious hand, an inventory of everything lost: saris, shirts, trousers, shoes, cooking pots, chickens, people.

While the headmaster performed, a man who was an organiser of the Awami People's League, the Bengali nationalist party of East Pakistan, told me angrily about an emergency evacuation plan which had not been implemented and a radio warning that had spoken only of severe winds and protective embankments, which the government in Islamabad had promised to build but had not. 'We are not animals,' he said. 'There is no reason why we should be the objects of God's hatred year after year.'

He led me to a woman called Nurunnessa, whose madness, he indicated, would illustrate what he was saying. For five years, during five natural calamities, she had watched her immediate family decline from six members to one – herself. In May 1965 her eldest son, Oli, had been drowned in a flash flood. In December of the same year her second son, Khan, had been one of 10,000 killed in a cyclone. In October the following year her mother-in-law had died from her injuries after her home collapsed in a cyclone; and in the floods only twelve months before, her six-year-old daughter, Moli, had been swept away while on an errand. During the harvest, he said, it was common for farmers to work around the clock and her husband, Seraj, had been in the paddies at midnight on Black Friday, the 15th, and he was still missing.

I had read nothing about these disasters. It was as if the London Blitz happened twice a year and the rest of humanity had not noticed or were not notified. Later, in Karachi, I looked at the files of a newspaper at the time of the 1965 cyclone, when 10,000 Bengalis perished, and the front pages were concerned with the crash of a Pakistani Boeing on an inaugural flight to Egypt. A party of 122 middle-class Punjabis, mostly journalists, had died in the crash. On an inside page there was a small item with the headline, 'STORMS LASH EAST WING. THOUSANDS LOST'.

This indifference was partially an imperial legacy. Pakistan's absurd boundaries had been drawn up by British civil servants and a constitutional lawyer during one frantic weekend just before independence in 1947. The Pakistan ruling class, dominated by those Punjabis who had run the Army of the Raj, regarded the new Islamic nation's Bengali majority, a thousand miles to the east, as a source of labour; and there was a racist edge to this. For the Bengalis, the callousness displayed by their current masters bore a long tradition. On December 12, 1876, *The Times* had confined its report of a cyclone which killed an estimated quarter of a million Bengalis to the following:

> The calamity is not likely to give rise to much material distress among the people. Government relief centres have been opened and help will be given to those who really need it. But no large sums of money will be spent and care will be taken to leave everything as far as possible to private trade.

And so it was on many other disastrous occasions in Bengal. In 1943 as many as a million and a half Bengalis starved to death after the British had stockpiled, transported or destroyed two crops in order to deny food to the advancing Japanese Army. Western war correspondents knew about this, but either they neglected to report it or their newspapers decided not to publish their dispatches.

The disaster in East Pakistan in November 1970 was different in so far as it became an international 'event' almost immedately the enormity of what had happened was revealed by Ian Brodie of the *Daily Express*, who had flown to Dacca from his Hong Kong base and was the first foreign journalist to send a detailed eye-witness account. After Brodie's reports, followed by mine in the *Mirror*, television squads arrived and 'the story' gained momentum. It could easily have gone the other way: the international, mostly Western press is capricious by nature, especially in its troubled relationship with the third world, and had it been diverted by some other, more 'newsworthy' event or had a reporter less experienced than Brodie led the way, television, the medium of impact, might well have stayed away and Bengal's agony would have gone unrecorded once again. And yet, in spite of the headlines and the television pictures coming out of East Pakistan, the media's power to galvanise the governments of developed Western nations into immediate and imaginative relief action, to cajole the humming bureaucracies of the international charity industry into marshalling its resources, proved minimal.

A major reason for this was the selective, entirely political application of what is known as 'aid'. The aftermath of the 1970 cyclone told us much about the nature of Western aid and its purpose: preserving in power a political and economic order incompatible with the interests of those in greatest need of genuine assistance.

In 1970 the Pakistani regime and its bloated military were held aloft by the 'Pakistan Aid Consortium' – Britain, Canada, West Germany, France, Holland and Italy – and separately and decisively by the United States. The governments of these countries regarded the undemocratic, chauvinist and brutal regime in Islamabad as, in the cliché of the time, a 'bulwark'. Pakistan was a 'bulwark' against China, which was then known as 'Red' China and promoted internationally as being demonic in almost every respect. Considering the turn of events since then, the irony is self-evident.

In 1970 Britain contributed £9 million to the Pakistan Aid Consortium. When the cyclone struck, the government of Edward Heath, along with other Western governments, clearly did not want to upset the Pakistani generals by rushing to the aid of the Bengalis who, in local elections and disturbances, had demonstrated their loathing for colonial rule from Islamabad. There was a precedent. A year earlier, in 1969, the Labour government of Harold Wilson had not wanted to upset the Nigerian regime by sending emergency relief to the beleaguered Biafrans. Nigeria, a major supplier of British oil, was also a 'bulwark'. So the Biafrans starved.

In East Pakistan, a week after the tidal wave struck in November 1970, no aid had reached the worst affected areas. During this week the Pakistani junta kept its helicopters and transport aircraft idle in the western province. The Awami League were in no doubt that the purpose of this was to sustain the chaos in the east and throw into disarray an incipient Bengali rejection of the very notion of Pakistan. No aid came from members of the Aid Consortium or from the United States during this critical time, a week in which an estimated 150,000 people, most of them the very young and old, died from dehydration, cholera and their injuries. On the fifth day, the United States government announced it would send six helicopters, two from Nepal and four from Fort Bragg in North Carolina. The two in Nepal remained there with engine trouble; the four from North Carolina, two of them flying bubbles with barely enough space for the pilots, took four days to be dismantled and assembled. A few hours away, in Vietnam, America had more than 5,000 helicopters, many of them idle, and with crews trained to scramble and airdrop supplies.

The Soviet Union was said to be sending ships with supplies to Chittagong, although no one seemed to be sure about that and less sure about when they might arrive. The Swiss, the French and the other EEC countries promised money, which was of no immediate use. Tokens arrived: blankets, baby food, electric flush lavatories; and most of them stayed at Dacca airport for want of helicopters and lorries.

Britain's one relief plane arrived eight days after the cyclone. Shortly afterwards thirteen British motorboats arrived, but without crews. However, a week of headlines was having some effect, though not unfortunately the required effect. Eleven days after the cyclone, a 'task force' of two Royal Navy ships sailed into the Bay of Bengal from Singapore. Convivial press conferences were conducted in Dacca by genial Brigadier Roy Ovens, the marine commander; and the headlines back home changed their tone. 'Today you can be PROUD to be British', announced a *Daily Mirror* front-page leading article, thereby setting in motion a public relations stunt of the kind the British military are more adept at than most. The *Mirror* leader ran:

> It is a moment today for unashamed and unabashed pride in being British. Here's the news that must make everybody's heart swell just a little. Effective British help is now getting through to the cyclone disaster area of East Pakistan.

By the last paragraph the glee had subsided and truth made a brief appearance:

> People waiting for relief are still dying at the rate of a thousand a day, according to a Red Cross estimate. Could British aid have been greater or quicker?[1]

Clearly scepticism and facts were now out of step. Brigadier Ovens swept up the British correspondents, flew us in helicopters to HMS *Intrepid* and gave us yet another briefing. He said that we reporter chaps would fly out on the 'first mercy missions' so that we could get back to *Intrepid* in time to dispatch our heart-warming copy via the Royal Navy's new Skynet communications system, which bounced telex and voice signals off a British radio satellite and right into the Ministry of Defence in Whitehall. After all those sweaty trips to the Dacca telegraph office, Skynet was living! A 'Press only room' had been set aside on *Intrepid*, typewriters were waiting with piles of pink paper, sailors were standing by to rush our words to Skynet and a bar was at our disposal in the officers' mess.

So off we flew on our 'mercy missions', but contrary to what we'd been told to expect we saw no marines burying the dead and no engineers throwing bridges across hostile waters. My helicopter carried six bags of rice, some tea and sugar and two of the bags split when they were dropped to the ground. Nevertheless, the villagers were grateful for our crumbs and they cheered as we flew away.

In the *Daily Telegraph* David Loshak wrote, 'The British contribution to the relief of East Pakistan . . . is seen in defence circles as providing a brilliant justification and a highly valid role for a British presence east of Suez.'[2] Loshak had put his finger on it. The Royal Navy at that time was seeking to justify its old 'east of Suez' presence, and the heart-warming headlines could not have been more perfectly timed. In my dispatch to the *Mirror* I described the meagre nature of the 'rescue operation' and contrasted its dubious efficiency with the brilliance of the public relations operation. Somehow my report was the only one of eight which the wondrous Skynet failed to transmit in time for that evening's edition in London. It finally reached the *Mirror* office in Holborn Circus two days later, delivered by an elderly Ministry of Defence messenger on a bicycle.

Soon afterwards I was recalled to London, with most other reporters, as the story was then considered 'dead'. Within a few days of our departure, the Royal Navy task force, Skynet, the typewriters and the pink paper slipped out of the Bay of Bengal. Ten days later A. U. M. Fakhruddin cabled the *Mirror* wire room that hundreds of small fires were still burning across the islands of Patuakhali as 'desperate signals for help'.

27

'Watch out at the Oval!'

Calcutta: June 1971. The manicured voice on the telephone said, 'I say, you really can't miss it. It's the rather dilapidated house at the end of Judges Court Road. Come at ten.' My taxi turned into Judges Court Road, past high whitewashed walls topped with barbed wire and gates fussy with guards. The driveway, resplendent with bougainvillaea and poinsettia, stopped at a structure that might have been contrived by Louis B. Mayer; lace iron dripped over a gingerbread confusion of sandstone and teak; Corinthian columns held up a splendid portico and beneath it, carefully parked in the only shade, stood a black Chevrolet Bel Air convertible of the mid-1950s, as new, and with a coat-of-arms on its bonnet and a man wearing a beplumed turban, waxed moustache, gold lanyard and red sergeant's stripes at its side.

Another man in starched white appeared and asked me to wait in 'the receiving room'. This was a room of wealth and splendour, as if the dust covers had been removed only that morning. Two centuries of British royalty, vice-royalty and Indian nobility marched in oils down the white marble staircase. There was a Rembrandt and a Monet, the tapestries were woven in gold, the chandeliers, twenty of them, were of pure crystal, the figures around the teak-panelled walls were mostly of gold and alabaster and the goblets and their trays were of silver, studded with precious stones.

'His Highness will welcome you now,' said the man in white, who led me up the staircase at the top of which I was greeted by a large photograph of a young Prince Philip in his polo togs. The study door was ajar.

'Come in, come in. No formality here.' His Highness, the Maharaja Bahadur Sir Uday Chand Mahtab of Burdwan, Knight Commander of the Indian Empire, stood behind his desk wearing a pair of cream Bombay bloomers, spotted shirt and tennis shoes. The Maharaja is one of the corporate heads of India's aristocracy. His father was a twentieth-century Mogul emperor and the Burdwan Raj estate, near Calcutta, is described in the Family Handbook of 1938 as 'an area of 4,000 square miles with a population of 2,000,000 souls'. The present Maharaja describes it, not immodestly, as 'a small Constantinople'.

'I must tell you', he said, 'that I pay 85 per cent of my income in taxes and for all intents and purposes I have only this house. I don't keep a single footman now. Of course, I don't go as far as some. The Maharaja of Mymmesingh has gone completely Marxist.

'I have my clubs and my few horses – you must join me in my box at the races on Saturday – oh, and I'm on the boards of Brooke Bond and Dunlop. I occasionally motor to Burdwan; I'd really rather live there, you know. But there are difficulties. The common people still see themselves as my subjects and they attempt to touch me and to kiss my feet. It's good luck to kiss my feet, you see.'

We talked about his devotion to the British royal family, about the Mountbattens, Nehru and the price of a bottle of champagne. His Highness seemed the embodiment of the extraordinary effect the British had on India. Lunch would be at the Calcutta Club as usual, followed by a meeting of the English Speaking Union. 'Please give my affectionate regards to the British people,' he said. 'I do miss them so. And I do hope they can spare some charity to help out with this latest mess in Bengal. None of this would be plaguing us now, of course, if they'd left India as she was.'

The 'latest mess in Bengal' was the arrival in Calcutta of some 7 million refugees from East Bengal, where a campaign of terror was in progress. To the Bengalis, East Pakistan no longer existed and 'Bangladesh' – free Bengal – was struggling to be born. It was indeed, as the Maharaja had said, the logical end of a process which had begun with the dissolution of British India twenty-five years before. In insisting upon the creation of a separate and specifically Muslim state, Dr Mohammed Jinnah and his comrades of the Muslim League had created, instead, a pantomime horse: a nation divided by culture, language and the breadth of India. And since and partly as a result of the cyclone, the hind legs of East Pakistan had at last parted from the forelegs of the West.

In the beginning the Bengalis had not wanted to secede. They simply wanted to run their own affairs. They, too, distrusted Hindu India, but the perennial Pakistani quarrel with India over Kashmir was remote from them; and it was a quarrel that consumed Pakistan's revenues in military spending to which the Bengalis contributed the lion's share. Bengal's exports of jute alone accounted for nearly half Pakistan's total foreign earnings, yet the eastern province received less than a third of the central government's annual budget. Worse, an intensely political people, as the Bengalis were, had no political voice.

When long-promised elections for a National Assembly were held throughout Pakistan in December 1970, one month after the cyclone, Sheik Mujibar Rahman's Awami League was carried to an overwhelming victory on the tide of suffering in the province. (During the campaign evidence was produced which suggested that President Yahya Khan's regime had received satellite warnings of the cyclone in time to mount a partial evacuation of the most vulnerable islands.) Sheik Mujib, as he was known, was a lawyer with little administrative skill and the political charisma of a Nehru. His strength lay in his Bengali gift of crowd-stirring rhetoric. Pacing himself as expertly as any American revivalist, he would rouse his crowds to choruses of 'Yahya and those drunken fools in Islamabad!', then calm them to melodramatic silences. Clearly, the Sheik was the first real threat to a united Pakistan.

The Awami League had won 167 of the 169 seats allocated to the Bengalis in the National Assembly, which represented the majority vote of all Pakistan. So the Sheik found himself in the paradoxical position of being the potential prime minister of a country from which his own party had demanded home rule. For the west, Zuliqar Ali Bhutto, leader of the People's Party of Pakistan, had won a victory only marginally less decisive, taking 81 out of the 138 seats at stake. So the two wings were irreconcilably divided, and all that was left between them, the thread of Islam, snapped on March 25, 1971.

Bhutto, a natural conspirator, had flown into Dacca in mid-March to open apparently cordial negotiations of unity with Sheik Mujib, and after they had met he announced that accord was close. In fact, Bhutto was the eager decoy of the Pakistani Army which, a few days after he had bade farewell to the Sheik, attacked Dacca. Artillery, tanks, bazookas, phosphorous grenades and incendiary bullets were ranged against newspaper offices, the Hindu quarter and the university, while the students slept. The bazaar in Nagar Bazar Road was put to the torch, bulldozed and made into a mass grave. According to one eye witness, my friend Michel Laurent, the French war photographer, more than 7,000 people were slaughtered in two days and nights. He described it 'as I imagined the assault on the Warsaw ghetto'.

Almost all of them were civilians. The bodies of many of the nation's leading intellectuals were taken to the riverfront where they fattened squadrons of crows. Entire communities of Hindus and those who tried to protect them went before firing squads. Sheik Mujib was arrested and flown to Lyalpur gaol in West Pakistan.

East Pakistan was now sealed to journalists. Peter Hazelhurst, the India correspondent of *The Times*, kept a lone vigil in Calcutta, patiently reporting and analysing refugees' accounts of atrocities which at times seemed too barbaric to be true. In April, Colin Smith of the *Observer* and Dennis Neeld of the Associated Press made a hazardous overland journey from Calcutta to Dacca and encountered the first rag-tag forces of the Mukti Bahini, the recently formed 'freedom fighters of Bangladesh'. When Smith reached Dacca he immediately contacted British diplomats, who distinguished themselves by shouting at him that his arrival would get them all killed and, anyway, it was not in the 'interests' of the British people to know what was going on in East Pakistan. He reported that the Mukti Bahini, although led by the surviving officers of the East Pakistan Rifles, were irritants rather than serious opponents for the Pakistani Army which, soldier for soldier, was one of the ablest in the world.

Little else but dark rumour had been heard from inside occupied Bengal when photographer Eric Piper and I crossed the border in June 1971 and set out to find 'free Bangladesh'. Making contact with the freedom movement outside the sub-continent was simple. All that was required was a day return rail ticket to Birmingham, where the Bengali community had formed a hive of patriotic committees. Since March 25, I had been receiving regular phone calls at my flat in London, from Abu Sayed Chowdhury, the exiled Chief Justice of the High Court in Dacca, who was to become the first President of Bangladesh. He would ring from a pay phone and always late at night.

'Chief Justice Chowdhury speaking.'

'Yes, Chief Justice.'

'At this very hour terrible and wonderful things are happening in my country. Heroic victories are being won by my people, but we are fleas against the lion.' The pip-pip-pips of the eccentric British telephone system would invariably drown the Chief Justice's voice as his money ran out.

Indeed, the journey to unconstituted Bangladesh might have been scripted by Satajit Ray, Bengal's maestro chronicler of everyday madness. The point of departure was the Ganges restaurant in Gerrard Street in London's Chinatown, where the proprietor was 'the contact' and provided an obligatory curry and an 'important message' written in Bengali on the back of his card.

'What does it say?' I asked him.

'It says, "Hello. Greetings from the ladies' committee of Birmingham. Joi Bangla."'

'Is that a code?'

'No, it is a greeting from the ladies' committee of Birmingham. They are doing very good work. Raising funds. Tea parties, that sort of thing.'

'How do I get into Bangladesh?'

'Here is the card of my friend in Calcutta, four doors from Grand Hotel and second door on the right up the stairs. Very good rate. Careful Moudud Ahmed and Rhamat Ali are the people they are presenting themselves to be. Lights have gone out in my country. Miscreants, informers galore! *Joi Bangla!*'

Moudud Ahmed and Rhamat Ali were young Dacca lawyers who had defended Sheik Mujib during one of his previous incarcerations in West Pakistan. After much negotiation, Moudud Ahmed agreed to lead Eric and me across the Radcliffe Line which divided India from East Pakistan.

We left at four in the morning and passed through what Calcutta's *Statesman* had called 'our corridors of pain': the roads and paddy tracks along which millions of people had come since March 25, across the border into India. They came in mostly silent, ordered files; the very fortunate in rickshaws, the tinkling of their handlebar bells only occasionally heard because their human loads were such that they could barely keep pace with the people on foot. Seen from a car going without lights to the border the scale of the exodus was blurred. Then they would spill across the road and the Sikh driver would be obliged to throw his gears into reverse, and harried faces would press against the windscreen.

War was coming. Ten million had poured into India; and from the early summer of 1971 Indian diplomats had ranged Europe and Washington, talking to anyone who might bring pressure to bear upon Pakistan, the Pakistan Aid Consortium and the American administration. The Indians asked that the Consortium countries and America share with India the responsibility of coping with one of the greatest ever flights of refugees. They requested only the means: food and medicines. India's care for the refugees of Bangladesh was itself a historic feat of humanitarianism.

However, Bengali nationalism was not an issue close to the heart of Indira Gandhi, regardless of her public utterances of support for Bangladesh. She and her Congress Party conservatives wanted the Pakistanis quietly to compromise, to release Sheik Mujib and trust a form of autonomy to his Awami League. They did not want to force the disintegration of Pakistan because they feared that the secessionist virus would spread to West Bengal and further into India.

India's diplomatic campaign to prevent war with Pakistan came to an abrupt end when the Indian foreign minister, Swaran Singh, returned from Washington with an 'assurance' from President Nixon and his National Security Adviser, Henry Kissinger, that the United States would stop supplying arms to Pakistan. After deliberating on this assurance amidst cheers at Delhi airport, a scene evocative of Neville Chamberlain's 'triumphant' return from Munich, the foreign minister was handed a note which said that a large consignment of American arms had just been flown into Karachi. Before giving his assurance to Mr Singh, Mr Kissinger had written a memorandum to President Nixon, which was subsequently leaked and published, advising him to 'tilt in favour of Pakistan' and to rush more arms there.[3]

Eric and I marched at night behind Moudud Ahmed and a guide bearing a green and red Bangladeshi flag and a ragged file of guerrillas armed with 25-year-old Lee Enfield rifles and Bren guns. One morning we came upon a mosque blown up, shops looted and burned, a house without a wall, felled by a tank, from which its owner had not escaped.

People emerged cautiously, asking if we had food. The Pakistani Army, which had come the previous night, had left them two piles of coarse rice: forty pounds to feed 5,000 people. An old man with a goatee and the lace cap of a *maulana* lifted his shirt, revealing a neat lattice-work of bayonet cuts on his stomach. An eight-year-old boy's ear was caked with blood, the lobe having been shot away at close range. A woman sat alone in a field nearby, grieving the burial alive of her husband. The Punjabi soldiers had put him and his two brothers, who had refused to go with them, in a trench beside the river and filled it with mud that came up to their noses and the crows had done the rest.

And so the stories of systematic killing accumulated as we went from village to village, keeping well off the roads, waiting for a lone jet fighter to pass. Where there had been Hindu communities, whose ethnic place in Muslim East Bengal had been delicately but peacefully maintained since Partition, there were now deserted ruins. Whenever the Punjabis attacked, it was to the same pattern. Every young man in the village was ordered to display his penis. If he was circumcised and therefore a Muslim, he was taken away. If he was uncircumcised and a Hindu, he was killed and, depending on the soldiers' whim, his penis was cut off. Anybody connected with Sheik Mujib's Awami League was shot. Food and animals, watches and family trinkets were taken; and those Bengalis who remained were threatened with the firing squad if they left their village.

My subsequent report and Eric Piper's pictures provided substantial evidence that the Islamabad government was practising genocide. A campaign was hurriedly mounted by the junta to discredit it. Three Conservative Members of Parliament were invited to Pakistan by President Yahya Khan. They travelled by Army helicopter and used government interpreters, and the Hindu hostel at Dacca University, where as many as 1,800 students were killed during the March 25 assault with rockets and mortar, was rebuilt for their visit. Their tour ended with a lavish party given by Yahya Khan. On her return to Britain, Jill Knight, the Member for Edgbaston, reported to Parliament that stories of systematic killings in East Pakistan were grossly exaggerated and that the situation was back to normal.

'Excuse me, I would like to see Fakhruddin.'
  'Please go away.'
  'But this is his office.'
  (In a whisper) 'He is gone, in the countryside, in the middle of the fighting, I don't know where. Several of his family were shot. Please, but your presence will be like death to us.'

The offices of *Chitrali*, a mass-circulation weekly where A. U. M. Fakhruddin was editor of the Cultural Section, radiated the fear of occupied Dacca. In late June, when foreign reporters were allowed briefly to return to the capital, it was clear that Bengali journalists had been among the first targets. All but a few of those in the Dacca Journalists' Club on the night of March 25 had been massacred. The newspapers had been closed or infiltrated with Biharis, a Muslim community which had fled India at Partition and now collaborated with the Punjabis.

Journalism is a Bengali tradition. Bengali reporters are among the more tirelessly inquisitive news gatherers in the world. Their reports have a purple eloquence whose origins might be part-Raj and part-Tagore, the Bengali Byron. They are incorrigible romantics. *Chitrali* had shouted '*Joi Bangla*' louder than most; its editorial writers had beaten their breasts at the iniquities of the Punjabi regime long before the cyclone, calling upon the Prophet Himself to disown the 'heretics' who oppressed Bengal. 'Golden Bengal will never forget you, never forgive you,' trumpeted a fearless *Chitrali* front page at the Pakistanis. 'We shall never foreclose on our people's passion for freedom, for which they are striving with every beautiful fibre in their bodies.' That was A. U. M. Fakhruddin's style. After the cyclone struck, he wrote (in the culture section):

> The mortal attack of the tidal-bore has reversed the serene face of Bengal and reduced the area to an unknown map of a place of millions of years B.C. . . . We can helplessly mourn for those whom the cruel fangs of lethal waves have devoured. With tears in our eyes we can only wish: let them live who are still alive.[4]

Always immaculate, pomaded and umbrella-bearing, A. U. M. Fakhruddin lived in the Wapeda Building, in a room above the Head Assistant, Planning (Power). He had four telephone numbers which were seldom answered, yet he was as dependable as the sun. Several times a day I would find a note pushed under the door of my hotel room on which was written, 'I am here . . . with deeply sincerest wishes, Yours, A. U. M. Fakhruddin'. There would be a postscript from Shakespeare.

His favourite quotation during the days of oppression was from Hamlet's soliloquy:

> Whether 'tis nobler in the mind to suffer
> The slings and arrows of outrageous fortune,
> Or to take arms against a sea of troubles,
> And by opposing end them?

Every encounter with my friend Fakhruddin would lift me from the most doleful mood and be concluded with much guffawing and self-deprecation, followed by a final burst from the Bard or Shelley's *Prometheus Unbound* or Browning: 'One fight more, the best and the best'. There now seemed little hope that I would see him again.

Dacca, a city of 3 million, is one of those human concentrations whose noise is enjoyed by every citizen. It is not noisy like a Western city of equivalent size; there are not enough cars and construction sites. A siren is rare. Dacca's din is of voices; save for the tinkling handlebar bells and a minstrel's frenzied playing of the three-stringed *jurri*, the resonance of human voices actually can be heard and felt. Bengali is a lilting language with a vast vocabulary much given to rhetoric and hyperbole; its users invariably are in full cry.

They could not be heard now. The city was almost silent. The markets, once the producers of the very finest noise, were funereal. In Dhanmandi, the central rice market, Elephant Road, the ancient terminus for elephant trains, was still. Except for the mosque. Instead of a minaret the Elephant Road mosque has a small aeroplane mounted on its dome. Five times a day the bearded muezzin, whose eccentricity was legendary and loved, would clamber into the cockpit of his little plane and proclaim the greatness of Allah, his voice magnified by loudspeakers fitted to the fuselage. He was a brave patriot who dared to fly the emblem of Bangladesh from his cockpit, an act inviting summary execution by the Army. He did not stop there. On more than one occasion during the months of occupation his ear-splitting intonation ended with the unholy cry, '*Joi Bangla!*' Perhaps fearing the wrath of Allah, the Punjabis left him alone.

My pockets were now filled with scraps of paper pressed on me by the porters at the Intercontinental Hotel and by people in the streets whose faces I would barely glimpse as they ran away. They were mostly maps, meticulously drawn and with notations such as, 'Hindu family bayoneted here. One survivor still on second floor. Room under stairs.' They told how to get to villages where massacres were alleged to have taken place, and there were lists of names to be trusted.

With one of these maps and a boy who insisted on guiding us, Eric and I drove into the old city, through the rubble of Tikka Khan Avenue, named after the military governor of East Pakistan whose brutality was a byword.

The silence broke as fear overflowed. 'Get away from here!' people shouted. 'If you take pictures, the Army will come back!'

We attempted to drive away, but a mob had formed around our taxi and was bellowing a litany of reprisals our presence would bring down on them. The boy who had led us to the street sat between us crying. 'If they don't kill me for bringing you here,' he said, 'the Army will.'

As the taxi was about to be turned on its side, I singled out one of the leaders of the mob and asked him to come with us to the nearest Army post, where he could seek assurance that they would not be harmed. He accepted and the taxi bounced back to its four wheels and clattered away to a place where a Pakistani major endeavoured to phone his colonel. Finally reached, the colonel told me there would be no reprisals against the street. I doubted his word. The man from the mob certainly did not believe him. The boy stayed at our side until we reached our hotel. Shaking with terror, he disclosed that our taxi-driver was a Bihari who would inform on him to the Pakistanis, and the street would never forgive him. 'I am condemned,' he said.

I took the boy's address and reported the incident to a government information official who was shepherding a second (and less malleable) group of British MPs. I said that if the boy was harmed he would become a martyr for both the Bengali and British peoples, a symbol of their implacable opposition to the Pakistani government. His bored reaction to the threats of a reporter who would soon fly away forced me to face the truth that I was an accomplice to whatever befell the boy and the people in the street. I tried to shut this out of my mind during the convivial swapping of stories with colleagues at the hotel bar that night. But I could not. Journalism's victims go quietly.

On the day the MPs left Dacca, the Army commander in East Pakistan, Major-General Rao Farman Ali Khan, held a press briefing in the former British Governor's mansion, a miniature Versailles. Tea and biscuits were served to us on the green baize and there were Bengalis to fan us. 'Why don't you chaps open the batting?' said the General.

I told him I had seen evidence of the shooting and torture of civilians. 'Not by our chaps,' he said. 'They have the same honour as you Brits . . . solid up to here.'

'Why', I asked, 'were mortar and rockets used against densely populated areas?'

'Look here,' he replied, 'yes, of course, we used rocket launchers to frighten and bullets to create pockets of temporary panic. But these are normal dispersal tactics. We didn't aim at anybody.'

The briefing ended with a chat about cricket, which the General said was his great love. 'Our chaps', he said, 'have young spin bowlers coming up that will put the MCC to shame next season. Then they'll take on the best of Australia.'

The General, a tall angular man, stood up and mock-bowled to his aide-de-camp, who dutifully affected disaster at the stumps. 'You fellows mark my words,' he said. 'Watch out at the Oval, I say!'

28

'Thank you all so much for coming!'

Quemoy, Straits of Formosa: November 1971. I had spent a day and a night on Quemoy, Chiang Kai-shek's fortress island off the mainland of China, when I received a cable from the *Mirror* saying that war was about to begin on the sub-continent and to hurry back to India. It was appropriate to receive such a message in Quemoy; no place on the planet is better prepared for war, with troops and armour permanently entrenched in tiers of rock, and no place presents a finer puppet show of war with an exquisitely idiotic performance every day at two o'clock.

Out of convenience and weariness after twenty-two years of lethal ping-pong, the Nationalist Chinese of Chiang Kai-shek and the communist Chinese of Mao Tse-tung had agreed to bombard each other on alternate days, and on the day I was there it was the turn of Chiang's men. They fired capsules containing quantities of Y-fronts, jelly babies, photographs of beautiful girls and inflatable Donald Ducks, which were meant to represent the delights of the consumer society to which the faithless communist minions presumably wished to flee. The capsules also contained, a Nationalist officer told me sternly, 'a photograph of a very big gun'. This was a warning, he said, of the price the communists would pay if Mao did not come out with his hands up, so to speak, which was expected to happen any day now.

On the previous day, Mao's men, taking their turn, had fired capsules containing flower-patterned vacuum flasks, electric radiator fires, a box of Mao's Thoughts, toy boats and fire engines (the Chinese never forget children), posters of deliriously happy peasants and a photograph of a steel mill. These were displayed for me in front of the actual Very Big Gun.

As my plane approached Calcutta the progress of events during the five months since I was last in Bengal was clear. Beyond Dum Dum airport's sprawl of permanently incomplete terminal buildings lay a city of refugees which had grown almost to the size of Calcutta itself. Three million more had come from Bangladesh, the equivalent of Birmingham erected virtually overnight. They no longer lived in the large water pipes forever awaiting installation, but were in tents and huts or under corrugated iron, hessian and straw. The cholera epidemic, which had broken out among the first arrivals, had been contained as a result of strenuous Indian efforts, and the children were now dying from common diseases like chicken pox.

I set out for Flower Street in the Taltolla district. I had a message to deliver to Dudley Gardiner from a friend of his in London, to whom he had not written for fifteen years. Dudley was a rumbustious tank of a man, a former sergeant-major in the Royal Fusiliers who had come to Calcutta after taking part in the 1956 Suez invasion, which he saw as an attack by a rich country on a poor country and which so distressed him that he set out to make his own amends. He was sixty-one when we first met; and every day, for fifteen years, he had collected drums of porridge, curry and milk from a Salvation Army centre, loaded them on to the tray of his Land Rover and driven into an area of considerable danger – where Maoist Naxalites killed policemen and threatened him – and gave the food to people who would otherwise go hungry.

Dudley had an uncommon view of Calcutta. He saw it as a vivid expression of humanity and its citizens as immutable heroes; merely to survive in such a place was, he argued, heroic, and it was typical of his humility that he never saw himself in the same light. 'I chose to be here', he would say, 'and I might leave any day now!' But of course he never did.

Dudley believed that Flower Street was a microcosm of Calcutta. It was the size of a small town, with some 4,000 people living there, most of them under the sky and without work, education, sanitation or adequate nutrition. The water pipes, which Messrs Jessop and Co. had laid beneath Flower Street a century earlier, had long passed their life expectancy and had burst and were surrounded with sewage. The street's only water pump was inscribed, 'WASTE NOT, WANT NOT – 1914.'

'There he is!' Dudley shouted excitedly after we had driven the length of Flower Street. 'Look at the little bastard, lying in his piss. Jesus bloody Christ!'

The little bastard's name was Pabul Ran and he had been born in Flower Street twelve years before, on the same straw mat where he now lay and seldom moved, defended from the pariah dogs and the sky assault of crows by his mother wielding an umbrella's skeleton. He was severely handicapped. On sight of Dudley's hobbling hulk, he smiled. His mother had her two paint tins ready to be filled with milk.

'He was born on my birthday and I've been feeding the little bastard ever since,' said Dudley. 'The bloody trouble is, when I go, he'll go.'

Dudley suffered from a blood disease which caused gross swelling of his legs and he was often ill. When I called at his home, which was a room bare except for a bed, a chair and a few snapshots from his Army days, the door was bolted. Someone came up the stairs and said he had been ill and had been taken away; he did not know where. I left the letter under his door and walked to the corner of Flower Street, where Pabul Ran, the little bastard, lived. But he too was not there. (Dudley, after a long illness, died in 1981.)

For most people in Calcutta there was little to lose, and this stoicism (or heroism, as Dudley would have it) had been passed down since Clive of India began stripping *Sonar Bengal* – Golden Bengal – of what he described as its 'inexhaustible riches' and since the Victorian trading masters established on the banks of the Hooghly an Asian Manchester, where people with previously enough to eat were enticed from their land so that fortunes in manufacturing could be made on their labour.

However, as the days passed the street crowds listened more intently to their transistor radios and large groups squatted around those who read the newspapers to them. Once, on the pavement outside the Grand Hotel, there was an outbreak of cheering and when I asked why, I was told that the newspaper reported the Minister of Defence, a Congress Party Brahmin, as speaking passionately about his burning desire for the freedom of Bengal: something he had never mentioned before. 'The aloof are worried about Bengal,' said the reader. 'Once this thing starts they wonder where it will finish.'

Clive of India's heirs remained sanguine. Their Tollygunge Club, which had been considered slightly but significantly inferior to the Calcutta Club until the latter 'went native', was preoccupied with preparations for the Ladies' Rose Bowl swimming competition and the brains trust in the writing room and the poolside dance and bingo. The times and dwindling numbers had militated against the British exclusiveness of the club, which now admitted Japanese and Eastern bloc diplomats who shouted at each other in the swimming pool. The Naxalites had been blamed for hurling a bomb at the gymkhana horses in July. This was bad enough, then one of the bombers turned out to be 'that agreeable little wallah' who held aloft an umbrella on the terrace. Naturally, all the 'umbrella boys' had to go. No one could be trusted any more.

The refugee camps were only twenty minutes' drive from the Tolly-gunge, but no one at the club had initiated a 'collection' as sometimes happened for local charities. The received wisdom at the Tollygunge was that this was one of those seasonal interruptions, like famine and pestilence: nature's way of culling the herd, as it were.

On the following Saturday, Ladies' Rose Bowl Day, Indira Gandhi made a speech to the nation which referred directly to the growing anti-India campaign in Europe following a year of indifference toward the upheavals in Bengal. 'The times have passed', she said, 'when any nation sitting three or four thousand miles away or anyone in our midst could give orders to Indians on the basis of their colour superiority. India is no more a country of bungling natives.'[5]

This was certainly true of the Indian armed forces, which had 980,000 men under arms in three brigades, thirty divisions, thirty-five squadrons and forty-six warships. The former KCIOs, King's Commissioned Indian Officers, strutted as Sandhurst and its local equivalents had taught them, drilling the *jawan*, the Indian Tommy, in great sanitised enclaves which consumed almost half the nation's budget. These camps bespoke another India, in which hunger and disease did not exist. It was hardly surprising that there were permanent queues outside the recruiting offices.

The 'phoney war' produced memorable farce. Calcutta, which lives at night in an unrelieved brown haze caused by smoke from thousands of little wood fires mingling in the humidity with the unchecked industrial filth, was ordered to 'brown out'. Civil defence units, in soup-plate helmets and *lungis*, toured the streets announcing an air-raid warning practice during which, they said, 'everybody must stay indoors and remain in the face-down position until the siren has ceased to operate'. The fact that up to a third of the population had no doors to stay inside, let alone roofs to stay under or walls to stay between, apparently had not occurred to the relevant authorities.

The Grand Hotel is in the heart of Calcutta. It faces the *maidan*, a legacy of the Raj appreciated by those who take the evening breeze on it and those who live on it; it is parched and scalped and there are drains criss-crossing it but there is some green, and bourgeois families, who have a permanently beleaguered air, secure these patches on Sundays. When the humidity and haze lifted, which was seldom, it was possible to see the pear shape of the Empress Victoria from certain rooms of the Grand, which was now filling rapidly. The Press were arriving by the platoon. A Scandinavian contingent flew in by specially chartered plane. A wedge of Japanese television people arrived wearing blue baseball caps and puce windcheaters embroidered with the word, 'GO!' A Swiss radio man became a fixture in the foyer as he waited for the signal to go to war, with gas mask of Mons vintage and soup-plate helmet purchased in the market. A Soviet reporter, who had loudly protested that he was being denied the special privileges due to a representative of India's most powerful ally, fell over a beggar outside the hotel and was alleged to have kicked him. The beggar, who was of an élite specialising in the swallowing of fountain pens, hit the Russian over the head with his transistor radio.

Most of us lived a life we enjoyed, felt smug about, agonised over, affected cynicism about, grew weary of and at times hated. Those who took Trappist vows with themselves to remain 'observers' only protected themselves, for a time, from becoming involved in what they saw or were told or had orchestrated for them. To admit to being 'subjective', like other ordinary mortals, somehow was to break a professional code. Whatever the impact of Peter Hazelhurst's early reports in *The Times* of barbarities in East Pakistan, it was due as much to the reporter's incisive, fallible and honestly subjective style as it was to the news he reported first. For many of us, the events that had confronted us during a year in the 'corridors of pain' served at least to demystify the observer's holy grail. And these events and their aftermath were to have their effect on those, like myself, who had previously inflated the importance of the reporter. We were to learn that we were small fry who could be ignored or manipulated or banned or seduced or duped, with impunity, by those who held the power of war and peace and would flaunt it at us.

Colonel Clarence Proudfoot was one of those. 'The Indian Army is a damn fine Army!' said the colonel. 'The Indian Army never joins battle until hostilities are declared and everything is up above board! No, gentlemen, what you hear is not outgoing but ingoing. Our men are standing by their guns and are at peace, with all vigilance, until Delhi says they are not at peace! Let me assure you, gentlemen . . . ' Colonel Proudfoot, a reserve officer who the week before had been sitting at his desk in the public relations office of a Bombay cement factory, jammed his fingers in his ears and winced.

Crump!

'Colonel,' I said, 'that artillery we can hear is outgoing, which means that India is already at war.'

'Gentlemen of the Press,' said the Colonel, 'I am a trained military officer. What you hear is ingoing . . . that is, incoming going in . . . Pak artillery are coming in at us. Thank you gentlemen. Tea is to be served under the trees.' Our guided tour of the 'non-war' proceeded to a shady spot where there were long tables, white tablecloths, tea, biscuits and deckchairs. The ingoing shells of the Indian artillery rattled the cups, but none was lost.

The following week Indira Gandhi came to Calcutta and spoke to half a million on the *maidan*. Her father had spoken in the same setting on the eve of independence a quarter of a century before. On this occasion the crowd had formed in less than an hour. I remember only a burst of car horns and rickshaw bells, then a massive, disciplined convergence as people marched from out of the shops and warrens and gutters in large groups, silently. As if by a pre-arranged signal they had cast off their wretchedness and cowering and were now an unstoppable force. I was reminded of a passage in Geoffrey Moorhouse's fine book about Calcutta in which he describes the nightmare of the city's rich 'when every poor man in the city rises from his pavement and his squalid *bustee . . .* '

> There will be a signal for this nightmare to become reality and it will be given by the rickshaw men who have pulled so many rich people around Calcutta like animals all their lives. They will begin to pass it on when darkness falls, as the rich move away to their homes and their pleasures. All over the city and along the Hooghly there will be the sound of bells being tapped one after another against the shafts of motionless rickshaws or upon the sides of lamp posts. As any rich man walks the streets that night he will be followed wherever he goes, from one pool of light to the next, by this dull anvil ring of rickshaw bells. Tap-tap-tap, the signal will pursue him mysteriously down each street; and there will be no shaking it off. It will tell him that his time has come. The time for compassion will be past.[6]

It was apparent from her speech that Indira Gandhi had at last decided on all-out war. When I had talked to her in June, I had suggested that the United States and the Pakistan Aid Consortium countries would do nothing to prevent war. 'Wrong!' she replied. 'They will not allow it. There is too much at stake. The Great Powers themselves could become involved.' Now before her adoring masses – she was approaching the peak of her popularity which later venalities would erode – she was embittered and emotional. To the enthralled Hindus, she invoked the sanctity of Mother India, which she might not have dared to do in Bengal at another time. With her carefully chosen euphemisms she reminded the world that the unity of the sub-continent was not a British creation, that from the invasion of the first Aryan tribes India had absorbed and Hindu-ised those with whom it had gone to war; indeed, even Mahatma Gandhi had preferred Hindu ideology to a secular nationalism and this had caused the Muslims to take fright and Jinnah to hurry his plans for a separate Pakistan.

This fear of suffocation by India persisted in Pakistan and persists today. And although the immediate issue in 1971 was the sovereignty of East Bengal, a great many Pakistanis believed that India had never accepted dismemberment by the Raj and that the coming war would gravitate quickly to the question of *their* survival; and a great many

Muslims in East Bengal shared this fear, although it was not the time for them to say so.

'In-di-ra! In-di-ra!'

A helicopter came for her. And the crowd vanished.

Two days later, at twenty minutes past midnight, All-India Radio interrupted its incessant *sitars*, and the Prime Minister, speaking first in English, then in Hindu, regretted that the second most populous nation on earth was at war.

Eric and I went by taxi to the war behind the Indian Fourth Infantry Division, which, it soon became clear, was not the first division of Indian troops, supported by tanks, artillery and fighter aircraft, to have advanced into East Pakistan. Four divisions were already there, and the embarrassing truth dawned on us that a full-scale war had been going on for three or four days before Indira Gandhi had declared it to the world. Moreover it had been going on less than seventy miles from the Grand Hotel. India had begun to draw again the map of Asia under our noses and we, the world's vigilant Press, had missed it.

The war between India and Pakistan may have been the last great war in the traditions of the nineteenth century. That is to say it was a war of trench fighting, blitzkrieg, aerial dog fights, rapid tank assaults, preposterous honour in the field and scenes of joyous liberation. Ecstatic crowds chanting '*Joi Bangla!*' greeted us all the way from Krishnagar on the border to Sudiah in Bangladesh, which had been smashed by Indian Army twenty-five pounders in their pursuit of the Pakistani enemy. And while some villages grieved and picked through the smouldering remains of their houses, others cheered our convoy, throwing flowers and offering chapatis, of which they had few.

We waved down a jeep bearing a Sikh brigadier, who drove us to his front line which might have been Ypres or Flanders. I vividly remember boots. Boots among the yellow mustard flowers. Boots with their soles turned upward. Boots, it seemed, to the horizon.

The Pakistani troops, as tough as the hard hills of the Punjab, where villages had supplied whole regiments for more than a century, had remained in their trenches and had fought like lions until the Indian tanks rolled over them. Each soldier now lay spreadeagled with only his boots visible, as if resting out of sight of an officer. Beside one lay snapshots of his family, the women in *purdah*, the men with fine moustaches, and his orders to take leave the week the war had begun.

The war proceeded with only one result possible. Seventy thousand Pakistani troops were trapped. The Chief of the Indian Army Staff, General Sam Manekshaw, speaking as if to the defenders of Mafeking, addressed the enemy every half-hour on All-India Radio. 'Hear me, hear me!' he said with Edwardian fervour. 'Lay down your arms before

23 A U.M. Fakhruddin, *Daily Mirror* correspondent in Bangladesh, 1974 (*Photograph: John Pilger*)

24 Vladimir Slepak, Soviet dissident, 1977 (*Photograph: Eric Piper*)

25 Underground hospital, Eritrea, 1978 (*Photograph: Eric Piper*)

26 Cambodian child with worthless new banknotes which poured into the streets of Phnom Penh from the destroyed national bank, blown up by the retreating army of Pol Pot, 1979 (*Photograph: Eric Piper*)

27 Nam Phann, Khmer Rouge commander and former provincial governor under Pol Pot, known to Western aid officials as 'the butcher', Cambodia/Thailand border, 1980 (*Photograph: Eric Piper*)

28 Cars swept into a symbolic pile by the Khmer Rouge when they forcibly evacuated Phnom Penh at the start of 'Year Zero' (*Photograph: Eric Piper*)

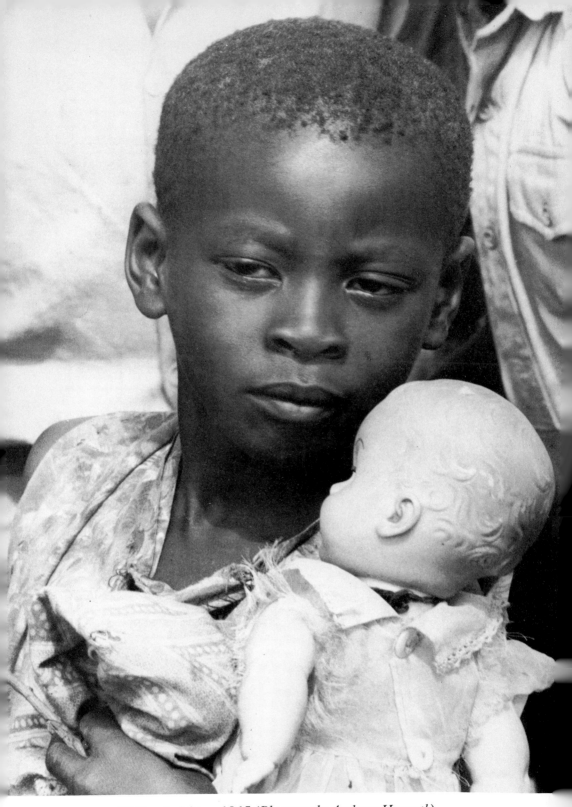

29 South Africa, 1965 (*Photograph: Anthony Howarth*)

it is too late. We have you surrounded. Your fate is sealed. Why die? There is no disgrace in laying down your arms to another soldier, and we will treat you as soldiers. For God's sake, do not lose time.'

Reporting the birth of Bangladesh became increasingly difficult. There were correspondents in Dacca, but they were trapped in the Intercontinental Hotel. In India the authorities did not need to impose censorship. They could control the Press in the time-honoured way. Every day there was a press briefing in Calcutta during which maps were unrolled and cricket scores of tanks knocked out, planes shot down and garrisons stormed were read out by an information officer. Whenever we became hyperactive on this diet of communiqués, jovial soothing would be applied by a General Jacob, who proudly billed himself as the Indian Army's only Jewish general. The final battle for Bangladesh was under way and none of us would see it. 'We simply have no transport for you,' said the information officer. But of course there was another way.

'Cash 'n' Carry' Harry had been in Vietnam, the Middle East, Biafra and other places of turmoil for one of the American television networks. A huge man who wore an 'Indy 99' T-shirt, he carried an attaché case at all times. In the attaché case were thousands of dollars. Cash 'n' Carry Harry was not a reporter or a cameraman. He had but one job: to buy. He bought politicians, civil servants and Army officers. He saw to it that his television team went to the war in their very own helicopter. 'The military', said Harry when the war was over, 'are always the cheapest.'

Unable to witness for ourselves the most crucial days of the fighting, we fell back on the second-hand. Among the first foreigners to be evacuated from Dacca by the Royal Air Force was a French official, whom I had known as a reliable 'diplomatic source' during the military occupation of Dacca. She told me that an orphanage near her home had been bombed by a Pakistan Air Force plane. I reported this and the *Mirror*'s headline was 'ORPHANAGE BOMBED BY PAKISTANIS'. I later learned that the Indians had bombed the orphanage. Perhaps for propaganda purposes of a diabolical nature, the plane had carried Pakistani markings, and this would not have been the first time this had happened in war. And perhaps it did not, and my source was simply mistaken. If there was ever a time I should have added the qualification, 'But I do not know the true facts', this was the time. But I did not. I retreated beneath the cover of a spurious objectivity. The need for a story, not the true facts, had triumphed.

I received a letter which had been forwarded from London, written in Dacca, spirited to India and posted to an address in Stepney. It bore the copperplate hand of A. U. M. Fakhruddin. 'By the grace of God I am still alive,' he wrote. 'Mind you, I have only the skin of my teeth left. Nevertheless, prepare yourself for my first report from liberated, democratic Bangladesh. P.S. *Richard III* is appropriate here, but my mind is blank. Sorry.'

With the Indians encircling Dacca, Eric and I finally reached Jessore,which had been the Pakistanis' Maginot Line. Jessore was a market town, as poor and flyblown as any. With the approach of the Indian Ninth Division, the 6,000 Punjabi troops who had brutalised Jessore for months had fled to the outskirts of nearby Khulna. Many of the officers had their wives and children with them. The Indians had brought up their heavy artillery, and if the Pakistani brigadier did not surrender, there would be carnage.

Two hundred yards separated the conquering Indian division and the trapped Pakistani division. Both armies were commanded by brigadiers who had been classmates at Sandhurst. The Pakistani brigadier was known affectionately to his Indian counterpart as 'Mo'. They had often played squash together, said the Indian brigadier, and Mo had always beaten him. 'He's a first-class chap; they come no better,' he said. 'But I fear the silly boy will not give up the ghost now and I shall have to teach him an old lesson. A shame.'

In nearby Khulna, the people were preparing to exact their revenge on Biharis who had collaborated with the enemy. The Biharis were roped together and made to stand with their hands on their heads and their heels against a wall. It was clear that the nature of their punishment had not yet been decided, but on the arrival of the foreign Press, and especially of two photographers, Eric Piper and freelance John Garrett, their guards began to beat them. Eric was trying to cover a war in which any orthodox 'news' picture had been difficult to find and could have commanded the front page. John Garrett, who paid his own hotel bills, could have had pictures for which any number of publications around the world would have competed to pay him handsomely. They both put away their cameras and walked away. The beating stopped.

The significance of this incident lay in the fact that it was not unknown for people to die for the camera. And indeed this happened two days after the Indians entered Dacca. While the Pakistani commander, General Amil 'Tiger' Niazi, was handing over his pistol in a final, flamboyant act of surrender in the centre of the racecourse, another less than gentlemanly ceremony was being stage managed for the Press a short distance away.

Abdul Kader Sidiqui was a self-appointed colonel and hero of the Mukti Bahini, who clearly craved a share of the publicity enjoyed by the foreign army which had liberated his country. Prostrate before him and his armed followers were four bound men described as 'anti-social elements who have molested women'. A crowd of several thousand had gathered, and several foreign photographers and a television crew from

ITN, London, had gone to see what was going on. Sidiqui's men began to strike their prisoners with the butts of rifles which were fixed with bayonets. Cameras were aimed, the crowd fell silent. Sidiqui strutted and made a speech about his right to judge and to execute on behalf of the people of Bangladesh. But there was a hitch; Richard Lindley, the ITN reporter, was horrified and he and his crew walked away.

Sidiqui's pique at the abrupt departure of his television stage might well have lapsed into boredom, leading perhaps to some sort of reprieve for his prisoners, had all the foreign Press walked away. But they did not walk away. They waited. And he noted the poised Nikons with obvious satisfaction. The four condemned men, together with a man who had tried to intervene, were bayoneted to death. The small son of one of the victims, who cradled his dying father's head in his arms, was trampled to death. A set of these pictures won a major press award. (This is not to suggest that the absence of cameras necessarily leads to the saving of lives. When the South African government barred journalists from the African townships in November 1985 the only effect seems to have been a sharp increase in the numbers of people killed by the police.)

'Three cheers for the victorious general!' shouted an Indian reporter at our final press briefing.

'Really, you are too kind,' responded Lieutenant-General Jagit Singh Aurora, GOC Eastern Command, Indian Army, conquerer of East Pakistan and liberator of Bangladesh, now before us rocking contentedly on his heels. 'Well, first off, I must say you press chaps made it easy. The Paks believed a newspaper story that said 5,000 of our paras had dropped near Dacca. That scared them to death. Actually, only a few hundred dropped. So thank you, boys! Thank you all so much for coming!'

29

Basket cases

The war ended colonial rule and a time of terror, and the map of the region made more sense. Sheik Mujibar Rahman came home from his Pakistani cell a hero, proclaimed himself *Bangabandhu* – Father of Bengal – and three and a half years later was murdered in a military *coup d'état*, which surprised no one.

During his rule, I came back to Bangladesh many times. In the first year of independence, the promise of a changing Bengal if not a golden one, with or without Sheik Mujib, still seemed possible to those like myself who admired the radical, vibrant strain in Bengali politics, not to mention the resilience of the people. To his credit, Sheik Mujib toiled at a constitution 'to embrace all the people', as he put it, and although 90 per cent of the population were Muslims, he declared Bangladesh a 'secular socialist republic' in which Hindu, Buddhist and Christian minorities would enjoy equal rights under the law. In the first elections, his Awami League won 307 of the 315 seats in parliament.

I got to know the Sheik well. He was a big man by Bengali standards, about five feet ten and robustly built. He always wore a black waistcoat over a starched white shirt and loose fitting pyjamas. He would prop himself on one leg and gesticulate with his bare foot. His charged intensity, his impetuousness and his sense of melodrama were difficult not to enjoy. Once, when I asked for his response to Pakistan's charge that the wartime atrocities had been exaggerated, he erupted, 'Okay, that is it! That is *it*! Put down your tea. We are going. Where is the car? Where is everybody? We are going. *Come!*' He scooped up a driver, a security man and a Belgian who was waiting to interview him; and with the prime minister sitting with his arms crossed and his bare left foot propping up the seat in front, we drove to the riverfront at Burhiganga, nine miles from Dacca.

The sight of the Sheik stopped everything. Sailing like a schooner under full sail above the crowd, he arrived at a jetty and proceeded to call people over to him, one by one. He asked them long questions and listened patiently to their answers. One man broke down and the Sheik held him until we left. 'They are telling me', he said to me, 'what I know very well. But I have asked them again for *you*. In the month of April the Pakistani firing squad killed 30,000 of my people in this one place. At every sunset they dragged men, women and children to this wharf, bound them up in human bundles and made them wade into the water. Then they shot them. This man lost his wife and two sons. His daughter was outraged and is in an institution. I have made her a Heroine of Bengal. Now your question is answered!'

The Sheik's tragedy was, as Anthony Mascarenhas wrote, 'that he never really got past the symbols and the flags'.[7] Although he left you in no doubt that he thought *he* was Bangladesh – 'my people, my government, my police, my army' – he was surrounded, isolated, manipulated and frightened by a legion of camp followers who were known widely by the epithet *Lallu panja*, which means Toms, Dicks and Harrys and is used on the sub-continent to describe hangers-on, time-servers and sycophants. These included bored old men, straight out of the boxwallah tradition of the Raj, a sprinkling of former Mukti Bahini, who enjoyed a feudal power in the countryside, and a Westernised clique whose members were more at ease in London than in Dacca and preferred the Queen's English to their native tongue. Indeed, their pride seemed to be that they had cultivated the British middle classes' abhorrence for emotion and of the ways of those of the station beneath them. Their wives would twitter at charity work, and they would speak of 'the masses' publicly with paternalism and privately with disdain.

Like the archetypal demagogue headed for disaster, the Sheik persecuted the best of his people for his own inadequacies. Moudud Ahmed was the young lawyer who had defended him in a Pakistan court, who had led Eric Piper and me into his occupied homeland, who had helped to form the Committee for Civil Liberties and Legal Aid and had defended ordinary people against the encroachment of the Sheik's draconian Special Powers Act. In the early hours of one morning Moudud's phone rang and a familiar voice shouted at him, 'If you keep opposing my will, I will get a gun and shoot you myself!' Moudud was imprisoned shortly afterwards and released only after I and other foreign journalists wrote to the Sheik threatening to mount an international campaign to shame him.

The Sheik grew more and more afraid of enemies, real and imagined. He abolished parliamentary government and suspended the constitution, and deeply hurt and angered the millions who had resisted and lost loved

ones in 'the cause of simple democracy', which was how the Bengalis
had described their struggle. Finally, he abandoned his earlier sobriquet
of Friend of Bengal for the megalomaniacal title of *Jatiya Pita*, Father
of the Race.

The famine in the autumn of 1974, and the total inability of his
government to cope alone with it, smashed any lingering hopes of the
Sheik's redemption. No single human being could manage a continuing
cataclysm, least of all Mujibar Rahman. The last time I saw him he tried,
pathetically, to cover up the scale of the famine, just as the Pakistanis
had attempted to cover up the scale of suffering following the 1970
cyclone. He blamed 'miscreants' at home, and the foreign Press, notably
myself, for 'stirring up trouble', just as the Pakistanis had done. When
I asked him why he had allowed the Bangladeshi Red Cross to appropriate
so much foreign aid and to account for so little of it, he became so
enraged he struck me on the knee with his fist. When I quickly withdrew
my knee he lunged for a second blow and fell to the floor. As I helped
him up he produced his watermelon smile. 'Shall we stay friends?' he
said. He was shot dead the following year.

Of course, Sheik Mujib's caricature of the national hero turned
corrupt dictator was one side of an all too familiar equation in much of
the impoverished or so called 'developing' world. The other side was
the nature of the 'development' itself and its tyranny of 'aid'.

In the weeks and months following independence the foreign aid
people would gather in the foyer of the Dacca Intercontinental, around
the murmuring fountain and the caged parakeets. The languages heard
were German, Russian, Japanese, Scandinavian, Dutch, Swedish,
Danish and the English of Americans, British, Canadians and Australians. In the parking lot, vans were lined up bearing the insignia of
the International Committee of the Red Cross, UNICEF, WHO, FAO, CARE,
USAID and other 'majors' of the international aid industry. All were
represented by experts on something or other: agriculture, flood control,
education, industry, health, birth control, money, God. Most seemed to
be in the country for only as long as it took them to compile their reports
which, I suspect, were read by others like themselves. I recall that one
of them took six months calculating that it cost twenty pence a day to
keep a Bangladeshi child alive.

The local patrons of many of these experts were foreign diplomats, in
whose homes the experts stayed or were frequent guests. In 1972 only
one member of the diplomatic community in Dacca spoke Bengali and
most of them had little contact with Bengali people other than the servants
in their air-conditioned, duty-free fortresses; Dacca was designated a
diplomatic 'hardship post', and the diplomats I met hated it.

Local corruption seemed to be the abiding concern of both experts and diplomats. Indeed for some it became their obsession, a lingua franca between the representatives of nations and institutions who otherwise had not a great deal to say to each other. And of course much of what they said was true, as hoarding and blackmarketeering were the unremarkable symptoms of a society racked by war, natural disaster, poverty in the extreme and a scarcity of almost everything taken for granted in the West. But it was a rare foreigner who could concede that it was the aid delivered by governments, international banks and agencies that helped to perpetuate corruption and poverty in countries like Bangladesh.

Far from helping people to achieve self-sufficiency, foreign aid tied the new nation's economy to a global system of 'aid dependency'. And far from helping the poor majority, foreign aid enriched a growing urban élite with imported luxuries and the opportunity to control outright markets such as food. In 1976 it was estimated that 5 per cent of a total 600,000 tons of foreign food shipped to Bangladesh reached hungry people; the rest secured a black market run by a corrupt few at the top.[8] Thus, aid reinforced the political position of a privileged minority and became the most powerful buttress against change.

In the first few years of independence millions of pounds, dollars, Deutschmarks, francs and yen in 'aid' vanished without trace. Everything was piecemeal. Not even the country's most pressing need – a system of flood control – was proposed as a programme to be begun and completed within a reasonable period of time. The World Bank's project for irrigation and flood control consisted of a few embankments here, a few bridges and canals there, and a bureaucracy to administer it. A World Bank official I interviewed in Dacca for a television documentary extolled the efforts his people were making in Bangladesh. When the camera was switched off, he said, 'The real problem is that these people are hopeless. Kissinger was right; what we've got here is another basket case.' I asked him to repeat this for the camera. Not surprisingly he refused, saying, 'I want to keep my job. It's a bloody fine job.'

For the 'hopeless' people of Bangladesh, who are one-hundredth of humanity, 'aid' meant not even a token version of the United Nations Relief and Rehabilitation Agency which had moved into Germany at the end of the war and dealt imaginatively with hunger, refugees and pestilence. In 1946 there were huge quantities of drugs to fight tuberculosis, insecticides to fight water-borne diseases like malaria, nutrition clinics for the children, a construction programme to rebuild homes, bridges, roads, railways.

Of course it is true that in so-called emerging countries, beset by the complexities of 'emerging' and prickly with the pride of independence, there are practical problems of how to distribute aid and through whom to channel it. Immediately after the war these problems existed in

Bangladesh but, compared with the experiences of other countries suffering the aftermath of extreme social upheaval, they were few. There was too much relief and sheer joy at having been liberated so quickly and too much eagerness to open up the country to a sympathetic world. What they got instead was ill-conceived, often unco-ordinated 'charity' which did them more harm than good and from which, as the model 'basket case', they continue to suffer.

Take, for example, the story of the Pill in Bangladesh. In 1972 the US Aid and International Development Agency (USAID) shipped to Bangladesh 22 million packets of oral contraceptives. These were dumped on an illiterate, rural people with no concept of chemical birth control. Directions were in English which few could comprehend, there was no village education programme and the pills were sold at market stalls. Three years later less than a million had been used by women; the rest were taken by men, children and chickens or collected in jars. During the three years of pill-pushing, according to some government officials, the population actually increased by ½ per cent. 'For some village women', wrote Ian Guest, 'the experience appears to have caused immense personal suffering and even suicides because of side-effects like bleeding which had been caused by irregular supply.'[9]

The culpability of the pill-pushers in failing to link effective distribution and education to their 'gifts' is equalled by an almost total neglect of the other half of the problem of population control: health. As in many countries, children are vital to the economic survival of every village. Eight-year-olds work in the fields and paddies; for families forever on the cusp of life and death, there is no other way. But in Bangladesh three out of every ten children die before the age of five from malnutrition, tetanus, dysentery and other preventable killers. An assault on these common diseases would save more young lives and convince people they need not breed merely to counter the loss of previous babies, and an interest in contraception, which is already shared by millions of women in Bangladesh, would spread.

The story of food aid to Bangladesh is also instructive. Most of the first foreign food to Bangladesh came from the United States in the form of surpluses. Under a policy laid down in 1973 by President Nixon's Secretary of Agriculture, Earl Butz – Butz called it 'Agripower' – American surpluses were dumped in Bangladesh in order to meet the demand of the 'food lobby' in Washington. This lobby is made up of a handful of conglomerates which between them control more than 60 per cent of all secondary cereals in the world, 50 per cent of the world's wheat and 95 per cent of soybeans: in other words, most of the world's trade in foodgrains.[10] Two of these companies alone account for more than 50 per cent of the world's whole-grain shipments.

Not surprisingly such a concentration of commercial interest works hard to ensure that world food prices remain high and 'stable' and regards the elimination of shortages as 'unstable' and falling prices as simply bad for business.[11] In other words, dumping surpluses in Bangladesh helps to keep the price of grain artificially inflated in the United States while guaranteeing a future market for manufactured agricultural products.

In 1975 this policy was given the backing of Congress, which called on the president to 'give special consideration to the potential for expanding markets for America's agricultural abundance abroad in the allocation of commodities or concessional financing'. Poor countries like Bangladesh were given 'concessional financing' – i.e. surpluses – until their economies became addicted to American wheat and their governments were forced to pay artificially high prices for imported food. This has happened to Bangladesh, forestalling plans for genuine development and helping to keep its governments politically weak, ineffectual, and malleable: a familiar pattern throughout the 'developing world'.

That 'Agripower' has nothing to do with the true needs of the recipient country was demonstrated in a report by the General Accounting Office in Washington, the 'watchdog' of Congress.[12] The GAO found that in the last three months of 1974, when there was generally acknowledged to be a 'global food crisis', less than half of American food shipments went to the countries in greatest need. Instead, those regimes which American foreign policy sought to prop up received substantial food aid, notably the military dictatorships in South Vietnam, South Korea and Chile. In 1974 almost half of all American food shipped abroad to the beleaguered regime in South Vietnam was diverted and sold on the world market for dollars, which brought arms and ammunition.[13] (In 1985 the country receiving more cash aid than any other in the world has never known starvation, is not 'underdeveloped' and is, per capita, one of the most prosperous in the world. It is Israel, which receives $212 per head of population per year from the United States.[14])

Some would argue that the most effective use of 'aid' is as a weapon. In 1973 the Office of Multilateral Diplomacy was established in the US State Department and became known as the 'zap office'. It was the child of Henry Kissinger, then Secretary of State, who believed that small countries had to accept a latter-day vassal's role if they came within the superpower's 'sphere of influence'. Those countries which tried to assert their independence – for example, by voting against American motions in the United Nations – were 'zapped'. Salvador Allende's Chile was one of the first to be zapped. All American food aid was withdrawn without notice and this contributed to the instability and finally to the overthrow of the Allende government by the army of General Pinochet. Within two years, a period which saw a democracy transformed to a state of siege and torture, American food aid to Chile reached a record level.[15]

During 1984 the television cameras turned on Ethiopia, the world's newest 'basket case'. And perhaps it was Ethiopia's televised suffering that educated many people about the uses of aid other than for humanitarian purposes. 'Over the next twenty years food can be the greatest weapon we have', declared President Reagan's Secretary of Agriculture, John Block, in 1982.[16] He did not have to wait long for an opportunity to use it. In January 1983 the Food and Agricultural Organisation's Global Information and Early Warning System gave clear warning of the tragedy about to envelop Ethiopia and the Sahel. Reporters doing the rounds of embassies in Addis Ababa in early 1984 confirmed that Western governments knew of the scale of the disaster but remained sitting on their hands. As a result, no effective food aid reached Ethiopia for twenty-two months and countless lives were lost. Ethiopia, whose regime proclaimed itself to be Marxist-Leninist, had been 'zapped'.

Dr Charles Elliott, the recently retired director of Christian Aid and a former Professor of Development Policy and Planning at the University of Wales, told the *Observer* in October 1984 that for the previous two years the long hostility of America and Britain to the Ethiopian regime 'caused them to refuse to release adequate funds or food'. The reason for withholding aid, he said, was that the last great famine in Ethiopia in 1972–4, when 200,000 had died, had brought down Emperor Haile Selassie. 'They thought that if there was a major catastrophe it would probably change the regime again,' he said.[17]

The British government's response to the Ethiopian famine is worth recounting, for it tells us much about the politics of 'aid'. Certainly, British officials in 1984 made no attempt to disguise the fact that 'political factors' influenced British policy of withholding aid from Ethiopia;[18] and Mrs Thatcher and her Minister for Overseas Development, Timothy Raison, went on record as being 'steadfastly against committing any long-term aid at all to Ethiopia'.[19] But then the television images became more and more alarming, and 'feeding Africa' became a great apolitical crusade which climaxed in Band Aid and the Live Aid benefit concerts. 'Famine', said Raison's parliamentary secretary, Tim Eggar, 'had become a domestic political issue to which we felt we had to respond.'[20]

As if sharing the public's concern and generosity the government announced in March 1985 that it was giving £60 million in emergency aid to Africa. What few realised was that this meant a *cut* of almost £40 million on the aid figure for Africa for the financial year just ending. Moreover, all of this money had been and continued to be 'old money', or funds deducted from aid already allocated to poor countries. This gave Britain the distinction of being the only industrialised country to *reduce* its help to the victims of probably the greatest famine in history.

Timothy Raison, said to be the 'human face' among Thatcher ministers, went to considerable lengths to defend the government's record. He had already admitted in the House of Commons that there 'may be a cut' in British aid; but then, mysteriously, the word 'cut' was deleted from Hansard and 'calculation' was substituted.[21] As if to demonstrate the government's readiness to give, he waved his own cheque book at a United Nations meeting in Geneva, a gesture which seemed to have little effect shortly afterwards when the World Bank launched a special fund for Africa.

The British government at first offered £75 million, but tied this 'gift' to the purchase of British goods. This was nothing new, of course. Contrary to popular mythology most British aid is commerce by other means or 'aid for trade' which, according to the *Financial Times*, 'helps UK exporters compete with subsidised competition'.[22] In the end, the World Bank refused to accept the strings to Britain's 'aid', although Timothy Raison claimed that Britain, with Germany and Japan, was giving 'a further $425 million' to the World Bank 'for Africa'. In fact, this money came from Germany, Japan and Switzerland. Britain had nothing to do with it.[23]

When American food surpluses began to arrive in Ethiopia at the end of 1984, they carried the slogan, 'A hungry child knows no politics'. They also carried the proviso that there would be no American support for development projects which might lead to self-sufficiency in Ethiopia. Britain and most of Europe – whose grain mountain in 1985 was increasing at a rate of more than 7,000 tonnes *a day* – followed suit. This meant that Ethiopia suffered twice over. Not only had it been 'zapped' by the initial, deliberate denial of emergency food, but it had also been drawn into the global system of 'aid dependency'.

The Soviet Union, although itself reliant on American grain surpluses, showed no more compassion towards its Ethiopian 'ally' than had Western governments. Apart from an estimated 10,000 tonnes of food, the Soviet contribution to the well-being of the Ethiopian people was the continued supply of arms and military technology to the Dergue regime in Addis Ababa, thereby allowing it to kill more starving Eritreans and Tigreans fighting for their independence. Soviet advisers had already helped to establish a system of collective farms emulating its own disastrous model and these are almost certain to aggravate food shortages in Ethiopia. 'It's not surprising', wrote the journalist Dr Enver Carim, 'that some analysts wonder whether the United States and the Soviet Union are actually in cahoots to keep Ethiopia in a state of dependency and underdevelopment. When food becomes a policy instrument, the

Cold War appears to be an elaborate ploy whereby poorer nations are held in thrall to the twin empires of East and West.'[24]

Every year there are 6,000 United Nations conferences and reports involving a million pages of documentation, many of them concerned with 'aid and development'.[25] The most ballyhooed and forgettable was the World Food Conference in Rome in November 1974, at which the delegates consumed three tons of pasta, two tons of meat, 12,000 eggs and 3,500 litres of wine and Henry Kissinger made a speech about every child in the world having the right not to go to bed hungry.

Then in 1980 there was the Brandt Commission which exchanged old jargon ('Third World') for new ('North versus South') and was, as author Teresa Hayter wrote, 'the product of an alliance between members of the ruling élite in the third world and enlightened sections of the ruling class in the north: enlightened mainly in the simple sense that they favour non-military solutions to the problem of containing unrest'.

And of course containing unrest is all important if raw materials and markets are to remain accessible. Teresa Hayter pointed out that

> between a quarter and a third of the exports of developed countries, and nearly forty per cent of US exports, go to the third world. Some of the major multi nationals make most of their profits, and even most of their sales, in the third world. The major banks lent multiples of their capital base to some third world countries and made fat profits in the process. Now the banks want their money back, or at least carry on making profits.[26]

Many of these lending banks have depended on the United States Treasury, which no longer wishes to underwrite them in the face of the greatest American deficit in the history of economics theory, most of it comprised of the greatest ever military budget. Willy Brandt was right, at least, when he warned that 'we are arming ourselves to death'.[27]

How the banks are persuading the poor to pay up is interesting. In 1985 the World Bank introduced a new 'aid' programme which, in effect, bribes countries to change their food production from local needs to export crops, regardless of the fact that one of the principal causes of the famine in Africa today is the rising proportion of money and land devoted to production for export only. Under the World Bank scheme, which is a copy of an American 'Economic Policy Initiative' for Africa, a £1,000 million 'special facility' loan is offered on condition that farms are privatised, wages are 'controlled', food prices are allowed to rise and produce is exported. More tea, coffee and cocoa, fruit and vegetables will go to European markets to earn the 'hard currency' which poor countries need in order to pay the interest charges on their debts to the banks.

It is ironic that India, the country which used to be caricatured as a 'basket case', with a begging bowl forever extended to the rich world, actually receives little aid relative to its size and has restricted foreign trade and investment. The benefits have been self-sufficiency in food, a technological capacity greater than that of many richer countries and probably more genuine 'non-aligned' independence than that achieved by any third world country.

The contrast in neighbouring Bangladesh, still riding the tiger of foreign aid, still trapped in indebtedness, is striking. And yet in Bangladesh there are some spectacular examples of what genuine foreign aid can do. I can think of village co-operatives whose needs have been assessed diligently and which have achieved self-sufficiency with fertilisers, water pumps and high-yield seeds, thus breaking the small farmers' cycle of debt and exploiting some of the most productive soil on earth. It is significant that several of these schemes have been assisted by small countries, such as Sweden, whose aid programmes are almost totally devoid of commercial and strategic strings.

Since the calamitous cyclone in November 1970 there has been a cyclone almost every year in Bangladesh and each accompanying tidal wave has met no resistance from the hypothetical barriers for which there is a perennial World Bank plan. After the last tidal wave struck, in May 1985, one of the experts calculated that a flood control system would pay for itself in increased food production. More than 11,000 people had just been swept to their deaths and their harvest and homes destroyed. The logic of real aid is immutable.

At the time of writing the storms are due again in the Bay of Bengal and the earth embankments, erected by farmers with their hands, are as soft as cake. In the foyer of the Dacca Intercontinental Hotel another generation of foreign experts gathers around the murmuring fountain, while in the markets, streets and villages poverty is still fought with ingenuity and enterprise: a beer can as a ladle, a battery case as a sink, a sewing machine still whirring after half a century of use. In spite of bloody coups, people still speak out and strike and go to gaol for their beliefs. In his last letter, A. U. M. Fakhruddin wrote, 'We still await simple democracy. We are undeterred.' And at the mosque in Elephant Road the *muezzin* still climbs defiantly into the cockpit of his aeroplane five times a day and proclaims the greatness of Allah, although he has not flown the flag and he has not cried *Joi Bangla!* since the bad old days.

VII

PALESTINE

30

Exodus

Jerusalem: Easter 1968. The last waves of the devout were arriving and to the accredited sceptic like myself, and to those toothless vendors of Pontius Pilate underarm deodorant ('Judge It For Yourself!') and Holy Sepulchre egg-timers, they were welcome relief from the upheavals of the past ten months. By legions of Jewish buses they came, knowing full well that if this was Easter, it must be Jerusalem.

'Oh yes, it *is* true: they are coming back to us,' said an Italian friar upon viewing the throng from the balcony of the Franciscan monastery deep in the Old City. 'You know, I am sending telex messages around the world saying, "No danger for Christians. Come please." But, alas, many choose to go instead to Lourdes.'

The Franciscans are the governors of what is surely the world's least known 'neutral state'. As Holy property millionaires, they have control over the *Terra Sancta*, the Holy Land, which extends into Israel, Jordan, Turkey, Syria and Cyprus; and it is they who carry the authority of the Vatican in negotiations with 'whomever may be in charge at the time', as they say. It so happened the Jews were now in charge of their capital and public relations were good. In return for water that was drinkable and lavatories that flushed, the friars had placed Hebrew on the curriculum of the monastery's small orphanage. Before June 1967, when the Arabs were in charge, the Arab Legion had used a loft in the orphanage as a sniper's nest.

So having been reassured by the Holy telex, though their numbers were less than half those of before the war, the pilgrims trudged up the Via Dolorosa, led by the friars bearing a mighty cross, past all fourteen stations. And when they reached the Church of the Holy Sepulchre, an asphyxiating smog of incense, sweat and drains descended upon those who could elbow their way inside. It had not cleared when the countdown

of anguish was completed and ritual bells were fired like artillery at
heaven and the word was wailed forth that God was dead and had not
yet risen.

It was generally agreed that Arabs lived here, although they preferred
to call themselves Palestinians; and it was even said that they had lived
here longer than anyone. But this fact, however obscure, should be
whispered, especially by the Palestinians themselves, lest they are roused
in the middle of the night and expelled from the city of their birth and
their house is bulldozed or taken over by the Custodian of Properties
and given to an American who has converted to Judaism. Today, those
who remain in 'united' Jerusalem must go quietly, for they are known
as the 'demographic problem': they won't, that is, simply fade away.

Ten miles away, in Kalandia camp, Ahmed Hamzeh said, 'I was a
street entertainer, first in Haifa, then in the Old City of Jerusalem. I
would play all kinds of musical instruments; I would sing in Arabic,
English and Hebrew; I am told I am gifted. I had a monkey, and because
I was rather poor, my small son would sell chewing gum while the
monkey did its tricks. One day a rich Kuwaiti stopped his car in front
of us. He was one of those who came to Ramallah for the summer. He
shouted at my son, "Show us how a Palestinian picks up his food
rations!" I made the monkey appear to scavenge on the ground . . . in
the gutter . . . and my son did the same. The Kuwaiti threw coins and
my son crawled on his knees to pick them up. He was a kind boy, but
hardened to street life, like me. When the Arab had gone, I could not
suppress an outburst of tears, and my son came to me and cried too.
What had happened seemed to be all our world . . . a world suspended
there in the gutter, and we were too weak, too alone to hit back at it. So
we wept.'

I had not seen a Palestinian refugee camp until then. The camps had
been fixtures on the horizons of two generations, and yet how many of
those who had been horrified by the hijackings since the Six Day War
and then dulled by their regularity on the TV news had seen one? How
many tourists and pilgrims to the Holy Land had seen one? How many
foreign politicians, pro-Israel or Arabist or pragmatist or Communist,
not to mention those who persistently called on the 'international community', whatever that was, to take action against terrorism, had seen
one? Of if they had, like Margaret Thatcher, what purpose did it serve
apart from an exercise in patronage? Most Israelis lived a Sunday drive
away from a camp, but only a tiny few had ever glimpsed one. Most
simply excluded the inhabitants of the camps from any context, and this
applied especially to the Israeli young, who did not remember the
European pogroms against the Jews, in which no Arabs were involved,
but nevertheless remained prisoners of their parents' fears.

One evening in Tel Aviv, in the pleasant garden of my friends Teddy and Shura Levite – Teddy, a journalist, was born in Warsaw and Shura was born in Vilna which was then in Poland – I set out to film for television a cross-section of young Israelis talking about how the camps could be emptied and the Palestinians could be satisfied. Instead I listened to the film turn in the camera as each struggled painfully to articulate the previously unthinkable.

Yuri, aged seventeen, had said, 'First, I think you can't turn history back. What has happened, happened . . . we are here now. They are in the camps . . . I mean you can't throw us out . . . history won't let you . . . I don't know . . . '

The aloneness which Ahmed Hamzeh, the street entertainer, had felt as a boy and the anger that frustrated his manhood were of course shored up not only by Jews but by his brother Arabs, from Kuwait to the Lebanon, and by Christians, whose charity came at Christmas and occasionally at Easter. Of the thousands besieging Jerusalem just two, a Lutheran and his wife, had driven across the valley to Kalandia with a Land Rover laden with blankets.

It was a bitterly cold and wet Easter. I had not worn a coat and the wind spun off the large rocks on the bare side of the valley and carried the stench of the sewer that had overflowed and merged with the mud. Some 3,000 people lived here, in sight of their homeland and in dwellings of mud, sacking and corrugated iron. Water trickled brown, if at all, from communal taps, and there were communal lavatories and communal illnesses, such as madness, blindness and gastro-enteritis. Each person was issued 2,300 calories of rations per day, which would drop to 1,500 in the summer: figures calculated by the United Nations Relief and Works Agency (UNRWA) as precisely the amount a human being needed to survive, no more and no less, and precisely the amount the agency could afford on its minuscule handout from the 'international community', with the notable exception of the Palestinians' shrill friend, the Soviet Union, which gave nothing.

The main meal at Kalandia was a tin plate of gruel in which a variety of nutrients were said to be expertly balanced, a brick of bread and a vitamin pill. Children under fifteen were supposed to receive a supplement of protein – rice, powdered egg, a vegetable – but this seldom reached all of them as UNRWA's money frequently ran out; and those who managed to get the food hurried back to the huts with it, where it was shared or put up for sale as the only defence against destitution. A quarter of the children were malnourished.

Two-thirds of Kalandia's men were unemployed; a generation had grown up who had never known work. They went nowhere. They walked up and down the camp's one undulating street. They huddled outside the administration block, listening to the broadcasts from Amman in which Palestinians throughout their Diaspora – in America, Europe, Latin America and the Arab world – sent messages to their families. These were followed by the melancholy songs of Oum Kalthoum, the beloved 'Star of the Orient', and the men hummed the refrains they knew well. Then they walked some more as they sat on small promontories jutting above the mud, which also served as places to scrub clothes and, when the weather allowed, to dry them. All of them exhuded a listless humiliation, as if waiting for some deity to come to their aid while they watched their women suckle the next generation.

'I have seen only two children in shoes,' I said to Mohammed Jarella, a gentle, sardonic Jerusalemite who had come with me to Kalandia and who, like most of the UNRWA people, was himself a Palestinian.

'I have seen the same two,' he said.

'But it is very cold.'

'Yes, I can feel it.'

'Well, what are you doing about it?'

'Well, my friend John, I have our budget in my briefcase . . . here it is . . . you see, in this column, is the money we have. In this next column is our expenditure . . . food for everybody and blankets for almost everybody. The two columns balance, you see. Three years ago we spent on food and roofs. In another three years . . . maybe we shall spend on shoes. That is our progress after twenty years.'

The highest hill above Kalandia rises in a mass of eroded limestone. Ahmed Hamzeh, the street entertainer, walked down the slope towards us, with his son holding the tail of his coat.

'He has sold the monkey,' said Mohammed Jarella. 'He doesn't go to Jerusalem any more. He broods; he reads. He is trying to perform a miracle and grow something on that hill.'

He arrived and gripped my hand and did not let go. His son stood very still at his side. 'You will forgive me', he said in good English, 'if after these years . . . twenty years I have been here . . . if I look like a peasant. Never mind. I could sing very well and even on the street I thought I was an artist, not a beggar . . . maybe I am not even a peasant now. Never mind.'

'After all this time,' I said to him, 'what do you feel? Do you feel hatred?'

'Hatred! What is that to a Palestinian? If you mean, did I hate the Jews? Well, I don't remember them much in Haifa. But after the 1948 war, when we came to Jordan, I remember the Arabs . . . the Arabs with jokes about Palestinians . . . the Arabs at the Aliens' Office who shouted and made you wait for weeks for a work permit . . . Yes, I hate the Jews, or maybe I pity them for their stupidity. They can't win, because we

Palestinians are the Jews now and, like the Jews, we will never allow them or the Arabs or you to forget. The youth will guarantee us that . . . is that not truth, Jarella?'

'My friend,' said Mohammed Jarella, 'I am here for the United Nations. I am meant to be neutral.'

'Neutral!' said Ahmed Hamzeh. 'What is neutral? Are you a Palestinian?'

'Yes, I am,' said Jarella.

'Then do or don't I speak the truth?'

'You speak it.'

When he walked away, I noticed he was leading his son, and that the son stumbled.

'It is trachoma,' said Jarella. 'In the early days it blinded hundreds of children in the camps. We have it under control now.'

In Kalandia's one substantial building, a group of teenage girls was learning to sew. The faces were bored and they ignored us, except for one girl who stood up behind her ancient machine and began to shout. The girl beside her pulled at her apron and admonished her, but still she shouted.

Mohammed Jarella put his voluminous overcoat around her shoulders, as if to protect her from the cold. 'Ah, this is difficult,' he said, embarrassed. 'She is asking you why can't she go to her home. She is saying, "Why? Why?" She is sixteen and was born here. You know, this is the only place she has known; I doubt if she has even been to Jerusalem. But she still believes this is not her home. In her imagination she knows she has a home elsewhere.'

I drove on to Ramallah, a few miles away. With Jerusalem, Jericho, Nablus, Bethlehem and Hebron, Ramallah, with its Christian majority, was at the matrix of the Holy Land on the West Bank of the Jordan taken from King Hussein the previous June; and already, there were voices in Israel claiming it as Israeli territory. To its 600,000 inhabitants, this was Palestine, adapted from *Falastin*, the Arabic corruption of the Roman name *Palaestina*, although Israeli historians insisted the Romans only used this name to wipe Judah from the map. Whatever the recent claims of territory and the biblical claims of convenience, the Palestinian Arabs had been the continuous majority here, living in flinty valleys terraced with olive and orange groves over which minarets rose and people moved about like butterflies in the fields; only the oak forests were missing and, Jew and Arab were agreed, it was the Turks who cut them down.

In Ramallah, the big clock in Mukhtaribine Square was stopped at seven minutes past ten. It had stopped on June 6, 1967. It had been one of the first targets hit by Israeli shells a few hours before Israeli troops occupied the town as the prelude to their lightning conquest of the West Bank. Ramallah and its sister town of El Bireh, 3,000 feet above sea level, were Jordan's holiday resorts. Money would start coming in at Easter in preparation for 'the season' and for the influx of thousands of wealthy middle-class tourists from the Gulf, on whom the towns' economies depended.

The streets were almost empty now. In a side street a distraught family picked over the ruins of their house blown up by the Israelis two nights before. Details were difficult to come by, but it seemed that a 'suspect' had slept there. This was now a common sight in the towns and villages of the West Bank and Gaza. Palestinians could become suspects if they were previously members of a political party, a trade union, a student society, a cultural association – all of which were banned. If they uttered a word of protest against the occupation, they could be arrested; striking, or even closing their own shops during normal business hours, was forbidden. And before they were tried or even charged, their families and often their neighbours – people they might have barely known and all of them innocent even in the eyes of the authorities – would be collectively punished. Indeed, they would be bundled out into the street regardless of the hour or the weather – women, children, the old, the sick – and marshalled to watch the destruction of their homes. This was to be their 'lesson'. It is not known if the Jewish soldiers who planted the explosives reflected upon the irony of their actions; for few peoples had known more collective punishment than the Jews.

Beneath the stopped clock in the square and outside the travel agent's, where 'Israel' on the globe in the window had been carefully covered with Plasticine, a long queue extended into the street. They were people going to America, where there was already a Palestinian community of some 5,000. The Israelis allowed them to take out their money in foreign currency, on condition that they signed a form declaring that their departure was voluntary and that they would never return. Most of the faces turned away when I approached them; their bitterness was touchable. They at least could arrange their own exodus.

Almost overnight Ramallah had been denuded of its teachers, lawyers, journalists, engineers and politicians. All but one of those to whom I had introductions had been deported from the land of his birth, including the mayor and the leader of the Evangelical Episcopal Community. Those left behind were the old puffing on their hookahs and listening to Al Fatah radio acclaim guerrilla victories no one believed, and the women and the young, of whom the street entertainer had spoken.

I drove south to Jericho where a mile beyond the walls of the world's first city, now swept into a neat neolithic pile, sprawled the world's largest ghost town: Aqabat Jabr, formerly a camp of 25,000 refugees from

Jerusalem, Nazareth and Haifa, all of whom had fled in a terrible
stampede on the night of June 12, 1967.

'Kill the Jews wherever you find them,' said King Hussein in his last
broadcast before the ceasefire on the sixth day of the war. 'Kill them
with your hands, your nails and teeth.' Now the Jews had won, they
would come and kill them all at Aqabat Jabr: that was the people's
conviction. By the dawn of the 13th they had gone, all 25,000 of them,
across the Allenby Bridge to what was left of the Hashemite Kingdom
of Jordan. All but one had gone. He was the mayor of the camp and he
approached me, marching stiff-backed and with a broom on his shoulder
as if it was a rifle. For ten months he had marched the empty streets,
guarding the empty houses with his broom, shouting orders to himself.
The convulsion of that night, caused by blind, contagious fear, had
apparently left him in this state. He had stayed to face the blood-thirsty
Jews, who came and were delighted by what they saw; they wanted not
blood, only the land.

'You, sir, are welcome!' bellowed the mayor. 'I, sir, am ready to receive
you . . . with all my people here!'

Inside the mud-walled houses there had been no alteration since the
night of June 12. The Israelis had left the camp exactly as they found it,
returning only to sweep the streets for mines. In one house was a crib,
unfinished basketwork, a table laid for breakfast. In another, a wedding
album lay open on the floor and two shy, out of focus faces peered up,
smiling, and beside it a carpenter's diploma bore the footprint of its
owner, left perhaps as he fled; a tattered copy of *First Steps in English
Grammar* flapped its pages; doors opened and shut in the breeze; flies
vibrated over cans of yeast which, said the label, were 'a gift of the
American people, not to be sold or exchanged'.

I picked up the wedding album and the carpenter's diploma and drove
away. Before I turned out of the valley I glanced in the rear-view mirror
and saw the solitary figure of the mayor. He was standing to attention,
presenting arms with his broom.

31

Unspeakables

Maoz Haim, Israel: February 1970. The children were inexplicably different: their eyes had a bland, almost adult look; and when at night the incessant noise began, like a great door slamming in the wind, they lay still in the chambers and they did not giggle. They were good children.

The chambers were their homes. They were underground and hermetically sealed against gas and lit by a soft violet light. The children were born here and would be preserved here until they were old enough to fight: such as the cycle of life at the front line of a war in the very heartland of Israel, the world's David, as Israelis would wish to describe their country, a nation in arms more than any nation in modern history, though others would describe her as Sparta.

Maoz Haim was a kibbutz that dribbled dangerously over the lip of the Jordan valley, half a mile from an electrified fence, beyond which was the River Jordan and the black basalt hills where, the Bible says, Jesus Christ multiplied the bread and fish. Maoz Haim had 350 members; the eldest was born in 1890 on the Russian steppes and the youngest was born the night before I arrived, during the eleven o'clock shelling, and given the name Shalom, which means, in literal Hebrew, peace and, in practice, ceasefire.

Maoz Haim was settled on July 7, 1936 by a dozen ragged Poles who came in a truck from Haifa and pitched their tents beside a malarial swamp, purchased from a sheik by the Jewish Fund. The Poles came at speed because the following day, July 8, the British Mandate authorities were to enact a law which proclaimed this Arab land and prohibited Jews from settling it.

'So what did we do?' said Itshah Carmel, one of the twelve. 'We *created the fact* that this was Jewish land!' He laughed from his belly, knowing that 'created facts' belong to his people's jargon.

Maoz Haim is the perfect image of Israel as many American Jews like to portray it, though without a notion of settling there themselves. The swamp and the brown folds of earth that surrounded it have long been converted to a lush profusion of datepalm, mango, olive, orange, jasmine and pomegranate; and were it not for another fact created long ago, the fact of Arab Palestine, the kibbutz might appear peacefully suburban, with its shade trees and rows of dolls houses and people cycling to the small plastics factory, which makes drinking straws and shower caps, and to the cotton fields and cow pasture. And were it not for the war, the cow pasture would not contain the mashed outline of a calf, which the day before had stepped on a mine meant for a man.

I arrived at the kibbutz at night, having driven the hundred miles from Tel Aviv, the breadth of Israel, past signs that read, 'If attacked leave your car and take shelter here'. At the last stop before the frontier, a town called Beit Sheam where, until 1948, Arabs had lived for at least a thousand years, I had a coffee and enquired where the original inhabitants had gone and what the town used to be called. No one knew. 'Shhh,' said the café owner, who was listening to the news with a worried expression; he had a boy on the Golan.

As I approached the kibbutz a spotlight picked up my car and guided me along the barbed-wire fence to the gate. Suddenly, the ground shook as explosions walloped it in firecracker succession. The spotlight left the car and swept out to the east; a siren sounded; a man came running with a torch. 'Get out of there!' he shouted. 'Get down here . . . Katyushas!'

A Katyusha is a 130 millimetre Russian cannon, which the Fedayeen fired usually every other night from the Gilead mountains. The shells smashed into the perimeter fence and one skidded through an orange grove, neatly laying it aside, and the rest merely furrowed the fields, as they usually did; they had a dependable inaccuracy.

Underground, in the chambers, the children were in a state of absurd calm, listening not to the explosions that shook their bunks but to a mounting argument among the adults as to whether they ought to watch *Bonanza* or *Mission Impossible* on a television recently donated by students in Salt Lake City. The adults were either parents or young women known as *metapelet*, which means roughly surrogate mother. At Maoz Haim, the rules regarding children are unwritten but strict. A mother may keep her newborn child with her only for the first four days. On the fifth day it is removed to a 'children's house' and given into the care of a *metapelet*. The mother is allowed to breast-feed her child for six months, and to play with him or her as long as she wishes, but only after she has worked the compulsory eight-hour day.

When the shelling had ended, I was taken to my hut, whose usual occupant, a single man called Yermiashu, was down at the electrified fence on patrol; after the Katyushas had furrowed the fields half a dozen Fedayeen would sometimes cross the Jordan and attempt to lay mines or ambush a patrol. Yermiashu had killed a guerrilla the week before and was regarded as a hero; to sleep in his bed, I was told, was a privilege.

I had often heard it said that whilst the kibbutzim enshrined the early ideals of the nation they no longer reflected the urban realities of Israel. There was much truth in this argument; the kibbutzniks were less than 4 per cent of the population. But they provided a quarter of all the Israeli casualties of the Six Day War (the proportion was even greater in the previous wars), and with their all-consuming self-belief, courage, discipline and isolation from the world around them, they remained an almost perfect microcosm of what Israel might become if she failed to sue for peace. Moaz Haim means fortress of life; most Israelis would accept this as a description of their country.

One morning at four o'clock I set out with a patrol almost to the edge of the River Jordan. The patrol was looking for two Fedayeen, who were the survivors of a raiding party that had come across in a rubber dinghy. Directly ahead was an Arab village called Zemaliah, surrounded by reputedly the richest soil in the Middle East. The original kibbutzniks, like Itshah Carmel, used to cross the river to hear the Arab farmers of Zemaliah sing in the fields; but only a goat coughed there now; everyone had gone. The heady smell of jasmine hung in the pre-dawn mist.

As the patrol's mounted machine-gun swept this emptiness, the young man in charge, whose name I was not permitted to know, said, 'It's like fighting mosquitoes: you never really *see* them.' He used the term 'them' a great deal; 'them' is how most Israelis refer to the Palestinians, terrorist or otherwise. 'The only one of them I ever knew to talk to', he said, 'was a boy I used to play with when my father took me into the fields.'

I asked all the young men on the patrol if they had ever known the enemy, 'them', as individual people. Each answered no.

When I returned to Tel Aviv, Dan Hadarni, an old friend who had photographed Kalandia, Akabat Jabr and Maoz Haim for me, said, 'I am full of confusion. I wish I had not seen the camps or the kibbutz. It is better for an Israeli like me not to be confused, because then we are at our weakest. At the refugee camp, I looked in a mirror; they were us, once again in the Diaspora; their bitterness was expressed with the words we used; their determination was our determination, which we grew up with in the ghetto. In my heart, I want them to be free, to go home, but I am afraid, and I know I have to stop them!'

Dan, with whom I have worked on other assignments, is a Pole, one of the 'human dust' as Ben-Gurion called the Jews of the Diaspora. He remembers, as a boy in Poland, the 'long black vans' of the Gestapo cruising the streets, and men in long overcoats getting out of them, enticing children to come for 'a joyride'. The rear compartments of the cars were sealed and the windows were opaque, and when each joyride began gas would pour from nozzles under the seat; it would take no more than a block or two of slow driving for half a dozen Jewish children to die. He had heard about the cars, so he ran when they came. Most of his family were gassed in Nazi camps.

Dan said, 'We do not want to live *together* with the Arabs because we don't trust them. I don't think the Jews trust anybody any more. That is a fact and a tragedy. I know we have passed this distrust, which I am afraid is essential for us, to the younger generation, so that they feel it even stronger than their parents.'

It was at this time that the fear and distrust was changing to a dependence on the Arabs as a captive labour force. Israelis were beginning to exhibit an anti-Semitism of their own; the Arabs, after all, were Semites, too. Sounding like a voice from out of the Jewish past, and using a familiar euphemism, Golda Meir had described the Palestinians as the communal problem. A few Israelis recognised the first signs of this racism and its dangers. While I was in Tel Aviv, a farmer's wife caused a minor commotion when she addressed the following anguished open letter to Moshe Dayan:

I am alarmed at the fact that with five Arab labourers, none of my family will mow the lawn or drive a tractor, on the grounds that 'Mohammed will do it'. Our treatment of the Arabs, right down to our personal dealings with workmen and others, sends shivers up my spine . . . because it reminds me of our past.[1]

Dayan replied, 'I agree this situation holds nothing good for Jews.' He made no mention of it holding nothing good for Arabs.[2]

'Unspeakables', such as compromise, were and are uttered in Israel by some of the most remarkable people I have met. Compromise has a very different meaning in Israel from that understood in much of Europe, because it dares to question Jewish exclusiveness. Israel Shahak is Professor of Organic Chemistry at the Hebrew University of Jerusalem, chairman of the Israeli League for Human and Civil Rights and an unofficial leader of the peace movement. Oded Pilavsky, a member of Matzpen, had said of him, 'Dr Shahak has seen true suffering. He was in the Warsaw ghetto and Bergen-Belsen and somehow managed to survive. Unlike most people who have suffered, his attitude is not "I've suffered enough, now it's their [the Palestinians'] turn". Rather, he decided that he himself would never be responsible for the type of suffering he underwent.'

I had several meetings with Israel Shahak in the clutter of his small flat in Tel Aviv. I sat on a chair; he sat on a pile of books. His face was terribly scarred by Nazi tortures. When his emotions rose I was transfixed by his eloquence. 'Peace,' he said, rolling it around his tongue, 'peace will come only when Jewish rights are no longer placed above human rights. Jewish culture has never been touched by the Enlightenment and is still ethically primitive. We never had a Martin Luther or a Calvin who said, "Wait a minute, we've been wrong about some basic principles for thousands of years." If Israel is a democracy . . . why are we so afraid to reform? Has Britain crumbled because it is no longer run by people beholden to the Church of England? France, until the Revolution, was built on the principle that only those who took the Catholic sacrament could be admitted to positions of power. This has changed. Has France left the map of Europe? The paradox of Israel is that her greatest weakness is the blinding force of Judaism, which has never been able to hear other opinions, criticisms. When people speak out for Jewish interests, they are regarded as people who have seen the light. When Zola defended Dreyfus he was not regarded by Jews as a man who loved justice but as a Jew-lover! Today, you only have to look in the Yearbook of Israeli Statistics, and you can see that everything in Israel is classified in Jewish and non-Jewish categories . . . vegetables! melons! babies! . . . and this means that non-Jews who now happen to be the majority here, the Palestinians, are not regarded in this country as human beings.'

I asked Israel Shahak if he believed Jews and Arabs would ever live together again in peace. 'Yes!' he replied. 'But only if there is security for both of us. I am working in Jerusalem. Two miles away a Palestinian lawyer was taken the other night and expelled, exactly like Solzhenitsyn from Moscow. It is not inconceivable that his house will be given to a Dutchman who has converted to Judaism, who will have all the rights the Palestinian never had in his homeland. We will never have security while we think *only* about Jews.'[3]

32

Diaspora

Amman, Jordon: March 1970. A month later I was on the other side of the River Jordan. Israel, which occupied the horizon, was a world away. The hill above us merged into a zinc sky; night had almost come when we reached the top and the bearers put his boy down on the rubble, and lifted him out and held him up, dead and still bloodied, to look at 'occupied Palestine'.

He was nineteen, a martyr now, or a fool, depending from which side of the Jordan you viewed his silhouette. I shall remember his bravery. His hearse, on which I had travelled to his funeral, was the same jeep, fitted with a machine gun, which had taken us down to the river the night before. The mourners included the four who had come back across the river with me, having achieved nothing, except his death. Our faces were still blacked up with a watery tar, and the mud which had almost consumed our ridiculous adventure still clung to our clothes; but my sorrow for him, his father and brother was eclipsed by my relief at having come back.

His name was Ahmed Jabit, son of Mohammed Jabit, a carpenter; and he was held up like a hanged man while automatic weapons spat into the air and his brother, Salah, shouted across the valley:

> 'Out of his crucified growth!
> Out of his stolen smile!
> Life will emerge!
> When he goes home . . . to Palestine!'

At this, he was laid in the box, which was then sealed and covered with stones; and when I asked why the body had not been buried in the Muslim way, in a shroud, his brother said, 'Because when we go home, each box will be reclaimed and carried ahead of us. No one will remain behind.'

I had met Ahmed Jabit in a tent in the Baqa'a UNRWA camp a week before his death. Baqa'a was one of ten camps hurriedly erected in the days following the Six Day War to accommodate the thousands who fled across the Jordan, many of them from camps to which they had fled after the 1948 war. When I arrived it had not rained for some days but the earth was still a slick of orange brown. The nylon beach tents, sent from abroad, were blue, yellow, orange and green: bright consolations, perhaps, for the winter snowstorms and the unrelenting sun that followed. Baqa'a camp contained 60,000 people and 6,000 tents, 3,000 fewer tents than were needed. Bathing sheds were not yet built; trench latrines provided the only sanitation. All the children, it seemed, had running noses and eyes. They included most of the 25,000 people who had fled Aqabat Jabr, the camp in the valley now guarded by a madman with a broom.

I had brought with me the wedding album and the carpenter's diploma, with its footprint still recognisable, which I had picked up two years before in a deserted mud house in Aqabat Jabr. The diploma belonged to Mohammed Jabit; and there were eight of that name at Baqa'a. After several days of inviting myself into tent after tent and showing the diploma and the wedding album, I found the owner.

He had sent his wife to live with a relative in Egypt. He lived on rations and was sometimes asked to do repairs in the camp, but there were hundreds of carpenters like him. He said proudly that his sons, Salah and Ahmed, counted themselves, like every young male in the camp over the age of eight, as members of the 'resistance', and that Salah had learned to lay explosives and wield a knife and to snipe with a long-barrelled Polish rifle, which was kept in a corner of the tent beneath an old sepia photograph of the house in Jaffa he had not seen since he and his bride of a few weeks had fled in 1948.

Both his sons were born at Aqabat Jabr and in recent months they had undergone training with the Popular Front for the Liberation of Palestine, which emerged after the Six Day War as one of the most politicised of the guerrilla groups, Marxist-Leninist in ideology and considerably less conciliatory in tone than Al Fatah, the largest group. Two evenings later I met Salah and Ahmed Jabit in a house in suburban Amman and prepared to join them and three others of the PFLP in a raid across the Jordan.

Unlike many reporters who have covered conflict, I have had consciously to leap out of character and abandon an ingrained sense of caution or simple cowardice. My friend George Jesse Turner, Granada Television's admirable and apparently dauntless *World in Action* cameraman, with whom I worked in Vietnam, has a similar lack of personal mission in war, which was reaffirmed when he preceded me across the Jordan and returned with an Israeli bullet in his bum. My own unease increased sharply during the briefing before the raid when Ahmed Jabit blew away the leg of a table in an attempt to load his automatic weapon. By the time we set out under darkness and painted liberally with tar, I knew I was on the wrong side in one important respect.

A jeep dropped us a few hundred yards from the river shortly before one o'clock in the morning. Burdened with the inner tubes of lorry and tractor tyres, all of them ancient and inexpertly patched, the six of us stumbled to the riverbank. The tubes were roped together and we splashed on to them in pairs: me with Salah, whom I had assumed was the leader, though I was never sure. When he ordered the others, who were talking as if we were going on a picnic, to shut up, they obeyed.

Our goal was also unclear. 'If you see an Israeli outpost', the portly PFLP briefer had said, 'you are to get through the wire and attack with grenades. If the track on the other side is clear, and there are no signs of patrols, you are to mine it.' I gathered that they had no advance intelligence and only the faintest idea of what to expect.

The tubes drifted erratically in the current; only Salah, in the lead, had a paddle, and after much inept and noisy splashing we reached the reeds on the other side, where we disembarked and all but disappeared in the mud. It now seemed a more than even bet that we would remain packed in the mud until daybreak when an Israeli patrol – one was expected then – would see us. Almost an hour passed before we extricated ourselves, only to hear a resounding splash as Ahmed fell backwards into the river. When I managed to drag him out, he was consumed by fear; and so, it occurred to me, was I. Ahmed, who spoke no English, was small and tubby and the opposite of his brother, who had build and instinctive bravado. When I first met Ahmed, he struck me as an intensely sensitive and shy young man; his watercolours of Jaffa, his father's birthplace which he had never seen, were proudly displayed in the family's tent.

There was no moon. But the floor of that part of the Jordan valley is flat and swept and, thus exposed, we walked for half a mile to a crop of rocks where the explosives were prepared. The Israeli kibbutzniks patrolling the perimeter of Maoz Haim had laughed about the guerrillas' attempts at mine-laying; one in five went off, they said, and usually killed Arabs and not Jews. The track was just ahead, and Salah and two others crept forward with the explosives.

Then there was a metallic chatter, the revving of a motor and a spotlight. Our file broke as we ran in all directions. The spotlight spread ahead of the man running in front of me who tripped as he jettisoned his bandolier of ammunition. I fell face first into the sand as automatic fire lifted it in little fountains; I drenched my pants. Salah fell back, swivelled on his belly and returned the fire, a brave and stupid act as he was blinded by the spotlight and had declared himself a target.

I found our marker at the riverbank and catapulted myself on to one of the tubes. There was a volley of grenade explosions, the roaring of the motor, then silence. The Israeli patrol had driven away at speed. They had been as surprised as we were; and perhaps their panic had matched ours, with the exception of Salah, whose furious detonations had doubtless given the impression of a force of formidable numbers. He stumbled towards us and into the mud, carrying his brother who was drenched in blood and crying.

We spreadeagled the tubby Ahmed across a tube and when I said, 'Where the fuck is the first aid?' there was no response; they had carried none. His right arm was in shreds; his left hand was a sponge. Salah and I set out to swim with him in the tube, but one leg dragged in the water and caused us to go round in circles. He had stopped crying when we got to the other side and hauled him out, and he was dead when we found the jeep. Salah nursed his brother's head until we reached a field hospital half-way to Amman and, after stretcher bearers had taken the body from him, he waved us on. It was dawn when I was dropped at the UNRWA office at Baqa'a camp and walked through the lines of tents to the home of Mohammed Jabit, the carpenter from Jaffa, and woke him and told him.

33

Going home

Allenby Bridge, Jordan: September 1973. In the three years since I had last
seen him, on the morning Ahmed had died in the raid across the Jordan,
the life of the carpenter Mohammed Jabit had stood still in time. Salah,
his surviving son, had grown disillusioned with the PFLP's attrition,
which he had never understood, and had defected to Al Fatah when it
moved its operations to the Lebanon immediately following Hussein's
rout of the guerrilla groups in September 1970, now known as Black
September. The last the carpenter had heard of his son was that he was
married, had twin boys and was training refugee children in Al Assifa,
The Storm, Fatah's youth wing.

Mohammed Jabit himself had barely survived the assault on the camp
by Hussein's Bedouin Army. Jordanian artillery had pummelled the
camp in order to drive home Hussein's edict that the Palestinians could
remain in his kingdom (of which Palestinians made up more than half
the population) only if they eschewed the guerrilla groups, which since
the Six Day War had flaunted their autonomous power in Amman. To
the Palestinians, Black September *was* Hussein, who had long kept his
end of a deal with Washington to expel the guerrillas in return for arms
and dollars and a tacit peace with Israel.

Mohammed Jabit's tent was only one of a dozen left standing on the
eastern perimeter of the camp after the Jordanians had opened fire
shortly after dawn. When he ran for his life it was the start of his third
flight since the day he left his small flat-roofed ochre-coloured house,
with its workshop and market garden, in Jaffa.

We had lunch and I said to him, 'I am going to Jerusalem tomorrow,
across the Allenby Bridge. Would you like to come with me? We can go
to Jaffa and see your house. There's a bus before daybreak. We can be
at your home before lunch.' His expression was incredulous.

I attempted to explain Israel's 'summer visits' scheme, which he had heard something about on the radio. The scheme was the idea of Moshe Dayan, now Israel's defence minister. Although on the surface it seemed a humanitarian gesture, allowing former residents of the West Bank to return for a limited period, the real purpose of the visits was to accelerate the expulsion of more and more Palestinians from their homeland. When brother was reunited with brother and father with child, their overwhelming desire was for permanent reunion. However, when they approached the Israeli authorities, they were told, 'Yes, of course, you can all be together again . . . on the other side of the Jordan!'

Although Mohammed Jabit came originally from Jaffa, as a former resident of Aqabat Jabr on the West Bank, he qualified as a 'visitor'.

'I can't go into Israel!' he said.

'Why?' I said. 'Thousands of West Bankers go there every day to work.'

'But I am afraid to go. What if my house is no longer there?'

He produced his wallet and took from it a key.

'This is the key to my home,' he said. 'I locked the door when I left in 1948.'

Early the next morning we boarded a vintage bus for the two-hour journey to the Allenby Bridge. On the other side, at the wired maze that is the Israeli checkpoint, we parted temporarily, as Arabs are scrutinised separately. Though I was not an Arab, the heels of my shoes were examined, my toothpaste was squeezed, my small cigars each ceremoniously broken in half and most of my papers read.

We hitched a ride in a fruit lorry to Ramallah, then gave a taxi-driver the address in Jaffa. The carpenter had sat in silence for most of the journey but now, as he directed the driver through a labyrinth of streets, past the boarded-up mosque where his family used to worship, he wiped his eyes.

'Yes, this is it . . . ' he said. Then for a moment he was not sure. 'Yes, yes, this *is* it!'

He got out of the taxi, walked to the front gate and kissed the ground. An old man, who had been pottering among the lettuces in the front yard, came over to us and I attempted to explain. But he was transfixed by the sight of the carpenter gazing upon the house which he had not seen for a quarter of a century. When Mohammed Jabit and his family had fled, the present owner was in a Russian labour camp, having lost four of his family in the war with Germany. He had acquired the house from the Custodian of Properties, the Israeli department which expropriates Arab homes and businesses.

'I have not made many changes,' he said to Mohammed Jabit. 'I have had to pull down the workshop . . . it was full of worm. But I have kept something . . . please wait a minute.'

He hurried inside and returned with a long wooden box. 'Here are tools I found,' he said. 'I have not disturbed them. They are as you left them. I cleaned them once.'

Mohammed Jabit sought to control his emotions and said nothing.

'I am so very sorry,' said the present owner, whose name he gave only as Ze'ev. 'Please, will you come inside for a cup of coffee?'

'No,' said Mohammed Jabit. 'Please . . . I have nothing against you, but I cannot accept an invitation to enter my own home.'

'I am so very sorry,' repeated Ze'ev. 'Please, what can I do?' And as if to redeem something, he added, 'You know I understand. Before the ceasefire I lost a son . . . '

He waved at us to wait, went inside and returned with a package of cake and fruit, which he asked Mohammed Jabit to accept; and he did. As we talked a woman held the screen door ajar but did not come out; her face was filled with concern and bafflement and was not without fear.

'There is no reason why we should not live together,' Ze'ev said. 'I am sorry. I cannot think of what else I should say.'

'There is no reason,' said the carpenter, whom I last saw when our taxi dropped me in Jerusalem and took him on back to the bridge. There he would wait through half the night for a bus back to the camp.

VIII

CAMBODIA

34

Year Zero

Phnom Penh: August 1979. The aircraft flew low, following the unravelling of the Mekong River west from Vietnam. Once over Cambodia, what we saw silenced all of us on board. There appeared to be nobody, no movement, not even an animal, as if the great population of Asia had stopped at the border. Whole towns and villages on the riverbanks were empty, it seemed, the doors of houses open, chairs and beds, pots and mats in the street, a car on its side, a mangled bicycle. Beside fallen power lines was a human shadow, lying or sitting; it had the shape of a child, though we could not be sure, for it did not move.

Beyond, the familiar landscape of South-East Asia, the patchwork of rice paddies and fields, was barely discernible; nothing seemed to have been planted or be growing, except the forest and mangrove and lines of tall wild grass. On the edge of towns this grass would follow straight lines, as though planned. Fertilised by human compost, by the remains of thousands upon thousands of men, women and children, these lines marked common graves in a nation where perhaps as many as 2 million people, or between a third and a quarter of the population, were 'missing'.

Our plane made its approach into what had been the international airport at Phnom Penh, towards a beaconless runway and a deserted control tower. At the edge of the forest there appeared a pyramid of rusting cars, the first of many such sights, like objects in a mirage. The cars were piled one on top of the other; some of the cars had been brand new when their owners were forced to throw away the ignition keys and push them to the pile, which also included ambulances, a fire engine, police cars, refrigerators, washing machines, hairdriers, generators, television sets, telephones and typewriters, as if a huge Luddite broom had swept them there. 'Here lies the consumer society', a headstone might have read, 'Abandoned April 17, Year Zero'.

From that date, anybody who had owned cars and such 'luxuries', anybody who had lived in a city or town, anybody with more than a basic education or who had acquired a modern skill, such as doctors, nurses, teachers, engineers, tradespeople and students, anybody who knew or worked for foreigners, such as travel agents, clerks, journalists and artists, was in danger; some were under sentence of death. To give just one example, out of a royal ballet company of 500 dancers, a few dozen survived; of the others, some escaped abroad, some starved to death or succumbed to illness related to extreme deprivation, and some were murdered.

During my twenty-two years as a journalist, most of them spent in transit at places of uncertainty and upheaval, I had not seen anything to compare with what I saw in Cambodia. 'It is my duty', wrote the correspondent of *The Times* at the liberation of Belsen, 'to describe something beyond the imagination of mankind.'[1] That was how I and others felt in the summer of 1979.

My previous trip to Cambodia had been twelve years earlier. I had flown across from wartime Saigon, exchanging venality and neurosis for what Western visitors invariably saw as the innocence of a 'gentle land' whose capital, Phnom Penh, had a beauty only the French could contrive. On Sundays the parade down Monivong Avenue was a joy: the parasols, the beautiful young women on their Hondas, the saffron robes, the platoons of well-fed families, the ice-cream barrows, the weddings, the hustlers. You awoke at the cavernous Hotel Royale, switched on your radio and, in all probability, heard the squeaky voice of Prince Norodom Sihanouk berating you or another foreign journalist for writing about the financial excesses of the royal family. This might be followed by a summons to the royal palace and an instruction to listen to the Prince's collection of jazz recordings, usually Oscar Peterson. Sihanouk, 'God-king' and a relic of the French empire, was his country's most celebrated jazz musician, film director, football coach, and juggler of apparently impossible options in Indo-China's cockpit of war. Such was his kingdom: feudal, unpredictable, preposterous and, in relation to events in the region, at peace.

The Cambodia which foreigners romanticised (myself included) belied a recent history of savagery between warring groups, such as those loyal to Sihanouk and the 'Issaraks', who were anti-French and anti-royalty but sometimes no more than murderous bandits. The atrocities which emerged from some of their skirmishes from the 1940s to the 1960s were of a ritual nature later associated with the Pol Pot period, but were probably common enough in a peasant world which few foreigners saw and understood. Sihanouk himself was a capricious autocrat whose thugs dispensed arbitrary terror when Westerners were not looking, or did not wish to look; and his authoritarianism undoubtedly contributed to the growth of the communist party, or Khmer Rouge. Certainly, his 'Popular Socialist Community', which he set up in the 1950s, had little to do with socialism and everything to do with creating suitably benign conditions for the spread and enrichment of a powerful mandarinate in the towns and ethnic Chinese usurers in the rural areas. But it is also true that the extremes of hunger were rare; indeed, so bountiful seemed the Khmers' lush, under-populated land that the Chinese coined a superlative: 'As rich as Cambodia!'

In 1959 a United States Defence Department report described the Khmers as a nation of people who could not be easily panicked, whose horizons were limited to village, pagoda and forest, who knew of no other countries, who respected their government, who feared ghosts and 'cannot be counted upon to act in any positive way for the benefit of US aims and policies'.[2] Cambodia then was regarded as 'neutral'; that is, it was allied to no bloc. However, Sihanouk later allowed Ho Chi Minh's Vietnamese to run their supply routes through his territory, and this fact was not unrelated to the Prince being divested of his kingdom in 1970 by a general called Lon Nol. The CIA denied that they had anything to do with the *coup d'état*. That may be so; but in that year Richard Nixon and his national security adviser, Henry Kissinger, were conducting their 'secret bombing' of Cambodia, aimed at Vietnamese 'sanctuaries'. Pilots were sworn to secrecy and their operational logs were falsified or destroyed. During 1969–70 the American public and Congress knew nothing about it. During one six-month period in 1973 B-52s dropped more bombs in 3,695 raids on the populated heartland of Cambodia than were dropped on Japan during all of the Second World War: the equivalent, in tons of bombs, of five Hiroshimas.

In 1977 a former member of Kissinger's staff, Roger Morris, described the way in which the President's foreign-policy advisers, known as 'the Wise Men', prepared the ground for the final destruction of Indo-China:

> Though they spoke of terrible human suffering reality was sealed off by their trite, lifeless vernacular: 'capabilities', 'objectives', 'our chips', 'giveaway'. It was a matter, too, of culture and style. They spoke with the cool, deliberate detachment of men who believe the banishment of feeling renders them wise and, more important, credible to other men ... [Of Kissinger and Nixon] They neither understood the foreign policy they were dealing with, nor were deeply moved by the bloodshed and suffering they administered to their stereotypes.

On the eve of an American land invasion of 'neutral' Cambodia in April

1970, according to Morris, Nixon said to Kissinger, 'If this doesn't work, it'll be your ass, Henry.'[3]

It worked, in a fashion. The bombing and invasion provided a small group of fanatical communists, the Khmer Rouge, with a catalyst for a revolution which had no popular base among the Khmer people. What is striking about the rise of Pol Pot, Khieu Samphan and other principals in the Khmer Rouge is their medievalism, which their principally Marxist pretensions barely concealed. Pol Pot and Khieu Samphan were both left-wing students in Paris in the 1950s, when and where other colonial revolutions were reputedly conceived; but neither admitted the existence of a Marxist-Leninist or communist organisation until 1977, by which time they were prime minister and head of state respectively of 'Democratic Kampuchea'. Indeed, in the movement they led all ideology, authority and 'justice' flowed from 'Angkar Loeu', literally the 'Organisation on High', which 'has the eyes of a pineapple; it sees everything'.[4]

Angkor was the capital of a Khmer empire which was at its zenith between the tenth and the thirteenth centuries. It reached from Burma to the South China Sea and was interrupted only by what is now central Vietnam; the equally nationalist Vietnamese having not long freed themselves from a thousand years of Chinese rule. Angkor, the place, was a tribute to the riches, energy and chauvinism of the dynasty, with its series of temples conceived as a symbolic universe according to traditional Indian cosmology, and built by slaves. There was an absolute monarch, a pharaoh-style figure, a bureaucracy organised by Brahmins, and a military leadership; and, like Egypt and Rome, the empire duly collapsed under the weight of its monuments and megalomanias, as well as its changing patterns of trade. The celebrated temples of Angkor Wat are all that remain of its glory.

'If our people can build Angkor Wat', said Pol Pot in 1977, 'they can do anything!'[5] This was the year Pol Pot probably killed more of his people than during all of his reign. Xenophobic in the extreme, he might almost have modelled himself on a despotic king of Angkor, which would perhaps explain his ambition to reclaim that part of the Mekong Delta, now southern Vietnam and known as Kampuchea Krom, over which the Khmer kings had once ruled. He was also an admirer of Mao Tse-tung and the Gang of Four; and it is not improbable that just as Mao had seen himself as the greatest emperor of China, so Pol Pot saw himself as another Mao, directing his own red guards to purify all élites, subversives and revisionists and to create a totally self-reliant state and one sealed off from the 'virus' of the modern world.

Cambodia is 90 per cent villages and the worsening imbalance in the relationship between peasant and town-dweller was one which Pol Pot and his 'men in black' were able to exploit almost with impunity. The

French had created Phnom Penh in their own remote image and had brought in Chinese and Vietnamese bureaucrats and traders. Those in power in the capital took from and taxed the peasants as if by divine right; and when three years of American bombing killed or wounded or dislocated hundreds of thousands of Khmer peasants and created many more as refugees, the Khmer Rouge, now operating from enclaves, swept into a power vacuum in the bloodied countryside. To understand the opportunities which the American bombing gave to the Khmer Rouge, one need not look beyond the story of Neak Long, a Mekong River town thirty miles from Phnom Penh. In August 1973 a B-52 unloaded its bombs on Neak Long and more than a hundred villagers were killed and several hundred wounded. The bombing was described as a 'mistake' and a crew member was fined $700. The American Ambassador to Cambodia, Emory Swank, subsequently went to the village and handed one hundred dollar bills to each grieving family as 'compensation'.[6]

At 7.30 on the morning of April 17, 1975, they entered Phnom Penh. They marched in Indian file along the boulevards, through the still traffic. They wore black and were mostly teenagers, and people cheered them nervously, naïvely, as people do when war seems to be over. Phnom Penh then had a swollen population of about 2 million people. At one o'clock the 'men in black' decreed that the city be abandoned by all except for a few thousand who would maintain its skeleton. According to witnesses interviewed later and journalists in Phnom Penh at the time, the sick and wounded were ordered and dragged at gunpoint from their hospital beds; surgeons were forced to leave patients in mid-operation. On the road out through the suburbs a procession of mobile beds could be seen, with their drip-bottles swinging at the bedpost; a man whose throat and mouth had been torn away by a rocket explosion was pushed along by his aged father. The old and crippled fell beside the road and their families were forced to move on. Crippled and dying children were carried in plastic bags. Women barely out of childbirth staggered forward, supported by parents. Orphaned babies, forty-one by one estimate, were left in their cradles at the Phnom Penh paediatric centre without anybody to care for them.

'Don't take anything with you,' broadcast the young troops through loudspeakers. 'The Angkar is saying that you must leave the city for just three hours so that we can prepare to defend you against bombing by American aircraft.'

The prospect of bombing was believed by many, but even among those on the road who knew it to be a lie, defeatism, fear and exhaustion seemed to make them powerless. The haemorrhage lasted two days and two nights, then Cambodia fell into shadow. When, on January 7, 1979, the Vietnamese Army came up the Mekong and drove into Phnom Penh, they found the city virtually as it had been left on the first day of 'Year Zero'.

This was how I found it when I arrived with photographer Eric Piper, film director David Munro, cameraman Gerry Pinches and sound recordist Steve Phillips of Associated Television (ATV). In the silent, airless humidity it was like entering a city the size of Manchester or Brussels in the wake of a nuclear cataclysm which had spared only the buildings. Houses, flats, office blocks, schools, hotels stood empty and open, as if vacated by their occupants that day. Personal possessions lay trampled on a front path, a tricycle crushed and rusted in the gutter, the traffic lights jammed on red. There was electricity in the centre of the city; elsewhere there was neither power nor a working sewer nor water to drink. At the railway station trains stood empty at various stages of interrupted departure. Pieces of burned cloth fluttered on the platform, and when we enquired about this it was explained that on the day they fled before the Vietnamese Army the Khmer Rouge had set fire to carriages in which as many as 200 wounded people lay.

When the afternoon monsoon broke, the gutters of the city were suddenly awash with paper; but this was not paper, it was money. The streets ran with money, much of it new and unused banknotes whose source was not far away. The modern concrete building of the National Bank of Cambodia looked as if it had sustained one mighty punch. As if to show their contempt for the order they replaced, the Khmer Rouge had blown it up and now with every downpour a worthless fortune sluiced from it into the streets. Inside, cheque books lay open on the counter, one with a cheque partly filled out and the date April 17, 1975. A pair of broken spectacles rested on an open ledger; money seemed to be everywhere; I slipped and fell hard on a floor brittle with coins; boxes of new notes were stacked where they had been received from the supplier in London five years ago.

In our first hours in Phnom Penh we shot no film and took no photographs; incredulity saw to that. I had no sense of people, of even the remnants of a population; the few human shapes I glimpsed seemed incoherent images, detached from the city itself. On catching sight of us, they would flit into the refuge of a courtyard or a cinema or a filling station. Only when I pursued several, and watched them forage, did I see that they were children. One child about ten years old – although age was difficult to judge – ran into a wardrobe lying on its side which was his or her refuge. In an Esso station an old woman and three emaciated children squatted around a pot containing a mixture of roots and leaves, which bubbled over a fire fuelled with paper money: thousands of snapping, crackling brand new *riel*: such a morbid irony, for these were people in need of everything money no longer could buy.

The first person we stopped and spoke to was a man balancing a load on his head and an arm on his son's shoulder. He was blind and his face was pitted from what might have been smallpox. His son was fifteen years old, but so skeletal that he might have been nine. The man spoke some French and said his name was Khim Kon and his son was Van Sok and that 'before Pol Pot' he had been a carpenter. 'This boy', he said, touching his son with affection, 'is my only child left. Because we came from the city, we were classified "new people". We had to work from three in the morning until eleven at night; the children, too. My wife and three others are all dead now.' I asked him how he had lost his sight. 'I was always blind in one eye,' he said. 'When my family started to die I cried, so they took out my other eye with a whip.' Of all the survivors I would talk to in the coming weeks, that man and his son, who had lost four members of their immediate family, were the least damaged.

My memory of Phnom Penh from twelve years before now told me where I was; I was in the middle of Monivong Avenue, facing the Roman Catholic cathedral. But there was no cathedral. In the constitution of Pol Pot's 'Democratic Kampuchea', article twenty stated that all Khmers had 'the right to worship according to any religion and the right not to worship according to any religion', but religion that was 'wrong' and 'reactionary' and 'detrimental' was prohibited. So the Gothic cathedral of Phnom Penh, a modest version of the cathedral at Rheims, a place where the 'wrong' religion was practised, was dismantled, stone by stone. Only wasteland is left now.

I walked across Monivong Avenue to the National Library which the 'men in black' had converted into a pigsty, apparently as a symbol, since all books published prior to Year Zero were also 'detrimental'. The library's books and documents had been burned, looted by the returning city dwellers, discarded as rubbish, or thrown into the street. Next door stood the Hotel Royale, whose stuffed crocodiles offered a kind of greeting; they at least had not been considered detrimental, although the garden aviary was empty and overgrown and the swimming-pool was festering and stagnant. I had swum in it long ago; now it was a cesspit.

Our billet was in the former Air France residence, a functional white building which a family of banana palms seemed to be reclaiming by the hour. Beneath many of these palms had been discovered human remains which, it was claimed, were used as human fertiliser. Like almost everywhere else in Phnom Penh, to enter this house was to intrude upon ghosts; an initialled pen, an opened packet of tobacco, a used air ticket lay in a drawer. David Munro unknowingly bedded down beside a nest of rats which ate our supply of candles through the night. The water in the shower ran yellow and the drains smelt rotten; corpses had been found wedged in wells. Whatever we touched, it seemed, had been polluted by the past. We heated our cans and boiled our water on a Primus stove in what had been somebody's sitting room. We ate little and spoke rarely and I found myself gulping neat whisky, without effect. On August 15 David Munro wrote in his diary: 'I don't know what to do to film what we're seeing, because all we're seeing is silence . . . and this smell. No one is going to believe us.'

For a fleeting moment, the normal and mundane would seem to return. One morning our interpreter, Sophak, was laughing with Eric Piper when she suddenly stopped and spoke, as if to no one, this horrific *non sequitur*: 'Can you imagine they take away friendship?' she said, still smiling. 'A young boy who used to be a student was taken away and beaten to death because he smiled at me while we husked the rice. He smiled at me, that's all.'

Sophak had been forced to live in a communal camp where people were fed according to how 'productive' they were. Those who fell sick were left where they lay in the fields or were attended, she said, by bogus 'doctors', usually teenage boys who would dispense tablets made from roots or give injections with filthy syringes. The 'serum' would leave their patients writhing in pain and often would kill them. Sophak said these 'doctors' would also perform 'operations' during which incisions were made with unsterilised instruments and without anaesthetic of any kind. Sometimes an organ would be removed and 'examined' on the grass while the victim screamed. These young 'doctors' earned food, which was also the reward for boys recruited as spies. The boys, said Sophak, would listen at night for 'detrimental' laughter or sorrow, and would report those falling asleep during a midnight 'ideological study'. Even the word 'sleep' itself was banned; from Year Zero there would be 'rest'. Only the camp controller could sanction marriage and people were married in large groups, having been directed to whom they might 'choose' as a partner; husbands and wives were allowed to sleep together only once a month. At the age of seven, children were put to work; at twelve, they were 'sent away'. There were, said Sophak, 'no families, no sentiment, no love or grief, no holidays, no music, no song'.

On another day, when we were filming several hundred Khmer Rouge prisoners at a barracks outside the city, I said to Sophak, 'Ask him how many people he killed.' In front of us was a man in his thirties who had an almost casual air. She put the question, he answered it briskly and she turned to me and said, 'In his group they kill 250.'

'How many were in his group?' I asked.

'Eight persons in each group,' she said.

'So eight of them killed 250 people,' I said.

'Yes,' she said, 'but this man over here says he killed fifty people on his own.'

We moved across to the second man, and when I asked Sophak to ask him who were the fifty people he had killed, she gave as his answer, 'Most of them were men, women and children from the city class, the middle class.'

'Has he children of his own?' I asked.

'He has one child', she said, 'and that child is very well.' She walked away and, out of sight, she vomited.

Two months earlier Eric Piper and I had followed Pope John Paul on his return to Poland, where we had seen Auschwitz for the first time. Now, in South-East Asia, we saw it again. On a clear, sunny day with flocks of tiny swifts, the bravest of birds, rising and falling almost to the ground, we drove along a narrow dirt road at the end of which was a former primary school, called Tuol Sleng. During the Pol Pot years this school was run by a Khmer gestapo, 'S-21', which divided the classrooms into an 'interrogation unit' and a 'torture and massacre unit'. People were mutilated on iron beds and we found their blood and tufts of their hair still on the floor. Between December 1975 and June 1978 at least 12,000 people died slow deaths here: a fact not difficult to confirm because the killers, like the Nazis, were pedantic in their sadism. They photographed their victims before and after they tortured and killed them and horrific images now looked at us from walls; some had tried to smile for the photographer, as if he might take pity on them and save them. Names and ages, even height and weight, were recorded. We found, as at Auschwitz, one room filled to the ceiling with victims' clothes and shoes, including those of many children.

However, unlike Auschwitz, Tuol Sleng was primarily a political death centre. Leading members of the Khmer Rouge Army, including those who formed an early resistance to Pol Pot, were murdered here, usually after 'confessing' that they had worked for the CIA, the KGB or Hanoi. Whatever its historical model, if any, the demonic nature of Tuol Sleng was its devotion to human suffering. Whole families were confined in small cells, fettered to a single iron bar. They were kept naked and slept on the stone floor, without blanket or mat, and on the wall was a school blackboard, on which was written:

1. Speaking is absolutely forbidden
2. Before doing something, the authorisation of the warden must be obtained.

'Doing something' might mean only changing position in the cell, but without authorisation the prisoner would receive twenty to thirty strokes with a whip. Latrines were small ammunition boxes left over from Lon Nol's Army, labelled 'Made in USA'. For upsetting a box of excrement the punishment was licking the floor with your tongue, torture or death, or all three.

When the Vietnamese discovered Tuol Sleng they found nineteen mass graves within the vicinity of the prison and eight survivors, including four children and a month-old baby. Tem Chan was one of them. He told me, 'For a whole week I was filled with water, then given electric currents. Finally, I admitted anything they wanted. I said I worked for the KGB. It was so ridiculous. When they found out I was a sculptor the torture stopped and I was put to work making busts of Pol Pot. That saved my life.'

Another survivor was Ung Pech, an engineer, whose fingers had been crushed in a vice. He wept as he told me, 'My wife, my sons, my daughter ... all are gone. I have only one child left. Five children dead. They gave them nothing to eat.'

The days now passed for the five of us as if in slow motion. Anxiety and a certain menace did not leave us. At Siem Reap, in the north-west, after trudging through a nightmarish mass grave filled with skulls, many of which had been smashed, Eric and Steve fell ill and did not recover. They worked most of the time in agony from dysentery. David's exceptional organising skills were much in evidence; he established a routine and saw everybody gently through it, a feat in itself.

Two concerns preoccupied us. Was it possible, we asked ourselves, to convey the evidence of what we had seen, which was barely credible to us, in such a way that the *enormity* of the crime committed in Cambodia might be recognised internationally and the survivors helped? And, on a personal level, how could we keep moving *away* from the sounds which pursued us? The initial silence had broken and now the cries of fleshless children tormented us almost everywhere.

This was especially so when we reached the town of Kompong Speu where 150,000 people were said to be 'missing'. Where there had been markets, houses and schools, there was bare land. Substantial buildings had been demolished, *erased* like the cathedral. The town's hospital had disappeared; Vietnamese engineers had erected a temporary one and supplied a doctor and some drugs. But there were few beds and no blankets and antiseptic was splashed urgently on our hands every few yards we walked; many of the people lying on the stone floor were dying from plague and anthrax, which is passed through the meat of diseased cattle and takes about a month to kill. It can be cured by penicillin, but there was no penicillin, except that brought by two French doctors, Jean Yves Follezou and Jean Michel Vinot, who had travelled down from Phnom Penh with us. The human sounds here, I recall vividly, had a syncopation, a terrible prosody: high and shrill, then deep and unrelenting, the rhythm of approaching death. In the 'orphan's war', the children sat and leaned and lay on mats, impassive, looking directly at us and at the camera lens. When a young girl died after begging us for help, I felt the depths of shame and rage.

Similarly, in the 'hospital' of an orphanage in Phnom Penh, laid out like a First World War field station in the Gothic shell of an abandoned chapel, there were children who had been found wandering in the forest, living off treebark, grass and poisonous plants. Their appearance denied their humanity; rows of opaque eyes set in cloth-like skin. Here Gerry put his camera on the ground, walked away and cried.

One of several adults in charge at the orphanage was Prak Sarinn, a former teacher, who had survived the Pol Pot years by disguising himself as a peasant. 'It was the only acceptable class,' he said. 'I changed my personality, and I shall not be the same again. I can no longer teach; my head is filled with death and worry.' I asked him what had happened on April 17, 1975. He said, 'I was in my classroom when they burst in. They looked like boys, not even thirteen. They put their guns on us and told us all to march north into the countryside. The children were crying. I asked if we could first go home to join our families. They said no. So we just walked away, and most of the little ones died from exhaustion and hunger. I never saw my family again.'

With Mr Sarinn interpreting I spoke to one of the children lying still on a mat in the chapel and asked him his age.

'I remember,' said the child. 'I am twelve years old.'

'What is your name?' I asked.

'I forget,' he replied.

'Where are your parents?'

'I forget . . . I think they died.'

In the main hospital of Phnom Penh, where modern equipment had been vandalised and destroyed and the dispensary was bare, 'No. 23' on a bare iron bed was Kuon, a ten-year-old who seemed to diminish by the hour; he was too ill to eat the crude rice for which the ration was then four pounds per person per month. On the day we were there he might have been saved; antibiotics and milk were all he needed, but there was not an aspirin. When we returned the next morning, his name, along with the names of five other dead children, were chalked on a blackboard in the hospital yard, beside a poster which read, 'The United Nations wishes to remind you that 1979 is the International Year of the Child'. The poster was put there by Dr Follezou 'much more in anger than in sorrow', he said. The United Nations recognised the ousted Pol Pot regime and the United Nations Children's Fund (UNICEF) had sent nothing to relieve the suffering.

My favourite symbol of international inaction was a large red cross on the roof of the hospital, remaining from the days when ladders of bombs from B-52s fell not far away. The red cross is, of course, the universal mark of humanitarianism and is said to transcend politics and frontiers. At this hospital it might have served to ward off evil spirits; no doctors or nurses of the International Red Cross (ICRC) had come, and the driblets of Red Cross supplied medicines had evaporated.

Shortly after our arrival in Phnom Penh, two men representing ICRC and UNICEF were preparing to leave. The UNICEF man, Jacques Beaumont, suitcase in hand, was in an emotional state and my interview with him was interrupted several times while he composed himself. I asked him how many people were threatened by famine.

He replied, 'The government [in Phnom Penh] has requested help for 2,250,000 people . . . this is the dimension of the problem . . . you see, 85 per cent of the women have stopped menstruating. Where is the next generation coming from? In Kompong Speu, in one of the very poor barracks with practically nothing, there were fifty-four children dying. I will always remember that I did not do anything for these children, because we had nothing.'

During the interview I asked Beaumont why UNICEF and ICRC had done so little. At this, he walked away from the camera, took David and me by the arm and led us to a Red Cross man sitting alone in the foyer of the Hotel Royale. '*He* will explain,' he said. 'Tell them what the truth is, François.'

François Bugnion, of ICRC in Geneva, was clearly distraught. He asked, 'What nationality are you? What government are you?' I told him I was an Australian national and a journalist.

'So you must have contacts in the Australian government,' he said. 'So you must go to them now please, and get them to send one C-130 Hercules aircraft here. The Hercules is important because all the forklifts at the airport have been destroyed. This plane can unload itself and one consignment of a truck, food and drugs will save thousands . . . The Australians have done this thing before. They paint out the military markings, and there is no problem. But you must not say this request has come from me . . . Geneva must not find out I have asked you to do this.'

I asked him why the Red Cross itself did not approach the Australian government; why was there this need for subterfuge?

'I am desperate,' he replied. 'In Geneva they are still studying the framework of a plan of relief for Cambodia, but the situation cannot wait. People are dying around us. *They* can't wait for the politics to be ironed out and for Geneva to say go.'

Bugnion tore a page from a yellow legal pad and laboriously wrote the names of those in the ICRC hierarchy responsible for 'Asia and Oceania'. 'Here', he said, 'are the people you will need to persuade.'

These raw interviews, conducted in Phnom Penh at a time of historic emergency for the Khmer people, are a guide to why this stricken society had to wait so long for Western relief to arrive. There were subsequent attempts, in Bangkok, Geneva and New York, to damage the credibility of both Beaumont and Bugnion; they were variously described as 'unreliable' and drunks. These were among the first of many smears mounted against those who told a truth unpalatable to some Western governments, to sections of the Western media, to the secular missionaries of the established aid industry and to ideologues of the right and far left. To understand this peculiar bigotry, which persists today, it is necessary to go back to the early spring of 1979 when the first refugees fleeing in advance of the Khmer Rouge crossed the border into Thailand. The Thai regime's immediate response was to describe the refugees as 'illegal immigrants' and to repatriate them forcibly into enclaves held by the Khmer Rouge. In one night in June 1979 the Thais 'pushed back' between 35,000 and 40,000 Cambodian refugees, many of them hungry and sick. They forced them down a hill and across a minefield. Some were killed or injured by the mines, although most were rescued by Vietnamese troops. Many of those who tried to cross the border again were beaten and shot by Thai soldiers.

A cross-section of these refugees was interviewed by the Australian Khmer scholar Ben Kiernan, one of the few Westerners to master the Khmer language, and by his wife, Chanthou Boua, herself a Khmer. Their conclusions are reflected in this one account. Kiernan wrote:

> Hong Var, whom Chanthou Boua and I interviewed at length in Aranyaprathet on April 2, fled to Thailand with her two daughters and 204 others on 24 March. She said every one of the peasants and people of other backgrounds in her village hated the Pol Pot regime bitterly, especially after the year 1978, during which she said half the population of the village, Andaung Khlong, died or were executed. When they arrived the Vietnamese troops were welcomed, and did not mistreat the people. There was a feast; the Vietnamese distributed food and medicine, and re-established freedom of travel. Then they withdrew.[7]

Kiernan and Boua interviewed at length Tae Hui Lang, an ethnic Chinese woman who fled Cambodia in May 1979. They recounted her story in detail because she had not only survived Pol Pot, but was a witness to the battles that followed. 'The rural people', she said, 'would gather together and then run behind the Vietnamese lines.' She described how the Vietnamese directed them to where they could find food and water, arranged transport for a woman who gave birth on the way and brought milk and medicine to her and found a place for her to live. Kiernan wrote:

> Lang herself, who had a two year old baby, was assisted in carrying her things by Vietnamese soldiers along the way. Although they couldn't speak any Khmer they still made a good impression on Lang's group. 'I don't know what their politics was about, but from what I saw they did good things', Lang said.

She said this also applied to the Vietnamese treatment of prisoners, who were not killed but even 'fed to the full'. She told how the Vietnamese tried to damp down Khmer racial feeling against Chinese residents of Cambodia, who had become the targets for abuse and attack because China had supported the Khmer Rouge.

There were many such stories, both from inside Cambodia and along the Thai border. They were recounted by people who had no motive to lie; indeed, the persuasion was the other way; the Thais certainly did not want to hear tributes to the Vietnamese, neither did the Americans reporting from the border, nor many of the aid people and assorted Western 'fundamentalists'. The facts of aid, such as they were known then, were equally unacceptable to ideologues in the West; up until August 1979, when I arrived in Cambodia, Vietnam had sent to Cambodia civilian aid estimated at 10,000 tons of rice seed, 20,000 tons of rice, 9,000 tons of fuel and 5,000 tons of other goods, such as condensed milk. These figures seemed quite likely given the amounts I saw arriving and were the result of a system of coupling Vietnam's Mekong provinces with provinces in Cambodia. For example, Kompong Speu was 'tied' to Cuu Long province in Vietnam, where many families contributed three kilogrammes of rice: a very considerable burden during a period of economic hardship in Vietnam, including hunger.

One memorable morning before dawn we were awakened by an unfamiliar sound rumbling over the emptiness of Phnom Penh: *traffic*, moreover the roar of traffic. At the southern end of Monivong Avenue the first, swaying, snorting, venerable, festooned Ford could be seen, then another and another, then a ribbon of them with no end in sight: Fords, Dodges and Internationals laden with rice, building materials, utensils, agricultural tools, tents and clothing. This was a civilian convoy from Vietnam whose drivers, from Saigon, included former members of the defeated Saigon Army. They told us in American-accented English that their final destinations were Kompong Cham, Kratie and Stung Treng in the north-east, Komgpong Chnang and Pursat in the north-west, and Kompong Speu to the south-west. The next day we happened to be at Kompong Speu when the convoy arrived; and we watched lines of hungry people receive enough rice to keep them alive. That the Khmer population had not been decimated was due to its own initiatives and resilience, but it was also due to convoys like this.

A month earlier, July 1979, most of the senior tier of the US State Department had given evidence before a Senate hearing on Indo-Chinese refugees. The witnesses explained that because the United States did not recognise the new government in Phnom Penh, led by Heng Samrin, it was prohibited by law from giving direct aid to Cambodia: that is, America was prevented from legally sending a single relief aircraft to a country over which it had illegally sent waves of B-52 bombers. Stories began to appear in the American Press that the International Red Cross had been told by the Phnom Penh authorities that no food was needed.

The opposite was true. The ICRC had been asked by the government in Phnom Penh for 100,000 tons of food, 15,000 tons of sugar and 8,000 tons of butter oil, as well as medical supplies. The request, in writing and dated July 3, was handed to François Bugnion and Jacques Beaumont in Phnom Penh. Prior to that, in May, the journalist Wilfred Burchett had visited Phnom Penh and described in graphic articles in the *Guardian* the overwhelming needs in Cambodia. Accompanying Burchett on that trip were Doctors Follezou and Vinot, representing the Comité Français d'Aide Medicale et Sanitaire, who returned to Paris with a 'shopping list' of emergency relief drawn up with the Phnom Penh government. Follezou and Vinot showed the list to all who might help, principally French government officials and journalists, but the interest expressed was minimal. The European Economic Community had confined its compassion to £425,000 as part of a development grant to the United Nations High Commissioner for Refugees which was destined for refugees *outside* Cambodia.

Wilfred Burchett, who was based in Paris, brought the list to London and read most of it out at a packed all-party meeting at the House of Commons. He described a trauma so profound that 'the very fabric of Khmer society has begun to unravel'. He said that not only food but basic equipment was needed, like hoes and fishing nets. When asked about difficulties in getting relief to Cambodia, he replied that the problems were inside the country, that there was no heavy transport and there were no roads; wharves and communications had been vandalised or had fallen into disrepair and therefore trucks were a priority. He said there was nothing to stop civilian relief aircraft flying into Phnom Penh, and that both the Vietnamese government and the government in Cambodia had assured him relief would be welcomed. 'I want to impress upon you', said Burchett, 'that a great many human beings are starving and need your help.' It was a moving speech. Nothing happened.

That is, nothing happened at the level of government; Margaret Thatcher had come to power only a few weeks earlier and one of her first acts as prime minister was to join the American boycott of Vietnam and suspend all food aid there, including powdered milk for Vietnamese children. To the British government, as to Washington, Cambodia was now in the 'Soviet/Vietnamese camp'.

At the House of Commons meeting was Jim Howard, technical officer of Oxfam. Oxfam had been set up in 1942 as the Oxford Committee for Famine Relief with the aim of arousing public interest in the suffering of civilians in Europe who were denied food because of the Allied blockade. The unfolding events of 1979 were not dissimilar, as Ben Whitaker recounts in his book about Oxfam, *A Bridge of People*:

> It was thought intolerable – a prelude to the cry 'people before politics' heard at the time of the recent Cambodian operation – that even at the height of the war the Allies should say to innocent children in Greece, 'Sorry, you've got to die'.[8]

Jim Howard, an engineer, is Oxfam's senior 'fireman', a veteran of disaster relief in Biafra, India, the Sahel, Latin America and Asia. He had spent most of that year in the camps of Malaysia and Hong Kong setting up Oxfam programmes to help the boat people. He saw the tragedy as the inevitable consequence of a war which had laid to waste much of Vietnam and that any boycott 'punishing' Vietnam was no more than an extension of the war. What is striking about Jim Howard is that he tends to see every problem he is sent to solve not from any Messianic complex or career prospect or opportunism but from the point of view of the people in need. It was this quality and perspective of events in Indo-China which, at a meeting in Geneva that year, had helped to conclude an agreement with the Vietnamese for an 'orderly departure' of several thousand Vietnamese refugees.

Howard was much touched by Burchett's speech in the Commons and believes that if any one individual deserves the credit for triggering the international rescue of Cambodia it was Wilfred Burchett. Two weeks later Jim Howard and other representatives of British voluntary agencies went to the Ministry for Overseas Development where an official informed them that the British boycott of Vietnam now applied to Cambodia. They were also warned that the Vietnamese were 'obstructing' attempts by ICRC and UNICEF to send and monitor aid, and that the voluntary agencies would encounter 'grave difficulties' if they mounted a relief effort of their own; they were told that aircraft would not be able to land at Phnom Penh and might even be 'fired upon'.

Oxfam ignored these warnings and Jim Howard flew to Paris to meet

Drs Follezou and Vinot and others of the French medical committee. He took £20,000 with him and got in touch with an air charter company, Cargolux, in Luxembourg, whose Icelandic and Danish pilots had a reputation for flying 'anything anywhere', and were prepared to fly a DC-8 to Phnom Penh for £16,000 cash. The French committee supplied drugs, Oxfam gave milk and vitamins. On August 19 Howard sent his passport to the Vietnamese embassy in Paris, where it was stamped and returned to him that afternoon. A few hours later he took off for Cambodia with the first Western relief of any significance.

During June and most of July I had been receiving phone calls, usually very early in the morning and late at night, from an elderly lady who lived alone in Oxfordshire. Her name was Madame Louise Vidaud de Plaud. The 'de Plaud' was a French aristocratic title, although it was not clear whether she herself was French. She told me that she and her late husband had lived in Phnom Penh and had cared for orphaned children there and that she was deeply distressed by the news of famine and suffering. She was clearly a lady of compassion and energy, and she insisted that I leave for Cambodia that day or night. Indeed, she was unrelenting, incorrigible and, although I never met her, we spoke constantly. 'Madame Vidaud here!' she would say. '*Why* haven't you gone yet? *Answer me John!*' She applied the same pressure to Oxfam and to anyone else whom she thought could bring succour to the Khmer people. It was she who put me in touch with the French doctors and set in train my journey to Cambodia.

At the end of July I flew to Vietnam. David Munro and I had filmed in Vietnam the previous year, 1978, and I had reported the war and its aftermath since the mid-1960s. Vietnam was a country I felt I knew well; certainly, my sympathy and admiration were with the Vietnamese, in both the North and South. I also felt that historic injustices were being done to those Vietnamese who had had the temerity to eject the Americans from their homeland, and that these injustices were being compounded by the perversity of Western attitudes to the liberation of Cambodia. But Vietnam was no longer a media 'story' in the West; the Western media had lost interest when the last Americans flew off from the rooftops of Saigon on April 29, 1975. Within a week of their departure, on May 1, the Khmer Rouge Army invaded Vietnam from Ha Tien to Tay Ninh, murdering and laying waste villages near the border. On May 4 Khmer Rouge forces landed on Vietnam's Phu Quoc island and throughout May occupied other Vietnamese islands, abducting more than 500 people from Tho Chu Island.

The Vietnamese attempted to placate the regime of Pol Pot; the last thing they wanted was another all-out war; but the attacks continued. In 1978 they asked the United Nations to establish and police a demilitarised zone along their border with Cambodia; the UN refused. In the same year they made unusual efforts to extricate themselves from the Sino-Soviet conflict by seeking to 'normalise' relations with Washington, going so far as to drop the question of war reparations. The Vietnamese foreign minister, Nguyen Co Thach, flew to New York to conclude an agreement. He waited until it was apparent that an agreement was now out of the question, that the United States preferred to 'normalise' only with China, Pol Pot's principal backer. These momentous and melancholy events were hardly noticed or reported in the West.

Then, in February 1979, less than a month after the Vietnamese Army had driven the Khmer Rouge to the Thai border, China invaded Vietnam from the north. The United States had been told in advance of the Chinese invasion; Washington and Peking were then in the first phase of their new 'friendship'. For the Vietnamese, America and China were now the senior members of an unholy trinity ranged against them. The third member was of course Pol Pot's 'Democratic Kampuchea'. Even after the regime ceased to exist China and the United States saw to it that Cambodia's seat at the United Nations remained occupied by Pol Pot's man, who now represented the remnants of a murderous Army and the legacies of a nightmare. In addition to this, the principal Western nations, America, Britain, most of Western Europe and Australia, continued to recognise Pol Pot's defunct government, which President Carter had described as 'the world's worst violator of human rights'. Such was the nature of a so-called 'policy of inconvenience', the goal of which was simple: the bleeding of a country which occupied an ancient bridge between China and the rest of Asia. The Vietnamese, to their cost, also stood between America and so many of its national myths, notably that of its invincibility.

When we arrived in Vietnam en route to Phnom Penh, David Munro and I set about arranging our freedom of movement inside Cambodia. We were aware that we might be accused of being 'shepherded'. We laid down three pre-conditions to the Vietnamese. We wanted our own van, our own fuel in Cambodia and the right to travel anywhere we wanted. Considering the state of Cambodia, which had no fuel, almost no transport and ruined roads, bridges and communications, our requests bordered on the outrageous. After a week's negotiations we got all that we had asked for.

The day before we left for Phnom Penh I interviewed Vietnam's foreign minister, Nguyen Co Thach. I asked him why Vietnamese troops had gone into Cambodia. He replied by describing the Khmer Rouge attacks, which had persisted for almost four years, and the 'final menace' of the encirclement of Vietnam by China. I said that Vietnam had once supported an armed Pol Pot when it had suited Vietnam's interests to do so. To this, he said, 'We were wrong. I would like to be clear. We did not go into Cambodia to save them. We went there to save ourselves. But what we found shocked even us who have seen so much war. Go and ask any soldier there.'

On August 26, 1979, the Cargolux DC-8 with medicines, milk and Oxfam's Jim Howard on board stopped to refuel at Bangkok, where a charade ensued. The Thai authorities refused to allow the aircraft to fly on to Phnom Penh. This, they argued, would 'legitimise' the new Vietnamese-installed government. Curiously, the Foreign Office in London had not mentioned the Thai regime as a source of 'obstruction', nor did the episode create indignant headlines in the West. Of course, the Thais were the 'right people on the right side' whose military leaders had provided bases for American bombers during the Vietnam war and a variety of comforts for American GIs. Jim Howard told me, 'We told them okay, we'll fly somewhere else; we'll fly to Saigon instead. So they finally let us take off, we circled out over the South China Sea and indeed flew overhead Saigon on our way to Phnom Penh. The Danish pilot couldn't believe his eyes. There was nothing at the airport. He couldn't even be sure the runway would take our load. We did one low run and decided to go in. We landed at eleven in the morning, got a few bods to help with the unloading and by four o'clock that afternoon the milk and antibiotics were being given to children in the hospital.'

When Jim Howard arrived at the Hotel Samaki, as the Royale had been renamed, I was working by candlelight in my room. The afternoon monsoon had been so powerful that rain had poured through the louvres of the french doors and two rats scampered to and fro, across the puddles. I watched them, feeling my mood plummet; I was endeavouring to compile a list of urgently needed items – milk, vitamins, antibiotics – which I intended to hand to the Australian Ambassador in Bangkok in compliance with François Bugnion's extraordinary request.

Jim Howard arrived like a one-man cavalry. 'Where do I start?' he said: words which would make him a fitting epitaph. To him, as to me, the first revelation was the sharp contrast to stories of 'obstruction' (none of which had emanated from inside Cambodia); the situation was a relief agency's dream. There were then few bureaucrats of the new Cambodian regime to 'interfere' because few professional administrators had been found alive, and those who presented themselves to us as officials of the new government were emaciated and hungry former students or shopkeepers or travel agents or waiters, who seemed too unused to or frightened of authority to exercise it. Like everybody else, they were so traumatised that their first conversation invariably centred upon a roll-call of the deaths and disappearances in their families. However, bureaucracy has a life force of its own and this innocence would change.

I gave Jim Howard a list of names and places and directed him to the Ministry of Health, which then operated from the former Volkswagen showrooms and consisted of a minister with three years' basic education, a deputy prime minister, an interpreter and an ancient Renault with no tyres and a flat battery. The next day he found one exhausted man trying to care for fifty starving children in a school which, like the National Library, had been converted by the Khmer Rouge to a pigsty. The children were naked or in rags, and without mats, blankets and food. His first cable to Oxford, which began one of the biggest and boldest rescue operations in history, read as follows:

FIFTY TO EIGHTY PER CENT HUMAN MATERIAL DESTRUCTION IS THE TERRIBLE REALITY. 100 TONS OF MILK PER WEEK NEEDED BY AIR AND SEA FOR NEXT TWO MONTHS STARTING NOW REPEAT NOW.

David and I decided it was time to leave. Our film stock was running low, and there was a macabre repetitiveness to our work each day. In our last days we filmed at 'regroupment centres' where thousands of people waited on the outskirts of Phnom Penh to be allowed to enter the city. Very few were reclaiming homes they had been forced to abandon more than four years earlier; most of the owners had fled or were dead. The people in the camps were country people seeking shelter, food and medicines and others seeking news of family members. Officials came here every day with the government's only battery-run megaphone and asked those with skills to come forward. One of them shouted, 'Who is a teacher? Who is a water engineer? Don't be frightened . . . you are needed.' At first there was silence. Then in one day three young men, vibrating with fear, revealed for the first time in four and a half years that they had been college students. Gerry Pinches's camera seemed to help restore confidence. At first they shook their heads when Sophak, our interpreter, asked them if they spoke any English or French. Then a few words tumbled out; knowledge of a foreign language, they said, had meant death.

A young woman told me in French how sixteen members of her family had been executed in one day. 'They were declared to be unproductive,' she said. 'They were killed with tree branches and their throats were slit . . . one by one. My baby was left in the heat while I was forced to husk the rice. When I came back he was dead.' She said this without emotion, as if her grief and shock were in suspense. She was accompanied by a young man, her brother, who seemed too afraid to speak. He wrote down for me the address of their uncle in Paris, their only surviving relative. 'He believes we are dead,' he said in English as we left, 'please give him the news of our living.'

We drove out of Phnom Penh on the highway to Vietnam, weaving through convoys of empty food lorries on their journey home. Shade trees which once had flanked the road, planted by the French, were now mile upon mile of stumps; the Khmer Rouge had cut them down during their assaults across the Vietnamese border, and on each stump were the marks not of saws and axes but of machetes and knives, the only 'modern' instruments permitted for such a task. Gangs of people in bondage slicing mindlessly at great trees was another cameo of Pol Pot's Cambodia.

When we crossed the border into Vietnam's Tay Ninh province, laughter, clatter, colour, crowds, children and dogs under feet and a female voice singing in the back room of a roadside café came as an interlude rather than the normality we had almost forgotten existed. That night, in hot Saigon, I slept in the hotel I had lived in until the last hours of the war more than four years earlier. My room had no window, the ceiling fan turned painfully, and the cistern wheezed through the night: I lay sleepless, paralysed in sweat.

We caught the weekly Air France flight to Bangkok. It was a Saturday afternoon when we arrived and I phoned the Australian embassy immediately I had a hotel room; François Bugnion's plea for an aircraft 'to save thousands' was weighing on my mind. A duty officer answered. I said I wanted to speak to the Ambassador urgently, and I endeavoured to explain why. I was told I would be called back. I waited. I rang again and was told, 'Sorry, sir, the Ambassador is preparing for a function and is unable to speak to you.'

I walked down to and circled the magnificent foyer of the Oriental Hotel, with its chandeliers and slightly manic string quartet and rows of postcard-poring tourists. My sense of disorientation was complete when I ran into David, who had taken the following message from June Peacock at ATV in London: 'SORRY. FORGET IT. YOU ARE ON STRIKE.' In our absence the television technicians' union, ACTT, had struck for more money and had blacked out Britain's commercial network. Our film could not be transmitted, not even edited.

This did not apply to Eric Piper's photographs and my reports for the *Daily Mirror*, which on September 12 and 13 devoted eleven pages to Cambodia: a feat of tabloid newspaper design. These issues of the *Mirror* were syndicated in many countries. I wrote a separate piece which I telexed to *The Age* in Melbourne telling of François Bugnion's appeal. I wrote:

I was asked to make this appeal simply because I am an Australian. I hope this is read by those Australians who have the political power to help save the children of Cambodia – for they now have before them an unprecedented opportunity to include our country in the ranks of truly civilised nations.[9]

In Britain the response was instantaneous. More than £50,000 arrived in a few days, most of it in small amounts: money orders, single pound notes. This was more than enough to pay for two fully-laden relief aircraft; and as Cargolux did not have any of their planes available, I sat down with a telephone and began to search much of the world for one. Insurance seemed to be the charter companies' main concern; no underwriter would give them cover for Phnom Penh, they said, and it became their reason for saying no. A Miami company with one old Convair was set to fly when the owner rang back to say the pilot had suffered a heart attack.

Sir Freddie Laker's 'Skytrain' was then enjoying considerable public goodwill and profit. I recalled that Laker's fortunes had begun with the Berlin airlift; a fraction of that enterprise would save the most vulnerable in Cambodia. And just one of Laker's DC-10s could achieve that. So I phoned Laker's personal assistant and winced as I outlined the 'positive public relations advantages' that would accrue from such a manifestation of compassion on Sir Freddie's part. I supplied lists of the aid needed, cargo weights, even maps; I secured a verbal guarantee from the Vietnamese that the aircraft could land. All of this seemed to generate enthusiasm in Laker's office, but I received no reply from Laker himself. My phone calls were not returned.

British Midland Airways agreed to consider the lease of a Boeing 707, then a representative phoned back to say they had been advised to consult the Foreign Office, which had warned them they might face 'a hostile reception by Vietnamese troops'. All of this suggested disinformation, or 'black propaganda', at work. Journalists receiving 'background briefings' at the Foreign Office were told that Oxfam had been 'duped by the communists'.

Hundreds of people who wanted to help Cambodia wrote to the prime minister. They were assured that the government was doing all it could, but that there were 'grave difficulties' because the Vietnamese-imposed regime was 'every bit as bad as the genocidal Pol Pot'. The Tory MP Sir Anthony Royle went further. The British government, he wrote to a constituent, 'has of course sent a great deal of aid into Cambodia and their efforts certainly have my full support'.[10] This was entirely false; the British government had sent nothing to Cambodia.

'Fly anything anywhere' Cargolux had a DC-8 available. On September 28 an aircraft filled with enough penicillin, vitamins and milk to restore an estimated 69,000 children took off from Luxembourg, all of it paid for by *Daily Mirror* readers. It was of no small significance that during the same week the British government voted in the United Nations to legitimise the most murderous regime since Hitler and Stalin. A majority of the UN credentials committee, including almost all the Western democracies, supported a Chinese motion that Pol Pot's 'Democratic Kampuchea' continue to be recognised as the government of Cambodia. As the American representative, Robert Rosenstock, rose from his seat after voting for Pol Pot, somebody grabbed his hand and congratulated him. 'I looked up and saw it was Ieng Sary [Pol Pot's foreign minister],' he recalled. 'I felt like washing my hands.'[11]

International 'legitimacy' would thus be denied to the government the Vietnamese had brought to power, regardless of the fact that it had freed the Khmers from their charnel house and governed 90 per cent of the territory of Cambodia. By contrast, the Lon Nol government, which the Americans had sustained from 1970 to 1975, controlled only the towns and main roads, yet received full international recognition. The cynicism of this was such that had the Thais, the right people on the right side, liberated their Khmer neighbours under the auspices of the Americans, the sky over Phnom Penh would now be crowded with American relief aircraft and Pol Pot's man would not be taking Cambodia's seat in the world assembly.

The UN vote for Pol Pot meant that stricken Cambodia was denied almost the entire international machinery of recovery and assistance: the United Nations Development Programme, the Asian Development Bank, the International Monetary Fund and the World Bank could not legally help. At the World Health Assembly in Geneva, the British delegate, Sir Henry Yellowlees, voted for Pol Pot's man to take Cambodia's seat. This meant that the resources of WHO, the World Health Organisation, were now denied to Cambodia. Shortly after the Geneva meeting a WHO official telephoned me. 'That picture with your Cambodia story of the pock-marked man,' he said, 'can you tell us if that was caused by smallpox?' I said I did not know, but if smallpox had reappeared during Pol Pot's time, surely a WHO investigator should go to Cambodia to find out. 'We can't do that,' he said. 'They're not recognised.'

Fortunately, the charter of UNICEF permits it to operate in territories that are not 'recognised'. UNICEF had formed a partnership with the International Red Cross for the purposes of their 'joint mission' in Cambodia. By October 1979 this 'mission' existed in name only. UNICEF and ICRC, between them, had sent to Cambodia 100 tons of relief; or as Alan Moudoux, the head of Red Cross public relations in Geneva preferred it, 'more than 100 tons'. More than three months had passed since the foreign minister of the Phnom Penh government, Hun Sen, had handed François Bugnion and Jacques Beaumont a modest list of needs, including 100,000 tons of food. A month went by without even a reply from the two top agencies.

As criticism grew, the Red Cross protested that it could do no more under the terms of its constituted 'neutrality'. This meant that unless the Red Cross continued to supply 'the other side' it would not mount a relief programme in Cambodia itself, where the overwhelming majority of people lived. 'The other side' consisted of camps on either side of the Thai border where the Thai Army had encouraged the Khmer Rouge to take refuge and regroup under cover provided by refugees who had fled the famine and had been driven ahead of the Khmer Rouge virtually as hostages.

On the face of it this 'neutrality' sounded proper, even commendable; it always does. The International Red Cross deserves its reputation for life-saving work, of which there are many celebrated instances, but there have also been times when the impossible goal of 'neutrality', as interpreted in Geneva with the multitude of prejudices that afflict all human enterprise, especially those in which 'geopolitics' is a major ingredient, is little more than benign fraud; the Cambodia emergency was such a time.

The Red Cross and UNICEF 'joint mission' had two rules: one for the way it would conduct its relief operation inside Cambodia and another for its work on the Thai border. Both agencies' headquarters, in Geneva and New York respectively, would not say 'go', as Bugnion had said, until the Phnom Penh government accepted a long caravan of conditions, guarantees and strings. These amounted to, according to one relief official quoted by Brian Eads in the *Observer*, ' . . . absolute licence, a radio station, diplomatic status. They want powers and assurances that would make them more powerful than the government in Phnom Penh.'[12] Moreover, according to the *Guardian* these conditions were designed ' . . . to structure aid to Cambodia in such a way as to give minimum legitimacy to Heng Samrin and maximum help to Pol Pot . . . and to pursue the unrealistic aim of using an army of aid officials in Cambodia as a means of "internationalising" that country and opening it up to Sihanouk.'[13]

In short, this was gunboat relief: arrogant and, above all, hypocritical. In a secret meeting on September 17, arranged by Ieng Sary, Pol Pot's 'foreign minister', Red Cross officials gave Khmer Rouge leaders guarantees of relief supplies, knowing that all talk of preconditions and monitoring was fruitless. When I asked a senior Red Cross official in Geneva if the Khmer Rouge had agreed to the same conditions imposed on Phnom Penh in the cause of 'neutrality', he said, 'Of course not. We're dropping the stuff over the border and getting out quickly.' As Brian Eads reported in the *Observer*, monitoring what the Khmer Rouge did with Western charity was 'in the hands of the Thai Army' at a time when the Thais were doing everything in their power to restore the Khmer Rouge as a military force.[14] The international aid organisations knew this. The World Food Programme knew this; nevertheless it shipped huge quantities of food to the Thai Army without preconditions, whereupon the food was promptly handed out to Khmer Rouge troops.

Jim Howard had estimated that one tanker filled with rice could feed the entire population of Cambodia for two months. On September 18, 1979, Oxfam's deputy director, Guy Stringer, flew to Bangkok with £50,000. He was told by the Thai authorities, as Howard had been told, that no relief could go directly into Phnom Penh by sea or air. Stringer flew on to Singapore where, in a frenzy of organisation, he arranged a barge the size of a football field and a tug to pull it all the way to Cambodia. On board would be Stringer and Chris Jackson of Oxfam, eight Filipino crew, an Indonesian cook, an Irish captain and 1,500 tons of seed, special high-protein food for malnourished dockworkers, plus tools and wood for gangways (as Stringer rightly guessed, there would be no conveyors or cranes at the port of Kompong Som). After sailing into the north-east monsoon, Stringer's barge arrived on the evening of October 13. He recalled to Ben Whitaker:

We wondered what sort of reception we might receive. We attempted to raise the radio station with a call sign we had been given. Silence reigned. From courtesy we ran up the Kampuchean flag we had bought in Singapore, forgetting that Singapore still continued to recognise the Pol Pot government. When the sun rose the next morning, nothing moved. But eventually the one tug which the port possessed moved out to us and twelve officials stepped aboard. They were all extremely young and carried only a penny notebook and a biro. On pieces of cardboard they had written their various duties – *douane* and *santé* – and these were pinned on their breast pockets. When we berthed – the first vessel from the West to bring supplies to this desperate country – it was one of the most agreeable moments that I can remember in my life. On the quay was a high level reception committee: the Minister for Economy and Reconstruction, the Minister for Health, the Minister of Agriculture . . . together with practically every truck remaining in Cambodia. Everything had to be carried off by a collection of emaciated young men and women, some of whom were really boys and girls. We had more typewriters in Oxfam's head office than they did in the entire country – in fact a typewriter and carbon paper were the first things I gave the Minister of Economic Development . . . [15]

The ACTT gave us dispensation to make the film, which was completed when the strike ended. On October 30, the eve of transmission, I phoned UNICEF in Geneva and asked how much relief they and the Red Cross had sent to Cambodia. I then recorded this postscript:

> Since this film was made, more relief has reached Cambodia from Vietnam, the Eastern bloc countries, Australia, Britain's Oxfam and some other Western charities, and the food situation has slightly improved. But throughout Cambodia hunger and disease are widespread. Three months ago the Cambodian government requested 100,000 tons of emergency food. As of yesterday, the total Western aid sent through the Red Cross and UNICEF amounted to 1,300 tons of food.

'Year Zero: the Silent Death of Cambodia' had a memorable public response. 'A solidarity and compassion surged across our nation,' said Oxfam's director, Brian Walker. Forty sacks of post arrived at ATV in Birmingham; 26,000 first-class letters in the first post alone. £1 million was reached quickly and, once again, most of it came from those who could ill afford to give. 'This is for Cambodia', wrote an anonymous Bristol bus driver, enclosing his week's wage. An elderly lady sent her pension for two months, endorsed to 'the children of Cambodia'. There were many pensioners. A young mother phoned with her flock kicking up in the background. 'I've only got £50,' she yelled. 'I've been saving it for three years. Where do I send it? . . . *Listen, I'm not starving, am I?*'

People stopped me in the street to write cheques. They came to my home with toys and letters, and petitions for Margaret Thatcher and poems of indignation for Pol Pot. Not only did they express that unremitting sense of decency and community which is at the core of ordinary British society, but it was clear they had not forgotten the years of television pictures of the suffering of innocent people in South-East Asia. The 'geopolitics' which had contributed to the wasting of Cambodia was a complex story and one of many ironies, but a great many people understood its basics. This taught me once again that it was not enough to produce television that assaulted the public's emotions; it was essential to present the plight of people in a historical context and thus seek an explanation of events, while not pretending to be the bearer of all the available truths. The reward was both a compassionate and an informed public response.

On November 1, 1979, the day after 'Year Zero' was shown, the BBC children's programme *Blue Peter* announced an appeal to help Cambodia's children. It was the first time the BBC had begun such an enterprise as a direct result of a programme broadcast by its commercial competitor. *Blue Peter* asked children to 'bring and buy' toys at Oxfam shops throughout the country. By Christmas they had raised an astonishing £3,500,000. ('Year Zero' raised almost $80,000 in world sales, all of which, including my share, went to the Cambodia Fund.)

There was also a political result; under the weight of letters, telegrams, phone calls and petitions, the British government became the first Western government to 'derecognise' the Pol Pot regime, although Britain continued to vote for the seating of Pol Pot's representative at the United Nations. Following the showing of 'Year Zero' in Australia a few weeks later, the Australian government also withdrew recognition from the Pol Pot regime. This was due in large part to the efforts of the then Minister for Foreign Affairs, Andrew Peacock, who persuaded the conservative coalition cabinet of Malcolm Fraser to make an uncharacteristic gesture against US foreign policy.

'Year Zero' was shown throughout most of the world, but not in the United States. News clips were much in demand, but no prospective American buyer would agree to one condition of sale: that the film be shown as it was made.[16] PBS, the Public Broadcasting Service in Washington, showed interest in 1980 after David Munro and I had made a second film, 'Year One'. The director of news and current affairs programming, Barry Chase, said he wanted to transmit both programmes together but that he was 'worried', although he would not say what he was worried about. David and I were so anxious that a view of Cambodia's tragedy other than that from the Thai border be shown in America that we agreed to fly to New York to edit the two films into one, for no payment. Months passed without word from PBS. Then we heard that Barry Chase had decided to have the two films 'journalistically evaluated'. The person charged with this task was the Washington correspondent of the *St Louis Post-Dispatch*, Richard Dudman, one of the few Westerners to be 'invited' to Cambodia during the Pol Pot period. Dudman's 1978 invitation had been part of an attempt by the Khmer Rouge to regain some international credibility just prior to the Vietnamese invasion. His articles reflected little of the savagery then enveloping the Khmers and little of their true misery. He not only cast doubt on the atrocity stories of refugees, but wrote that people were 'reasonably relaxed' and 'the physical conditions of life may well have improved for many peasants and former urban workers – possibly for the vast majority of the population, as the regime claimed'. He offered observations such as: 'On the bright side . . . I found the country in the midst of one of the world's great housing programs.'[17]

To Barry Chase of PBS, the author of this apologia was to be the 'objective observer' who would resolve his dilemma about whether to show what was then the only complete filmed report from Cambodia since the demise of Pol Pot. Not surprisingly, Dudman turned his thumb down on our films. In a memorandum to Chase he wrote that, contrary to the impression gained from 'Year Zero', he had seen in Pol Pot's Cambodia 'many thousands of evidently healthy people living a life of extreme regimentation but clearly possessing the physical necessities of food, clothing and shelter'.[18] I telexed a list of Dudman's inaccuracies to PBS, but there was no reply. Some months later one of Barry Chase's assistants at PBS, Wayne Godwin, told me, 'John, we're into difficult political days in Washington. Your films would have given us problems with the Reagan administration. Sorry.'

By the end of November 1979 UNICEF and the Red Cross finally had begun to marshal their enormous resources, almost four months after the original request for relief and two months even after the Phnom Penh government had dropped its demand that the agencies stop supplying the Khmer Rouge enclaves on the Thai border. In Britain the local Red Cross saw the recent behaviour of its international organisation in quite a different light.

The British Red Cross Society has roots deep within the British establishment; its patron and president is the Queen, its office bearers knights and colonels. To criticise the Red Cross, let alone to accuse its august world body of cynically playing politics with lives, is to invite the wrath of Sir Evelyn Shuckburgh GCMG, CB. As chairman of the British Red Cross, Sir Evelyn wrote to The Lady Plowden DBE, then chairman (*sic*) of the Independent Broadcasting Authority, to complain about 'Year Zero' and about 'allegations' that the Red Cross had not done its all for Cambodia. He wrote:

> You will understand that the Red Cross is in a delicate position as regards publicly denying such allegations. It must do nothing to upset the hard won consent of the Phnom Penh government to its relief operation which is now in full swing and it is hard to explain the delays which have occurred without criticising them. The only thing one can hope, therefore, is that partial and biased criticisms will not be given wider circulation than they have already received and/or that people will not believe them. I do not think I can ask for more than that the Authority should weigh these considerations in considering the future use of this material.[19]

Sir Evelyn was trying to halt distribution of the film abroad. At the time of his writing, November 1979, the total Red Cross and UNICEF effort in Cambodia, which he described as 'now in full swing', was 1,300 tons: a scandal by no other name.

Back from Lady Plowden came a reply agreeing that the programme was unsatisfactory 'in certain respects' although she omitted to say in which respects. Prior to transmission two IBA officers had viewed 'Year Zero', studied the commentary and sources, asked for several points to be clarified and pronounced themselves satisfied. The 'unsatisfactory respects' had to do with the truth. As for preventing 'wider circulation' and 'future use' of the film, Lady Plowden could not further reassure Sir Evelyn. 'The IBA's writ', she wrote, 'does not, of course, run in other countries.'[20]

Perhaps the degree of opportunism in a year of lost opportunities was best expressed in a letter written by Colonel J. T. Palmer of the British Red Cross to the senior IBA television programme officer, Neville Clarke. In his capacity as secretary of the Disasters Emergency Fund, a consortium of British voluntary relief agencies, Colonel Palmer wrote:

> Further to our discussions on the subject of the use of the balance of the 'Cambodia Fund' set up by ATV I have pleasure in detailing below plans put forward by our member agencies for the expenditure of the money accrued. As you know, Oxfam will not be claiming a share of this sum since it has already received an allocation for approximately £250,000.[21]

Oxfam had not agreed to withdraw any 'claim' to the Cambodia Fund, neither could any combined Disasters Emergency Fund Appeal proceed without Oxfam. The plans put forward by the Red Cross and other voluntary agencies were mostly for work on the Thai border, where a plethora of voluntary agencies already ministered to a small percentage of the population of Cambodia and where the Khmer Rouge, reported Ian Guest in the *Guardian*, were now being 'fattened' on Western aid.[22]

35

'Is there no pity?'

On January 8, 1980, John Gittings reported in the *Guardian* that the previous November US State Department sources had revealed

> . . . their intention of mounting an international propaganda offensive to spread atrocity stories about Vietnamese behaviour in Kampuchea. Within days, presumably on White House instructions, US journalists in Bangkok and Singapore were shown the appropriate 'refugee stories' and Dr. Brzezinski himself verbally briefed a distinguished foreign correspondent and a Washington columnist over lunch on the contents of 'the latest CIA report'.

The 'distinguished Washington columnist' was James Reston of the *New York Times*. Under the emotive headline 'IS THERE NO PITY?' he wrote:

> The latest US intelligence report to President Carter on the Soviet Union's role in South-east Asia indicates that Moscow is not merely refusing to relieve the suffering of the Cambodian people but is actually blocking the distribution of food and medicine from other countries.
> This intelligence report notes that large amounts of desperately needed supplies are reaching Cambodia but they are being diverted from the people who need them most and into the hands of pro-Soviet Vietnamese and the Heng Samrin military.[23]

Reston went on to say that 'there have been verified reports, according to this report to the president, that chemical warfare is being used against Pol Pot forces and Kampuchean civilians'. He quoted an impassioned

plea by President Carter in which he called upon 'Moscow and Hanoi
... not to feed the flames of war, but use aircraft and airfields to ferry
food to feed the people of Kampuchea'. Reston ended his piece by
quoting Carter as asking, 'Is there no pity?'

Reston is regarded as something of an elder statesman among journalists in the United States and in that cultivated role he has access to
presidents and their advisers. In this case he must have suspended critical
judgment; his information was simply untrue.

Moreover, it could be shown to be untrue from US government
sources. In 1980 the State Department published an assessment, not
an 'intelligence report', of international aid reaching Cambodia. The
Russians were listed as the biggest single donor and the 1982 Food and
Agricultural Organisation report indicated that Soviet aid to Cambodia
between 1979 and the end of 1981 amounted to $300 million.

Since 1979 the United Nations Under-Secretary General in charge
of humanitarian operations in Cambodia and Thailand has been Sir
Robert Jackson, a distinguished international civil servant and veteran
of many disaster emergencies. When asked about the diversion of aid,
he replied:

In terms of the Vietnamese army living in say, Kampuchea, we have
never had one complaint from anywhere nor have any of our people.
There's been all these allegations; governments come to us and say,
'Our intelligence sources indicate this' – always in very general terms.
We've said, 'Look, for heaven's sake, will you give us the time, date
and place and we'll follow through.' We've never had one response
when we've asked that question.[24]

Reston's was not the only platform for 'the latest CIA report'. Other
leading American columnists and editorial writers printed extracts and
embroidered them with their own indignation. One Emmett Tyrell Jr
wrote in the *Washington Post*, 'The lesson of Cambodia is the lesson of
the Nazi concentration camps and the Gulag. Some people are immune
to Western decency.'[25]

To my knowledge, no journalist publicly questioned the 'facts' of this
mysterious CIA report, even speculated that it might be in the tradition of
the 'disinformation' so prevalent during the Vietnam war and Watergate
years. The report was 'Kampuchea: A Demographic Catastrophe' released by the CIA in May 1980 (a draft copy was leaked in November
1979). Much of it was warmed-over propaganda which replaced an earlier
CIA analysis from which only opposite and unpalatable conclusions could
be drawn. An author of the original report told a Washington source,
'They [the CIA] misrepresented everything I wrote'.

Shortly after Reston's column appeared, I was asked by a Western foreign minister for my observations on the situation in Cambodia. I began by asking him, 'Have you seen the CIA report?' 'Yes,' he replied. 'The State Department advised us to ignore it, that it was only for the media.'

The 'distinguished foreign correspondent' who, wrote John Gittings, had lunched with Brzezinski and Reston, was Alistair Cooke. In his BBC *Letter from America* broadcast on December 28, 1979, Cooke spoke of 'a document that has been delivered into the hands of the President of the United States and one that made him *furious*'. With 'the latest CIA report' as his source, Cooke accused the Vietnamese and the Russians of plotting to block 'great supplies and medicines that could save unaccountable lives in Cambodia'. Cooke had been misled; none of this was true.

Cambodia's suffering spawned a flourishing cottage industry of 'sidelines reporting' and punditry, especially among those to whom the true nature of events inside Cambodia since the liberation presented an often infuriating challenge. To Western ideologues and active cold warriors, the fact that the 'wrong people' had rescued the Khmer nation from a 'communist hell' was embarrassing. It was embarrassing because both conservatives and liberals in the West found themselves supporting those who had sustained arguably the most extreme communist movement in history. Their confusion was at times almost comical as events in Indo-China made a mockery of that venerable demon known as monolithic communism from which American ideology and strategy had drawn inspiration since 1945. Clearly, new demons had to be invented before the facts eroded such an important myth.

One of the most prolific and influential writers on Indo-China was the British freelance journalist William Shawcross, who during the critical period of 1979–80 was given considerable space in the American Press as the acclaimed author of *Sideshow: Kissinger, Nixon and the Destruction of Cambodia*, published in early 1979. To many of its readers, *Sideshow* had represented a frontal assault on the American political establishment and its military conduct in Indo-China. But this was not the case, neither was it the reputation sought by Shawcross. His prime target was not the system which had underwritten war in Indo-China, but Kissinger and Nixon, whom the eastern liberal establishment held in contempt. Indeed, in his foreword to *Sideshow*, Shawcross clearly implied that in his opinion 'the world's most vital democracy' had been led astray by the influences of Nixon and Kissinger.

In a long five-part series in the *Washington Post* Shawcross wrote that 'one-half of all the international aid reaching the port of Kompong Som [in Cambodia] ... was being trucked into Vietnam'. His source for this damaging and, as it transpired, entirely false charge was an unnamed 'defector' who had been immediately shipped off to Paris and 'put under wraps'.[26] In a sensational and widely-quoted article entitled 'The End of Cambodia', published in the *New York Review of Books*, Shawcross gave credence to a set of unsubstantiated stories passed to him by François Ponchaud, the author of a book about the Pol Pot era, *Cambodia Year Zero*. According to Ponchaud, who had got the stories from Khmer Serei (anti-communist) groups in the Thai border camps, the Vietnamese were behaving in a barbarous way in Cambodia. They were mining ricefields, shooting farmers and sending young Khmer men off to fight the Chinese on Vietnam's northern borders.

Although Ponchaud had tried to cover himself by adding that 'the provenance of these reports should be remembered when they are assessed', he used the stories as the basis for accusing the Vietnamese of committing genocide in Cambodia. Ponchaud described this as 'subtle genocide', and Shawcross appeared to endorse him. At the very least the effect of Shawcross's 'exposé' was to blur the difference between Cambodia under Pol Pot and Cambodia liberated by the Vietnamese: in truth, a difference of night and day. Shawcross wrote:

> . . . it seemed possible that they [the Vietnamese] were a lesser enemy of the Cambodian people than the Khmer Rouge. Now the awful possibility arises that they may not be. Indeed, there have been reports that they are treating the Cambodians with almost as much contempt as the previous regime did . . . if there is a famine in Cambodia today it is principally the Vietnamese that must bear the immediate responsibility.[27]

Shawcross had not been to Cambodia for almost nine years. Nevertheless, publication of rumours of this kind can have devastating results. Their very appearance in the work of an author and commentator of stature causes readers to translate them as fact. Coming on top of Reston's tales from the 'secret CIA report', they soon came to represent, to many people, the general situation in Cambodia. As a direct consequence, there was a burst of editorials whose frequently hysterical tone said less about Cambodia than about the frustrations in the American Press of seeking justification for the American 'loss' of Indo-China. That most emotive and evocative of words, 'genocide', united conservative and liberal commentators. Communists could be damned and lumped together again – Pol Pot with Ho Chi Minh. And now that there was 'evidence' that the Vietnamese communists were practising genocide in Cambodia, surely America's war against them had been justified. After all, one of the principal accusers, William Shawcross, bore impeccable liberal credentials.

It was not long before President Carter was referring to the 'genocide' in Indo-China: not the genocide of Pol Pot, who was being erased from official memories with uncommon alacrity, but that of the 'invaders' of Cambodia. US officials now had further 'proof' to add to their black propaganda that conditions in Cambodia were intolerable to those trying to organise the Western relief effort. And they had further justification for concentrating 'humanitarian aid' on the Thai border, where American officials could 'monitor' the supplies. It is reasonable to suppose that this new 'proof' gained support for the American strategy of 'bleeding' Vietnam and supporting Pol Pot's 'legitimacy' in the United Nations.

That the Vietnamese genocide story was false and could be proven false by an abundance of available, substantiated evidence, hardly affected its propagation, by government and media, during the Cambodia emergency in 1980. There were other voices, but they were barely heard. For example, Shawcross's assertions contrasted with the unpublicised, meticulous research of Ben Kiernan, the Australian Khmer scholar, and his wife, Chanthou Boua. In 1979 they interviewed refugees on the Thai border, which had been the source of the Shawcross/Ponchaud genocide stories, and in 1980 they recorded some 500 interviews inside Cambodia.[28] They found not the slightest evidence to support Ponchaud's claims.

Moreover, journalists who visited Cambodia in 1979 and early 1980, when the emergency was at its height, found no evidence to confirm such claims. They included Michael Beckham of Britain's Granada Television, Anthony Barnett of the *New Statesman*, myself, and a string of European, American and Japanese journalists, some of them quite hostile to Vietnam. Jim Laurie, the prize-winning producer of American ABC News, travelled extensively in Cambodia in January 1980 and reported for both ABC and the *Far Eastern Economic Review*. He found nothing to support charges of theft or denial of crops and relief supplies, which underpinned the stories of 'subtle genocide'. He wrote:

At no time during 26 days in Kampuchea did this correspondent find any indication of wilful obstruction in the delivery of international relief supplies. Nor did there appear to be any basis for allegations that food was being diverted to either Vietnam or Vietnamese troops . . . Vietnamese charter companies from Ho Chi Minh City appear to handle the bulk of the aid sent by road to Phnom Penh . . . Interviews revealed no complaints of Vietnamese troops preventing the harvest of rice as alleged in some Bangkok reports.[29]

In a later report Laurie quoted complaints by foreign aid officials in Phnom Penh that 'confused and negatively biased reporting ... has begun to undermine relief efforts'.[30]

During the next three years Shawcross made several visits to Cambodia, and in response to a letter I wrote to him in 1983, he retracted his suggestions of genocide.[31] But he subsequently made other damaging assertions. The most serious of these, repeated in articles and in his 1984 book, *The Quality of Mercy: Cambodia, Holocaust and Modern Conscience*, was that Khmer Rouge torturers were 'actually being promoted by the new [Vietnamese-backed] order into positions of authority' over their former victims. His evidence for this is the following story: 'In one fishing village ... I met an old woman who described with great passion how the Khmer Rouge murderer of her son was living, unpunished, in the neighbouring village.'[32]

Ben Kiernan accompanied Shawcross on this particular trip. He interpreted for him at the village and tape-recorded the interview. Kiernan wrote:

> The woman actually said that the killer had 'run away' to a neighbouring *district*. This rather suggests that he at least feared punishment, and there was certainly no suggestion that he had been 'promoted' to 'new authority'.[33]

Shawcross also claimed that when he was in Phnom Penh 'no Cambodian was supposed to talk to foreigners without permission'. I interviewed dozens of people without permission and at random, as indeed have countless journalists, researchers and others, including Kiernan who was in Phnom Penh at the same time as Shawcross. Shawcross accused the Vietnamese of allowing 'no exhaustive examination of the records of the Khmer Rouge'. Much of the *New Statesman* of May 2, 1980, was given over to the translations by Ben Kiernan and Chanthou Boua of a welter of Khmer Rouge documents brought back from Phnom Penh by Anthony Barnett. Kiernan himself later copied 5,000 pages of documents; Steven Heder, an American scholar on a research grant from the US State Department, was allowed to copy thousands of pages. As Grant Evans has pointed out, a theme of Shawcross's 'Cambodia campaign' was that it was always the communists who allowed 'politics' to thwart Western 'humanitarianism' in Cambodia; the converse was apparently unthinkable.[34]

The fact that most Western 'aid to Cambodia' never reached Cambodia, but instead went to Thailand's south-eastern border with Cambodia, was not generally understood in the West. This aid included food, which fell into four categories: food which fed starving people; food

which was sold on the black market long after the famine had passed
and was often bought back by the aid agencies; food which was handed
over to the Thai Army and never accounted for, together with millions
of dollars given to the Thai regime for 'Thai Affected Villagers' and
never accounted for; and food which restored the Khmer Rouge as a
fighting force.

According to an internal UNICEF report I was given, 84 per cent of
food supplied to the Thai border during 1979–80 never reached those
for whom it was intended. In short, most of the fears expressed in Phnom
Penh about the effect, if not the aims, of Western aid to the Thai border,
were proven to be justified. Moreover, the apparent generosity of most
Western governments and the principal aid agencies was not quite as it
seemed in 1979 and 1980. According to one estimate[35] the United
Nations High Commission for Refugees (UNHCR) and the International Red Cross (ICRC) were given $134.9 million to spend on just
120,000 people chiefly because Western donors preferred their charity
'for Cambodia' to be spent entirely in Thailand. More than half of the
funds of the UNICEF and ICRC Joint Mission were spent on the Thai
border, paying for the needs of some 300,000 people while between 6
and 7 million people, who represented the population of Cambodia,
received the other half, roughly $50 a person. This imbalance was sharply
demonstrated in 1983 when Western governments pledged $70 million
for work on the Thai border and less than $2 million for all of Cambodia
itself.

The principal town on the Thai-Cambodian border is Aranyaprathet.
From 1979 to 1981 it accommodated newly prosperous Thai families
whose pick-up trucks and polythene-wrapped Hondas, tape decks and
chubby children reflected the entrepreneurial opportunities presented
by the unique tragedy across the border. Westerners abounded in 'Aran':
men and women of good intentions and others with less altruistic motives.
Indeed, 'Aran' resembled in some ways Saigon before it 'fell': the latter
being familiar to and mourned by many of the foreigners who came to
the border. The mainstays of old Saigon, brothels and a black market,
were faithfully reproduced. In Prol's restaurant, memories were stirred
by Simon and Garfunkel on tape, burgers, Tom Collins and martinis
with a twist, served by children and consumed by a rich assortment of
'cowboys' and 'freelancers', not unlike the *paparazzi* who followed the
Americans in Vietnam, and doctors relaxing after a day's work on the
'refugee valium programme'. Attitudes brought from old Saigon were in
evidence, both genuine and affected. Those camp followers and others
who had known the war in Vietnam, or were disappointed to have just
missed it, assumed a world-weary, almost proprietorial view of the West's
latest stand in the East. 'Man, this will go on for years' was a sort of

catch-cry, as if 'this' was a permanent roadshow for an occidental audience. As in old Saigon, roots, causes and solutions were not often considered part of the entertainment.

Almost everybody who was anybody lived in a fine house on piles: that is, when they were not shuttling to and from the comforts of Bangkok. The Catholic Relief Services had a house, a place of urgency commanded by a former US Green Berets officer turned Jesuit priest. UNICEF, *Newsweek* and *Time* each had houses; the American television networks had a house. And Colonel Prachak Sawaengchit had a house from which he commanded the Royal Thai Army's second infantry regiment and the border itself. Prachak was the warlord of the border; not to give his men kickbacks on demand, such as a truck fully laden with relief, was to incur his famous indignation and wrath. In November 1979 he ordered the shelling of a refugee camp on the Cambodian side of the border; the following year he stopped all food and water going into another refugee camp.

The United States government also had a fine house on the border. It was known as the 'Taphouse' and was distinguished by an imposing radio transmitter on its roof. From here men of KEG went forth in a fleet of unmarked Holden station wagons, also with transmitters. The men of KEG, or Kampuchean Emergency Group, were attached to the US embassy in Bangkok and, according to the State Department in Washington, were 'a special monitoring force'. Lionel Rosenblatt, formerly of the United States embassy in Saigon, was 'refugee-co-ordinator' of KEG. He told me:

> I feel that what we're doing is an appropriate extension of our war in Vietnam. I think it's important for America to remember its responsibilities in this region, even though it doesn't have the high security threshold that we used to have with half a million men there. I think that actually the only problem with America in this part of the world is that, having fought the Vietnam war, most people at home have retired completely in terms of involvement. Well, the people who are working here with us, some are old Indo-China hands and some aren't, are people who are interested in seeing that humanitarian effort continue, who are concerned about the life-threatening processes here. Okay, so the general inclination is forget South-East Asia, that was the Sixties, early Seventies. Now *we* say we need to be involved, and there will be an increasing US involvement in South-East Asia in the 1980s. And the new line, if you like, is right here in Thailand, okay?

For Rosenblatt to describe the Vietnam war as 'humanitarian effort' seemed premature; recent history in South-East Asia was being rewritten in academic institutions across America but surely not that quickly. However, the mission of KEG was indeed the 'appropriate extension' of the war in Vietnam, for it was to oversee the distribution of Western supplies to the border, to the proxies in the latest Indo-China war, the 'guerrilla forces' or 'resistance movements' which operated from the border, principally the Khmer Rouge. The importance of the Khmer Rouge to US strategy cannot be underestimated. With Pol Pot as its military commander, the Khmer Rouge was to become the fighting arm of the new 'Democratic Kampuchea' coalition which had Prince Sihanouk as its 'president' and included Son Sann, a former head of the National Bank of Cambodia and Khieu Samphan, Pol Pot's mouthpiece.

Two American relief workers, Linda Mason and Roger Brown, spent six months working in refugee camps on the border, where they learned Khmer and talked to a wide range of officials. In a book published in 1983 they wrote:

> The US Government, which funded the bulk of the relief operation [on the border], insisted that the Khmer Rouge be fed ... The US was interested in the resistance movements for its own strategic objectives. Like Thailand, the US preferred that the Khmer Rouge operation benefit from the credibility of an internationally-known relief operation.
>
> Throughout 1980, their health rapidly improved ... The Khmer Rouge had a history of unimaginable brutality, and having regained their strength, they had begun actively fighting the Vietnamese.[36]

These 'strategic objectives' were spelt out in July 1980 when President Carter and Chairman Hua Guofeng of China met in Tokyo for the first time. It was a 'historic meeting', as their spokespeople effused; for here was the seemingly unlikely alliance begun by Nixon and Kissinger in 1972 being consummated with the following communiqué:

> There is essential agreement between the United States and the People's Republic of China with regard to strategic perspectives and particularly as they relate to ... the invasion of Cambodia by Soviet-backed Vietnamese.

Thus America abandoned the relatively cautious position taken by Secretary of State Cyrus Vance before his resignation over the Iran hostages 'rescue' fiasco – that Washington supported neither the Phnom Penh government nor the Khmer Rouge – and gave its full approval to China's Indo-China policy, which was to subdue Vietnam, by force or attrition, and to imbue 'Democratic Kampuchea' with a new, internationally respectable image, preferably in the guise of a 'non-aligned' coalition led by Prince Sihanouk or another equally pliable.

For American policy, then guided by the president's national security adviser, Dr Zbigniew Brzezinski, and not substantially changed by the Reagan administration, the following results were desired: the total economic isolation of Vietnam; the retrospective discrediting of a generation of Vietnamese resistance, so that US intervention in Indo-China and its use of Vietnam as a laboratory of war technology could be justified historically, and future 'Vietnams' (as in Central America) be accorded renewed 'moral purpose'; revenge for the humiliation of a 'lost' war; and the deepening of the differences between the Soviet Union and China and of the obsession of each with the other's 'expansionism'.

So the 'new line' in this new war was the Thai border with Cambodia, where the American side of the bargain with China would be implemented by the men of KEG. The identity and career of the chief of KEG underscored the continuity of American intervention in Indo-China. In 1969–70 Michael Eiland was operations officer of a clandestine Special Forces group code-named 'Daniel Boone' which was responsible for the reconnaissance of the secret and illegal American bombing of Cambodia.[37] By 1980 Colonel Eiland was running KEG from the American embassy in Bangkok. He was also responsible for interpreting satellite surveillance pictures of Cambodia and in that capacity was a valued informant of a number of resident members of Bangkok's Western press corps who described him in their reports as a 'Western analyst'. Indeed, the Colonel was one of their main sources of 'news' from inside Cambodia. And perhaps this was why so little was written about the activities of KEG. It must be presumed that journalists knew that Eiland's speciality was disinformation. In 1983, Eiland was appointed Defence Intelligence Agency (DIA) chief in charge of the South-East Asia Region, one of the most important jobs in American espionage.

The American presence in Thailand was headed by the Ambassador, Morton Abramowitz, a foreign service officer who had worked inside the Pentagon as a China specialist. Abramowitz was one of those who felt passionately about the 'loss' of Vietnam and about events across the border in Cambodia. He devoted much of his energy to getting aid to refugees in the border camps. He had little patience with relief agencies which objected to their supplies going to 'the guerrillas' (the Khmer Rouge) and he was frequently accused of interference. He regarded Oxfam as a dupe of the communists and, although he may not have been responsible, his embassy was the source of a false and damaging rumour that rice sent into Cambodia by the Oxfam/Non-Governmental Organisation (NGO) Consortium had been treated with a deadly mercury-based fungicide which would poison Khmer peasants handling or eating the seed.[38] And this was only one example of virulent 'black propaganda' emanating from the US embassy. However, Abramowitz did dismiss reports of Vietnamese 'genocide' in Cambodia and said that embassy intelligence had found no evidence of the Vietnamese blocking food aid.[39]

Bangkok and the Thai border were medialand. So ubiquitous was the media on the 'sidelines' of the Cambodia tragedy in 1980 that Khmer children in Kao I Dang camp produced a piece of theatre which told the story of their country's suffering beginning with soliloquies about murder and starvation and ending with a tableau of foreign television crews gaping emptily at the dead.

Among the many 'media events' staged on the border was the 'March for Kampuchea's Survival' in February 1980. This attracted publicity around the world because it was led by former 1960s American civil rights singer Joan Baez, Swedish film star Liv Ullman and others including Conservative MP Winston Churchill. The march was reportedly organised by Médecins Sans Frontières, a group of Paris doctors. In an interview in the *Observer* Joan Baez was quoted as saying, 'We are able to present the case to the world that there are no doctors in Cambodia'.[40] Ian Hopwood, deputy director of UNICEF in Phnom Penh, dismissed Baez's remarks and said that there were medical teams in every province in Cambodia. 'We need many things,' he told me, 'what we don't need is more medical teams. They may look good in headlines and to donors in the West, but they are far from top priority.'

(The reasoning was lost in the potent 'white angel' image of Western doctors and nurses saving people in a third world country: an image assiduously promoted by some Western charities in order to raise money. The charities seldom if ever explain that medical teams are not always the answer. They need a complex support structure – refrigeration, for example – and what they achieve at great expense can often be matched by local 'bare-foot doctors', who are familiar with the people and their environment and capable of dispensing basic drugs and inoculations.)

Reports from the border made much of the contention by Joan Baez and Liv Ullman that they and their entourage of 'medical teams' were being prevented by the Phnom Penh authorities from marching straight into Cambodia. What was not reported was that the entire operation was a propaganda stunt set up and run by the US government. In a letter in the Paris Press, Doctors Jean-Marc Dumas and Jean-Christophe Rufin of Médecins Sans Frontières disclosed that the march had been conceived on December 18, 1979, at a meeting with three US senators, and representatives of the White House and the State Department, and it was agreed that 'in order for it to be more acceptable', an American agency, the International Rescue Committee, would be given the responsibility of driving over a 'land bridge' into Cambodia twenty trucks of food and medical teams. The doctors wrote:

> The French supporters of the march committee knew nothing of all this ... Thus, for the first time in our history, our association has been deliberately involved in a remote controlled operation for which it served as a cover [for] the initiatives of political forces.[41]

The Times of February 6, 1980, published a picture with the caption, 'Joan Baez, the American folk singer, cuddling a Kampuchean child at the Sa Kaeo refugee camp in Thailand before joining a march for the survival of Kampuchea'. What was not mentioned was a fact known to every aid official and journalist on the border: Sa Kaeo, although flying the flag of UNHCR, was controlled by the Khmer Rouge, whose cadres dispensed Western aid, enforced discipline (such as black dress and short hair for women) and intimidated dissidents with beatings and burial up to the neck. The Khmer Rouge leaders had special quarters in the camp, just inside the main gate, and were on hand with waxen smiles to greet the thirteen American missionaries of the Assembly of God who came regularly with gifts and to inform them that Jesus Christ would save them, if not their victims. And they were on hand for all 'media events', such as the visit of Mrs Rosalynn Carter, wife of the President of the United States, who came to say that America would save them, which was more to the point.

At night, when there were no visitors and no television cameras, Khmer Rouge wounded from battles over the border with the Vietnamese would be ferried to Sa Kaeo camp by the secretive Thai military unit, Task Force 80, which was 'advised' by an official of USAID, Jack Williamson. Foreign surgical teams, which had been sent to care for civilian refugees, were frequently called out to treat the soldiers of Pol Pot's Army; this was known among some young doctors as 'getting third world tropical/emergency experience'.

One of the critics of the 'March for Survival' was the UNICEF information officer in Bangkok, Jacques Danois. A caring man, Danois knew Indo-China well, though not as the archetypal 'Asia hand'. In his spare time he wrote children's books based on his experiences in Indo-China and which he described as 'stories of the East for children of the West'. He resented deeply the political manipulation of the aid agencies. Unlike most aid officials and journalists based in Bangkok he had travelled widely in Cambodia and Vietnam during the emergency. The picture he brought back from Cambodia was an unpopular one in Bangkok: that of a people making a courageous effort to recover and of a government working with great difficulty but in good faith.

In his travels Danois had come upon Vietnamese distributing rice to Khmer peasants, and he spoke and wrote about this on his return to Bangkok. He also suggested that much of the Thai border operation was having the effect of diverting farmers in north-western Cambodia from sowing their crops and de-stabilising the country and therefore should be closed down. This stand made Danois enemies in Bangkok, including one American newspaper correspondent who reported him to UNICEF in New York for being 'pro-Hanoi'. UNICEF had just appointed a new executive director, James Grant, an assistant administrator of the American AID agency in Vietnam during the 1960s and an enthusiastic supporter of the American war. Danois was told that if he continued to speak his mind his job would be in jeopardy.

'Sidelines reporting' from the border did not necessarily mean a poor and prejudiced coverage of Cambodia. Because the border produced a narrow perspective and determining the truth required considerable skill, the best and wisest journalists excelled. The *Observer*'s coverage was unequalled, thanks in large part to its Hong Kong based correspondent Brian Eads, who spent much of his time on the border. Eads's ability to resist the pressures of 'consensus' reporting made his journalism a consistent counter to the work of those who used the tragedy to echo their simplistic view of the wider cold war. In an *Observer* piece which drew on Eads's reporting and was signed by him, Laurence Marks, Robert Stephens, Denis Bloodworth and Geoffrey Lean, this final paragraph evoked that which I had seen and felt in Cambodia:

> It is as if the world's statesmen contemplating the problem of Cambodia, had, between them, arrived at a final solution of extraordinary elegance: militarily secure, ideologically incorruptible, diplomatically irreproachable – a dead child.[42]

For the *Guardian* Ian Guest warned of the restoration of the Khmer Rouge from as early as the spring of 1979. The reporting of the *Boston Globe*, the *Philadelphia Inquirer* and other, smaller American papers outstripped that of their more venerable rivals in New York, Washington and Los Angeles.

Although it was common knowledge on the Thai border that a number of the refugee camps were actually Thai-run military bases, few journalists tried to get inside them. One who did and was imprisoned by the Thai military was Rod Nordland of the *Philadelphia Inquirer*. Nordland discovered 'Camp 42' which, he reported, was 'run by Thai military men in civilian clothes who were commanding Cambodian guerrillas on Thai territory' and who 'murdered a Cambodian refugee not 100 yards away from us, and even beat children who tried to sneak food to us and other prisoners'.[43] Nordland found ample proof that the 'guerrillas' – in this case the Khmer Serei, who were generally regarded as anti-communist bandits – controlled 'the rice shipments brought in by refugee agencies, much of which they confiscated and carried back into the war-ravaged Cambodian interior, where they trade it for gold'.

36

Year One

In June 1980, almost a year after I had reached Phnom Penh, I went back with Eric Piper, David Munro, Gerry Pinches and Steve Phillips. I had asked Jim Howard of Oxfam and the two French doctors, Jean Yves Follezou and Jean Michel Vinot, to return with us in the belief that perhaps only those who had seen Cambodia in 1979 could make a fair assessment of the changes during the first year of liberation. The main aim of this second trip was to account for the estimated $45 million which my documentary, 'Year Zero', had raised around the world.

Shortly before I left London I received a phone call from Paris. A familiar, husky voice came quickly to the point. 'Can you postpone?' he said. 'I've heard about a Khmer Rouge list and you're on it. They're waiting for you, and I'm worried.' That Wilfred Burchett was worried about the welfare of another human being was not surprising. I have not known another journalist who, through half a century of risk-taking, demonstrated as much concern for others. The quintessence of the man lay in what he did not say on the phone: that he himself was on the same list and that a few weeks earlier, at the age of seventy and seriously ill, he had narrowly escaped death in Cambodia in an ambush laid for him by Khmer Rouge assassins.

Wilfred's warning certainly worried me, if only because I had become somewhat superstitious. Having made my way intact through half a dozen wars and other calamities I felt only respect for the laws of averages and luck. I was also concerned that, as a companion travelling with Wilfred had been hit, the same might happen to those travelling with me. So I launched an eccentric scheme to protect us all from Pol Pot and sent off for half a dozen armour-plated vests. I had never worn one of these things, not even a flak jacket, and I was assured by the supplier in

Hertfordshire that I would be receiving 'the new lightweight jobs as used by the SAS . . . nothing at all like your Crusaders' breastplates'.

It was when I opened my front door in South London and found the delivery man spreadeagled across two crates, his back temporarily broken, that I began to question the wisdom of my decision. Indeed, by the time I had unpacked one of the vests, picked it up and dropped it on my foot, thereby spraining my ankle, I knew this was an idea whose time had passed.

We flew to Saigon, where once again we insisted upon having the means of free movement inside Cambodia: a van and fuel. It seemed this time even more important to demonstrate our independence from both the Vietnamese and the Heng Samrin government in Phnom Penh. In his subsequent report to Oxfam, Jim Howard wrote:

> It was made clear by Pilger that they wished to film where they liked on the aid programmes and the general situation, and they would not work to a pre-planned schedule as this was too limiting and they would decide daily what to film and where. This arrangement was partly . . . to avoid 'set pieces' arranged by the authorities.

'Listen,' said David Munro as we drove into Phnom Penh. The tinkling of bells on hundreds of pony traps carrying people and food and goods was a new, rich sound. Compared with the emptiness of the year before Phnom Penh was a city transformed, with a population grown to around 100,000 people. There were traffic accidents, two bus routes, restaurants, raucous markets, re-opened pagodas, telephones, a jazz band, a football team and paper money. And there were freedoms: uncoerced labour, freedom of movement and freedom of worship. I had never seen so many weddings, nor had I ever received as many wedding invitations – four in a day. Marriage had become a mark of resilience, of freedom restored, and was celebrated with as much extravagance as was possible in the circumstances, with long skirts and brocade tops and hair piled high with flowers, and with the men bearing gifts of precious food arranged on leaves, their necks craning from makeshift and unaccustomed collars and ties. These were peasant people – most of the city people were dead or 'missing' – and for all their apparent joy, they bore an air of transience.

There was electricity now and a supply of fresh water, paid for by British people and connected by an Oxfam engineer. Virtually everywhere we went we found the results of the millions of pounds given to the Khmer people. Through a separate fund set up by Doctors Follezou and Vinot, and paid for by the British viewers of 'Year Zero', a pharmaceutical factory had opened, which meant that ready-made drugs, like penicillin, no longer needed to be imported.

The generosity of donors in Britain had literally put colour back into people's lives. Oxfam had reopened a textile factory, so that people could shed the hated black the Khmer Rouge had often forced them to wear; £30,000 worth of dyes had come from Britain, 280 tons of cotton yarn and 60,000 knitting needles, producing sixty designs. The plant employed some 300 people, most of them widows who had lost all their immediate families. And this was just one of several development projects paid for by money which had flowed to Associated Television following the showing of 'Year Zero'. In all, Oxfam received and spent some £6 million. Of this a final total of £3,710,823 came from children selling and buying toys in BBC's *Blue Peter* appeal. What placed Oxfam in a class of its own was that not only did it manage to deliver help swiftly, but it accounted for every pound and held administrative costs at around one per cent.

'My name is Cham,' said an eight-year-old. 'Are you a friend?'

The interpreter frowned as she put his words into English. Cambodia was probably the only place on earth where a child would ask that question so disarmingly, as if adults were no longer to be trusted and the young no longer assured of their protection. Cham carried a plastic briefcase filled with books, paper and pencils, of which there had been none the year before. These were the product of Guy Stringer's ingenuity: 'Orphanage kits' he called them, and designed them to help restore a recovering child to normality. Each kit contained a drawing book, crayon set, pencil sharpener, pencil, mosquito net, sleeping mat, soap, toothbrush, bowl, spoon, football, bright-coloured shirt, toilet paper, water purifying tablets.

I met Cham at the school where one year earlier Jim Howard had found fifty sick and hungry children. Now it was a school again, the largest primary school in Cambodia, packed with 2,000 rowdy youngsters in hot pursuit of a cheated childhood. In less than a year some 900,000 children had been enrolled in rudimentary schools throughout Cambodia and 19,000 new teachers given a two-month crash course, an astonishing achievement.

In Phnom Penh, in the chapel converted to a field hospital in an orphanage, where children had been brought from the forest, I was greeted by Prak Sarinn, the former teacher who had lost all his pupils and his family on the day Phnom Penh had been emptied by the Khmer Rouge, the day of Year Zero.

'But you don't recognise Ock!' he said.

I looked down at a pudgy, impassive Buddha of about twelve years of age.

'He was on that bed there. You filmed him, and I spoke to him for you . . . ?'

'But that child was dying,' I said.

'Yes. He could not sit up he was so weak. But look at him now! I think he is fat! People should know that Ock would have died without the drugs, milk and mosquito nets that came to us so quickly.'

The realisation that this child and the wasting small figure in our film were one and the same was one of the most welcome moments of my life. (The most undernourished adults we saw were Vietnamese soldiers, whose rations no longer included the staple of dried fish but were now mostly rice and salt, with banana stalks made into a soup. Their condition made nonsense of the stories of food aid being diverted for the Army.)

During 1980 several of the aid agencies were critical of the Phnom Penh government's decision to stockpile and ration food and to give priority to feeding people in the cities and towns. Some of this criticism was justified; but Oxfam's chief representative in Cambodia in 1980–81, Bill Yates, believed that the government had taken a calculated gamble in emphasising seed over food distribution. He told me, 'They have trusted the peasants' instincts to live off the land, and everyone who needs to work and has no source of food, from nurses to bridge repairers, is receiving rations. All the villages I have seen have subsistence plots. I haven't seen a sow that isn't pregnant. I think the aid agencies have been outguessed by the government and seriously under-estimated the resources of people themselves.'

We decided to try to verify the distribution of seed. Unannounced, we watched seed unloaded from the Oxfam consortium's twentieth barge in Phnom Penh, followed it to the railyards, then drove the 250 miles to Battambang to see it unloaded and trucked to warehouses. The next day a moving belt of ox carts, donkey traps and cycles delivered the entire consignment of 390 tons to villages. From barge to soil took just three days.

In Phnom Penh, the frustrations of some of the Western aid contingent grew in relation to a new and burgeoning bureaucracy which spawned its fair share of obdurate officials. There was, as some had charged, a degree of 'political interference' in the distribution of aid. But given the chaos in Phnom Penh that was hardly surprising. In those days the government was barely a government at all. It was a collection of survivors and amateurs, a confusion of the remnants of the educated class, of anyone with skills and of those who had formed the resistance within the Khmer Rouge and had fled for their lives to Vietnam. One of these was Heng Samrin, the new president of Cambodia, a distant, taciturn figure, whom I met in 1979. His regime is described as socialist, yet encourages one of the freest consumer markets in Asia, and the impression I got was that its crash-course cadres understood very well that their bored audiences wanted little to do with any political evangelism. However, the more prolonged Cambodia's international isolation and the threat from the Thai border, the greater the risk of authoritarian ways becoming habitual.

By June 1980 foreign aid officials in Phnom Penh outnumbered the staff of the Ministry of Health. In the Hotel Samaki, where most of them were billeted, a monastic claustrophobia led to a certain paranoia, especially during the afternoon downpour. This would be relieved by the arrival of a new colleague, laden with welcome duty-free bags or, when the rain had eased, by the sport of the new Cambodian Army's recruits who, with their newly issued automatic weapons, would mount an assault on bullfrogs in the stagnant hotel pool; bullfrogs, it was rumoured, were guilty of stealing the moon. Beneath the infrequently turning fans in the great colonial rooms of the Samaki, a month might seem like a year for those aid industry men who seldom ventured far and for others who complained incessantly and railed against the 'incompetence of communism' and believed their rooms to be bugged. Few of these secular missionaries had been to Cambodia before, or had attempted to comprehend the past and see the precarious state in which the whole of Khmer society was suspended. For some the great ideological struggle of East and West had to go on regardless of local difficulties.

These people were in the minority, but they were such a vocal minority that when they were replaced, aid programmes which had been their responsibility and had seemed mired in local bureaucracy were implemented quickly. 'For some of us in the relief business', said Jim Howard, 'the old colonialist fervour dies hard. How can the natives *possibly* have a government which might, just might, know its own people best. The attitude is that the West knows best. Well, the truth is that real corruption here has been negligible. All the supplies we've been putting in have got through; none of them are on sale in the market. In the circumstances, they have done an historic job of recovery.'

But it was a recovery which could not be sustained without international development aid on a scale comparable with the rescue of European agriculture following the Second World War. Sir Robert Jackson, the UN Under-Secretary General whose responsibility was emergency relief to Indo-China, had been in charge of flying aid to Europe during 1944. He recalled:

As to tractors, my first recollection of tractors was flying them in to Tito. The whole post-war [operation] in Europe, Asia, China, USSR was tractors, tractors, tractors. Here . . . the Kampucheans want them, they're crying out for them, but were simply told by the donors that would be regarded as development aid.[44]

In the critical months of 1980, with one harvest expected and another waiting to be planted, I came upon rows of rusted, immobile tractors in sheds in Battambang. They had not been replaced and parts had not arrived, because tractors were classified as development aid. Like Vietnam, Cambodia is classified as 'Category Z' by the US State Department, which enforces a First World War-vintage Trading with the Enemy Act. Export licences have been denied to American charities which have wanted to send tractor parts, animal vaccine, fish nets, a sawmill to make school furniture, school pencils and paper. Oxfam was prevented from sending an irrigation pump, which had been made in Britain under licence to an American company. The consequences of the embargo have been devastating. In 1983 the World Bank listed Cambodia as the poorest country in the world. Since 1981 malnutrition has increased and, says one estimate, affects 53 per cent of children; and almost half of Cambodia's population are children.[45]

To this burden is added fear. Fear threads almost every conversation. 'Will Pol Pot come back?' is a question put incessantly to foreigners, especially Westerners whose governments continue to underwrite him. Because of this fear most traditional Khmer antipathy towards the Vietnamese has been shelved for the duration. Vietnamese soldiers are a common sight in the markets; they go unarmed and their discipline is respected. Whatever the qualms people have about the presence of a foreign army, they believe that the Vietnamese stand between them and another Khmer Rouge regime, no matter its disguise.

The tenuous nature of this 'normality' was demonstrated to me during a 'disco night' I attended at the Monorom Hotel in Phnom Penh. The women and the children sat on one side of the room, *palais* style, the men on the other. It was a lot of fun, especially when a competing jazz band next door struck up with 'Stompin' at the Savoy'. But when a cassette of the much-loved Khmer singer, Sin Sisamouth, was played, people stopped dancing and walked to the windows and wept. He had been taken to Battambang, forced to dig his own grave and to sing the Khmer Rouge anthem, which was about blood and death. After that, he was beaten to death.

These reminders of the immediate past, and of the possibility of the past becoming the future, were constant. There was an old steam train which carried seed to the north-west. On its return journey it was a moving human ant-heap, conveying between five and ten thousand passengers, slung in hammocks between the wheels, embracing the funnels, sardined in the driver's cabin. The station master did me the honour of speaking his first English in five years. A sardonic man, he explained that the train could not proceed all the way to Phnom Penh central station 'because the driver is no good; he is learning, you see. He does not know when to put on the brake, and when it is raining cats and frogs he is even worse!' Two days later the Khmer Rouge, operating from their Thai border sanctuary, ambushed the train with rockets and automatic weapons; at least 150 people were killed.

Returning to Phnom Penh one evening we approached the bend in the road where Wilfred Burchett had been ambushed two months earlier. We were travelling in our van followed by an Oxfam Land Rover. Ahead, where the road narrowed, a covered truck was parked at an angle, almost blocking our way. The Vietnamese driver of the van accelerated as he and the escort reached for their automatic weapons shouting for those behind to get down. Both vehicles lunged into the verge and in an eruption of dust we cleared one end of the truck. It was over in seconds; and the snapshot I carry in my mind is that of armed men in black lying on their bellies aiming point blank at us.

We flew to Bangkok and drove to Aranyaprathet on the Thai side of the border, almost within sight of where we had camped a few nights earlier. From here we travelled in a UNICEF Land Rover at the head of a convoy of forty trucks: seventeen loaded with food, seventeen with seed and the rest with 'goodies', which was the term the agency people used for their assorted largesse. We were headed for Phnom Chat, a Khmer Rouge operations base set in forest just inside Cambodia and bunkered with land mines about every fifteen yards. The mines had been laid by the Thai Army, which kept a commando unit encamped on the perimeter. The base itself had a Thai Task Force 80 'liaison officer', who was worried and displeased by the presence of foreigners other than those bearing supplies. The UNICEF official leading the convoy, Phyllis Gestrin, a University of Texas psychology professor, was also worried and clearly disliked what she was doing. 'I don't want to think what this aid is doing,' she said. 'I don't trust these blackshirts.' She could barely suppress her fear and demonstrated it by driving us across a suspected minefield and into a tree. 'Oh man,' she said, 'this place gives me the creeps. Let's get it over with.' At that she turned the Land Rover around and pointed it back along the track. 'I got to make a quick getaway,' she said.

The forty trucks had dumped their 'goodies' at sheds in a clearing and Phyllis nervously solicited the signature of three Khmer Rouge who had watched in bemused silence from a thatched shelter. 'Well, I guess what I got here is a receipt,' she said, with a little laugh. 'Not bad, from a butcher like *him* . . . '

The 'butcher' was the base commander, a senior Pol Pot man who liked the foreign aid people to call him '*Monsieur le President*', which they did. Although he was middle-aged his face seemed to have regressed to that of a small boy; his eyes were static. In 1979 I had seen in Siem Reap province the mass grave of several thousand people, many of whom had been beaten to death; the splintered skulls attested to that. Now, smiling before me, here was Pol Pot's governor of the province at the time the people were beaten to death. His name, he told me, was Nam Phann, which was probably a military alias. He was eager to confirm that Western aid had indeed nourished and restored the Khmer Rouge. 'Thank you very much and we wish for more,' he said.

On June 8, 1984, there was a small item in *The Times* which quoted the vice-president of the coalition 'Government of Democratic Kampuchea', Khieu Samphan, as promising that a Cambodia free of the Vietnamese would have a 'liberal capitalist regime'. Khieu Samphan, said the report, 'wrote a radical economic study on Cambodia while he was studying in France'. The report neglected to mention that this man, with Pol Pot, still ran the Khmer Rouge and that the 'radical economic study' was an omen of the genocide of the Khmer people. According to *The Times*, 'Mr. Samphan said the switch to capitalism was necessary to preserve national unity at home and abroad and preserve and increase support for the coalition government at the United Nations.'

'Mr. Samphan!' How respectable, how almost eminent he appears in *The Times*. For 'author of a radical economic study' read the apologist for the mass murder of perhaps a quarter of his people. In 1984 the *Far Eastern Economic Review* reported that the representatives of Khieu Samphan's revised 'liberal capitalist' ideology were ambushing and killing their allies in the 'coalition' led by Prince Sihanouk, just as they are seeking the 'increased support' of the United Nations.[46] In other words, the pretence of a 'popular resistance' or 'third force' based in Thailand is crumbling.

In November 1984 the Vietnamese began a long-planned campaign to eradicate the Khmer Rouge from the Cambodian side of the Thai border. By March 1985 they had captured all twenty Khmer Rouge bases, including Phnom Chat, which I had visited, and Pol Pot's stronghold of Phnom Malai. This was the most grievous setback to the Khmer Rouge since the Vietnamese drove them into Thailand more than six years earlier; but they may well have moved their 'front line' deeper into Cambodia. On May 26, 1985, Jon Swain reported in the *Sunday Times* that between 150 and 200 people had died when the Khmer Rouge attacked a train forty-seven miles from Phnom Penh: a repetition of the ambush I had encountered five years before.

Then in September 1985 the Khmer Rouge announced that Pol Pot was 'retiring' as military commander and would be replaced by Son Sen, whom Thailand's foreign minister rushed to describe as 'a very good man'.[47] This 'very good man' was Pol Pot's defence minister during 1975–9. In September 1977 his troops killed nearly 300 Vietnamese civilians in a single raid across the border. The following year he was implicated in the greatest massacre of the Pol Pot period, when at least 100,000 people were murdered in the eastern zone of Kampuchea.[48] Son Sen, like Khieu Samphan, is another Pol Pot. In any event, Pol Pot had announced his 'retirement' once before, in 1976, but neglected to announce his resumption of power.

Can there ever be peace in Cambodia and in all of Indo-China? Perhaps there can. In January 1985 the Vietnamese offered to withdraw their troops from Cambodia in return for the 'exclusion' of the Khmer Rouge from the 'Democratic Kampuchea Coalition'. They made no mention of their previous condition that total withdrawal was possible only if the 'threat from China' was ended. They have also said that they are prepared to allow 'an act of self-determination' involving elections scrutinised by international observers and a measure of democracy which would not suffer by comparison with that of most ASEAN countries.[49] In addition to this, in a meeting with Australia's Minister for Foreign Affairs, Bill Hayden, in Saigon in March 1985, Cambodia's prime minister, Hun Sen, said he was 'ready to make concessions to Prince Sihanouk and other people . . . '

In the spirit of such a regional agreement – which would have to exclude the United States, the Soviet Union and United Nations, for each is compromised – the Vietnamese would leave Cambodia as the Thais, under international supervision, disarmed the Khmer Rouge on their territory. This is not as distant a prospect as it might seem. At a United Nations conference on Cambodia in 1981 the ASEAN delegates proposed that a settlement must include the disarming of the Khmer Rouge; and this condition would have appeared in the conference's final resolution had the Chinese and American delegates not insisted upon a declaration of support for Pol Pot.

Of course, it would be naïve to think that the Vietnamese are not doing everything in their power to cultivate a leadership in Cambodia which will be friendly to them and will co-operate with them in all of Indo-China. Equally, it is clear that Vietnam, with five times the population of Cambodia and Laos combined, will be the most influential of the three. But as John McAuliff has argued, it is also 'naïve to think the relationship is simply one of domination or that it will remain static and cannot be affected by the positive initiatives of Western countries'.[50] The most positive of these initiatives so far is that of Bill Hayden, whose Labour administration's policy, alone among Western and South-East Asian governments, is to restore economic aid to Vietnam. If implemented, this would establish a clear Australian independence from the United States and China and might create a credible negotiating position among all the nations of South-East Asia with which Australia has sound relations.

That there is still only speculation about the *possibility* of peace in Indo-China after a generation has suffered so much is itself an indictment of those who have arranged and maintained the present *impasse*. While the Khmer Rouge are given sanctuary in Thailand, together with American dollars, Western supplies and Chinese arms, while the United Nations continues to give them respectability of a kind and the international 'lever' of representation in the General Assembly, while the Western media continue at best to obscure the role of the Khmer Rouge and at worst to rejuvenate them, these fanatics will not wither in exile as they ought to have done long ago. When asked how such a state of affairs could exist, Sir Robert Jackson reflected:

I know of no parallel to the conditions which have been experienced in Kampuchea over the last decade . . . In the case of post war Europe there's the vast tragedy of the concentration camps: Dachau, Auschwitz, Buchenwald, but thank God, the world had an immediate reaction to that situation and to this moment there has been a sensitivity as to what happened virtually forty years ago. In the case of Kampuchea, for some extraordinary reason, I'm left with the strong impression now that the world wants to forget the tragedy that happened . . . they want to forget it.[51]

If the Khmers were white-skinned or, like the Thais, 'the right people on the right side', they would not be forgotten. In 1986 they are in their eighteenth year of depredation: of bombing, war, genocide, starvation and now isolation. They deserve better; and they deserve better than occupation by a foreign army.

Neither history nor Hollywood nor pseudo-historians can alter the fact that it was the Vietnamese who saved Cambodia. But without the Khmer Rouge threat and a justification for remaining in Cambodia, the Vietnamese presence in their country would soon be intolerable to the Khmers. At the same time the social cost to the Vietnamese of the border war and the occupation has been immense. It is a mockery of the sufferings of these two nations to pretend that they do not both want the opportunity finally to be at peace.

IX

AT THEIR RISK

37

A Prague spring

Czechoslovakia: May 1977. We were to cross the border at Gmünd in Austria. Several miles from the checkpoint we turned into a country lane and stopped on the edge of a field where we hoped the vagaries of the rite we were about to perform (conceived with some levity in a Vienna bar) would not be observed. There were three of us: film cameraman John Davey, sound recordist Christian Wangler and myself. We were travelling in an old camper with GB plates, and in our guise as itinerants we had been granted a three-day transit visa by the Czech embassy in Vienna.

So we set about joyfully scattering cornflakes and the grease of freshly fried eggs on the camper's floor. The theory was that declared squalor would underline our harmlessness, as well as deter the border guards from inspecting beneath the floor, where a film camera and film stock were hidden. We also papered the camper with centrefolds of *Playboy* and *Penthouse*, which, according to another theory, would further divert prying official eyes. A veteran colleague had recommended this method of gaining entry to those countries with little fondness for foreign journalists and limited access to the alleged delights of Hugh Hefner's product. It was a not very subtle form of bribery; the offending material would be 'confiscated' and the foreigner hurriedly waved through while the confiscating official furtively stuffed the booty in his pocket. (The ruse had worked once before for me, on entering Ghana during a *coup d'état*.)

Inevitably, farce ensued. Two Czech guards, in shape and demeanour not unlike Bud Abbot and Lou Costello, examined our passports and indicated that they wanted to inspect the camper. On opening the rear door they recoiled at the human swill, but quickly averted their eyes to Misses January, February, March, April, etcetera. The tubby one appeared to be beside himself and drew his colleague aside to discuss the need for expediency. But the thin one was reluctant to let us go that easily and clearly wanted to take the camper apart. They argued, with Bud gesticulating at the floor of the camper and Lou at the glossy bodies almost within his reach.

No agreement seemed possible, and as Bud began to examine the floorboards, Lou set about removing the centrefolds while taking impressive care not to damage them. Fortunately the two of them could not perform these duties without falling over each other in the egg grease and cornflakes. So Bud withdrew; but by the time Lou had claimed his booty and the two of them had taken time to study its contents and sniggers were exchanged, it was clear we had been saved by the skin of Miss January and her friends. The thin one, however, could not leave it there. He wanted to explain why. *Penthouse*, he said, was illegal in Czechoslovakia because it was 'porno', but *Playboy* was 'very illegal' because it was both porno and 'political'.

It was a Friday. We had to be out by midnight on the Sunday as our presence as a film crew would almost certainly be revealed by the time the STB, the Czech secret police, were back on the streets in force. The filming that followed had taken many months to prepare and it resulted in a television documentary entitled 'A faraway country . . . a people of whom we know nothing'. This was Neville Chamberlain's dismissal of Czechoslovakia in 1938 before he had helped to arrange its deliverance to Hitler; and more than a generation later it remained an epitaph to Czech democracy, felt deeply by those who had tried and were still trying to create socialism that would mean humanism and democracy. Some of these people, at great risk to themselves, appeared in my film; and this chapter is dedicated to them.

In 1977 they were signatories to Charter 77, which had been published in the West in January of that year and banned in Czechoslovakia. Distributed clandestinely, the Charter was a distant echo of the 'Prague spring' of 1968 when Alexander Dubček and his revisionist communist party pursued a bold, sophisticated and immensely popular conversion of the country's rigid bureaucratic class system, imposed by the Soviet Union in 1945, to 'socialism with a human face'. In 1977 the spirit of the Prague spring had long been crushed, first by the Warsaw Pact tanks which rolled into Prague in August 1968, and since then by the suffocation of 'normalisation'; freedoms to speak, to write, to sing, to object, to oppose, to travel had all come and gone as if in a tantalising dream by Franz Kafka, who himself had been 'normalised': that is, his work had been 'erased'.

Charter 77 was a modest and subtle document. It did not suggest an ideology or a political programme of opposition. Neither did it originate from former members of the Dubček government. Indeed it called upon the Soviet-sponsored regime of Gustáv Husák to honour the legal, constitutional and international obligations to which Czech law specifically subscribed. Hence, the drafters hoped that the Charter would attract wider support than the communist opposition alone. 'Our rulers', wrote the philosopher Jan Patocka, 'can now never be quite sure who it is they are dealing with. They must ask themselves whether those who still obey them today will be willing to do so tomorrow . . .'[1]

Within two months some 700 people had signed the Charter, representing many who did not and dared not. They were teachers, journalists, clerks, factory workers and housewives. They were Marxists and those who rejected Marx, Christians and those of no special commitment. One of their deepest grievances centred upon a system of political apartheid which denied jobs, housing and higher education to the children of those who did not give unqualified support to the regime. Husák's dynastic ambitions were little different from earlier imperial élites of the Jesuits and Austria.

The regime's response was panic. A campaign of abuse and intimidation reflected an official hysteria reminiscent of the mass denunciations of the 1950s. People were ordered to sign an anti-Charter condemning a document most of them had not seen. In one factory all but twenty-two of the 14,000 workers refused to attend a government rally against the Charter. Prominent Chartists were stripped of their identity documents and were issued with slips of paper with which they could not even post a registered letter. Their driving licences, marriage certificates and other official papers necessary for daily function in an authoritarian state were withdrawn. Their telephones were cut off and they no longer received normal postal deliveries. Some lost their jobs and flats and their children were expelled from classes.

By the spring of 1977 the pressure on prominent Chartists became intolerable. Of the three original spokesmen, the writer Vaclav Havel was forced to give an undertaking to keep out of politics and to resign as spokesman for the Chartists as a condition of his release from Ruyzne prison, where he had been held for four months. Jiri Hajek, foreign minister in the Dubček government, was held under house arrest, as was Frantisek Kriegel, who had accompanied Dubček to Moscow in 1968 and was virtually held as hostage by the Kremlin.

And Jan Patocka was dead. The gentle philosopher's ringing 'Last Testament' had warned his compatriots that

> . . . no conformity has yet led to any improvement . . . The greater
> the fear and servility, the more brazen the authorities have become,
> are becoming and will become . . . what is needed is for people to

behave at all times with dignity, not to allow themselves to be frightened and intimidated, and to speak the truth.[2]

For speaking the truth, this much-loved man, who was almost seventy, was harassed mercilessly. His phone was disconnected and his family subjected to constant police surveillance. On March 1, fully aware of the risks he was taking, he paid a call on the visiting Dutch foreign minister, Max van der Stoel, in the minister's hotel in Prague. It was the first meeting between a prominent Chartist and a Western statesman and it led to a campaign of vilification against Professor Patocka and to a chain of police interrogations, the last of which went on for almost eleven hours.

The next week he suffered a heart attack and the police pursued him to hospital where they continued to bully him until he became partially paralysed. A brain haemorrhage, and death, followed quickly. At his funeral, which thousands attended, a police helicopter droned over his grave and police motorcycles were deliberately revved to drown the blessing at the greatest outpouring of grief for Czech democracy since 1968.

We drove into Prague in the late afternoon. Ed Harriman, the film's researcher, had arrived by train from Vienna earlier that day with concealed film stock. (It was Ed's journalistic and organisational skills, together with those of Jan Kavan in London, which were most responsible for the success of the filming.) Others had flown into Prague with more film stock and a second camera. We were to meet Alan Bell, the director, in Wenceslas Square, and by deploying prearranged signals and aliases we were to find out where we were to go from there. So confusing were our semaphors that only one of us, Alan, had mastered them and he was their author.

Prague is a supremely ironic city. Its sculptured Renaissance beauty – the thirty Christian statues on the Charles Bridge, the Old Town, the Little Quarter and the panorama of palaces from the cathedral at Hradcany – ill deserves to be a backdrop to rituals of Stalinism.

What does fit comfortably in Prague is its youth. On some days it seemed an exclusively young city, with all the urgency of the young, but tinged with a sort of mass furtiveness: an averting of the eyes from foreigners, and a greyness contrived between people in public. Where had the last generation of youth gone? Where were those millions of Czechs who in 1968 had expressed their desire to live as free human beings, who stood against the foreign tanks, who marched to honour the memory of their martyr, Jan Palach? A few weeks before I arrived in Prague, Vilem Precan, the Czech historian and one of the authors of the 'Black Book' which documented the Soviet-led invasion in August 1968, wrote that the same millions 'have not vanished without trace, but have merely been pacified for a time . . . ' He went on:

> The ruling class had to resort to a massive application of power to suppress this movement: in the years that followed it succeeded in enforcing or buying the obedience of some, including apathy in others, and depriving many among the rest of hope . . . This majority is the submerged larger part of the iceberg. They have gritted their teeth and adopted the mimicry of officially proclaimed lies and hypocrisies in order to lead a comfortable life but also because they can see no other way out.
>
> Afraid to lose the little they have, they turn up at sham elections, attend May Day parades, put out Soviet flags, and some even sign statements condemning Charter 77 without so much as having read it . . . In their subconscious there is a growing anger and hatred directed at those who humiliate them and at themselves to be corrupted. This is the explosive charge waiting for the next acute outbursts of crisis.[3]

I wondered about this 'explosive charge', because the complement of 'normalisation' surely was powerlessness and cynicism. 'We', Praguers tell each other, 'are the most non-aligned people in the world. Why, we don't even interfere in the internal affairs of our own country any more.'[4]

I did see the word 'Charta' scribbled on a suburban wall, like a political icon, until someone informed the authorities and they came quickly to scrub it out. And I was told that very occasionally '*Rus – hnus*' ('Russian – nausea') or '*Husak – Rusak*' ('Husak is a fucking Rusky') would appear, too. Someone had stood outside Kafka's birthplace that morning with a banner demanding that the great man's works and those of Kundera, Caculik and others who had inspired the visionaries of the Prague spring be allowed to circulate again. But even the plaque outside Kafka's birthplace, which had been restored in 1968, was missing. Not even the Good Soldier Svejk, 'the quintessential prole', as Geoffrey Moorhouse called him,[5] is allowed into the bookshops.

It was the silence of the millions who made the men and women of Charter 77 such heroic individuals. People did not touch them in the street and whisper encouragement. The eyes averted from foreigners were averted from them. This was not always the case, as in the factories where workers refused to condemn the Charter and at Jan Palocka's funeral. But as time wore on, in the words of one Chartist, 'The air around us gets thinner.'

The Chartists I met and filmed in secret were chosen by their own underground organisation in Prague. Some had known and suffered from publicity in the past; others had experienced no publicity before they met us. The risk they incurred was ill defined, and there was nothing to reassure them, or ourselves, that having touched their lives we had not condemned them. Only their insistence to speak as free Czechs, and their courage, were certain. 'If I knew', said Julius Tomin, a teacher, 'that tomorrow I go into prison for it, I shall talk with you anyway.'

Look-outs were on the block of flats where one group of Chartists waited for us. Shy at first and their faces guttered from calculating every step of the way, they spoke politely, hesitantly and watched us carefully. After a while Julius Tomin remarked, 'I think we are now beginning to be normal.'

At thirty-eight, Tomin had endured much. He had refused the military draft and had been sent to a psychiatric clinic for two years. After 1970 he was prevented from teaching his speciality, philosophy, and the only work he could find was as a nightwatchman at Prague zoo. He eventually lost this job. His wife was also denied work and their eldest son was barred from any form of higher education or apprenticeship. Summoned regularly to interrogations by the secret police, Julius Tomin refused to answer questions 'on the ground that the legal requirements for such an interrogation were not fulfilled; I myself had not committed any crime'. Inevitably, there would come a point when the interrogators would exclaim, 'Mr Tomin, you commit a crime with every step you make and with every word you say.' 'One morning', he was told, 'you will be found dead in a ditch.'

Like most of the other Chartists, he described the Charter as 'the start of the experiment of combining freedom and socialism' and, like most of them, he qualified this by saying that 'it doesn't mean to impose on us the kind of freedom you are living with. We must develop new concepts of freedom which come from our own situation.' None would be drawn into endorsing what they called 'certain freedoms in the other camp'. Like people in most small nations they wanted to go a third way. 'If you come from Britain and you don't understand this,' one of them said, 'I suggest you go to see the principal exhibit in the Klement Gottwald Museum just below Wenceslas Square.' I went to see it: a large photograph of the Munich Agreement in 1938, fine print and all.

Jitka Bidlasova, in her twenties, lost her job as a clerk in a food-processing plant when she signed Charter 77. She described herself as 'apolitical'. I asked her if signing the Charter had made her an outlaw in her own country. 'Yes,' she replied. 'I am now an outlaw. But the Charter was *true*. So why shouldn't I sign it?' I asked her what would now happen to her young daughter. Would she be refused a proper education because of her mother's stand? 'I hope my child will have a chance,' she replied, 'but even if she doesn't, something else will have to be arranged, because I don't share the view of most of the people in this country that one should keep quiet on account of the children. It's on account of the children one should speak out!' How isolated did she feel? 'I try to draw strength', she said, 'from what one old man said to me: "You know, thirteen million people here think the same as you do, but only a few have your guts." '

Jiri Pallas, aged twenty-eight, an electrician, related what he called his 'saddening experience'. 'I was the only signatory in my small town,' he said. 'At first my friends expressed support, but [later] they tended to keep their distance and slowly they began to be afraid to greet me. Their fear followed me . . . I was completely alone. I'll give you an example. When I became ill, [the management] at my factory proposed to twenty people, my colleagues, that I should be expelled from their working team. A vote was taken: the three managers were for it, one young girl was against it and fifteen abstained. So the vote turned out badly for me. The manager then addressed the others, reminding them that they were employees of the head office and that they should remember their duty as trade unionists and as politically committed members of the work force. He reminded them that I was "bad", that I had an illegitimate child.

'A second meeting was held and I was expelled from the trade union. The young girl spoke again in my defence. She said, "We haven't read the Charter. It's never been published here, so how can we condemn him for it?" No sooner had she finished speaking when the chairman began to shout at her, "What's the idea? If that's what you think, we'll have to have a little talk about it elsewhere." When I objected that this was intimidation, I was shouted down. No one else dared to speak.'

Jiri Pallas was eventually dismissed and could not get another job. He tried to put an advertisement in a newspaper. 'Willing to accept any kind of employment', it read, and was signed, 'A signatory of Charter 77'. The rest might have been from Kafka.

He said, 'I was passed from one newspaper employee to another, right up to the editor-in-chief. Each one refused to accept the ad and refused to explain why he wouldn't accept it, and also refused to confirm in writing that he had refused to accept it! . . . The only work I eventually got was a fortnight's washing up.'

The Chartists' courage was personified in one man, author Zdener Urbanek, who has translated Dickens into Czech and whose own books have been banned since 1948. Alone in his small house, his shelves cluttered with ageing titles and not one new paperback among them, he welcomed us with our film equipment at his front door in broad daylight, defiantly, utterly unafraid. He spoke good English but with a stutter; his price had been a nervous collapse.

'We had twenty years of freedom', he said, 'from 1918 to 1938. A faraway democracy perhaps, but one that functioned quite well. It is a pity to have to remind the British people of that.'

I asked what happened to him after he signed the Charter.

'I was interrogated for twelve hours, my flat was searched and my typewriter was taken away to be registered in the official files. Whatever I write, they know who wrote it. In this way they control me. The next thing that happened was I was asked by the police to take a new driving test. Well, I was quite unprepared for this, so they took away my driving licence. Bit by bit they whittled me down.

'But let me make one thing clear. I am *not* frightened. I write what I wish when I start to write, and that's exactly why I can't get it published! My problem is that, without publication, without a response of the public, the writing tends to deteriorate . . . My other problem, and I should say it honestly, is that I have lived with censorship so long that the censor is no longer at his desk; he is in my head.'

But how had he preserved a vision of freedom after more than thirty years without it? 'I believe that freedom without the inner freedom of oneself is almost nothing,' he replied. 'If you don't decide inside yourself about what you wish to do, then the outer freedom is nonsense. I've tried to keep free inside.'

When we had finished filming he drew back the blinds and produced a large, menacing bottle. 'This is Wild Cat,' he said. 'Wild Cat is Czech Scotch whisky distilled in Scotland and bottled in Czechoslovakia. It's only ten in the morning, but shall we try some?' We did. 'Here's to my wish,' he said, 'to see just one day of freedom in Czechoslovakia!'

On Sunday morning a secret police car, known in Prague as a black locust, appeared as we moved our van from a campsite across the river to the centre of the city. It was a reminder that we had only a few hours to find where Marta Kubisova lived in the country. I had wanted to meet Marta Kubisova since I saw her sing at Olympia in London in the sixties. Her deep, slightly harsh voice evoked Edith Piaf. Small and delicate like Piaf, she was a thrilling singer, and many regarded her as the 'nightingale' of the Dubček period.

In September 1968, one month after the Soviet invasion, Marta Kubisova gave a concert in Prague and sang, 'O my country, let not fear and violence establish themselves on your soil; keep yourself faithful and true to yourself'. This became known as 'Marta's Prayer' and the new rulers of Prague did not like it. In 1969 photographs of a nude woman said to be Marta were circulated and scandalous stories were told about her. She found it impossible to get work as a singer and all her records were banned. They had done to her as they had done to Zdener Urbanek; they had whittled her down.

In February 1977 Marta compounded her problems by signing the Charter. This brought her more isolation and impoverishment. When we met she had a temporary job glueing bags together at home. Like the other Chartists she had forfeited her passport, her identity papers, her driving licence. When I found her village near the Austrian border, mention of her name was enough. 'Yes, yes she lives over there,' said a man, shaking his head.

I asked her how she contained her despair and fear and she replied, 'No . . . it is *they* who are afraid.' She asked me to read the words of a song written by a Czech group called the Plastic People of the Universe, who were also banned and treated brutally by the regime. The song was one of the group's last before their arrest; the words refer to their oppressors.

They are afraid of the old for their memory.
They are afraid of the young for their innocence.
They are afraid of the graves and flowers people put on them.
They are afraid of those not in the Party.
They are afraid of singers, tennis players, Santa Claus, archives,
   each other . . .
They are afraid of truth. They are afraid of freedom.
They are afraid of democracy. They are afraid of socialism.
So why the hell are *we* afraid of them?

At the end of the interview I asked her if she would sing 'Marta's Prayer'. We were sitting in her garden and she took off her glasses and pushed back her hair and sang her banned anthem with all the power of her lungs. When she had finished, she said, 'You see, I am still free.'

After the film was shown on television in Britain, a ritual denouncement on Prague Radio allowed me to share a small distinction with the Chartists. But I had merely come and gone, leaving them to bear the consequences of agreeing to meet me. I could not tell myself that they would be all right, because in all probability they would not be all right and, anyway, I would not know; the minds in the locust cars would beset them with some further constraint or penalty; at the very least they would continue to whittle them down. I cannot rationalise this. Is one television programme worth the price *they* must pay? Although they might believe it is, I am not so sure.

In August 1980 Julius Tomin asked permission to study abroad, and this was granted. In May 1981 he was called to the Czech embassy in

London where his passport was confiscated and he was told that he and his wife were deprived of Czech citizenship. Today Julius Tomin teaches at St David's University College in Wales. Generously, he wrote to me, 'Every visitor from abroad brought with him an oasis of normal, non-frustrated human communication. In a sense, our interview and similar publicity in the West was the price to pay, and it was worth it. To refuse an interview would have meant giving in and accepting the unfreedom as an integral part of my life, and I was not prepared to live unfree.'

Jitka Bidlasova and Jiri Pallas are now exiled in Sweden. Zdener Urbanak still lives in Prague and remains, with his 'registered' typewriter, both a state and cultural prisoner.

Marta Kubisova suffered many more pressures in her life which led her, among other things, to divorce her husband. She is now living alone, looking after her small daughter. She can find little work and endures a great deal of hardship; her songs remain banned.

38

Heroes of the Soviet Union

Moscow: June 1977. At nine o'clock in the morning they did precisely as they had forewarned foreign journalists they would do. They converged from all directions trying not to run, and when one of them signalled with a handkerchief, they swept past the Soviet militiamen whose principal job was to prevent Soviet citizens from entering the West German embassy. They were nine ethnic Germans from Kirgizia in Central Asia and they were seeking sanctuary and emigration. One of them, Jakob Schultz, was still shaking from the audacity of their action when he spoke from inside the embassy. 'We are the little peoples of the Soviet Union,' he said. 'We represent thousands who cannot live any more in exile, banished. This is our last chance.'

The following day the nine left the embassy 'voluntarily' and I watched them arrested by four carloads of KGB officers. The last I heard of them was that they were either in prison awaiting trial or on their way back to exile in Central Asia. Their act of bravado received no acknowledgment in the Soviet Press and very little in the Western Press, compared with the coverage then being given to Andrei Sakharov and the other celebrated Soviet dissidents.

The 'little peoples' of the Soviet Union, forgotten and unheard from except for an occasional incident like at the embassy, are those millions of Soviet citizens belonging to national and religious minorities, such as the ethnic Germans and the Crimean Tartars. Stalin had them deported in cattle trucks from their respective homelands along the Volga and in the Crimea and Khrushchev pointedly excluded them from his 'de-Stalinisation' of the mid-1950s.

The stigma of 'untouchable', with its overtone of treachery to the Soviet state and its burden of day-by-day discrimination, has never been erased from these people. The Tartars' leader, Mustafa Dzhemilev, is largely unknown abroad, and although barely forty he has served eighteen years in labour camps. When I heard of him in Moscow he was in a camp on the Soviet Pacific coast, where the sun rises as it sets on his homeland in the Crimea. At the most recent of his many bogus trials (1976), at which he was charged with 'anti-Soviet slander', the catch-all used to convict dissidents, even the prosecutor was said to be visibly astonished by the sight of the judge receiving instructions on how to rig the case.

'For most of his incarceration', I was told, 'Dzhemilev has been the only political prisoner in camps of criminals, many of them violent, who are encouraged to mete out their own ill-treatment to him in return for favours. They do to him anything they want, because the outside pressure to spare him is not great.'

It was Ida Nudel who told me this. Ida, small and cherubic and seemingly calm, was known as the 'guardian angel of the prisoners'. Before her own rebellion she had been an economist at the Moscow Institute of Hydrology, where she reported on the standards of hygiene in food stores. Her father, a Commissar in the Red Army, had fought at the front during the Second World War and died in the battle for Stalingrad. Her 'credentials' were respected; she enjoyed the privileges of the state. But at the back of her mind was the memory and influence of her grandfather, who had been murdered by the Nazis when they entered the Crimea. He had been teaching himself Hebrew with a group of Jews, who were intending to emigrate to Palestine. In 1971 her own Jewishness prevailed and she applied to emigrate to Israel. Within six months she had lost her job, and her application to leave was refused.

This made Ida, in the jargon, a 'refusenik'. What was unusual about her, and others I met with her, was the adoption of other 'prisoners of conscience' who were neither Zionists nor remotely linked to Jewish causes. Of Dzhemilev she said, 'He is at everyone's mercy. He gets food that is rotten and he is punished with devices like special handcuffs that tighten when you move even a little. At his camp prisoners are forced to cut glass without face protection, and it is the rule that political prisoners are barred from the prison hospital. Every day is a war for them; they must fight to keep their dignity or they die spiritually. If just a whisper reaches them that they are not entirely forgotten, they go on.'

I met Ida Nudel at the flat of scientists Vladimir and Maria Slepak in Gorky Street. Eric Piper and I had left our hotel shortly after dawn and after a withering climb to Apartment 77, we were greeted by the great bearded head of Vladimir Slepak beaming at us. He said he knew it was us; foreigners generally came before the morning KGB shift took up position on the stairs.

In 1977 the brief period of tolerating certain dissidents – if tolerance it was – was then past, and the KGB relentlessly harassed the Slepaks. Their telephone was disconnected and their flat had been raided and books and letters confiscated. When I met them Vladimir (who came from a family of devoted communists and was named after Vladimir Ilyich Lenin) and Maria had already served short terms in prison for 'anti-Soviet activities'. It was clear they had been singled out because of the help they had given others and specifically for Vladimir's work as an adviser to the beleaguered monitoring committee on the 1975 Helsinki agreement on human rights. (At the European Security Conference in July 1975 Leonid Brezhnev signed an agreement to 'respect human rights and fundamental freedom, including freedom of conscience, religion and belief, equal rights and self determination of peoples', all of which were guaranteed by the Soviet constitution.)

'What is bizarre', said Maria, 'is that those of us who call on the state not to break its own laws are known as dissidents and law breakers!'

As the Slepaks' files had been confiscated, they now drew on formidable memories. 'My head', said Vladimir Slepak, 'is much too crowded these days.' This was also true of Ida Nudel, who last saw her shelves of books and correspondence being bundled into a KGB van. Nevertheless they spoke in detail about 'the forgotten ones', as Vladimir Slepak called them. He mentioned the 'loss' of Vladimir Klebanov who, like himself, had been arbitrarily arrested and charged under the Criminal Code with 'deliberately and systematically spreading slanders against the Soviet state and social system in oral and written form . . . ' Klebanov was a miner in the Ukraine who had refused to demand overtime from his workers or to send them down pits when he believed that safety regulations were being ignored. In a statement which reached Amnesty International in 1978, Vladimir Klebanov wrote:

Since 1958 I had actively spoken out against gross violations of the Labour Code [the implementation of the decree of 1956 about the six-hour working day and the thirty-six-hour working week]. I demanded correct wage payments, and in particular an end to the concealment of industrial injuries in official reports; the correct definition of invalid categories, and proper compensation for miners who suffered injuries through the fault of the management. I demanded the prosecution of the criminals who stole valuable materials, men in important industrial and Soviet positions; an end to bribery and so on . . . [6]

His crime was that he had objected to twelve to fifteen deaths and 700 injuries at one colliery and that he had tried to form a free trade union.

He was detained in a mental hospital and demeaned publicly as an 'untouchable'.

'Klebanov is not an intellectual; he is an ordinary worker,' said Vladimir Slepak, who believed that the Western campaign to focus on dissidents among the Soviet élite had allowed the authorities to move harshly against more potentially serious rebellions, such as that represented by Vladimir Klebanov and his worker supporters. 'Unlike them', he said, 'the Jewish refuseniks are not a threat to the state; we just want to leave.' Had the Slepaks and Ida Nudel and others like them remained simply refuseniks they might have evaded much of the vindictiveness of the state. That they chose to speak for others and perhaps to dash any hope of being allowed to leave, was a measure of their valour.

I realised this only when Eric and I left the Slepaks' flat that morning. At the bottom of the stairs was a pack of KGB men. They all had apparent curvature of the spine and an air of melodramatic sullenness. They stared at us, blew cigarette smoke in our faces, and when we were almost out of the door, one of them made several inept attempts to trip me up from behind and to grab Eric's camera bag. Such harassment and intimidation were intended to provoke a reaction, but Eric wisely restrained me from providing it. The Slepaks endured this almost every day.

During all of one Sunday in Leningrad, Eric and I rode in buses, cruised in taxis and walked in driving rain with two young teachers. Staying on the move was often the only way we could talk. Their main concern also was for a friend, a young Greek Orthodox priest, Father Lev Konin, who had been summoned to a police station six weeks earlier, bundled into an ambulance and taken to Leningrad Psychiatric Hospital No. 6.

Lev Konin had written just one article criticising the Soviet government on its record of human rights. For this, he was declared 'temporarily insane'. Such a method of silencing had several advantages for the Soviet authorities over conventional prosecution in the courts. A person deemed to be mentally incompetent had no right of appeal or of any judicial review of his case. If he was sent to a 'special' psychiatric hospital it was likely that his physical and mental integrity would be systematically degraded by anti-psychotic or wax-based drugs, so that either he would recant or end up truly insane.

Eric, the two teachers and I covered a great deal of Leningrad that day. We pretended to be tourists and they our guides. We inspected the Hermitage, the Admiralty and St Isaac's Cathedral, Nevsky Prospekt with its network of canals and hump-backed bridges. We stood in the room in the Winter Palace where the Tsar had interrogated the

Decembrists, and at noon heard the gun on the cruiser *Aurora* which signalled the storming of the Winter Palace. We were reminded constantly that more than a million people died in the siege of Leningrad by the Nazis, who were driven back by deeds of incredible heroism. That the modern state which evolved from this heroism should feel so threatened by the nonconformity of individuals seemed to me a defeat.

It was in Leningrad that I met the unsinkable Ilya Levin. At twenty-eight and a languages scholar, Ilya Levin's troubles began when he was offered a year's postgraduate study at an American university and applied for an exit visa. In his application he said he had no intention of emigrating.

'I was ordered immediately to the KGB office, and told that a visa was out of the question,' he said. 'I was also told that I must have no contact with foreigners, especially journalists, and I was read a decree which said I had committed crimes against the state. I asked, "What crimes?" They said, "We can't tell you; it's a secret."

'I was interrogated many times – I can't remember how many – and after each session I stood and told them they were breaking Soviet law by their actions. They scoffed at this. "The law", they said, "is not for you."

'The tactics changed. I was set upon in the street by thugs, beaten up pretty badly, and when I reported this to the police station I was arrested for "resisting arrest" and sent to the old St Petersburg prison. I was put in cell 141 and the guard told me: "Do you know who was in cell 138? Lenin! The Tsar's secret police put him in there." He didn't see the irony in what he was saying.'

In between prison stretches, Ilya could not return to his university job because his internal passport, which all Soviet citizens must carry, was stamped with the equivalent of 'politically unreliable'. The only job he could get was as a lift watchman. And in the following months, he was brought back, again and again, to the KGB office: to sit, to stand, to be shouted at, to be ordered to sign lies about himself.

He was beaten by KGB gangs in the street, given fifteen-day sentences for 'resisting arrest' and followed constantly. His crime remained the same. He had wanted to go abroad. He had spoken up for friends similarly intimidated. He had spoken with foreigners. And he had stood up to his inquisitors.

'I am not a scientist or a great writer,' he told me. 'I am merely a little fry; but they bothered to stamp on me.' When I left Ilya Levin's small flat, there was a KGB car parked diagonally opposite. 'Hello there Boris!' shouted Ilya mischievously, waving his walking stick.

I asked Valentyn Turchin, the brilliant computer scientist who, with Andrei Sakharov, had written an open letter to Brezhnev calling for a drastic democratisation of Soviet society, how much support he believed the dissidents had among the Soviet people. He replied, 'The majority of Russians have been drilled to remember the past and are grateful for the flats and jobs, so many will regard us as spiritual traitors. But we also know that many are secretly with us.

'You see, in private the Soviet personality will want to talk openly, to protest, read books and newspapers, see films, travel . . . Russians are not children, you know . . . but the public personality will be obedient and silent, and very, very cynical, because it knows it will never take the risk and speak out. For us, the ones who speak out, there is no such confusion. We are not split in two.'

How this split personality is developed was demonstrated when I visited School No. 62 in Moscow. In an English class, a girl of fifteen called Rina stood up and said, 'We have been discussing the international situation today. We agree with what Comrade Brezhnev said, that an arms limitations accord is imperative for peace . . . ' And so she went on. A boy, impatient at the desk next to her, asked me: 'Tell us about the political situation in Britain. Please explain . . . What are the British saying about us? Why do your newspapers always say there is a Soviet threat? Tell us!'

More hands signalled more questions. But for every inquiry, there was someone, like Rina, with a little recitation. The bold used my presence to grope for the limits, glancing back at the teachers as they did, and the obedient did precisely as they had been told. And often the same boy or girl would play this dual role.

At Moscow University I sat with half a dozen students selected to talk to me. A vice-rector was there, stiff and obviously irritated that I was asking them the questions and not him. It looked an impossible situation, as the students were clearly intimidated by his presence, until I asked them, 'Why do you think *Pravda* has criticised some of your generation for being "ideologically indifferent"? Why does Soviet youth seem to be obsessed with rock music and most things Western?'

A young man who belonged to Komsomol, the Communist Youth League, said, 'You are talking about the outer self, which can absorb rock music and blue jeans and things like that without any interference to the inner self . . . because that is dedicated to Marxism and Leninism.'

At this, the vice-rector's irritation began visibly to fade. I was getting the correct message; and while I was getting the correct message, the student seated next to me leaned behind my back and whispered, 'Mister . . . he is talking shit. We are divided here . . . but for me, the spirit of my generation is the spirit of the Helsinki agreement . . . of human rights.'

I asked two senior journalists, Melor Sturua, a columnist of *Izvestia*, and a senior editor of *Pravda* (whose name I have since misplaced) why so much information was denied to the Soviet public. The *Izvestia* man said, 'We have no censorship. We tell our readers about the shortcomings of our politicians.' The *Pravda* man made a remark to be relished. 'You must understand', he said, 'there would be no Russian dissidents if the Western Press ignored them.' Did this mean, I asked, that if people and events could be ignored then they did not exist or they did not happen? 'If you like,' he said.

On the day before we left Moscow Eric and I set out to say our goodbyes to Vladimir and Maria Slepak. We walked along Gorky Street and turned into the courtyard of their block of flats. The KGB guard had changed, and these played no games. '*Nyet*,' said one of them as we started for the stairs. We kept going. A pincer of arms shot out, spun us around and ejected us back into the courtyard. And there we stood for an hour, looking up into the vicinity of the eighth floor, hoping to catch sight of the Slepaks. We were about to leave when an object fell out of the sky. It was a tin mug and taped inside it was a note, which read, 'Good voyage to you! Please remember us.'

In June the following year, 1978, Vladimir and Maria Slepak were arrested for displaying an 'anti-Soviet' banner on their balcony. Vladimir was given a five-year sentence of exile for 'malicious hooliganism' and was sent to the Buryat autonomous republic on the Mongolian border. Maria was given a three-year suspended sentence and joined her husband in exile. In December 1982 Vladimir completed his sentence and he returned to Moscow, with his health impaired. In his absence both his sons, Alexander and Leonid, had been allowed to leave the country.

In January 1984 the Slepaks were told by the Moscow emigration authorities that they could not leave the Soviet Union because they were a 'security risk'. Vladimir Slepak is today seriously ill.

Ida Nudel, the 'guardian angel of the camps', was arrested at the same time as the Slepaks. In June 1978 she was sentenced to four years' exile in a village in Siberia. On her release in March 1982 she returned to Moscow only to be told that she would not be allowed to live in the capital, as she was an 'undesirable character'. She was eventually permitted to settle in Moldavia, some 600 miles south of Moscow, where the KGB has kept her under surveillance and threatened her whenever friends have visited her. She, too, is seriously ill; she has been told she has cancer.

Valentyn Turchin, the scientist and tireless civil rights campaigner, was allowed to emigrate in October 1977 and was stripped of his Soviet citizenship. He now lives in the United States.

Lev Konin, the Greek Orthodox priest committed to a psychiatric prison for 'slandering' the Soviet Union, was allowed to emigrate in 1978 and is now living in France.

In July 1977, one month after I left the Soviet Union, I received a phone call at two o'clock in the morning from Vienna. The voice said, 'Hello, it is me! Look, I am free!' It was Ilya Levin. He told me that during the week my article about him had been published in London he was once again summoned by the KGB and told that if he renounced his Soviet citizenship he could leave Russia within nineteen days. He said that on the day of departure at Leningrad airport a KGB photographer had tried to hide behind an artificial palm tree while he took his picture.

'Even as I walked up the steps to the plane there was one of them with a camera clicking at me,' he said. 'I took my last look at my homeland, then I looked back at the camera and right into the lens and put my two fingers up in the air. I trust that will be the last picture in my dossier. It is appropriate.'

X

THE AMERICAS –
VIETNAM AGAIN

39

The attack on El Salvador

San Salvador: July 1981. The airport sign read, 'Welcome to the World of Pan Am'. But Pan Am did not, or dared not, fly any more to the one country on earth named after the reputed Saviour of Mankind. Outside it was early evening and an empty, unfinished motorway swept through mist beneath a dead volcano. The taxi-driver's foot was pressed to the boards of his Toyota. He missed the toll booths by inches. There was no one in them.

San Salvador was announced by an incandescent Marlboro Man, the one with stetson and moustache, who died from lung cancer, and a McDonald's, Rexona underarm deodorant, Coca-Cola and a strip of sweatshops known as a 'free economic zone', many of them run by phone from Miami. One of the largest sweatshops was said to be the world's biggest manufacturer of beach towels. Beyond the sweatshops was a street of smart and very empty restaurants with the tables laid and the candles flickering, and the discothèque where the sons and daughters of the 'fourteen families', El Salvador's recently expatriated oligarchy, used to dance around a fountain of champagne. We turned eventually into a long road reminiscent of a road in Vietnam, from Saigon to Bien Hoa; both are of coffin-makers.

In the city centre a surprising number of pedestrians wore running shoes and roller skates. Curfew was at eleven o'clock, after which you were likely to be shot or mutilated by the forces of law and order. The traffic now jarred to a halt. Steering wheels were turned instinctively as drivers looked for a way out, but there was none, no sanctuaries, no neutral corners. No one was safe and everybody knew it.

We were enveloped by sirens and trucks of jack-booted, black-helmeted National Guard. They pulverised their way through the traffic, to where two armed men had been caught as they prepared to mount an attack on the American embassy, which rose over the city like the Bastille. One of these men was now dead; the other was wounded and lay in the gutter beneath a takeaway chicken sign, where he was finished off with an automatic round in the brain; and his blood glistened on the face and uniform of his killer who nonchalantly waved the traffic past.

The Camino Real was the 'secure' hotel for media people. The United Press man, John Newhagen, who lived on the second floor, printed, issued and 'authorised' a 'Press Card' which, he said, was less likely to cause the bearer to be shot than the government-issued credential. The other modern hotel was the Sheraton which, like the American embassy, stood on high ground. The Sheraton echoed with Vietnam. On the top floor was Colonel Moody Mayes and his 'secret' contingent of US Green Berets. On the floors below was a 'rural pacification team' led by 'Blowtorch' Bob Komer, who had run the same programme in Vietnam during the 1960s and was assigned to El Salvador for the same purpose. Then there was Professor Roy Prosterman, famous for his 'land redistribution programme' in Vietnam known as 'Land to the Tiller' and who also had his old job back in El Salvador. As Jenny Pearce wrote in her definitive study, *Under the Eagle*:

> In Vietnam, Land to the Tiller had been part of a rural pacification programme known as Operation Phoenix. Prosterman believed that this kind of land reform, which basically rewarded loyal peasants with small plots while others were often terrorised and murdered (Prosterman denies being involved in the repression), would pave the way to a non-Marxist road to social change. As one US official commented on Land to the Tiller: 'There is no one more conservative than a small farmer. We're going to breed capitalists like rabbits.'[1]

Occupying two floors of the Sheraton were teams from the United States Agency for International Development (USAID) and the American Institute for Free Labour Development (AIFLD). Both organisations were instruments of US foreign policy and had played important parts in the invasion of Vietnam. In El Salvador, as in Vietnam, USAID had provided the means of sustaining an economic structure on the American model. At the same time its Office of Public Safety trained local police in methods of 'combating subversion' i.e. torture. AIFLD, which had worked closely with the CIA in Vietnam, established the Salvadorean Communal Union in 1968. In the guise of promoting 'land reform' the American-led UCS infiltrated and sought to control (sometimes successfully) genuine peasant organisations and trade unions and to stifle 'social unrest'.

The Sheraton was 'protected' by the National Guard which also 'protected' the American embassy. In the lobby were photographs of the Miss Universe contest of 1976 which was described as 'our most spectacular event to date', although some might say that, in this category, Miss Universe paled against the killing of José Viera. In December 1980 Viera, president of the El Salvador Land Reform Institute and a former *campesino*, accused the latest junta of undermining attempts at land reform after he discovered that wealthy estate owners were being paid double the true value of their properties and that the colonels in the junta were taking their cut, leaving the peasants nothing. 'We are tricked', Viera announced, 'and they [the colonels] are shooting our people like dogs.' On January 3, 1981, while having coffee at the Sheraton Hotel with two officials of USAID, he was hit by thirty bullets, three of them around the mouth.

Viera's murder was not unexpected. He was one of two agrarian reformers whom the junta had briefly tolerated in order to claim some popular acceptance and to impress liberal politicians in the United States. The other was Enrique Cordova, who as agriculture minister had set out to break up 3,000 acre estates and to establish co-operatives. He, too, was shot.

Night-time at the Camino Real bar was commanded by 'Colonel' Bob Poos. Pukka in moustache and pressed combat khaki, Bob Poos had flown to San Salvador from Boulder, Colorado, 'in my capacity as executive editor of *Soldier of Fortune*', which he described as a journal 'all about war and manly adventure'. A former US marine in the Korean war and a reporter in the Vietnam war, Bob Poos said repeatedly, 'We sure as hell are not losing this one. All President Reagan's got to do is send in more helicopters, artillery, M-16s and morphine, lots of morphine, and lots more of our guys to tell them how to do it right and we can win this one.'

The next morning the San Salvador newspapers described the National Guard as heroes for apprehending the two 'terrorists' beneath the takeaway chicken sign near the American embassy. This was a minor item; the main headline was devoted to a 'scandal' about uncollected rubbish, but there was no mention of what the rubbish might have contained. Six weeks earlier, children scavenging on a rubbish tip had found a victim of the night. A pregnant woman had been slit open, the foetus torn away and the head of her lover inserted in its place. A priest, who had seen this, related it to me and, while watching me recoil, he said, 'Open your notebook and write it down please; I would wish to God that those who give sustenance to the criminals should see what the children saw; at least they should read about it.'

Within a few days of this crime, Peter Thomas, the British Conservative MP for Barnet, Hendon South, wrote to Nicholas Ridley, then

Minister of State at the Foreign Office, on behalf of two constituents who had asked why the British government could not discourage the United States government from interfering in the affairs of small countries, such as El Salvador. Ridley replied to Thomas:

> It is understandable that the US government feel the need to resume military assistance in addition to their very substantial economic aid to the government of El Salvador. Their interest in countering Soviet and Cuban subversion in Central America is one which we share.[2]

Thomas forwarded this to his constituents, adding that he hoped it 'clears up any misunderstandings and I think I should make it clear that I fully support the policy of our government'.[3] Brush-off letters from the Foreign Office are often written for the minister by a 'desk' man, and are common enough; however Ridley's brush-off not only compounded an especially dishonest piece of propaganda, but effectively offered the support of his government to those who perpetrated and sanctioned the crimes described above. I have sometimes wondered if apologists like Nicholas Ridley and Peter Thomas, however minor, however supine, are ever confronted by the human consequences of policies to which, at great distance, they give their 'full support'.

According to the United Nations Commission on Human Rights, between January 1980 and April 1981 20,000 civilians were murdered by 'death squads' related to or part of the 'security forces' of El Salvador. The death of people 'in industrial quantities', as one American reporter wrote, was therefore well known, yet the Reagan administration in its first year increased its initial $25 million in military aid to the El Salvador regime to $523 million without congressional approval and after 'laundering' it through the international banks. To give one example of this 'back-door' aid: the Inter-American Development Bank in 1981 gave the El Salvador regime $45 million out of a 'special operations fund' in which Washington held sixty-two per cent of the capital.[4] The West Germans, Canadians and Danes strongly objected to the loan on the grounds that it violated the Bank's charter, because it could not be implemented properly. The Americans said it was for 'land reform'. The Europeans suspected it was for 'counter insurgency equipment'. 'We are giving away blood money', a European representative at the Bank told me.

One Sunday morning, with church bells peeling in relays, I travelled in an ambulance of the El Salvador Green Cross, an organisation which originated in France during the Second World War 'to give human warmth as well as first aid'. The Green Cross volunteers, many of them teenagers as young as fifteen, go into those areas of El Salvador where the Red Cross, including those of the international committee, don't go. They wear white and green jumpsuits and exude a bravado which includes the singing of patriotic songs at National Guard checkpoints. 'When you speak to people', said Juan Francisco Zamora, the Green Cross president, 'do not take down their names, not even the name of a simple *campesino*, not even the name of a child.'

We approached the Guazapa volcano, which the guerrillas controlled. Troops of the regime were grouped beside the road, apparently awaiting orders and looking extremely frightened. Two American 'advisers' saw us and dissolved into the bush. Like the Vietcong, the resistance controls the countryside and the roads by night. Like the Vietcong, they are dug into tunnels, from where they ambush. Like the old Saigon Army, the government troops are weighed down like miniature GIs and dependent on machines and tactics imparted to them by Colonel Moody Hayes and his Green Beret veterans of Vietnam. Like the old Saigon Air Force, the El Salvador Air Force is trained and led by Americans, using tactics and 'anti-personnel' bombs designed originally for Vietnam whose purpose is to terrorise civilians. Just as the bombing in Indo-China was the greatest ever recorded, so the bombing in El Salvador is now the most intense ever known in the Western hemisphere. Its effects are seldom reported in the United States and elsewhere.

At the foot of the Guazapa volcano, the Green Cross had established a camp of 1,600 people, most of them from a nearby village, San Raphael, which now was ashes. The army had burned it down, said the people in the camp, and told them that to go back was a 'crime'. The camp was centred around an abandoned *hacienda*, called La Bermuda, which the previous week had seen the arrival of a caravan of *abandonados* – orphaned or displaced children who had banded together and walked through the forests, picking up others on the way. Beneath a banyan tree was a circle of rocky mounds: the fresh graves of some of the children. What had defeated most of them in the end was common diarrhoea and the rules of 'aid'.

The Green Cross, which has no money to speak of, had appealed to the International Committee of the Red Cross for funds and medicines for La Bermuda. The ICRC replied that it could not co-operate unless it could take over the camp completely, in accordance with ICRC 'procedure'. However, the ICRC knew that only the Green Cross was trusted by the people in the camp, who associated the local Red Cross with the regime.

I enquired about this *impasse* when I met the Swiss head of the ICRC mission in San Salvador, Arturo Mangotti. 'Yes', he said, 'there is a great need at La Bermuda; I have seen it. But our rule number one is that we must be trusted by both the government and the guerrillas . . .

What if some of our food goes to the guerrillas? And rule number two is we won't go anywhere without guarantees of safety. We are not Boy Scouts or kamikazes.'

For the return journey from La Bermuda I had accepted a lift in a car which drove ahead of the Green Cross convoy. This proved a mistake. It was now dark and the road ahead was lit only by the rattling Datsun's one working headlight. Then what looked like a film arc light blinded us. Voices shouted for us to stop, to turn off the road, get out and get our hands up. With one of its armoured personnel carriers straddling the road, topped by a searchlight which fanned the surrounding bushland, the Salvadorean Army had set up a roadblock.

Photographer Eric Piper, the driver and I were thrown backwards against the car, then told to turn around with our hands on the roof. The driver had not closed his door and a uniformed shape drew pleasure from slamming the door against the man's fingers. He did not scream; he signalled to Eric and me to do exactly as we were told and not to argue. Only after a while did we realise that somebody was having the life beaten out of him or her. We could see only the glow of cigarettes and hear thuds of boots, and laughter. Before we were allowed to go, we were punched in the kidneys and robbed.

Two weeks later, the Army descended upon La Bermuda, selected 500 people and loaded them into trucks. The *New York Times* reported the officer in charge as saying the selected people were being taken elsewhere 'for their own safety'. 'Many could be subversives,' he said. They included old men, women and sick children, who were prevented from speaking to reporters. The camp was burned down and the selected people were taken to a prison; many of them have since 'disappeared'.[5]

'Under the constitution of the United States,' said the chief security officer at the American embassy, 'the Stars and Stripes must be lowered every day at sunset. Only one place on this earth is excluded: our embassy right here in El Salvador. And that's by the executive order of President Reagan himself.'

The embassy has electronically-controlled doors every few yards, as in a maximum security prison, and US marines bunkered on the roof, as well as troops of the El Salvador National Guard in the courtyard and at roadblocks within a mile radius, and groups of thugs in reflecting glasses and running shoes and 'Rolls-Royce' T-shirts circling it. The thugs are called Operation Shark.

Howard Lane, the press attaché, sat in a windowless panelled office, the Stars and Stripes behind him, Ronald Reagan on the wall and a magnum in an open drawer. A grey, rumpled man in his forties, he spoke at first the Official Optimism. 'The guys in the bush', he said, 'have no more than 5,000 human assets and a comparative support structure.'

Translated, that meant that there were only 5,000 guerrillas and 5,000 civilian supporters. But, surely, the previous year there had been more than 300,000 people crowding the centre of San Salvador in support of the opposition groups? That left 295,000 'support structure' unaccounted for, minus the twenty-one who died when the forces of law and order opened fire on the crowd.

The press attaché described himself as a leftover from the Carter administration's diplomatic appointments and said that he had been proud to serve the previous American Ambassador to El Salvador, Robert White, who had taken the courageous step that January of going before a congressional hearing to say that 'the chief killers of Salvadoreans are the government security forces. They are the ones responsible for the deaths of thousands upon thousands of young people who have been executed merely on the suspicion that they are leftists'.[6] For saying that, White paid with his career.

Howard Lane's Chevrolet had armour plating and a galleon-style porthole through which an automatic weapon could repel boarders. Like Old Glory never furling, this apparently was another first for El Salvador. He drove through the embassy gates, smiling at the National Guard and the 'sharks' in their reflecting glasses.

'They're your allies,' I said.

'Assholes,' he said.

Apart from 'Rough Time at Jericho' on San Salvador television and a reputedly rougher time at Gloria's, a brothel 'checked out' by the embassy's doctors, there was not much fun for the Americans 'in-country'. Cocktail parties, with their distasteful task of entertaining members of the regime, were grim, heavy-drinking affairs. Robert White's successor, Deane Hinton, a career diplomat expelled from Zaire in 1974 after allegations of a coup attempt against President Mobutu,[7] was a Reaganite who liked to scare newly arrived reporters. 'I could pick up a phone right now and say into it you're a communist, right?' he boomed to a photographer at a party. 'And sure enough some guy would drop by and – pfff – he'd kill you, right? But I know you're not a communist, don't I . . . don't I?' (Hinton was later removed, apparently for being too liberal.)

When President Reagan assumed office in 1981 nationalists fighting United States-sponsored tyrannies throughout Central America were described variously as Marxist-Leninists, communists, leftists and terrorists. In El Salvador, where the American assault had been concentrated, the Frente Democratico Revolucionario, formed in April 1981, sprang entirely from popular resistance organisations which date back to the nineteenth century. It unites peasants, trade unionists, priests, teachers, students, businessmen, Christian Democrats, social democrats, social-

ists, Jesuits and communists. It includes groups such as the Union of
Slum Dwellers and the Christian Peasants' Association. Only the Union
Democratica Nacionalista, one of the smallest coalitions, is of communist
inspiration. As in Vietnam, the aim of American propaganda is to cast
El Salvador into the wider arena of the cold war and so deny the true
nature of the resistance movement.

Tatters of resistance flags still hung from San Salvador's unfinished
cathedral. On the steps, beside a bundle of humanity swathed in plastic
sheeting and pummelled by rain, were splashes of red paint with which
someone had replaced the blood of those massacred at the funeral of
Archbishop Oscar Romero. As a microcosm of the human struggle in
Latin America and of the forces opposing it, El Salvador is where the
Catholic Church is said to be 'on fire'. It might also be said that there
is in El Salvador, and elsewhere in the region, a trinity of Rome and
Reagan and the colonels. At the time of his murder by an 'unknown
assassin', as he held up the chalice at Mass, Archbishop Romero had
publicly set aside the strictures of the Vatican and sided politically with
his flock, preaching that their enforced poverty and their landlessness
was not God's will, and that they should resist.

One year after his death the power of Archbishop Romero's following
was still much in evidence. In the garden of the archbishop's palace in
San Salvador, some 600 frightened people had taken refuge against the
terror of the National Guard. They were unarmed and all that separated
them from the black helmets and black boots outside were two rickety
gates of corrugated iron. Perhaps it was the presence of foreign journalists
which kept the Guard at bay. No one was quite sure.

A twelve-year-old boy, Domingo García, whose job was to open and
shut the gates quickly, told me how the Guard had killed his father for
belonging to an agricultural workers' union. 'They killed my three
brothers and they thought I was dead, too,' he said. He had scars on his
scalp, neck and arms, caused by machete 'chops'. It was a familiar story.
Between January 1980 and April 1981 the Legal Aid Service of the
Archdiocese had documented 322 cases of children assassinated.

The Legal Aid Service, the Socorro Juridico, was established in 1977
by a group of lawyers as a means of defending the poor in the courts.
Carrying their files they move constantly; I found them in a shed at the
end of a vegetable allotment between the American embassy and the
morgue. On the wall was a photograph of Maria Henriquez, director of
the Human Rights Commission, who was kidnapped on October 3,
1980, and tortured to death with razorblades. The administrator, Ramón
Valledares, was taken three weeks later and nothing has been heard of
him since. 'We have noticed,' a young woman said, 'since Reagan's
election and the increase in US aid, new methods of torture have been

introduced; previously people were simply shot.' To underline this, she produced a sheaf of photographs of victims who had been found recently on rubbish tips. She spread the photographs on a picnic table outside the garden shed, but hurriedly gathered them back into their waterproof folders when a man emerged and whispered something to her.

On my last day in El Salvador I happened on Conception Street which has a wrestling stadium but is otherwise a street of funeral parlours. It was early morning, the curfew had ended and Perez Dominguez had returned with his first 'catch', a body for his funeral parlour. He switched on the Muzak, which played 'Strangers in the Night' and 'Yesterday', and he waited. Soon a man came enquiring about his friend, Antonio Majano. 'They always look in my shop first,' said Perez. 'I am the quickest; everybody knows that.'

Antonio Majano was twenty-four when he was shot and mutilated. He had worked in a shoe factory for the equivalent of £12 a week, then he had been made redundant. 'I don't understand; he had no political ways,' said his friend. Across the street, on the wall of the wrestling stadium, was graffiti which had defied a number of attempts to erase it. I asked Perez to translate the words for me. He read, 'To hold down people for ever is like putting a hand up to the sun'.

From 1980 to 1986 the United States sent more than $2 billion to El Salvador as 'aid'. Eighty-five per cent of this has paid for arms, planes, helicopters, incendiary bombs, oxygen-reduction bombs, phosphorous bombs, Napalm bombs, cluster bombs, 'anti-personnel' weapons and munitions, electrified wire, surveillance equipment, more conscripted troops, more black helmets, more black boots and 'the continued involvement', wrote Amnesty International in 1984, 'of all branches of the security and military forces in a systematic and widespread program of torture, mutilation, "disappearance" and the individual and mass extrajudicial execution of men, women and children from all sectors of Salvadorean society . . . '[8]

In 1983 President Reagan 'certified' that the El Salvador regime had satisfied the 'human rights criteria' required by the Congress for American military shipments to continue. In 1985 a report by the Congressional Arms Control and Foreign Policy Caucus said that a four-month investigation had shown that the Reagan administration had misled and lied to Congress about the situation in El Salvador, even claiming that most of the US 'aid' money had gone to improve social conditions when, in fact, it had gone to the military. The United States, the report concluded, was becoming more deeply involved in El Salvador, in a manner that was 'reminiscent of Vietnam'.[9]

40

'Basta!'

Q: Mr President, have you approved of covert activity to destabilise the present government of Nicaragua?

A: Well, no, we're supporting them, the – oh, wait a minute, wait a minute, I'm sorry, I was thinking of El Salvador, because of the previous, when you said Nicaragua. Here again, this is something upon which the national security interests, I just – I will not comment.

President Reagan's press conference, Washington
February 13, 1983

Managua: July 1983. The Boeing 720 is an antiquity of the jet age and there are few still in service; one of them, having already been retired by three airlines, represents the entire long-haul fleet of Aeronica, the airline of Nicaragua. It flies every day and night, proving, I was assured, that 'God protects even the butterfly on the wheel'.

Having waited and suffered with many airline passengers, I cannot recall another group applauding, if sardonically, news of an open-ended delay, but they did that evening at Miami airport. There were no ground staff; Aeronica could not afford them. People spread picnics on the polished floor, a guitar was produced and a party proceeded, interrupted by visits from the American pilot who was cheered when he announced, 'Sorry folks, maybe another hour.' This spirit continued in the air. With the lights dimmed, my fellow passengers sang, 'Nicaragua, Nicaragua' and a barely whispered version of '*No Pasarán!*', the national hymn which means, 'They shall not pass'.

Only when disaster strikes does attention focus on ordinary people who live in the 'under-developed' world. An earthquake, a flood, a war and they are news, though invariably of a short-lived kind, from which they emerge as victims, accepting passively their predicament as a precondition for Western charity. The Western perspective on the Ethiopian famine, that of people denied fundamental control over their lives, complied with the stereotype, and the 'consensus' was to give surplus food and cash to them. Their need was deemed 'above politics'. That their predicament had political causes, many of which were rooted in the 'developed' world, was not widely considered a central issue. Since 1979, against historically impossible odds, the Nicaraguans have smashed the stereotype.

The *depth* of what has happened in Nicaragua and its wider implications, in particular the very real threat posed to the United States and its global system of 'development', struck me when I stayed in a frontier community, El Regadio, in the far north of the country. Like everywhere in Nicaragua, it is very poor, and its isolation has made change all the more difficult. However, since the Sandinistas threw out the dictator Anastasio Somoza in 1979 a 'well baby clinic' has been established, including a rehydration unit which prevents infants dying from diarrhoea, the most virulent third world killer. When I was there no baby had died for a year, which was unprecedented. More than 90 per cent of the children have been vaccinated against polio and measles, with the result that polio has been wiped out. The production and consumption of basic foods has risen by as much as 100 per cent, which means that serious malnutrition has disappeared; and a co-operative has been established on part of the land of a former wealthy *Somocista* politician, whose sons have also been given part of the land, and they and the *campesinos* have been advanced credits by the government. And there is a new school attended by children who, before 1979, would have laboured in the fields; and eighty-seven people, mostly middle-aged peasant women, have learned to read and write.

Petrona Cruz, aged fifty-three, is one of them. A mixture of jolliness and shyness, she mentioned to me a word, *pobreterria*, for which there is no precise translation. 'It is the equivalent of people calling themselves the scum of the earth,' she said. 'It was a view of ourselves based on shame, on believing that things could never change. The word doesn't exist now.'

I asked Susan Veraguas, a Chilean midwife teaching at the clinic in El Regadio, about this new sense of esteem. 'I can speak best as a woman', she said, 'for it is the women who have seen the most dramatic changes ... in themselves. For instance, they have discovered their bodies, discovered for the first time how they can conceive, how their vagina and insides, the whole thing, works. Now they've got 50 per cent of the responsibility to conceive a child! Imagine! Can *you*? And I ask them, "How do you feel now?" and they say, "We feel different. We feel people. We feel women with dignity because we know exactly how we are, and now we can share this knowledge with our children and with the future generation, because we don't want them to be ignorant like us. And, listen, now we feel more sure, and more proud."'

Nicaragua, minuscule, impoverished and facing an invasion by the most powerful and richest nation, is indeed a threat. It is a threat to American foreign policy, not because its people and their leaders want to create 'another Cuba', isolated and with the Russians ensconced. It is a threat for the opposite reason: that Nicaragua offers an *alternative* model of development to anything the Soviet Union would want to impose. This is why American policy and propaganda are aimed at severing Nicaragua's ties with its neighbours and 'pushing' it towards the only available benefactor, Moscow. It is the same policy and propaganda employed against Cuba in 1960 and 1961 and against Vietnam since May 1975.

Of course, the gravest threat posed by Nicaragua to the United States is that it offers to those nations suffering under American-sponsored tyrannies, such as El Salvador and Guatemala, a clear demonstration of regional nationalism at last succeeding in the struggle against hunger, sickness, illiteracy and *pobreterria*. And when the Reagan administration and its 'New Right' supporters say that the United States is in danger of 'losing' Central America, they are right. It is no coincidence that since the Sandinistas came to power the nationalist guerrillas in Guatemala have enjoyed a dramatic increase in support among people in at least nineteen of the country's twenty-two provinces. The same is true of the resistance in El Salvador, which has grown in strength not because of some imaginary Ho Chi Minh Trail of arms supply masterminded by Russians and Cubans, but because one 'good example' in the region has survived against all odds. As Noam Chomsky has pointed out, 'The weaker the country, the greater the threat [to US policy], because the greater the adversity under which success is reached, the more significant the result.'[10] Unlike Vietnam, Nicaragua is neither isolated from its neighbours, nor has it felt obliged to embrace the Eastern bloc; more than 75 per cent of its foreign trade is with Western and non-aligned countries and only 11 per cent with the Soviet Union and Eastern Europe.[11]

For five years Nicaragua has fought an invasion directed by United States military officers and government officials in Honduras, where the full panoply of American 'small war' technology has been installed. In addition, Nicaraguan airspace is invaded almost every night by United States AC-130 attack aircraft, based in Panama, and every week by

AWACS surveillance aircraft based in Oklahoma. American Naval task forces are on permanent station off both the Caribbean and Pacific coasts of Nicaragua. In 1983 the CIA mined Nicaragua's harbours and blew up its main oil storage depot at Puerto Corinto.

In the same year the United States successfully brought pressure on the Inter-American Development Bank to stop a loan of $34 million to Nicaragua. The loan, already agreed, would have revitalised the Nicaraguan fishing industry and provided a substantial and cheap source of nutrition.[12] In 1985, just as the same international bank seemed ready to approve $58 million in agricultural credits to Nicaragua, the United States Secretary of State, George Schultz, warned the Bank's president that the loan risked a complete withdrawal of American contributions. Despite its non-political charter, the Bank set aside the loan.[13] A total American embargo now operates against everything Nicaraguan, denying its raw materials their most important market. The old Aeronica Boeing is no longer allowed to land in Miami.

Against this is ranged what President Reagan has called the Nicaraguan 'war machine' which, at the last count, centred upon forty-five old T-54 and T-55 Soviet-built tanks, designed for use on the North German plain and not in dense tropical terrain. In addition there are a few anti-aircraft batteries and the Nicaraguan Air Force's 'strike command', which consists of three American Korean war vintage T-28s, two of them flown by the same dapper Chilean pilot with a honed sense of humour. 'I am ready', he informed me at a party in Managua, 'to take on the entire US Air Force. Let us say I am the pigeon attacking the buckshot!' (The Sandinista revolution has its own Woody Allens. Tomás Borge, the only original Sandinista to survive, told *Playboy* magazine that the leadership had been seriously trying to get copies of *Bedtime for Bonzo*. 'The movie deals with a monkey', said Borge, 'and the monkey's master is Reagan. So this is a wonderful allegory ... almost a premonition!')[14]

The lines of Bertholt Brecht slip into mind in Nicaragua: 'By chance I was spared. If my luck leaves me I am lost.' What has happened in Nicaragua all seems so tenuous. How *did* they slip the leash and 'triumph', as they say, on July 19, 1979, when the Sandinistas swept into Managua after Somoza had fled to Miami? For a brief moment American foreign policy had paused; Jimmy Carter's consuming obsession was the American hostages in Iran. And for once Washington found it difficult to contrive an intervention on behalf of a dynasty of banana Napoleons so outrageous their sponsors knew they could be relied upon to surpass their monstrous reputation and 'embarrass' a president who had sought to build his reputation as the guardian of 'human rights'.

The Somozas were handed Nicaragua in 1933 by the US marines

who had occupied the country for twenty-one straight years. In 1934 César Augusto Sandino, whose guerrilla army had forced the marines out, was invited to Managua for 'peace talks' with Anastasio Somoza, whom the Americans had put in command of their creation, the National Guard. When Sandino arrived in Managua he was murdered on Somoza's orders. Two years later Somoza appointed himself president for life. The Somozas went on to run Nicaragua like a family business. During the 1940s a calypso popular in American nightclubs began:

> A guy asked the dictator if he had any farms. The dictator said he had only one . . . It was Nicaragua.

The Somozas owned almost half the arable land. They controlled the coffee, sugar and beef industries. They owned the national airline outright. If you bought a Mercedes car you bought it from a Somoza company. If you imported or exported, you did so through Somoza 'kickback' agencies. The first Somoza had begun his career as a sewerage inspector and went on to own the sewers of Managua, right up to the manhole covers. Even the paving stones in the street were made by a Somoza cement factory which got the contract from a ministry run by a Somoza, and of course the profits ended up with El Presidente.

Nothing was overlooked; most Nicaraguans recall the 'House of Dracula', which was the name they gave to a blood plasma factory in Managua called *Plasmaferesia*. The poor would go to this place to sell their blood for as little as a dollar a litre and the company would export it to the United States for ten times that amount. In January 1978 the editor of the newspaper *La Prensa*, Pedro Joaquin Chamorro, was murdered while he was conducting a campaign against the blood traffic. The company was registered in the name of a Miami-based Cuban exile, but evidence published by *La Prensa* suggested that this was merely a front for Somoza. Certainly, most Nicaraguans would have been surprised had El Presidente not been selling his people's blood. During the anti-Somoza demonstrations which followed Chamorro's death, the 'House of Dracula' was burned to the ground.

The National Guard was Somoza's private 'death squad'. Paid and armed as part of America's 'aid' programme, the dreaded *Guardia* was the instrument of American policy in Nicaragua for almost half a century. Senior officers were trained at the 'School of the Americas' in the US-run Canal Zone in Panama (known throughout the Americas as '*escuela de golpes*', the school of coups), where they were taught to equate social unrest with communist subversion. They were above the law. They could murder at will. Somoza called them 'his boys' and, if repetitive reports by human rights organisations are an indication, they tortured almost as a sport. For example, one of the delights of Somoza's 'boys' was to drop his political opponents from helicopters into the Masaya volcano. Said President Roosevelt of the first Somoza, 'That guy may be a son of a bitch, but he's our son of a bitch.' Said President Nixon of the second Somoza: 'Now that's the kind of anti-communist we like to see down there.'[15]

In 1972 an earthquake struck Nicaragua, destroying Managua and killing an estimated 10,000 people. Officers and troops of the National Guard went on a looting spree, and one senior officer tried to blow open the national bank. When relief supplies arrived from all over the world, a National Emergency Committee was set up under Somoza's control and run by the National Guard. This, wrote Dianna Melrose in her book on Nicaragua for Oxfam, 'institutionalised the misappropriation of emergency relief':

> . . . Realising that relief supplies were being syphoned off and sold by the National Guard, Oxfam's Field Director talked Mrs. Somoza into giving permission to bypass the official distribution system. This meant waiting in the air traffic control tower for the right plane to be spotted, then careering onto the tarmac to get the trucks loaded before the National Guard arrived on the scene.[16]

Following the earthquake, the United States gave $57 million in emergency aid to Nicaragua; but the Nicaraguan Treasury reported receiving only $16 million. By April 1979, with Somoza near the end of his reign and now bombing his own people, he received a loan of $40 million from the International Monetary Fund. There were no binding conditions. A few weeks later the IMF, urged on by the Carter administration, gave him a further $25 million.[17] After Somoza had fled to Miami, the Sandinistas found less than $2 million in the national treasury.

Barrio Riguero bore the brunt of the 'final offensive' against the National Guard. During six weeks of street battles, more than 50,000 Nicaraguans were killed, from a population of only 3 million. Lupita Reyes Montiel lost her two sons. Beneath her small dirt garden lies Julio, whom she herself buried, having carried his tortured body under fire back from the lines of the Guard. He was twenty. Her other son, aged seventeen, 'simply disappeared'. 'We said "*Basta!*" to Somoza,' she said. ('*Basta*' means 'We've had enough'.)

Near Lupita's home is the grave of seven people who were killed when the Guard threw a grenade into a house. There are other graves, of other sons, some of whom died fighting only with slingshots loaded with ballbearings, some of them with their bare hands. In Barrio Colonia Nicarao, Norma Gallo lifted the floorboards in her house and displayed part of the tunnel network through which their sons had escaped. All the mothers I spoke to said that the Sandinista leadership 'kept their promise and died with us'. This was a revolution from the bottom up, a quality which sustains it.

From the *barrios* there are lines of white crosses at the roadside all the way to the Bank of America and the pyramid-shaped Intercontinental Hotel, the only tall buildings to withstand the 1972 earthquake, and the only tall buildings standing today. Somoza stole the money which would have rebuilt the capital, and there is no money for building now, with the result that Managua retains a surreal quality, with its centre and commercial district still flattened, the rubble surrounded by rusted barbed wire. A lone art deco cinema withstood the earthquake and today it advertises American macho movies, John Wayne and Burt Reynolds, its ancient pink neon blinking across a wasteland dotted with crosses.

The crosses mark victims both of the earthquake and of the 'final offensive'. On a street corner in Barrio Riguero stands a cross and monument to the memory of an American television reporter, Bill Stewart. On June 20, 1979, less than a month before the 'triumph', Bill Stewart was murdered by the National Guard. His cameraman continued filming as Stewart, his hands up, was ordered to lie face down on the ground by a Guard officer, who casually put his rifle to the reporter's head and killed him.

The film of Bill Stewart's death was shown on American television and helped finally to put Somoza beyond the pale in the United States and to break the pattern of American intervention. Nicaraguans understand this. The plaque on Bill Stewart's monument reads, 'In memory of Bill Stewart. He didn't die on foreign soil and we keep his memory alive because he is part of a free Nicaragua.'

In Nicaragua there is a war and a siege, but there is no curfew. Neither are there roadblocks (none that I could find), nor truckloads of black helmets and black boots, nor 'sounds of the night', nor 'waking up dead', nor death squads working their shifts, as in El Salvador. Nicaragua is one of the few countries in the world in which Amnesty has found no torture practised or condoned by the state.[18] Equally, Nicaragua is one of the few countries, perhaps the only country in Latin America, where the United States Ambassador apparently feels secure enough to stroll through the streets to his barber or to indulge in his hobby of amateur dramatics. When the German writer Günter Grass visited Nicaragua he wrote:

The French, the North American and the Russian Revolutions all resulted in vengeful violence, murder and mass liquidation. Indeed all known revolutions have wanted to appease their ideals and make their people happy with theories soaked in blood. Yet in this tiny sparsely populated, powerless land, where Christ's words are taken literally, the Sandinista revolution provides a different example . . . [19]

The Sandinistas began by abolishing the death penalty and setting free some 2,500 National Guardsmen (which angered many of those Nicaraguans who had lost loved ones to the Guard's brutality) and putting others to work on the cotton harvest. 'Consider our dilemma,' said Tomás Borge, now the Interior Minister. 'The more humane our ideals the higher the price we had to pay. How many of the National Guard we let go went straight to the border and signed up with the CIA's Contras?'

I accompanied Tomás Borge to Tipitapa maximum-security prison near Managua where, before 1979, he himself had been kept naked, hooded and half-starved, 'so much so that I welcomed the return of the torturer'. In a country which has no Castro, no pictures of the leadership in public places and no streets named after them, Tomás Borge is as close to being the accredited national hero as any. This is no doubt due to what he suffered and to his refusal, under torture, to betray other leaders of the Frente de Liberación Sandinista. While he was imprisoned his wife was gang-raped and murdered by the National Guard, and shortly after the 'triumph' he had to identify her body in a mass grave.

At Tipitapa Borge led me among the prisoners, seeking complaints. They shouted that they wanted books and more 'conjugal visits'. One man claimed to be a distant relative of his. 'So what is it you want?' said Borge. 'To visit my mother . . . our relative,' said the man. Borge threw his head back and laughed. Twenty minutes then passed as the two men negotiated this proposal like carpet salesmen until the prisoner had won a brief freedom the following Monday.

'This is my old cell,' said Borge. 'My torturer is in it now Believe me, it is a coincidence. He is sorry now, I think. Hello, how are you? . . . you want books? Okay, I'll get them. And this fellow here . . . he would scrape off the skin of his victims . . . and this man gouged out eyes with a spoon . . . and here is the murderer of Pedro Chamorro, the owner of La Prensa.'

In April 1983 special courts, known as the Tribunales Populares Anti-Somocistas, were set up to try 'crimes of war and against humanity', ranging from acts of violence to 'political subversion'. These courts did not fall within the jurisdiction of the Supreme Court and gave a defendant only two days in which to prepare a defence. They were repressive, and what was striking was not that the Sandinistas admitted the mistake but that the human rights commission, an independent body established by the Sandinistas, singled out most of those unjustly imprisoned and the Interior Ministry pardoned them.

For most of my time in Tipitapa I was free to talk to anybody I wanted. All the prisoners, regardless of their crimes, are eventually eligible for places in the six open and semi-open prisons. At Granja Abierta prison there are no fences and no guards. The staff consists of two agricultural teachers and the only potential weapons are machetes, which the prisoners were trusted to use in the fields. In two years one man had walked away. Since Granja Abierta opened in 1982 seventy-six inmates have been released into the community and, according to research by Irish psychologist Benny McCabe, there has been less than 15 per cent recidivism.[20]

One of the Sandinistas' most public 'mistakes' concerned the Miskito Indians, the indigenous population of the Atlantic coast who, until 1979, had little contact with the 'Spanish' population on the Pacific coast. In 1982, as President Reagan intensified his 'secret war' of Contra attacks against Nicaragua from Honduras, the Sandinistas evacuated several isolated Miskito communities along the River Coco. They gave little warning to the Miskitos themselves and destroyed their crops and homes so as to prevent them from being used by the Contras. As a consequence, some 10,000 Miskitos fled north across the border, and ended up in camps where many were recruited by the CIA for the Contras. This was enough for the administration in Washington to accuse the Sandinistas of genocide. In her book on Nicaragua for Oxfam, Dianna Melrose wrote:

> While criticism must be made of the situation, Oxfam feels that genuine efforts were made to help the 8000 or more Miskitos who were resettled inland. In contrast to the totally inadequate resettlement provisions made for the Miskitos 20 years before, the Government took steps to try to provide the five new settlements at Tasba Pri with housing, agricultural and public health services.[21]

Nicaragua's economy is based on the highly conventional wisdoms advocated by the United Nations Economic Commission for Latin America since the 1960s. For example, land reform is modelled partly on the venerable ideals of the Co-operative Movement, as bemused British visitors are constantly reminded. 'This began in Rochdale,' they are told, 'didn't *you* know? . . . The Toad Lane Co-op in 1844.' There is no state farm monopoly as there is in Cuba. Individuals can own as much land as they can work, provided they produce, re-invest and pay union-agreed wages. The law says that you are subject to having your land taken over only if you have 850 acres lying idle. 'Fortunately', an official of the Land Reform Institute told me, 'Somoza owned so much land that taking it over was a universally popular move. We were able to divide it quickly and go a long way to satisfying the yearning of people for land.' Of the land which was taken over, 65 per cent is now owned by individual farmers, 21 per cent by state farms and 14 per cent by co-operatives.[22]

However, according to critics on the left in Nicaragua, the Frente Obrero in particular, the people's need for land has not been met and the Sandinistas have been too cautious. Private ownership is responsible for more than 60 per cent of national production and most of the principal exports – coffee, cotton, sugar and beef. And yet in spite of being offered interest rates well below commercial rates, most of the big private owners had ceased to invest in Nicaragua, blaming their 'lack of confidence' on American hostility to the regime.

This lack of confidence has not been shared by the international aid agencies. And therein lies perhaps the bitterest irony for Nicaragua, for no country has handled aid funds more diligently. Reviewing an urban reconstruction programme completed in 1983, a confidential World Bank report called it 'probably one of the most effective urban projects supported by the Bank'. Government teams, said the report, 'completed the necessary technical studies with remarkable speed' and 'achieved twice quantities of road improvements – paving and drainage' as envisaged.[23] American pressure has since meant that World Bank assistance to Nicaragua has been scaled down.

In 1984 Nicaragua held the first democratic elections in its history, and international observers agreed that the voting process and count were scrupulously honest.[24] The Sandinistas won 66.7 per cent of the vote and 61 seats in the 96 seat National Assembly. On the right, the Democratic Conservatives, the Independent Liberal Party and the Popular Social Christian Party took 29.3 per cent of the vote and 29 seats, while the three left-wing parties won 4 per cent and 6 seats.

The Reagan administration, having campaigned to ensure that a coalition of three right-wing parties did not participate in the election, denounced the election as a farce. (The 75 per cent turnout of registered voters contrasted with the 1980 United States presidential election in which more than 48 per cent of the voters abstained and fewer than 27 per cent voted for the winning candidate, Ronald Reagan.) The US Ambassador, Harry Berghold, personally visited two opposition party leaders, one of whom later accused an embassy official of offering his campaign manager a bribe. Two days after the election the US administration accused the Sandinistas of importing MiG fighter aircraft from the Soviet Union. This had the effect of diminishing news and discussion of the election in the media. As journalists in Nicaragua soon discovered, the story of the Soviet planes was false.

Indeed, not since the Vietnam war has disinformation, or black propaganda, been used as a principal weapon, and perhaps no modern president has assumed outright the role of propagandist as has Reagan. In numerous speeches and statements since 1981 he has accused the Sandinistas of 'repression' as the agents of international communism. The source of this rhetoric is said to have been intelligence reports concentrating on the Nicaraguan opposition parties, the church and the media. From 1981 the author of these reports was David MacMichael, a senior CIA analyst. In 1985 MacMichael said:

All the time . . . my conclusion was that there was significant space for these groups to operate. They were in no danger of suppression. Compared to any other Central American country, Nicaragua has by far the liveliest opposition press and media. Over two-thirds of forty-odd radio stations are still privately owned and generally speak their mind.[25]

For speaking his mind, MacMichael was sacked from the CIA.

There are Stalinists, Maoists, even followers of the dead Albanian dictator Enver Hoxha, among the Sandinistas, but the dominant strain is that of genuinely non-aligned radicals, who are probably closer to Mexico than they ever will be to Havana or Moscow. 'We're like a drug store,' said José Perera, of the Liberal Party, 'we've got everything here. Only the pressure from America will change this, and turn us into something that is alien to all of us.' I asked Xavier Gorostiaga, a Jesuit economist and head of the Institute of Economic and Social Research in Managua, why Nicaragua was different. 'When the North Americans reduce our uniqueness to a jargon they themselves do not understand', he replied, 'they deny the power of our nationalism. Augusto Sandino himself was not in any way "anti-North American". Nor did he know anything about Karl Marx. He was a Nicaraguan first, a *nationalist*.

'Marxism is embraced here in a variety of ways, but by far the most powerful influence is Christianity and our Indian heritage. In Nicaragua today to be Christian can mean you have a real option for the poor. This has caused a dramatic division in the church. It's not a theological division; it's a social and political division and it's between the hierarchy and the people, between the Archbishops, the ones who pontificate and wish to control, and those who see the logical Christian extension of being with the people, fighting for them and with them if necessary.' I asked him what side the Pope was on. 'Ah, the Pope,' he said, 'he is with the poor in Poland!'

The Pope prays for the leadership of every country he visits. He prayed for the regime of General Jaruzelski in Poland and for the murderous regime of El Salvador, but he refused to pray for a Nicaraguan government which has the support of the majority of its people and three priests in the cabinet. In January 1985 the Vatican told the three priests they must stand down from the government or be unfrocked. They have decided to continue, regardless of the consequences. That the United States, abetted by the Vatican, is doing to the Sandinistas what the Soviet Union has done to Solidarity in Poland is an irony upon which the Pope may have reflected.

Accompanied by film director Alan Lowery and a crew I drove north towards the border with Honduras, where the Contras were. At Esteli our Land Rover had a flat tyre and needed a new tube; but not surprisingly Nicaragua in wartime classifies such things as essential items. Permission in writing was needed from the Ministry of Internal Trade before the garage could make the repair. 'This is no problem,' said the owner of the garage, summoning a phalanx of children to guide the Land Rover and its occupants to the local office of the Ministry and the relevant official and back again. This was accomplished in an hour. No one would accept payment. The children were persuaded to take a few foreign coins. Everyone at the garage shook hands and waved us on our way.

At Ocotal, the former US marines barracks stands as it was abandoned half a century ago. Carved in the belfry of the cathedral are 'Buster Baker, the Minnesota Kid', 'Clyde Atkins, Williamsburg, Kentucky, May 1st, 1927', 'T. L. Davie . . . the Real Big Man . . . ' A plaque says that the first 'organised aerial bombing in the history of warfare took place here on July 16, 1923'. At 2.30 that afternoon a formation of five British-made de Havilland biplanes, machine guns firing, dived on Sandino's troops as they laid siege to the barracks. Sandino lost at least 100 men and escaped to the mountains. Colonel José Antonio Ucles Marin escaped with him. Now eighty, and with his military bearing unaltered, he met me in the square at Ocotal and saluted. 'The general', he said, referring to Sandino, 'learned a lesson on that day. You fight from cover, you fight by stealth and surprise. That's how we will fight if they dare to come again.'

On the Pan American Highway we were flagged down by a distressed woman, who said that Julio Moncarda, the regional director of land reform, had been ambushed and killed on the road up ahead. A gang of Contras had ordered him out of his car and shot him, then disfigured his body. He was unarmed. Like most of the Sandinistas in charge of eradicating the legacies of Somoza, he was in his early thirties. That day, whenever people we met were told about his death, they wept. 'He performed many ceremonies here', they would say, meaning that he had transferred land back to people. Two days later the town of Esteli stopped for Julio Moncarda's funeral and people hummed his name in the Nicaraguan way.

At El Regadio, a frontier community, we were told about Celestina Ugarto, a recently qualified midwife, a woman given new skills in her fifties, who was loved and respected. She was abducted by Contras and murdered. She was one of five midwives from the same valley murdered by an organisation comprised of former National Guardsmen and those trained to a CIA manual of throat-cutting and other forms of gangsterism in military camps in Honduras and Florida. President Reagan has described the Contras as 'our brothers' and 'the moral equal of our Founding Fathers'.[26] Since 1982 Contra death squads have murdered 3,346 children and teenagers and killed one or both the parents of 6,236 children. During one year, 1984, the Contras caused an average of more than four deaths every day.[27] When Reagan commands headlines around the world by describing Nicaragua as 'the new version of Murder Incorporated', a country which gives a 'haven to the IRA' and whose 'acts of war against the United States' justify US military action to defend itself,[28] some may feel an uncontrollable urge to laugh at such apparent disingenuousness. But that would be to miss the point. 'So obsessed is the Reagan administration', wrote Charles Maechling from Washington,

> . . . that it has not hesitated to twist through redefinition the meaning of human rights in order to downgrade the most basic right of all, the right of life. Its acquiescence in patterns of torture, murder and other forms of state terrorism . . . comes close to condoning the kind of crimes against humanity condemned at the Nuremberg war crimes trials.[29]

XI

MEDIA GAMES

41

A question of balance

'Well, we've heard two points of view for and against capital punishment, and probably the truth lies somewhere between the two
extremes.'

Chairman, 'Any Questions', BBC Radio 4

As the 1960s drew to a close a rash of surveys confirmed that television
had usurped the Press as the main source of information for most of the
Western world. Not only had television become the dominant medium,
but in the cliché of the age, the medium itself had become 'the message'.
This was especially so in Britain where the concept of 'public service
broadcasting' was first developed. It was this 'tradition' which allowed
the BBC, and later commercial television, to distance itself from the
unseemly partiality of British newspapers and to claim a certain mysterious authority. As Michael Tracey put it, 'Broadcasters had convinced
the public that the words they spoke may have been few [compared with
the Press] but, by God, they had been touched by the beauty of truth.'[1]

The 1960s jargon for this authority was the 'consensus view', which
was served and buttressed by 'objectivity', 'impartiality' and 'balance'.
These of course are words resonant with fair play, decency, moderation.
They are sacred words in the lexicon of broadcasting, having been
handed down by way of Lord Reith, founder of the BBC. Above all,
they are words which do not mean what they say.

There is no such thing as a genuine consensus view. Britain is not
one nation with one perspective on events and with everyone sharing
roughly the same power over their lives. 'Consensus view' is often a
euphemism for the authorised wisdom of established authority in Britain.
Reith understood this; and it says much about the stamina of myths

about objectivity and balance that the behaviour of the BBC at its birth in 1922 and the nature of Reith's work for the Tory government of Stanley Baldwin during the General Strike are apparently so little known and their implications for the subsequent development of public service broadcasting are so little understood. To Reith, impartiality in broadcasting was a 'principle' to be suspended when the established authority was threatened. It is necessary only to examine the television coverage of the two great upheavals of the 1980s, the Falklands war and the miners' strike, to understand how faithfully the Reithian code has been followed. Reith himself demonstrated this when he became Baldwin's propagandist, writing parts of his speeches to the nation and broadcasting them on the BBC, while refusing to allow Labour leaders to put their side until after the General Strike was over. In his book about the General Strike, Patrick Renshaw wrote:

> In the false mood of euphoria and national unity which suffused Government supporters at the end of the strike Reith emerged as a kind of hero, a young man who had acted responsibly and yet preserved the precious independence of the BBC. But though this myth persisted it had little basis in reality . . . the price of that independence was in fact doing what the government wanted done . . . Baldwin . . . saw that if they preserved the BBC's appearance of impartiality, it would be much easier for them to get their way on important questions and use it to broadcast Government propaganda.[2]

Today, Reithian 'balance' remains the point of reference for the most powerful medium. And this, wrote Carol Campbell in her study of television, inevitably

> . . . gives the impression that there is a point of balance somewhere between contending extremes, and from that point society can be surveyed in a neutral fashion . . . as if this centre is non-political, is somehow not a political position. A more subtle aspect is that broadcasters are required to take note of public opinion and yet the medium of TV is such a powerful force in society, it is simultaneously creating that climate of public opinion. This is achieved by holding fast to the form of objectivity/neutrality/impartiality and balance to the prevailing bias.[3]

My first documentary for television was called 'The Quiet Mutiny', made in 1970 for Granada Television and transmitted under the *World in Action* banner. This was one of the very few times *World in Action* abandoned its anonymous 'voice-over' style, in which an announcer reads the words of a producer and researcher. In 'The Quiet Mutiny' I, the reporter, was seen 'on camera' stating what the documentary was about and interviewing its witnesses. The film told the story of the collapse of morale within America's Army in Vietnam following the arrival of conscripted troops, or 'grunts', of the 1960s anti-war generation. The 'Green Machine', as the greatest land army in history was called, was disintegrating because of the nature of the war and because its frontline men had no stomach for a war without apparent winners or laurels or purpose. 'The Quiet Mutiny' was the first of several films I made about Vietnam in which young American soldiers were represented as much victims of the American invasion as the Vietnamese.

I made this film with director Charles Denton, who had learned his craft at the BBC when Hugh Greene was Director-General and a flowering of 'personal view' programmes, satire and irreverence, had briefly disturbed the 'consensus view'. With cameraman George Jesse Turner and sound recordist Alan Bale, we had filmed a patrol of 'grunts', ostensibly in search of the Vietcong enemy. We did not see any Vietcong. What we did see was a chicken, which the sergeant presumed to be a Vietcong chicken and therefore worthy of mention in his dispatches as an 'enemy sighted', if not a 'body counted' The appearance and designation of the chicken seemed to underline the farce of the war, and I later recounted the incident in the film's commentary.

That chicken provided me with my first encounter with the guardians of 'objectivity'. A Granada executive, concerned about involving the Independent Television Authority, wanted to know the source of my statement that the chicken had communist affiliations. Could it not have been a pro-American chicken? After some enjoyable discussion along these lines it dawned on me that he was serious. 'Be objective!' he urged. Discussion about the chicken's politics proceeded for most of one day and was resolved finally in favour of the chicken remaining in the commentary as a fellow-traveller, if not an all-out card carrier.

The day after 'The Quiet Mutiny' was transmitted the American Ambassador to Britain, Walter Annenberg, a close friend of President Richard Nixon, complained to the Director-General of the ITA, Sir Robert Fraser. Sir Robert had previously been a senior civil servant at the Ministry of Information. Although he had not seen 'The Quiet Mutiny' Sir Robert described it as 'grossly unbalanced' and 'in serious breach of the code of impartiality' and 'anti-American'. This puzzled Granada's chairman, Lord Bernstein, who wrote to the *Sunday Times* to point out that no one had complained to the company and he saw nothing wrong with the film and indeed he commended it. As for it being anti-American, which Americans was it anti? Certainly not American soldiers, whose profound despair it had featured sympathetically.

However, the ITA (later to become the IBA) insisted that Granada make a 'balancing programme' in order to comply with the 'due impartiality' clause in the Broadcasting Act. As it happened, *World in Action* had pioneered a means of satisfying this section of the Act; as long as 'balance' could be achieved elsewhere in a series, a single programme could be transmitted as a 'personal view'. The problem for Granada was that it did not wish to make a programme defending a war which seemed indefensible, so *World in Action* set about making a programme about Prime Minister Edward Heath's love of yachting. In the nautical world of 'balance', the subject of Ted Heath's yacht was considered to contain enough ideological ballast to correct 'listing' caused by a film critical of the American war in Asia.

My second documentary for Granada was 'Conversations with a Working Man'. This was the story of Jack Walker, a dyehouse worker from Keighley in Yorkshire. Jack's job was monotonous, filthy and injurious to his health, yet he derived a pride from 'doing it well'. He is close to his wife Audrey and daughter Beverley; he loves cricket and growing prize-winning marrows and leeks. He is a gentle man with tolerant, principled views, and a loyal member of his (now defunct) trade union, the Dyers and Bleachers. In other words, he is not unlike millions of Britons.

'Conversations with a Working Man' was to be a documentary given over to the views of an articulate trade unionist without intrusion by those who often claimed to speak for him. Indeed, it was so unusual to see an ordinary trade unionist speaking virtually on his own terms, that the film I made with director Michael Beckham began to receive special attention during its editing.

One Granada executive worried a great deal about 'what the Authority will think'. I said that I did not understand why he should be worried about what the IBA would think of my film, which was factual and non-controversial. He shook his head, took me aside and, like a doctor telling me I had cancer, said that my film was 'committed'. But committed to what? There were dark hints, but no details. What was made very clear was that the commentary would have to undergo numerous changes to be 'acceptable to the Authority'. Two of the changes are unforgettable.

The Authority, I was told, would not tolerate the term 'working class' because it had 'political implications'. It would have to be changed to 'working heritage'. Then there was the problem of the term 'the people', which was a 'Marxist expression' and was therefore anathema to the Authority. I had not read much Marx, so I did not know. But surely 'the people' had existed before Marx?

Behind this nonsense was, of course, serious purpose. Twelve years

later the film director Ken Loach, whose films about trade unionists
were to be the object of censorship, wrote:

> Working people are allowed on television so long as they fit the
> stereotype that producers have of them. Workers can appear pathetic
> in their ignorance and poverty, apathetic to parliamentary politics, or
> aggressive on the picket line. But let them make a serious political
> analysis based on their own experiences and in their own language,
> then keep them off the air. That's the job of professional pundits,
> MPs and General Secretaries. They understand the rules of the
> game.[4]

In 1973 Charles Denton became deputy head of documentaries at
Associated Television (ATV) and he and I began a long association with
ATV, which became Central Television. I first met Charles in 1969
when he and two other young directors from the BBC's Hugh Greene
years, Richard Marquand and Paul Watson, asked me to join them in
setting up an independent production company. The aim, in Paul
Watson's words, was 'to take documentaries beyond the limit laid down
for BBC staff and to get on to television subjects unpalatable to hierarch-
ies'. Charles had directed 'One Pair of Eyes', Richard had worked with
the journalist James Cameron, and Paul had refined what became known
as television's 'fly on the wall' method. David Swift, a successful actor
and businessman, was to be our manager. I was fortunate to be in
their company; but the concept was ten years too soon. At that time
'independents' had no influence on the content of the BBC or ITV.
Most of us, however, have since worked together for ATV and Central.

As a newspaper journalist I learned much from the producers, directors, cameramen and film editors I worked with, and I am indebted to
them. I learned that the broadcaster whose work was informed by no
opinion, no irony, no humour, no compassion and no 'commitment'
lacked a very serious dimension and that these ingredients were no less
important than 'objectivity'. I also learned that my ordinary mortal's
fallibility did not change for the better when I stood in front of a television
camera. I did not ascend to some nirvana of neutrality; and it seemed to
me that all any journalist could do was to seek truthfully to report and
interpret events and experience, rather than believe that attaining the
whole truth was possible. Perhaps it is time journalists and broadcasters
redefined 'objectivity'. T. D. Allman, the distinguished American reporter, described 'genuinely objective journalism' as journalism that

> . . . not only gets the facts right. It gets the meaning of events right.
> Objective journalism is compelling not only today. It stands the test

of time. It is validated not only by 'reliable sources' but by the unfolding of history. Objective journalism is reporting that which not only seems right the day it is published. It is journalism that ten, twenty, fifty years after the fact still holds up a true and intelligent mirror to events.[5]

This would accurately describe the first documentary-makers in British television. In the early 1960s the work of John Grierson, Denis Mitchell, Norman Swallow and Richard Cawston owed nothing to bogus 'balance'. They presented people and places as they saw them; and their work was rich, moving and often brilliant. Neither did they present people as stereotypes, as 'moderates' or 'militants', but as men and women in specific situations, with lives and needs as real and worthy of fair description as anybody's. They understood and used television as the medium in which experience could be shared. For them, the issue was not so much 'personal bias' as illuminating those areas in society which had long remained in shadow. Today they would be called campaigners; and perhaps they were. They dared to put cameras and microphones in front of ordinary people and to allow them to talk. And what they revealed was another Britain. John Grierson, for example, was the first to give people the opportunity to tell of what it was like to live with rats, damp and cold. Norman Swallow's documentary about a northern mining community and Denis Mitchell's portraits of a street and a prison campaigned implicitly for greater understanding of people's lives across the divides of class. If today's standards of 'objectivity' had been applied then we might never have had documentaries. In 1985 Denis Mitchell said that throughout his career he had remained 'absolutely astonished . . . at people's quality of strength and dignity'.[6] Indeed, it was the blood, sweat and tears of ordinary people that gave us the documentary.

The Independent Broadcasting Authority showed little interest in my first series of documentaries for ATV when they were shown at noon on summer Sundays. But when they were moved to a peak hour and began to draw high ratings, the official arbiters of 'objectivity' and 'balance' were quickly on the scene. In 1976 I made several films in the United States with producer Richard Creasey and director Richard Marquand. One film, 'Zap, the weapon is food', examined the political manipulation of American food aid. It included evidence that the US Secretary of State, Henry Kissinger, was behind a policy to withdraw food aid from impoverished countries which did not vote with the United States in the United Nations, and that the voting record of these countries was monitored by a 'zap office' in the State Department. The programme challenged important myths about the 'generosity' assumed in the American policy of dumping food surpluses in the third world.

Before the film was completed the IBA demanded a preview and took what was then the unusual step of mounting its own investigation, using US government sources. The IBA, as Geoffrey Robertson has pointed out, 'has no legal obligation to scour programme schedules and preview current affairs programmes'.[7] Nevertheless, the official making the enquiries expressed concern about a report by the General Accounting Office, the US Congressional 'watchdog', which I had quoted in the film. The report gave statistical evidence that most American food aid went not to the neediest, but to US client regimes: a fact with which few, including the US administration, would argue today. According to the IBA, the Nixon administration had not suspended food aid to the Allende government in Chile, even though there was abundant evidence to the contrary. What was revealing about this episode was the manner in which IBA civil servants had involved themselves in the creative and editorial processes of documentary-making: for example, the parallel investigation using official sources. It was clear that the IBA, with its appointed officials and appointed board, aspired to much more than regulatory status. Indeed, the then Director-General of the IBA, Sir Brian Young (ex Eton, ex headmaster of Charterhouse), saw the Authority as a 'thoughtful editor', previewing, vetting, balancing and possibly banning. 'We are given teeth for biting, not gnashing,' he said.

ATV were told that my programmes in future would have to be 'balanced',[8] but just how this 'balancing' might be achieved became an apparently insoluble problem. The IBA ordered ATV, in effect, to counter each of my programmes, no matter their content, with another programme. However, questions of logic were raised. What if viewers who saw the first programme missed the 'balancing' programme? Surely they would be left seriously unbalanced! In some desperation ATV asked me to suggest someone whose work was the antithesis of mine. This was put to me, I thought, as a joke and so I nominated Auberon Waugh. The joke became a television series, and Waugh's subsequent and contrived encounters with working people in pubs and northern clubs so bemused his subjects that they appeared to treat him with affectionate concern, humouring him as one does a person recuperating from a particularly disturbing illness. The series was watched by few and his contract was not renewed. There was, however, a legacy. It was a caption which the IBA had instructed ATV to place before and after my and Waugh's programmes. It read:

IN THE PROGRAMME THAT FOLLOWS THE REPORTER IS EXPRESSING A PERSONAL VIEW

The words, in large black type, were intoned by an anonymous voice. As well as opening and closing the half-hour of transmission time, the caption was originally intended to interrupt the film's progress after fifteen minutes – rather like God intervening during a discussion on Darwinism. (ATV successfully protested against this.)

Censorship of the most popular medium is not necessarily as ham-fisted and open to ridicule as the above might suggest. The Broadcasting Act, Section 22, reads: 'The Minister may at any time, by notice in writing, require the Authority to refrain from broadcasting and it shall be the duty of the Authority to comply with this notice.' The closest a peacetime government has come to invoking this was in July 1985 when the then Home Secretary, Leon Brittan, effectively banned a film in the BBC's *Real Lives* series, which included an interview with Martin McGuinness, reputedly chief of staff of the IRA. In withdrawing the film as a result of government pressure, the BBC ignored the protestations of its producer, Paul Hamann, that he had made a meticulously 'balanced' film in the BBC tradition, that he had set the interview with McGuinness against an interview with Gregory Campbell, a committed Loyalist who advocated a shoot to kill policy against the IRA. But what Hamann apparently had not understood was that there were numerous exceptions to the rule of 'balance', and at the top of the list was the war in the north of Ireland.

If the style of the Thatcher government had been different, it is unlikely there would have been a public controversy of the *Real Lives* episode, because the BBC would have discreetly done the government's job. This was part of the 'tradition'. In 1937 Lord Reith wrote that he had 'fixed up a proper contract between Broadcasting House and the Home Office . . . I made it clear that we must be told ahead of things that might cause trouble'.[9]

Commercial television is less coy. In the IBA's guidelines, under a section headed 'Crime, anti-social behaviour, etc.', there is this:

> Where a programme gives the views of people who use violence *outside* the British Isles to attain political ends, managing directors of programme companies . . . may go ahead without consultation with the Authority . . . Any plans for a programme item which explores and exposes the views of people who *within* the British Isles use or advocate violence or other criminal measures for the achievement of political ends must be referred to the Authority before any arrangements for filming are made. A producer should therefore not plan to interview members of proscribed organisations, for example members of the Provisional IRA or other para-military organisations, without previous discussion with his company's top management. The manage-

ment, if they think the item may be justified, will then consult the Authority.[10]

In television jargon this is known as 'prior restraint'. It means that interviewing members of foreign para-military groups may be allowed, but interviewing members of Irish para-military groups is certainly not allowed. From summer 1977 to spring 1978 the journalist Peter Taylor made four documentaries in Northern Ireland for Thames Television. As a result of direct intervention by the IBA and by the then Secretary of State for Northern Ireland, Roy Mason, Taylor's reports were banned on the eve of transmision, delayed or emasculated. Taylor himself was vilified by Roy Mason for 'aiding and abetting' the IRA and it was suggested to his producer, David Elstein, that another reporter should cover Northern Ireland. Peter Taylor is one of Britain's most professional television journalists; without his responsible and courageous reporting there would be little to recall from the media coverage of a particularly turbulent period in the affairs of Northern Ireland. Those who doubt the scope and tenacity of the censors might consider the following list compiled by Liz Curtis.[11] Since 1959 *forty-eight* television programmes on Ireland have been banned, censored or delayed. Here are a few of them.

1959, BBC
See It Now (A talk show presented by Ed Murrow)

Lord Brookeborough, prime minister of Northern Ireland, personally intervened to secure the banning of a programme in which the actress, Siobhan McKenna, referred to IRA internees as 'young idealists'.

1959, BBC
Tonight

Seven ten-minute reports by Alan Whicker were dropped after the intervention of Lord Brookeborough. The programmes made passing reference to the political situation.

1966, ITV
This Week

A programme critical of Ian Paisley was banned in Northern Ireland.

1970, BBC

The BBC commissioned Jim Allen to write a contemporary play about Northern Ireland, to be directed by Ken Loach and produced by Tony Garnett. The BBC stopped the project when the script was partially written.

1971, BBC
24 Hours

Senior BBC executives prevented *24 Hours* from doing an in-depth programme about the IRA and its roots.

1971, Granada
World in Action: 'South of the Border'

The IBA banned the programme before it was completed. It included interviews with the IRA Chief of Staff and Sinn Fein President.

1973, ATV

Lord Grade banned a film by Kenneth Griffiths and Anthony Thomas about the life of Michael Collins, the IRA leader in the war against Britain in 1920.

1975, Thames

A programme about IRA fund-raising in America, timed to be shown on the day of the elections for the Northern Ireland Convention, was delayed by the IBA because, it said, 'the subject matter could have an unfortunate impact on opinions and emotions in the North of Ireland'.

1976, BBC

A play commissioned by the BBC from Brian Phelan was about torture and mentioned Northern Ireland in passing. It was recorded and banned.

1978, BBC

Director Colin Thomas made a film, 'A City on the Border', about Derry. He was ordered to cut sequences including one showing a tombstone which read, 'Murdered by British Soldiers on Bloody Sunday'. Another Thomas film about Ireland was cut substantially. Thomas refused to make the changes and resigned.

1978, Thames
This Week

The IBA banned a programme about the Amnesty report on the ill treatment of suspects by the Royal Ulster Constabulary.

1979, BBC
Panorama

The BBC filmed an IRA roadblock in County Tyrone. The film was seized by Scotland Yard under the Prevention of Terrorism Act. The item was never completed.

1981, Granada
World in Action

Granada withdrew 'The Propaganda War' rather than make cuts ordered by the IBA.

1983, Yorkshire
First Tuesday

Following pressure from the IBA, Yorkshire TV stopped production of a film about plastic bullets.

This last example probably typifies the insidious nature of television censorship. The *First Tuesday* programme was banned as a result of pressure similar to that applied to the BBC over *Real Lives*. In both cases the Press alerted the authorities. In March 1983 the *Irish Times* quoted a Yorkshire TV researcher as saying a film he was working on would be critical of plastic bullets.[12] Both the Royal Ulster Constabulary and the deputy director of the IBA, David Glencross, wrote to Yorkshire TV's managing director, Paul Fox. Glencross wrote:

> I take it you will be keeping a close eye on this programme referred to in the enclosed cutting from the *Irish Times* . . . Presumably when the researchers say they are on the side of people suffering from injustices and hardship, they include in that category those who are the victims of the IRA and INLA? Or don't those kind of victims count?[13]

According to Liz Curtis, who helped to arrange witnesses and research material for the *First Tuesday* programme, 'the project was dropped like a hot potato. The producer was put on another project and the researcher was exiled to paperwork. The proposed interviewees were told by phone that the programme was off.'[14]

Television in Britain may still enjoy more credibility among the public than television in other countries. This is probably because in other countries bias in broadcasting is understood, if not always acknowledged. In Eastern Europe many people regard the bias of the state as implicit in all its media and a conscious or unconscious adjustment is made by the viewing (and reading) public. This is not so in Britain where the bias of the state operates through a 'consensus view' that is broadly acceptable to the established order. Perhaps in no other country has broadcasting held such a privileged position as an opinion leader. Possessing highly professional talent and the illusion of impartiality, as well as occasionally dissenting programmes, 'public service broadcasting' has become a finely crafted instrument of state propaganda.

The propaganda has seldom been bellicose – although television news in the Thatcher era is drifting that way – and it still relies on a shared assumption among management and broadcasters that the prevailing establishment view is the correct view. In his memoirs Sir Ian Trethowan, Director-General of the BBC from 1977 to 1982, told of his devotion to the establishment and politicians and of his loathing for 'contemptibly unfair' political satire and his support for 'D' Notices and the strictures of the Official Secrets Act. Sir Ian gave this flavour of his blithe days as 'DG': 'Phillip would do research. Jennifer would fix the appointments. There seemed an endless supply of bright young men with good degrees, and charmingly efficient girls'.[15]

This attitude was reinforced in the news room by the predominantly middle-class background of the newscasters, the choice of interviewees (overwhelmingly establishment accredited), the angle of the camera, the repetitive use of labels and clichés, such as 'moderates' on the right versus 'extremists' on the left; trade unions and other groups 'dominated' by the left, never by the right; and the current favourite, 'Marxist'. For example, a BBC television reporter at the scene of the volcanic eruption in Colombia in 1985 said that relief supplies had been held up because the 'Marxist' regime in Nicaragua had prevented flights from crossing Nicaraguan airspace. Thus, in a few minutes, he was able to instil a series of attitudes by using a catch-word. At it turned out, the story was completely untrue.[16]

The BBC Charter and Licence says that 'for the BBC to take sides in any controversial issue would in any case be contrary to its own long established policy of impartiality . . . ' Set against the list of banned and censored programmes about Northern Ireland such a statement of principle has the ring of self-mockery. The statements of the assistant Director-General of the BBC, Alan Protheroe, are similarly divested of self-doubt. 'BBC news', he wrote to the *Guardian*, 'will continue – as in the past – to tell the truth, without distortion or suppression.'[17]

In this instance Protheroe had been challenged by letter writers to the *Guardian* about the BBC's coverage of the American invasion of Grenada in 1983. Readers and viewers had wondered, given the claim that the BBC neither distorted nor suppressed, how the newsreader Sue Lawley came to describe Eric Gairey, the former Prime Minister of Grenada, as a 'moderate' and the assassinated Prime Minister of Grenada, Maurice Bishop, as a 'communist', when Gairey had been a leader of the notorious and murderous 'Mongoose gangs', as well as being a UFO spotter and religious fanatic.

In his numerous letters to newspapers defending the independence of the BBC Alan Protheroe did not once mention that it was the British secret service that decided who would or would not be the tellers of truth at the BBC. From an office in Bush House, a brigadier passed on names of applicants for editorial jobs in the Corporation to MI5 for 'vetting'. Journalists of repute, such as Isabel Hilton of the *Sunday Times* and Richard Gott of the *Guardian*, were refused BBC posts because they were not considered 'safe'. This secret process went on for more than forty years and would still be going on if the *Observer* had not exposed it in 1985.[18]

A more subtle form of staff 'moulding' is achieved by the powerful Weekly Programme Review Board which is often chaired by Alan Protheroe. According to BBC producer Chris Johnson:

> It is [the Board's] duty to interpret policy handed down from on high and apply it to the daily output. Who is to be branded 'militant' and who 'moderate'? It is this body that decides when to stop calling Robert Mugabe's supporters 'terrorists' and switch to the more neutral 'guerrillas'. The minutes of these meetings were marked 'confidential' and circulated to department heads. But they were encouraged to leave them overnight in unlocked drawers. Knowledge thus gained, surreptitiously by the night shift, spread like wildfire. It was marvellously effective in inducing self-censorship.[19]

Whenever Independent Television News is accused of being less than objective (usually by the Glasgow University Media Group), its publicity machine responds by saying that ITN's impartiality is 'a matter of public record', although it does not say where the public might view this record. Once again, the tellers of truth are above the subjectivity and self-interest which they do not hesitate to criticise in others. Much more than canned applause or fake soundtracks, it is this specious authority that is television's most enduring trickery.

Today, due to growing public interest in the secret lores of the media and in particular to the work of monitoring organisations, television's 'authority' is being challenged. A catalyst for this was the rejuvenation of the nuclear disarmament movement. For the fifteen years to 1980 Parliament did not once debate the nuclear arms race. An almost parallel silence existed in the media. This silence was identified in Peter Watkins's remarkable film, 'The War Game', which reconstructed the aftermath of an attack on London with a one-megaton nuclear bomb. The commentator in 'The War Game' said:

> On almost the entire subject of thermo-nuclear weapons, on problems of possession and effects of their use, there is now practically total silence in the Press, official publications and on TV. There is hope

in any unresolved or unpredictable situation. But is there real hope to be found in this silence?

The irony of this statement was equal to its accuracy. On November 24, 1965, the BBC banned 'The War Game'. The official reason for the ban was the nanny-view that the Watkins film would be bad for the faint-hearted or, as a BBC press release put it, 'the effect of the film has been judged by the BBC to be too horrifying for the medium of broadcasting'. The BBC insisted that the decision had been entirely its own and had been taken 'after a good deal of thought and discussion, but not as a result of outside pressure of any kind'.[20] Both these statements were false.

The then chairman of the BBC Board of Governors was Lord Normanbrook, formerly Secretary to the Cabinet. On September 7, 1965, he wrote the following to his successor in the Cabinet, Sir Burke Trend:

[The War Game] is not designed as propaganda: it is intended as a purely factual statement, and is based on careful research into official material. I have seen the film and I can say that it has been produced with considerable restraint. But the subject is, necessarily, alarming; and the showing of the film on television might *have a significant effect on public attitudes towards the policy of the nuclear deterrent*. In these circumstances I doubt whether the BBC ought alone to take the responsibility of deciding whether this film should be shown.[21]

My italics indicate the real reason for the ban. The BBC subsequently surrendered its editorial control over 'The War Game' to the government. On September 24 the film was viewed at Television Centre by Sir Burke Trend and senior officials from the Home Office, the Ministry of Defence and the Post Office. Lord Normanbrook kept a minute of the comments of these officials. He wrote, 'The officials agreed . . . that the major question of policy was whether it would be expedient, in the public interest, that any film of this kind should be shown on television.'[22]

Most of the officials vetoed this 'factual' and 'restrained' film for the very reason Lord Normanbrook had outlined. The Director-General, Hugh Greene, concurred with the decision. In a speech in February of that year, Greene had said, '. . . censorship to my mind is the more to be condemned when we remember that, historically, the greatest risks have attached to the maintenance of what is right and honourable and true.'[23]

Most of the Press at the time swallowed whole the official version. There was little speculation that the BBC's motives were political. And there the career of Peter Watkins in British television virtually ended. Isolated and embittered, he launched himself upon a crusade against censorship, which he continues to this day. The BBC prolonged the ban on his film until 1985. Sir Ian Trethowan told an audience in 1981 that he had refused to lift the ban on 'The War Game' because he feared for its effect 'on some elderly people living alone' and on people of 'limited mental intelligence'. He made no mention of the Normanbrook letters.[24]

As well as keeping 'The War Game' from the gaze of those of 'limited intelligence', Trethowan withdrew an invitation to the anti-nuclear campaigner E. P. Thompson to give the 1981 Dimbleby Lecture on BBC television. 'Disarmament is all right for a discussion', said Trethowan, 'but not a lecture.'[25] This wisdom was passed to Thompson, who changed his subject to the cold war; but the veto stood.

Of course, the BBC has covered the 'nuclear debate' since the nuclear arms race was exhumed as an issue in 1980. For example, in its coverage of the United Nations Special Session on Disarmament in June 1982, BBC television news described the million people who came to New York to demonstrate for a nuclear 'freeze' as 'pacifists' and 'against defence'. The biggest public demonstration in American history had been labelled and its aims distorted. In May 1983 BBC Television broadcast the 'Great Nuclear Arms Debate', made originally for the American CBS Network. It was a pristine exercise in Reithian balance, with perspectives held comfortably within the framework of the 'consensus' view. The debaters were the Secretary of Defence, Michael Heseltine, the former US Secretary of State, Henry Kissinger, former American SALT negotiator Paul Warnke, and the chief opposition spokesperson for the Social Democratic Party in Germany, Egon Bahr. They talked for ninety minutes about NATO policy. Warnke offered reservations, Bahr scepticism; but as neither the disarmament movement nor the nuclear freeze lobby had been asked to participate, there was no one to oppose NATO policy. The presenter, Walter Cronkite, sought to reinforce the illusion of an informed and fair debate by saying at the end that 'any conclusion will have to be left perhaps to history'.

Britain has more nuclear bases per head of population and per square mile than any other country on earth. It can be reasonably presumed that they are all Soviet targets. Such is the efficacy of censorship that this fact is unknown to many of the British people. On June 18, 1980, Bob Cryer, then a Labour MP, asked the Secretary of Defence, Francis Pym, to provide a complete list of United States bases in Britain. Pym obliged with a dozen. Over the next two months and under further questioning from Cryer, Pym's list grew to fifty-one. Cryer asked Pym if he would like to tell the House about any omissions from his earlier lists. There were three more bases, Pym replied, including the largest underwater surveillance base in the world. But that was not all. In the *New Statesman* the journalist Duncan Campbell listed another forty-seven bases, making a grand total of 103, a long way from Pym's dozen. (By 1984 the total number of bases, installed or planned, had risen to 135.) Apart from Duncan Campbell's reports and one Thames Television programme, the struggle to air the truth about the bases received no coverage in the national media.

Opinion polls in Britain have consistently demonstrated people's serious misgivings about nuclear defence. A clear majority did not want Cruise missiles brought to Britain; almost half the population does not want the country's defences dependent on nuclear weapons. These views have found scant expression on television. Since 1980 a handful of programmes, such as Jonathan Dimbleby's 'The Bomb', and 'The Truth Game', made by David Munro and myself, have rejected the assumptions of the cold war. None of these programmes reached the television screens without a struggle. Denis Postle's 'Nuclear State' set out to discuss whether nuclear weapons had terrorised people into passivity and whether policies which excluded feeling and emotion could be regarded as rational. It was an original concept and highly relevant to arguments that 'anti-nuclear' programmes are 'emotional'. Postle's film was kept off the air for six months and only after protracted negotiations was it finally shown on Channel 4 in January 1984, with minimal publicity and at eleven o'clock at night when the smallest possible audience was assured. This all but nullified its impact.

Independent Television's grandiose equivalent of the BBC's 'Great Nuclear Arms Debate' was shown during Channel 4's 'Nuclear Week' in May 1983. The 'experts' were affiliated with the following institutions: Oxford University, the Institute of Strategic Studies, the Institute of International Affairs and the Royal United Services Institute. The political spectrum was represented by Michael Heseltine, David Owen and John Silkin of the Labour Party's right wing. The interviewer was Brian Walden, who projects himself as a man of the dead centre. As a member of the right wing of the Labour Party Walden consistently opposed unilateral attempts at influencing the nuclear arms race. He made no mention of this on the 'Nuclear Week' programme. No speaker fairly represented the fears of the majority about Cruise and Trident missiles.

1983 was election year in Britain and the issue for the political parties was the imminent arrival of Cruise and the Tories' commitment to Trident. The issue was not the already operative Polaris. However, because of a relatively minor wrangle in the Labour Party about the future of Polaris, this became the media-designated 'nuclear issue' of the election campaign. The terms 'defence' or 'multilateral disarmament' were used to describe government policies while the opposition was said to be for 'unilateral disarmament'. This gave a clear impression to many people that the Labour Party wished unilaterally to disarm Britain, which was untrue. The word 'nuclear' was often dropped and the distinction between a powerful, conventionally-armed Britain and a Britain reliant on nuclear weapons was seldom made.

Mrs Thatcher gave three main television interviews during the campaign: to Robin Day, Alistair Burnet and Brian Walden. None asked her why the government had vetoed or ignored so many opportunities for 'multilateral disarmament'. Indeed, the British record spoke for itself. In 1981 and 1982 there were forty-six resolutions put forward at the United Nations concerning multilateral limitations on nuclear and chemical weapons, and weapons of 'mass destruction'. Britain voted for only six of these resolutions. By contrast, the Soviet Union voted for thirty-eight resolutions. Britain voted against a resolution which merely condemned nuclear war as being 'contrary to human conscience and reason'.[26]

Robin Day confessed to *The Times* that he might have tried harder during his interview with Mrs Thatcher; certainly, his was the least obsequious of the three interviews.[27] Both he and Burnet were knighted by Mrs Thatcher. And both have projected themselves as men of reason and balance: firm, fatherly figures.

In December 1983 Alistair Burnet wrote an 'open letter' in the *Guardian* to Tony Benn.[28] He was affronted by Benn's charge that he and ITN were deeply biased and spread cold war propaganda. Brian McNair of the Glasgow Media Group responded with a question. Was it not as propaganda, he asked, that ITN chose to report a recent Soviet disarmament proposal in this way: 'Well, our defence correspondent says it's merely another attempt to drive a wedge between America and Europe over Cruise and Pershing.'[29] McNair wondered how ITN's defence correspondent knew that the Soviet proposal – on this occasion to remove and dismantle a number of SS20 missiles – was merely 'another attempt to drive a wedge' between NATO allies. Were not these words, he asked, the very language of the White House and the Thatcher government? He wrote:

> Governments and politicians generally have opinions and can be relied upon to express them. But when journalists present *some* opinions – such as the view that all Soviet proposals are 'wedge-driving' exercises – as 'truth', and when people have a high regard for those journalists, as they do for Mr. Burnet, a grave disservice is being done.[30]

When David Munro and I set out to make 'The Truth Game', it

seemed to us that 'wedge-driving' and the like were not simply examples of media bias. Language was being used to sell the nuclear arms race; and this use of language was part of the 'modes of thinking' which Einstein predicted would allow us to drift toward 'unparalleled disaster'. We decided to ignore images and look principally at language and ideas; the pictures would come later. The first aim of our film was to decode the language of nuclear inevitability, to reveal the doublethink which the linguist Paul Chilton has called 'Nukespeak'.

The origins of Nukespeak were the testing of the atomic bomb and its devastation of two Japanese cities. By using reassuring, even soothing language which allowed politicians, scientists and the public to distance themselves from the horror of nuclear war, a new kind of propaganda created acceptable images of war and the illusion that the world could live securely with nuclear weapons. The first atomic test in the New Mexico desert was given the code name 'Trinity'. The official report of the explosion was overflowing with Christian imagery, almost mystical in its reverence. These are the words President Truman read at his meeting with Churchill and Stalin at Potsdam:

> It lighted every peak, crevasse and ridge of the nearby mountain range with a clarity and beauty that cannot be described but must be seen to be imagined. It was the beauty the great poets dream about but describe most poorly and inadequately ... Then came the strong, sustained, awesome roar which warned of doomsday and made us feel that we puny things were blasphemous to dare tamper with the forces heretofore reserved to the Almighty.[31]

When Hiroshima was bombed, Truman expressed satisfaction that 'the experiment' had been 'an overwhelming success'.[32] 'Experiment' and 'success' went well with the innocent comic-book names given to the two bombs dropped on Japan: 'Little Boy' and 'Fat Man'. And it was not long before bombs were not bombs at all, but 'devices' and 'hardware' with names like 'Mule' and 'Sow' and 'Little Bambi'. Bigger and more lethal weapons were called 'modernised systems'. Above all, people were conditioned to accept a strategy of possessing nuclear weapons called 'deterrence', which although appearing to be logical could not be explained rationally and blurred the fact that the nuclear arms race was under way.

During the late 1970s, NATO developed and introduced a revised 'defence strategy' (war plan) known as 'flexible response', which was Nukespeak for a contingency plan to attack first with nuclear weapons. In 1979 the decision was taken to introduce 'modernised systems' in Western Europe, such as Cruise and the short flight-path Pershing II.

Pershing was designed not as a defensive weapon, but to attack. On August 17, 1982 the *Guardian* reported that the Pentagon had completed a 'strategic master plan' to give the United States the means of winning a nuclear war. This was called a 'limited' nuclear war and would be fought with 'theatre' weapons, like Pershing II.

The most important success of Nukespeak has been the Soviet threat. 'Once a nation pledges its safety to an absolute weapon', wrote Professor P. M. S. Blackett, the physicist, 'it becomes emotionally necessary to believe in an absolute enemy.'[33] It also becomes necessary, as Phil Bralthwaite has pointed out, to exaggerate Soviet crimes and mistakes, as well as Soviet military might and intentions. The 'mode of thinking' contends that the Soviet people are no longer people. They are worse than 'militants' and 'extremists'; they are an evil force. They are not the people who lost 20 millions in the struggle against Hitler, and whose sacrifices helped to win the war. They are the 'Soviet threat', the 'wedge-drivers' whose tanks will reunite the two Germanies, thus abrogating their deepest fear and defying their own history. Although the rhetoric softened following the summit meeting in Geneva in November 1985, the essence remained unchanged.

There is an analogy of events today with those prior to the First World War. The same calculations, the same misperceptions, the same fears and reactions are abroad in the 1980s as those which combined to send German troops on a 'pre-emptive strike' against France on the morning of August 14, 1914, precipitating devastation no one had imagined. The euphemisms then were only slightly different. The First Sea Lord, Admiral Fisher, talked of 'Copenhagening' the German fleet in its berths before it could challenge the Royal Navy. For 'Copenhagening' read 'first strike'. Admiral von Tirpitz talked of a 'zone of inferiority'; Caspar Weinberger talks of a 'window of vulnerability'. In 1914 the 'them' and 'us' mentality became dominant. 'Our' actions were justified by national interests; 'theirs' were not. Pressure grew to the point where any compromise was construed as humiliation. Somewhere in the sequence of steps that each government took to guarantee its 'national security', steps that seemed justified at the time, a watershed was crossed. As the slope got steeper, and the pace quickened, journalists made so many accommodations with government that they became part of the war process itself. In an aside to the editor of the *Manchester Guardian*, C. P. Scott, the wartime prime minister, David Lloyd George, said, 'If the public knew the truth, the war would end tomorrow. But they don't know and can't know.'[34]

'The Truth Game' traced the history of the nuclear arms race at two levels: that of 'official truth' and 'unofficial truth'. The history of nuclear weapons was a history of the exercise of secrecy, of keeping information not from an enemy but from the people the weapons were meant to 'defend'. The few journalists who had tried to draw out this information at the beginning became the objects of smear. In 1945, Wilfred Burchett, then of the London *Daily Express*, was the first Western correspondent to reach Hiroshima after the atomic bombing. While American public relations officers were shepherding his colleagues to the formal surrender ceremonies on board the USS *Missouri*, Burchett was on a perilous train journey to Hiroshima. After persuading the Japanese secret police not to shoot him, Burchett inspected the city's two remaining hospitals. He told me, 'The deputy head of the hospital, Dr Katsubi, explained to me, "We don't know what we're dealing with." People come in, the symptoms are of dizziness, internal haemorrhage, diarrhoea, and then later there are spots and before death the hair falls out and there is bleeding from the nose.'[35]

Burchett described this in his *Daily Express* dispatches as an 'Atomic plague'. It was the effects of radiation, a phenomenon of the nuclear era. The occupation authorities denied his reports. A military spokesman said that people had died only as a result of the blast, itself a historic lie. Nevertheless this 'official truth' was widely accepted and given credence in the Western Press. The *New York Times* published a report with the headline, 'NO RADIOACTIVITY IN HIROSHIMA RUIN'.[36] The writer W. H. Lawrence quoted Brigadier General Thomas Farrell as denying 'categorically' the presence of radioactivity. Wilfred Burchett had his press accreditation withdrawn and was issued with an expulsion order from Japan, which was later rescinded. Strict censorship was introduced. The hospitals Burchett had visited were declared out of bounds to the guided press party which followed in the wake of his reports. Japanese film shot in the hospitals was confiscated and shipped to Washington where it was classified secret and not released until 1968. American film shot shortly afterwards at Nagasaki was also classified and has still not been shown in its entirety.

'The Truth Game' took eighteen months to make. All but one of our requests to the Ministry of Defence for filming facilities and interviews were refused. Ian McDonald, the ministry's public relations man who later became famous as the spokesman, or speaking clock, of the Falklands war, arranged for me to have a 'non-attributable' interview with a ministry boffin. McDonald met David Munro, researcher Nicholas Claxton and me at reception and the conversation that followed was entirely about how you cook duck. The boffin told us nothing we had not read in the newspapers; but so secret was this encounter that it ended with McDonald saying, 'You realise none of this happened.' However, he did offer us twenty-year-old film of a Polaris submarine. When we asked for something more current, a Navy PR man interrupted, 'Oh come on, the public will never know the difference.'

The 'rough cut' of 'The Truth Game' was seen at various stages of production by executives of Central Television, who agreed that its subject matter and interviews were so important that the film should run to an hour and a half in a peak evening 'slot'. 'The Truth Game' adhered to the IBA's 'personal view' guidelines. Moreover, the majority of its witnesses were establishment figures, including the former Pentagon chief scientist Dr Herbert York and Paul Warnke. I also interviewed Caspar Weinberger, and this was used uninterrupted and uncut.

On September 24, 1982, 'The Truth Game' was viewed by David Glencross, then Deputy Director of Television of the IBA. Glencross has since risen to Director, a position of considerable power in British television. He is accountable only to a politically appointed IBA board of the great and good, and not in any way to the broadcasters whose work he and his officers scrutinise and 'pass' or 'fail', often on the basis of guidelines which they have written. Neither is he accountable to the viewing public, although he would argue that the IBA is merely an instrument of the Broadcasting Act, itself a creation of Parliament. David Glencross is commercial television's chief censor.

After the viewing he made two comments, both of them related to Hiroshima. Historians 'knew', he said, that the atomic bomb was not dropped for experimental reasons. He offered no evidence in support of his assertion. In any event, he said to us, 'when I was growing up we believed the Japanese had got what they deserved'.

On October 5 Charles Denton, Central's director of programmes, saw a 'rough cut' of the film and approved it. Transmission date was set for November 23. At nine o'clock on November 4 the full board of the IBA viewed 'The Truth Game' on David Glencross's recommendation; it was, he said, 'out of my hands'. At noon the film was taken out of the television schedules and a promotional article in *TV Times* was cancelled. That afternoon an IBA press release launched a new euphemism. 'The Truth Game' would not be shown, it said, until a 'complementary programme' was made.

IBA officials attempted to explain that a 'complementary film' was *not* a 'balancing film'. It was merely an extension of the 'debate' to which 'The Truth Game' had made a 'valuable contribution'. But this did not square with guidance given to journalist Max Hastings, who, along with the Bishop of London and others of pro-Bomb persuasion, had been canvassed to make the 'complementary film'. According to Hastings, the IBA had not asked him to contribute to a 'debate', but wanted a point-by-point rebuttal of 'The Truth Game'. Hastings said that if this had gone ahead, 'I think [the IBA] would have made themselves look ridiculous in a film which said, "And in the 14th minute, Pilger said Blah, blah, blah".' This, Hastings told Glencross, would be 'unwatchable television'. Instead he proposed a film which would see that the IBA did not look ridiculous. His film would be 'sensible'; it would argue the government's case, with mild reservations about American leadership and some criticism of the government's tactical handling of the Cruise issue. 'I got them off the hook,' said Hastings.[37]

The result, entitled 'The War about Peace', was mostly interviews with government spokesmen on both sides of the Atlantic. Its overall effect was reassuring, to which its visual effects offered no small contribution. A Polaris submarine slid silently, gracefully through the water over which classical music played. Hastings himself addressed the camera while stroking a sleek mock-up of a Trident missile.

The IBA was delighted with Hastings's film which David Glencross described as indeed 'sensible' and 'adult'. In the meantime, the controversy over the delay of 'The Truth Game' guaranteed its stereotyping as a 'committed' and 'unilateralist' view which needed to be balanced by a 'sensible multilateralist' view. Such caricaturing can be effective and words like 'multilateralist' and 'unilateralist' serve to cloak the real conflict between unilateral *armers*, like the British government, and disarmers of many varieties, from the American nuclear freeze lobby in the United States to the Campaign for Nuclear Disarmament in Britain.

By the time the two programmes were transmitted they had been trivialised into a gladiatorial contest between Max Hastings and me. Herbert Kretzmer wrote in the *Daily Mail*, 'Max Hastings versus John Pilger – the decision has to go to Max Hastings on points!'[38] A charade such as that which enveloped 'The Truth Game' has a significant, chastening effect within the industry. Max Hastings said later that he did not believe 'that particular situation will be repeated', and I agree with him.[39] No ITV company will want to make another 'Truth Game', knowing that it will have to spend more than £100,000 making a 'complementary' programme while putting at risk its substantial investment in the first programme should it prove impossible to fill the 'empty chair' as part of a facile exercise in balance. Such an affair also subdues programme makers who might otherwise resist and it causes programme managers to believe that by placating government and its allies 'in these difficult times' they are somehow ensuring the survival of public broadcasting. They are wrong. And even if they are right, the price is too high to pay, for silence is contagious.

For some television people deference to institutional authority, and to the government itself during the Thatcher years, has been a conscious process, the way to pursue their careers. For others, it has been the outcome of a sequence of events and lost opportunities in which they have seen themselves as helpless before the onrush of 'reality'. They include people who once propagated liberal ideas and argued, indeed fought, for television to be 'opened up', and who now remain silent as they pursue the very goals they condemned.

There is a myth that many of these people are or were of radical mind, and it is true that during the 1960s a group used to delight in proclaiming their membership of such organisations as the International Socialists; but once that trend had passed and career and dilettantism seemed attractive alternatives, these faded subversives were secured in open-plan offices with hot line telephones. However, the radical or left-wing myth persists, leading to claims by the truly paranoid that television is one quivering Red plot. For example, in 1985 freelance Red-catcher Chapman Pincher wrote that television producers and writers are 'most often the victims of contacts whom they trust but who are Soviet-inclined agents of influence such as left-wing politicians'. Well, who are these agents and their victims? 'The laws of libel', wrote Pincher, 'make it difficult for some of the most blatant to be named.'[40] Indeed, the laws of libel are a problem when nonsense has to be substantiated as truth. This is not to deny that there is a strong humanist streak through television, although it is is not necessarily 'left wing'. Presumably some Tories regard themselves as humanists. Before Thatcher, most of them did.

The most radical period in television was the 1960s, and it is significant that it was then that 'The War Game' was banned. Peter Watkins made an interesting observation about the nature of this 'radicalism' when he described

> . . . the liberal repression which has been emerging as a phenomenon on TV over the past fifteen years . . . and that what one has to fear is not only the conservatism and political timidity at the managerial level, but a particular kind of jealousy [of commitment] that cuts in from the ranks of one's own radical colleagues . . . Using the names of 'quality' and 'professionalism' and 'objectivity' and 'standard' the middle echelon of television are now exercising a repression which is even more severe than that of the political bosses who they like to claim are responsible, but in fact whose only guilt often is that they (the bosses) provide an excuse, or a front, for the middle echelon to carry out a wave of censorship and self-censorship unparalleled since the inception of public television broadcasting. The result: the personal, subjective, committed, individual programme or film making is being openly stamped out in the name of, and for the sake of 'authoritative' and 'objective' programming.[41]

Watkins's 'War Game' was eventually shown in July 1985, during a BBC 'week' to commemorate the fortieth anniversary of the destruction of Hiroshima and Nagasaki. The opening programme was a documentary about Group Captain Leonard Cheshire's 'return journey' to Nagasaki which, as Britain's observer, he had watched being destroyed from the air. This made him an accessory, according to many people in Nagasaki, who were offended by his anniversary trip and asked him to stay away from their memorial service. Moreover, he sought to justify the bombing. This programme was shown on BBC1 at a peak viewing time. 'The War Game' was introduced by Ludovic Kennedy, who said it had been kept off the screens all these years because it was 'too shocking and too disturbing to transmit'. He made no mention of the true reason. 'The War Game' was shown on BBC2 to a minority viewing audience. The next day there was the repeat of a dramatisation of a nuclear attack on Sheffield, entitled 'Threads'. The British prime minister in 'Threads' spoke about 'reckless Soviet actions'. The American president called for a joint Soviet/American withdrawal from the flashpoint, Iran. It was clear that the Western allies had tried their best to avert war; the Soviets, of course, fired the first nuclear missile. Like the Cheshire film, 'Threads' was shown to BBC1's majority viewing audience.

It was significant that Mrs Thatcher did not like the BBC's commemorative week. She regarded it as unbalanced and said so in Parliament. Clearly, she had come to expect a higher standard of 'objectivity' in matters of vital national interest. The television coverage of the Falklands war had set such a standard. During that small war both the BBC and ITN competed to demonstrate their patriotism, to be 'on side'. Giving evidence to the Parliamentary Defence Committee on the reporting of the Falklands war, ITN explained that its approach was to give a 'nightly offering of interesting, positive and heart-warming stories of achievement and collaboration born out of a sense of national purpose'. No mention was made of 'objectivity' or 'balance'.

Being 'on side' did not necessarily mean making statements of patriotism; it meant leaving things out and shifting the emphasis of the news. For instance, it is now clear that the Peruvian plan for a negotiated settlement with Argentina came close to success, certainly closer than the British public ever knew. On May 13, 1982, in 'News at Ten Falklands Extra' Edward Heath said:

> It is now appearing quite plainly in a statement from the Peruvian government that what the Argentines did was to suggest three amendments to the Peruvian proposals. Now this is negotiation. Personally, looking at those three amendments I find it very difficult to see how we could have rejected them.

Heath's criticism of the government's handling of the negotiations was ignored by the interviewer; and that interview was the only occasion on television news, ITN or BBC, that reference was made to the Argentine amendments and the British government having a case to answer on the failure of the Peruvian peace plan. According to an analysis by the Glasgow Media Group, in eighty-four TV news programmes between May 1 and May 15, 1982 only four references were made to interpretations of the negotiations which did not place blame on the Argentines for their failure.[42] Using the results of an opinion poll, ITN claimed that '70 per cent [of the public] want to launch an invasion'. But, as Greg Philo has pointed out, the same poll showed 76 per cent of those questioned wanting the United Nations to occupy the Falklands while Britain and Argentina negotiated. This went totally unreported and the poll results were interpreted on the news as showing public opinion as 'hardening' and that 'more people are now prepared to accept British casualties'.[43]

The Falklands war gave the game away. Broadcasters who had defended their objectivity as 'a matter of record' were now almost truculent in their praise of their own subjectivity in the cause of Queen and Country as if the war was a national emergency, which of course it was not. If they had any complaint it was that they had not been allowed sufficient freedom to win the 'propaganda war', as several of them described it. Alan Protheroe, who had proclaimed that the BBC would 'tell the truth without suppression or distortion', chaired the Weekly Review Board during the war. The minutes of these meetings show that the BBC had decided that its reporting of the war was to be shaped to suit 'the emotional sensibilities of the public', and that the weight of BBC coverage would be concerned with government statements of policy and that an impartial style was felt to be 'an unnecessary irritation'.[44]

Even when the war was won and the excuse of withholding news and analysis so as not to give comfort to an enemy or to endanger lives no longer applied, the truth did not burst or even trickle forth. It is difficult to forget a post-war BBC extravaganza called 'Task Force South', billed as a documentary special. It opened with Richard Baker describing the iniquities of Argentine propaganda ('a class of its own') and it had Admiral 'Sandy' Woodward playing Jack Hawkins ('I'm not for blowing people's heads off. Equally, as a military man, if my job is to start blowing heads off, I'll do it in the most effective and efficient way possible'). There was Brian Hanrahan losing his beard on the voyage south and limbering up for counting them out and counting them in ('It was time to start learning about the hardware of war') and there were marines saying hello to their mums and to their dogs and singing, 'We're all going on a summer holiday' followed by 'Rule Britannia!' Finally, there were magnificent funeral sequences in the pale winter sunlight, dominated by the Union Jack and by tired, but supremely fit-looking young men. There were no bodies on show, no bits of scalp and brain and severed legs. The enemy was merely the 'Argies', beaten and stupid. There was nothing about the results of the waves of British cluster bombing. There was nothing about the implications of the war for the British economy and the commitment of national resources in order to maintain the islands as a 'fortress'. As Albert Hunt so drily noted in *New Society*, the BBC's documentary special was, like the pursuit of the war itself, 'a continuation of British Second World War movies by other means'.[45]

It seems no coincidence that the two outstanding innovative talents to emerge in British television during the past twenty-five years, Peter Watkins and Ken Loach, have had to struggle to have their work shown. Whereas the banning of 'The War Game' became a *cause célèbre*, the banning of Ken Loach's series *Questions of Leadership* was a Kafkaesque affair. Loach's distinction as a film-maker goes back to the 1960s when his 'Cathy Come Home' crystallised the desperate situation of homeless families in Britain. His other films include 'Up the Junction', 'Family Life', 'Days of Hope' and 'The Price of Coal'. In 1981 he was asked by the embryonic Channel 4 to make a series of films about the trade unions. The commissioning company, Central Television, agreed to four 55-minute films and these were shot in the summer of 1982. Loach was told by Central executives that they were delighted with the result and there was no reason to expect 'trouble'.

To understand the power of Loach's films to disturb and contradict the 'consensus view', and the 'trouble' that awaited him, one need only consider the opening sequence of *Questions of Leadership*. Over archive film of a mass meeting of trade unionists during the 1930s Depression the sound-track begins to play the chorus from Gilbert and Sullivan's *Iolanthe*:

> Bow low ye lower middle classes;
> Bow, bow ye tradesmen;
> Bow ye masses . . .

As the mockery continues, the pictures dissolve to a parade of earnest young men, standing on platforms, exhorting the masses. Then they grow older, florid, comfortable and become portraits of self-satisfaction, dressed in the ermine of the House of Lords. They are Joe Gormley, Vic Feather, Richard Marsh, all former trade union leaders. The commentary, honed with irony, says, 'There are some trades union leaders who are so prosperous that they have in their own person achieved the harmony of the classes'.

Throughout the Loach films, rank and file trade unionists speak about democracy within the large and powerful unions, such as the electricians' and the engineers', then the preserves of Frank Chapple and Terry Duffy. They complain about 'small bureaucratic, centralised groups of people who have a disciplined, well organised stratum within the organisation that prevents individual members from playing a role within the policy of the union, the rule changes within the union and the general direction in which the union is going'. Are not those the familiar words of right-wingers complaining about 'militants' infiltrating their 'democratic' institutions? Yes, but in Loach's films they come from ordinary trade unionists analysing the undemocratic hold of the trade union establishment on the organisations and fortunes of millions of working people. The films demonstrate how the leadership not only works against the interests of the members but collaborates with a government determined to circumscribe shop-floor power and to subordinate the workforce. Nothing like this perspective of the trade unions had been seen in a sustained form on television.

When David Glencross saw the Loach programmes in the summer of 1983 he said they were in breach of the Broadcasting Act. He said that as the union leadership had been criticised, there would have to be 'balancing material'. Loach pointed out that Frank Chapple had been given the opportunity to state his side and had walked out on an interview. (One of the films showed him walking out.) In any case, argued Loach, the trade union leadership enjoyed so much access to television that his films *were the balance*. But Glencross was adamant, and Loach reluctantly agreed that one of the four programmes be dropped. Channel 4 would commission another company to make a half-hour 'balancing' programme to back on to each of the three Loach programmes and yet another, longer programme would be made to 'balance' what had already been 'balanced'. Such a convoluted arrangement is, of course, in the nature of censorship.

By Christmas 1983 Loach was given a new ultimatum. He would have to cut his three programmes down to two, and each would be followed by thirty minutes of 'balancing material'. Central Television, which had made the Loach films, now would have to make 'balancing' programmes in which the union leadership would appear. However, Frank Chapple, Alex Kitson and others made it clear they would not take part, creating a Catch-22 situation known as 'the empty chair'. For his part Glencross denied vehemently that the union leaders had a right of veto. He said he was confident the programmes would be shown. Channel 4's Controller of Programmes, Paul Bonner, wrote to Ken Loach to reassure him that the Chief Executive, Jeremy Isaacs, 'is resolutely in agreement with you that censorship by non-appearance is unacceptable'.[46]

Every major decision concerning Loach's films was taken in secret; delay and prevarication were common. While Loach worried that industrial disputes he had highlighted in the films were becoming dated, the source of the delays eluded him. Finally, it seemed, it was agreed that a panel of MPs would replace the union leaders in a 'balancing discussion'. This discussion was filmed on April 5, 1984, but still no transmission date was scheduled. So who was stalling now? Ken Loach wrote in the *Guardian*:

> Censorship is not achieved by an outright ban, but by bureaucratic manoeuvres. No one has formally banned any one of the films. Yet they remain unseen. [The films] touched the most sensitive nerve in the current political arena. [The government's strategy] means allowing unemployment to rise, legislating against trades unions and relying on union leaders to prevent any serious challenge to the government . . . [47]

The chairman of the board of the IBA is George Thomson, or Lord Thomson of Monifieth, and the chairman of the board of Channel 4 is Edmund Dell. Both are former leading figures on the right wing of the Labour Party and both are former political associates of the trade union leaders in the films.

On April 17, 1984 Ken Loach and representatives of Central Television saw a leading Queen's Counsel. The films had already been scrutinised by a firm of solicitors expert in defamation cases, the interviewees had been seen, statements and documents had been checked. The Queen's Counsel is a specialist in libel and during the meeting with him it emerged that one cut should be made. Loach made the cut and was assured that the films were now cleared of all remaining obstacles. On July 31, 1984 Central Television issued the following statement:

> The Board of Central has been advised that the programmes 'Questions of Leadership' are defamatory and would have no adequate defence in law. The Board regrets that these programmes cannot, therefore, be offered to Channel 4 for transmission as originally planned.

To many miners on strike during 1984 and 1985 television took on a distinctly 'Falklands' role, with themselves cast as the 'Argies'. Of course the views of striking miners were heard, though generally in the context of television news which, with the honourable exception of Channel 4 news, devoted itself to dramatic scenes of picket-line disturbance. These scenes were filmed mostly from behind police lines, and so who was responsible for the disturbance was often unclear. When asked why they did not film from the other side of picket lines, television crews expressed understandable fears for their own safety. But what was not explained was why crews crossed sides as a matter of professional routine in more dangerous situations abroad, such as Beirut, where they are targets.

When the strike was over, the National Council for Civil Liberties produced a report on the role of the police. The NCCL had, incidentally, stood fast for the right of working miners not to strike. The report said that 'contrary to the impression inevitably created by the media, most of the picketing during the strike has been orderly and on a modest scale'.[48] But what distinguished the television coverage of the longest industrial upheaval in Britain this century was a familiar set of potent assumptions. At the Edinburgh television festival in August 1984 one of the speakers in a debate on the coverage of the strike, Martin Adeny, industrial editor of BBC news, described trucks bringing coal to a steelworks as having made a 'successful run'. It was, of course, a successful run if you were on the side of the National Coal Board, not a successful run if you were a striking miner.

These assumptions are hardly surprising when television is structured to represent one side in a 'them' and 'us' society and the subject of work, its conditions and meaning to people's lives, is related to the 'them' category and relegated to archival film and nostalgia. As Jeremy Isaacs, chief executive of Channel 4, confirmed, 'Work is the great unreported subject on British television over the past twenty years.'[49] So, too, is poverty, which is associated with so many working lives. Today there may be as many as 18 million people, or more than a quarter of the population, living on or below the poverty line. They include more than a quarter of all children, some 3.7 million. The number of people living in poverty increased by a quarter between 1971 and 1981 and the number of children in poverty increased by 90 per cent.[50] As unemployment grows and trade unionism is emasculated and its compliance with government assured, the British workforce is becoming increasingly female and unskilled and in or near the 'poverty trap'. In other words, the largest category of poor people is that of people *at work*.

As the Thatcher government has effectively scuttled this quarter of the British population, so too, it seems, has television, with honourable exceptions (such as the two most innovative companies in documentaries, Central Television and Yorkshire Television). Why? Is it because 'the people who are thinking interesting things are on the radical right', as one senior television executive has said? Or is it because a true reflection of the vandalism of many lives, plus a glimpse into the future of many other lives, might have a 'significant effect on public attitudes', to quote Lord Normanbrook on 'The War Game'. As Peter Golding asked in the *New Statesman*:

> Since the heroic days of Cathy Come Home, what has happened to the one medium able to translate the grand scale of isolated privations into the public drama of common experience? Where are the dramatic explorations of the growing schism between comfortable and poor in contemporary Britain? Of course there are honourable exceptions: Bleasdale's Boys from the Blackstuff, Loach and Garnett's Spongers . . . But television drama has become all upstairs and no downstairs, a wholesale abandonment of any attempt to engage with the social calamity of Thatcher's Britain.[51]

There are television programmes about unemployment, and ITN lights up its jobs lost-and-found map once a week; but it is a rare programme that captures the impact of poverty and dares to place it in its proper political context. To those of us who are not poor, 'modernised' poverty can be disguised and isolated in enclaves where outsiders seldom go and which are beyond the reach of Reithian notions of impartiality and balance. How can the 'impartial' camera possibly describe the shredding of spirit, the loss of self-esteem, the frustration and rage not articulated by the unemployed and the impoverished employed who are forced to watch their possessions borne away by bailiffs? How can 'impartial' television news, so enamoured with dramatic pictures, represent the uprisings in English inner cities in terms other than racial, when the truth is that the issue of race serves as a distraction, that the street battles have largely been between ordinary, angry people and policemen pushed into the front line? When does television tell us that the problems are scarcely racial at all and that black people just happen to be at the dirtiest end of an authoritarian stick being wielded across racial lines?

Television is changing fast. On the majority-audience channels schedules have been revised so that 'light entertainment' is dominant. Among the soaps, the anodyne sitcoms, the cowboys-and-Indians in a variety of disguises and the routine violence, the new prince of British television is the 'game show'. This type of entertainment, says the BBC's head of variety, James Moir, 'will not employ creative writers. It will not expand our talent base by employing artists and performers in any significant way . . . it will, of course, work for television. But at what price? The price is to permit the Americanisation of a significant proportion of what is produced, in tone, in style and in the name of the popular audience. I venture to say the price is not right; the price is far too high.'[52]

The advance of such 'light entertainment' coincides with the orderly retreat of peak-hour mass-audience journalism, for which British television used to be renowned. The successors to *Tonight* and *24 Hours* have long ago gone to the minority-audience second channel. *Newsweek* and its successor, *People and Power*, have been killed off, along with *Platform One* and *Saturday Briefing*. *The Money Programme* struggles for a budget to allow it to be shown all year round. *Panorama* has been pushed to the end of the news. Most ITV documentaries are now shown at 10.30 or later when most of the viewing audience are said to be in bed or on their way there, although at the time of writing there are encouraging moves by Central Television to bring back the 9 o'clock slot. Certainly, this is 'what the public wants'. According to a MORI survey, more than 55 per cent of the public want news and documentaries and only 35 per cent want quiz shows. 'Royal events', which news editors believe to be close to the hearts of most viewers, hold an attraction for only 22 per cent of the public.[53]

In recent years it has become practice for the IBA to demand that the independent companies and Channel 4 show 'controversial' programmes to vested interests before the public is allowed to see them. This arose partly as a result of a case brought by Mary Whitehouse in the High Court, in April 1984, over a film about Borstals, called *Scum*, which she said she found shocking. The judge ruled that in future the entire board of the IBA would preview and approve all such programmes before they are shown. This led to injunctions against television companies by corporations and governments featured in controversial programmes. It meant that ITV factual programmes were prone to courtroom battles before they were shown.

Before a *World in Action* programme about Oman was completed, lawyers acting for the Omani regime took the IBA to court alleging that the programme 'might be unfair' – even though the regime had refused to allow television cameras into Oman or to answer questions on film. The court granted the injunction and ordered the IBA board to 'vet' the programme. However, the court ruling was less significant than the nature of the IBA's vetting. Even after lawyers had approved the programme, the IBA ordered material linking Mrs Thatcher and the Trafalgar House company, then owners of the *Daily Express*, removed from the film. The censored material gave details of how Trafalgar House had given £40,000 to Conservative Party funds before Mrs Thatcher came to power, how the *Express* had campaigned vigorously for Mrs Thatcher's election, how Mrs Thatcher had subsequently given Lord Matthews his peerage, how a celebration lunch on the day of her 1979 victory was organised by Trafalgar House at the Ritz Hotel, which is owned by the company. All this was true; none of it was libellous.

The IBA did not publicly disclose that it had ordered sections of the programme dealing with Mrs Thatcher to be cut. According to the *Observer*, the IBA 'refused to give reasons beyond saying that the excised material was not considered impartial'.[54] Such a transparent act of censorship to protect the political interests of the prime minister ought not to be repeated if the IBA adheres to the spirit of an Appeal Court decision which overturned the original ruling on the *Scum* case. The Court, wrote Geoffrey Robertson, 'paves the way for the IBA to adopt a less interventionist role in television programming' and makes unnecessary 'the line-by-line scrutiny of certain current affairs programmes'.[55]

These events may well have been in Denis Forman's mind when he addressed the 1984 Edinburgh television festival. Chairman of Granada Television and (with David Plowright) keeper of Granada's tradition of challenging censors, Forman said:

> In the 1960s we were confident that we were holding our ground in the endless struggle against censorship and repression. We were wrong: during the last decade the opposing forces have made great advances . . . The protection of government information has become undiscriminating and obsessional, with the resulting suspicion that frequently the motive is not so much to protect the security of the state as the political comfort of ministers.[56]

Unless the whole question of censorship is addressed – direct, indirect and self-imposed censorship – and venerable myths are challenged and structures are changed, the majority channels may quietly discard their last fig leaves. For example, in spite of the Appeal Court judgment, the IBA's censorious impulses show no sign of waning. Therefore the most pressing reform in commercial television must be the IBA, which was never intended to be a censoring body, nor to adopt its present over-legalistic role. This was made clear by the Annan Committee on the Future of Television in 1977. As Geoffrey Robertson has pointed out:

> Annan deplored the fetters on initiative and imagination caused by IBA meddling with programmes prior to broadcast. It recommended that the Authority should intervene only when it had good reason to believe that its policy was being flouted. Post-censorship should replace pre-censorship . . . The ultimate sanction – loss of licence – would be sufficient to ensure that television companies did not repeatedly outrage public feeling.[57]

My own view is that the IBA ought to be disbanded, or at least relegated to its rightful place overseeing such matters as the factual content and frequency of advertisements. If there are to be IBA guidelines at all, these ought to be the result of democratic discussion inside and outside the industry. The day of the nannying 'quangoes' of the 'great and good', be they unelected BBC governors or IBA board members, are past. That a civil servant should hold secret sway in one form or another over the destinies of programmes seems to me ridiculous in a mature broadcasting service. Parliament needs to rewrite the 1981 Broadcasting Act and to provide for an elected public complaints body comprised equally of members of the industry and members of the public; and that does not mean the great and good by divine right. And unlike the Press Council, it ought to have teeth and the resources to make its own speedy professional enquiries. This could serve both ITV and the BBC.

At the BBC those occupying places of public power and trust on the sixth floor of Television Centre ought to be elected by all members of the Corporation. They might even campaign for office, as politicians do, for their power is indeed political, and they could be held to their promises as politicians ought to be. Indeed, freedom of speech, glimpsed at the BBC during the 1960s, could be implicit in the manifestos of those who might seek to replace for ever the unaccountable legatees of Lord Reith's accommodations with officialdom and to create a genuine public broadcasting service before it is hijacked by a new generation of game show zealots. And why does the BBC have to compete for 'ratings-approval' in every field? As Anthony Smith has suggested, a leaner BBC 'could offer us its independence of operation as the chief return on our annual investment in the licence fee; the larger the increase it demands the more politically vulnerable it renders itself'.[58] Surely, if programme makers and managers agree with Denis Forman that the forces of censorship have indeed made 'great advances' and that reforms are necessary, then at the very least let us begin seriously to debate them with the public. What was remarkable about Forman's warning was that it was rare.

42

'You write. We publish'

Newspapers serve their noblest purpose when they are popular news-papers. A newspaper which is read by just a few of the so-called influential figures of the establishment is like an inter-departmental memorandum of the élite. It is a bloodless thing. Newspapers are also about crusading. They are part of people's lives. That is what the great popular newspapers were in the past and should be now.

A. J. P. Taylor, July 1984

At the time of writing, in February 1986, the television news showed journalists alighting from a Rupert Murdoch company bus at Wapping in East London. They moved forward to show security guards their new identification cards on which they were described as 'consultants'. They passed through ten-foot electronically operated steel gates, in spiked walls topped with coils of barbed razor wire. Several tried to hurry inside without running; they squinted into searchlights covering the perimeter of their new workplace. They were journalists of *The Times*, the *Sunday Times*, the *Sun* and the *News of the World* who, between them, commanded the greatest newspaper readership in the English language. They had been ordered to go to Wapping or be sacked. They had not been consulted; and all their agreements with the management had been dishonoured. On the news they appeared like so many Pinocchios, driven to a magic place where the hated print workers and their 'restrictive practices' were finally extinct, where shining new 'direct input' and 'user friendly' machines stood ready, where there was the promise of more money and a private health-care scheme. As Pinocchio's nose and ears grew, the longer he remained on his magic island, so at Fortress Wapping the heads of some journalists had noticeably bowed as they came and went. Others admitted to depression and to rising cynicism, to a feeling, as one of them said, 'of defeat and loss'.[59] This was a strange attitude in those embracing what their proprietor viewed as a new freedom of the Press.

For many, no sense of defeat and loss would be evident; for the move behind the razor wire at Wapping was merely the latest step in a process which had less to do with technological change than with the sickening of press freedom in Britain. Some will argue that death is imminent. Not only is Fleet Street itself physically dying, but traditional Grub Street is going too. Among the raucous, the mischievous, the decorously sentimental and the naming-of-guilty-men there was always a certain humanity. That certainly has gone.

This is not to suggest that the Press was ever truly 'free'. The structure of the British Press has always prevented that. There is simply another kind of Press now, a new spirit which is reflected more obviously in the tabloids but is shared by those so-called quality newspapers produced under the same roof by the same owner and for the same aims.

For the meaning of these changes we must first go back to 1969 when the International Publishing Corporation, then owners of the *Daily Mirror*, sold the title of the *Sun* to Rupert Murdoch. The subsequent development of Murdoch's *Sun* is much misunderstood. Contrary to Fleet Street lore, Murdoch did not set about plagiarising the successful post-war *Mirror*. His new *Sun* mined none of the *Mirror*'s political populism, which was founded on its benevolence: its sympathy for the ordinary person and its crusading tradition.

The *Sun* was a new invention, a hybrid. At a glance it looked like a tabloid newspaper, even at times like the *Mirror*; but most of its content was drawn from the past: from the English 'penny dreadful' and the American 'yellowback', whose tales of shock and horror were thought to have expired with the death of *John Bull* in the 1960s and *Reveille* in the 1970s. The new *Sun* dressed up the lurid to look like news, added sexism, racism, violence and the kind of moral indignation reminiscent of the 'hate organs' of the 1920s. Initially, critics of the *Sun* dismissed it as merely a comic. But it was much more. As the 1970s progressed, the *Sun* became, as Jeremy Seabrook has argued, 'intensely ideological' and presented a 'positive, coherent world view' of society in the latter part of the decade and beyond.[60] This of course is the society of the Thatcher Revolution, or the *Sun* version of it, in which you stand on your own two feet and pull yourself up by your bootstraps and trust nobody, except Lady Luck. Money is all that matters, not to mention fun, such as looking on at misfortune, sex and violence, especially violence. And those who oppose this society are 'loony'; Mrs Thatcher has said as much.

In the 1980s the *Sun* performs a state functionary service with great professional skill; for all the extremism it expresses overtly, such as in its leader page tirades, it is the *Sun*'s covert message which is the most powerful and, above all, anti-human. There are myriad examples: the racism, the pillorying of powerless people, the gloating over dead Argentine sailors, the 'world exclusive' fabrication of an interview with the widow of a Victoria Cross winner,[61] the daily subversion of the most fundamental news values. In this way information is distorted and denied with impunity, which is dissimilar only in style to the part played by the Press in Eastern Europe. Repeated censure by the Press Council and libel actions have had little effect; and the infection has spread to the point where the British Press now displays, according to Harold Evans, former editor of the *Sunday Times* and *The Times*, 'more political bias and plain dishonesty than at any time in the last forty years'.[62] These sentiments were echoed by Jack Jones, former leader of the Transport and General Workers' Union and a man not given to hyperbole, when he warned that a 'new wave of Goebbels-type methods is beginning to spread in our country'.[63] All of this is what I would call anti-journalism.

The *Sun* and the *News of the World* are giving Rupert Murdoch the profits with which he plans to start an American television network and to beam direct satellite television to Britain. His 'dream' is said to be a 'world newspaper'. Whether or not this is so, Murdoch's manifest desire for more and more control over information channels in the Western world makes nonsense of the current worship of 'new technology' simply as progress. Technology, never neutral, is always the tool of the controlling power. Of course the 'direct input' terminals at Fortress Wapping are capable of expedient wonders and of course they *are* part of the future, but the way they have been imposed on people is part of a demoralising and dehumanising process in a country where millions of citizens have been forced into unemployment and the single capital asset of millions of others, their skill, has been declared expendable. The correlation of this is the impoverishment of up to 18 million people, or more than a quarter of the British population.[64]

This mass impoverishment, the most urgent issue in Britain for a generation, occupies little space in the Press most people read. This is hardly surprising. In 1986, three conglomerates control 90 per cent of the 18 million Sunday newspapers and 75 per cent of the 15 million daily newspapers in Britain, and two men, Rupert Murdoch and Robert Maxwell, between them exercise personal control over the majority.

None of this ought to be confused with genuine popular journalism. I agree wholeheartedly with A. J. P. Taylor's sentiment that 'newspapers serve their noblest purpose when they are popular newspapers'.[65] Indeed, that quotation is from an article about the *Daily Mirror*, for which, until recently, I worked for most of my adult life. The article was nostalgic, which itself says a great deal, for it is the decline of the *Mirror*, once the greatest-selling newspaper in the Western world and the only mass-circulation paper to offer consistent political dissent in Britain, that most demonstrates the erosion of press freedom, and other freedoms. When Maurice Edelman wrote, 'The history of the *Daily Mirror* is the history of our times'[66] he was exaggerating, though not by much.

Edelman wrote his history of the *Mirror* in the mid-1960s when there was a great deal of hope and expectation in Britain, which the *Mirror* reflected. Throughout the 1960s the *Mirror* had been changing perhaps as no British popular newspaper had tried to or wanted to or dared to; from Harry Guy Bartholomew's brash and crusading paper was emerging a new *Mirror*, still brash, but now beginning to analyse the world about it. It was as if for the first time a map of the world was spread before many readers of the *Mirror*, who in 1964 were estimated at some 14 million, or about a quarter of the British population.

During the political upheavals of the late 1960s – Paris, Prague, Chicago, Saigon – the coverage and presentation by the *Mirror*'s staff of major foreign events was frequently, in my view, more incisive than that of the 'quality' papers. And not only was the *Mirror* the newspaper of most working people but its readership included more so-called 'A' readers than the entire readership of *The Times*. According to a survey by the National Union of Students, the *Mirror* in 1968 was the most widely read national newspaper in the new redbrick universities, where class realignments, however minor, were taking place. This breadth of readership represented an achievement unprecedented in the history of the British Press. The *Mirror* had crossed class frontiers without deserting its roots: indeed, by reinforcing them. When the *Mirror* was named as 'Newspaper of the Year' for 1968, no paper deserved the recognition more than Hugh Cudlipp's 'great adventure', as he once described it. (Like the *Mirror*, its editor-in-chief had little time for false modesty.)

Under Cudlipp and the benign editorship of L. A. Lee Howard, the new *Mirror* encouraged its journalists to abandon what Dr Johnson called 'the tyranny of the stock response' and to try new approaches. Much of this enterprise fell to several young Cudlipp-bred executives, notably Tony Miles, an exceptionally skilled journalist who started 'Mirrorscope', a twice weekly four-page feature of background news, profiles and analysis, and Mike Molloy, whose graphics talent made him one of the finest tabloid designers in post-war Fleet Street.

These were exhilarating days for me. It was 1965; I had not long returned from two years in the North of England when I was summoned by Hugh Cudlipp and told to prepare a list of story ideas about young volunteers for a series called 'Youth in Action'. The prospect of writing about variations on the Scouts and Guides did not fill me with enthusiasm. However, in the *Mirror* library I discovered a remarkable organisation called Voluntary Service Overseas, begun by Alec Dickson, which sent volunteers throughout the world and on which President Kennedy based the American Peace Corps. With the aid of a *Daily Telegraph* map of the world I charted a journey that would take me across every continent, from Rio to Lake Titicaca in the Andes, from the islands of Polynesia to Papua, Laos, India, the Levant, Africa, and included almost everywhere in the world I wanted to go. I regarded the memorandum I sent the next day as little more than an exercise in the audacious and expected Welsh scorn in return. Instead, it came back with 'Yes!' scrawled on it. One year later I returned from my journeys, during which, in a series of dispatches, I was able to tell something about the nature of the political and economic divisions between rich and poor in the world, as seen through the eyes of young volunteers from all backgrounds in Britain. Certainly, that year helped to shape my own politics.

Thereafter I was assigned to write about apartheid in South Africa, the conflict in the Middle East, the revolution in Cuba, the rise of Japan as a manufacturing power and the unending war in Indo-China. I went to live and travel in the United States, to write about an America beyond Hollywood. In response to a cable I sent asking what I should do next, I got back the reply, 'YOU WRITE. WE PUBLISH.' That was a measure of the *Daily Mirror* then.

Hugh Cudlipp's encounter with Rupert Murdoch was a turning point for Fleet Street. Cudlipp knew well the rapacity of the Australian newspaper proprietors, the 'wild men of Sydney' like Frank Packer and Ezra Norton. But he did not understand the younger, colourless Murdoch, who seemed to offer little threat to Fleet Street's dinosaurs. That Murdoch had already established in Australia his own relentless style of newspaper management and takeover, which was aimed at and capable of taking over at least one Fleet Street title and destroying the *Daily Mirror* in the process, clearly was not a consideration when Cudlipp, as chairman of IPC, sold the title of the old, ailing *Sun* to him. Of course, hindsight is easy for those like myself who were not privy to the deliberations at the time; but it seemed as though, once Cudlipp saw a 'dummy' of the new *Sun*, he knew he had made a ghastly mistake.

This was evident during one forlorn night on the eve of the new *Sun*'s birth. Cudlipp had called about a dozen of us together for dinner at his favourite restaurant, the Ivy in Soho. There was Sidney Jacobson, former editor of the *Daily Herald* and the old *Sun* and now editorial director of the Mirror Group, Lee Howard, the *Mirror*'s editor, Marje Proops, Peter Wilson, Donald Zec, Tony Miles, myself and others. Lee Howard, who disliked such occasions, spoke briefly and dutifully about the *Sun* sinking without trace in a few months' time, then sat down looking decidedly unwell. Cudlipp's performance was vintage, but equally unconvincing in one respect and deeply convincing in another. He mocked 'the dirty digger', by listing the regular features the *Sun* had stolen from the *Mirror*: 'liveliest letters' from the *Mirror*'s 'live letters', a strip called Scarth similar to the *Mirror*'s Garth and, most contemptuous and wounding of all, the *Mirror*'s old masthead slogan, 'FORWARD WITH THE PEOPLE.' He went on to outline the *Sun*'s character and its potential, radical appeal in a climate of reaction and intolerance; the supreme journalist that Cudlipp was, he had unwittingly defined the threat which his scorn could not conceal. He had done it so well that when he had finished speaking there was no murmur of approval, just silence and foreboding. Lee Howard looked as if he was about to have cardiac arrest and his pallor represented the feelings of us all.

During the months that followed Cudlipp conducted a series of unhappy staff seminars in his ninth-floor suite during which he attempted, without success, to explain the undermining of his vision, which was now characterised by the nightly spectacle of an almost breathless wait on the editorial floor for the arrival of the first edition of the *Sun.*

As the columns of trivia and voyeurism (and, finally, bingo) in the *Mirror* increased, a vocabulary of justification was introduced. 'The readers' were constantly evoked. 'The readers' were no longer interested in real news and serious issues; 'the readers' cared only about doing the pools and the price of a pint of beer. 'Lively', 'fun' and 'frothy' were euphemisms employed to describe stories which were patronising junk, and in any case was not as 'good' as the *Sun*'s junk. Few had their heart in the changes, but at the same time few acknowledged that fighting Murdoch on his own low ground, then justifying it by saying that it was what the readers wanted, was a disaster; and the circulation continued to dive. In my view, more than any single factor it was this loss of faith in the readers, which derived from an eroding self-regard at the *Mirror*, that was the most grievous error. Somebody in charge had to decide whether the *Daily Mirror* was to be a popular newspaper or a popular comic, to retain its humanity or be a copy of the *Sun*. It was not possible to be anti-Thatcher *and* like the *Sun*; the two were incompatible. But nobody made that decision, and the *Mirror* deteriorated.

There were those who argued that it was too risky, in a suddenly volatile market, to reinforce those characteristics of the *Mirror* that seemed to be going against the grain of Murdoch's rapid success. I can sympathise with that viewpoint, because I know most of those who in good faith held it. But that does not alter the fact that the one option never consistently pursued at the *Mirror* was keeping the paper's nerve.

No one said, 'There is another way of seeing human affairs. The *Daily Mirror* can give a *different* vision of British society, which is not as the *Sun* portrays it.' The debate, such as it was, soon petered out, and an embarrassed silence hung in the editor's office whenever the issue was raised. As a consequence, many *Mirror* readers simply gave up reading any newspaper.

Whenever the *Mirror*'s nerve returned, the result was incomparable, such as the 'shock issues' on unemployment, class and the prospect of nuclear war. In 1979 only the *Mirror* could have devoted eight pages to a report from faraway Cambodia and cause an almost immediate humanitarian and political effect, as well as increase the paper's readership on the day of publication.

Other strengths remained: the treatment of staff, for one, and the support given to journalists like myself and Paul Foot who not in-frequently attracted establishment wrath and smear. For example, in 1982 a Thai government official accused me and the author of a United Nations report on child labour in Thailand of fabricating the case of one child. This was later proved to be a lie and a frame-up, and the *Mirror* backed me all the way in what could have been a very expensive libel action.[67] Over a period of almost two years the United Kingdom Atomic Energy Commission and the Central Electricity Generating Board sought to discredit articles of mine about the dangers of radiation leaks at the nuclear plant at Windscale in Cumbria (now Sellafield) and at Three Mile Island in the United States. Those were days when the nuclear establishment in Britain would blithely mount expensive, strident public relations campaigns to 'prove' the safety of their product. Since then, Sellafield's leaks have become so numerous that the plant has rightly fallen into public disrepute, and its operators prosecuted and fined for putting the public at risk.[68]

In 1983 the *Mirror*'s fortunes began to improve. Not only was circulation gaining, but there was the prospect of a new kind of ownership which might guarantee the independence of the paper for many years. The chief executive of the Abbey National Building Society, Clive Thornton, was appointed chairman of the Mirror Group with a brief from the owners, Reed International, to prepare the company for flotation on the stock market the following summer. Thornton was an interesting maverick who had grown up in poverty on Tyneside. He had left school at fourteen and become a solicitor the hard way. While at the Abbey National he was credited with breaking the building societies' cartel and financing inner city housing. Certainly, I shall remember his time at the *Mirror* as a return to the freedom to work that had characterised the paper's best days.

Thornton, like the rest of us, had a straightforward commitment from

the Reed chairman, Sir Alex Jarratt. This is Reed's press release dated
October 13, 1983 and signed by Jarratt:

> The Reed International Board has decided to realise its investment
> in Mirror Group Newspapers by making an offer of sale to the public.
> It is not seeking, nor will it seek, offers for Mirror Group which
> would result in its coming under the control of a single individual or
> corporation since the Board believes such offers would not be con-
> ducive to maintaining the traditions, character and independence of
> the newspapers.

Thornton wasted no time. He drew up a 'protective structure' in
which no single shareholder could own more than 15 per cent of the
company. He also proposed that the company launch a 'serious left-wing
tabloid' in addition to the *Mirror*, together with a second London evening
paper. On top of this, he said he intended to give the workforce a
substantial share of the company. Reed were taken aback: they had hired
Thornton on the implicit understanding that he would 'cut the unions
down to size' and instead he was winning them over. Thornton found the
unions co-operative and the real canker in the management; moreover, he
said so.

For this he was criticised as 'naïve' by managers and journalists alike.
There was no 'gap in the market' for a radical tabloid, they said, which,
if true, amounted to a bleak condemnation of the British popular Press
and implied that only a newspaper that was sexist and racist and on the
right could survive. In fact, market research commissioned in 1985 for
a new left-wing Sunday paper, *News on Sunday*, suggests the opposite:
that the gap in the market is so wide that as many as 1,500,000 new
readers could beckon.[69]

When it appeared that Jarratt was about to de-sanctify Reed's pledge
not to sell to a 'predator' and indeed to sell the *Mirror* to Robert Maxwell,
the unions, including the journalists, met hurriedly and gave Thornton
a commitment to industrial peace for a year, so that he might finally
secure the company against the fast-approaching Maxwell. It was an
unheard of agreement, though short-lived. At the journalists' meeting a
number of impassioned speeches were made, notably one by Joe Haines,
the *Mirror*'s talented leader writer and former press secretary to Prime
Minister Harold Wilson. Haines had been active in the office in trying
to rally anti-Maxwell forces; and now, red-faced and shaking his fist,
Haines said he would have to be 'dragged through the door to work for
a crook and a monster like Robert Maxwell'. A few hours later Maxwell
was swivelling in Thornton's chair on the ninth floor which, along with
all the other floors, he now owned. Two days later Joe Haines accepted

promotion from Maxwell to assistant editor and today holds the title of 'Mirror Group Political Editor' and has a seat on the board. In at least one article Haines has written Maxwell's 'philosophy', under Maxwell's name, and is widely regarded as Maxwell's most trusted journalist on the *Mirror*, and is probably the most powerful. Speaking on *What the Papers Say*, Haines said, 'Mr Maxwell doesn't believe in doing things by halves.'[70]

Such an observation might well have applied to the *Mirror*'s circulation, which was staging a recovery just as Maxwell took over. In June 1984 the *Mirror* was selling 3,487,721 copies daily. After one year under Maxwell the *Mirror* had lost 350,000 sales. After eighteen months under Maxwell the *Mirror*'s circulation was down to an all time low of 2,900,000 and falling.[71] The number of readers of a newspaper is often more than double that of the circulation figure. It therefore can be conservatively estimated that since Robert Maxwell's arrival at the *Daily Mirror* at least a million people have stopped reading it. One observer quoted by *Marketing Week* noted that 'it takes something close to genius to lose so much circulation so quickly'.[72]

The now rapid decline of the *Mirror* under Maxwell – he may well have delivered the *coup de grâce* – has meant a significant change in character for the paper. In its leading articles the *Mirror* continues to oppose the Thatcher Government and to give its traditional support to the right wing of the Labour Party; but little more than tokenism now appears in the *Mirror* dissecting the issues and challenging the assumptions upon which the Thatcher Revolution and the impoverishment of so many *Mirror* readers are based. The dismantling of much of the welfare state, the demoralising of the state education system, the tearing down of protective barriers for working people, such as the Wages Councils for people under twenty-one, the erosion of ordinary civil liberties and the growth of centralised government and the Americanisation of British foreign and defence policies – except for a brief leader, an item in Paul Foot's column, or an occasional piece by Roger Todd, these issues are rarely discussed in Maxwell's *Mirror*.

One of Maxwell's numerous 'solemn pledges' on taking over the *Mirror* was that 'under my management editors in the Group will be free to produce their newspapers without interference with their journalistic skills and judgement'.[73] This was a remarkable statement, for since Maxwell's move to Holborn Circus he has intervened at almost every level of the editorial process. Indeed, he clearly relishes his role as owner/editor-in-chief (although he prefers the suitably all-embracing title of publisher). The fate of a column by Geoffrey Goodman, the *Mirror*'s industrial editor, is a case in point. On July 27, 1984 Goodman disclosed that at a Cabinet meeting during the 1974 miners' strike

Margaret Thatcher had opposed Prime Minister Edward Heath's decision to hold an election, wanting instead 'to take on the miners, fight 'em to a finish and win . . .' 'She has never forgotten', wrote Goodman, 'and clearly never forgiven the miners for that [election] defeat'.

The implication was clear: Mrs Thatcher's need to 'take on the miners' had as much if not more to do with the origins of the 1984–5 strike as any concern about 'uneconomic' pits. Maxwell struck these paragraphs from the first edition proofs and ordered the headline, 'DIGGING INTO A VENDETTA', scrapped. It was late; the editor, Mike Molloy, had gone home. When he was told the next day that Goodman was threatening to resign, Maxwell said that he had cut the column because it looked 'too grey, with too many words'.

During the week of Maxwell's arrival there was press speculation that Paul Foot and I might no longer be welcome at the *Mirror*. I mentioned this to Mike Molloy, who suggested a meeting with the publisher. On the ninth floor we were greeted by one of Maxwell's sons, Ian, a slight, diffident young man. 'Oh you're the one your father sacked,' said Paul Foot, setting the tone. Much hollow laughter all round. 'He's a good boy,' said Maxwell. 'Everybody deserves one more chance.' More laughter.

Exuding much charm, Maxwell offered us 'guarantees' that our work would not be 'interfered with' and that his door was always open. 'We want no hierarchy here,' he said. I asked him if we would have the freedom to dissent from the paper's line. 'Of course!' he replied.

The Maxwell 'line' was expressed in the new slogan under the *Mirror*'s masthead. 'FORWARD WITH BRITAIN', it said. 'FORWARD WITH LIECHTENSTEIN' might have been more appropriate, for that was where the ultimate holding company of the *Daily Mirror* was based. Indeed, the real ownership of Britain's only pro-Labour national newspaper remains a mystery. One who might be regarded as the owner occupies an office at No. 5 Aeulestrasse, in Vaduz, capital of the minuscule principality in the Alps. He is Dr Walter Keicher, a local lawyer and the resident director of Pergamon Holding Foundation (PHF). According to the *Financial Times*, PHF has neither '"members, participants nor shareholders", as the local legal textbook puts it. But if ownership is identified as control, then Dr Keicher is as close to being the owner as either UK or Liechtenstein law can allow . . . "I publish the *Mirror*" [said Maxwell]. "Ownership is a separate issue." But who controlled PHF Maxwell refused to say. "I am not in the business of disclosing other people's business."'[74] A few days later the merchant bankers Henry Ansbacher, speaking for the Pergamon holding company in Liechtenstein, put out a statement that the bank

. . . is able to say categorically that, as is well known, the persons ultimately entitled to [*sic*], comprise a number of charities and relatives of the respective grandparents of Mr and Mrs Robert Maxwell, not resident in the United Kingdom . . . there is no further information which the Pergamon foundation needs to release.[75]

Whatever the editorial 'line' of the new *Daily Mirror* under Robert Maxwell, its commercial roots were to remain foreign and secret; or, to quote Maxwell himself, 'other people's business'. Nevertheless, it was soon clear that the *Mirror*'s publisher saw himself as doing and knowing what was best for Britain in its current difficulties. He had a Plan for unemployment; he would be a great conciliator, a Solomon if necessary; he would unite warring parties and knock heads together. And his 'good offices' would be available for these pursuits in the national interest. For, above all, Robert Maxwell saw himself as a patriot, even to the point of questioning the influence of his Czech origins. 'I am British! I think British!' he told Russell Harty. And the acquisition of the *Daily Mirror* and four other national newspapers would give him that which had been denied him for too long: the power to act *for* Britain. Not even a substantial stake in Central Television, or ownership of the largest cable TV operation in Britain, or control of radio, book publishing and magazine contract printing could match being a latter-day Beaverbrook or Hearst, even if others perceived a Lord Copper. It is a truism that prime ministers seldom come to lunch with one who prints the labels on cans of baked beans, no matter how many labels one may print, or how rich one may be. But prime ministers do come to lunch with the owner, the publisher, of the *Daily Mirror*, no matter how rude that day's leading article may have been.

Maxwell came to power at the *Mirror* in the midst of the longest industrial crisis this century, the 1984–5 miners' strike. So it was not surprising that he quickly applied himself to this 'terribly damaging dispute', as he called it. He phoned me at home on a Saturday afternoon and told me to arrange a 'secret' meeting with the miners' president, Arthur Scargill (whom I had never met, although I had many links with the miners).

I did not like the role of fixer; but the miners needed every ally they could get and, more important, their case urgently needed a fair hearing in a national newspaper. The meeting was to be held near the NUM headquarters in Sheffield, preferably in a hotel with a heliport on it or nearby, as the publisher wanted to arrive and leave by this form of transport. This did not seem to me commensurate with secrecy. Nevertheless, a bemused Peter Heathfield, the NUM's general secretary, suggested the Hallam Tower Hotel, which is on the edge of a wood outside Sheffield. It did not have a heliport, he said, but Sheffield had an airport.

The *Mirror* 'team' was Maxwell, Robert Edwards, then editor of the *Sunday Mirror* and a longstanding trustee of the publisher, Geoffrey Goodman, Joe Haines and myself. I received several calls from the publisher's personal assistant about the availability of 'No. 1' and 'No. 2' helicopter and whether the smaller one could accommodate us all. I said I would prefer to travel by train (which, anyway, was faster). At the newsstand at St Pancras Station the front page of the *Daily Mirror* was triumphant:

ONLY in the Mirror
The <u>REAL</u> £ million
Here it is – the *Mirror*'s REAL £1 million. IN CASH.

And tax free to the winner of our Win a £Million game in Mirror Group Newspapers. MGN Publisher Robert Maxwell saw a million in banknotes for the first time yesterday. He admitted he was impressed and beamed: 'I'm itching to give it to one of our readers.' He went on: 'This is it – one million in cash which will make someone a millionaire.'

Mr. Maxwell's pretty daughter, Ghislaine, 22, was on hand to see the cash. Ghislaine said: 'It pleases me to know it will make one of our readers happy.'

Dominating the front page was a large picture of Robert Maxwell leaning on a trolley loaded with a million pounds in bundles of various denominations. I was admiring this when a familiar baritone boomed over my shoulder: 'Well, what do you think of it?' It was my publisher no less, attended by Robert Edwards; both the No. 1 and the No. 2 helicopters had been grounded in the fog and the three of us would now journey together to Sheffield. Goodman had gone by car; Haines had been assigned to wait for the helicopter, so that the publisher could fly back in it.

Maxwell was clearly delighted with a front page on which there were images only of himself and money. He held it up and seemed to be reading the few words on it again and again. When the British Rail waiter serving us breakfast showed interest Maxwell said, 'Do you want us to sign it? Yes, of course you do; it'll be a collector's item.' The waiter seemed grateful, though perplexed, especially when the publisher opened his attaché case and passed around one of the bundles of £50 notes which had appeared in the front-page picture. Edwards and I were invited to hold it, then return it.

On the way to Sheffield Maxwell spoke about his 'deep concerns'; the need for propriety and self-discipline 'in the country'. The young, above all, lacked this discipline; standards had fallen; selfishness was rampant. And everything was linked: drug-taking, violence on the terraces, violence on the picket lines. A new commitment to morality was needed, a new patriotism.

The meeting in the penthouse of the Hallam Tower lasted almost four hours, during which Arthur Scargill and Peter Heathfield, with patience, skill and sustained good humour, laid out the miners' case, explaining why the union could not agree to closing pits on ill-defined 'uneconomic' grounds. They based their argument on an agreement in the 1974 Plan for Coal which allowed closures only when coal reserves were exhausted. They showed us evidence of the Coal Board's manipulation of the Colliery Review Procedure and of the union's attempts to compromise, few of which had received national publicity. For his part, Maxwell told them of his 'fears for the country': of a 'breakdown in law and order and civilised values' and the spectre of revolution on the streets. It was up to them to prevent this, he said. As the afternoon wore on, the miners' case – the destruction of communities, the need to keep open the coalfields as North Sea oil dwindled, the burden on society of tens of thousands of redundant miners, the duplicity of the Coal Board under its Thatcher-appointed chairman, Ian McGregor – seemed increasingly irrelevant to the real purpose of the meeting; and at times a certain incredulity would slip across the faces of Heathfield and Scargill as they were lectured, now incessantly, on their 'responsibilities to the nation'.

The next morning I phoned Maxwell and said that we had been given at the meeting substantial evidence that the Coal Board and the Government were not telling half the truth about their dealings with the miners, and that the *Mirror* ought to run the story. I proposed that I write it. 'You mustn't be taken in,' said Maxwell. 'I'll get Haines to do a leader.' However, he did authorise a major piece by me about police violence in the coalfields, which was one of the issues that Scargill had raised at the meeting: an indication both of Maxwell's quixotic temperament and his assumption of the role of editor.

I was not on Maxwell's 'team' three weeks later when he met Scargill at Brighton during the Trades Union Congress conference. Maxwell was in his element. Following the 'secret' negotiations that the *Mirror* trumpeted each day, Maxwell, in shirt sleeves, gave impromptu press conferences on the seafront. He was merely offering his 'good offices' he said, and doing what had to be done in the national interest. Shortly afterwards, on September 10, Maxwell's efforts in the national interest seemed to have paid off. The *Mirror*'s front page read:

SCARGILL TO BALLOT MINERS
ON FINAL OFFER

by Terry Pattinson

Peace talks aimed at settling the miners' strike ended after only two hours last night.

But the *Mirror* can exclusively reveal that whatever the outcome, miners will be asked to vote on the Coal Board's final offer.

Both sides were non-committal last night . . .

On page two the *Mirror*'s revelation was described as an 'astonishing development' and there were several columns of detail about the 'final package'. This second story was 'by a special correspondent'.

Almost none of it was true. Terry Pattinson, the *Mirror*'s respected industrial reporter, had indeed filed from Scotland that 'peace talks had ended after only two hours' and that 'both sides were non-committal'. This much was true. The second paragraph, in which 'the *Mirror* can exclusively reveal' that the miners were to hold a ballot, was inserted into his copy, and the first he heard about his 'scoop' was when he returned home the next morning and was congratulated by his wife. The night before, the *Mirror*'s wire room had received a telex message direct from Maxwell House, the head offices of Pergamon Press which owns Mirror Group Newspapers. There was no name on the telex, which was marked 'MUST'. Assuming it was sent by Maxwell, *Mirror* executives decided to publish it. A leader, written by Joe Haines, entitled 'A vote for sanity' and lauding the non-existent decision to ballot, was published alongside it. The identity of the 'special correspondent' was not revealed.

In the following weeks and months the leading articles in all the Mirror Group papers had a recurring theme of personal and vitriolic attack on Scargill. 'Arthur Scargill has lost the miners' strike', read the *Mirror*'s front page on January 28, 1985. 'No one else is to blame. Not the men. Not the miners who struck. Not those who stayed at work. Not those forced by poverty to go back. Neil Kinnock didn't let him down. Nor did the TUC. He let himself down. Every move he made was wrong . . .' Many would agree that Scargill made wrong moves during the strike, and that the union ought to have balloted its members. But the words quoted above, which were typical, carried the assumption that more than 100,000 miners had followed Scargill like sheep, too dull to understand for themselves the issues involved and too craven to act upon their own considerations. Such outbursts indicated, in my view, just how far the *Daily Mirror* had strayed from the heart of its readership; among the million who have stopped reading it are, I know, many miners and their families. Moreover, Maxwell *knew* from the experience of his 'secret' meetings at Sheffield and Brighton that Scargill was prepared to negotiate seriously *and* to compromise, and that the Coal Board in the person of Ian McGregor and in the shadow of Thatcher was not. The prime minister's position had been made clear, after all, in the paragraphs Maxwell had cut from Geoffrey Goodman's column. Bogeyman Scargill, who had dared not to heed the *Mirror* publisher's call for 'discipline' and 'patriotism' (i.e. capitulation) was also blamed for much of the violence on the picket lines, in spite of a report by the National Council for Civil Liberties which concluded that 'contrary to the impression inevitably created by the media, most of the strike had been orderly and on a modest scale'.[76] When, in August 1985, the courts finally dropped charges against all ninety-five miners arrested during mass picketing at the Orgreave coking plant near Sheffield, the *Mirror* gave the story four paragraphs at the bottom of page eleven, beneath earwigs invading a seaside town and a TV show getting a 'wicked J. R. type character'.[77] In the latter part of the strike only the uncompromising reporting of Paul Foot saved something of the *Mirror*'s grace.

In the foyer of the *Mirror* building in Holborn Circus, London, there are four front pages of the *Daily Mirror* set in the wall opposite the lifts. It is almost impossible to miss them. They are said to represent the sweep of twentieth-century history as chronicled by one of Britain's most famous newspapers. Next to victory in the Second World War, the assassination of President Kennedy and the 1984–5 miners' strike, there is a 1985 front page two-thirds of which is covered by the image of Robert Maxwell. Not unlike the Shah of Persia, whose newspapers *knew* which photographs of him to use every day, Maxwell has converted the *Mirror* to something approaching a family album. There is Maxwell with a million pounds, and Maxwell with Maudie, the granny who won it, and with Maudie's family and Maudie's dog, Thumper, and Maxwell in Ethiopia and with the President of Sudan, and the President of Bulgaria, and the ex President of the United States, and with Chairman Gorbachev and Chairman Deng Xiaoping, and receiving an honorary degree from the Polytechnic Institute of New York, and so on.

'I am not on an ego trip,' the publisher told the BBC, whose cameras he allowed to pursue him almost everywhere.[78] When the interviewer asked Maxwell if his ubiquitous presence at the *Mirror* actually improved the paper, he replied that it 'improves the adrenalin throughout the building [and] helps journalists to do their job better'. Indeed, the film showed Maxwell helping journalists to do their job better: there he was approving pages hot from the editorial floor, giving orders to Joe Haines and changing Geoffrey Goodman's column while the columnist looked on (the changes were for the camera; Goodman later rescinded them). What was the effect of his image on the sales of his papers, asked the interviewer. 'I don't think that has any effect on sales!' replied Maxwell. Around that time the combined loss of sales of all Mirror Group newspapers since Maxwell took over was 700,000, an unprecedented fall.[79]

When Maxwell arrived at the *Mirror* he fully expected opposition from the guardians of its tradition of brash editorial independence. That he encountered none, that no 'tank traps' lay on the editorial floor 'astonished him', according to a former associate. As whims were speedily translated into commands, the 'hot line' calls became more frequent. There were days when most of the *Daily Mirror*'s photographic staff were unavailable for news assignments as they were either in the publisher's suite on the ninth floor or elsewhere in the Maxwell empire taking pictures of the publisher with 'visiting dignitaries' or pictures of the publisher with adoring fans at the Oxford United Football Club, which he owns; or they were on 'special Cap'n Bob missions'.

One such mission was a special *'Mirror* train' which had a picture of a growling lion (the *Mirror*'s new symbol) and 'FORWARD WITH BRITAIN' emblazoned on its engine. This train bore the publisher and his entourage on a progress through Southampton, Bristol, Birmingham, Nottingham, Sheffield, Manchester, Liverpool and Newcastle. The stated purpose of the mission was for Maxwell and his senior editorial people to 'listen to the people, our readers'. If listening to the readers had been the real intention, the accompanying circus would have been more than justified. The *Mirror*'s publicity people and local correspondents worked hard to ensure that enough 'dignitaries' turned up at town hall receptions to meet the publisher and to listen to him, and enough readers left the warmth of their homes to sit in cold, often half-empty local halls.

At most places Maxwell was flanked by a selection of editors and writers. After he had finished speaking, he would invite people to criticise the *Mirror* and to make suggestions. 'Don't be afraid,' he counselled, 'speak up!' It was a rare opportunity: here was Fleet Street confronted by its readership and by none of its stereotypes. Both men and women asked why contorted, naked bodies and pubescent smut were essential in a great newspaper, why real news had been replaced by page upon page of pop stars, why great issues which were altering the shape of people's lives were barely acknowledged. In Newcastle a bus driver proposed a *Mirror* campaign to illuminate the Government's plan to sell off the national bus system. A woman whose family had read the *Mirror* for a quarter of a century suggested a series of articles making sense of the morass of welfare regulations and benefits, which many people can no longer understand.

Neither of these excellent ideas has seen print. While on Tyneside I enquired into a common complaint of young readers: that the Government's Youth Training Scheme was little more than a cover for cheap labour. The article I subsequently wrote was delayed for almost two months, then published only after Maxwell had sent a copy to the Secretary of State for Employment, Tom King, who was responsible for the Youth Training Scheme. King's remarks were published on the same page: the first time in my experience that an investigative article has had to be first seen by a member of the Cabinet. The piece produced an instant response from readers, with letters running five-to-one in favour and most of them giving examples of how employers were using YTS to exploit the young unemployed. Instead of this ratio being reflected on the letters page, which was usually the case, a 'Public Opinion Special' was dominated by a second, longer letter from the Minister. On our journey to Sheffield Maxwell had expounded on his support for many forms of 'youth training' as a means of restoring 'discipline' to the nation.

Of course, there was much more to owning a great newspaper than mere egocentric pursuits. There was the opportunity to use journalists for ends other than journalism. In January 1985 I was assigned to go to Bulgaria. Bulgaria? An appointment had been made for me to see the Bulgarian Ambassador in London, who would explain my assignment; he had recently been to the *Mirror* for lunch with the publisher. The Ambassador came to the point quickly. 'Mr Maxwell tells me you will fly to Sofia next week and write the truth about the Pope affair,' he said. The 'Pope affair' was the coming trial in Rome of a Turk who had attempted to assassinate the Pope and who had implicated three Bulgarians as part of an alleged plot by the Bulgarian KGB to kill the Pope on behalf of the Kremlin. I told the Ambassador I had not agreed to go to Bulgaria. He said, 'But Mr Maxwell *himself* is going soon. And he says you are a good communist.' (Laughter) I said that I was not a communist, good or bad, and that I had no intention of doing a whitewash job for the Bulgarian government. Back at the office I wrote a memorandum to Maxwell proposing that 'if the *Mirror* really wants to pursue the story, there seems to be only one way to go about it: to investigate all the available evidence from all sides – Italy, Bulgaria and Washington. I am sure it will be appreciated I do not wish to be associated with the Bulgarians at this stage. And I strongly recommend that the *Mirror* avoids any Bulgarian initiative on the Pope story'.

Shortly afterwards, in February 1985, Maxwell flew to Sofia accompanied by a *Daily Mirror* reporter and photographer. The report that followed in the *Mirror* described how the publisher dined at

> ... the court of a modest Communist King [who] brought forth caviar, then consommé, then soufflés, then veal. Vodka vied with

brandy, white and red wines – with champagne twinkling through cut-glass crystal. But the 'king' leaned back and quietly ordered a swift light ale. When you're the Boss – and everyone knows it – you can do things like that.

Today Todor Zhirkov, President of Bulgaria, professional revolutionary and – after 30 years – the longest-serving leader in the Soviet bloc, was gently easing back the curtain on his iron image. 'I don't really approve of champagne,' he said. 'But we serve it for protocol's sake and to remind us when it's time to make speeches.'

He laughed softly and looked longingly back through thick, gold-rimmed glasses to his light ale. That jokey style last month bowled over Sir Geoffrey Howe, the first British foreign secretary to visit Bulgaria for more than 100 years. It contrasts clearly with his country's image as the heart of the Balkans, the Kremlin's stooge, infamous for poisoned umbrellas and the alleged plot to kill the Pope.

Not surprisingly it's an image the President indignantly dismisses as propaganda. Bulgaria for him should be seen by the West as a tourist top-spot, a go-ahead place with one of East Europe's most successful economies and virtually no foreign debt. Science, technology, profits and peace are his keys to Bulgaria's future . . .

And so it went on until it reached the president's 'special guest across the table, Robert Maxwell', and got to the point:

> The Mirror Group publisher had just struck a huge deal with the Bulgarian Government to help update the country's printing and packaging industries.[80]

This report occupied half the *Mirror*'s centre pages and was illustrated by a picture of President Zhirkov and Robert Maxwell with their arms on each other. It was published on Monday, March 4, the day after the end of the miners' strike, Britain's longest industrial upheaval since the General Strike. Clearly, updating the printing and packaging industries in Bulgaria was considered more important.

Three months later Robert Maxwell flew to Poland, where he also has printing interests, to negotiate the publication by his Pergamon Press of the speeches of General Jaruzelski, the Polish leader. On May 31, 1985 he gave the following interview to Warsaw Radio:

> Interviewer: I get the impression, sir, that you got on rather well with the Prime Minister [Jaruzelski]. Is that correct?
> Maxwell: Yes, that is correct. But you can't have a discussion with the Prime Minister of a large country like Poland without getting on well

with him. I'm an admirer of his. Otherwise, they wouldn't have decided
to publish his book in the 'Leaders of the World' series. He has done
great services to Poland in recent years . . .

Interviewer: Poland's sullied image might change a little bit now.
Poland has been having a very bad press in the West, in Britain in
particular perhaps, over the past three-and-a-half years. There has
not been much of the much-lauded unbiased reporting about Poland.
Poland has been given the stick and has not been perhaps allowed to
reply. Any comment on that?

Maxwell: Yes, I have. One of the things I hope as a result of our
publication of this book and my visit will change because the problem
of Solidarity is now solved . . .When I suggested to the prime minister
that in the interests of economic reform that why doesn't he adopt a
very small percentage of unemployment, he said in Poland everybody
had a right to work . . .

Interviewer: Does your visit here and what you've said suggest
that perhaps there might be a change in the tone used against
[Poland]?

Maxwell: Well, I can't talk for anybody else. I can talk for our
own newspapers and they – the Mirror Group Newspapers, are very
large – with the *Daily Record* in Scotland and the *Sunday Mail* we sell
about 35 million copies a week. We certainly will be devoting less
space to Solidarity and more space to improving relations and trade
between Great Britain and Poland because we both need, in the
interests of our own and your prosperity, to do more trade and that's
exaggeration of what Solidarity now represents in Poland . . .

Interviewer: But don't you tell them just to toe the editorial line no
matter what?

Maxwell: If I told my 600 journalists to toe the editorial line they'll
tell me to get stuffed.[81]

In a letter to *The Times* of June 25, 1985 Robert Maxwell wrote that
he had 'no intention of censoring the work of MGN [Mirror Group
Newspapers] journalists. Events in Poland, including the activities of
Solidarity, will be reported on their merits'. But of course as Maxwell
said in Warsaw, 'the problem of Solidarity is now solved'. So what
activities are there left to report? Perhaps the fact that the number of
political prisoners and detainees in Poland rose sharply during 1985 is
an 'activity' worthy of publication, especially as the dissidents being
imprisoned these days are relatively unknown men and women
– teachers, young people, factory workers: the Polish counterparts
of *Daily Mirror* readers – whose fate is less likely to stir protest in
Poland and abroad.[82] Their plight has not been given an inch in the

Mirror. No, that is not absolutely correct. On July 23, 1985 precisely one inch of space was given to a pro-Solidarity demonstration outside the Polish embassy in London. On the same night, reported the *Mirror*, 'publisher Robert Maxwell co-hosted a reception with the Polish Ambassador to launch the publication of a book by the Polish leader, General Jaruzelski'.[83]

The following week Robert Maxwell was in China, accompanied by the *Mirror*'s political editor, Julia Langdon, whose assignment was to report 'an exclusive interview with Deng Xiaoping, leader of a quarter of mankind' by 'the first British or European businessman to be received as a guest'. The main headline on her report read, 'CHINA SAYS "NO" TO STAR WARS'; and Deng Xiaoping did offer some mild criticism of American ambitions in space. But the real purpose of the Maxwell trip, like the trips to Bulgaria and Poland, was revealed only near the end of Julia Langdon's piece. 'This open discussion', she wrote, referring to the meeting between the Chinese leader and Maxwell, 'came at the end of a successful week's negotiations between Robert Maxwell's printing and publishing interests and a number of Chinese Government and printing organisations.'

Julia Langdon added that Chairman Deng 'cheerfully expressed his regret that he had not met the *Mirror* publisher before – for all the world as if Robert Maxwell had been free to drop in for tea anytime in the past 20 years'.[84] For a journalist who used to be political correspondent of the *Guardian* there was a certain poignancy in a subsidiary headline on her report. 'As we say in China', it read, quoting Chairman Deng, 'boats rise with the water . . . '

Today's *Mirror*, under its new, Maxwell-appointed editor, Richard Stott, features royalty scrapings, sexism, voyeurism and what are little more than handouts from the pop music and TV soap industries: anti-journalism. Apart from Maxwell's journeys abroad to tie up new, enriching deals, the paper's foreign reporting is now conducted mostly from a desk in London. And from this desk Soviet troops are sighted in Cambodia and Nicaragua, although they continue to elude reporters on the spot. On January 28, 1986, a fairly typical day, the *Mirror*'s front page read, 'WHAM! Win George Michael's bed . . . £50,000 twingo bingo' and 'Finger lickin' free . . . a Super lip-smackin' offer from Kentucky Fried Chicken'. The only serious story was Mrs Thatcher's role in the Westland helicopter saga. On page three the main headline was 'My boobs are too big, by Sammy' (Samantha Fox is a *Sun* page three pin-up). Next to this story was the *Mirror*'s own 'Page Three Cutie'. Across the centre pages was 'day two' of a series about Princess Diana, entitled 'Five years that rocked the royals'. And on page fifteen there was a story about a 'super plan to help the poor feed themselves'

which 'has brought together three remarkable men – President Jimmy
Carter, Japanese multi-millionaire Ryoichi Sasakawa and *Mirror* publisher Robert Maxwell'. The page was dominated by a picture of the
three men, of whom Maxwell was the most prominent.

Every day now Maurice Edelman's remark that the 'history of the
Daily Mirror is the history of our times' gains currency. For me, one of
the joys of working for the *Mirror* was its readers. Letters to the *Mirror*
were generous, eloquent, angry, passionate and seldom boring. People
expected us to listen and respond to them, to take up those issues that
touched their lives. In later years most of my investigations originated
with readers; and what I learned was that even at its best, the paper's
knowledge and understanding of the world it claimed to represent was
inevitably two steps behind those of its readers. During the Second
World War the Daily Mirror Readers' Service was set up to help families
while the breadwinner was away at the war. Guiding people through the
bureaucracy was a speciality. Anybody could use the Readers' Service,
which after the war gained a reputation for extracting justice from 'the
system' and became something of an ombudsman for countless thousands
of powerless people: the old, the handicapped, single parents, people
who simply could not fathom the fine print of their lives. It was entirely
free of charge and what the *Mirror* got in return was a depth of goodwill,
loyalty and affection which no market research could ever gauge and no
bingo could ever buy.

On New Year's Eve 1985 the Daily Mirror Readers' Service was cut
by Maxwell after more than forty years. It was one of the last direct links
with the readers. On the same New Year's Eve I was 'purged', precisely
as Maxwell had given his word I would not be. I was in Australia on
holiday and had planned to resign in the week of my return. My position
on the paper had become untenable; my ideas and stories were no longer
accepted. Among others, a major three-part series commissioned by the
previous editor, Mike Molloy, about the cold war, which I wrote entirely
from British and American establishment and independent sources, was
considered too kind to the Russians and 'too anti-Reagan', and was
scrapped. Unless I joined Maxwell's travelling PR team or, as the new
editor, Stott, had put it, unless I allowed myself to be 'given new
direction', I could not work. When I heard that I was out, I felt some
sadness but a huge relief. The paper had long ago abandoned what, for
me, was one of its main purposes: to warn its readers when they were
being conned – conned by governments or by vested interests or by
powerful individuals. The spectacle of the leader of the Labour Party at
a lavish party which Maxwell gave to celebrate the first anniversary of
his takeover of the *Mirror* not only underlined this abandonment of
purpose but cast it into a wider political context. Neil Kinnock does not

approve of Maxwell, but his deputy, Roy Hattersley, has told him to keep smiling, to say little. This, believes Hattersley, is the sound, pragmatic way; of those who control the majority Press in Britain, Maxwell is all they have got. Put another way the tragedy becomes clearer: Robert Maxwell and the present Labour leadership are all that *Mirror* readers and Labour voters have got.

The plummeting circulation of the *Mirror* demonstrates that people are aware of this. 'By turning their back on Maxwell in this way', said Donald Trelford, editor of the *Observer*, 'the old *Mirror* readers have underlined an important point: that readers want to feel that papers represent the honestly held views of free men and women. Honest political views and honest news values. Those are not always the same as sensible or even reasonable views, of course; often far from it. But they have to be authentic. Readers can sniff out the fake like dogs sniffing out drugs . . . '[85]

That may be so, but it also may be argued that the real power and influence of anti-journalism are insidious. Take, for example, three issues which in the popular papers carry potent stereotypes: race, Northern Ireland and drug-addiction. In a revealing piece in the *Guardian*, Charles Donington, press officer of the Commission for Racial Equality, wrote:

> . . . when the Metropolitan Police first issued an ethnic breakdown of crime in London, the popular press seized the figures on street crime (2 per cent of London crime) and produced front page headlines such as 'Black crime: the alarming figures' (*Daily Mail*) and 'Black crime shock' (*Sun*). Yet when the Home Office produced figures which showed that for every one racial attack on a white person there were thirty six on Afro-Caribbeans and fifty on Asians, there was no coverage in the popular press, with the exception of a short article in the *Daily Mail*.

Charles Donington referred to two 'major stories' concerning black people in June and July 1984. They were a Department of Employment report which showed that black unemployment was now double that of white unemployment, and a campaign of terror against the Bengali community in the East End of London which had forced Tower Hamlets housing department to rehouse the families under attack. Neither of these stories was given a line in the popular Press.[86] Moreover, this distortion in the coverage of minorities – in particular the inflation of 'black crime' – has had a direct political effect, giving rise in the 1970s to armed police 'special patrol' and 'support' groups and their harassment of and attacks on black people. In 1984 these groups graduated to work in the coalfields where they were controlled from Scotland Yard in what is now, effectively, Britain's first highly mobile national police force.

Britain is 90 per cent white and many white people have never actually met a black person. Therefore the way black people and 'race' issues are reported, argues Donington, crucially affects the way white people perceive their black fellow citizens. For example, Enoch Powell's inflammatory 'rivers of blood' speech, which was given wide coverage in the late 1960s, undoubtedly affected the way many white people perceived blacks. According to Derek Jameson, former editor of the *Express* and the *Star*, Powell told him that he delivered that speech twice before it finally made headlines. 'Both times his words went unnoticed!' wrote Jameson, who also noted that, 'normally you don't get any change out of £1000 for running an article by Enoch'.[87]

In an analysis of the reporting of Northern Ireland in the mid-1970s, when 'the troubles' were seldom out of the news, Philip Elliott of Leicester University found that 'most stories in the British media were about acts of violence or the enforcement of the law. Overall, only one third dealt with politics and other subjects'.[88] In other words, there was minimal explanation of events and of the roots of the conflict, let alone of the 'silent issues', such as the imposed poverty of the North of Ireland, which in 1986 was the poorest region in Europe after Calabria. This neglect unquestionably helped the British government put through parliament, in the place of any coherent policy, historically repressive legislation. The rights of freedom of speech and freedom of movement for certain citizens were abolished, juries in criminal courts were abandoned and replaced by the so-called 'Diplock courts' and the role of the British Army underwent a radical conversion to that of an instrument of civil and political repression. Bereft of real information about these changes, the popular reporting of Northern Ireland became, as Elliott called it, merely 'a new dressing every day for the wound suffered there'.

Anti-journalism is always concerned with youth. Young people, in spite of mass unemployment, are still important consumers and the advertising industry competes for their favours. For example, in 1986 the *Daily Mirror* launched a £2.8 million television campaign with the aim of presenting a youthful image and attracting young readers. 'Look forward to tomorrow', was the campaign's slogan. None of this is new; patronage of teenagers, their fads and private lives, is almost as old as Fleet Street. What is new is the level of exploitation. On December 4, 1985 the *Mirror* devoted ten pages to what it called the 'JUNK GENERATION'. Wrapped around the front and back pages were two huge pictures. The headline captions read, 'THIS GIRL IS ON HEROIN' and 'THIS BOY IS FOR SALE'. Inside there was 'Debbie is a dosser' and 'Jackie is a racist' and 'Joey Lamb is a thug' and 'Darren is a no hoper'. Under the headline 'RENT BOY', Paul Blake, a homosexual prostitute, told 'his story'. Paul, 'like many other thousands of drop-out kids who trudge the streets every day . . . falls into the twilight world of drugs, crime . . . and sordid homosexuality'. Paul's 'relatives do not know of his plight'. They do now, of course.

On the centre pages was a picture of two teenaged girls who, read the caption, 'look just like schoolgirls'. The headline read, 'CHERYL AND MANDY ARE EIGHTEEN AND ON THE GAME'. Their 'story' began as follows:

> Mandy and Cheryl pulled the nearly white sheet over the old stained mattress and apologised for the bed not being made.
>
> An hour earlier they'd been rolling around on it with a fat middle-aged tax inspector.
>
> He paid them £15 each for what the girls call a 'straight sex' session.
>
> That's the going rate for 18-year-olds in the red light district of Bristol.
>
> 'We only do straight sex. No perverted stuff. The older girls do all that,' explains Mandy, who has been a prostitute for about two years.
>
> 'I hate the word prostitute,' she says, spitting the word out
>
> 'It's so old fashioned. It's so common. I wish someone would think of another name for us . . . '

Cheryl assured the writer of this, Christina Appleyard, that 'We always work on top. That way we're in control. And it stops them trying any rough stuff' . . .

> Looking around the room Cheryl proudly points out what the money has bought her after five months of selling herself. There's a dried flower arrangement, a wok from Habitat, a few Wedgwood ornaments, the picture of Lassie and two small teddy bears.
>
> 'Those bears only cost £7.99,' she says.
>
> And in almost the same breath she reels off the girls' price list . . .
>
> '£10 for a full strip and a relief job. £15 for sex (usually takes about 15 minutes). £50 for a full hour,' she says with a smile.
>
> 'If they want to slap our bum or anything like that, it's extra. All extras are £10.'

Apart from a few asides which described the girls' 'cold, dead eyes that stand out like dark holes in their lovely young faces' and pitied the fact that they 'have given away the best toy in the world because they didn't know how it worked', the article and most of the 'junk generation' issue of the *Mirror* were no more than an exercise in voyeurism and junk journalism. No serious attempt was made to explain *why* some young people found themselves in such distressing circumstances, or to set their distress in a social and political context. That is the nature of exploitation.

Drug-taking was featured prominently in that particular issue. Drugs are the 'serious' issue for the popular Press in the 1980s, and the coverage of the 'drugs menace' has complemented a Government public relations campaign aimed at showing the young victims of drugs as hopeless, helpless and depraved, and without choices. The myth is extended that the pushers are 'Mr Big' types when, in fact, most pushers are addicts themselves. This myth allows ministers and leader writers to extend pity or impute shame to the hopeless addicts and to rail against the 'evil crime bosses' while all but ignoring the fact that Government policies have caused drug dependency clinics to close.

Those I have spoken to who work with young addicts are most critical of what they see as the glamorising of drug-taking, either subliminally or openly in the Press. During September 1985 the *Mirror* published a 'world exclusive' series about the Rolling Stones. On the first day the headline read, 'Ah, cocaine . . . such an amusing drug don't you think'. This was allegedly Princess Margaret's response to the sight of the Rolling Stones' Keith Richard sniffing cocaine 'from a silver spoon'.[89] On another day readers, presumably young readers, were invited to admire the romps of 'Count Keith' . . . whose passions 'were music, fun and drugs' and who is 'a truly exotic character who sees himself as a kind of debauched, elegantly waisted European aristocrat . . . Keith always looked glamorous . . . Despite his drug problem, Keith remained a witty man.'[90]

Regardless of bingo and other circuses, the Press in Britain will always be deterred from being an effective 'fourth estate' while secrecy is organic and the laws of libel, the Official Secrets Act and a maze of 'guidelines' and accepted practices negate any notion of press freedom as it is understood in North America. Indeed, the American Press is often held up – and holds itself up – as the boldest and freest in the world. It is interesting to draw a comparison.

Certainly, the Press in the United States and Canada seem as free as it is theoretically possible to be. Both countries have Freedom of Information Acts; in America the right to know is written into the constitution. But has this freedom really inspired journalism less enamoured with government, institutions, and the tactics of politicians than in Britain? Has it bred journalists manipulated less by the propaganda of authority and vested interests than in Britain?

Watergate is the *Arc de Triomphe* of modern journalism. The Watergate scandals developed in the early 1970s when I was reporting from America. Some 1,500 journalists then lived in Washington; and yet in the beginning only two of the least experienced reporters, Carl Bernstein and Bob Woodward of the *Washington Post*, sustained any curiosity about the Watergate burglary.

Moreover, with the hated Nixon in disgrace, the Press seemed to avoid the implications of Watergate as if Nixon's demise could be explained away, in writer Nicholas Van Hoffmann's words, 'by defining him as a unique moral deviant'. The accepted wisdom was that other presidents were not like Nixon. Newspaper editorials pronounced that 'the system works!'

Perhaps America's greatest investigative journalist, Seymour Hersh, believes that, contrary to the myth of a fearless adversary Press, 'the Press did an awful lot to bring us Watergate'. Hersh contends that some of the most disturbing episodes of the Nixon/Kissinger years – the secret bombing of Cambodia in 1969, widespread, illegal wire-tapping, Washington's 'destabilising' operations against the Allende regime in Chile in 1970 and the CIA's domestic spying campaign – were not disclosed until after Nixon was elected for a second term in 1972.[91]

Today, with corruption running deep in the Reagan administration ('the sleaze factor') the president is *protected* by sections of the Press, which nurture the image of an attractive 'nice guy', a little slow maybe, even ignorant, but not for example a politician immersed in religious quackery of the kind that says the good guys will survive the apocalypse. This is not surprising. Far from being a liberal redoubt, 75 per cent of the American Press in the last forty years have endorsed Republican candidates.[92] In an article in the ultra-conservative magazine *Public Opinion*, the editor of *Fortune*, Walter Guzzardi, wrote that the flow of news in America was 'essentially benign' and that 'the Press has become a tremendous – and often unappreciated – force for legitimising govern-ments, institutions and free enterprise'.[93]

Apart from formidable loners like Hersh and I. F. Stone (who said, 'Every government is run by liars and nothing they say should be be-lieved'[94]) it seems doubtful that many American journalists stray far from assumptions that put them as comfortably 'on side' with 'the system' as their British colleagues. And if this is true in a Press with *constituted* freedoms, it suggests that real freedom of expression may remain as much a quality of attitude in individual journalists as a reflection of the structure of the Press itself. For, as Henry Fairlie has pointed out, 'Men such as Murdoch can operate only if they can find pliant men to assist them. Their power will always be found to rest ultimately, not only on their resources, not only on the extensiveness of their organisations, but on their gift for searching out men to do their will.'[95]

Pliant men and women are of course not difficult to find. But neither are journalists who reject the notion of themselves as functionaries and sycophants, of barkers in one man's circus. Among them are some of the best journalists in Britain: Phillip Knightley, Hugo Young, John Shirley, Stephen Fay, Peter Gillman, Peter Dunn, Paul Eddy, Patrick Forman, John Whale, Elaine Potter, Rosemary Righter, Stephen Aris, Eric Jacobs, the cartoonist Michael Heath and the photographer Donald McCullin. These are just a few of the names in the exodus of journalists since Murdoch took over the *Sunday Times* in 1982. The stand of less well-known journalists during the enforced transfer of Murdoch's papers to Wapping in February 1986 – with those like Martin Huckerby, Eric Butler, Richard Davies, Kim Fletcher, Ian Blunt, Don Berry, Paul Routledge, Greg Neale, Don Macintyre, David Felton, Barrie Clement, Pat Healy, Pam Spooner, Ian Griffiths, Derek Pain, Fred Meachin, Miles Hedley and Mike Topp displaying considerable courage – brought about a rare public debate on the vandalism being done to journalism today: a fact that has been overshadowed by the apparent hypnotic effect of the direct input terminals, as if 'new technology' is an end in itself. After visiting the picket lines at Fortress Wapping Neil Ascherson wrote in the *Observer*:

> The new way of production will change British newspapers more radically than anything since the abolition of stamp duty in 1855. The fall in production costs may break the financial dependence on advertising. It may soon be possible to launch and profitably maintain a first-class 'quality' daily paper with a circulation of 100,000 or perhaps far less – until now, the vain dream of those who long to see a politically varied and responsible Press in Britain.
>
> All fine hopes. But then I see again those figures hunched in shame, the wire and the guards, the violence done to the independence of journalists and the integrity of editors. It is easy to sneer at 'the hacks who caved in to save their mortgages'; they have little chance of finding another job when they join the 5,000 dismissed printers and the four million unemployed. And yet that new free Press of the possible future will need men and women with guts and high spirits to write it.
>
> The self-respect and confidence of this journalistic generation are hanging on the old barbed wire down at Wapping and bleeding to death.[96]

Perhaps reform of the structure of the British Press will have to wait until the excesses of the present owners and their 'pliant men' *forces* a future government to rewrite the monopolies laws, so that ownership of more than one daily and Sunday newspaper is illegal, and to legislate the right of employees to share ownership of their newspapers and the right of editorial freedom. New technology can lead to a more diverse

Press only if the substantial capital investment necessary is made available to those without friends in the City of London. And there is a case for providing public funds to underwrite the widest possible access to the latest technologies by which public opinion is moulded, and for a state-supported but entirely independently run fund of 'seed money' to back those seeking to realise the 'vain dream' of a Press which reflects the political, sexual and racial complexion of Britain.

Until that happens, responsibility surely rests with journalists themselves. 'One of the main reasons for the general weakness of the British Press,' wrote the playwright David Hare, 'appears to be the readiness of journalists to conspire in the massacre of their own work.'[97] It is hardly surprising that outsiders like Hare are perplexed that some journalists should adopt such a role. My own view is that, far from conspiring to do so, many journalists are unaware of their own malleability and the *effects* of what they do. Take the stereotyping of black people. As Charles Donington pointed out, few journalists are consciously racist, but fewer still appear to have thought seriously about the basis of their 'news sense' and its 'stock response', or to have even the most fundamental knowledge of their black fellow citizens. How many consider the end result of their reporting and how it is presented on people's lives?

Attitudes are passed on. Anti-journalism is contagious. Like many young people to whom the word 'career' derives from some ancient lexicon, many young reporters are not given the chance to apply their natural idealism and curiosity and instead affect a mock cynicism which they believe ordains them as journalists. And what they gain in cynicism they lose in heart by having to pursue a debased version of their craft. A teacher at a post-graduate course in journalism told me about one of her class who submitted an assignment filled with inaccuracies. When these were pointed out, the student said, 'What does it matter? It reads better that way. That's what the papers do these days, isn't it?'

An Australian friend, a newspaper executive, once said to me, 'Look, we're *only* journos.' *Only journalists.* Morgan Philips Price of the *Manchester Guardian*, who remained in the Soviet Union after the 1917 revolution, almost alone, almost starved, trying to report the Allied invasion and to warn of its grave implications for the future, was *only* a journalist. Ed Murrow, the American reporter, dared to report Dunkirk as a near-disaster and in later years repelled smear upon smear in his campaign against the vendettas of Senator Joe McCarthy; and he was *only* a journalist. Martha Gellhorn, who reported the Great Depression from the heartland of America and the Spanish Civil War from the viewpoint of its victims, went, not long ago, in her seventies, to report bloody events in El Salvador; she said she wanted to 'set the record straight'; and she is *only* a journalist. James Cameron broke the silence of functionary reporting from the Korean war and described the atrocities of 'our side'; and he was *only* a journalist. Robert Fisk proved that, for all the special difficulties facing a British reporter in Northern Ireland, events could be reported honestly and given meaning, powerfully and eloquently; and he is *only* a journalist.

One of Fisk's earliest predecessors on *The Times* was William Howard Russell who reported from the Crimea, a war described by Queen Victoria as 'popular beyond belief'. Once, when I returned from Vietnam, Cecil King gave me an early edition of Russell's Crimea diaries, and they are a precious possession. Not for that reporter the 'patriotic' propaganda of the Falklands war. He wrote about the sacrificial battles, the waste, the blunders. 'Am I to tell these things?' Russell wrote to his editor, John Delane, 'or am I to hold my tongue?' To which Delane replied, 'Continue as you have done, to tell the truth, and as much of it as you can.'[98] Both of them were accused of treason; and they were *only* journalists.

XII

RETURN TO AUSTRALIA

43

Beyond the frontier

T. S. Eliot wrote that the whole point of a journey was to come back to the place you left and see it for the first time. I have been coming back to Australia since shortly after I left some twenty-three years ago as if pursuing an illusion which, with every journey 'home', becomes more compelling, yet more abstruse. I used to think this was merely the fate of the expatriate beset by age and nostalgia, but I now believe that to be only part of the explanation; the greatest island and the most ancient continent is a uniquely secret place with a secret past and a future of unusual possibilities: a place where universal questions have been raised and their resolution is not, as elsewhere, predetermined.

My mother and father had gone their separate ways before I left Australia, but my links with both remained strong, although finding Elsie at home in Sydney was not always certain. In her sixties, with little more than her state pension, she had set out to discover the world. (I once sent her a cable which found her travelling in the Solomon Islands.) On her first trip to London she shared my eight feet by six feet garret next door to a strip club and brothel in Old Compton Street, Soho, where she could be found conducting regular and convivial conversations with the working women who occupied my doorstep. 'Do you know my son very well?' she would ask. I never heard the reply, just her laugh.

In Sydney she lived in a two-room flat of 'veneer brick' on top of an Armenian laundry, an Italian hairdressers' and an 'antique' shop which announced itself with a cigar-store Indian standing defiantly to attention in the back of an old pick-up parked outside. This shop was one of her favourite places and my birthday was invariably celebrated with an item of indispensable, if obscure, Australiana of which she would say: 'What d'you reckon? I got it down from twenty dollars.'

From her flat it was just possible to glimpse the dark blue swell of the Pacific at Sydney Heads, through which Francis McCarthy, her great-grandfather, had sailed in leg irons more than a century and a half earlier. From her back porch, facing north-west, in late January and February, which are the height of summer, it was possible to see a ring of fire. These fires, which lick the edges of Australia and cause seasonal havoc, are unpredictable; light planes and helicopters are sent to 'bomb' them with water and chemicals, often to no avail. The wind which drives them on is a westerly which, 'like a blast from an oven', as Elsie would say, carries the flames into corners of contrived gentility, where they incinerate manicured gardens. Sand is whipped from the beaches; ocean currents become neurotic. There is a vaguely suicidal edge to these days, and the faces coming home on the commuter buses and trains tend to have the look of the condemned. At the very least cats are kicked and the breweries' profits rise. Watch the flames with your back to the sea, feel the 'blast' of wind coming off unseen deserts beyond a frontier unimagined by many Australians and you have been served with a reminder that the European is no more, and no less, than an interloper in this secret country.

But these are exceptional days in Sydney, which is protected by sea breezes. The 'southerly buster' at the end of an otherwise still and sweltering day, or the gentle nor'easter, reinforce the illusion for most that there is no Australia other than this southern Arcadia. Certainly, with each journey back, it became increasingly clear to me that I had grown up in one of the most fortunate cities on earth, which not only had resisted urban decay but had improved as it had grown. Why Australians still bother to measure Sydney against San Francisco and Rio I don't know; it is so much more beautiful, more generous and endearing. In 1983 *L'Express*, the Paris weekly,[1] was moved to effuse over 'modern Australian civilisation' as 'perhaps the last dream of the decade . . . no other Eldorado in the world can express or incarnate the hopes, the aspirations of the old world.'

I doubt if such a munificent observation would have fallen from the lips of great-great-grandfather McCarthy when he was brought up on deck to await a long boat to his prison home. However, I recall one recent midsummer's day in Sydney when there was Joan Sutherland and Tchaikovsky in the park, free; and a production of *Twelfth Night* acclaimed as the most imaginative in the history of the modern theatre; and new plays and good jazz; and, afloat on the harbour, a barge on which a symphony orchestra played, oblivious to the swell. And at dusk, sitting on the sanctity of 'The Hill' at Sydney Cricket Ground, I was advised on the historical meaning of cricket by Elsie, who earlier that day had batted and bowled against her grandson and whose unforgiving view of the 1932–3 English side of 'bodyline' bowlers was summed up in one of her favourite expressions, 'that iniquitous mob', to which she would add that 'their bowling tactics, aiming for the man and not his bat, almost got us out of the empire! But it didn't . . . pity.'

Many of my expatriate generation dismissed Australia as a second-hand Europe. They believed that 'the world' and its cultural riches did not exist in the southern hemisphere. Some of them longed for visions of England as only the truly colonised can. They relished stale English newspapers, mediocre English writers and the prospect of their talents being 'recognised' on arrival in London; indeed, as one of them later wrote in his memoirs, he was 'born again' as his ship passed through Sydney Heads on its way to the motherland. That so many judged their homeland as all but worthless and 'so far away' said much about the self-esteem of our society then.

The present Sydney had not been built when the exodus to Europe was at full flow. A tram depot stood where the Opera House now dominates the Harbour; and the perennial presence of R. G. Menzies, a fundamentalist mentality called 'wowserism' and the 'White Australian Policy' kept the nineteenth century close at hand. Few of us who left, like most of those who stayed, ever saw past the city's western suburbs and beyond the frontier which ran as much through our consciousness as it did across the desert plains.

Beyond this frontier lived another, invisible Australian nation. There was virtually no reference to them in the chronicles of my own pioneer family; and yet throughout the nineteenth century and as recently as the 1950s, wars and massacres were visited upon them in the name of the Christian God, the English king, anthropology, 'phrenology',* money and land. These terrible and epic events were recorded by few white historians. The anthropologist W. E. H. Stanner called it 'historical amnesia',[2] although it was much more a conspiracy of silence. An anonymous Aboriginal poet wrote in the Aboriginal paper, *Bunji*, in 1971:

> At the white man's school, what are the children taught?
> Are they told of the battles our people fought?
> Are they told how our people died?
> Are they told why our people cried?
> Australia's true history is never read,
> But the blackman keeps it in his head . . . [3]

At the white man's school there was *The Squatting Age*, in which Professor Stephen Roberts wrote, 'It was quite useless to treat them [the

---

* Phrenology was a pseudo science which drew on Darwinism. It provided popular, bogus theories for 'explaining' Aboriginal inferiority.

Aborigines] fairly, since they were completely incapable of sincere and prolonged gratitude.'[4] Growing up, I was given to understand that we whites were merely innocent bystanders to the slow and 'natural' death of people whose time had come, rather than the inheritors of a past as bloodthirsty as that of the United States, Spanish America and colonial Africa and Asia. That the jolly swagman was not especially jolly was unmentionable; that genocide was all but colonial policy in Australia was a secret. 'The barriers which for so long kept Aboriginal experience out of our history books', wrote Henry Reynolds, one of Australia's new wave historians,

> . . . were not principally those of source material or methodology but rather ones of perception and preference. Much of the material used in this book has been available to scholars for a century or more. But black cries of anger and anguish were out of place in works that celebrated national achievement or catalogued peaceful progress in a quiet continent, while deft scholarly feet avoided the embarrassment of bloodied billabongs.[5]

In Tasmania the First Australians were said to have died out. In fact, they were hunted, along with kangaroos, and wiped out: poisonous baits being a popular method. The tribe which had watched Captain James Cook sail into Botany Bay in 1770 was reduced by slaughter and imported disease to three women and a man. An Aborigine, known as Old Mr Birt, related this story told to him by his mother:

> They buried our babies with only their heads above the ground. All in a row they were. Then they had a test to see who could kick the babies' heads off the furthest. One man clubbed a baby's head off from horseback. They then spent most of the day raping the women; most of them [the women] were then tortured to death by sticking sharp things like spears up their vaginas until they died. They tied the men's hands behind their backs, then cut off their penis and testicles and watched then run around screaming until they died. I lived because I was young and pretty and one of the men kept me for himself, but I was always tied up until I escaped into another land to the west.[6]

Growing up in Australia I knew nothing about this; none of us did. Our history was one of suppression, omission and lies. For example, in 1966 an unusually adventurous Apex Club in the small New South Wales town of Bingara proposed putting up a monument at the site of the 1838 massacre of twenty-eight Aboriginal men, women and children,

known as the 'Myall Creek Massacre'. The response was apoplexy. In a
letter to the *Bingara Advocate* J. T. Wearne expressed a peculiarly
Australian view of history:

> Why should we carry the stigma of an event which occurred 130 years
> ago and for which not one of us could be held responsible? . . . The
> pity of it is that the Myall Creek massacre was practically forgotten
> and the great bulk of the people had never even heard of it![7]

It was not until 1968 that I went beyond the Australian frontier for
the first time and saw that which I had not imagined. Charlie Perkins
went with me. Charlie was born on a table-top in a disused telegraph
station near Alice Springs in 1936 or 1937; he is not sure which. His
brother killed himself, he says, as a result of the pressures and confusions
of being a 'half-caste' Aborigine seeking the acknowledgment and respect
of whites. Charlie was taken from his parents so that he might be
'protected' from the 'paganism' of his people; his 'saving grace', in the
eyes of the missionaries who educated him, was that he had European
blood.

In 1963 Charlie led a group of Sydney students on a series of 'freedom
rides' through the outback of New South Wales, with the aim of ending
segregation in cinemas, swimming pools and other public places. He
and white students, notably Jim Spigelman, had borrowed the idea from
the freedom rides to the American southern states a few years earlier;
and they stood – Charlie with his 'one bung kidney' – at the entrance to
the municipal baths at Moree, gripping the turnstile bar and refusing to
let go until Aboriginal children were allowed to swim there; and eventually they were. In 1965 he became the first Aborigine to graduate from
an Australian university. As a result of his efforts and those of many
other courageous black Australians and their white allies, a referendum
was held in 1967 in which almost 90 per cent of the Australian electorate
gave the federal government special powers to legislate justice for the
Aboriginal people. This meant that the original inhabitants of Australia,
who had occupied their country for at least 20,000 years, were now
considered worthy of inclusion in the national census: that is, they were
now 'citizens'.

We set out from Sydney for what was then known by whites as the
'nowhere land' west of Alice Springs in the Northern Territory, where
Charlie's people, the Aranda, lived in the country of their 'dreaming'.
We had flown over great salt lakes which to Aranda and Pitjantjatjara
peoples are tears from heaven, shed for all people. At The Alice, Charlie's
mother, Heddy, was waiting; she is a queen of the Aranda and she was
wearing her best black hat.

'Listen,' she said to Charlie, 'you should take on plenty of water . . . dinkum.'

The temperature was 115°F and on the track we passed a car abandoned in the dust; Charlie wrote on the bonnet: 'Coming back this way soon – Charlie'. When we arrived at Santa Teresa mission, it was covered in the crisp, stinking carcases of millions of recently expired locusts. 'A cloud of them bastards hung over us for a week', said a forlorn Irish priest, 'then dropped like shit, right on us.' He gave us water and walked away. In the black square shadow of the water tower, Aboriginal stockmen stood like the silhouettes of lynched men. They lived in the 'blacks only backyard', in igloos of mud and sandstone and with open fires into which their children would roll. There was no power, no sanitation and little water. Andy Ross had just come home to find his youngest child with her back badly burned. Andy was paid £7 a week and got some food from the priest. 'One little fella o' mine may go down to Adelaide school,' he said, 'we don't know which fella yet.'

Back on the track, facing the horizon, we reached the government reserve at Jay Creek. The barbed-wire gate was locked, so we reversed the Ford Falcon, revved it and drove through the gate. This you were not supposed to do; there was a Department of the Interior form to fill out and a permit to be granted. Jay Creek was part of Australia's Gulag. Some 300 people lived beneath corrugated iron and car bonnets, tree bark and newspapers propped in the dirt. Apart from the administration compound on the other side of a dead creek, there was only one building, a Nissen hut, which was said to be a church. The Lutherans had this reserve on lease, and an Aborigine called Leslie was allowed to be pastor as long as he collected all the garbage, for which he was paid £14 a month.

The white manager had seen us now and came running. He was a small man whose trousers were not quite on. He had a nervous way and a Yorkshire voice and was worried that we did not have an appointment and a permit. Then he said suddenly, 'Oh, bugger it. What do I care?' His job, he said, was to 'phase these people into our society', for which he was paid £22 a week, '. . . and that's less than a bloody counter jumper in Alice'. He said there were three stages of housing through which people were 'phased'. The first stage was the 'housing' we could see, the iron and bark things which he described, without conviction, as 'the blacks' natural, primitive home'. The second stage was a silver corrugated-iron and oven-hot shed where the people were 'house broken'; and the third stage was a 'modern' two-room cement block with fly screens and running water, of which there was none at Jay Creek. The week before there had been no water either, he said, and last winter the hoses and the people had frozen. 'We gave them firewood,' he said.

'We don't get many complaints, no trouble really, just the usual drunk or wife-beater and I fix them quick-smart by sending them back to the bush for thirty days.'

The manager excused himself. He said he had to finish the auditing before tomorrow when two busloads of American tourists would come and stay an hour, watching boomerang throwing and camel riding.

'Aborigines on camels?' I queried.

'Do the bloody Yanks know the difference?' he said. 'Anyway, without them, we couldn't afford the little extras, now could we?'

The light was falling when we took a winding road to The Palms. Against a blazing sky galahs fell and ascended and blue cranes drifted and stood. We took a short cut across the plain, over corrugations of red dirt on which the dust of erosion seemed suspended, unmoving. Then a crunching noise was beneath us, like the sound of snapping branches. We were driving over a landscape of bones. In the half-light whole skeletons sat up grotesquely, as if waiting for life to return. This was the graveyard of tens of thousands of kangaroos, their flesh long canned as pet food, their coats now admired in Sydney, London, Paris.

'Where are the live ones?' I asked Heddy.

'Gone . . . shot . . . done in,' she replied. 'The big red roo's gone altogether. Lotsa dollars in roos. But they'll come back. Everything comes back.'

The Palms, run by the federal government, was designated an Aboriginal 'pensioners' camp'. Its grey sheds gave the surreal appearance of village lavatories, which was appropriate, for they leaned on the side of a treeless hill overlooking a sewer stream and a rubbish dump. We wondered about the person who had named it 'The Palms'.

'Must've been some sort of joke, eh Mum?' said Charlie.

'Whole thing's a joke,' said Heddy. 'Pity y'can't laugh much about it.'

The old people at The Palms walked four miles to buy bread and treacle and tea at a shop owned by a man known as The Pig, because of his rudeness to blacks. And if they were lame and could not make the journey, they crossed the sewer to the rubbish dump and scavenged with the crows and dogs. In the middle of the dump, which was always smoking, one family lived in an overturned water tank, with brown water resting in it: two women, four children, six dogs and one old copy of the *Australasian Post* which was torn open at: 'Are You Satisfied With Your Exam Results?'

As the 1960s ended, the shadows beyond the Australian frontier began to recede. Extraordinary events began to unfold. Having disturbed the silence contrived around them by white Australia, many Aborigines no longer saw themselves merely in relation to white society, as victims.

Their anger, organisation and the public eloquence of their protagonists began to grow as white Australians were made aware that the 'poor old Abos' were not at all 'dying out', that their exclusion from the national census had covered up the fact that the black population was *increasing*. The exposure of this historical lie excited renewed interest in Australia's 'passive' original inhabitants and led to other 'discoveries', notably that the cultural denigration of the Aboriginal people had obscured the uniqueness both of the Australian past and the nature of the first Australians.

The Obiri Rock stands as a testimony to this. The Obiri is a cathedral to the Gagadju and Kunwinjku peoples and overlooks the paper bark swamps of the East Alligator River which flows along the escarpment of Arnhem Land in the Northern Territory, east of Darwin. Although a 1948 expedition into the East Alligator established the scope of the gallery of paintings beneath the Obiri and at other sites, it was not until the 1950s and 1960s that their significance was understood. Their discovery has been compared with the finding and deciphering of the Rosetta Stone with which the secrets of ancient Egypt were unlocked.

That Australian civilisation predates the pharaohs by at least 20,000 years was confirmed by the Obiri paintings, which are considerably more sophisticated than the cave drawings at Lascaux in France, by which the European tribes have measured their civilisation. Unlike the European preglacial sites, the Australian figures are dynamic portrayals of life in the remote millennia before the glaciers melted, when it was possible to walk from Tasmania to India. There are animals long extinct, such as the Tasmanian Tiger, and spirits and human figures such as the spectacular 'Lightning Man' who, with a fan of magpie geese feathers in one hand, appears to be shouting to the heavens. In later paintings there are figures in broad-brimmed hats, nineteenth-century British man, the invaders; or as Thomas Keneally aptly described them, 'the people from outer space, the Venusians and the Martians'.[8] The span of these paintings is some 25,000 years; and that remains a conservative estimate. Having been included belatedly in the World Heritage List, the Obiri gallery is now said to be 'perhaps the oldest and the most significant expression of human creativity ... the longest historical record of any group of people'.[9]

Shorn of the racism which distorted much of nineteenth-century and early twentieth-century anthropology and historiography, another kind of Australian scholar began to listen to the Aborigines; and discovered that oral histories were still alive in several linguistic groups and clans. The Bunggunditj people in South Australia knew about the eruption of Mount Muirhead 20,000 years ago and of Mount Gambier a mere 5,000 years ago when Australia was a land of volcanoes and of convulsive change. There is this passage in Geoffrey Blainey's *Triumph of the Nomads*:

> We have long believed that during the time of the aboriginal possession of Australia their way of life did not change and nor did their landscape. They were said to be static people in a static environment. But . . . their world was violently affected by volcanoes. For all the peoples living within one mile of the ocean . . . a more shattering change was to affect their landscape and way of life: that change was the rising of the sea and the drowning of their hunting grounds. Nothing in the short history of white men in Australia can match these physical changes. The recent clearing of extensive forests, the building of a million miles of fences, the making of railways and roads and artificial lakes – none of these changes which dominate the modern history of Australia can be compared with the ancient rising of the seas, the shaping of thousands of new harbours, the swamping of scores of tribal territories . . .[10]

Not only did the Australians survive these multiple holocausts, they evolved a society which Europeans tied to racial stereotypes never saw or never acknowledged. A myth which persists today is that the first Australians were and are 'primitive' people. This is not so. They were often more sophisticated than those who came in ships and, again contrary to myth, they were immensely adaptable. They learned languages better than whites. They displayed an intimacy with their environment which produced knowledge and skills of which the whites had no concept. Moreover, they lived lives whose intrinsic value was not understood by whites whose European background was that of brutality and deprivation. In their 'one family' society the First Australians' nature was generous, and reciprocity was taken for granted. European observers, wrote Henry Reynolds,

> . . . were struck by the importance of sharing in Aboriginal society. 'They are truly generous among themselves', wrote William Thomas of Port Phillip blacks in the 1840s. 'Meanness is rarely found among these people', noted Donald Thompson while on Cape York a hundred years later. Both men observed that reciprocity was so fundamental to Aboriginal society that the clans they knew had no word meaning 'thank you'.[11]

The Aborigines had no appreciation of the extremes of wealth and poverty, and were unable to fathom the nineteenth-century European model of 'equality': of freedoms negotiated by and confined to élites. The native Australians, wrote the West Australian Protector of Aborigines in 1841, are a nation of 'owning no chief, a literally pure democracy'.[12] A clergyman in the colony of Victoria wrote in exasperation, 'The Aborigines do not understand exalted rank. In fact, it is difficult to get into a blackfella's head that one man is higher than another!'[13]

Above all was their reverence for the land, which they held as sacred as life itself and which they could never presume to 'own'; and that is as true today as it was then, for they regard themselves as related to the land and recognise it as 'mother'. Members of each clan belonged to a particular part of the land, believing that their spirits had pre-existed in it since the creative epoch and would travel in it again after the death of the body. Thus, land was crucial to the Aborigines retaining their identity. They had no objection to the Europeans trespassing, rather to the European assertion 'of exclusive proprietorial rights often heard from the first day of occupation'.[14] Viewed against the nightmare of the British invasion – the introduction of smallpox and other infectious diseases, followed by war, massacres and finally dislocation and dependency – today's Aboriginal renaissance is a phenomenon, perhaps even a marvel of the twentieth century.

Within a few years of their officially-endowed emancipation following the referendum in 1967 Aborigines began to change Australian politics. In 1972 the first Australian Labour government to be elected for twenty-three years drafted land rights legislation under which 'inalienable' land and proven sacred sites would be returned to the Aborigines. The Act was to include the power of veto over the exploitation of certain resources, such as mineral wealth. In a ceremony in the country of the Gurindji people, prime minister Gough Whitlam became the first white Australian to hand back part of the continent to its original owners.

The land involved was minuscule, but the faith was good and this first gesture has never been forgotten. In my own journeys I have found that the names of other prime ministers, Robert Menzies and Malcolm Fraser (who was not indifferent to Aboriginal demands) and even the current Bob Hawke, are unknown or 'unaccepted'; only Whitlam is acknowledged. The dismissal of the Whitlam government by a British viceroy, the Governor-General, in November 1975 extinguished what was left of radical 'land rights' legislation. However, justice for the Aborigines remained popular, at least until the 1980s; it offered no perceived threat and was therefore politically fashionable. A land rights Bill, with only a partial veto over resources, was enacted in 1976, but only in the Northern Territory for which the federal government had direct responsibility.

The decade that followed saw the first national Aboriginal health programme, including the first co-ordinated scheme to combat trachoma. I had seen trachoma in Africa; I had not imagined such a thing in

Australia. It is one of the ancient eye diseases, which, if not treated, scars the eyelids and causes ulcers and eventual blindness. Trachoma is found only in the impoverished, overcrowded conditions of the 'developing world'; Australia is the exception.

The anti-trachoma programme was primarily the initiative of one man, Professor Fred Hollows of Sydney's Prince of Wales Hospital, a bluff, square-shouldered New Zealander whose knowledge of and respect for the Aboriginal way of life led him into many battles on behalf of black Australians, chiefly against the state authorities of Queensland. What Fred Hollows found among the Gurindji people in 1971 affected him deeply. He told me:

> It was an appalling situation. Every child had some sign of trachoma. Twenty per cent had the sort of trachoma that if it persisted would lead to premature blindness. It attacks mostly the kids and the old people. I'll never forget finding an old Aboriginal woman paraplegic, crippled from the waist down, lying on a dirt floor with no possibility of being cleaned or ablutions; and she was blind.[15]

During the 1970s Aboriginal power grew with the establishment of medical and legal services, and land councils based on the traditional structure of the clans and linguistic groups. Their flaw was that in one form or another they were drawn into a system of government patronage. Only the Federal Council for the Advancement of Aborigines and Torres Strait Islanders operated entirely without government funds and its effectiveness is often compared nostalgically with the confused and emasculated authority of 'development' bodies which became instruments of official manipulation and, inevitably, vehicles for black careers and opportunism.

But the renaissance had a momentum of its own. Aboriginal artists, writers and playwrights were recognised and wecomed in the white cities. A national Black Theatre was formed and the first all-Aboriginal production, *Basically Black*, opened in Sydney. The book of the Aboriginal writer and artist, Dick Roughsey, was published, along with the writings of Kevin Gilbert, whose *Because a White Man'll Never Do It* was probably the first major political work by an Aborigine. To understand the price paid by Aborigines for their survival and the heroic nature of their renaissance – for example, the painful abandonment of the victim's mentality and of acquiescence – one must read this book of Gilbert's.

> Price of survival. Bewildered by the strange new conditions of life, the Aborigine bowed to his forced removal from his tribal area even though he knew that if he were to die in a strange area his spirit would

be lost forever. He bowed to the ward system by which the various authorities could split families and assign him, his wife or his children to separate areas as servant-slaves to white squatters. He bowed to the apartheid-style policies that kept him apart on reserves. He bowed to the nightly curfews that kept him out of towns. He bowed to segregation rules of hospitals that ensured that his kind would not receive proper medical attention or humane care. He bowed to the power exercised by squatters over every facet of his life, diet and actions. He bowed to the demands of stockmen and squatters for 'black velvet'. He bowed to the fact of his women having to prostitute themselves for the food that would allow the children to survive, or for the alcohol that would yield the oblivion that was so much more desirable than the daily reality . . .[16]

The late summer of 1975–6 was a strange, embittered time for many Australians. Gough Whitlam's call to his supporters to 'maintain your rage' following the unconstitutional dismissal of his government had not been heeded; a conservative government had been elected in its place, with a large majority. And it rained and it rained, breaking the longest drought in memory with floods of equal devastation.

Charlie Perkins and I decided to go back to the Northern Territory. At Alice Springs the airport buildings were two feet under, and the road through the MacDonnell Range was cut. 'Go back,' said a policeman at a point where the usually sand-dry River Todd now surged across the road. We didn't go back; we slewed to the other side and drove across a plain of red mud to The Palms. The little iron shelters, in which the old people lived, had been painted pink since we had been there seven years earlier; and the pink paint represented the sum total of benefits flowing from emancipation under the Australian constitution. The mud lay inside the shelters, almost up to the level of beds.

On our return to Alice the rain had eased and we stopped at the bowling club where we spoke to Aboriginal people camped in tents at the end of the bowling green. The tents were sodden and silt coursed through them; the coughing of children who lived in them seemed relentless. A trench of beer cans and other rubbish, in which the bronchial children scavenged, divided the tents from a group of club officials on an inspection tour of the green. I remember that they never looked our way, though they were barely a dozen feet from us. And as the children's coughing became almost a chorus, the men on the green raised their voices almost unconsciously, so that their deliberations on the prospects for play could continue.

In 1979 the New South Wales Health Commission reported that 20 per cent of male Aborigines who had reached the age of twenty would be dead by the age of forty, and that Aboriginal infant mortality was fifty per 2,000 compared with twelve per 1,000 of the white population. These statistics, said the report, 'are at a level found only in underprivileged countries'.[17]

New South Wales is said to be an enlightened state compared with the *veldt* of Joh Bjelke-Petersen, the Queensland premier. 'Joh' is frequently portrayed in the media of the southern states as a benign and amusing old rogue. He is about as benign and amusing as a Transvaal farmer with his bull whip barely concealed behind his back. He reminds me of Alabama Governor George Wallace in the 1960s; the fake bonhomie, the intimidation and the menace are not dissimilar. Bjelke-Petersen has distinguished his long jerry-mandered tenure in public office by defying most federal laws related to the advancement of Aborigines. No federal government has confronted the racism in his state; Bob Hawke, champion of 'bringing all Australians together', which was his electoral slogan, has done little to make Australian democracy's writ run in Queensland.

In 1983 two researchers made a discovery in the records of the Queensland Health Department: Aboriginal deaths from preventable, infectious diseases were as much as 300 times higher than that of the white average in the state and among the highest in the world.[18] Epidemics are common on Palm Island, twenty miles out from Townsville on the edge of the Great Barrier Reef. Palm Island was established in 1918 as a concentration camp for Aboriginal 'troublemakers', who were men, women and children convicted of such 'crimes' as homelessness, rebelliousness and drunkenness. They were forced to live in single-sex dormitories and to work for food hand-outs. This did not change until the 1960s, and although people today are 'citizens' and free to come and go, overcrowding, malnutrition, alcoholism and venereal and other diseases remain.

I have been twice to Palm Island. Like so much in Aboriginal Australia, its physical beauty belies that which is just beneath the surface. When I was there in November 1980 an epidemic of gastro-enteritis had hospitalised 130 people. Four years later little had changed. In the cemetery, a circle of palms beyond which long rolling waves break on the reef, a disproportionate number of the headstones bear the names of children. This is true of all Aboriginal graveyards. A young man called Jack, who had helped to mend the island's water supply, said, 'The water in the reserve tank is so putrid you can't even bathe in it. The kids get the bug, and that's it . . . they don't make it.'

In 1977 Bjelke-Petersen personally stopped Fred Hollows' anti-trachoma programme in Queensland when he learned that the medical teams were also explaining to Aborigines that they had a right to vote.

In 1981 I met the artist Fred Williams in Melbourne. A small, stout man in a grey suit, white shirt and tie he was not at all what one might expect of Australia's most original and perhaps greatest artist. His wife, Lyn, told me they both knew Fred was dying from cancer and that he was gathering his failing strength to complete a series of oil pictures and *gouaches* known as 'The Pilbara Series'. These pictures were the product of two journeys Fred had made to the Pilbara region of north-west Australia. Coming to terms with the nature of the Australian continent, its fickle harshness and its ghostliness, has always seemed an impossible goal for white artists, as remote as white understanding of the native Australian people. Sydney Nolan and Russell Drysdale achieved international fame by combining European forms in order to describe the 'nowhere land' of Australia. Their work was rich, but it also served to reinforce European visions of Australia. Since then it has been *passé* to paint the Outback, and one suspects that the reason for this is that ancient Australia has defeated them all, with one exception. Fred Williams' pictures, on which he worked in the shadow of his own death, capture his secret country. He saw beyond the images of harshness and death a spectacle of beauty and vitality.

Fred Williams died in 1982. Today, Australian tourists on their way to Singapore or London and glimpsing the Outback from their jumbo jet, often for the first time, fly directly over where Fred Williams painted his Pilbara pictures and where he became the first white man to establish an Australian aesthetic. I saw his Pilbara pictures only once, but they so moved me that they became one of the spurs for another journey beyond the frontier.

In November 1984 I returned to the Northern Territory with fellow Australians Alan Lowery, the film director, and Jerry Bostock. Alan and I had filmed in Nicaragua the previous year and Jerry, an Aborigine, had worked as a producer on 'Lousy Little Sixpence', Alec Morgan's superb documentary about the Aboriginal 'protection' acts.

I went first to Darwin. In the Regency Room of the Darwin Hotel the waiter wore a wing collar which caught his sweat. The ceiling fans were like vintage aeroplane propellors and the furniture tried to be art deco. The hotel, more than a hundred years old, had withstood the Japanese bombing in 1943 and a cyclone which razed the city in 1974. Darwin has a Chinese mayor by tradition; and Indonesia is half an hour's flight away. On the hotel steps, when I arrived, lay an Aboriginal woman crippled with the booze. Here was the starting point.

The spine of the Australian Outback is the 'track' from Darwin in the North to Adelaide in the South, by way of Alice Springs in the 'red centre'. Once past 'civilisation', as announced by a lone billboard with the warning that there were 280 miles to 'your next cold beer', a landscape

I had not seen anywhere else in the world unfolded. If the Aborigines thought the Europeans were Venusians, what did the white explorers make of this? It must have seemed to them another planet. Great anthills rose like warts on the exposed crust of the earth and ghost gums clustered in petrified forests with fine sand, coloured ash white and ochre, shifting among them like mist. There seemed to be no life; the silence was sepulchral. This was Fred Williams country; it was not what it seemed.

Peter Fuller, the London critic, once wrote that what Fred Williams perceived 'extends far beyond the shores of the Antipodes . . . We live, even those of us who are not Australian, on the periphery of a potential desert'.[19] He was referring to the forests of nuclear missiles in the English countryside, although for a perspective of the nuclear past, present and possible future, one must come to Australia. From Jibaru in Arnhem Land to Ranger, south of Alice, some of the largest deposits of uranium have been mined and made into nuclear weapons. This has given Australia the distinction of being the only country in the world to have supplied the ingredients for nuclear bombs which its leaders allowed to be dropped by a foreign power on their own people, without warning.

In the 1940s the British were looking for somewhere to explode and test their new nuclear weapons. The central and western deserts of Australia were said to be ideal because they were 'empty', just as more than 150 years earlier the British had declared all of Australia *terra nullis*: the empty land. At Maralinga and Emu Junction between 1952 and 1957 the British government, in collusion with the Australian government of Robert Menzies, exploded nine nuclear bombs with almost five times the power of the two atomic bombs dropped on Hiroshima and Nagasaki. Dr Keith Lokan, director of the Australian Radiation Laboratory at the time, said, 'There was the view in the back of everybody's minds that the land was unoccupied and likely to remain so.'[20]

This 'view' was rapidly converted into a self-serving 'fact'. The scientists drew maps of land where three peoples, the Ngaanyatjara, Pitjantjatjara and the Yankunytjatjara, had lived since long before the arrival of Captain Cook. The scientists wrote across their maps: 'VACANT: NO ABORIGINES'. This lie was integrated into one of the more spirited propaganda campaigns of the cold war. This was the *News of the World* in May 1957:

TESTS WILL HARM NO ONE

Churchill's War-Time Adviser
Condemns 'Scaremongers'[21]

In the *Daily Express* Chapman Pincher identified the opponents of Britain's 'harmless' tests as 'those who hate or envy the British . . . [such as] Jap business tycoons who are already using underhand methods to beat Britain in the export markets'.[22]

The *Daily Graphic* published this open letter to William (now Lord) Penney, the British scientist in charge of the testing programme:

> The fact that you and your team have made it possible for Britain to make and store atom bombs has made the country a world power once again ... American scientists who worked with you believe that a world of wealth, luxury and leisure beyond human dreams will be possible when atom power is properly harnessed for our welfare.[23]

Glimpsing this nuclear Nirvana the *Graphic* described how food grown in radioactive seas would put an end to famine for ever and 'it will be as though we were stepping out of the Ice Age into a world of permanent sunshine'.

For many years Aboriginal people tried to tell the world what had been really done in Australia, but few listened. It was only when British and Australian servicemen and others who had worked on the tests began to suffer and die from cancers that the horror of the bombs began to emerge. Dr Hedley Marston, the scientist who researched the fallout patterns, disclosed that 'extensive areas of Australia have been contaminated'.[24] Patrick Connolly, who served in the RAF at Maralinga, was threatened with prosecution by the British Special Branch after he had disclosed that 'during the two and a half years I was there I would have seen 400 to 500 Aborigines in contaminated areas. Occasionally, we would bring them in for decontamination. Other times we just shooed them off like rabbits.'[25]

I met Yami Lester in Alice Springs. When two bombs went off at Emu Junction Yami was a young Yankunyatjara boy living about 100 miles away. He and his people received no warning and were told nothing. He told me, 'I remember one early morning the bomb going off. It was a warm morning, the sun was coming up and I was out playing. There was this bang, really loud. I don't have any times and hours when it went off; I didn't go to a white man's school. It was coming south of where we were camping and I thought it were dust storm but it was too quiet for a dust storm, and black smoke came rolling through the trees and above the trees and passed right over us. I don't know how many days after that, but most of the people became sick and we all got skin rash and diarrhoea, and sore eyes and red, red eyes. You couldn't open them because they were hurting so much, and tears were coming from them; and some people died.'

I asked Yami if anyone came to help them. He replied, 'No, nothing. Nothing like that were coming ... I got sick, and through that sickness

I went blind in one eye; I still had a bit of sight in the left eye; I don't really know how much per cent. But I still went tracking. I could see the tracks and track animals, but it wasn't any good; it gave trouble and later on, I think in '57, I went blind then.'

I asked Yami why those of us who lived in Australia never heard about these things. He said, 'Yeah that's a mystery to ordinary people. I think only the government people know. They wanted to make a weapon, I suppose; they worried about some other countries; so they come over to Australia. I don't know why they pick Australia, but they did; and they just wanted to make something big and powerful and blow somebody up.'[26]

The town of Katherine, on the 'track' between Alice and Darwin, is one of the hottest places on earth, where the temperatures often reach their highest when the sun is down. On the day I arrived in Katherine there was a partial eclipse of the sun, and the sky looked as it might have looked to Yami Lester on the morning the bomb went off at Emu Junction. The 'road trains', hauling as many as four wagons, began braking on the rise in a shimmering detonation of dust. And when the dust had settled at the weigh station there appeared a man wearing long white socks and carrying a yellow plastic rubbish bin. His job was to pick up chewing gum wrappers, beer cans, cigarette ends and eucalyptus leaves by gloved hand. Katherine, proclaimed the words on his T-shirt, was 'The Top End's Champion Tidy Town Winner'.

Katherine has a substantial black population, although you are not aware of this until you turn right at the Tidy Town sign and drive into the bush to a camp of the Walpiri people, run by Katherine Council, which is all white. Here there are corrugated-iron shelters of the same architectural school which produced The Palms, and in these too the occupants broil and the infants have flies on their eyes and ear infections, and there is a system of drainage and plumbing which mocks the term 'running water', not to mention 'Tidy Town'. Farther on there is a slaughterhouse, from which meat is 'put out' for the people in the camp. The meat, say the people, is sometimes diseased and they have to cut away the maggots. Hind pieces are mostly put out and the scrub around, where the tails are discarded, has a permanent haze of flies. Hungry people gnaw at these tails, in Australia, in the 1980s.

Nearby is the Tindal Air Force Base which will be re-opened in 1988 to accommodate Australia's FA-18 Tactical Fighter Force, and American B-52s whose function is to remain in the sky with nuclear weapons. It is said they will refuel at Tindal; and if the implications of that are incomprehensible to the Walpiri people, the coming changes at Katherine are not. Contractors and servicemen and those to service them will more than double the population of the town. The Aborigines will become a minority and vulnerable, yet again, to the imported disease of alcoholism and to prostitution and to a dismemberment of their society – a society now in the first stages of restoration.

Indeed, all the frailty and hope of the Aboriginal renaissance is at Katherine. Past the Council's wretched camp and the slaughterhouse and the fly-blown scrub, all of which represents the past and too much of the present, is Bamyili, the future. Bamyili is a place owned and administered by black Australians. It, too, has won 'Top End Tidy Town' awards and these are displayed in the office of Robert Lee, a founder of the town's all Aboriginal council, who describes himself modestly as 'a sort of town clerk'. No doubt, as the nineteenth-century clergyman observed, he 'does not understand exalted rank'. Like many of the men here he was a stockman, once the only skilled trade for blacks in the white man's Outback, and he still wears big-heeled boots and he still leans on his hips.

Bamyili is funded modestly by the Northern Territory government and white-run Aboriginal bureaucracy in Canberra: the Department of Aboriginal Affairs and the Aboriginal Development Council. With less than a million pounds Robert Lee and his people have transformed a former mission into a community they cherish: houses designed for extended families, a clinic, a school, a bus and a truck. Some white influence prevails, in education for example, but the first Aboriginal teachers have qualified.

There are two Bamyilis: a 'wet' Bamyili where you can live if you drink the ration of four cans a day, and a 'dry' Bamyili where alcohol is not allowed. 'We didn't say they had to do this,' said Robert Lee. 'We talked about it a hell of a lot, then we voted on it.' The bush, its sacred sites and clear spring billabongs, its kangaroo, fish and duck, is all theirs to the horizon.

Far west of Bamyili are the outstations, some of the most imaginative developments in the Aboriginal renaissance. Until the 1970s most Out-back Aborigines were concentrated on 'reserves', such as at Jay Creek and The Palms. These were run by white managers and missionaries. After the referendum of 1967, Aboriginal elders throughout Australia began to move back to their tribal lands, and the clans followed. Three-quarters of the 700 people of the Hermannsburg mission went back to their 'country' and established outstations, where they now live a modified traditional life, free from the dependency of booze and 'the welfare'. Many run their own cattle and are self-supporting. They have short-wave radio, several have their own air strip and one has running water powered by solar energy. Twenty years ago all of this would have been unthinkable.

In 1980 Bobby Randall, whose father was a Scot and mother a Pindara woman, wrote a song called 'My Brown Skinned Baby':

> Between her sobs I heard her say:
> 'Policeman takin' my baby away;
> From white man boss
> that baby I have;
> Why he let 'im take baby away?'[27]

This lament, which Bobby recorded during the search for his mother, became something of an anthem to those children of mixed blood (that is, with white fathers) who were taken from their families. Today, the search for family across Australia and the reclaiming of roots and identity has become an important aspect of the Aboriginal renaissance.

Bobby Randall was taken from his family in the 1940s when he was seven years old and sent to a mission on Bathurst Island, north of Darwin. Bobby is now forty-three. Sitting beneath a tree in a park in Darwin, with the Timor Sea behind us, he told me, 'I was playing with a group of children when Constable Bill McKinnon came on his trip, you know doing the rounds and checking up on everything, and picking up any part-coloured kids and taking them and placing them in Alice Springs. Well this first time my grandpa said to him, "You don't take that kid, you know." So I was left. But then the following year he came back when I was playing away from the house. So Constable McKinnon put me on the camel and took me.'

When Bobby arrived at Bathurst Island he was told his Aboriginal language was 'pagan' and he must not speak it. 'Here was I', he said, 'born under the sky and now finding myself in a closed room on a stinking rotten mattress. It was like coming from heaven to hell. And I was screaming out, "Someone save me from this hell" in my Pindara language and not being able to understand because none of the others could speak my Aboriginal language; they were all Aranda people. I tried to run away many times, back to my people, but they caught me.'

Thirty-two years later, in 1980, Bobby's odyssey began. He was living in Darwin and he began to 'look around for somebody who knew me, to tell me who I was, where I came from . . . Every year I took my annual leave from this job I had and went down the track, to Katherine; and because of our Aboriginal kinship system you are always somebody's child, you belong to *somebody*, so it's easy to be tricked with so many mothers saying, "Yes you are my son". But I'd look around and I'd say to myself, "No this isn't the place I come from; I come from further south." You see, inside I had the picture of my country, and I knew I'd come home when I drove around this corner and I saw the two hills meeting like two breasts of a mother. Our old camp had gone; the trees were overgrown; but the valley was the same. I was home; and the people there knew me, and I knew them! They told me my mother knew I was coming, so she waited for me, but she couldn't wait longer than a year before I came. She died then.'

What puzzled me about Bobby Randall and Yami Lester and most of the Aboriginal men and women I met on this journey was their generosity towards whites. It was odd, because it did not in any way dilute the anger of blacks or trim their commitment to 'self-determination'. In Sydney I asked Fred Hollows about this. Professor Hollows's anti-trachoma programmes have made him one of the most trusted white allies of black Australians. He replied that the generosity came from 'Aboriginality'. 'It's difficult to put into words', he said, 'because Aboriginality is about being a human being. Does that sound trite? I hope not. You see, I like Aboriginal people. They have taught me that people are much more important than any product of people, that a motor car, no matter how much it costs, is something you should never cry about, but you should always go to your uncle's funeral; you should always look after your brother's children when they're crook; you should forsake your job to go and attend to an ailing relative. There is another thing they have taught me. I've seen in traditional law and the Aborigines themselves a truly non-neurotic people. If an arm works, whether it causes you pain or not, it is of no consequence. Pain and apprehension about any part of your body only come in when it fails to function. Then there is their attitude toward other people. They don't consider other people according to their class, rank, dress, demeanour. Other people, to them, have an existence that's just warranted by their very existence. Then there's their attitude toward children. They don't think of children as being special or little models; children are just children and there's none of that special hu-ha and absurd indulgence that tends to occur in the small white family. That is what they've taught me; and what they have goes beyond this country. It is something that can be universally applied; it is the skill and confidence of living in peace.'

There are other universal questions and hopes raised by the Aboriginal struggle. Is it possible for the dominant Western societies to grasp that their current ascendancy is only one-dimensional in its power, which is material, and that this is not an end, not an ideal, but merely a means? Is it possible for 'us' not only to learn from 'Aboriginality' in its widest sense, but ultimately to come to terms and to share with 'them'? In his book *On the Other Side of the Frontier* Henry Reynolds offered this alternative:

In the long run black Australians will be our equals or our enemies. They will identify with a radically altered historiography or they will seek sustenance in the anti-colonial, anti-European history of the third world. Unless they find an honoured place in the story we tell of

Australia's past their loyalties will increasingly lie with 'the wretched of the earth'.[28]

What is tantalising about events in Australia in the 1980s is that the possibility and opportunity still exist for a reconciliation between the two Australian nations, people of the 'first' and 'third' worlds sharing one country. I realise that those who will dismiss this as romanticising can point to the massacres, duplicity and lies touched upon in these pages, and to the racial fears and myths which are part of the white experience in Australia. The doubters' case is further strengthened by the manoeuvres of the present government of Bob Hawke, whose 'pragmatism' and 'economic management' of Australia include a review of the 1976 land rights legislation.

When Bob Hawke came to power in 1983 his Minister of Aboriginal Affairs, Clyde Holding, spoke of Aboriginal land rights as a restitution for white Australia's genocidal past, a final healing of the wounds. A national land rights Act was to be drafted at last: one, it was hoped, without strings to snatch the land back. But mining, much of it foreign controlled, was central to this. Justice Woodward of the Australian High Court, whose commission set up by the Whitlam government had laid down the principles of land rights, said that to deny Aborigines the right to prevent mining on their land was to deny them basic rights and justice.

During the 1984 election campaign powerful mining interests conducted an openly racist campaign which included television commercials showing a black wall built across the state of Western Australia. In October 1984, during the last critical weeks before the election, the West Australian Labour premier, Brian Burke, met Prime Minister Hawke. They talked about the 'problem' of land rights and marginal seats and of being 'fair' to mining interests which had 'invested in the future of Australia'. After the meeting Hawke effectively cancelled Labour Party policy which would have given Aborigines the right to control resources on their land. An Aboriginal friend of mine later remarked that 'the betrayal this time at least wore a smile'.

However, there is a catch to this. Hawke's dream is to preside over the 1988 bicentenary of white settlement in Australia, an occasion which cannot proceed, unless as farce, without the co-operation of those whose land was taken from them. If their land rights are not honoured and restored, the Aborigines promise to reduce the bicentenary to a series of dog days: days of mourning, anger and civil upheaval, days of shame to which international attention will be drawn. Fred Hollows says this will happen if the government balks at anything less than 'self-determination' before 1988. 'The government will be shocked by the strength of the counter bicentenary,' he told me. 'They won't expect the organisation, and they won't expect the white support. The average white Australian *knows* that the Aborigines are entitled to justice, and when the time comes and the battlelines are drawn up, a lot of whites will stand on their side.'

Should that prove to be true, it will defy present forebodings about a 'white backlash'. In 1985 Australia was one of the few Western countries enforcing serious economic sanctions against the apartheid regime in South Africa. Since the Second World War Australia has absorbed more cultures than the United States and without major disturbance or disaffection of the kind still turbulent in American cities. Indeed, Australia is now the most multi-cultural nation on earth after Israel. In the mid 1980s four out of every ten immigrants to Australia came from Asia, and there is one Asian settler for every two from Europe.[29]

These are sensational facts, as Bill Hayden, the Australian foreign affairs minister, commented in an historic speech. Hayden said:

> I think inevitably we'll become predominantly a Eurasian country. I'm talking about twenty years' time perhaps. That is a process which is under way . . . the very fact that I've been able to say this so often without the flood of letters one used to receive for expressing views critical of the White Australia Policy in the 1960s is an indication that it [Australia] is already in that process.[30]

This is the source of my optimism. During the 1984 general election a deep seam of youthful idealism was struck in Australia, in contrast to trends of resurgent 'conservatism' in youth elsewhere in the world. Having been persuaded that his 'charisma' embodied the good fortunes of Australia, Bob Hawke missed the real point that his deference to corporate interests and to the strategic policies of Washington was profoundly at odds with a national confidence and a yearning to 'grow up' as a nation. One in fourteen Australians gave their first preference vote in the Senate, the Australian upper house, to the Nuclear Disarmament Party, which had gathered its organisation together in less than three weeks. Had Hawke's Labour Party campaigned on a policy of nuclear disarmament, it would have won the Senate and become the first Labour government for a generation to control both houses of parliament. Only one government, New Zealand's, has ever attained political power on such an explicit 'peace' platform.

It is in the grain of these changes and possibilities, unimagined such a short time ago, that the opportunity of reconciliation exists between white and black. That is all one can say now. If Australia is 'the last dream', *that* is the dream.

Flying back to Sydney from Alice Springs, my aircraft banked across the MacDonnell Ranges into the heartland of the Aranda, Charlie Perkins' people and one of the oldest human communities. Below was Australia's spiritual heart, into which has been implanted 'Pine Gap'. The pilot had kept to the Civil Aviation Authority's regulation of flying no closer than four kilometres to Pine Gap, which belongs to someone else. Just as the British in the late eighteenth century had presumed they could do with Australia as they wished, so the Americans in the late and precarious twentieth century have presumed they can do as they wish in twelve important spy bases in Australia.

Since I first came to Alice Springs I have watched Pine Gap grow. In the 1960s there were two giant silvery radomes; now there are six. These are made of perspex and are designed to protect the enclosed antennae from the elements and from 'unfriendly' observation. Officially, Pine Gap is a joint Australian/American installation but in reality it is run by the US Central Intelligence Agency, and, together with Nurrungar and North West Cape in Western Australia, it is one of the most indispensable American spy bases in the world. What the Russians do in Europe, Pine Gap is told by satellite directly overhead. It is also one of the most important potential links in the American Star Wars system; and, not surprisingly, the Russians have indicated that it is a prime nuclear target. What Pine Gap and the other bases mean is that Australia has positioned itself on the front line of a prospective nuclear war on the other side of the world.

Beyond Pine Gap there is a brush track leading to a clearing and a square of corrugated-iron buildings. This is the Yrprinya school where children are taught Aranda and Luritja, languages from the millennia. They are children whose forebears were forced off their land by squatter farmers, and at Yrprinya they are being taught their roots. As my plane turned east to Sydney there was a fleeting moment when the cloud parted and Yrprinya and Pine Gap were framed as one: an instrument of the Apocalypse together with a place for those people with, in Fred Hollows' words, 'the skill and confidence of living in peace'.

Notes

I AUSTRALIA

1   This is Michael Cannon's description of the conditions under which the six Tolpuddle Martyrs were transported to Australia in 1834: conditions which were the norm during the 1830s. See *Who's Master? Who's Man?, Australia in the Victorian Age: 1*, Nelson, Melbourne, 1971, p. 51.

2   Cannon cites this testimony of a convict (p. 51), originally published in *A Complete Exposure of the Convict System*, Lincoln, *c.* 1841.

3   *The Times*, October 3 and 5, 1833. See *Settlers and Convicts*, A. Harris, London, 1847.

4   Cited by Cannon (p. 69), originally published in *Settlers and Convicts*.

5   Cited by Cannon (p. 68), originally published as above.

6   As cited in *The Macquarie Book of Events*, Bryce Fraser and Kevin Weldon, Macquarie Library, Sydney, 1983, p. 59.

7   Cited by Cannon (p. 60), originally published in *Reminiscences of Australia*, J. T. Ryan, Sydney, 1894.

8   Ann Summers, *Damned Whores and God's Police*, Penguin Books Australia, Ringwood, Victoria, 1975.

9   The march was later abandoned and women were taken by boat along the Parramatta River.

10 Cited by Cannon (p. 56), originally published in *The Prisoners of Australia*, London, 1841.

11 Cited by Cannon (p. 56), originally published in *Reminiscences of Thirty Years of Residence*, London, 1863.

12 See *Reminiscences of Thirty Years of Residence*.

13 Cited in 'Island of Dreams', broadcast by Channel 7, Sydney, on June 12, 1981.

14 Ibid.

15 See *The Quest for an Australian Identity*, Manning Clark's James Duhig Memorial Lecture delivered at the University of Queensland in 1979, published by University of Queensland Press, St Lucia, 1980, p. 18.

16 See W. S. Parkes, Jim Comerford and Dr Max Lake, *Mines, Wines and*

People, published by The Council of the City of Greater Cessnock, 1979, p. 183.

17   Ibid., pp. 193–201.
18   Cited in 'Island of Dreams' (see n. 13).
19   See *Mines, Wines and People*, p. 195.
20   General MacArthur was addressing Federal Parliament in April 1942. Cited by Humphrey McQueen in 'The Sustenance of Silence', *Meanjin Quarterly*, June 1971, p. 162.
21   There is a family disagreement about this. My father says we were already in Silverdale when the Japanese struck.
22   *Australian*, December 31, 1983.
23   *Australia's Yesterdays*, Reader's Digest, Sydney, 1974, p. 196.
24   Robert Drewe, *The Bodysurfers*, James Fraser, Sydney, 1983.
25   I am indebted to Meg Stewart's essay, 'Beachstruck on Bondi', for this detail. It appeared in *Bondi*, James Fraser, Sydney, 1984.
26   Cited in 'Island of Dreams' (see n. 13), from a research paper 'Australian Racism: one people, one prejudice' by Andrée Wright, 1980.
27   Ibid.
28   David Denholm, *The Colonial Australians*, Penguin, Harmondsworth, 1979, p. 28.
29   From Cyril Pearl, *Wild Men of Sydney*, W. H. Allen, London, 1966.

II VISITOR TO BRITAIN

1   A. J. P. Taylor, *English History, 1914–1945*, Oxford University Press, 1965.
2   Hugh Cudlipp, *Walking on the Water*, Bodley Head, London, 1976, p. 243.
3   *Daily Mirror*, October 14, 1964.
4   *Guardian*, May 9, 1983.
5   See A. B. Atkinson, *Unequal Shares: wealth in Britain*, Allen Lane/Penguin, Harmondsworth, 1972.
6   *Standard*, January 15, 1985.
7   See Francis Wheen, *The Sixties*, Century Publishing in association with Channel 4, 1982, pp. 114–29.
8   See the book of the TV series, *All our Working Lives*, by Peter Pagnamenta and Richard Overy, BBC Publications, London, 1984, p. 268.
9   George Orwell, *The Road to Wigan Pier*, Penguin, Harmondsworth, 1982.
10   See the Sunday Times Insight Team, *Suffer Little Children*, Futura, London, 1979, pp. 33, 34.
11   Letter from John Cater to Alfred Morris, cited in the *Daily Mirror*, January 16, 1978.
12   *Daily Mirror*, September 22, 1969.
13   See Shelter report on Northern Ireland, 1981.
14   See Home Office report, 'Racial Attacks', November 1981.
15   See Manpower Services Commission report, August 1985, cited in *The Times*, August 1, 1985.
16   See report by School of Applied Social Studies, Bristol University, 1981, author Professor Peter Townsend, cited in the *Daily Telegraph*, August 9, 1984.
17   *New Society*, January 19, 1984.

18 Analysis by CHAR, Campaign for the Single Homeless, cited in the *Daily Mirror*, March 13, 1984.
19 Analysis by Shelter, cited in the *Daily Mirror*, March 13, 1984.
20 This estimate, cited in the *Daily Mirror*, April 4, 1984, is almost certainly only a small proportion of the true amount accruing to 'bed and breakfast' landlords from DHSS funds. It was calculated from totalling DHSS payments from major centres; there is no official national figure.
21 An examination of Namecourt's accounts revealed that in 1978 the company bought Duke's Lodge in Earls Court, London – another 'hostel' for the homeless – for £63,516. In 1981 the company sold Duke's Lodge for £254,913. See the *Daily Mirror*, March 19, 1984.
22 Letter from DHSS, Dodd Street, East London, to John Blackwell, March 1, 1984.
23 See *Daily Mirror*, March 22, 1984.
24 Letter from G. Bethell, Chief Assistant, Environmental Health, London Borough of Tower Hamlets, to Simon Brooke, Convenor of Tower Hamlets CHAR, November 15, 1983.
25 Report on Princes Lodge for the Tower Hamlets Law Centre by Shelter environmental health officers John McQuillan and Mel Cairns, February 1984. Cited in the *Daily Mirror*, March 13, 1984.
26 Medical report by Dr R. J. D. Harris, sent to Councillor Paul Beasley, cited in the *Daily Mirror*, April 17, 1984.
27 Referred to in 'Progress Report on Princes Lodge', cited in the *Daily Mirror*, April 17, 1984.
28 The poor, for whom the Labour Party is meant to speak, may number some 18 million people in Britain, 7 million more than in 1979, according to Professor Peter Townsend in Fabian Tract 500, 1984.
29 Report of DHSS appeals tribunal, cited in the *Daily Mirror*, July 31, 1984.
30 With acknowledgment to John Saville for a precise reminder of these working-class struggles: *New Socialist*, July/August 1984.
31 See Jim Coulter, Susan Miller and Martin Walker, *State of Siege, Miners' Strike 1984: Politics and Policing in the Coal Fields*, Canary Press c/o Housmans, 1984.
32 Brian Simon compared the position of comprehensive schools in 1981–2 to that in 1970–1 and found that the percentage of pupils gaining no passes at whatever level in GCE or CSE has dramatically declined – from 44 per cent in 1970–1 (or almost half) to 12.9 per cent eleven years later. *Marxism Today*, September 1984.
33 Cited by Brian Simon in *Marxism Today*, September 1984. It comes from Stewart Benson's 'Towards a Tertiary Tripartism: new Codes of Social Control and the 17+', in Patricia Broadfoot (ed.), *Selection, Certification and Control*, Falmer Press, London, 1984.
34 *News at Ten*, ITN, September 19, 1985.
35 *Marxism Today*, February 1985.

III AMERICA

1 Reagan, as head of the Screen Actors' Guild, appeared eighteen times before the House of Representatives Un-American Activities Committee

as a 'friendly witness'. His principal function was to 'acknowledge' Red 'plots' in the major studios, and to identify the 'plotters'. His refusal to allow the Guild to fight the blacklisting of Karen Morley, the star of *Scarface* and *Our Daily Bread*, effectively ended her career.

2   The effects abroad of this rhetoric are interesting. In Britain there appears to be something of a crisis in confidence in United States 'idealism' and leadership. In 1985 the Gallup Poll found that more than half those interviewed had 'very little' or no confidence at all in the Reagan administration's ability to deal with world matters.

3   Martha Gellhorn, *The Face of War*, Virago, London, 1986, p. 254.

4   *Time*, April 26, 1963.

5   Matt Herron, 'A proposal for the Southern Documentary Project', 1964.

6   From notes and the *New York Times*, May 30, 1979.

7   Interview for 'Heroes', Associated Television documentary, broadcast May 6, 1981.

8   Ibid.

9   Ibid.

10 Interview for 'Frontline: the search for truth in wartime', Associated Television documentary, broadcast July 19, 1983 (interview recorded but not transmitted).

11 Reagan was addressing the Veterans of Foreign Wars convention in Chicago, August 18, 1980.

12 *Daily Telegraph*, May 28, 1983.

13 This is the estimate of writer Peter Martin, cited in the *Far Eastern Economic Review*, May 2, 1985; also cited in 'Heroes', Associated Television documentary, broadcast May 6, 1981.

14 Marshall Frady, 'The Return of George Wallace', *New York Review of Books*, October 30, 1975.

15 Garry Wills, 'Can Wallace be made respectable?', *New York*, March 6, 1972.

16 In an interview with the author in Montgomery, Alabama, August 1968.

17 Stephen Brill, 'George Wallace is Even Worse than You Think', *New York*, March 17, 1975.

18 Ibid.

19 *Parade*, August 14, 1983.

20 *Observer*, April 21, 1985.

21 Robert Scheer, *With Enough Shovels*, Random House, New York, 1982, p. 42.

22 *Newsweek*, September 15, 1980.

23 Cited in Alvin M. Josephy Jr's excellent article in *American Heritage*, June 1970, entitled 'Here in Nevada a terrible crime . . . '

24 Ibid.

25 Ibid.

26 Ibid.

27 Ibid.

28 Ibid.

29 My interview with Warren Toby, Carl Dodge and others at Pyramid Lake was conducted for my 1977 ATV documentary, 'Pyramid Lake is Dying',

directed by Richard Marquand and produced by Richard Creasey. Richard Creasey also researched the film.

30 John Steinbeck, *The Grapes of Wrath*, Pan, 1975, first published 1939.
31 *New York Times*, November 12, 1983.
32 Wyatt is not his real name, which I changed to protect the family from possible action by state welfare authorities.
33 Study based on report by the Congressional Research Service and Congressional Budget Office, cited in the *Guardian*, May 25, 1985.

IV VIETNAM

1 *New York Times* survey, cited on BBC Radio 4 *Today* programme, January 1, 1985.
2 Archimedes L. A. Patti, *Why Vietnam? Prelude to America's Albatross*, University of California Press, Berkeley, 1980. Ho Chi Minh's independence day remarks are on p. 250 and Patti's reasons for delaying his book are in the preface.
3 Interview with Michael Charlton in BBC Radio 4 series *Many Reasons Why*, cited in the *Listener*, September 22, 1977.
4 Cited by Archimedes L. A. Patti in 'The Development of a Vietnam Policy', a paper presented at a conference, 'Vietnam Reconsidered: Lessons of a War', at the University of Southern California, February 1983
5 Interview with the author, November 5, 1982.
6 Cited by Patti in 'The Development of a Vietnam Policy' (see n. 4).
7 Ibid.
8 Letter from Ed Hoyt in the *Far Eastern Economic Review*, June 8, 1979.
9 From *Why Vietnam? Prelude to America's Albatross*.
10 Noam Chomsky, 'The Vietnam War in the Age of Orwell', *Race & Class*, spring 1984, p. 44.
11 See report of the Library of Congress, a four-part analysis on decisions which led to American involvement in the Vietnam war, submitted to the Senate Foreign Relations Committee May 1984, and cited in the *Guardian*, May 7, 1984.
12 Dwight D. Eisenhower, *The White House Years: Mandate for Change 1953–1956*, Doubleday, New York, 1963, p. 372.
13 *New Statesman*, February 23, 1979.
14 Alexander Haig, *Caveat*, Weidenfeld & Nicolson, London, 1984, p. 202.
15 See National Security Memorandum 5429/2, cited in the *Pentagon Papers Volume I*, Beacon Press, New York, 1971.
16 In an interview for the Central Television programme 'Frontline: The search for truth in wartime', broadcast on ITV, July 19, 1983.
17 Ralph W. McGehee, *Deadly Deceits: My 25 Years in the CIA*, copyright © 1983 by Ralph W. McGehee, Sheridan Square Publications Inc., Box 677, New York, NY 10013, pp. 131–3.
18 Cited in *The Backroom Boys* by Noam Chomsky, Fontana/Collins, London, 1973, p. 155.
19 Cited in 'The Vietnam War in the Age of Orwell' (see n. 10), p. 46, from a study by George Kahin in *Pacific Affairs*, winter 1979–80.
20 David G. Marr in 'Burchett on Vietnam', his chapter in the forthcoming

(spring 1986) book on the life of Wilfred Burchett, to be published by Quartet Books.

21 The account and sources of the 'Gulf of Tonkin Incident' used in this chapter derive from an investigation by Robert Scheer of the *Los Angeles Times* and syndicated in the *International Herald Tribune*, May 8, 1985.

22 *Aggression from the North: the Record of North-Vietnam's Campaign to Conquer South-Vietnam*, US State Department, 1965.

23 Cited in 'The Vietnam War in the Age of Orwell' (see n. 10), p. 46.

24 Senator Nelson made this statement in a speech to Congress on August 25, 1970. Source: US Senate library.

25 According to Peter Henriot, of the Center for Concern, a Washington foundation specialising in monitoring US food policy, almost 50 per cent of American food distributed under PL480 went to South Vietnam and Cambodia in 1974 'for military reasons'. See also General Accounting Office report cited in the *Washington Post*, February 1, 1975.

26 Cited in *The Times*, April 7, 1975.

27 Frank Snepp, *Decent Interval*, Random House, New York, 1977, p. 302.

28 *Daily Mail*, April 7, 1975.

29 *New Statesman*, May 11, 1985.

30 See 'Hanoi's bitter victory' by Paul Quinn-Judge, in the *Far Eastern Economic Review*, May 2, 1985.

31 General William C. Westmoreland, *A Soldier Reports*, Doubleday, New York, 1976, p. 340.

32 The Third Force comprised professionals, students and others who were close to the NLF but believed there was a way between total communism and total Americanism.

33 *Daily Mirror*, December 7, 1979.

34 John McAuliff was addressing a conference, 'Vietnam Reconsidered: Lessons of a War', at the University of Southern California, February 7, 1983.

35 Nguyen Co Thach said this to a delegation from the Hong Kong Chamber of Commerce in Hanoi in June 1979. Cited in the *New Statesman*, July 20, 1979.

36 See 'The Chinese Invasion' by Anthony Barnett, in the *New Statesman*, February 23, 1979.

37 O. T. Barck and H. T. Lefler, *Colonial America*, Macmillan, New York, 1958, p. 679.

38 John McAuliff's address to a conference, 'Vietnam Reconsidered: Lessons of a War', at the University of Southern California, February 7, 1983.

39 *Guardian*, December 20, 1984.

40 See 'Behind Barbed Wire', a Policy Statement by the British Refugee Council, December 1984.

41 *The Times*, April 18, 1983.

42 Stanley Karnow, *Vietnam: A History*, Viking Press, New York, 1983.

43 Phillip Knightley, *The First Casualty – From the Crimea to Vietnam: The War Correspondent As Hero, Propagandist and Myth Maker*, Quartet Books, London, 1978, p. 380.

44 Ibid., p. 380.

45 Ibid., pp. 379–80.

46 Ibid., p. 396.
47 In an interview with the author during a conference, 'Vietnam Reconsidered: Lessons of a War', Los Angeles, February 1983.
48 Cited by Noam Chomsky in 'US media and the Tet Offensive', *More* magazine, June 1978, reprinted in *Race & Class*, 1978, p. 25.
49 Cited in *The First Casualty*. The quote is reporter Kevin Buckley's (p. 400).
50 This was made clear in a memorandum by counter-insurgency specialist John Paul Vann. Cited in 'The Vietnam War in the Age of Orwell' (see n. 10), p. 46.
51 A 1968 US State Department study found that the 325th Division of the PAVN was composed entirely of South Vietnamese 'at least until 1959'. Cited in 'The Vietnam War in the Age of Orwell' (see n. 10), p. 50.
52 Interview with the author during a conference, 'Vietnam Reconsidered: Lessons of a War', Los Angeles, February 1983.
53 Anthony B. Herbert, *The Making of a Soldier*, Hippocrene Books, New York, 1982.
54 My own file of Anthony Lewis's prodigious writings, in which he sought to call the American government and public to account for the bombing, is thicker than that of any individual reporter. Anniversaries never escaped him. 'Remember the Christmas Bombing' read the headline on his column on December 24, 1982, when it was ten years since B-52s had bombed Hanoi and Haiphong.
55 *The First Casualty*, p. 383.
56 David Halberstam, *The Powers That Be*, Chatto & Windus, London, 1979, p. 490.
57 In an interview with the author during a conference, 'Vietnam Reconsidered: Lessons of a War', Los Angeles, February 1983.
58 Martha Gellhorn's articles appeared in the *Guardian* during September 1966. The passages quoted were cited in *The First Casualty*, pp. 389–90.
59 *Sunday Times*, April 4, 1985.
60 *New York Times Magazine*, February 3, 1983.
61 *New York Times Book Review*, October 16, 1983.
62 See *Vietnam: A History*.
63 Noam Chomsky, *Manifesto: Vietnam Retrospectives*, April 21, 1985.
64 Cited in the *New Statesman*, July 20, 1979.
65 Letter from Deirdre English, Editor of *Mother Jones*, cited by Christopher Hitchens, *New Statesman* Diary, April 17, 1981.
66 *Daily Express*, July 2, 1985.
67 *Radio Times*, March 31, 1985.
68 Michael Herr, *Dispatches*, Alfred A. Knopf, New York, 1977, p. 8. Published in Great Britain by Picador Books, London, 1978.
69 *New Statesman*, April 7, 1978.
70 *Dispatches*, pp. 67–8.
71 *Newsweek*, April 15, 1985.
72 Charles Mohr, 'Reagan Seems Confused on Vietnam's History', the *New York Times*, February 19, 1982.
73 Cited in 'The Vietnam War in the Age of Orwell' (see n. 10), p. 59, from 'American Opinion: Continuity not Reaganism' by John E. Rielly, *Foreign Policy*, spring 1983, issue no. 50.

74 *Manifesto: Vietnam Retrospectives* (see n. 63).
75 Cited by Anthony Barnett in the *New Statesman*, August 22, 1980.
76 Joel Charny and John Spragens Jr, *Obstacles to Recovery in Vietnam and Kampuchea*, Oxfam America, 1980.
77 'Documents Concerning the US Government's Pledge to Contribute to Healing the Wounds of War and to Post-war Reconstruction in Vietnam', *Vietnam Courier*, June 1977.
78 Letter to *The Times* from Alfred McCreary, June 3, 1982.
79 Alexander Haig, *Caveat*, Weidenfeld & Nicolson, London, 1984, p. 32.
80 From *Nuremberg and Vietnam* by Telford Taylor, cited by Alex Carey in the Sydney *Sun-Herald*, June 30, 1985.

V AFRICA

1 *Guardian*, January 15, 1973.
2 As told to Jonathan Steele, the *Guardian*, July 22, 1975.
3 René Caillé, *Travels through Central Africa to Timbuctoo*, edited by E. F. Jomard, Volume II, Frank Cass & Co. Ltd, London, 1828, p. 49.
4 See Market International Report (Ethiopia summary), January 1977, cited in *Behind the War in Eritrea*, edited by Basil Davidson, Lionel Cliffe and Bereket Habte Selassie, Spokesman, Nottingham, 1980, p. 39.
5 Letter from Sir Kennedy Trevaskis to *The Times*, March 15, 1978.
6 For an understanding of land reform in Eritrea, I am grateful to the Minority Rights Group booklet, 'Eritrea and Tigray' by Colin Legum and James Firebrace, London, 1983, p. 13.
7 *Spectator*, December 1, 1984.

VI JOI BANGLA!

1 *Daily Mirror*, November 23, 1970.
2 *Daily Telegraph*, November 25, 1970.
3 Henry Kissinger, *Years of Upheaval*, Weidenfeld & Nicolson and Michael Joseph, London, 1982, p. 806; see also p. 677.
4 Quoted in a letter from A. U. M. Fakhruddin to the author, March 30, 1977.
5 Translation quoted in letter as above.
6 Geoffrey Moorhouse, *Calcutta*, Weidenfeld & Nicolson, London, 1971.
7 *Sunday Times*, August 17, 1975.
8 See 'The Food Aid Conspiracy' by Kai Bird and Susan Goldmark, in *New Internationalist*, March 1977.
9 See 'The Great Pill Push' by Ian Guest, in *New Internationalist*, March 1977.
10 Statistics from 'The Profits of Doom', a War on Want investigation into the 'world food crisis', by Christopher Robbins and Jayed Ansari, London, 1976.
11 See 'Economics of Hunger' by R. Dennis and R. Lendness, in *Science for the People*, March 1975.
12 See the *Washington Post* analysis of a General Accounting Office report by Dan Morgan, January 31, 1975.

13 Analysis by Center for Concern, a Washington agency set up to monitor US food policy (Director: Dr Peter Henriot), 1975.
14 From an OECD Development Co-operation Review, cited in *New Internationalist*, September 1985.
15 From the North American Committee on Latin America, cited in *New Internationalist*, September 1985.
16 Cited in Granada Television's *World in Action*, 'The Politics of Starvation', broadcast November 12, 1984.
17 *Observer*, October 28, 1984.
18 Ibid.
19 Cited by Dr Enver Carim in 'Pawns in the Game', in *New Internationalist*, September 1985.
20 See *Seven Days*, November 16, 1985.
21 *Hansard*, November 22, 1984, p. 493.
22 *Financial Times*, March 24, 1984.
23 In a letter from Timothy Raison to Douglas Hurd, MP, February 14, 1985.
24 'Pawns in the Game', in *New Internationalist*, September 1985.
25 See report by David Tonge on the Brandt Commission, in the *Financial Times*, February 13, 1980.
26 'AID – the West's false handout', *New Socialist*, February 1985.
27 From a speech by Willy Brandt at a public meeting in Oxford, May 28, 1980.

VII PALESTINE

1 Letter and response from Dayan originally published in the *Jerusalem Post* and cited in 'Palestine is still the Issue', Associated Television documentary, broadcast July 1974.
2 Ibid.
3 Interview filmed for 'Palestine is still the Issue', Associated Television documentary, broadcast July 1974.

VIII CAMBODIA

1 *The Times*, April 19, 1985.
2 Cited by William Shawcross in *Sideshow: Kissinger, Nixon and the Destruction of Cambodia*, André Deutsch, London, 1979, p. 55.
3 Roger Morris, *Uncertain Greatness: Henry Kissinger and American Foreign Policy*, Quartet Books, London, 1977, pp. 7, 147, 151.
4 Cited by Denis Bloodworth, 'The man who brought death', *Observer* magazine, January 20, 1980.
5 Ibid.
6 *Vietnam: a Television History*, Programme 9, 'The secret war: Laos and Cambodia', broadcast in Britain by Central Television, June 6, 1983.
7 *Bulletin of Concerned Asian Scholars*, vol. 11, no. 4, October–December 1979, pp. 19–25.
8 Ben Whitaker, *A Bridge of People. A Personal View of Oxfam's First Forty Years*, Heinemann, London, 1982, p. 14.
9 *The Age*, Melbourne, September 21, 1979.

10   Letter from Sir Anthony Royale, MP, to John Clive, November 1, 1979.
11   Gareth Porter, *Kampuchea's UN Seat: Cutting the Pol Pot Connection*, Indochina issue no. 8, July 1980.
12   *Observer*, October 7, 1979.
13   *Guardian*, September 25, 1979.
14   *Observer*, October 7, 1979.
15   *A Bridge of People*, p. 5.
16   This rule was broken once when we allowed ABC Television, New York, to use selected clips in its evening news.
17   *St Louis Post-Dispatch*, January 15, 1979.
18   Memo from Richard Dudman to Barry Chase, December 16, 1980.
19   Letter from Sir Evelyn Shuckburgh to Lady Plowden, November 6, 1979.
20   Reply from Lady Plowden to Sir Evelyn Shuckburgh, November 19, 1979.
21   Letter from Colonel J. T. Palmer to Neville Clark, December 5, 1979.
22   *Guardian*, April 10, 1980.
23   *New York Times*, December 12, 1979.
24   Interview in 'The Eagle, the Dragon, the Bear and Kampuchea', Central Television documentary for Channel 4, directed by John Sheppard, broadcast April 28, 1983.
25   *Washington Post*, December 24, 1979.
26   *Washington Post*, March 18, 1980.
27   *New York Review of Books*, January 24, 1980.
28   Ben Kiernan and Chanthou Boua, *Peasants and Politics in Kampuchea 1942–1981*, Zed Press, London, 1982, pp. 370–7.
29   *Far Eastern Economic Review*, January 4, 1980.
30   *Far Eastern Economic Review*, January 18, 1980.
31   Letter from William Shawcross to the author, January 27, 1983.
32   William Shawcross, *The Quality of Mercy: Cambodia, Holocaust and Modern Conscience*, André Deutsch, London, 1984, p. 359.
33   *New York Review of Books*, September 27, 1984.
34   *New Left Review*, no. 152, July–August 1985.
35   *The Quality of Mercy*, pp. 391–3.
36   Linda Mason and Roger Brown, *Rice, Rivalry and Politics: Managing Cambodian Relief*, University of Notre Dame Press, Indiana, 1983, pp. 135–6.
37   See *Sideshow*, p. 25.
38   See Joel Charney and John Spragens, Jr, *Obstacles to Recovery in Vietnam and Kampuchea*, Oxfam America, 1984, p. 90.
39   See 'Cambodia the Hostage' by Jean Lacouture, *New Republic*, January 5 and 12, 1980. Also Oxfam officials as sources.
40   *Observer*, November 4, 1979.
41   Original of letter dictated to author and translated by Wilfred Burchett, Paris, May 27, 1980.
42   *Observer*, November 4, 1979.
43   *Philadelphia Inquirer*, May 6, 1980.
44   Interview in 'The Eagle, the Dragon, the Bear and Kampuchea', 1983 Central Television documentary for Channel 4, directed by John Sheppard, broadcast April 28, 1983.
45   *Obstacles to Recovery in Vietnam and Kampuchea*, p. 116.
46   *Far Eastern Economic Review*, August 30, 1984.

47 *The Age*, Melbourne, September 3, 1985.
48 See Ben Kiernan on Pol Pot's 'retirement', *Inside Asia*, no. 6, November–December 1985.
49 *Australian*, March 12, 1985.
50 John McAuliff in a paper on US policy in Indo-China for the American Friends Service Committee, Philadelphia, September 8, 1982.
51 Interview in 'The Eagle, the Dragon, the Bear and Kampuchea', Central Television documentary for Channel 4, directed by John Sheppard, broadcast April 28, 1983.

IX AT THEIR RISK

1 From 'What Can We Expect of Charter 77', also known as Jan Patocka's 'Last Testament', written in Prague, March 8, 1977, cited in *The Times*, March 15, 1977.
2 Ibid.
3 *The Times*, April 13, 1977.
4 Geoffrey Moorhouse, *The Great Cities – Prague*, Time-Life Books, London, 1977.
5 Ibid.
6 Text supplied by Amnesty International, August 14, 1978.

X THE AMERICAS – VIETNAM AGAIN

1 Jenny Pearce, *Under the Eagle: U.S. Intervention in Central America and the Caribbean*, Latin America Bureau, London, 1982, p. 234.
2 Letter from Nicholas Ridley to Peter Thomas, May 19, 1981.
3 Letter from Peter Thomas to Mr and Mrs L. Thompson, May 21, 1981.
4 Statistics from Center for International Policy Aid memo, Washington, April 1981. See also *New York Times*, April 1, 1981.
5 *New York Times*, July 7, 1981.
6 Robert White's speech before the Senate Foreign Relations Committee shown in 'Heroes', Associated Television documentary, broadcast May 6, 1981.
7 *Under the Eagle*, p. 184.
8 Amnesty International Report, London, 1984, p. 148.
9 *Daily Telegraph*, February 13, 1985.
10 *Guardian*, July 22, 1985.
11 Statistics from Ministry of Foreign Trade, Managua, 1983.
12 Dianna Melrose, *Nicaragua, The Threat of a Good Example*, Oxfam, Oxford, 1985, p. 42.
13 Ibid., pp. 42–3.
14 *Playboy*, August 1983.
15 Cited in 'Nicaragua, a special report', Central Television documentary, broadcast November 15, 1983.
16 *Nicaragua, The Threat of a Good Example*, p. 7.
17 *Under the Eagle*, p. 125.

18 Amnesty International Report on Torture 1984; see also *New York Times*, June 16–17, 1984.
19 *Guardian*, January 29, 1983.
20 *Nicaragua, The Threat of a Good Example*, p. 26.
21 Ibid., p. 29.
22 *Comment*, 'Nicaragua', Catholic Institute for International Relations, London, May 1985, p. 8.
23 Jim Morrell, 'Nicaragua's War Economy' in *International Policy Report*, Washington, November 1985.
24 *Comment* (see n. 22), pp. 11–13.
25 *Diverse Reports* for Channel 4, broadcast November 30, 1985.
26 *The Times*, February 28, 1985.
27 *Nicaragua, The Threat of a Good Example*, p. 37.
28 *Guardian*, July 9, 1985. See also *The Times*, July 13, 1985.
29 *New York Times*, September 4, 1983.

XI MEDIA GAMES

1 *UK Press Gazette*, April 29, 1985.
2 Patrick Renshaw, *The General Strike*, Eyre Methuen Ltd, London, 1975, p. 207.
3 Carol Campbell, 'Guardian of Unity: the Concept of Balance in Television', a thesis, University of Bristol, 1984.
4 *Guardian*, October 31, 1983.
5 T. D. Allman, 'Eulogy to Wilfred Burchett (1911–1983)', March 31, 1984. Read at a New York memorial service.
6 *Television*: Episode 8, 'The Rise and Fall of the Documentary', Granada Television, 1984; directed by Michael Beckham, broadcast April 2, 1985.
7 From 1985 Edinburgh Television Festival magazine, cited in *The Stage and Television Today*, August 8, 1985.
8 E. S. Turner wrote one of the funniest rebuttals of 'balance' I have read. See *Punch*, September 29, 1976.
9 Lord Reith's diary for March 5, 1937, cited by John Ezard in the *Guardian*, August 22, 1985.
10 Guidelines of the Independent Broadcasting Authority, London, 'Crime, anti social behaviour etc', p. 11, item 7.
11 Liz Curtis, *Ireland the Propaganda War: The British media and the 'battle for hearts and minds'*, Pluto Press, London, 1984, pp. 279–90.
12 *Irish Times*, March 17, 1983.
13 Letter from David Glencross to Paul Fox, March 23, 1983.
14 Letter from Liz Curtis to the *Guardian*, copy to the author, August 15, 1985.
15 Ian Trethowan, *Split Screen*, Hamish Hamilton, London, 1984.
16 See Paul Foot's column, *Daily Mirror*, December 5, 1985.
17 *Guardian*, November 9, 1983.
18 *Observer*, August 18, 1985.
19 *New Internationalist*, April 1985.
20 BBC press release, November 24, 1965.
21 Letter from Lord Normanbrook to Sir Burke Trend, September 7, 1965,

cited by Michael Tracey. See *Sanity Broadsheet* no. 6, 1980; also *Guardian* article and letters, September 1, 3 and 6, 1980.

22 Lord Normanbrook's note of TV Centre meeting, September 24, 1965, cited as above.

23 Hugh Greene's speech, 'The Conscience of the Programme Director', delivered to the International Catholic Association for Radio and Television, Rome, February 1965.

24 Ian Trethowan's address to the University of East Anglia, quoted in the *Morning Star*, March 13, 1981.

25 *Sunday Times*, October 18, 1981.

26 G. Crossley, *Disarmament Negotiations – the way forward*, CND Publications, London, 1984.

27 *The Times*, June 2, 1983.

28 *Guardian*, December 19, 1983.

29 *Guardian*, December 24, 1983.

30 Ibid.

31 Cited by Nicholas Humphrey in his Bronowski Memorial Lecture, 'Four Minutes to Midnight', published in the *Listener*, October 29, 1981.

32 *The Times*, August 7, 1945.

33 *New Statesman*, December 12, 1959.

34 Phillip Knightley, *The First Casualty: From the Crimea to Vietnam: The War Correspondent as Hero, Propagandist and Myth Maker*, Quartet Books, London, 1975, p. 109.

35 In an interview with the author for 'The Truth Game', Central Television, broadcast February 28, 1983.

36 *New York Times*, September 13, 1945.

37 In an interview on January 13, 1984 with Carol Campbell for her thesis (see n. 3).

38 *Daily Mail*, April 22, 1983.

39 In an interview with Carol Campbell (see n. 3).

40 *The Times*, October 22, 1985.

41 Peter Watkins, *Cine-Tracts*, vol. 3, no. 1, winter 1980.

42 *New Internationalist*, January 1983.

43 *Guardian*, September 23, 1985.

44 *Sunday Times*, September 22, 1985.

45 *New Society*, August 12, 1982.

46 Letter from Paul Bonner to Ken Loach, August 24, 1983.

47 *Guardian*, October 22, 1983.

48 NCCL, *Civil Liberties and the Miners' Dispute*, cited in the *New Statesman*, April 19, 1985.

49 *Did You See . . .?*, BBC Television, broadcast April 22, 1984.

50 Professor Peter Townsend, *Why are there many poor*, Fabian Tract 500, Fabian Society, London, 1984; also see report by School of Applied Social Studies, Bristol University, cited in the *Daily Telegraph*, August 9, 1984.

51 *New Statesman*, May 25, 1984. Peter Golding was analysing *Poverty? What Poverty?*, Child Poverty Action Group fact sheet.

52 *The Stage and Television Today*, September 6, 1984.

53 *The Times*, November 5, 1985.

54 *Observer*, July 29, 1984.

55 Article in the 1984 Edinburgh Television Festival programme, cited in *The Stage and Television Today*, August 8, 1985.
56 Denis Forman, 'Will the Centre Hold?', MacTaggart Memorial Lecture, Edinburgh, August 26, 1984.
57 *The Stage and Television Today*, August 8, 1985.
58 *Guardian*, June 17, 1985.
59 This mood was especially striking to former colleagues of those who had decided to go to Wapping. Greg Neale, ex Father of Chapel at *The Times*, said that there was a general feeling that had the journalists remained together they would have been able to negotiate at the very least a civilised transfer to the new premises.
60 In conversation with the author.
61 A Press Council adjudication published on August 8, 1983 said, 'The world exclusive interview with the widow of Sergeant Ian McKay VC, which *The Sun* boasted of having obtained, never took place. In pretending that it had, the newspaper practised a deplorable and, in these circumstances, insensitive deception on the public.' The Press Council was told that, according to *Sun* journalists, some of the 'quotes' came from secretaries at the *Sun* who were asked how they would feel if their husbands died winning the VC.
62 Harold Evans said this in a lecture to the Worshipful Company of Stationers, London, June 1979.
63 *Tribune*, April 6, 1984, an edited version of Jack Jones' lecture to the Workers' Educational Association, Hastings.
64 This statistic is given in *Why are there many poor*, Fabian Tract 500.
65 *Daily Mail*, July 15, 1984.
66 Maurice Edelman, *The Mirror: a political history*, Hamish Hamilton, London, 1966, p. 1.
67 I was hoaxed in Thailand. To be 'stitched up' is an occupational hazard facing any journalist, with or without enemies. There is no doubt that I have made enemies in South-East Asia, not the least of them the Thai regime and its Western supporters and apologists. This is the background:

It is almost impossible to travel through South-East Asia without observing the conditions under which children have to live and work, although Thailand manages to conceal the suffering of a great many of its children behind a façade of tourism and a dynamic consumer economy. Thailand was a loyal American ally during the Vietnam war; US bombers flew from Thai bases and an army of GIs enjoyed themselves in Bangkok's 'massage parlours'. That many of the girls in these brothels were, and are, children was never, to my knowledge, an issue in the United States or elsewhere during the extensive media coverage of the war.

In 1980 the United Nations Working Party on Slavery in Geneva accepted two reports on child slavery in Thailand. One was compiled by the London-based Anti-Slavery League; the other by Timothy Bond, a case worker for the Swiss aid agency, Terre des Hommes. Bond estimated that 200,000 Thai children had been sold into the sweatshop industries and massage parlours that are the staple of Thailand's cheap export and tourist trades with the West. In his evidence on behalf of the Minority Rights Group, Bond described how he had bought two children in Bangkok and returned them to their homes in the impoverished north-east. As a result of the two reports, the Thai authorities promised to take action to stop the trade in children.

Two years later I asked Bond to return to Thailand with me to see what had changed. He now estimated that up to 500 children were being sold in and around Bangkok railway station. Through a 'fixer' he and I arranged to buy an eight-year-old girl, whose name was Sunee, for 3,500 Thai Baht, then about £85. Accompanied by a case worker from a Thai human rights group, who also acted as our interpreter with the child, we traced Sunee's mother to a village some 400 miles north of Bangkok and returned Sunee to her.

My report in the *Daily Mirror* was published shortly before the arrival in London of a Thai trade delegation led by the Prime Minister General Prem Tinasulandonda on his first visit to Europe. I had urged that buyers of Thai products, especially textile goods in well-known retail stores, enquire about the age of the products' makers and the conditions under which they were forced to work, often for nothing. My report was quoted extensively in the Thai Press, and the Thai regime was said to be 'embarrassed', especially the director-general of the Labour Department, Vichit Saengthong, who was then a leading figure in the International Labour Organisation. The ILO had campaigned vigorously against child labour, and Vichit would soon fly to Geneva to chair an important regional board meeting.

On the eve of his departure for Geneva Vichit called a press conference in Bangkok and produced Sunee and her obviously frightened mother, who said that her real home was in Bangkok, and she thought they had been acting in a movie. Tearfully, she apologised for 'defaming Thailand'. Her 'confession' was received with scepticism by Thai reporters. This was the third such 'show trial' of a foreign reporter investigating child slavery that this particular official had staged. A few months earlier, the South-East Asia correspondent of *Stern* magazine, Dr Eric Follath, wrote a cover story about child slavery in Thailand, similar to mine. In his absence, the mother and child involved in his story were wheeled out to say it was all a fake and to apologise tearfully for 'defaming Thailand'.

In London, Auberon Waugh repeated Vichit's accusations against me in his column in the *Spectator* and, supported by the *Mirror*, I sued him and the *Spectator* for libel. Waugh subsequently changed his story, writing that Bond and I had been the victims of a 'cruel hoax'. This was supported by an article in the *Far Eastern Economic Review* which produced evidence that our 'fixer' had conspired with Sunee's mother and another woman to hoax us. The case was settled finally with Waugh and the *Spectator* paying their own costs and the *Spectator* publishing a statement that they never intended to suggest that I had fabricated the story.

I later learned that Sunee's father, whom the mother had told me was dead, was, in fact, in Thai military intelligence. Certainly if the exercise was for profit it is difficult to see that the effort involved was worth the reward. Little more than the £85 paid for Sunee was involved. Split among the three hoaxers it would have come to nothing after expenses; indeed they would have made a loss. It was a highly competent frame-up.

68 British Nuclear Fuels were fined £10,000 with £60,000 costs on July 23,

1985 for 'failing to minimise the exposure of persons to radiation and failing to keep radioactive discharge as low as reasonably possible'.

69 Research carried out in October 1985 by Research Surveys of Great Britain Ltd found that 'estimates of the sale of *News on Sunday* . . . range from a pessimistic level of 800,000 copies weekly to a maximum potential of some 1.5 million copies'.

70 *What The Papers Say*, Granada Television, July 27, 1984.

71 Audit Bureau of Circulation figures cited in *Media Week*, July 19, 1985; and the *Guardian*, October 28, 1985 and January 27, 1986.

72 *Marketing Week*, January 31, 1986. At the height of Murdoch's difficulties in distributing the *Sun* from Wapping, the *Mirror* claimed on February 11, 1986 to have attracted 'six million [extra] readers in the past two weeks'. There was no mention of sales figures.

73 Cited in 'Commercial Breaks', BBC Television, broadcast July 12, 1985.

74 *Financial Times*, December 8, 1984.

75 *Financial Times*, December 14, 1984.

76 NCCL, *Civil Liberties and the Miners' Dispute*, cited in the *New Statesman*, April 19, 1985.

77 *Daily Mirror*, August 6, 1985.

78 'Commercial Breaks', BBC Television, broadcast July 12, 1985.

79 *Media Week*, July 19, 1985, based on Audit Bureau of Circulation figures.

80 *Daily Mirror*, March 4, 1985.

81 From Robert Maxwell's interview with Warsaw Radio transmitted (in English) on May 31, 1985 and monitored by the BBC, transcribed as heard.

82 *International Herald Tribune*, September 27, 1985.

83 *Daily Mirror*, July 23, 1985.

84 *Daily Mirror*, August 6, 1985.

85 Donald Trelford was giving the Kenneth Allsop Memorial Lecture, cited in the *UK Press Gazette*, November 25, 1985.

86 *Guardian*, August 6, 1984.

87 *UK Press Gazette*, September 30, 1985.

88 *New Society*, November 25, 1976.

89 *Daily Mirror*, September 16, 1985.

90 *Daily Mirror*, September 18, 1985.

91 Seymour Hersh was addressing a conference, 'Vietnam Reconsidered: Lessons of a War' at the University of Southern California, Los Angeles, February 1983.

92 *Guardian*, February 24, 1986.

93 Ibid.

94 I. F. Stone said this in the documentary film, *I. F. Stone's Weekly*, cited by Phillip Knightley in *The First Casualty*, p. 373.

95 *New Republic*, January 9 and 16, 1983.

96 *Observer*, February 2, 1986.

97 *Guardian*, August 15, 1981.

98 *The First Casualty*, pp. 4, 7, 12.

XII RETURN TO AUSTRALIA

1   *L'Express*, December 30, 1983, no. 1695.
2   W. E. H. Stanner, *White Man Got No Dreaming, Essays 1938–73*, Australian National University Press, Canberra, 1979.
3   Cited in 'Aboriginal Australians' Minority Rights Group Report no. 35.
4   Professor Stephen Roberts, *The Squatting Age*, 1964, cited by Jan Roberts in *Massacres to Mining: The Colonisation of Aboriginal Australia*, Dove Communications, Melbourne, 1981, p. 68.
5   Henry Reynolds, *The other side of the frontier: Aboriginal Resistance to the European Invasion of Australia*, James Cook University of North Queensland, 1981, p. 163.
6   *Massacre to Mining*, p. 20.
7   *Bingara Advocate*, January 20, 1965.
8   Thomas Keneally, *Outback*, Rainbird Publishing Group Ltd for Hodder & Stoughton, Sevenoaks, 1983, p. 198.
9   D. Gillespie, *The Rock Art Sites of Kakadu National Park – Some Preliminary Research Findings for their Conservation and Management*, Australian National Parks and Wildlife Service Special Publication 10, 1983, pp. 3–5.
10 Geoffrey Blainey, *Triumph of the Nomads*, Sun Books, Melbourne, pp. 13–14; first published by Macmillan, London, 1975.
11 *The other side of the frontier*, p. 56.
12 Ibid., p. 113.
13 Ibid., p. 119.
14 Ibid., p. 54.
15 Interview recorded for 'The Secret Country', Central Television documentary, broadcast May 21, 1985.
16 Kevin Gilbert, *Because a White Man'll Never Do It*, Angus & Robertson, Sydney, 1973.
17 Cited in 'Island of Dreams', Channel 7 Sydney documentary, broadcast June 12, 1981.
18 *Courier Mail*, Brisbane, April 19, 1983.
19 *New Society*, June 7, 1984.
20 *New Statesman*, November 30, 1984.
21 *News of the World*, May 10, 1957.
22 *Daily Express*, May 1, 1957.
23 *Daily Graphic*, October 14, 1952.
24 Adrian Tame, 'Maralinga: Britain's atomic legacy', in *Penthouse*, November 1980.
25 *Massacres to Mining*, p. 47.
26 Interview for 'The Secret Country', Central Television documentary, broadcast May 21, 1985.
27 Copyright Bobby Randall.
28 *The other side of the frontier*, p. 166.
29 *Far Eastern Economic Review*, May 10, 1984.
30 Ibid.

Index